www.wadsworth.com

www.wadsworth.com is the World Wide Web site for Thomson Wadsworth and is your direct source to dozens of online resources.

At *www.wadsworth.com* you can find out about supplements, demonstration software, and student resources. You can also send email to many of our authors and preview new publications and exciting new technologies.

www.wadsworth.com
Changing the way the world learns®

5th EDITION

Taking Charge of Your Career Direction

Career Planning Guide, Book 1

Robert D. Lock

Jackson Community College

THOMSON

BROOKS/COLE

Australia • Canada • Mexico • Singapore • Spain
United Kingdom • United States

THOMSON

BROOKS/COLE

Executive Editor: *Lisa Gebo*
Acquisitions Editor: *Marquita Flemming*
Assistant Editor: *Shelley Gesicki*
Editorial Assistant: *Amy Lam*
Technology Project Manager: *Barry Connolly*
Marketing Manager: *Caroline Concilla*
Marketing Assistant: *Mary Ho*
Advertising Project Manager: *Tami Strang*
Project Manager, Editorial Production: *Catherine Morris*
Art Director: *Vernon Boes*

Print/Media Buyer: *Emma Claydon*
Permissions Editor: *Kiely Sexton*
Production Service: *Scratchgravel Publishing Services*
Copy Editor: *Linda Purrington*
Illustrator: *Christopher H. Lock*
Cover Designer: *Brenda Duke*
Cover Image: *Digital Vision/Getty Images*
Compositor: *Scratchgravel Publishing Services*
Text and Cover Printer: *Edwards Brothers, Incorporated*

For more information about our products, contact us at:
Thomson Learning Academic Resource Center
1-800-423-0563

For permission to use material from this text or product, submit a request online at
http://www.thomsonrights.com.
Any additional questions about permissions can be submitted by email to **thomsonrights@thomson.com.**

Library of Congress Control Number: 2004108521

ISBN 13: 978-0-534-57426-0
ISBN 10: 0-534-57426-2

Thomson Brooks/Cole
10 Davis Drive
Belmont, CA 94002
USA

Asia
Thomson Learning
5 Shenton Way #01-01
UIC Building
Singapore 068808

Australia/New Zealand
Thomson Learning
102 Dodds Street
Southbank, Victoria 3006
Australia

Canada
Nelson
1120 Birchmount Road
Toronto, Ontario M1K 5G4
Canada

Europe/Middle East/Africa
Thomson Learning
High Holborn House
50/51 Bedford Row
London WC1R 4LR
United Kingdom

Latin America
Thomson Learning
Seneca, 53
Colonia Polanco
11560 Mexico D.F.
Mexico

Spain/Portugal
Paraninfo
Calle Magallanes, 25
28015 Madrid, Spain

To my family, students, and colleagues

Contents

Chapter 7   Cultural, Personal, and Work Values   251

Preface

The unexamined life is not worth living.—Socrates

The examined life is no picnic.—Robert Fulghum

You *can* choose to go through life without examining it. Plenty of people simply react and remain indifferent to experiences, letting events mold them. There is even something to be said for this attitude; sometimes it is best to bend so you don't break. But when people consider their careers, that's different because work is so central and fundamental to our lives. Career planning *does* call for examination of what is happening around you and within you. This book can be a great help in your survey of the occupational environment as well as in an examination of the personality that makes you a unique individual. Based on a study of yourself and the occupational world, career decisions can be made that *will* make your life "worth living."

Taking Charge of Your Career Direction is the first of a two-book series on career decision-making and the job search. The books are intended to be used by students as comprehensive texts in career-planning courses or by individuals with the help of a counselor. Each chapter can stand on its own. The first book has an introductory chapter followed by three major themes. The first is *career awareness*—knowledge of the world of work and the occupational alternatives you can derive from it (Chapters 2 and 4). The second is *self-study*— knowledge of your personality, interests, needs, achievements, abilities, and values (Chapters 3, 5, 6, and 7). The third theme is *career decision making*—making wise occupational choices and setting realistic career goals (Chapters 8–10). For those who prefer to study personality first, move ahead to Chapters 3, 5, 6, and 7, and then come back to Chapters 2 and 4 for the material on occupations. (I prefer to start with a study of the world of work, using the interests aroused by it to generate a list of occupational prospects, thus giving students time to research several major alternatives while they are engaged in self-study.) A fourth theme, covered in the second book (entitled *Job Search*), is implementing the career decision by learning the skills needed to find a job in the occupation of your choice.

To the Student or Client: The Task at Hand

You were born for a purpose. Figuring out who you are and why you are here is a lifelong project. Your career is not all of your life, but it is a major part of it. This book is about how to decide the direction your career will take. It's like unraveling a mystery. You are a career detective, looking for clues to find the work that is meaningful, brings satisfaction, and is a service to others. Those clues can be found in the chapters of this book. Some of the evidence will enable you to develop a number of prospective occupations and learn about them. Other observations will help you understand more of your own personality. Then you can bring this material together and get to work on solving your career mystery.

We know some things about career decision making—the subject has been heavily studied. Career decision-making skills and degrees of "decidedness" can be assessed. A state of decidedness develops over time. Factors such as gender, socioeconomic status, educational level, and ethnic background affect career decisions. Career indecision does not automatically disappear once a decision has been made. Decision-making processes are complex, not simple. Counselor interventions help people decide about careers; longer, more intensive interventions such as career courses help even more (Krieshok, 1998).*

This text also represents an effort on the part of the author to develop a program or course in career planning that is worthy to stand with other academic subjects in the arts and sciences. At the same time, we want the text to be practical and useful—characteristics that are not outside the bounds of good scholarship.

In many ways, career planning has become a survival skill in today's world. The economy can deliver unexpected surprises in the form of recessions, plant or office shutdowns, mergers, business takeovers, or bankruptcies—all of which could force you to consider a new occupation or a change in career direction at any time. A bewildering array of job opportunities has become available. New occupations are created, and others become obsolete. If the outside world isn't confusing enough, your inner nature is subject to changes as well. The job that was once so challenging and exciting can become dull, monotonous, and deadening. New values and interests may compete with ones that have always characterized your personality. The average worker now makes seven to ten job changes over a career lifetime and is likely to change occupations two or three times before retiring from work. The career choice you make is not likely to last forever. Helping you set an occupational goal is an important part of *Taking Charge of Your Career Direction*, but its larger purpose is to equip you with a set of career decision-making skills you can use as often as you need them.

This book is indeed a guide for your career planning. It will not tell you which career to choose; that decision is your responsibility. But it will guide you through the steps needed to make the decision. Use it, keep it for reference, and use it again when another occupational decision must be made.

Changes in the Fifth Edition of Taking Charge of Your Career Direction

The greatest change between this fifth edition and its predecessor is an integration of the "old" *Student Activities* manual into the text, and this accounts for the larger size of the text and the inclusion of several appendices at the back of the book. A number of exercises had appeared in both books. Combining the manual with the text saves space. The same pattern of chapters has been retained. Several recently developed theories of career choice have been added to Chapter 1: cognitive information processing, self-efficacy, social cognitive, personal construct, and integrative life planning. The older theories of career choice and development of Roe, Holland, Ginzberg, Super, and Krumboltz have been retained because they continue to undergo revision, be very relevant, and are often cited in the career literature. Chapter 2 always presents a challenge to the writer; the economy is volatile and constantly changing. The occupational-trend data of Chapter 2 have been revised—and revised again! A section on new and emerging occupations has been added. A condensed version from the U.S. Department of Labor's "Job Outlook in Brief" was devised to present a lot of information in a shorter space. Chapter 3 on interest and personality inventories and generating occupational prospects remains substantially the same. Brief descriptions of six more inventories have been included.

Reorganized information on practically all sources of occupational information appears in Chapter 4. The latest edition of the *Occupational Outlook Handbook (OOH)* always calls for an update. More material on the electronic *O*NET (Occupational Information Network)* has been inserted into the chapter. The Canadian *National Occupational Classification (NOC)* has been added; American as well as Canadian students have access to it through the Internet. The *Dictionary of Occupational Titles (DOT)* has

*T. S. Krieshok (1998), An introspectivist view of career decision making, *The Career Development Quarterly*, 46(3), 210–229.

been kept because that weighty tome is still being sold by distributors of occupational information and it is still used in many career centers. The *Guide for Occupational Exploration (GOE)* is now in its third edition. Brief descriptions and exercises for each of the OOH, NOC, DOT, O*Net, and GOE systems appear in Chapter 4; more detailed exercises for them appear in Appendices B, C, D, E, and F—which gives this text greater flexibility of use. (I am aware that counselors and teachers will not want to inflict all these career information systems on their students and clients. However, not knowing which systems are used at particular institutions, it is safer to put all of them in the book; then choices can be made by those using this text.) Worksheets on which to write information about occupational prospects can be found in the last appendix of the book, Appendix I.

Chapter 5 on achievement motivation has stayed basically the same. The Origami game, an achievement motivation exercise, appears in Appendix G. The portfolio section, introduced in the fourth edition, has proven very worthwhile. Chapter 6 introduces the Ability Profiler, a replacement for the General Aptitude Test Battery. A number of reviewers asked for more material about cultural diversity and that fascinating subject is now included in Chapter 7. The title of Chapter 8 has been changed and the material on the nature of decisions and types of decision makers has been shifted into it from the next chapter. Narrowing occupational choices, as in earlier editions, completes Chapter 8. Making a career decision remains the same for Chapter 9. Updated information about education can be found in Chapter 10. Appendix A has the usual concise material on the job search, the subject of the second book in the *Career Planning Guide* series. The other appendices (B through I) are attachments to Chapters 4, 5, and 6.

Acknowledgments

The influences on my writing have been many and varied. My family comes first. I have witnessed the resolute dedication of my wife, Barbara, as she entered a new career teaching art history at the age of 52. My father was a model of integrity in his work and was living proof that a tax collector could be known for his charity. I watch my three children as they struggle with and grow in their assorted occupations of interior design, teaching, and social work. My mother worked long hours as a secretary and still longer hours as a political campaigner. My sister gives honor to the occupation of homemaker and is a dedicated animal rights volunteer. Can one family include so many different occupations? The answer is yes, and most families will be even more diverse in the future.

My colleagues and students have given me much support and assistance. Over 3,000 students at Jackson Community College have made important contributions to this book through their evaluations and suggestions for the career-planning course I have taught for the past quarter-century. Counselors Elaine Galoit, Woody Wilson, Mike Killian, Bob Hanlin, Thelma Bowles, Gina Alfaro, and Ellen Schneider have taught and/or counseled students about their career plans and have guided many students into my class. My associate Mark Schopmeyer helped me with an exercise, and I am grateful to Bill Lundberg, track coach at Hillsdale College, for his inspiring story of achievement. My professors at Michigan State University, the University of Maryland, and San Francisco State University have made significant impressions on my learning, particularly Willa Norris, Jim Costar, and the late Buford Stefflre at Michigan State University.

I would like to acknowledge the writers and researchers in career development from whom I have borrowed. Part of Chapter 1 is based on the career choice and development theories of Donald Super, John Krumboltz, Anne Roe, and John Holland. Chapters 2 and 4 draw much material from the work of economists and occupational researchers in the U.S. Department of Labor. Chapter 3 includes some of the most widely used vocational interest inventories, those inspired by Holland and C. G. Jung, such as the *Self-Directed Search,* the *Strong Interest Inventory,* and the *Myers-Briggs Type Indicator.* Chapter 5 has a foundation based on the achievement motivation research of David McClelland, the human needs hierarchy of Abraham Maslow, and the career management ideas of Bernard Haldane. Chapter 6 is based on the skills analysis and prioritizing models of Richard N. Bolles in his workshops and best-selling *Parachute* books. Chapter 7 is grounded in research on human values by Louis Raths, Sidney Simon, and others in the values clarification movement, and on the research of work values by Donald Super. Chapter 8 is based on career indecision research summarized in an article in the *Career Development Quarterly* by Virginia Gordon and on the ideas of Lee Isaacson and Elwood Chapman. Chapter 9 takes much of its inspiration from the decision-making model of Robert Carkhuff, H. B. Gelatt, Irving Janis, and Leon Mann. Chapter 10 uses material on trends in college education from the Labor Department's *Occupational Outlook Quarterly* and an exercise adapted from force field analysis of Kurt Levin. The writing of this book, being guided by several outstanding leaders in the field of career development, gives it a strong theoretical and practical background.

I am indebted to the following reviewers for their helpful comments: Janet Corcoran, Ohlone College; Patricia Crowe, North Iowa Area Community College; Carrie DeLeon, Columbia Basin College; Margo Jackson, Fordham University; Jill Jurgens, Old Dominion University; William Kolodinsky, Northern Arizona University, Yuma; Nancy Levine, Mitchell College; Robert Spier, Hartnell College; Myra Swanson, Raritan Valley Community College; Timothy Thomason, Northern Arizona University; Jan Wencel, University of Southern Florida; and Laurie Williamson, Appalachian State University.

Robert D. Lock

Introduction to Career Planning

You may be saying to yourself as you open this book, "Is learning about career planning and decision making really worth it? Nothing seems to last very long in today's world. The uncertainties we face—economic downturns, massive layoffs, accelerated change, corporate corruption, disappearing benefits, bankruptcies, terrorist attacks, family problems, and so on—how can anyone plan in a time like this?" Could this be why so many people give so little thought to making career plans? A nationwide survey for the National Career Development Association found that only 32 percent started their present job or career where they had made a conscious choice and followed a definite plan (Miller and Vetter, 1999). Apparently, the 68 percent who did not make career plans relied on luck to rescue them. Luck, however, usually involves being prepared for opportunity, one of many benefits of career development programs.

There is plenty of evidence that career planning can be effective. After reviewing extensive studies, Herr and Cramer (1996) assert that the impact of career counseling is perhaps stronger than any other kind of psychological influence on individuals. The same two authors cite research from a survey of 47 articles that positive gains and improvements in career maturity and decision-making skills are reported in 93 percent of long-term (course) programs. I can give personal testimony to the positive gains of career planning from course evaluations (voluntary and unsigned) of over 3,000 community college students. Not all these students could make a definite choice of an occupation at the end of the course. Making a firm career choice is nice, but that never can be a promise from the beginning. What is important is that you learn a career decision-making process you can use at any time in your life. This process takes time and effort. It means considering social forces and labor trends (Chapter 2); examining your personality, interests, achievements, abilities, and values to create reasonable occupational prospects (Chapters 3, 5, 6, and 7); getting information about occupations that interest you (Chapter 4); learning the skills of decision making (Chapters 8 and 9), and reality-testing your choices (Chapter 10).

Is learning about career planning and decision making worth it? The answer, in a word, is—yes! Consider what is at stake: by far the largest part of your waking hours,* a personal identity, a source of income, and most of your physical and mental well-being. The work you do in life involves your best years, gives you a living, and describes who you are. It determines much of your lifestyle as well as your physical and emotional health. Few aspects of life are as important as work. If you don't think so, ask anyone without a job—he or she will quickly tell you how important work is.

Few people will say career decisions are easy. How often have you thought how nice it would be to have a career, or simply a job, fall directly into your lap? But the "real world" seldom works that way. Common to all career problems is a gap between the reality that prevails and things we hope for. We would like our career problems to be plain and straightforward; instead, they are likely to be complicated by internal desires and outside pressures. An answer to a career problem is often not a single clear choice, but one involving multiple options. Some uncertainty almost always accompanies the expected outcome of a choice; no solution to a career problem automatically promises success and satisfaction. A decision about a major career problem usually leads to another, unforeseen, set of problems (Reardon, Lenz, Sampson, and Peterson, 2000). Making a career decision is a challenging task, no way around it.

A note about language: The words *career, occupation,* and *job* are terms that mean the same to a lot of people. A *career* is a sequence of a person's work experiences over time (Arthur, Hall, and Lawrence, 1989); it is the broadest concept of the three. An *occupation* is one's vocation, business, calling, profession, or trade. Many people change occupations in mid-career. The term *occupation* takes a middle place between *career* and *job.* A *job* is a position of employment within an occupation. A person can

---

*To be exact, 76,900 hours for the average American, according to Patterson and Kim (1991).

have a succession of jobs in the same occupation. Thus a career spans a period of time that may involve one occupation or several, in which a person can hold a series of jobs. For example, network administrator is a job. Information technology is an occupation. The progression from data entry operator to network administrator shows a career.

How do you go about planning a career? It may help you to know that logical, systematic methods exist, and this book suggests one. The process is rational, although there is plenty of room for imagination along the way. This chapter outlines several theories of career choice and development, providing an overview and an underlying logic for the book's career-planning program. Chapter 1, like those that follow, contains exercises to stimulate your thinking. For example, in the "Ideal Job Description" you describe a working situation that you believe would be perfect for you. That may sound impractical now, but later you can compare your dream job with the real jobs you are researching. Some career planners have used the closest approximation to their ideal job as a basis for creating another prospective occupation.

GETTING STARTED

Have you ever found yourself in one of the following situations?

Which direction? You are registering for the next semester of school. A counselor asks, "What are you planning to major in?" You really don't know—it's such a troublesome subject that you've always managed to put it off. You feel pressure to choose an occupational goal. Your friends seem established in their programs, and now the counselor is asking that tough question just because you have to get some courses approved for the next term.

The wrong job. You are caught in a job that is not right for you. You have known this for some time, but you can't seem to get out. You'll miss the money, but there has to be more to life than the 8-to-5 grind you have now. Other people listen to your problem, offer suggestions, and tell you to change—but change to what? You know that some other work might give you even less satisfaction, so you don't want to change just for the sake of change. Still, you've got to do something. Staying in the same deadening job you have now is simply too depressing.

Back to school. You have been out of the workplace for several years. Going back to school for training is sort of frightening because you've been away from it so long. You or your family could use the extra money work could bring, and you need a new challenge to get more out of life. You must conquer your fears and "get on with it." The question is, "Get on with what?"

Laid off. You've been a faithful worker for a company for many years. Suddenly, it merges with another company, goes bankrupt or out of business, or downsizes and lays off people. You are forced to make a career change—something you never expected.

All these situations involve people who are stuck, immobilized, undecided, or unable to get moving in their careers. This happens to just about everyone, sooner or later. The need for work has a central place in people's lives, and the career and educational choices we make are just as important. When we identify who we are to others, we usually do so in occupational terms—student, parent, farmer, teacher, cook, forester—or one of thousands of titles we use to describe the way we work. Because of the significance of making appropriate career decisions, you enroll in a career-planning course or seek career counseling. The reasons for doing so are many and varied, leading some career researchers to classify people into types of career decision makers based on their degree of decidedness. Can you find yourself in any of these groups, described in the three paragraphs that follow?

1. You have already *decided* on a career goal or educational major; even so, you are *uncertain* about how suitable this choice is for you. Maybe you were pressured into deciding because the school asked you to declare a major or you wanted to satisfy your parents (or someone significant in your life). Or you may have accepted a new job immediately after the old job ended, simply because the opportunity presented itself. Whatever happened, you have some doubts about the choice you made, and now it's time to "check it out" through counseling or a course in career decision making.

2. You acknowledge you are *undecided* about making a career decision, but you believe you are ready and able to make one. You may worry about committing yourself to one option. You may realize you do not know enough about yourself and the occupational world, but you are willing to do the necessary exploration of these subjects. Whatever your reasons are for being undecided, you believe the problem can be solved or at least alleviated through a program of career development.

3. A third group of reasons people seek help for career *indecision* comes from an overpowering sense of anxiety and tension surrounding the experience of trying to make a career decision. You may feel apprehension and uneasiness about the way life is going. You may regard yourself unable to make decisions in *all* aspects of your life, not only about a career, and believe you are inadequate in coping with life's problems. You may constantly run into all sorts of barriers or feel controlled too much by others. You may see your life as aimless and become unmotivated to do much of anything about your problems. Many issues need to be worked on and resolved before you can be productively absorbed in something such as career decision making. Perhaps your personal concerns could be better handled in a one-on-one counseling relationship before getting into a course or group working on the subject of career development.

A career-planning course or career counseling can definitely be helpful to people in the first two groups but can be problematical for people in the third group. Career indecision has been widely studied over a long time. Researchers at first classified people as either decided or undecided. That method of dealing with career decision making has given way to a "multidimensional" concept (Multon, Heppner, and Lapan, 1995; Savickas, 1995), meaning we are now aware of a number of subtypes within both decided and undecided groups. These types are described in Chapter 8.

The concept of *career maturity* often comes up before starting on a program of career planning. Career maturity is your ability to make appropriate and informed career decisions, becoming aware of what is required to make career choices, and the degree to which those choices are realistic and consistent over time (Levinson, Ohler, Caswell, and Kiewra, 1998). Career maturity involves making truthful self-estimates of one's abilities, sufficient experience with the social environment, family togetherness, and personal characteristics such as self-respect and being thoughtful. Certain risk factors have been uncovered and identified; among them are low intelligence, poor education, social isolation, low self-esteem, and low or high intelligence compared with family or peers (Gottfredson, 1986). Another indication of career maturity concerns your willingness to plan for a career, explore occupations, gather information, and engage in making decisions (Super, 1983). Several assessment inventories exist to help you determine the degree to which you are ready to embark on a project of career decision making. A career counselor can help you identify, complete, and interpret an appropriate career-maturity inventory. Examine your readiness for enrolling in a career development course or for seeking career counseling, so you and your counselor or teacher can determine the extent to which you will effectively concentrate your attention on career-planning activities.

CHOICE AND FREEDOM

One problem of living in a free society is that we must make choices—but are you really free to choose your occupation? There is a lot of debate on this question. One side says yes, emphasizing you can take charge of your life by using reason and logic. This approach is called a *rational, systematic* process of making career decisions. You get as much information, knowledge, and understanding as you can about yourself and work that interests you, bringing them together in a meaningful way that allows you to make a commitment to an occupation.

Another answer is no—you are not as free as you might think when making career choices. People are subject to forces they cannot control. This can be called the *sociocultural determinant* approach, because it focuses on social and cultural conditions you cannot influence. These include family background, income level of parents, parents' occupational and educational level, where you grow up, race, ethnicity, sex, and age. According to this theory, the kind of work you do is basically determined by environmental factors; the job chooses you more than you choose the job. Evidence shows that sociocultural factors do affect people's occupational choices. However true it may be, this deterministic view essentially denies people the freedom to choose.

A third view on occupational choice is the *accidental* or the *happenstance* approach. The world is so complex, why figure it out? Better to take life as it comes. Alan Watts (1975) tells a wonderful Taoist story about a farmer whose horse ran away. The neighbors commiserate with him over his bad luck, but he says, "Maybe." The next day, the horse returns with six wild horses. The neighbors proclaim his good fortune, but he says, "Maybe." His son then tries to tame a wild horse, gets thrown, and breaks a leg. The neighbors express great sympathy, but the farmer says, "Maybe." The next day, conscription officers come to the village to seize young men for the army. Because of the broken leg, the farmer's son is rejected. When the neighbors say how fortunate the farmer is, he says (naturally), "Maybe." Sometimes life seems to confirm the accidental approach. There is even a theory of "planned happenstance" where a person can take advantage of the opportunities presented by unpredictable events using the skills of curiosity, persistence, flexibility, optimism, and risk taking (Mitchell, Levin, and Krumboltz, 1999). To depend *entirely* on chance and luck involves enormous risks, but unplanned events are normal occurrences in life, and accidents have led to great discoveries.

Although I draw heavily on the rational, systematic approach to choosing occupations, I acknowledge the strength of social factors and the existence of luck and circumstance. Don't despair just because social forces exist and unplanned accidents occur. There is still plenty of room for conscious, reasoned planning. You have literally thousands of occupational prospects. This book can help you make a career decision, either through a class in career planning or independently with the help of a counselor. More importantly, it can show you how to generate numerous occupational alternatives, narrow them to a manageable few, and arrange them in order of preference.

The rapid pace of change today complicates career planning. With all the changes "out there" in the working world, a job in an occupational choice made early in life will probably not last an entire career lifetime. And if the nature of work weren't confusing enough in today's volatile economy, there are also changes going on within your own personality.

Career counseling is a profession that has evolved to help people plan for work that will use their abilities creatively, appeal to their interests, and express their important values at any point in their working lives. For much of the 20th century, career counseling was based on matching workers to jobs using logical, straightforward decision-making strategies. Now, career counseling takes a life span perspective rather than a single career choice point. A newer term for career planning is *career development*, meaning it takes into account more complex matters such as the influence of

What's in a Name?

Abbott	Carter	Fowler	Mason	Sexton
Archer	Chamberlain	Fuller	Master	Shephard
Armour	Chandler	Furman	Meyer	Shoemaker
Arrowsmith	Collier	Gardner	Miller	Skinner
Baker	Constable	Glover	Miner	Singer
Banks	Cook	Goldsmith	Noble	Smith/Schmidt
Barber	Cooper	Groom	Packer	Snyder/Schneider
Barker	Coppersmith	Hacker	Painter	Steward
Bauer	Corder	Hammersmith	Palmer	Tanner
Bellman	Cutler	Heater	Pargeter	Taylor
Bishop	Cutter	Hunter	Plummer	Tinker
Blocker	Dean	Judge	Pope	Turner
Boardman	Draper	Keeler	Porter	Tyler
Bookbinder	Duke	Kellner	Powdermaker	Waggoner
Bowman	Dyer	King	Priest	Waterman
Brewer	Falconer	Leatherman	Richter	Weaver
Butcher	Farmer	Lehrer	Sander	Webster
Butler	Fisher	Lerner	Sawyer	Wheeler
Carpenter	Fletcher	Locksmith	Saylor	Wright
Carrier	Forester	Marshall		

What do all these names have in common? These surnames—names that people have in common with their families—can be traced to occupational sources, as is true for about 15 percent of all American names. This list is only a sampling; there are many more family names with occupational roots. The connection between occupations and names is obvious in many cases, but with other names modern spelling disguises their occupational source.

psychological issues on career concerns and the impact of family, community, and social systems on a person's career choices (Brott, 2001).

You can easily be tempted to let someone (friend, parent, counselor) or something (inventory, test, computer) choose an occupation for you. Tell yourself that your career decision is too important to be left to someone or something else. Accept the responsibility of choosing an occupation and then be willing to live with the consequences of that decision. Of course, these words are easy to say but difficult to practice. At times you'll want to escape the responsibility that freedom of choice brings, but no good counselor, parent, friend, or test interpreter can encourage you to refuse that responsibility.

The main objective of this book is to help you develop career-planning skills that you can use as often as you need them, which will probably be several times during your life. A lot is at stake here. The effort you put into planning a career can lead to great rewards, both psychological and financial. You gain an identity from your occupation. You can fulfill yourself as a worker and contribute something to the world. There is a big investment in time: If you average 40 hours in 40 weeks for 40 years on the job, that's 64,000 working hours. If your yearly income averages $50,000 in that time, your total earnings will be $2 million. What you do at work determines much of what you do with the nonwork parts of your life. Work is at the very heart of life. The French writer Albert Camus remarked, "Without work all life goes rotten. But when work is soulless, life stifles and dies."

THE CAREER DECISION-MAKING PROCESS

An exact step-by-step sequence for a career-planning or problem-solving process is difficult to establish, because we all have our own individual differences and preferences. Bergland (1974) and Kinnier and Krumboltz (1984) have included these steps:

Define the problem, generate alternatives, gather and process information, assess self, investigate probable outcomes and select goals, start action, and evaluate plans. The process in this book has evolved from previous sources (among them are the two cited). In this book, the following eight sections of a career-planning process are identified and explained.

1. *Become aware and committed.* In this phase, realize that you are confused and undecided about your career future and become willing to dedicate yourself to a program of action toward resolving this problem.
2. *Study your environment.* Examine the social, economic, political, and geographic setting around you to consider the environmental factors that influence your career choice.
3. *Study yourself.* Analyze and process data about your personality characteristics—your interests, needs, achievements, abilities, and values.
4. *Generate alternatives.* Create several goals, plans, or courses of action to solve the problem of career indecision. These are called *occupational prospects.*
5. *Gather information.* Collect and study accurate information about your occupational prospects.
6. *Make the decision.* Determine a career goal from judgments you make about yourself and the characteristics of your occupational prospects.
7. *Implement the decision.* Put the career decision you have made into action by developing your own job search campaign.
8. *Get feedback.* Evaluate how well the career decision is working. If there is too much negative feedback, the process starts over again.

Let's next look at each of these eight sections in a little more detail.

1. Become aware and committed. You begin to solve a problem, such as career indecision, only when you recognize that the problem exists. Some students think they'll just take a few courses and somehow everything will fall into place. Many of these students never finish school, but even those who do may go on making one costly mistake after another. Once you become aware of the need to establish a career goal, commit yourself to a career-planning process and become an active agent in charting your own future.

Commitment to your own career planning cannot be emphasized enough. Lack of commitment defeats more people than any other single factor. A student may start a career-planning course, come faithfully to class for a few weeks, read the assigned material, and complete several inventories and exercises. A number of occupations begin to emerge as prospects, and the student is asked to investigate them. Research takes time; the student's commitment begins to waver. After missing a few classes, the student has gaps in learning; the whole career-planning process makes less and less sense. Eventually the student drops out. Time and money have been wasted, with nothing to show for it. Commitment, dedication, purpose, involvement, and persistence are qualities essential to career planning. Without them, little or nothing is going to happen.

2. Study your environment. Many aspects of your social environment affect career decisions. Among them are home, other people, school, place of worship, community, the economy, and political institutions. Geographic factors in your physical environment also influence decisions. The nature of the economy usually has a greater direct impact on career planning than any other single environmental factor; therefore Chapters 2 and 4 are devoted to studying work in the economy.

3. Study yourself. Honestly assessing yourself is one of the most difficult things you can do in life. You need self-knowledge to make judgments about your occupational prospects. Ask yourself questions such as, Do I have the ability and the energy to complete the education required for the occupation? Do my major work values correspond to those expressed in the occupation? What insights can I get from my previous experiences and achievements? You can start to answer these questions in Chapter 3 through individual exercises and group activities and the results of personality inventories. Your self-study continues in Chapters 5, 6, and 7. The fundamental question of identity is raised here: "Who am I—*really?*" As with the career decision itself, you have the ultimate responsibility for answering that question.

4. Generate alternatives. In career planning, alternatives are different potential occupations that look attractive. Many ways of generating occupational alternatives exist; you will encounter them in Chapter 3. Whether you examine a deck of career cards, use a computer-based guidance system, take interest inventories, analyze your daydreams for occupational content, engage in fantasy exercises, glance through career books and pamphlets, or talk with workers about their jobs, you will begin to get suggestions for occupations to put on your prospect list. An *occupational prospect* is simply an occupation that interests you enough to motivate you to spend some time researching it.

5. Gather information. As you work on expanding your list of occupational prospects, remind yourself that one of those occupations could provide you with a livelihood. Because you could spend a lot of time in that occupation, it deserves thorough research. Will the pay and benefits be enough to enable you to live the kind of life you wish to live? Will this job deliver the psychological satisfaction you want from your work? Do you have the resources to meet the challenges and responsibilities of the occupation? Can you cope with its demands and frustrations? What are the typical characteristics of people who enter such an occupation? Will there be a steady demand for workers in this field? How much and what kind of education is needed? Information to answer these and other questions is available if you know where to look and whom to consult. This subject is covered in Chapter 4.

6. Make the decision. You need a way to arrange all the information you gather about yourself and your occupational prospects so you can arrive at some tentative or definite conclusions about future career direction. You can use Chapter 8 to reduce the number of your occupational prospects to a manageable size. In Chapter 9, you are guided through a set of career decision-making exercises, finishing with a preferred occupational choice, a next most-preferred choice, and so on. You are in charge of all the judgments and evaluations that go into ranking your occupational prospects. In the final analysis, you are responsible for your own decisions. You can learn how to make a decision from this book, but only you can make the decision itself.

Understand from the outset that your career decisions may change as you receive new information. Decisions about jobs are not made for all time, nor will your ranked order of occupational prospects necessarily stay the same. A second or third choice may become your first choice at some future time. Your personality and the environment continue to change, so the original ranking of your occupational alternatives will need to be re-examined.

7. Implement the decision. Implementing means putting your career decision into practice. Some career-planning programs stop with the decision itself. For some students, that may be enough for the time being—but what good is a choice if you don't act on it? The following activities and skills are involved in this action phase of career planning:

- *Education and training.* Determine the educational majors and degrees (if any) that are needed for the occupational choice, the costs, the length of the training, where the education is available, and how (and how much) financial aid can be obtained.
- *Work experience.* Part-time and summer job experiences can give you direct knowledge of the job world you will enter after school. If your temporary

work experience can be related to a definite career goal, so much the better. For example, being a summer playground director is excellent for a person going into the fields of recreation, physical education, or teaching.

- *Job leads.* Learn how to obtain information about job openings from a variety of sources—personal contacts, the Internet, school career services, employment agencies, and publications.
- *Writing skills.* Learn how to write job search materials such as cover letters, résumés, follow-up letters, and applications.
- *Research skills.* Learn how to determine where you want to live and work by investigating geographic areas and workplaces before you move to a community and start work.
- *Speaking skills.* Learn how to manage job and informational interviews with potential employers and people who have special knowledge about jobs.
- *Keeping a job once it has been obtained.* Develop skills and attitudes that will help you hold a job in an occupation you have chosen.

Education and a brief summary of job hunting are covered in Chapter 10 and Appendix A: *Implementing Your Career Decision—The Job Search.* A thorough treatment of job hunting is the subject of the second book in this series, *Job Search.*

8. Get feedback. Feedback involves awareness of your emotional reaction to how well your career decision is working as you move into a job and continue with it. When your personal characteristics fit well with those of the job, your internal feedback messages are more positive than negative. You experience more personal satisfaction, feelings of accomplishment, and increased self-esteem, along with the external rewards of money and status a suitable job can bring. However, even the best career decision can lead to frustrations and disappointments. You change, and your environment changes. The job that once looked so good may begin to produce more negative than positive internal feedback messages. Perhaps this is a signal to set the career decision-making process in motion again. (Actually, the career development process is never finished; experiences can restart it again at any time.) When negative feelings about a job situation become overwhelming, you find yourself back at the beginning; you are aware of a career problem and need to commit yourself to repeating at least part of the decision-making process. You can stay temporarily in a bad job while recycling this career-planning process, but you must eventually change jobs for the sake of your health and emotional well-being. Feedback renders our career decision-making model more dynamic and open-ended. Life today is more likely to embrace a series of starts and stops, improvisations, and new commitments that may seem disconnected at first but perhaps later can be seen to compose an integrated whole (Bateson, 1989).

Awareness and commitment, knowledge of the social environment, self-knowledge, occupational alternatives, information about occupational prospects, decision making, implementation, and feedback or re-evaluation are the chief components of the career-planning process. Look at Figure 1-1 on the next page for a graphic overview of this career-planning model.

THEORIES OF OCCUPATIONAL CHOICE AND CAREER DEVELOPMENT

"There is nothing more practical than a good theory" (Stefflre, 1965). Some people don't believe this statement; they think theory is unrelated to real life. Nothing could be further from the truth. Theory seeks to give us guidelines for action and bring order out of chaos. This book is based on theory and its practical applications. As you read the brief outlines of the career theories in the pages ahead, relate these theories to your own life.

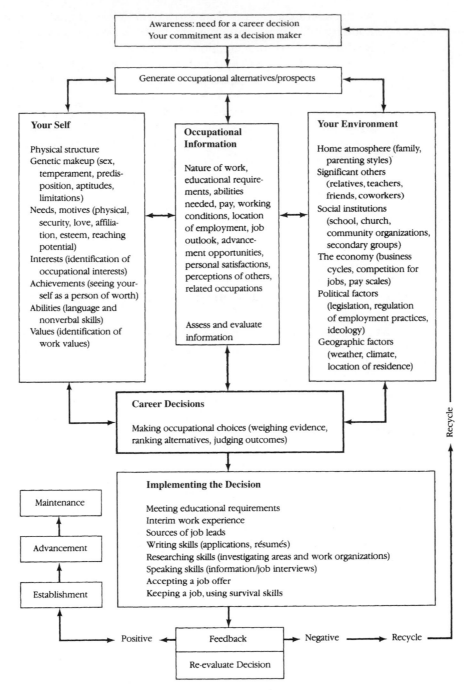

Figure 1-1   A comprehensive model of career planning

Roe's Theory of Occupational Choice

In "The Rainbow," the poet William Wordsworth wrote, "The Child is father of the Man." Sigmund Freud, father of psychoanalytic psychology, taught that the first few years of childhood mold the personality for the remainder of life. Anne Roe, a clinical psychologist, proposed the idea that early childhood experiences are strongly related to occupational choices. Think of the home atmosphere in which you were raised. Was it mostly "warm" or "cold"? How would you describe your parents? Were they attentive or neglectful? Accepting or rejecting? According to Roe's theory, your answers have implications for the career you choose (Roe, 1956, 1957). In her theory, Roe uses psychologist Abraham Maslow's hierarchy of human needs. According to this hier-

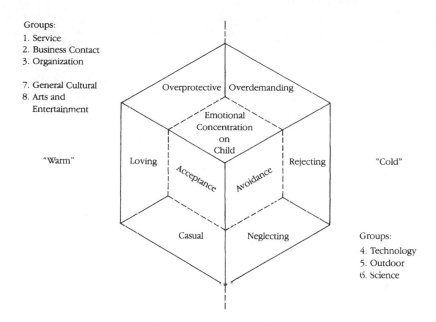

Figure 1-2 Roe's theory of career choice. *Source:* Based on Roe (1957).

archy, people start with physiological needs such as food and shelter, followed by needs for security and safety. Once these basic needs are met, we advance to more psychological needs—love and friendship, esteem and achievement, and finally, self-actualization, the realization of one's full potential. As each need is met, the next higher one moves into awareness. Needs that are not fully satisfied can be important motivators in occupational choices. A person aware of a need for security, for example, is likely to search for work providing a safe environment.

Roe outlines early parent–child relationships from the standpoint of need satisfaction or frustration and analyzes three basic attitudes children experience with their parents: emotional concentration, avoidance, and acceptance. *Emotional concentration* on the child ranges from an overly protective style to an overly demanding one. A balance between these two extremes may show itself as anxiety over a first child, followed by less worry about a second child. (This may account for personality differences between children in the same family.) Roe believes that both overprotective and overly demanding parents put conditions on their love and approval. Whereas physical needs are readily met, psychological needs are often withheld if the child does not measure up to the parents' expectations. The overprotected child, learning that conformity to the desires of others brings rewards, thus becomes dependent on others for gratification. An overly demanding parent sets exacting standards for behavior and expects high achievement from the child, withdrawing approval for failure to perform as the parent wishes. People who adopt extremely high standards from their parents may develop a high degree of perfectionism. This can cause them to experience more difficulty in making career decisions because of anxiety that they might show themselves to be less than perfect (Leong and Chervinko, 1996).

A second style of parenting is *avoidance,* ranging from neglect to rejection. Within limits, both physical and psychological needs of the child are ignored, although not intentionally in the case of neglect. Roe uses the term "emotional rejection" to indicate that not all rejection means actual physical neglect. The third style of parent–child interaction is *acceptance* of the child, either on a casual or a loving basis, where physical and psychological needs are met. Independence and self-reliance are encouraged in either an unconcerned, noninvolved way or an active, supportive one. See Figure 1-2 for an illustration of the dynamics of Roe's theory.

According to Roe, you are likely to choose a work situation that reflects the psychological climate of the home in which you grew up. If your home was warm, loving,

Table 1-1 Roe's Classification of Occupations and Levels

Groups of Occupations	Occupation Levels
I. Service	1. Professional and Managerial—1
II. Business Contact	2. Professional and Managerial—2
III. Organization	3. Semiprofessional and Small Business
IV. Technology	4. Skilled
V. Outdoor	5. Semiskilled
VI. Science	6. Unskilled
VII. General Cultural	
VIII. Arts and Entertainment	

Source: Roe (1956).

accepting, or overprotecting, you will probably choose an occupation in the categories of service, business contact, organization, general cultural, or arts and entertainment, where the orientation is toward people. A career choice in the technology, outdoor, or science groups indicates that you may have experienced a colder, neglecting, rejecting, or overly demanding home climate, because these occupations deal with things, plants and animals, or ideas more than they do with people. Roe has developed a two-way occupational classification system with *eight groups of occupations* and *six levels of ability and motivation*, forming 48 cells into which a specific occupation may be placed. Look at Table 1-1 and circle the *group* and *level* in which you believe you belong. More information about the eight groups and six levels is available in Exercise 4-5 of Chapter 4.

Roe and others subjected her theory to testing and research. The relationship between childhood experience and adult occupational choice was not found to be as strong as Roe had anticipated. Parents are not as consistent as the theory would require. Were your parents always consistent in their relationships with you? More likely, there was a mixture of attention, acceptance, and avoidance. Also, your mother and father may each have had different parenting styles; one might have been mostly accepting whereas the other was basically overly demanding. Another drawback to Roe's theory is that it does not take into account many events in normal human development between early childhood and adult career outcomes (Osipow and Fitzgerald, 1996).

Nonetheless, Roe's theory has importance. Her model was one of the first theories to suggest personality factors, childhood events, parental influences, and psychological needs could be significant in making career choices. Roe's ideas stimulated a great deal of research about how and why people choose their occupations. Her classification of occupations has influenced the measurement of people's interests. Finally, Roe's theory asks you to examine your early life. It seems reasonable to propose that your experiences as a child will have lasting effects on who and what you become as an adult.

Holland's Theory of Careers

John Holland advances the hypothesis that career choices are an expression of personality. "The choice of an occupation is an expressive act which reflects the person's motivation, knowledge, personality, and ability. Occupations represent a way of life, an environment rather than a set of isolated work functions or skills. To work as a carpenter means not only to use tools but also to have a certain status, community role, and a special pattern of living" (Holland, 1997, p. 9).

Holland believes people develop stereotypes or typical images of occupations. "Just as we judge people by their friends, dress, and actions, so we judge them by their vocations. Everyday experience generates a sometimes inaccurate but apparently useful knowledge of what people in various occupations are like. Thus we believe carpenters are handy, lawyers aggressive, actors self-centered, salespeople persuasive, accountants precise, scientists unsociable, and the like" (Holland, 1997, p. 9). Research studies demonstrate that many vocational stereotypes have some validity.

Holland makes the assumption that most people can be classified as having one of six types of personal orientation to life: realistic, investigative, artistic, social, enterprising, or conventional. These types are models against which we can measure the real person (Holland, 1997). The *realistic* types (mechanics, farmers) prefer activities that require physical strength, motor coordination, and the handling of objects such as machines and tools. *Investigative* types (chemists, biologists) prefer scientific thinking, solving problems, and scholarly activity. *Artistic* types (musicians, artists) like free, unstructured pursuits that call for the creation of art, writing, music, drama, dance, and so on. *Social* types (social workers, teachers) seek contact with people in teaching and helping situations. *Enterprising* types (salespeople, managers) prefer situations where they can persuade and control people to attain organizational goals or economic gains. *Conventional* types (accountants, clerks) like activities that call for the orderly, systematic handling of data and materials.

By comparing your personal traits with the characteristics of each of the six model types, you can determine the one you resemble most. After this is done, Holland suggests, make a hierarchy of types in descending order. For example, you might resemble the realistic model most, then the investigative, and then the others, on down to the type you resemble least. Your pattern of six types is what Holland calls your *personality pattern* (Holland, 1997). The six categories combine into 720 possible personality patterns, one of which best describes you. Holland has constructed an inventory called the "Self-Directed Search" to measure your resemblance to each personality type.

Holland uses the same six labels for work environments, each of which is dominated by the corresponding personality type. In the realistic work environment, for example, the largest percentage of people would reflect the realistic personality. This same matching occurs in each of the five remaining types. You search for work environments that will let you use your skills, express your values, and take on compatible roles. If you are blocked from going into your most appropriate work environment, you could move to an occupation or work role that is appropriate to your second-strongest orientation.

Ask yourself, "What personality type do I most closely resemble?"

Write that type in this space: _____   _____

Which type would be second? _____

Third? _____

More information about Holland's theory is given in Chapter 3.

Theories of Career Development: Ginzberg and Super

The vocational theories of Eli Ginzberg and his associates (1951) and of Donald Super (1957) are based on developmental stages through which everyone progresses. Other writers have conceived of life as a series of stages. For example, William Shakespeare, in *As You Like It* (Act II, scene 7), has one of his characters describe the seven ages of a person's life:

> All the world's a stage,
> And all the men and women merely players.
> They have their exits and their entrances,
> And one man in his time plays many parts,
> His acts being seven ages. At first the infant,
> Mewling and puking in the nurse's arms.
> Then the whining schoolboy, with his satchel

Table 1-2 Ginzberg's Stages of Career Development

1	2 a b c d	3 a b c
Fantasy period	Tentative period a. Interest stage b. Capacity stage c. Value stage d. Transition stage	Realistic period a. Exploration stage b. Crystallization stage c. Specification stage

> And shining morning face, creeping like snail
> Unwillingly to school. And then the lover,
> Sighing like furnace, with a woeful ballad
> Made to his mistress' eyebrow.
> Then a soldier, Full of strange oaths . . .
> Jealous in honor, sudden and quick in quarrel . . .
> And then the justice, In fair round belly . . .
> With eyes severe and beard of formal cut . . .
> The sixth age shifts
> Into the lean and slipper'd Pantaloon
> With spectacles on nose and pouch on side . . .
> Last scene of all,
> That ends this strange eventful history,
> Is second childishness and mere oblivion.

Ginzberg views career development as a long-term process divided into three periods—fantasy, tentative, and realistic—with career decisions being an optimal adjustment between your ideal preferences and the available job opportunities (see Table 1-2). Ask yourself, "Where am I now on Ginzberg's career development line in Table 1-2?"

The *fantasy* period is illustrated by children's play as they imagine themselves in work roles they see adults performing. Children become famous athletes, astronauts, movie stars, and cowboys for the simple delight of the activity, ignoring realistic considerations of ability and potential. The *tentative* period is divided into the stages of interest, capacity, value, and transition. The interest stage begins when you become aware of things you like or dislike. The capacity stage shows itself when you discover that you can do some things better than others. The value stage appears when you become conscious that some things are more important to you than others. A transition stage is marked by more self-reliance and awareness of occupations and brings you to the *realistic* period. The exploration stage of this period begins when you enter college or full-time work for the first time and investigate several occupations, even though a specific choice is not needed for some time. The next stage is crystallization, when a career pattern emerges and you declare a college major or commit yourself to a particular kind of work. Finally, a specification stage is reached, when you specialize in graduate school or select a specific job. Ginzberg cautions against interpreting his theory too rigidly; variations in the pattern are possible. Some people select an occupation early in life and never change from it, whereas others make widely different occupational choices before establishing themselves in a clear pattern. Some may never complete the process, or never determine a pattern at all (Osipow, 1983; Zaccaria, 1970).

Psychologists are well known for their identification of stages in human life. Sigmund Freud detected five stages of psychosexual development. Erik Erikson set out eight psychosocial stages of human life. Donald Super has developed a theory that emphasizes stages of vocational development. "Choice is, in fact, a process rather than an event. The term should denote a whole series of choices, generally resulting in the elimination of some alternatives and the retention of others, until in due course the narrowing down process results in what might perhaps be called an occupational choice" (Super, 1957, p. 184).

Super conceives of vocational development as one part of your total growth over your life span. In addition to the role of worker, you play a variety of other roles at certain ages, including child, student, citizen, spouse, parent, homemaker, leisurite, and pensioner (Osborne et al., 1997). Super divides the vocational part of life into the following stages:

1. *Growth stage.* This is a period of general physical and psychological development, when you form attitudes and behaviors that shape your *self-concept* for the rest of your life. (*Self-concept* in simple terms means "the characteristics you ascribe to yourself.")

   a. *Prevocational substage.* No interest in or involvement with careers and occupational choices is expressed.
   b. *Fantasy substage.* Needs and fantasy are the bases of vocational thinking.
   c. *Interest substage.* Thoughts about occupations are based on your likes and dislikes.
   d. *Capacity substage.* Abilities and career requirements are considered.

2. *Exploration stage.* You become aware that a career will be a major part of your life, and you begin to explore occupations in school, part-time work, and leisure activities.

   a. *Tentative substage.* Needs, interests, abilities, and values become the basis for occupational choices.
   b. *Transition substage.* As you enter the job market or seek further education and training, realistic considerations about employment opportunities in the world of work characterize your thinking.
   c. *Trial substage.* You find and try out a beginning work role you believe is a potential life's work, but at this point you have not made a final commitment.

3. *Establishment stage.* You believe you have found your appropriate field of work, and you try to create a permanent place in it.

   a. *Stabilization (or second trial) substage.* One or two career changes may mark this period, but there is greater commitment to an occupational choice. (For some people, it may become clear that work could possibly be a series of unrelated occupations.)
   b. *Advancement substage.* As the career pattern becomes clearer, you put forth efforts to make a secure place for yourself in the world of work. For many, this is a time of creativity and promotion.

4. *Maintenance stage.* Your major concern is continuation in your chosen occupation, holding onto the gains you have established.

5. *Disengagement stage.* Physical and mental activity decrease; work slows down and, in due time, stops.

   a. *Deceleration.* This is a time of declining work activity. Some people take on part-time work to replace their full-time career.
   b. *Retirement.* Work stops—easily, with difficulty, or only with death.

Ask yourself, "Where am I now in Super's design of vocational development?" Look at Table 1-3, and mark approximately where you are on the career development line. Your answer could give an indication of your *vocational maturity*, to use Super's words. Vocational maturity here means developing attitudes, performing behaviors, and completing tasks that are appropriate at various stages in life. Accomplishing vocational developmental tasks at certain stages does not always occur in well-ordered sequences. For example, a person reaching the maintenance stage may experience new growth, decide a job change is needed, and recycle the exploration stage (Zunker, 2002). These tasks, attitudes, and behaviors are summarized in Table 1-4.

Table 1-3 Super's Stages of Vocational Development

Stages	a b c d	a b c	a b		a b
	Growth	Exploration	Establishment	Maintenance	Disengagement
Substages	a. Prevocational b. Fantasy c. Interest d. Capacity	a. Tentative b. Transition c. Trial	a. Stabilization b. Advancement		a. Deceleration b. Retirement

Table 1-4 Vocational Developmental Tasks

Life Stage	Vocational Development Task	Description	Attitudes and Behaviors Appropriate to Vocational Developmental Tasks
Early adolescence	*Crystallizing* a vocational preference	Developing ideas about work that are appropriate for yourself	Awareness of the need to crystallize, use of personal resources, noticing environmental factors, distinguishing interests from values, awareness of present/future relationships, developing a generalized preference, obtaining information on and planning for the preferred occupation, and wisdom of the vocational preference
Middle adolescence	*Specifying* a vocational preference	Narrowing a general career direction into a specific one	Attitudes and behaviors similar to crystallization task, but relating to the need for specification
Late adolescence	*Implementing* a vocational preference	Completing training and entering suitable employment	Awareness of the need to carry out the vocational preference, planning to implement the preference, accomplishing plans to qualify for job entry, and obtaining an entry-level job
Young adulthood	*Stabilizing* in a vocation	Settling into a field of work showing appropriateness of choice	Awareness of the need to stabilize, planning for stabilization, becoming qualified for a stable regular job (or accepting the inevitability of instability), and obtaining a stable regular job (or acting on resignation to instability)
Middle adulthood	*Consolidating* status and advancing in a vocation	Creating a secure job position for yourself	Awareness of the need to consolidate and advance, gaining information on how to consolidate and advance, planning for consolidation and advancement, and carrying out these plans

Sources: Osipow (1983); Super (1957); Zaccaria (1970).

Super has studied career patterns that can be seen in workers' lives. The career patterns described next are adapted from Super's work. Ask yourself which career pattern is—or will be—most descriptive of you, and circle it. Which pattern do you believe is most prevalent in the economy today?

- *Occupation-stable career pattern.* School, then a series of jobs in the same occupation, but for different employers
- *Organization-stable career pattern.* School, then employment in one organization in different occupations within the company
- *Conventional career pattern.* School, then one or more trial jobs, then stable employment
- *Double-track career pattern.* School, then two occupations pursued at the same time

- *Interrupted career pattern.* School, then work experience, then suspension of work, then return to school (possibly) or work (most common to people who drop out of the labor force for such reasons as being laid off or caring for children)
- *Unstable career pattern.* School, then an alternating sequence of trial and unstable jobs with no permanent occupation, or one potential career sacrificed for another
- *Multiple-trial career pattern.* School, then a series of occupational changes in unrelated trial jobs without really establishing a career. (Adapted from Srebalus, Marinelli, and Messing, 1982; Super, 1957; Zaccaria, 1970)

Super writes, "In choosing an occupation one is, in effect, choosing a means of implementing a *self-concept*" (Super, 1957, p. 196). A self-concept can be described as a set of beliefs you have about yourself. It is your answer to the question "Who am I?" A healthy self-concept emerges as you progress through the tasks and master the crises of each stage of vocational development. When you choose an occupation, you say in effect, "I am this or that kind of person." When you work in and adjust to an occupation, you discover whether your work is agreeable and lets you play the role you want in life. Working in an occupation is one way to test your self-concept against reality and to see if you can live up to the image you have of yourself (Super, 1957).

Krumboltz's Social Learning Theory

Social learning theory is linked to stimulus–response behaviorism, which, to many people, raises the threat of external control and loss of personal freedom. Although the theory does state that certain limits to freedom must be recognized, it emphasizes that human behavior can be controlled by the individual as well as by the environment. Most behavioral programs call for self-management.

John Krumboltz, a social learning theorist, identifies four types of influences on making career decisions (Mitchell, Jones, and Krumboltz, 1979). First are *genetic characteristics* (race, sex, physical appearance, handicaps), which can expand or restrict your career preferences, and special abilities, such as intelligence, musical and artistic ability, and muscular coordination. Second are *environmental conditions and events*, such as job entry requirements being determined by employers or government officials, labor laws and union rules, natural forces (floods, dry spells, earthquakes, hurricanes), availability of and demand for natural resources, and new developments in technology. Countless *past learning experiences* also influence career decisions. Krumboltz identifies two kinds of learning experiences—those where you act on the environment, and those where you respond to the environment. The fourth type of influence is the variety of *skills, performance standards, and values* you develop as you approach each new task or problem.

As a result of these influences, you make observations about yourself, use learned skills to work on tasks, and take actions to manage problems. Your *self-observations* can be recorded and measured using interest inventories, which ask whether you like, are indifferent to, or dislike certain activities. Adjective checklists, where you select words you believe describe you, and value surveys, where you indicate the relative importance of things, are other ways of making observations about yourself. You *learn skills* to interpret and cope with your environment and make predictions about the future. In career planning, your skills are used in clarifying values, setting goals, predicting future events, generating occupational alternatives, seeking information, interpreting past events, and eliminating and selecting alternatives. *Actions* are behaviors you have learned and put into practice. Examples of actions in career planning are applying for jobs, accepting a job offer or promotion, and starting a program of study.

Why do you express preferences for certain occupations and not for others? Your preferences reflect learned responses, say the social learning theorists. When you get positive reinforcement, such as praise or recognition for doing something associated with an occupation, you are more likely to express a preference for that occupation. If you get an *A* in chemistry, you are more likely to be encouraged to become a chemist than someone who gets a *C*. Other examples of positive reinforcements are observing someone with whom you identify, succeeding in an occupation, being directly encouraged into an occupation by someone you admire, and encountering positive words and images about it. Positive reinforcement also works for learning skills and taking actions that are necessary in career planning.

Receiving no reinforcement and being punished for your preferences, skills, and actions are negative influences that can weaken an occupational preference or eliminate it entirely. Some illustrations of negative reinforcement are low grades in school, observing others unable to find jobs in their chosen fields, hearing parents or others ridicule and degrade certain occupations, and seeing a movie or reading a book that depicts a particular kind of worker as corrupt. Still others are being overruled when making your own career plans, concluding you have no control over your future, being unable to locate information, and being denied access to the training necessary for entrance into an occupation (Mitchell, Jones, and Krumboltz, 1979).

One aspect of social learning theory as it applies to career planning is to identify troublesome beliefs you might have about making career decisions and searching for jobs (Krumboltz, 1983). Albert Ellis calls these thoughts "irrational beliefs" (Ellis, 1962) and Aaron Beck labels them "faulty reasoning" (Beck, 1972). Confront or test the validity, rationality, or accuracy of your career thoughts, either by yourself or with the help of a counselor. Some of your beliefs may be self-defeating. If you don't challenge them, you might choose an unrealistic occupation or fail to recognize a possible occupation that would be satisfying to you. Because decision making is stressful and sometimes painful, people may react to this pressure by becoming rigid and defensive. Instead, we can analyze ourselves, seek career guidance, and commit ourselves to a decision process. Several troubling thoughts about career decision making and the job search are listed next. You may have slipped into a pattern of self-defeating thinking because you have at times felt frustrated, depressed, guilty, bored, vulnerable, worthless, resentful, or anxious. Check any of these thoughts that you have had at any time. Restructure each into a more rational, productive way of thinking.

____ 1. Something is terribly wrong with me because I don't know what I want to do.

____ 2. All the others seem to have goals and know the occupations they want.

____ 3. Somewhere there is an expert or a test that will tell me the right occupation (or educational major) to choose.

____ 4. I will probably end up failing in my major field or a course of study that I really want.

____ 5. If the economy goes into a downturn or competition increases, I'll never get a job.

____ 6. Making a list of occupations to explore is a waste of time.

____ 7. I must find the one and only occupation that is just right for me.

____ 8. No one will hire me because I'm _____ (fill in the blank space).

____ 9. I'll never be successful in a career because I'm _____ (fill in the blank space).

____ 10. You really can't plan your career because the world changes too fast.

____ 11. No woman (or man) would enter an occupation like that.

____ 12. I can't work for a boss who is male (or female).

Any of these beliefs, if you hold them, can be challenged. Use three key questions when examining your beliefs: (1) How do I know this is true? (2) What steps could I take to find out if this is true? (3) What evidence could convince me that the opposite is true? (Mitchell and Krumboltz, 1990). Here are just a few bits of information that could dispute some of the beliefs just stated:

- There is more than just one right occupation for you; thousands of occupations, divided into groups with similar, related interests and abilities, are available.
- It is normal for people to be undecided about what they want to do; more than half of all students change their educational goals in the first year of college, and the average person now changes jobs 7 to 10 times over a career lifetime. In fact, career counselors usually prefer to work with people whose career goals are uncertain, because they are more willing to generate occupational alternatives to explore.
- Job seekers do land jobs, even in the hardest of times.
- Many employees do work willingly for a male (or female) boss.
- Thousands of people do succeed in occupations once "reserved" for the opposite sex.

When you think clearly, you can overcome the irrational thoughts that could defeat you in your career planning.

Cognitive Theories of Career Development

Cognitive information processing (CIP) theory is constructed on the idea that your brain takes in, codes, stores, and uses information in solving problems and making decisions. (The term *cognition* refers to the way you think and process information.) Career decision making is a problem-solving activity. You come up with an answer to a career problem in much the same way you figure out a solution to a mathematical or scientific problem. Career choices are based on how you think and feel about experiences in life. Your ability as a career problem solver depends on knowledge of yourself and occupations. Career development requires the use of long-term memories and a desire to become a better career problem solver, all part of your lifelong learning and growth. The quality of your vocational life is based on how well you make career decisions and solve career problems; you can improve these abilities by improving your cognitive information-processing skills (Reardon, Lenz, Sampson, and Peterson, 2000).

CIP theory focuses on how you make decisions. Five information-processing skills are used. They are known by the acronym CASVE: communication, analysis, synthesis, valuing, and execution. *Communication*, both internal and external, makes you aware of a gap between an ideal condition and the current situation, which can no longer be ignored. For career planning, the messages you receive may be an anxious feeling about being unsure of your career plans (internal communication). Parents or friends may ask you questions concerning a career after graduation (external communication). As a result, you recognize a need to make a career choice. *Analysis* requires information, gathered from research and observation, to improve the knowledge of your own interests, skills, and values and the knowledge of occupations, fields of study, work organizations, and so on. *Synthesis* brings together the accumulated information you have collected about yourself and occupations, expanding and then narrowing down your options to remove the gap that started the decision process. *Valuing* involves using your best judgment to set priorities on your remaining options and to choose an occupation, job, or college major. *Execution*, the final part of the CASVE cycle, means converting your thoughts into positive action and solving the career problem identified in the communication stage (Reardon et al., 2000).

Self-efficacy theory concerns a person's judgments about his or her ability to plan and take courses of action required to produce desired outcomes (Bandura, 1986). How you assess your competence to accomplish your goals influences your educational and career choices. If you think you cannot be effective in some part of career behavior, this belief may become detrimental or harmful to making a beneficial career choice (Betz and Hackett, 1986). Low self-efficacy might convince you to avoid enrolling in certain courses needed to prepare for a given occupation, despite evidence that you could succeed with effort in those courses. Some gifted women may underestimate their abilities in considering careers that employ men in greater numbers, or may make insufficient use of their abilities in male-dominated occupations (Betz, 1992). Likewise, minority people with different cultural backgrounds living in a larger population must often deal with negative images and misleading ideas about their abilities or potential, detracting from their sense of self-efficacy. Nonetheless, self-efficacy theory teaches that an honest or appropriate appraisal of your abilities can give you the confidence needed to establish a career goal and achieve it.

Social cognitive career theory (SCCT) emphasizes how thinking processes and beliefs control and direct a person's actions, rather than focus on the behaviors themselves. SCCT studies three concepts that markedly affect the career decision-making process: self-efficacy, outcome expectations, and personal goals. *Self-efficacy* beliefs center on an internal question, "Can I take this action—such as enroll in a particular course and complete it or enter a certain occupation and perform in it successfully?" By contrast, *outcome expectations* lead you to ask, "If I do this activity, what will happen?" Here you enter a set of personal beliefs about the results of an activity. You may anticipate a reward coming from outside of yourself (a good salary, an award, high praise, and so forth), or you may be motivated by the good feeling you expect to experience within yourself for an excellent achievement. When you believe the outcome of an activity will be successful, your interest in it will be higher. If you think some activity will end in failure, you will tend to lose interest in it. *Personal goals* are guides that support and maintain a given activity over a period of time. Some long-term goals require setting subgoals (or short-term goals). If the subgoals are accomplished, they in turn reinforce the long-term goal. Self-efficacy, expected outcomes, and goals are related to each other and influence each other in many ways. Although confidence in your abilities directly affects the achievement of your career goals, SCCT recognizes that environmental factors beyond your ability to control (such as few jobs, lack of money) have an impact on your career choices (Sharf, 2002).

Personal Construct Theory (PCT)

We humans are scientists, constantly examining our ideas about the world (making hypotheses and testing them) through actions (experimenting), and coming up with discoveries (findings) that lead us to make conclusions and construct concepts (theories) about the world we live in. From very early on in life, we look at the world and try to make sense of it by creating *constructs* that organize and structure events, other people, and the environment. Constructs are hypotheses or assumptions we use to test ideas and behavior we think will be effective (Ivey, 1980).

All of us have our own set of constructs by which we try to make sense of the world. Constructs are not the same as events; instead, they are sentences and groups of sentences we use to structure the world we experience. Personal construct theory (PCT) has been around for a while, but only recently has it been applied to career decision making. PCT is based on the work of George Kelly (1955). He reasoned that we view, or construct, the world differently from each other. Constructs apply to all aspects of life, among which is a career construct system that Kelly described as those ideas and concepts relating to career choices and work roles. We learn more about ourselves and the world of work as we grow and mature; this development allows our career constructs to become clearer and more apparent to ourselves. Our constructs are likely to change as we experience life events (marriage, working in various jobs, graduating, being laid off, receiving a job promotion, and so on).

Kelly devised the Repertory Test (or RepTest) to aid counselors and their clients in identifying the personal constructs used by the client. This test has been adapted for career counseling by Greg Niemeyer (1992). Clients furnish constructs that are connected to a number of occupations (usually 10) that interest them. The occupations are presented in sets of three at each time. The client is asked to indicate any way in which two occupations are alike, but different from the third. For example, two occupations are described as "allowing for creativity," whereas the third is viewed as "noncreative," and this distinction becomes a *vocational construct*. This compare and contrast technique continues with more combinations of three occupations until a number of constructs are elicited. The occupations are then ranked according to each construct by using a rating scale, which may be a seven-point scale (+3, +2, +1, 0, −1, −2, −3) or a 1-to-10 scale. Occupational preferences are determined, and the basis for those preferences can be revealed by examining the values expressed in evaluating occupations (Sharf, 2002). When you rank occupations in the career decision-making exercises of this book in Chapter 9, you will notice some strong similarities with this theory of personal constructs.

Integrative Life Planning

Integrative Life Planning (ILP) is a holistic career-planning model that goes beyond a linear process of choosing a vocation to viewing work in its relationship to other roles in life, or work within a life (Hansen, 2001). Career-planning practices concentrate on education and choosing an occupation for self-satisfaction. (Lately, planning for leisure has been added to the list.) ILP does not reject those approaches but insists they are not enough. Integration means bringing many different parts together. ILP seeks to include many pieces that should be linked with career planning—life roles of love, learning, labor, leisure, and citizenship; the multiple dimensions of body, mind, and spirit; family relationships; and connecting people to a mission of the larger society (Hansen, 1997).

The Integrative Life Planning approach is based on six interactive, critical life tasks. (1) *Finding work that needs doing.* Hansen (2001) finds 10 kinds of work particularly important: preserving the environment, constructive use of technology, understanding changes in the workplace and families, accepting changing gender roles, understanding diversity, reducing violence, reducing poverty and hunger, advocating for human rights, discovering new ways of knowing, and inquiring into spirituality and purpose. (2) *Weaving our lives into a meaningful whole*—one that embraces the social, intellectual, physical, spiritual, and emotional parts of human development as our occupational role. (3) *Connecting family and work*—emphasizing the need for men and women to share provider and nurturer roles in equal partnerships. New roles have risen with the occurrence of more two-income families, gay and lesbian families, single adults without children, single parents with children, and delayed marriages and parenting. (4) *Valuing pluralism and an inclusive worldview*—helping people to understand and adapt to growing diversity in the United States and other countries. (5) *Managing personal transitions and organizational change.* Making decisions is a big part of this task. The rational, logical, linear model of decision making may no longer be sufficient. Newer approaches to career planning prepare people for uncertainty, instability, ambiguity, and complexity. This task also emphasizes social change and the need for individuals to function as a change agent in their personal lives, families, and organizations. (6) *Exploring spirituality and life purpose.* Spirituality assumes a higher power outside of one's self, a sense of the inter-relatedness of all life. Increasingly, people are seeking greater purpose and balance in life, not wanting to give their entire lives over to their jobs and making money. There is a trend toward simplifying our lives and redefining success.

Enlarging on the last task, Hansen (1997) acknowledges the impact of other counseling theorists, psychologists, and theologians for their work on the connection between work and spirituality. Abraham Maslow developed the concept of "peak experiences" in which people get in touch with the spiritual part of their lives, allowing them to see the world as an integrated whole. Carl Rogers saw human wholeness as a pattern of interpersonal relationships and understanding the self from within. Gordon Allport wrote of the mature human being as having an ability to find a meaning or purpose that gives life unity despite tensions, ambiguities, and paradoxes. Viktor Frankl's therapy grew out of his experiences in Nazi concentration camps; he found that those who were not mentally destroyed from their horrifying ordeal searched for meaning, even though they were trapped in completely degrading and utterly humiliating circumstances (Frankl, 1963). Matthew Fox (1994) calls for a "re-invention of work" where life and livelihood are not separated; they flow from the same source, Spirit. Individual lives can be lived with meaning and purpose along with a sense of contributing to a larger community.

Now that you have read brief accounts of several career development theories, ask yourself, "Which one makes the most sense? Which is the most useful? Can I use pieces of several theories?" Construct your own personal theory of career planning and decision making. Parts of many theories are interwoven into the reading and exercises of this book to give you a comprehensive approach to career planning.

The theories described in this chapter illustrate or reflect several major schools of thought in vocational psychology: psychoanalytic (Roe), person–environment fit (Holland), developmental (Ginzberg, Super), behavioral (Krumboltz), cognitive (CIP, self-efficacy, SCCT), humanistic (PCT), and holistic or integrative (ILP). Theories provide guides for action, but they don't solve all problems. Because they always seem to leave something out, they receive their share of criticism. Career theorists themselves acknowledge their work is far from complete. And, when you consider how far they have come from the early days of the 20th century when Frank Parsons (1909) wrote *Choosing a Vocation*, the progress made in career development theory is a remarkable accomplishment in itself.

CHAPTER 1 EXERCISES

EXERCISE 1-1 IDEAL JOB DESCRIPTION

Joseph Campbell (Campbell with Moyers, 1988) describes the mission of life as realizing its potential. How do you do this? Campbell's answer is "Follow your bliss [and] you put yourself on a kind of track that has been there all the while. . . . I say, follow your bliss and don't be afraid, and doors will open where you didn't know they were going to be" (p. 120).

Be imaginative, use creative thinking, let your thoughts wander, and dream about what your ideal job or work situation would be like. Write your thoughts on blank sheets of paper, or write in the blank spaces provided. Describe the characteristics of your dream job. It is better *not* to have any particular occupation in mind at this point. This is a fantasy exercise; reality can be considered later. Don't think about obstacles and problems for now. Come back to this exercise later and add new insights. Here are some things to consider. In this exercise, always keep in mind: *This is my ideal job.*

1. *Nature of the work activities.* The term *work* has a negative meaning for some people, so use the word *activity* instead. What activities would be like a calling to you—a mission, a labor of love, a passion—things in which you could immerse yourself and give of yourself, in which you would be so deeply involved you would not notice the passage of time. (You've had experiences like these. Write them down!) Are there products you would like to make or services you would like to perform? What responsibilities would you be willing to take on? Remember, it's best to think of work as a putting forth of energy, something that you would do because of the nature of the activity itself, even if you were not paid for it—something you want to do more than anything

else. It could be tinkering with a mechanical thing, or putting ideas on paper and analyzing them, or cooperating with other people, or any of a million other possibilities, as long as it is something you naturally look forward to doing. When you think of work this way, it's more like play—activities you would throw yourself into without thinking of the energy or work involved.

2. *Education/training.* How far do you want to go in school? The range can extend from "stop now" to "*x* number of years." If school is not in your ideal plans, think about work experiences outside school and on-the-job training (OJT). Most community colleges offer one-year certificate and two-year associate-degree programs. Technical institutes and business schools have programs that vary in length of time. College bachelor's degrees take four years, master's degrees take five years, and doctorates (Ph.D.) take seven or more years. State an educational major if you can. Would you rather have a combination of school and work activity? School could be part time. What kinds of preparation experience do you want to have?

3. *Skills/abilities.* What skills do you have or could you develop that you would enjoy using while working? Notice the word *enjoy*—remember, you are thinking about your ideal job. Reflect on the things you have learned or hope to learn in school and from hobbies, family relationships, and other experiences. Think of physical skills (assembling things, motor coordination, strength, and so forth). Think of intellectual skills (solving problems, analyzing, and so on) or self-management skills such as dependability. Consider relationship skills such as teaching and controlling your emotions. Think of using numbers, writing, leadership experience, reading, musical talents, artistic skills, preparing food, designing, operating machines, and on and on. The possibilities are endless.

4. *Pay and fringe benefits.* What would be your ideal beginning, average, and top salary per year (or week or hour)? How much money do you need for the kind of life you want to live? Use the value of today's dollars to measure the cost of your desired lifestyle. There is more to this dimension of your ideal job description than first meets the eye, because it involves possible family obligations, major expenses such as housing and transportation, and other costs of living such as food, clothes, taxes, furniture, appliances, health care, and recreational activities. For an estimate of average expenses, consult the Consumer Expenditure Survey of the U.S. Bureau of Labor Statistics, in Figure 1-3.

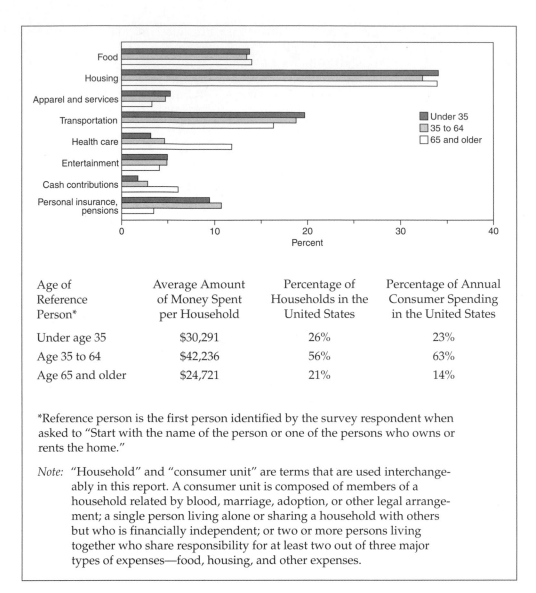

Age of Reference Person*	Average Amount of Money Spent per Household	Percentage of Households in the United States	Percentage of Annual Consumer Spending in the United States
Under age 35	$30,291	26%	23%
Age 35 to 64	$42,236	56%	63%
Age 65 and older	$24,721	21%	14%

*Reference person is the first person identified by the survey respondent when asked to "Start with the name of the person or one of the persons who owns or rents the home."

Note: "Household" and "consumer unit" are terms that are used interchangeably in this report. A consumer unit is composed of members of a household related by blood, marriage, adoption, or other legal arrangement; a single person living alone or sharing a household with others but who is financially independent; or two or more persons living together who share responsibility for at least two out of three major types of expenses—food, housing, and other expenses.

Figure 1-3 Consumer Expenditure Survey in households grouped by age of reference person (reported in 1998). *Source:* Adapted from *Issues in Labor Statistics*, U.S. Department of Labor, Bureau of Labor Statistics, Summary 00-16. Washington, DC: U.S. Government Printing Office, August 2000.

5. *Ideal working conditions.* What kind of physical environment do you want at work? Indoors or outdoors? Office? Factory? Home? Store? Work schedule— what part of the year, week, day? Air conditioning and heating? Management style preferred? Work for yourself? Union membership? Type of clothing worn? Degree of quiet or noise?

6. *Location of employment.* Where do you want to work? Think in terms of the following:
    - *Type of work organization.* Big or small company, institution, agency? Private or government? Company of one (self-employment)?
    - *Geographic area.* Region? State or province? City? Part of the world? Size of community? Rural, suburban, or urban area?

7. *Personality characteristics.* What are the characteristics of typical workers in your ideal work activity? What kind of people do you want to work with? Age ranges? Percentage of males and females? What are their interests? Mechanics, technology? Scientific, intellectual? Literary, musical, artistic creativity? Social problems? Business, politics? Being organized?

8. *Employment and advancement outlook.* Does it matter to you whether there will be many or few job openings in your ideal occupation? How much competition for the job are you willing to encounter? (A lot of competition often means greater challenge and higher pay.) At what level do you want to start in this work? How much responsibility are you willing to accept? How far and how fast do you want to go up the career ladder? Is career advancement important to you?

9. *Personal satisfaction.* What values do you want expressed in your work? What will it take in your ideal job to give you personal satisfaction? In addition to pay, think of such values as independence, creativity, prestige, security, close relationships, achievement, helping others, challenge, time to be with your family, health, variety of duties, recognition, stability, inner harmony, and travel, as well as many other values not mentioned here.

10. *Advantages and disadvantages.* What positive characteristics do you want your ideal job to have? Are there any good things to add that have not been suggested before? What negative characteristics do you want to avoid in your

work? You may have read or heard of some bad things workers have encountered and said, "I don't want that happening to me!" Perhaps you have had some experiences you don't want to repeat. If so, mention them here.

If you are having trouble getting started with this exercise, try responding to this fantasy: You are going to your own retirement party. What would you like said about you? What people are present? A newspaper article has been written about you. What would you like to see in it as a review of your career? Write a headline that summarizes your life story.

Now start writing your ideal job description in the spaces provided or on blank sheets of paper. Come back to it as you move through your career-planning process. Use a pencil; you may want to change or add to some of your ideas at a later time. After you have written your ideal job description, you can use it to compare with real job descriptions later. If you prefer to use a more specific or structured set of directions to this exercise, complete instead the "Ideal Job Description: Detailed Directions" exercise that follows.

IDEAL JOB DESCRIPTION: DETAILED DIRECTIONS

Describe the ideal characteristic of your "dream job"—one in which you could "lose yourself" once you have found it. Consult the instructions for each of the 10 sections of Exercise 1-1. Below are ideas in each category to stimulate your thinking. Check or circle possibilities. Make additions; fill in blanks. *Be more specific.* (Many ideas are expressed in general terms.) Use a pencil so changes can be made.

1. *Nature of the work activities* (ideally). In what activities can you put forth a lot of energy and not think of it as effort or "work"? What activities would you want to do more than anything else? Check any possible ideas:

   ____Talking with people   ____Creating designs

   ____Organizing people/ideas/things   ____Reading about _____

   ____Making _____ with my hands

   ____Helping others with _____

   ____Planning _____   ____Growing _____

   ____Assembling (parts of) _____

   ____Acting roles   ____Analyzing data or people

   ____Operating machines

   ____Drawing/composing _____

   ____Writing _____   ____Producing _____

   ____Teaching _____   ____Arranging _____

   ____Studying _____   ____Computing numbers

   ____Supervising others

   ____Tending, repairing _____

____Guiding, advising people about _____

____Collecting information   ____Driving vehicles

____Using color   ____Negotiating

Other: _____

2. *Education/training* beyond high school (ideally). How much? What kind?

____None   ____On-the-job training

____Apprenticeship (for _____)   ____Certificate (one year)

____Associate degree (two years)   ____Bachelor's degree (four years)

____Master's degree   ____Doctorate (Ph.D.)

____Technical institute   ____Business school

____Beauty or barber school

____Full-time program   ____Part-time with work

____Ideal major in college: _____

____Other: _____

3. *Skills/abilities.* Which ones (that you have or can learn) would you most enjoy using?

____Operating/driving machines   ____Using hands/fingers

____Coordinating eyes/hands/feet   ____Using physical strength

____Constructing/building things   ____Using tools/objects

____Getting information   ____Diagnosing/solving problems

____Using numbers   ____Researching

____Knowing/expressing languages   ____Knowing facts/data

____Reasoning logically   ____Drawing/sketching/painting

____Producing music   ____Visualizing in 2 or 3 dimensions

____Writing/dramatizing ideas   ____Entertaining people

____Acting   ____Speaking/conversing

____Teaching people   ____Communicating with people

____Advising/coaching/helping people ____Diagnosing illness

____Healing   ____Cooperating with others

____Studying people   ____Leading/directing/managing people

____Getting things done   ____Motivating people

____Promoting programs   ____Persuading/convincing others

____Initiating ideas   ____Organizing things neatly

____Paying attention to detail   ____Spelling correctly

____Keeping records accurately   ____Using office machines

____Typing rapidly, accurately

____Other: _____

4. *Pay and fringe benefits* (ideally, in terms of today's dollars). Ideal salary or income per:

    ____year   ____month   ____week   ____hour (check one)

    Beginning/entry-level amount: $ _____

    Average: $ _____   Top: $ _____

    Benefits (list them): _____

    Estimated expenses: _____

    ____Single?   ____Family?   Number of children (ideally)? ____

    Home/apartment: How many rooms? ____

    Major appliances (list them): _____

    Car expenses: _____

    Furniture:_____

    Clothes: _____

    Food: _____

    Recreation, entertainment:_____

    Tools: _____

    Church/synagogue/mosque/religion: _____

    Education/books:_____

    Repairs around house:_____

    Other: _____

5. *Ideal working conditions* in your occupation:

    Physical setting:

    ____Office   ____Factory   ____Home   ____Store

    ____School   ____Hospital   ____Outdoors   ____Garage

    ____Restaurant   ____Library   ____Church   ____Museum

    ____Theater   ____Lab   ____Studio   ____"On the road"

    Other (specify): _____

    ____Quiet   ____Work alone   ____Lots of people

    Schedule: ____8 to 5   ____Morning   ____Afternoon

    ____Evening   ____Night   ____Anytime   ____Weekend

    Management style: Be my own boss? ____   Join a union?____

    Clothing worn (suit, casual, uniform, etc.): _____

    Other: _____

6. *Location of employment* in your occupation (ideally):

    a. *Type of work organization*
        Ideal number of employees:

        ____1–20   ____21–50   ____51–100   ____101–500

        ____501–1,000   ____1,001–5,000   ____5,001–10,000   ____Over 10,000

    Industry (name): _____

Privately owned? ____   Government? ____

Self-employed?____   Nonprofit? ____   Profit-making? ____

Name of organization (if known): _____

Other: _____

b. *Geographic area*

Country: _____   Region: _____

State/province: _____   City/village: _____

____Rural   ____Suburban

Ideal distance of workplace from home: ____ miles

Climate: _____   Terrain: _____

Size of community: _____

7. *Personality characteristics* of work associates and customers. What kinds of people would you like to work with and serve?

Ratio of women/men: ____% female   ____% male

Age range preference:

____16–21 ____22–30 ____31–40 ____41–50 ____ Over 50 ____Even mixture

Children: ____0–1 ____1–2 ____3–5 ____6–10 ____11–15

____Elderly   ____Aged

Particular ethnic background (specify): _____

Interests of others:

____Mechanically inclined   ____Likes the outdoors   ____Electronics

____Athletics   ____Technical subjects   ____Machines

____Cars   ____Abstract ideas   ____Science

____Mathematics   ____Research   ____Problem solving

____Reading books/publications   ____Music

____Art   ____Design   ____Creative things

____Writing   ____Literature   ____Drama

____Problems of society   ____People in general   ____Children

____Adolescents   ____Adults   ____Elderly/aged

____Psychology   ____Business   ____Leadership

____Politics   ____Economics   ____Buying/selling

____Organizations   ____Clerking   ____Filing

____Organizing data   ____Efficiency   ____Traditions

Other personality characteristics of people you would like to be around:

____Practical   ____Realistic   ____Analytical

____Rational   ____Expressive   ____Idealistic

____Supportive   ____Sociable   ____Energetic

____Persuasive   ____Dependable   ____Orderly, neat

Other (list): _____

8. *Employment and advancement outlook* (ideally) in your occupation. How much competition do you want to encounter for a job in your occupational choice?

____Little   ____A lot

(In general, more competition means greater challenges, higher pay.)

Are you:

____a risk taker?   ____looking for security?   ____"turned on" by challenges?

How much do advancement and promotion mean to you?____Little ____A lot

How far and how fast do you want to go up the "career ladder"?_____

How much responsibility do you want in your job?   ____Little ____A lot

9. *Personal satisfaction* (ideally) from working in your occupation:

____Feeling secure	____Sense of achievement
____High income	____Being creative
____Meeting challenges	____Having time for family
____Developing new friendships	____Getting recognition
____Having the support of others	____Power/influence
____Maintaining good health	____Being independent
____Helping others	____Being close to nature
____Gaining prestige/status	____Inner peace
____Learning new things	____Traveling
____Furthering a mission	____Producing beauty
____Being close to home	____Excitement
____Using my skills	____Competing with others
____Discovering truth	____Showing my agility or strength
____Solving problems	____Being part of a team
____Expressing a lifestyle	____Getting bonuses
____Keeping clean	____Helping those less fortunate
____Expressing my religious and moral values	

Other (list): _____

10. *Advantages.* List positive characteristics you want that are not mentioned elsewhere. (Examples: training opportunities, organizing your own time, privacy, fair supervision.)

Disadvantages. List negative characteristics you would like to avoid. (Examples: conflict, monotony, danger, dullness, disorganization, confinement, health hazards.)

EXERCISE 1-2 AUTOBIOGRAPHY

Unstructured Autobiography

Take seven (or more) sheets of blank paper. At the top of each sheet write, "Who Am I?" On each sheet, write an answer to the question. (For example, "I am sensitive to other people's needs.") Then write about half a page of detail explaining your answer. Just writing "I am sensitive" is not enough; provide details of experiences. Look at your answers and explanations. Below each one, write what appeals to you about each response. Finally, arrange your "Who Am I?" essays in order of priority from the one you like most or that seems most important (that one goes on top) to the one you like least or is least important to you.

Structured Autobiography

(1) Use as many separate sheets of blank paper as you need, or (2) use the spaces provided in the outline that follows these directions and jot down your ideas and remembrances as you read through the instructions for each part of your autobiography.

Personal data. Start with your full name, address, age, height, weight, telephone number, and other basic information. Then indicate how your age, sex, physical characteristics, community, and region of the country have influenced your career thinking.

Work experience. Start with your latest work experience and work back in time. Include all work (not just full-time), with dates, name of organization, duties and responsibilities, titles, special achievements, and names of supervisors. Mention part-time, summer, and volunteer work experiences. What did you like most (and least) about your work experiences in working? How were decisions made? Describe your relationship with work associates and your supervisor. What did you learn about yourself and about jobs and working through these experiences?

Education. List all high schools and colleges attended, with dates and locations. What courses did you enjoy most (and least)? Who was your favorite teacher? Why? Describe special abilities acquired (writing, research, speaking, using numbers, organizing activities, playing music, foreign language, and so on), skills used (refer to previous list or the skills section of Exercise 1-1 for examples), and achievements (awards, high grades, significant reports, athletic accomplishments, outstanding projects, and the like).

Leisure-time and extracurricular activities. List memberships in clubs, organizations, and professional groups (including offices held), hobbies, recreational pursuits, and sports. What are you most proud of or most satisfied with in these activities? Why? What books have you liked best? Why?

Parents and significant others. What is (or was) your father's career? Mother's career? Would these careers interest you? Why? What do your parents want you to be? How have they communicated this to you? Who have been the most influential people in your life so far? (These can be historical figures as well as people you know.) In what ways have they been influential?

Childhood interests. As a child, what did you dream (or daydream) about becoming? What were your major interests early in life? Do these things still interest you? Why?

Life roles. Think of all the roles you play in life. You are a son or daughter, brother or sister, mother or father, student, worker (in what kind of work?), grandson or granddaughter, wife or husband, club member, consumer, athlete, musician, driver, and so on. List several roles you have played or functions you have fulfilled so far in life. Which role or function do you like or value the most? What sources of satisfaction and dissatisfaction come with each role? What skills have you used for each?

Self-assessment. Name seven or more positive things you have accomplished in the past. Name seven or more abilities or skills that you have; try to provide evidence for each skill. Name seven or more values that are important to you; try to define the meaning of each value. List five or more occupations that interest you now or have interested you in the past. What values would be expressed in each one? What skills could you bring to each one?

(If you don't like writing so much, try talking into a tape recorder instead. Afterward, write down key phrases and ideas from what you have said.)

STRUCTURED AUTOBIOGRAPHY

Consult Exercise 1-2 for more complete instructions.

1. *Personal data.*

   Name _____ Telephone ( ) _____ Age _____

   Address _____ City _____ State _____

   What, if anything, and/or who, if anyone, has influenced your career thinking? How?

2. *Work experience.* Start with your latest experience and work back in time.

Dates	Name of Organization	Titles, Responsibilities, Achievements
____	_____	_____
____	_____	_____
____	_____	_____
____	_____	_____
____	_____	_____
____	_____	_____

3. *Education.* Current and previous schools attended.

Dates	Name of School/Location	Best Subjects, Achievements, Skills Learned
____	_____	_____
____	_____	_____
____	_____	_____
____	_____	_____
____	_____	_____
____	_____	_____

4. *Leisure-time and extracurricular activities:* hobbies, clubs, groups, sports, etc. (Include satisfactions received and what you learned from these activities.)

5. *Parents and significant others.*

   Father: _____ Occupation: _____ Influence: _____

   Mother: _____ Occupation: _____ Influence: _____

   Others: _____ Occupation: _____ Influence: _____

                              Occupation: _____ Influence: _____

                              Occupation: _____ Influence: _____

                              Occupation: _____ Influence: _____

6. *Childhood interests.*

7. *Life roles.* These are personal roles such as son or daughter, brother or sister, mother or father; educational roles such as student, club member, musician, or athlete; and occupational roles such as full-time, part-time, or volunteer worker. With each role, indicate the satisfactions and the skills you have learned.

Role	*Satisfactions*	*Skills Learned*
_____	_____	_____
_____	_____	_____
_____	_____	_____
_____	_____	_____
_____	_____	_____
_____	_____	_____
_____	_____	_____

8. *Self-assessment.*

Accomplishments. Include any you have already mentioned, plus any new ones you can think of.

Skills or abilities used in and acquired from the accomplishment. (What did you know/do to achieve it?)

Values expressed in the accomplishment. (What satisfactions did you get from the accomplishment?)

EXERCISE 1-3 LIFE LINE

This exercise can be done alone or in a small group. Its purpose is to help you know yourself better and, if you are in a group, to get to know other group members better. Your life line can provide a framework for an overview of your life and work. You will need a large sheet of blank paper and a pen, pencil, crayon, or felt-tip pen for this exercise.

Draw a line on the sheet of paper to suggest where you have been in your life, where you are now, and where you are going. The beginning of this line represents birth; the end of the line is death. In between, your life line expresses your life with its good times and bad times, relationships with people, and experiences of all kinds. Your life line can be any shape and can move in any direction; you can think of it as a road, path, river, map, object, simply a line, or anything else you can imagine. Mark where you are now; it doesn't have to be a time mark, but rather an indication of how much living you have done and how much you have left to do.

Look to the past to see where you have been. Place on your life line some details from your past, branching out from the main line. Use the autobiography exercise (Exercise 1-2) to help you note some important events in your life.

Project yourself into the future as much as you can. Draw what you would like to become during the rest of your life. Use symbols, signs, pictures, colors, cartoons, labels, and so on. Be creative! The path can branch off in a number of directions. Where do you think you are going? Let yourself go, experiment, and see what happens.

If you are in a small group, share your life line experience with the others, but remember that you have the right to pass should you prefer to say nothing. This exercise is a lot of fun once you get into it, but the important thing is to be comfortable in letting other people know something about yourself.

SUMMARY

1. Various kinds of people need career planning, including undecided students, people caught in the wrong job, those who have been away from work for a long time, and workers whose employers have gone out of business.

2. Three broad approaches to career planning are the rational approach, the sociocultural determinant approach, and the accidental approach.

3. It is important to make your own occupational choice, not allowing others to do something you ought to do for yourself. Too many people abandon their own career choice, usually with bad results.

4. Career planning can be defined as a process in which you (a) become aware of your need to make a career decision; (b) study your environment; (c) study yourself, particularly your interests, abilities, and values; (d) generate occupational alternatives; (e) gather information about your occupational prospects; (f) make a tentative choice or definite decision, ranking your prospects; (g) implement your career decision through training and job search methods; and (h) use feedback to evaluate the decision, positively or negatively. Too much negative feedback can start the career-planning process in motion again.

5. Roe's theory of occupational choice is based on the assumption that your choice of occupation is strongly influenced by your experiences in early childhood.

6. Holland proposes that your choice of work is primarily an expression of your personality pattern. He presents six basic types of personality, with many possible combinations, and corresponding work environments.

7. According to Super's theory of career development, movement through vocational development stages is needed to attain a healthy self-concept and a mature, appropriate role in the world of work.

8. Krumboltz's social learning theory states that you should take into account genetic factors, environmental conditions, learning experiences, and decision-making skills in making self-observations, developing skills, and taking action in your career planning. Irrational personal beliefs need to be challenged and reconstructed. If left alone, they could obstruct or damage your career thinking.

9. Cognitive theories of career development focus on how our minds work in handling information and the thought processes we use to make career choices. Cognitive information processing (CIP) theory views career decision making as a problem-solving activity; you solve a career problem by making a decision as you would furnish an answer to a mathematical or scientific problem. Self-efficacy theory studies how you make evaluations of your abilities when you need to make plans and take actions required to produce a desired outcome such as a career decision or getting a job in a preferred occupation. Social cognitive career theory (SCCT) examines how our thinking and belief systems influence our actions that affect the way we make career decisions.

10. Personal construct theory studies the way people view the world and create constructs that structure events, other people, and environments in which we live. Constructs are words, sentences, and groups of sentences we form within ourselves to make sense of the world around us. When we assume there are certain characteristics that describe occupations in terms of their similarities and differences with other occupations, we make a vocational construct for ourselves.

11. Integrative Life Planning is an approach to career planning that not only focuses on choosing jobs, but also views work in its relationship to other life roles considered to be as important as our occupational role.

12. Vocational theories are imperfect and subject to much criticism, but theory, reason, logic, and intuitive thinking along with planning will certainly help in mapping your future career.

REFERENCES

Arthur, M. B., Hall, D. T., and Lawrence, B. S. 1989. Generating new directions in career theory: The case for a transdisciplinary approach. In M. B. Arthur, D. T. Hall, and B. S. Lawrence, eds., *Handbook of career theory*. Cambridge, UK: Cambridge University Press.

Bandura, A. 1986. *Social foundations of thought and action: A social cognitive theory*. Englewood Cliffs, NJ: Prentice Hall.

Bateson, M. C. 1989. *Composing a life*. New York: Atlantic Monthly.

Beck, A. 1972. *Depression: Causes and treatment*. Philadelphia: University of Pennsylvania Press.

Bergland, B. W. 1974. Career planning: The use of sequential evaluated experience. In E. L. Herr, ed., *Vocational guidance and human development*. Boston: Houghton Mifflin.

Betz, N. E. 1992. Counseling uses of career self-efficacy theory. *The Career Development Quarterly*, 41, 22–26.

Betz, N. E., and Hackett, G. 1986. Applications of self-efficacy theory to understanding career choice behavior. *Journal of Social and Clinical Psychology*, 4, 279–289.

Brooks, L. 1990. Recent developments in theory building. In D. Brown, L. Brooks, and Associates, *Career choice and development*, 2nd ed. (pp. 364–394). San Francisco: Jossey-Bass.

Brott, P. E. 2001. The storied approach: A postmodern perspective for career counseling. *The Career Development Quarterly*, 49, 304–313.

Campbell, J., with Moyers, B. 1988. *The power of myth*. New York: Doubleday.

Ellis, A. 1962. *Reason and emotion in psychotherapy*. New York: Stuart.

Fox, M. 1994. *The reinvention of work: A new vision of livelihood for our time*. San Francisco: Harper.

Frankl, V. 1963. *Man's search for meaning*. Boston: Beacon Press.

Ginzberg, E., Ginsburg, S. W., Axelrad, S., and Herma, J. L. 1951. *Occupational choice: An approach to general theory*. New York: Columbia University Press.

Gottfredson, L. S. 1986. Special groups and the beneficial use of vocational interest inventories. In W. B. Walsh and S. H. Osipow, eds., *Advances in vocational psychology*. Hillsdale, NJ: Erlbaum.

Hansen, L. S. 1997. *Integrative life planning: Critical tasks for career development and changing life patterns*. San Francisco: Jossey-Bass.

Hansen, L. S. 2001, March. Integrating work, family, and community through holistic life planning. *The Career Development Quarterly*, 49, 261–274.

Herr, E. L., and Cramer, S. H. 1996. *Career guidance and counseling through the life span: Systematic approaches*, 5th ed. New York: HarperCollins.

Holland, J. L. 1997. *Making vocational choices: A theory of vocational personalities and work environments*, 3rd ed. Odessa, FL: Psychological Assessment Resources.

Ivey, A. E. 1980. *Counseling and psychotherapy: Skills, theories, and practice*. Englewood Cliffs, NJ: Prentice-Hall.

Kelly, G. A. 1955. *The psychology of personal constructs*. New York: Norton.

Kinnier, R. T., and Krumboltz, J. D. 1984. Procedures for successful career counseling. In N. C. Gysbers, ed., *Designing careers: Counseling to enhance education, work, and leisure*. San Francisco: Jossey-Bass.

Krumboltz, J. D. 1983. *Private rules in career decision making*. Columbus: National Center for Research in Vocation Education, Ohio State University.

Leong, F. L. T., and Chervinko, S. 1996. Construct validity of career indecision: Negative personality traits as predictors of career indecision. *Journal of Career Assessment*, 4, 315–329.

Levinson, E. M., Ohler, D. L., Caswell, S., and Kiewra, K. 1998. Six approaches to the assessment of career maturity. *Journal of Counseling and Development*, 76, 475–482.

Miller, J. V., and Vetter, L., project directors. 1999. *National survey of working America*. Alexandria, VA: National Career Development Association.

Mitchell, A. M., Jones, G. B., and Krumboltz, J. D. 1979. *Social learning and career decision making*. Cranston, RI: Carroll Press.

Mitchell, K. E., Levin, A. S., and Krumboltz, J. D. 1999. Planned happenstance: Constructing unexpected career opportunities. *Journal of Counseling and Development*, 77, 115–124.

Mitchell, L. K., and Krumboltz, J. D. 1990. Social learning approach to career decision making: Krumboltz's theory. In D. Brown, L. Brooks, and Associates, *Career choice and development*, 2nd ed. (pp. 145–196). San Francisco: Jossey-Bass.

Multon, K. D., Heppner, M. J., and Lapan, R. T. 1995. An empirical derivation of career decision subtypes in a high school sample. *Journal of Vocational Behavior*, 47, 76–92.

Neimeyer, G. J. 1992. Personal constructs in career counseling and development. *Journal of Career Development*, 18, 163–174.

Osborne, W. L., Brown, S., Niles, S., and Miner, C. U. 1997. *Career development, assessment, and counseling: Applications of the Donald E. Super C-DAC approach.* Alexandria, VA: American Counseling Association.

Osipow, S. H. 1983. *Theories of career development,* 3rd ed. Englewood Cliffs, NJ: Prentice Hall.

Osipow, S. H., and Fitzgerald, L. F. 1996. *Theories of career development,* 4th ed. Boston: Allyn and Bacon.

Parsons, F. 1909/1989. *Choosing a vocation.* Garrett Park, MD: Garrett Park Press.

Patterson, J., and Kim, P. 1991. *The day America told the truth.* New York: Penguin.

Reardon, R. C., Lenz, J. G., Sampson, J. P., and Peterson, G. W. 2000. *Career development and planning: A comprehensive approach.* Belmont, CA: Wadsworth-Brooks/Cole.

Roe, A. 1956. *The psychology of occupations.* New York: Wiley.

Roe, A. 1957. Early determinants of vocational choice. *Journal of Counseling Psychology,* 4, 212–217.

Savickas, M. L. 1995. Constructivist counseling for career indecision. *The Career Development Quarterly,* 43, 363–373.

Sharf, R. S. 2002. *Applying career development theory to counseling,* 3rd ed. Pacific Grove, CA: Brooks/Cole.

Srebalus, D., Marinelli, R., and Messing, J. 1982. *Career development: Concepts and procedures.* Pacific Grove, CA: Brooks/Cole.

Stefflre, B., ed. 1965. *Theories of counseling.* New York: McGraw-Hill.

Super, D. E. 1957. *The psychology of careers.* New York: Harper & Row.

Super, D. E. 1983. Assessment in career guidance: Toward truly developmental counseling. *The Personnel and Guidance Journal,* 61, 555–562.

Watts, A. 1975. *Tao, the watercourse way.* New York: Pantheon.

Zaccaria, J. 1970. *Theories of occupational choice and vocational development.* Boston: Houghton Mifflin.

Zunker, V. G. 2002. *Career counseling: Applied concepts of life planning,* 6th ed. Pacific Grove, CA: Brooks/Cole.

The Changing World of Work

Imagine you work at XYZ, a company with 2,000 employees. Like many businesses, XYZ faces pressure from domestic and foreign rivals. You are constantly called on to improve the quality of your work and increase productivity so that your job and the company will survive in a competitive world. Occasionally you receive a nice letter of recognition from the boss and a write-up in the company bulletin, but your wages have been frozen for the past two years. XYZ cites priorities other than your pay increases, such as buying new equipment, meeting debts, and paying dividends to stockholders. The company has begun to draft plans for moving its operations to another part of the country, where labor costs and taxes are lower. You begin to feel insecure about your future at XYZ. The company has been good to you, at least until now, and your job, demanding as it is, has given you personal satisfaction as well as a livelihood. Thoughts of the disruption you and your family would have to endure if XYZ were to leave your community make you worry. You start to feel resentful and say to yourself (and maybe a few close friends), "This is the reward I get for all my years of dedication to the company?"

Why does something like this happen? That it has happened to plenty of workers is a fact. Throughout history, the forces of economic, social, and technological change have acted on workers, compelling them to make adjustments to those changes. Usually we don't notice these forces until they affect us directly. By then, the time may be too late or too difficult to prepare for and make the adaptations dramatic change brings to our lives.

Changes in work have always been with us, even in primitive times, when the two sexes developed different work roles. Women performed the kind of work that allowed them to raise children, a valuable occupation in any age. Men were occupied in food gathering, hunting, and fighting. More changes came in ancient times. Manual labor was done by people designated as the "lower classes"—peasants, artisans, and slaves. Intellectual and cultural pursuits such as politics, music, philosophy, and athletics were largely the province of the "upper classes." The Middle Ages brought greater respect to skilled craftsmen, although the pious, contemplative life of priests and monks was considered the ideal. For centuries, the household was the unit of production. The entire family was involved in the enterprise, whether it was farming or baking. In preindustrial society, work and family were just about the same thing (Curry, 2003).

The modern era laid the foundations for a view of work that resulted in an industrial society. A predominantly agricultural way of life was transformed into a manufacturing society, which today is an economy largely based on service and information. In modern times, two fundamental changes affected all workers. First, merit, talent, and ability became more important in the workplace than an individual's social position—a decisive factor in earlier times. More able and productive workers got better jobs, higher pay, and advancement on the job. Second, the location and organization of work changed. Jobs were moved to the factory site, and craft skills were divided into many separate tasks. Machines did more of the work. The activities of workers and machines were coordinated into an efficient flow of production (Cosgrave, 1973).

Industrialization, however, created its own share of problems. Men, women, and children left their farm homes for cities and a factory where their movements were coordinated with that of machines. Workers labored long hours for low pay. Jobs were all too often dull, dangerous, and monotonous. Many companies were impersonal organizations, designing work without regard for the people who did the job. The changes wrought by the machinery of the Industrial Revolution brought economic crisis, psychological shock, and violent disruption—as in the early 1800s when a group of English workers known as Luddites (named after Ned Ludd, their leader) smashed the machines that had replaced them in manufacturing woolen goods. Since then, the displacement of workers by advancing technology has been a constant concern all through the industrial age (Bix, 2000).

Work is not as simple today as it was when labor was less specialized. Most people once knew at an early age, by watching Mom or Dad, how their own lives were going to be spent. There were few options. When young Abraham Lincoln chose not to follow his father's footsteps into farming, he tried nearly every other career the frontier offered: carpenter, riverboat man, store clerk, soldier, merchant, postmaster, blacksmith, surveyor, lawyer, politician. Experience eliminated all but the last two (Donald, 1995).

Futurists such as Alvin Toffler speak of the three waves of occupational history (Toffler, 1981). The first wave was agricultural. The second wave, beginning in the 1700s, was industrial. Now the third wave, the electronic, high-technology revolution, is sweeping the world. Think of all the changes that have recently appeared or are now taking place. New methods of production emerge. Renewable energy sources are developed. Computers and robots have become standard tools in business and industry. Space stations circle the globe. Genetic engineering shapes many characteristics of humans. The means by which you get information and entertainment are highly specialized. Products are more customized. You could be working in an "electronic cottage" (that is, your home) for much of your working day. More organizations are less centralized. These are just a few of the ongoing changes occurring today.

This chapter begins an examination of the world of work that extends into the next two chapters. You will read about economic forces and employment trends that influence the growth or decline of various occupations and create new and emerging occupations. A discussion of trends occurring in several occupational groups can give you information as well as an appreciation for the diversity of the world of occupations. At the end of Chapter 2, you can take part in an exercise based on the scenario described at the beginning of the chapter.

OCCUPATIONAL TRENDS

In Arthur Miller's play *Death of a Salesman*, protagonist Willy Loman asks his Uncle Ben for occupational advice. Uncle Ben responds "diamonds" and "Alaska." Somehow, those magic words are supposed to unlock the door to fulfillment and riches. In the 1960s movie *The Graduate*, occupational success was summed up in one word: "plastics." Later, the word was "computers." Today, the new key to career success might be "biotechnology" or "Internet." Does selecting a growing occupation guarantee getting employment and being happy in it? There are no guarantees in the career game. To be sure, the growth of certain occupations creates jobs. However, hiring trends are only part of the total career-planning picture.

Planning a career may seem strictly an individual effort, but it is part of a larger picture too—our social environment and the world. Think of the events in our society of the recent past. The cold war ended with the triumph over Soviet-style communism. U.S. citizens had poured $11 trillion of their wealth into the political, economic, and military competition (Johnson, 2002). Already offering the highest standard of living in the world, the U.S. economy zoomed to still higher levels in the boom years of the 1990s. The best of all economic worlds existed: low unemployment, low inflation, high productivity, and record high profits. U.S. dominance was supreme in science, technology, medicine, and military power.

No depression or global war threatened. Wall Street markets soared, setting one record after another. The Internet fostered a new era. Computerized trading transformed the business world, operating at a pace and on a scale once thought impossible. New companies, particularly the dot.com businesses, could make an initial public stock offering having never shown a profit and could see their value triple or quadruple by the end of that day. A startup company such as Netscape would become worth as much as or more than old Wall Street titans within hours; it took only months to overshadow the titans.

In his interviews with entrepreneurs in Silicon Valley, Haynes Johnson (2002) chronicles the spirit of the last half of the 1990s.

They exuded confidence in their ability and destiny. They believed they made their own breaks through talent and perseverance; they subscribed to the Darwinian law-of-the-jungle, winner-take-all school of life. . . . Their rejection of rules and authority at times bordered on anarchy, but they were convinced that, for all its failings, American society was by far the best. In their energy, their acquisitiveness, their arrogance and conceit, their blend of selfishness and idealism, their lack of interest in the past, their studied casualness edged with cynicism, their infatuation with—if not worship of—youth, their behavior reflected the larger society. (pp. 24–25)

And yet, with all the genuine achievements and prosperity, an uneasy anxiety shadowed the good times. There were enough disturbing incidents across the cultural scene to make thoughtful people wonder whether all was well. The media published disturbing reports about corruption, self-destruction, illegal drugs, sexual exploitation, abuse, road rage, violence, and suicide. The speed and pressures of life in the "go-go times" were simply too much for too many people, many of whom could sense they were being left behind. A wave of scandals undermined confidence in U.S. economic and political life. Once-respected corporate leaders were tarnished with greed and graft. Voter participation declined—not a healthy sign for democracy. People distrusted their leaders more than ever; they became more cynical and turned their attention away from public affairs. They focused more on their own personal concerns or lost themselves in the trivia of electronic entertainment, perhaps as a way of avoiding the indications of trouble that were brewing in society. Whether the signs were renewed racial tensions in the past week and random shootings this week, followed by a crisis in public health or a report of a widening gap between rich and poor, attentive people recognized, however vaguely, these were signs of social corrosion. The disturbances seemed endless: alienation among youth, disintegrating families, worn-out parents, child neglect, spouse abuse, poverty, depletion of natural resources, proliferation of guns, hate crimes, outbursts of rage and violence, lack of common courtesy, increasing coarseness in language and entertainment—all this and more.

If these incidents weren't enough, then came "9/11," September 11, 2001, and the war on terrorism. The attacks on the World Trade Center in New York and the Pentagon in Washington brought a new outlook in the people of the United States. The view of the world we thought existed and the world that really surrounds us had changed. Television brought to the entire world the horrifying scenes of a second plane blasting into the trade center's other tower, billowing smoke, blazing fire, bodies falling helplessly from upper-story windows, twisted metal and broken glass, and terrified people on the ground running for their lives. Suddenly, on that day, Americans lost their complacency about security and realized they were as vulnerable as any other people on earth.

The pictures of 9/11 will remain fixed inside the heads of Americans for a long, long time. So many aspects of life were instantly changed. People were afraid, where they hadn't been before, as the terrorists intended. The travel industry was badly hurt. Airport security tightened markedly; long lines greeted passengers, who had to arrive hours before flight departures. People moved out of offices in skyscrapers and apartments in high-rise buildings, and visitors thought twice before going into such buildings. Letters containing anthrax powder arrived in the mail—was this the opening round of a chemical/biological war with terrorism? Would the water that poured out of our faucets be safe? Alerts became commonplace as officials became uneasy about the safety of bridges, subways, tunnels, water systems, electrical generating plants, nuclear facilities, sewer systems, and other elements of U.S. infrastructure.

The following year, 2002, brought the debacle of Enron, an energy company based in Houston that had become the seventh largest corporation in the United States. Enron went bankrupt, but it represented more than the largest bankruptcy in United States history up to that time. It became a symbol of corporate greed, corruption, and the buying of political influence. Enron covered up more than $1 billion of debt through insider deals, hidden partnerships, and lax regulation by its auditors.

This manipulation allowed Enron's executives to make hundreds of millions of dollars in profits by selling overvalued stock to an unsuspecting public that included the company's own employees (who eventually lost their life savings as their stock became worthless). A succession of similar occurrences at other corporations began to produce a lack of confidence and trust in U.S. business.

The events of the last few years have left Americans mystified, confused, and upset over the state of the economy and the culture. The economy and the markets often seem bewildered, trying to forecast how things will sort themselves out. How can one make predictions regarding economic and labor trends in an atmosphere of such volatility? Yet all kinds of experts try to tell you what the economy will do. Sar Levitan (1987) warned us to be careful with "trendy" forecasts. Louis Rukeyser (1988), commentator for television's *Wall Street Week*, remarked, "Who knows? Nobody really does."

Forecasting occupational trends is a difficult art at best. No one can predict with 100 percent accuracy. Many unexpected factors are involved; in addition to those already mentioned there are shifts in population, political decisions, technological advances, geographical changes, and changing values of the culture. A time lag is built into all predictions. When you read a forecast for an occupation, several years may have elapsed from the time the prediction was made to when it got into print. The proverbial pendulum is always swinging between two points on the occupational scale. On one side are shortages of workers in a given occupation, on the other, an oversupply of workers. No one knows exactly how far the pendulum is going to swing, when it will stop moving one way and start moving in the opposite direction, how fast it is moving, and where it is going to be when you want to enter an occupation. By the time you become aware of an occupational forecast, the position, direction, and speed of the pendulum may have changed.

Labor forecasts usually fall into one of three categories: optimistic, middle (a blending of the other two), or pessimistic. *Optimists* look to the future with great expectations. The coming workplace is often visualized as one of high technology, computers, robots, constant innovation, expanding imagination, greater worker--management interaction, rapid job change, and exciting new occupations spawned by a knowledge explosion. A *middle position* can be represented by government forecasts (McDaniels, 1989). The U.S. Department of Labor publishes a new *Occupational Outlook Handbook* every two years, an *Occupational Outlook Quarterly*, and a *Monthly Labor Review*. The government's projections assume, among other things, that there will be no major war, social upheaval, or significant changes in work patterns during the projected period (Toossi, 2002). No one can assure you that these assumptions will always hold, and it is safe to say that forecasts will not be completely accurate. *Pessimists* emphasize high rates of unemployment and underemployment, creation of more low-paid jobs than high-paid ones, a declining middle class as the gap between rich and poor widens, the growth of an underclass of underpaid workers, and increasing numbers of temporary and part-time workers (McDaniels, 1989).

Should you only choose an occupation where the number of employed workers is increasing, or in which the demand for workers is greater than the supply? Some people say, "Yes—there's no sense picking an occupation that is declining and won't offer you a job." That statement is true only when the chosen occupation will cease to exist altogether; it fails to account for the need to replace people who leave their work. Jobs in an occupation come from two sources: growth needs and replacement needs. Obviously, an occupation that is new or rapidly growing in number of workers will create more jobs. In most occupations, however, replacement needs provide the majority of jobs. Even when the number of workers in an occupation is declining, positions are still open to replace those who retire, quit, die, are promoted, get injured, develop poor health, or change to another job for any reason. You could overlook an occupation you would enjoy and find meaningful if you based your career decision solely on favorable job trends. Another consideration is the number of people who are preparing to enter a specific occupation. It's a pretty safe guess that if the supply of workers has been greater than the demand, the number of people preparing to enter the occupation will decline. This starts the pendulum swinging toward a shortage of workers, thereby lessening the competition for you at some point. In short, *make occupational projections a part of your career planning, but not all of it.*

GENERAL ECONOMIC FORCES AND LABOR TRENDS

The following forecasts in this paragraph were made by trend analyst John Naisbitt (1982): An industrial economy is being replaced by an information society where a majority of workers create, process, and distribute data. The centralized factory system of industrialized society will give way to the decentralized workplace of the information age. National economies will evolve into an interdependent world economy that will experience a global economic boom. People will take on more responsibility for their own health, education, jobs, and general well-being instead of relying on corporations and government agencies. Workplace communication will require more networking instead of waiting for messages to flow down from the top. All these predictions of the future were not evident to the average person 25 or 30 years ago, but they are now well confirmed. People who based their decisions on these and other forecasts benefited from that information. A number of economic forces and labor trends that will influence the occupational picture over the next several years are described in the pages to come.

Demographic Trends

The high growth rate of the U.S. labor force from 1950 to 2000 will be much lower in the next 50 years. The government's definition of the *labor force* includes both people employed in paid jobs *and* those currently looking for work. The civilian labor force was 62 million in 1950, grew to 141 million in 2000, and is projected to reach 192 million in 2050. Growth rates in the workforce were high between 1950 and 2000, averaging 1.6 percent each year. This rate of increase will drop to an average of 0.6 percent per year in the 2000–2050 period (Toossi, 2002). The dynamic growth of the labor force from 1950 to 2000 was caused largely by natural population increases, more women working or seeking work, and a wave of immigration, particularly Latino or Hispanic and Asian. Immigrants have furnished significant scientific and technical talent, started thousands of new companies (especially in Silicon Valley), and helped hold down prices by filling low-wage jobs (Baker, 2002). Look at Table 2-1 for a breakdown of the labor force by age, sex, and race between 1950 and 2050.

More people over age 16 will participate in the U.S. labor force than in previous years; however, these rates will fall after 2010. The population of the United States *16 years of age and older* was 168 million in 1980 and is forecast to be 234 million in 2010 and 312 million in 2050. The labor force participation rate (the proportion of an age group in the labor force) was 59.2 percent in 1950 and 67.2 percent in 2000. The forecast is for the labor force participation rate to drop in 2050 to 61.5 percent, as the 65-year and older proportion of the U.S. population increases to 24.5 percent (Toossi, 2002). For the 10-year 2000–2010 period, the *percentage rate* of increase in the U.S. labor force is expected to be about the same, 12.0 percent compared with 11.9 percent for the previous 10 years. The *numeric* increase is projected to be 17 million more workers between 2000 and 2010 than in the previous 10 years, when the labor force grew by 15 million (Fullerton and Toossi, 2001).

The number of women in the labor force will continue to increase, but the proportion will slow markedly in the next 50 years. Ten million more women are forecast to be in the U.S. workforce by 2010 than in 2000. The 70.6 million women projected to be working and looking for work in 2010 will account for 47.9 percent of the entire labor force (Fullerton and Toossi, 2001), up from 29.6 percent in 1950, 42.5 percent in 1980, and 46.6 percent in 2000. After 2010, the proportion of women to men is projected to level off and stay about the same. Why are so many more women working than in 1950? Economic

Table 2-1 U.S. Civilian Labor Force by Age, Sex, Race, and Hispanic Origin, 1950, 2000, and Projected 2050

Group	Level (in thousands)*			Percent Change		Percent Distribution			Annual Growth Rate (percentage)	
	1950	2000	2050	1950–2000	2000–2050	1950	2000	2050	1950–2000	2000–2050
Total, 16 years and older	62,208	140,863	191,825	126.4	36.2	100.0	100.0	100.0	1.6	0.6
Men	43,819	75,247	100,280	71.7	33.3	70.4	53.4	52.3	1.1	0.6
Women	18,389	65,616	91,545	256.8	39.5	29.6	46.6	47.7	2.6	0.7
16 to 24	11,522	22,715	31,317	97.1	37.9	18.5	16.1	16.3	1.4	0.6
25 to 54	40,017	99,974	124,443	149.8	24.5	64.3	71.0	64.9	1.8	0.4
55 and older	10,669	18,175	36,065	70.3	98.4	17.2	12.9	18.8	1.1	1.4
White	—	117,574	143,770	—	22.3	—	83.5	74.9	—	0.4
Black	—	16,603	27,094	—	63.2	—	11.8	14.1	—	1.0
Asian and other	—	6,687	20,960	—	213.5	—	4.7	10.9	—	2.3
Hispanic origin	—	15,368	45,426	—	195.6	—	10.9	23.7	—	2.2
Other than Hispanic origin	—	125,495	146,399	—	16.7	—	89.1	76.3	—	0.3
White non-Hispanic	—	102,963	102,506	—	-0.4	—	73.1	53.4	—	0.0

*Remember to add three zeros to numbers reported in thousands.

Note: Dash indicates data not available. The "Asian and other" group includes (1) Asians and Pacific Islanders and (2) American Indians and American Natives.

Source: M. Toossi (2002, May), A Century of change: The U. S. labor force, 1950–2050, *Monthly Labor Review,* p. 16.

necessity is one reason; a single income is not enough for many couples. A second reason is that more women find themselves heading single-parent families. Divorce or separation often requires women to live on their own incomes. Another reason is the need for achievement beyond the home and family, particularly among college-educated women. In former male bastions such as science, engineering, management, banking, skilled trades, and politics, women are making inroads as never before.

The average age of the U.S. labor force is getting older. Between 2000 and 2010, the number of people age 55 and older in the workforce will grow by 46.6 percent. In the same time span, they are also expected to have the largest numeric increase of any age group in the U.S. labor force. This group will experience the most sweeping changes in the years to come, primarily because of the aging "baby-boom generation"—those born in the 18 years between 1946 and 1964. They will be 46 to 64 years old in 2010 and age 86 to 104 in 2050 (Toossi, 2002). By 2010, the median age of the labor force will be 40.6 years, a level not reached in the United States since 1962 (Fullerton and Toossi, 2001). The median age is expected to stay in the 40-year range to 2050 when workers age 55 and older will make up about 19 percent of the entire labor force (Toossi, 2002). The U.S. Bureau of the Census revealed in 2002 that of the 33.8 million people age 65 and over, almost 4.5 million (13.2 percent) were holding jobs or looking for work (Armas, 2003). As life expectancy increases, many workers will retire later or stop for a while and then begin again in another occupation. Reasons for the return to work are varied, but they include needing more money, boredom in retirement, and the desire for another challenge in life. Even though legislation bans age discrimination in hiring and all other aspects of employment, hidden bias against older people can still be a problem. Some employers think older people are "over the hill," more resistant to change, less educated, less trainable, and more demanding of benefits and pensions. Despite these fears, largely unsubstantiated, an expanding number of over-50 people will participate in the labor force as consultants, temporary workers, and part-timers—not as traditional 8-to-5 employees in full time jobs (Drucker, 2002).

The youth workforce will increase in numbers in the next 10 years more than it has in the past 30 years. The "youth labor force," ages 16 to 24, is projected to grow 14.8 percent or by 3.4 million between 2000 and 2010. This group will comprise 16.5 percent of the labor force in 2010, and that proportion is expected to remain close to that figure through 2050. In 1950, the youth labor force was 18.5 percent of the total. By 1980, the percentage was 23.7. Perhaps social scientists should include work experience at ages earlier than 16. Studies have shown that young people working at ages 14 and 15 were more likely to be working two years later. Even about half of the 12- and 13-year-olds engage in some sort of work (Huang, Pergamit, and Shkolnik, 2001). The U.S. Bureau of Labor Statistics (2003b) reports that about 60 percent of 16-year-old students were at work in the beginning of the 1999–2000 school year; this proportion rose to 68 percent for those age 17 and to 77 percent for the 18-year-olds.

America's labor force will become more diverse than ever before. In 1980, minorities made up 18.1 percent of the U.S. labor force. By 2010, the minority portion is expected to be 30.8 percent, and in 2050, it is projected to be 46.6 percent. Soon after 2050, the "minorities" when added together will become a majority, according to estimates by the U.S. Bureau of the Census. Of the anticipated 157.7 million people in the labor force by the year 2010, 20.9 million (13.3 percent) will be Hispanic or Latino, 18.9 million (12 percent) will be African American, and 8.7 million (5.5 percent) will be Asian, Pacific Islander, American Indian, and Alaska Native. A total of 128 million white people, including Hispanic or Latino, will make up 81.2 percent of the workforce; without Hispanics or Latinos, the white share drops to 69.2 percent. The "Asian and other" and Hispanic or Latino labor forces will increase faster than other groups (Fullerton and Toossi, 2001). Fast forward to 2050. Of the 191.8 million people expected in the U.S. labor force then, 45.4 million (23.7 percent) will be Hispanic or Latino, 27.1 million (14.1 percent) will be African American, and nearly 21 million (10.9 percent) will be Asian, Pacific Islander, American Indian, and Alaska Native.

White people, including Hispanic or Latinos, will number 143.8 million (74.9 percent); without Hispanics or Latinos, the white share drops to 53.4 percent. In the 40 years between 2010 and 2050, the number of Hispanics or Latinos in the labor force is projected to more than double (Toossi, 2002).

Foreign-born workers are playing an increasingly important role in the U.S. economy. Between 1996 and 2000, the foreign-born made up nearly half of the net increase in the U.S. labor force. Their share of the U.S. workforce expanded from about 1 in 17 in 1960 to 1 in 8 workers today. During the 18th and much of the 19th centuries, immigrants generally came from northern Europe and Africa. Large numbers of the Irish fled starvation and disease and the African slave trade continued through the first half of the 19th century despite laws that attempted to ban their coming to America. Asia provided a large source of immigrants after 1848 as Chinese contract laborers came to work in the gold mines and on the transcontinental railway; this ended with exclusionary legislation that banned Chinese immigration. The early 1900s saw European immigration shift, with the majority coming from southern and eastern countries. In 1917, Congress started applying immigration quotas based on nationality; this was eliminated by the Immigration and Nationality Act of 1965. The act led to a substantial increase of immigration and a change in the national origin of immigrants. The proportion of foreign-born from Europe dropped from 74.5 to 15.3 percent between 1960 and 2000. During the same time, the proportion coming from Latin America increased from 9.3 to 51 percent. In 2000, the 10 top nations of birth for the foreign-born population in the United States were Mexico, the Philippines, India, China, Cuba, El Salvador, Vietnam, South Korea, Canada, and the Dominican Republic (Mosisa, 2002).

Labor Trends

More people will make mid-life career changes. People now expect to be working in second and third occupations during their career lifetimes and make major career changes on an average of every 10 years. A recent Louis Harris poll discovered that only 39 percent of all workers intend to hold the same job 5 years from now, and 31 percent say they plan to leave their current work (29 percent do not know). Most people will study for their next occupation as they continue with their current work. One person or the other in two-earner couples will often go on a sabbatical to prepare for a new occupation (Cetron and Davies, 2003).

Two-income families are becoming standard in today's world. This trend has been a long time in the making. By 1992, both partners worked full time in 63 percent of U.S. households, and this figure is projected to be 75 percent in 2005 and for some time beyond (Cetron and Davies, 2003). The labor force participation rate of working-age women is beyond 60 percent, up from 33.9 percent in 1970 (Toossi, 2002). Today, lower rates of around 40 percent are found in more traditional countries such as Italy, Spain, and Mexico. When children are involved, two-income families create higher demands for child care and extended parental leave. Employers worry that family-oriented benefits could erode profits unless they are matched by equal gains in productivity (Cetron and Davies, 2003).

White-collar work will continue to grow while the proportion of blue-collar workers in the labor force will continue to drop. In the late 1970s, the United States became a white-collar economy for the first time in its history. White-collar workers have jobs in the professional, technical, managerial, sales, and clerical fields. Blue-collar workers include manual laborers and construction, craft, and factory production workers. Skilled-craft work offers the best employment prospects within the blue-collar ranks. The blue-collar workers in greatest jeopardy are factory operatives and the unskilled. Not even an increase in manufacturing production will reverse the trend. Manufacturing production keeps on rising in the United States, yet the number of blue-collar workers employed in manufacturing will continue to decline (Franklin, 1997).

Manufacturing is following the same path that has been traveled by agriculture. Farm production is four or five times greater than it was 100 years ago, with far fewer agricultural workers. That same drop in numbers of farm workers is now characterizing blue-collar workers in manufacturing and goods-producing industries (Rifkin, 1995). Manufacturing productivity has probably tripled in volume since World War II, although it involves smaller proportion of the workforce (Drucker, 2002). These productivity gains keep the economy healthy, but they force many workers in agriculture and manufacturing to seek other kinds of employment.

Employment will continue to shift toward knowledge-based industries and away from labor-based industries as the pace of technological change accelerates even faster. One consequence of new technology and the current information explosion is the greater need for a strong mind than for a strong back. Pharmaceuticals, analytical instruments, telecommunications, and information processing are examples of knowledge-intensive industries. Collectively, knowledge workers account for more than 50 percent of the U.S. workforce. They are members of skilled manufacturing teams, information system designers, managers, professionals, educators, scientists, and the like (Halal, 1996). The most rapidly growing industries hiring knowledge workers are microelectronics, biotechnology, new material sciences, telecommunications, civilian aircraft manufacturing, machine tools and robots, and computer hardware and software (Thurow, 1996).

Knowledge workers will continue to be the dominant group in the workforce, the center around which many other kinds of work will revolve. Even in manufacturing, knowledge workers outnumber blue-collar workers. Forty years ago, about 30 percent of the costs in manufacturing were for labor; today, they are down to 12 to 15 percent. In automobile manufacturing, the most labor intensive of the engineering industries, labor costs in the most advanced plants constitute no more than 20 percent. One of the main characteristics of "knowledge workers" is *borderlessness*, because knowledge travels so easily in the information society. Another trait is upward mobility, available to all through education, which can be easily obtained. The "knowledge society" will be highly competitive, with potential for failure as high as for success (Drucker, 2002).

Knowledge as an instrument of production, once owned almost entirely by employers, is now increasingly owned by knowledge workers. When the corporation was invented in the late 1800s, it owned the means of production—the factory, machines, tools, know-how. Workers depended on the corporation to make a living. With knowledge workers, this dependency no longer exists. Today, corporations rely on knowledge workers to survive and make their living. To produce their goods and services, company managers do not have the kind of technical and scientific expertise they need, so they must hire that knowledge. Because of this trend, the knowledge worker is becoming an equal partner with the company (Drucker, 2002; Pink, 2001).

Creativity is becoming the driving force of the economy. In the minds of a number of social and economic analysts, people who are creative have become the dominant group in society. Taking figures from the *U.S. Statistical Abstract*, Richard Florida (2002) calculates the workforce devoted to technical creativity has increased from 42,000 in 1900 to 625,000 in 1950 and 5 million in 1999. The number of people making a living from artistic and cultural creativity has increased from 200,000 in 1900 to 525,000 in 1950 and 2.5 million in 1999. Core industries of the "creative economy" are research and development, publishing, software, television and radio, design, music, film, toys and games, advertising, architecture, performing arts, crafts, video games, fashion, and art (Howkins, 2001).

The number and percentage of jobs in the service-producing industries will continue to greatly outpace the number of jobs in the goods-producing industries. By 2012, the service-producing sector (health care, professional and business services, retail and wholesale trade, transportation, education, finance, and the like) will employ over five times as many workers as the goods-producing industries (manufacturing, construction, and mining). Table 2-2 gives the figures. Service industries are expected to contribute 20.8 million of the 21.3 million projected increase in nonfarm wage and salary jobs between 2000 and 2012. The service-producing sector now accounts for three out of every five new jobs in the U.S. economy (Berman, 2004). The services division already

Table 2-2 Employment by Major Industry Division, 1992, 2002, and Projected 2012 (numbers in thousands of jobs)

Industry division	Employment			Percent distribution		
	1992	2002	2012	1992	2002	2012
Total[a]	123,325	144,014	165,319	100.0	100.0	100.0
Nonfarm wage and salary	109,526	131,063	152,690	88.8	91.0	92.4
Goods-producing, excluding agriculture	22,016	22,550	23,346	17.9	15.7	14.1
Mining	610	512	451	0.5	0.4	0.3
Construction	4,608	6,732	7,745	3.7	4.7	4.7
Manufacturing	16,799	15,307	15,149	13.6	10.6	9.2
Service-providing	87,510	108,513	129,344	71.0	75.3	78.2
Utilities	726	600	565	0.6	0.4	0.3
Wholesale trade	5,110	5,641	6,279	4.1	3.9	3.8
Retail trade	12,828	15,047	17,129	10.4	10.4	10.4
Transportation and warehousing	3,462	4,205	5,120	2.8	2.9	3.1
Information	2,641	3,420	4,052	2.1	2.4	2.5
Financial activities	6,540	7,843	8,806	5.3	5.4	5.3
Professional and business services	10,969	16,010	20,876	8.9	11.1	12.6
Education and health services	11,891	16,184	21,329	9.6	11.2	12.9
Leisure and hospitality	9,437	11,969	14,104	7.7	8.3	8.5
Other services	5,120	6,105	7,065	4.2	4.2	4.3
Federal government	3,111	2,767	2,779	2.5	1.9	1.7
State and local government	15,675	18,722	21,240	12.7	13.0	12.8
Agriculture[b]	2,639	2,245	1,905	2.1	1.6	1.2
Nonagriculture self-employed and unpaid family workers	9,009	9,018	9,162	7.3	6.3	5.5
Secondary wage and salary jobs in agricultural production, forestry, fishing, and private household industries[c]	178	143	128	0.1	0.1	0.1
Secondary jobs as a self-employed or unpaid family worker[d]	1,973	1,545	1,434	1.6	1.1	0.9

[a]Employment data for wage and salary workers are from the BLS Current Employment Statistics (payroll) survey, which counts jobs, whereas self-employed, unpaid family workers, and agriculture, forestry, fishing, and hunting are from the Current Population Survey (household survey), which counts workers.
[b]Includes agriculture, forestry, fishing, and hunting data from the Current Population Survey, except logging, which is from the Current Employment Survey and government wage and salary workers, which are excluded.
[c]Workers who hold a secondary wage and salary job in agricultural production, forestry, fishing, and private household industries.
[d]Wage and salary workers who hold a secondary job as a self-employed or unpaid family worker.
Source: U.S. Bureau of Labor Statistics, 2004. *News, USDL 04-148.* Washington, DC: U.S. Department of Labor.

contributed more than half of the U.S. job growth between 1988 and 2000 (Goodman and Steadman, 2002). Three-fourths of all workers provide a service rather than produce a material good. Pay rates vary greatly in services, from the low-paid helpers in fast-food establishments to the high-paid workers in managerial, legal, communications, and computer services. In manufacturing, anxieties have long been expressed about the shift of basic technology overseas, short-term benefits at the expense of long-term gains, and the loss of the blue-collar jobs that have given millions of people entry into the middle class (Bluestone and Harrison, 1982; Kuttner, 1983). Another perspective: If companies, industries, or even countries do not sharply increase manufacturing production and, at the same time, reduce the blue-collar workforce, they cannot hope to remain competitive (Drucker, 1986).

A larger share of all new jobs will continue to be created by small businesses. Large businesses were the source of most new jobs for the first two-thirds of the 20th century; then they began a contraction of employment that hasn't stopped (Hopkins, 1997). The "small companies create the most new jobs" message began with researcher David Birch (1987). Since then, Birch's investigations have revealed that growth companies, a tiny subset of productive small businesses, have become the major creator of jobs within the United States (Richman, 1997). Between 1994 and 1998, companies with fewer than 20 employees created four out of every five new jobs in the economy (Pink, 2001). Perhaps these findings should not be surprising: 91.5 percent of all establishments employ fewer than 50 workers, and 97.9 percent have fewer than 100 employees (U.S. Bureau of Labor Statistics, 2002a). The specialization that is spreading throughout industry and the professions creates new "niche markets" to be served by small businesses. Old specialties become outmoded as new ones appear even more rapidly, creating more career choices (Cetron and Davies, 2003).

Large companies are getting smaller. No one expects large companies to disappear; however, they are "disintegrating" or restructuring into confederations where one division is entirely responsible for producing a part of a given product. The rationale for production that prevailed until recently was for a company to bring all activities needed to turn out a product under one management. Now, a company *"outsources"* those activities (computer programming, data processing, and so on) to other companies and suppliers both in the United States and in foreign countries. A growing number of workers with full-time jobs will be employed on the edge of an organization; that is, they will be working for an outsourcing contractor and strategically arranged where their specialized knowledge can make the greatest contribution. The growth of a business today develops through alliances, partnerships, agreements, and joint ventures. The corporation of the future will be reduced to its top management; every other activity can be outsourced. The corporation has been a creator of jobs and wealth, but now the biggest challenge for the large company (especially the multinational) may be how it validates itself through its values, mission, and vision (Drucker, 2002).

Large companies will still be attractive for many workers. Would you rather work for a large company or a small company? Small companies claim they offer more flexible work rules, creative problem solving, personalized training, and a less intimidating work environment (Wegmann, Chapman, and Johnson, 1989). The average size of the effective work organization is dropping, sometimes drastically, as companies adopt automation and new information technologies and abandon the old hierarchical structure for a smaller, weblike arrangement of divisions within the larger corporation. However, others see another side to small businesses: They offer a lot of jobs, but also let a lot of workers go. When you subtract one from the other, the small-company advantage disappears. Risks are assumed to be greater in small business; many fail and shut their doors. Small firms generally pay lower wages, offer fewer benefits, lag in adopting new technology, and depend on the large corporations for whom they serve as contractors or suppliers (Harrison, 1994). Large businesses are perceived as paying higher wages, providing better fringe benefits, offering more opportunities for advancement, and having greater job security.

The aftermath of the 9/11 attack in New York and Washington, D.C., is creating more security-oriented jobs. Until September 11, 2001, Americans felt insulated from devastating terrorist invasions on their homeland. The deliberate seizure of domestic airplanes and crashing them into the World Trade Center and the Pentagon has changed all that, bringing a much greater interest in security and the military. Various news sources tell us that employment in security-oriented work is expanding; we read or hear of the emphasis on homeland security, creating a need for more airport screeners, air marshals, border patrols, immigration agents, cargo ship monitors, hazardous waste protectors, and reference checkers of criminal records. In the private sector, defense contractors need systems engineers, software developers, project managers, and company security workers. Database surveillance has been stepped up. Another illustration is the growth of the U.S. Secret Service, originally created in 1865 to combat counterfeiting. The agency expanded when it began providing part-time security for President Grover Cleveland and assumed full-time responsibility for the president's protection following the assassination of President William McKinley. Added to the Secret Service's duties was the protection of diplomatic missions in Washington, D.C., in 1970 and throughout the nation in 1975 ("Bogus bucks," 2002). Employment has been cut in industries negatively affected by 9/11; among these are airline companies, hotels, car rental companies, and local economies that depend on tourism and conventions. The response to terrorist strikes within the country presents a dilemma: how to prevent them without damaging the values and freedoms we have come to rely on for our quality of life (Hughes, 2002).

More jobs will continue to be available from replacement needs than growth needs. Where do jobs come from? According to the U.S. Department of Labor, they come from replacement needs and growth needs. "Replacement" means a new person is needed to fill a job position that a former worker has left because of promotion, retirement, death, illness, injury, termination, or some other reason. "Growth" means more job positions are created from an increased demand for a product or service that the occupation provides. Between 2000 and 2010, 58 million jobs are projected to open. Of these, 35.8 million job openings will be for replacement and 22.2 million will come from employment growth in the economy (Hecker, 2001). With all the attention given to new or rapidly growing occupations, job seekers could overlook more traditional occupations, which emphasize replacement needs. The pattern of replacement and growth needs varies among major occupational groups. The professional and related occupational group provides more job openings from growth needs than from replacements. However, within this group, replacement openings are expected to exceed growth openings in three slower-growing occupations: architecture and engineering; education, training, and library occupations; and social science occupations. All other major occupational groups are expected to provide more job openings because of replacement needs rather than growth needs, although the rapidly growing health-care support occupations should have more openings from job growth than replacement needs (Berman, 2001).

New (or Re-Emphasized) Work Values

Meaningful work is replacing money as a standard for success for an increasing number of people. Money can provide the means to a livelihood, but many people are asking more from work than a paycheck. A research adviser for AARP (American Association for Retired Persons) and a native of the Philippines recalls her father's mantra:

> Money can buy a house, but not a home.
> Money can buy medicine, but not health.
> Money can buy fun, but not happiness.
> Money can buy sex, but not love.
> Money can buy a church, but not heaven. (Delehanty, 2000, p. 6)

A former U.S. secretary of labor writes about a paradox: Many people are earning more money and are living better in material terms than they did a quarter of a century ago. Nonetheless, we find our personal lives growing poorer and the time and energy for the nonworking part of our lives evaporating as we work longer and more frantically than before (Reich, 2000). Money is important, but a lot of people want to put more significance on their family and personal time. As for work, people hope for jobs in which they can grow, express their values, and set their own priorities. They want occupations about which they can be passionate. Their *search for meaning* indicates that a lot is being asked from work nowadays. What gives meaning to work? People ask for the freedom to have more control over their work. They want the kind of employment that is authentic, where they can be true to themselves, not become a stranger to themselves or something they're not, just to survive. They are willing to be held accountable for whatever they produce at work; traditionally, this was the job of the manager or employer. Success in work, then, is defined on the individual's own terms rather than society's evaluations (Pink, 2001).

The definition of work is changing for many people. Many people will have periods of intense work interspersed with periods of unpaid activities that are more meaningful to them. We often think there is only one kind of work—paid work on the job. This narrow definition of work puts the economic needs of society ahead of all the other purposes of life (Handy, 2002). Beyond paid work, there is the work needed to sustain a home, raise a family, take on volunteer projects, update skills, and keep up with developments in your field. To attract talented people, organizations will be required to allow their employees time for essential home-type work, study work, and charitable work in their local communities. About 59 million or over one in four people age 16 and over in the United States did volunteer work at some point from September 2001 to September 2002, according to a news item reported by the U.S. Bureau of Labor Statistics (2003a).

Alternative Work Styles: Free-Agent Independent Workers and Nonstandard Workers

"Free agent" or independent workers are increasing in the U.S. economy. "Free agents" are described as independent workers who are free from the attachments of a large institution and are agents of their own futures (Pink, 2001). They represent a shift in power from the organization to the individual. In the 1950s, the "organization man" was a type of worker who submerged his identity in serving a big company that rewarded faithfulness with a regular paycheck, a pension, job security, and a place in the corporate world (Whyte, 1956). The organization man had replaced the entrepreneur—an individualist long honored in U.S. business life but not equipped to fit the corporate mentality. Now the entrepreneurs have come back in the form of free agents. Their substructure consists of copy and print shops, bookstores, coffee shops, the Internet, executive suites, office supply superstores, postal service centers, and overnight package delivery services. Three types of free agents are soloists, temporary workers, and microbusinesses. Pink (2001) gives four basic reasons for the rise of free agency. (1) The "social contract" (loyalty for security) that organizations once offered to individuals has been withdrawn. (2) Workers rather than companies increasingly own the tools needed to produce wealth. (3) Prosperity is reaching more people. (4) Organizations have shorter lives—many of us will outlive the company for which we work.

Some researchers see the percentage of "nonstandard" workers growing at a faster pace than the total labor force; others do not. The change in the U.S. economy from a stable work environment to an uncertain, fiercely competitive one is most visible and dramatic in the "nonstandard" segment of the labor force. Many organizations want to hire people to get a project done and then wave goodbye to those workers until they are needed again. Employers defend these practices as survival tactics in a dog-eat-dog world of global competition; critics point out that the human costs to some people are enormous. "Standard work" means full-time work, just as a standard career once meant lifetime employment with the same company. "Nonstandard" work arrangements include part-time work, working for a temporary help agency, on-call labor, day labor, and independent contracting and self-employment—the free-agent type of work (just mentioned) that is growing more common. In 1995, the first year data were available for nonstandard work, the Economic Policy Institute (EPI) classified 29.4 percent of all jobs as nonstandard with 34.3 percent of all female workers and 25.3 percent of all male workers in these kinds of jobs (Kalleberg et al., 1997). The U.S. Bureau of Labor Statistics (BLS) 2001 Contingent and Alternative Arrangements Survey came up with a figure of 4.0 percent of all jobs under BLS's broadest measure of contingent work and a total figure of 9.4 percent for people in "alternative work arrangements." The BLS appears to have a narrower definition of "nonstandard work" than the EPI; the BLS definition consists of independent contractors, on-call workers, temporary workers, and contract company workers—but not self-employed workers and day laborers. Some people regard part-time and temporary work positively. DiNatale (2001) found the proportion of these workers who prefer alternative work arrangements has increased since the mid-1990s. Independent workers reported in 1999 that 84 percent preferred their arrangement to a traditional, standard one. Many nonstandard workers see their job as a way of supplementing income, obtaining a full-time position, trying out a job for experience, handling child care problems, or creating time for further education. Other workers don't see it that way. Compared to core or full-time workers, nonstandard workers on average face less pay, more unpredictable hours and work days, fewer benefits, and less advancement and job security. Employers see advantages in nonstandard work arrangements; they can lower their labor costs, expand or contract their supply of labor as they adjust to changing demands for their products, and screen potential candidates for permanent jobs. Nearly four out of five employers in the United States use some form of nontraditional staffing (U.S. Department of Labor, 2000).

Self-employment, or running your own business, will attract increasing numbers of people into entrepreneurial work roles. Owning a business has been a persistent American dream. The entrepreneurial spirit is vital to starting a new business. Typically, the image of the entrepreneur is of a self-confident, hardworking, competent, creative risk taker. Peter Drucker (1985) writes that entrepreneurial activity is a process that is systematic, managed, and based on purposeful innovation. Entrepreneurs can be "intrepreneurs"—that is, they operate from within a company that employs them but function in an entrepreneurial role. About 8 percent of the U.S. workforce meets the rather narrow definition of the Bureau of Labor Statistics' definition of self-employment: workers who rely on their businesses for their primary source of income. An expanded definition would raise the figure to about 13 percent, or 17.3 million in 1997 and projected to increase by over a million in a decade (Silvestri, 1999). Another study puts self-employment in the United States at 17.5 percent in 1993, up from 6.7 percent in 1973 (Frenkel et al., 1999). Although it is beyond the scope of this book to cover the details of starting a business, here is a short list of subjects involved:

- Creating or buying a business and assessing its risks (over half of all entrepreneurial businesses fail within the first five years)
- Analyzing the market
- Budgeting
- Determining location
- Financing (lack of capital is a major cause of failure in the early years)
- Borrowing (if necessary)
- Organization—sole proprietorship, partnership, or corporation
- Designing the place of business
- Rental space
- Merchandising
- Assessing customer needs
- Advertising
- Naming the business
- Pricing strategy
- Finding employees
- Cash flow
- Obtaining credit
- Inventory control
- Accounting
- Payroll and taxes
- Buying computers and equipment
- Insurance and security
- Managing the business

Ask yourself: Do I have the qualities of an entrepreneur? Am I willing to work long hours? Do I have ideas that could fill people's needs, and can I describe them to others? Plenty of help is available from bank loans to courses and workshops to information in books, newspapers, and magazines.

An increasingly popular way to run your own business is to purchase a franchise from an established company. Over 33 percent of U.S. retail businesses are franchise operations, which account for 50 percent of all retail sales, reports the International Franchise Association. Over 300,000 franchise stores together employ 8 million people. Even during an economic downturn at the beginning of the 2000s, franchising expanded 4 to 5 percent in the United States (Folks, 2003). Franchises are permissions granted by producers to sell their products. You, the franchisee, operate the business within a specified territory. You must raise enough money to buy and equip a building and pay wages, taxes, insurance, and bills. The franchiser may give you a plan to run the business and help solve problems. As with the startup of any new business, you work long hours and must provide enough money to keep the business going before the profits begin to come in. To get an idea of what's happening in the franchise world, click on Franchise News Briefs at www.franchise.org/news/newsbriefs.asp sponsored by the International Franchise Association. The top 10 franchise industries in 2003 were fast food, retail, service, automotive, restaurants, maintenance, building and construction, retail food, business services, and lodging. The top 10 franchise companies in the same year were McDonald's, 7-Eleven, Subway, H&R Block, Burger King, Jani-King, Taco Bell, Radio Shack, Pizza Hut, and Domino's Pizza. However, franchising is not all burgers and fries. Franchising is growing in other categories such as financial services, Internet services, and bioenvironmental services (Franchise News Briefs, 2003).

More women will become self-employed than men. The rate of self-employment for women is an astounding 12 times that of men (Pink, 2001). Perhaps this should not be surprising. Women have always had to rely on self-employment more. Their career paths as paid employees typically have been interrupted by giving birth to babies, having greater child-raising responsibilities, and caring for elderly parents. These disruptions, along with lingering sexism, may account for lower pay rates for women (about 76 percent of men's pay rates at the present time). Women's career patterns are more complex than men's.

Self-employment has problems that will require time and effort to solve. As exciting as working independently can be, free agency has a downside. Because you are self-employed, you must pay for your own health insurance; people who work for an employer receive full or partial benefits—declining these days, to be sure, but helpful nonetheless. Because you are your own boss, you pay both the employer's and employee's share of your Social Security payroll tax, double the amount of other workers. Being self-employed, you must estimate your income tax four times a year to the federal government—and four times annually to the state if it has an income tax; traditional workers have their taxes automatically withheld from each paycheck by their employer (Pink, 2001).

"Career ladder" and "career lattice" concepts will be replaced by other metaphors for the working patterns of many individuals. The "career ladder" indicated a way to move up in a company through promotions and pay raises. The concept of "career lattice" signified a pathway within an organization when companies became less hierarchical and resembled more of a weblike structure. Moving alongside or taking the place of those images will be other metaphors. One such concept is the "LEGO career," Daniel Pink's (2001) metaphor from a "LEGO set" where you assemble your skills, connections, interests, and opportunities as pieces of a work arrangement, then disassembling the structure when it has outlived its usefulness, and reassembling the pieces in a new arrangement to meet a new need. Pink believes "ladder careers" are likely to decrease, "lattice careers" may become less typical, and " LEGO careers" will be more abundant.

Education and Job Training Trends

The mismatch between available jobs and people's ability to do them will continue. Too often, workers are not in the right place with the right skills. A labor shortage exists for many occupations requiring technical skills. Employers have reported positions staying vacant for months because they could not find skilled people to fill them. Some labor analysts believe the skills–jobs mismatch could worsen as large numbers of employees begin to retire and the shortage of skilled labor forces U.S. companies to attract educated immigrants (Judy and D'Amico, 1997). Of companies with 100 or more employees, 57 percent have had difficulty hiring workers with the required skills (Van-Horn, 2002). By 2010, more than 10 million additional workers will be needed in the United States, particularly in the fastest-growing occupations that require a postsecondary education (Herman, Olivo, and Gioia, 2003).

You will be asked to perform more functions, be more productive, and use more skills in tomorrow's work. Because the global market is demanding more of the companies that participate in it, your employer is going to expect more of you as a worker. Just as 2 percent of us produce enough food for the nation, in contrast to the 90 percent once engaged in agriculture, workers in all fields must now increase their productivity so that they and their companies will survive. Not only will you need to produce more in goods and services, but the quality of what you provide must improve. Flexibility, adaptability, mobility, knowledge, commitment, excellence, accountability, self-direction, and self-management are your keys to future success. Pay will be increasingly linked to job performance. The transformation of the working world is so extensive that "the job" as we have known it throughout the industrial era could all but disappear (Bridges, 1994). Many workers will hire out their skills to several organizations on a contract basis. If they still work for one company, they will use a number of skills on a series of projects, doing whatever work needs to be done. Jobs change so rapidly today that the skills used in them could become outdated. In electronics, half of the knowledge first-year students learn is obsolete by senior year (Cetron and Davies, 2003). Unless workers can adapt to the challenges of the working world, many of them may become obsolete as well. Author Isaac Asimov, in his story "Profession," portrays a future in which specialists, instantly trained by connecting educational tapes to the brain, are able to function for only a short time before being discarded by new workers whose advanced skills will also become obsolete in time.

Your need for training and retraining will increase. Forget the notion of "finishing" your education: A college education is only a springboard to further education. In all likelihood, you can anticipate lifelong learning experiences that will involve returning to the classroom several times over your working life. Continuous learning will be required in any job where people want meaningful work. The drive for greater productivity translates into rewards for those who prepare themselves. Over the past 25 years, real wages (which account for inflation) have risen for college-educated workers, whereas they have fallen for people who never got beyond high school. The greatest source of inequality today is the difference between those who have skills employers need and those who don't. Educational requirements for many jobs are increasing, and young people without any college education or postsecondary training must often settle for poorly paid retail trade and service jobs. People lacking developed skills will see the purchasing power of their wages erode and will face more likely job loss from automation and other technological advances (Judy and D'Amico, 1997). Male college graduates average about 70 percent more in earnings than high school graduates. For women, the difference is even more dramatic: Female college graduates earn more than twice as much as female high school graduates (Buchholz, 1996). Many factory production jobs now require postsecondary education; 32 percent of precision production and craft workers have been to or graduated from college, and the number is much higher for recent hires (Thurow, 1996).

Most jobs in the United States require some on-the-job training, but the fastest-growing jobs call for a college degree. Projected figures for 2008 from the U.S. Department of Labor (2000) indicate that 39 percent of all employment will need short-term on-the-

Yes, Stewart, I _do_ think it's time for job retraining.

job training, 13.7 will require moderate-term on-the-job training, and 9.1 percent will need on-the-job training on a long-term basis. _Short term_ is defined as 1 month or less, _moderate term_ from 1 to 12 months, and _long term_ as over 12 months. You can see the distribution of employment by education and training in Figure 2-1. Three out of every four U.S. workers are in occupations that do not require a bachelor's degree, a

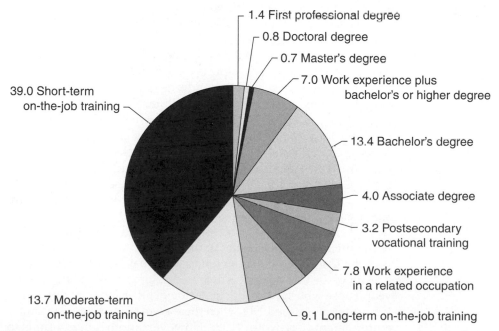

Figure 2-1   Employment distribution by education and training category, projected 2008 (percentages). _Source:_ U.S. Department of Labor (2000, Summer), Futurework: Trends and challenges for work in the 21st century, _Occupational Outlook Quarterly,_ p. 35.

distribution that is expected to remain about the same in the near future. The majority of new jobs being created call for knowledge other than that obtained from earning a degree. Good basic reading, communication, and mathematics skills will play an important role in developing a career. A 1998 American Management Association survey found over one-third of all job applicants deficient in math and reading skills, a sharp increase attributed largely to the higher literacy and math skills required for many jobs today.

The Internet will grow exponentially. As of 2003, about 500 million people in the world were Net users; that figure is forecast to be between 709 and 946 million in 2005. One reason for this rapid expansion is the increased use of the Internet in developing countries. In the United States, educational institutions are using the Internet more frequently. Colleges market their programs to distant students. Small and rural high schools supplement their curricula with material from the Internet (Cetron and Davies, 2003). In 2001, 72.3 million workers or 53.5 percent of all U.S. employees used a computer on their jobs. The industries where over 70 percent of all employees used a computer at work were managerial, professional specialty, technician, and administrative support occupations. The most commonly reported use was connecting to the Internet or accessing email (Hipple and Kosanovich, 2003). The impact of the Internet will be positive, significant, and sustained. The Internet will produce major cost savings in many sectors of the economy, meaning faster growth in productivity, lower prices for consumers, and an improved standard of living for average Americans (Litan and Rivlin, 2001).

Economic Forces

The global economy will have more influence in our lives than ever before. Look at the labels on your clothes and the shoes you wear. And where were the electronic gadgets made that you hold in your hand? Chances are good these products came from outside your country and are distributed by an international company. The growth of the interdependent, worldwide economy means international trade is more important for the United States and Canada. Free trade practices have overcome many protectionist impulses. *Protectionism* occurs when governments shield domestic industries from foreign competition through quotas and increased taxes (tariffs) on imports and/or subsidies and reduced taxes for home companies (Lee, 1987).

Importing more products than exporting them continues an unfavorable balance of trade. Since the 1970s, the United States moved from trade surpluses to trade deficits, as Europe and Japan became competitive with the United States in a number of industries (Scott, 1999). Since then, imports have remained steadily ahead of exports. Annual trade deficits have soared to hundreds of billions of dollars. In 2002, the U.S. trade deficit widened to a record $435.2 billion, as U.S. demand for foreign imports grew larger and U.S. exports slumped (Dukcevich, 2003). Americans have developed a fondness for foreign goods. There is a story about an American dressed in a British tweed coat, Korean shirt, and Hong Kong slacks; wearing Italian shoes and looking at his Swiss watch; glancing at his German car with four new French tires; pouring a hot cup of Colombian coffee into a Canadian mug; setting a Chinese place mat on an Irish linen tablecloth atop a Danish table varnished with linseed oil from India; filling his Austrian pipe with Turkish tobacco; watching the news on a television set made in Japan; reaching into a Moroccan briefcase and picking up a Taiwanese ballpoint pen with which he writes a letter to his representative in Congress demanding to know why the United States has an unfavorable balance of trade. The number of jobs lost as a result of the trade deficit is disputed. Estimates range from zero to 3 million jobs per year. Those who say trade deficits do not affect jobs cite the strong performance of the U.S. economy in the 1990s when there were rising trade deficits *and* falling rates of unemployment (Griswold, 1998). However, another study finds that if the U.S. trade deficit increases by $100 billion to $200 billion, 700,000 to 1.5 million jobs will be eliminated, particularly in manufacturing, where male blue-collar workers are hardest hit

What do you mean, "They're <u>moving</u> the plant overseas?"

(Scott and Rothstein, 1998). With an unfavorable trade balance, the difference between exports (which creates jobs at home) and imports (which loses jobs to other countries) produces more unemployment in the United States (Scott, 1999). The trade deficit may have a negative effect on wages as well. Rising exports created about 4.1 million jobs between 1992 and 1999, but rising imports lost 7.3 million jobs for a net loss of 3.2 million jobs. Because most foreign trade is in the manufacturing sector where pay related to both imports and exports tends to be higher than average, loss of manufacturing jobs had the effect of depressing U.S. wages (Scott, 2000).

National, corporate, and personal debt will threaten jobs and standards of living. The U.S. debt is measured in trillions of dollars. Annual deficits in the billions were recorded all through the 1980s and into the 1990s. With a stronger economy, balanced budgets and surpluses were finally achieved in the late 1990s. The weaker economy and battle against terrorism of the early 2000s brought a return to federal spending beyond the revenue taken in. Interest payments on the national debt take money that could go toward building and repairing infrastructure and programs to alleviate pressing social problems—these expenditures would normally create more employment. Corporate debt is troubling; it blocks new investments that typically produce new jobs. Personal bankruptcies are at an all-time high, their number rising 7.4 percent and totaling 1,573,720 in March 2002 to March 2003, up from 1,464,961 in the previous 12-month period (Associated Press, 2003). People paying their way out of debt don't have as much money to spend for goods and services that keep other people working. Some say the impact of this debt is small because we mostly owe ourselves. However, concerns are expressed about passing on a reduced living standard to future generations.

For better or worse, deregulation and privatization brings greater competition into the economy. Government became more involved in the regulation of private industries from the 1890s through the 1930s, resulting in numerous federal regulatory agencies. A reaction against government intervention inspired "deregulation" in the late 1970s and 1980s. Competition increased, starting in telecommunications, transportation, and finance. Survival meant doing more with fewer people. Layoffs became an important feature of corporate strategy. Middle management and staff are reduced as companies reorganize. Deregulation is credited with better products, lower prices, improved efficiency and productivity, and greater innovation and creativity. Its detractors cite job loss and instability, more business failures, and a growing concentration of business ownership after an initial spurt of competition. Some analysts predict a future "reregulation" in response to the turmoil created by deregulation. Terrorism and corporate crime are bringing back government's role as protector of the people and watchdog of the economy (Nussbaum, 2002).

Privatization occurs when government transfers responsibility for delivering certain services to the private sector. It is the opposite of *nationalization*, when government takes over a business or industry that has been owned privately (Lee, 1987). Advocates of privatization claim it contains the costs of government and increases competition, rewarding those companies that provide better services at lower prices to the public. Opponents of privatization say government employees are dedicated first and foremost to providing a high-quality public service, whereas the main goal of private business is to make a profit by paying its workers less and charging higher fees in the long run. Privatization has become a major issue in current political struggles.

Automation will increase the loss of jobs but will also add new ones that require higher skills. Ever since machine work was introduced early in the industrial revolution, improvements in manufacturing have drawn dire predictions of massive unemployment and plants emptied of workers. Digitally controlled robots, combined with advanced computers and software, have ushered in a system that requires progressively less human labor (Rifkin, 1995). Automation does cause many types of work to disappear. Gone are repetitive, mind-numbing tasks. Workers have the opportunity to take on more interesting and challenging work. People are recruited to design, manufacture, sell, transport, install, operate, and service the new machines. When computer-driven machines and robots are brought in, they aid design and manufacturing, crunch data faster, produce higher-quality goods, improve service, increase output, lower costs, and reduce "downtime" during model changes. Some jobs are "deskilled" as an operator controls a switch or button and a machine does a job formerly done by a skilled worker. However, most new occupations are upgraded and require more skill, training, and responsibility. Failure to automate can mean the loss of jobs because business is eventually lost to high-technology competitors. Career planners need to be aware of those occupations that can be easily automated in the years ahead.

Company restructuring in response to the pressures of competition will create opportunities as well as hardships for workers. Mergers, acquisitions, divestitures, takeovers, and buyouts are strategies that will continue to be used in business. The "shakeout" from reorganization means new jobs and promotions for some and layoffs for others. Some experts declare that frequent restructuring is healthy—businesses must be lean and mean to be successful in a competitive world. The essential feature of the capitalist system is "creative destruction," as Joseph Schumpeter (1962) observed long ago; it is an ongoing process of constant destruction and creation. Millions of workers have lost their jobs over the past century, but millions of workers today earn their living from occupations that didn't exist 100 years ago because of the destruction–creation process. Nonetheless, some critics see company restructuring as merely moving money around on a financial chessboard, with no gain in productivity and with workers getting mangled in the process. Stories abound of corporate raiders making off with millions of dollars while bitter workers end up with no job, no benefits, and no pension—no matter how good or loyal they've been. Harrison and Bluestone (1988) assail corporate restructuring strategies that focus on labor costs. They charge that these strategies create civil war between companies and regions of the country as they compete for investments that produce jobs, pit worker against worker, and further divide society into the "haves" and the "have-nots." *Downsizing*—reducing the size of a company's workforce—is an economic necessity to many corporate executives (they call it "rightsizing"). Albert Dunlap, former chairman of Scott Paper, reduced that company's workforce to 20,000 by laying off 11,200 employees. He justified this downsizing by saying, "If I hadn't saved the company, everyone would have been out of work. . . . But what I keep uppermost in my mind is not that I cut away 35 percent, but that I saved 65 percent. . . . the remaining 65 percent have a more secure future"

(Dunlap, 1996, pp. 21, 23). Business leaders claim that often no jobs are lost in downsizing. In the early 1980s AT&T employed around 950,000 people. By 1996 it had downsized to 300,000 employees, but its industry still numbered about 950,000 workers (Nocera, 1996). Nevertheless, to many workers, downsizing turns the American dream into an economic nightmare. Those workers who survive are usually forced to work longer and harder. This can increase stress, lower morale, and undermine company loyalty. One former "corporate executive" claims the idea that layoffs are good for companies is a myth. Not only is the loss of jobs a catastrophe for workers, but downsizing has been ineffective for most companies (Downs, 1995).

Location and Time Trends

More workers will do their jobs, or part of their jobs, at home. Imagine going to work in your pajamas, bathrobe, and slippers. If you are working at home, that idea may not be as far-fetched as it sounds. At-home workers are self-employed, run part-time businesses at home to supplement full-time jobs, or "telecommute"—they are connected to an employer by a computer modem, telephone, and/or fax machine. The U.S. Bureau of Labor Statistics (2002b) reported 19.8 million people usually did some work at home as part of their primary job in May 2001. These workers accounted for 15 percent of U.S. total employment. Four-fifths were employed in managerial, professional, and sales jobs. About 8 of 10 used a computer for the work they did at home. Half of those who usually worked at home were wage and salary employees taking work home from the job on an unpaid basis, mainly to finish or catch up on work usually done at the work site. Another 17 percent arranged with their employer to be paid for the work they did at home, and the remainder (30 percent) were self-employed (U.S. Bureau of Labor Statistics, 2002b). Be careful before you shell out money for access to a job that is done entirely from your own home. Complaints to the National Fraud Information Center about at-home schemes came in second only to bogus credit card offers (Harris, 2002).

At-home workers take up a pattern of working that has existed throughout human existence. Until the start of the industrial revolution at the end of the 18th century, people's work was generally home based. When mass-production manufacturing reshaped the economy, work moved out of the home and into factories. The increasing importance of information, the breakup of mass-production manufacturing industries, and the appearance of completely new industries have returned some work to the home. There are benefits and drawbacks to working at home. Living and working in the same place saves time in commuting. There may be fewer interruptions; you may be able to get more done. Money may be saved without expenses for gas and parking, rush-hour traffic jams may be reduced, and workers may have more time to spend with their families (Toffler, 1983). Drawbacks may be having a home too small to allow for adequate office space, feeling isolated or "out of the loop," and finding it hard to separate work and home life. Rules need to be established, such as no interruptions by family members, friends, or neighbors. A private place for working needs to be separated from the rest of the home. Occupations and industries in which you find many at-home businesses include construction, cleaning services, consulting, designing, computer services and repair, real estate, painting, lawn maintenance, arts and crafts, landscaping, automotive services and repair, remodeling and repairing buildings, management and business consulting, marketing programs and services, trucking, wholesale goods (nondurable), communications, and audiovisual production services. No one knows how many businesses that start at home stay home based (Friedman, 1997).

The percentage of people in the U.S. labor force holding more than one job ("moonlighting") is declining somewhat. Suppose your intended occupation does not pay enough to support yourself and your family. It may be that the skills acquired in your first job lead naturally to a second job. Whatever the reasons, one job may not be enough. Nearly 8 million U.S. workers, or 5.4 percent of all employed people, held more than one job in 2001 (U.S. Department of Labor, 2002), up from 3.9 million in 1975. "Moonlighting" peaked at 6.2 percent in 1996 and has edged downward since then. Moonlighting rates for males in 1995 had stabilized at around 6 or 7 percent. Rates for women have increased, growing from one-third of the male rate in 1970 to about the same as the male rate in 1994. Blacks and people of Hispanic or Latino origin moonlight at much higher rates, and more often, because of economic hardship, than whites (Kimmel, 1995). Although most people work multiple jobs in order to earn extra money to meet regular expenses and pay off debts, economic necessity is not the only reason. In many cases, moonlighting is a choice when a worker enjoys the second job or needs a flexible work schedule. A person may combine two or even three part-time jobs to schedule work hours around family obligations. Labor force studies show that the proportion of those holding multiple jobs actually increases with education. Workers in professional, technical, service, and clerical occupations were the most likely to hold multiple jobs. Hobbies and interests may lead to a part-time job different from one's primary occupation (Amirault, 1996–1997).

Hours on the job have lengthened as reactions against the longer workweek (or work year) take place. The average time spent at work by full-time workers in the early 1970s was 39 hours per week, a reduction from twice that number in the early days of the Industrial Revolution. Shorter working hours meant making labor more humane and distributing more jobs. Predictions were made that the standard 40-hour week would be lowered to 32 hours or even less (Cetron, 1984). From a lowest point reached in the early 1970s, however, the average working week for full-time workers increased to about 43 hours by the 1990s. Extended over an entire year, that increase came to about 164 more hours, or the equivalent of an extra month's labor for the average U.S. worker (Schor, 1993). The U.S. Department of Labor also reported a 43-hour average workweek for people who usually work full time, although the average went down to 39.2 hours when part-time workers were added (Rones, Ilg, and Gardner, 1997). The typical American now works 350 more hours a year than the typical European, and even more hours than the hardworking Japanese (Reich, 2000). Workers spend about 10 percent more hours on the job than they did a decade ago, and time is becoming the world's most precious commodity. Stress-related problems affecting employee morale and health will continue to grow (Cetron and Davies, 2003). The longer working week is producing a reaction; more people now believe there is too much emphasis on work. Companies have found shorter hours often produce happier, more productive employees (Saltzman, 1997). Why such growth in the number of working hours? Employers have found that paying premium wages such as time-and-a-half to regular employees for overtime work is more profitable than training and providing benefits for new employees. Many workers have found they need to work longer just to maintain their standard of living. Advances in labor-saving technology should cut workers' hours, but companies argue that competition forces them to use fewer people and extend their hours.

Boundaries between work and home are becoming blurred even though employers resist becoming a second home to workers. Workers' attitudes are changing; many people faced with time pressures at home seek a sanctuary at work. Work becomes home, and home becomes work (Hochschild, 1997). We cannot get away from work when we are at home, and we cannot get away from home when we are at work (Challenger, 2002). Companies are being asked to become "family-friendly" by providing regular or emergency day-care services for preschool children, care for aged parents, and flexible work schedules. Employers are quick to remind us, however, that the basic functions of business are to make profits, return dividends to investors, and create jobs for workers. Companies can most benefit families by being productive and profitable. Being family-friendly can mean losses in productivity. With all the pressures of competition and time on both workers and companies, the impact of family-friendly policies at the workplace is likely to be minimal (Boyett and Boyett, 1995).

Time boundaries at work are shifting. Less than one-third of Americans work a 9-to-5 day. "The social contract is changing as a fluid schedule demands more flexibil-

ity from everyone in the workplace" (Brady, 2002, p. 142). Workers are increasingly allowed to adjust work around their needs. Hours on the job have intruded into leisure
time, but free time has inched its way into the job with exercising, talking with friends,
Internet shopping, and other breaks being built into the work day.

Employee job security and loyalty to the organization are declining. Workers once
bought into an implied "social contract"—they gave their loyalty to the employer in
exchange for security from the company. This alliance has been shattered by practices
such as restructuring of companies, automation and new technology, downsizing, hiring temporary workers, and outsourcing. Survey data show increased feelings of job
insecurity even in times of economic growth and lower unemployment rates (Mishel,
Bernstein, and Schmitt, 1999). Ask older workers about the transformations in work,
and most will tell you they've never seen anything like it in their lifetime. The changes
can be viewed as exhilarating and stimulating or threatening and intimidating—or a
mixture of these feelings. When the organization indicates to the worker "You will be
employed only as long as you add value to the company," this message will not produce loyalty to the organization. Employers would like a "vertical" loyalty, where
workers offer allegiance to their company and its leadership. In return, workers
would like cradle-to-grave security. Both workers and employers are likely to declare
that loyalty is dead today. Writer Daniel Pink (2001) maintains loyalty has not disappeared, but has changed. Replacing vertical loyalty is a "horizontal" loyalty—faithfulness that moves laterally to colleagues, ex-colleagues, profession, industry, teams,
clients, customers, family, and friends. Talent, skill, performance, and results are
sought by organizations today, and workers must provide them.

Unemployment, Underemployment, and Turnover Rates

*Unemployment is higher than official figures indicate and it remains troublesome for mil-
lions of people.* Many economists consider "natural" rates of unemployment to be
around 6 percent of the labor force. In the 1950s, "full employment" was considered
achieved whenever the unemployment rate was around 3 percent. Now, "full employment" allows for a 6 percent unemployment rate (Rifkin, 1995). Official unemployment figures do not give the full picture. Dembo and Morehouse (1997) claim the
real jobless rate is almost twice as high as the reported rate. The government's
monthly figure doesn't count "discouraged workers"—those who want a job but have
given up looking for one. If laid off or fired people do not look for a new job in a four-
week time span, they are not counted in the unemployment rate. Not included are
people back in school because they can't locate the job they want or set up their own
businesses when unable to find work. The official unemployment rate does not adjust
for part-time workers who would prefer a full-time job, nor does it count those who
would like to work but have been forced into early retirement. If all these people were
included, a 6 percent unemployment rate would grow to 10 percent. Even a slight rise
in unemployment rates clobbers the lower-income portion of the population. The key
to improving living standards for the bottom half is and always has been full employment. During the boom years of 1995 to 2000, everyone gained, and the most affluent gained even more. With a mild increase in unemployment in 2001, everyone
lost except the top 20 percent of the population. Real prosperity requires full employment (Bernstein, 2002).

Widespread loss of jobs becomes disastrous in a free-market, competitive economy. Workers losing their jobs become displaced or dislocated. Finding a new job can take a financial and emotional toll; changes may include a pay cut, only part-time work,
pulling up stakes, selling the old house, buying or renting a new one, and adjusting
to a new environment. When displaced workers find new work, their new jobs pay
an average of 13 percent *less* than the jobs they lost, and more than one fourth who
had health insurance on their old jobs don't have it at their new ones (Mishel, Bernstein, and Schmitt, 1999). Unemployment causes a vast array of social and personal
problems. Homicide, suicide, crime, drunkenness, and domestic abuse all increase

when unemployment increases. Work disappears in the ghettoes of America's large cities. Places where the poor and jobless live are different from the neighborhoods of the working poor (Wilson, 1996). Work has a moral dimension; it is a part of the "social compact" individuals have with society. Work is too much a part of the human condition to be wished away (Wolfe, 1997). The absence of work all too often takes away the meaning of life itself.

Underemployment will continue to be a fact of life for some college graduates. The number of college graduates taking jobs not typically requiring a college degree rose from 11 percent in 1969 to 20 percent for the 1990s. Projections for the 1996–2006 time span were for the number of college graduates to be underemployed to be around 18 percent, remaining almost unchanged from the previous 10-year period (Mittlehauser, 1998). *Underemployment* means working in an occupation that does not use the worker's skills and training to the maximum. A graduate in forestry becomes a forester's aide, a social science major works as a teacher's aide, or someone with a master's degree in English accepts a job in a child care center. Although a job below expectations is better than no job at all, the situation is frustrating. In the minds of some students, it erodes the value of a college education. Some college graduates are underemployed because colleges have produced more graduates in certain fields than the labor market needs. There is no clear solution for this, but some recommendations can be made. (1) Gain work experience while attending school; it can give you an advantage when job hunting. (2) Consider dual majors in college, such as combining a liberal arts program with business, or a teaching degree in physical education with math or science. (3) Be willing to move to a location that offers a greater probability of gaining employment in your major occupational choice. (4) Adjust your attitude. Underemployment is not the end of the world. Being aware of the possibility of underemployment can take the shock out of the situation if it should occur. A more positive approach is to view underemployment as an opportunity to learn new skills and gain more work experience.

Turnover rates are turning higher in a volatile economy, costly to workers but increasingly costly to companies. The U.S. Bureau of Labor Statistics (BLS) finds there were 52.9 million "separations" of workers and their employers between May 2001 and May 2002. (52.3 million people were hired in the same time period, a slight downward trend in a time of recession.) Those figures mean over one-third of the U.S. workforce were coming to and going from jobs in one year's time. Let's look at "worker displacement," as the BLS calls it. The BLS defines *displaced workers* as people 20 years or older who left their jobs because their company closed or moved, there was insufficient work for them, or their position was abolished. Between 1999 and 2001, 4.0 million workers were displaced from their jobs they had held for at least three years, up from 3.4 million in the previous two years. Another 6.0 million workers were displaced from jobs they had held for less than three years; combining that number with the first figure would total 9.9 million, up from 7.4 million of the previous two years (U.S. Bureau of Labor Statistics, 2002b). High employee turnover is not only hard on workers, but also costly to companies. A job seeker may see only the difficulties of landing a job offer, but an employer faces a challenging environment in which to recruit, hire, and keep skilled employees. Financial analysts are paying more attention to the stability of a company's workforce. Uncomfortably high turnover of workers can cause a company's bond ratings and stock prices to drop. A stable, productive workforce is a competitive advantage for any company, always true but especially in the economy of the future (Herman, Olivo, and Gioia, 2003).

Miscellaneous Trends

Income inequality is growing in America. The gap between the educated, high-income "haves" and the less-educated "have-nots" is widening. The first group, mostly white and affluent, is increasing its advantage through their greater use of computers and the Internet, creating the so-called digital divide. The disadvantaged group, mostly people of color and poor, has less access to the new technologies and are falling further behind. Inequality in the United States has risen to levels not experienced since the Gilded Age of the late 1800s and the boom years of the 1920s. Both eras were followed by antibusiness backlashes (Lexington, 2003). U.S. Bureau of the Census (2003) data divides the household shares of combined income by fifths and the top 5 percent of the income distribution (2001 dollars, in percentages and average income):

Percentage of U.S. population	Percentage of Total U.S. Income	Average (Mean) Income
Lowest 20 percent	3.5 %	$ 10,136
Second 20 percent	8.7	25,468
Third 20 percent	14.6	42,629
Fourth 20 percent	23.0	66,836
Highest 20 percent	50.1	145,970
Top 5 percent	22.4	260,464

Alternative forms of education will proliferate. We see this trend already in home schooling, distance learning, and charter schools. Independent teachers will provide the tutoring for many of these kinds of learning experiences (Pink, 2001). Apprenticeship training will expand for more people, especially younger students who may be enrolled in two or three regular school courses and be apprenticed to a graphic design artist or an electrician for the rest of the school day (Botstein, 1997).

Membership in labor unions is declining in numbers and in proportion to the overall U.S. labor force. A creation of the industrial age, the union movement has been, in some ways, a victim of its own success. Almost all it fought for has been made law in modern countries—the right to bargain collectively, shorter working hours, increased pay for workers, overtime pay, and retirement pensions. Over all industries in 2000, the average weekly earnings for union workers were $696, or 28 percent higher than the $542 made by nonunion workers (Reinhold, 2000). Union membership in the United States reached a peak of 22.2 million workers in 1975, but since then it has fallen to its lowest point in six decades (White, 2001). In 2002, 16.1 million people were union members, or 13.2 percent of the U.S. workforce. However, "if middle-class people are indifferent to labor unions, they are increasingly hostile to corporations" (Wolfe, 1998, p. 236). Workers in the public sector had a union membership rate of 37.5 percent compared with 8.5 percent for private-sector employees in 2002 (U.S. Department of Labor, 2003). New initiatives to increase union membership may be tried—organizing temporary workers, for example.

More families will seek to blend work and family, instead of balancing them against each other. Contacts with both family and work will occur during the day. Fewer people want work only or family only; more people want both work *and* family and will try to develop a mixture that will work for them. The line between one's personal and occupational life is predicted to become more blurred in the future. With ringing cell phones, humming fax machines, and constant email, those who want a balance between work and home will need to work and plan well to achieve it. A study entitled "Shared Work—Valued Care" from Michigan State University reveals that the United States lags far behind many other nations in helping workers balance professional and home lives and addressing the pressures on working families. Too many employers expect their employees to function as if they had a partner or other care giver at home full time. The Netherlands, for example, helps workers adjust their hours of work. Most German employers allow their workers to bank extra hours in time accounts that can later be used as paid time off (Baba, 2003). The full report can be viewed at www.epinet.org/books/sharedcare.pdf.

"Soft, nontechnical skills" are valued just as highly, if not more so, by employers as the technical requirements for jobs. With today's competitive market comes the demand for higher standards, among which are "soft skills." These skills are explained as a cluster of personality traits, social graces, language fluency, personal habits, and

friendliness all of us have in varying degrees. Employers often advise job seekers not to worry so much about technical skills; they are more concerned about workers showing up on time, taking supervision well, and functioning well in teams. Soft skills include a good work ethic, courtesy, honoring commitments, self-discipline, and keeping to company culture in grooming, dress, appropriate body language, and language of the workplace. Training for soft skills may not be obvious; they seem to come from early childhood and family environment (Calvert, 2002).

Working harder and smarter does not automatically mean raises in the paycheck. Rewards in the economy of today may be praise and recognition from the boss, cheaper goods and services to buy, or a one-shot bonus, but not necessarily more money each payday. Companies have other priorities; among them may be new equipment, plant expansion, paying off debt, or increased dividends to stockholders. Competitive pressures multiply from such things as foreign imports, improved quality standards, increases in productivity, and deregulation—not to mention beating out the competition in the same industry. To stay profitable, companies today are more likely to contract out instead of producing in-house, replace workers with machines, and hire part-time or temporary workers. The "XYZ Affair" in Exercise 2-1 at the end of this chapter provides some insights into the point raised here.

NEW AND EMERGING OCCUPATIONS: DIFFICULTIES AND BENEFITS

Many occupations we now take for granted did not exist until recently. However, as the world of work changes, the tasks workers are asked to do on well-established jobs become so different that they develop into new occupations. Technology is only one force driving the creation of new occupations. Shifts in consumer needs and tastes, business trends, new research, higher levels of education, aging, and increased immigration are among other factors causing new types of jobs to emerge. In a fascinating article in the *Occupational Outlook Quarterly*, Olivia Crosby (2002) explains how new occupations develop, why they are hard to identify, and what rewards and risks workers face in newly created jobs.

New jobs emerge when employers need workers to do tasks never done before, such as managing Web sites in the early 1990s. A worker might simply add a new task as a specialty to an existing occupation, but if it is sufficiently different and becomes the primary job of enough workers, the new task may grow to become a new occupation on its own. Crosby (2002) cites the example of computer security as an emerging specialty. Workers setting up and managing computer networks also have the responsibility of keeping them secure. As security work becomes more complex, computer workers begin to specialize and a new occupation begins to emerge. When videoconferencing became widespread, workers who could establish, troubleshoot, and track the new technology were needed, and the occupation of videoconferencing technician was born. Improved computer graphics brought forth new multimedia and animation specialties. Advances in data management and networking capabilities led to geographic information systems technicians and programmers who manage data from global positioning satellites.

Changes in the law bring into being new occupations and specialties. Welfare-to-work legislation created the need for new types of job coaches and human services workers. Telecommunications laws that require closed captioning of television programs created the need for stenocaptioners, or closed captioners. Changes in Medicaid regulations meant new types of recordkeepers and record makers were needed. Population shifts and social developments are another source of new occupations. Because the aging population is growing, organizations are employing workers with geriatric expertise, including geriatric nurses, human services workers, and social workers. Changes in business practices also result in new occupations. As more people use health management organizations, restorative therapy and utilization coordinators examine patient records to make sure treatment met the organization's standards. Most new types of work result from a combination of reasons. For example, distance learning programs are now possible because of improved computer networking, the popularity of lifelong learning concepts, and competition between schools.

Career researchers try to distinguish existing occupations from those that are relatively new, emerging, or evolving. Fuzzy definitions make this difficult. *New* occupations are those that have appeared recently and have work activities, skills, and knowledge that are so distinctive they are not included in the most current occupational classification system. Recent examples are artificial intelligence specialist, employee wellness coordinator, ethics officer, and information technology specialist. *Emerging* occupations have few workers but are expected to grow in the future. Such occupations are easier to identify, because researchers notice an occupation that is growing. But growth can take a long time. For example, massage therapists formed a professional association in the 1940s, became identified as an emerging occupation decades later, and in 2000 received a specific title in the U.S. Standard Occupational Classification. An *evolving* occupation is an existing occupation where tasks and skill requirements are changing significantly. All occupations change to some degree, but *evolving* occupations are changing *dramatically*. At present, for example, animators are shifting from two-dimensional pen-and-paper work to three-dimensional computer modeling. Other occupational examples are data security engineer, grants specialist, health quality-assurance manager, and safety director.

Researchers grapple with the meaning of the word *occupation*. Most of us think of an occupation as a set of jobs with similar tasks requiring similar skills. A look at the work of geriatric social workers explains the difficulty in deciding whether it has enough unique tasks to be a new occupation. If there are not, the job becomes a specialty within the broad field of social work, which includes a few well-established detailed occupations such as mental health social worker and medical and public health social worker. Geriatric social workers take on functions of both of these occupations, providing counseling referral services, case management, and help to older patients with chronic medical problems. Are these tasks unique enough to make it a separate occupation, or are these workers part of an existing one? The answer depends on the judgment of the researcher (Crosby, 2002).

Building a career in a new occupation is a venturesome enterprise because the stability of a new occupation is so uncertain and its specialized nature can make it less secure than other, established occupations. Job seekers have modest opportunities in new and emerging occupations, which are small by their very nature. Most new occupations never do become very large. Horticulture therapy aide, for example, was recognized as an emerging occupation in 1976. It was still small enough over 25 years later to be listed as new and emerging in the popular literature. A new technology can become absorbed into existing occupations. Internet research technician is a new occupation that now has declining numbers of workers, as more people become skilled at making their own online searches. Another difficulty arises when organizations that once functioned without an occupation for many years decide they can do so again when budgets tighten. Occupations that have been regarded as expendable include employee morale officers and wellness coordinators. Workers can reduce this risk by learning skills useful in a number of different occupations.

Many career planners are intrigued by new occupations because the work is challenging and exhilarating. They can take advantage of the labor shortage that may exist in the new occupation before other people can get adequate training. Shortages can lead to high wages and good advancement opportunities for workers in the new occupation before it becomes well known. One thing to remember about new occupations is that they generally grow out of old occupations. Crosby (2002) refers to the case of a fuel cell technician who combined 20 years of experience as an auto mechanic with an associate degree in electronics. The work he does as a fuel cell technician is different from car mechanic work, but many parts of it are the same.

Readers interested in identifying emerging occupations can find occupations in the "Trends in Specific Occupations within Occupational Groups" section (just after the next section) of this chapter by selecting occupations that in 2000 had fewer than 50,000 workers and are expected to grow twice the average for all occupations over the 2000–2010 decade. These occupations are listed in the "much faster than average" and "faster than average growth" categories of the "Employment Prospects" column. Examples are landscape architect, biomedical engineer, diagnostic medical sonographer, and desktop publisher.

GROWING AND DECLINING OCCUPATIONS AND INDUSTRIES

Now that you have read about a number of economic forces, employment trends, and the nature of new occupations, we now look at growing and declining rates and numerical increases and decreases in occupations and industries. Table 2-3 lists 30 of the occupations expected to grow fastest between 2002 and 2012. Note that these occupations are listed in order of *percentage* increase. When reading occupational forecasts, it is important to consider the *number* of workers employed in an occupation. Table 2-4 lists the 30 occupations projected to have the largest job growth in *total numbers*. If you compare the 38 percent growth rate anticipated for environmental engineers from 2002 to 2012 with the 19 percent growth expected for accountants and auditors, you might conclude your chances of getting a job would be better as an environmental engineer. But when you look at the numeric change in employment forecast for these two occupations, you find that 205,000 new accountants and auditor positions are expected, compared with 18,000 new jobs for environmental engineers—a 187,000 margin for accountants and auditors. Of the 30 fastest-growing occupations projected for the 2002–2012 time period, 15 are health-related and 7 are computer-related occupations, as shown in Table 2-3 (Hecker, 2004).

The 30 largest job-growth occupations of Table 2-4 are from a much broader range of occupational groups than the fastest-growing occupations. Six are service occupations, and five are health related. Four each are in education, training, and library occupations and in sales and related occupations. Three occupational groups are in management, business, and financial occupations and in the office and administrative support category. Twenty-one on the list in Table 2-4 had employment of at least 1 million workers in 2002 (Hecker, 2004).

The job picture through 2012 in other fields is very different. Occupations facing a loss in total numbers of workers are listed in Table 2-5 in order of their projected numeric decline. Even though the percentage or number of workers is declining in an occupation, don't despair of finding work if that occupation is your favorite. Remember that there are always replacement needs, except in occupations being phased out entirely. There may not be as many new hires as there are workers leaving a declining occupation, but some job positions in the field will still be open.

Table 2-6 reveals the strength of the services division within the service-producing industries; here, it accounts for 10 of the 20 fastest-growing industries listed. All the industries shown in Table 2-6 are expected to grow at least twice as fast as the average (16 percent) between 2000 and 2010.

Table 2-7 shows projected employment changes in selected industries between 2001 and 2010. The 20 industries on the left side of the table are projected to account for nearly 60 percent of all employment growth. All are in the service-producing sector, and 15 of the 20 are in the services division. The first three industries will make up nearly half of the growth in the services division. Most industries projected to have the largest employment declines are in the goods-producing sector (with the exception of private households and federal government).

What causes declines in certain industries? Drops in consumer demand, increased imports, productivity gains from improved technology, and transfers of duties to different occupations are among the answers usually given.

Every two years, the U.S. Bureau of Labor Statistics prepares a new set of employment projections for the next 10 years, based on data collected by the U.S. Department of Labor and its state branches. The first report appears in the *Monthly Labor Review* during the fall of odd-numbered years (generally, the November issue).

Table 2-3 Fastest Growing Occupations, 2002–2012 (numbers in thousands of jobs)

Occupation	Employment 2002	Employment 2012	Change Number	Change Percentage	Quartile Rank by 2002 Median Annual Earnings[a]	Most Significant Source of Postsecondary Education or Training
Medical assistants	365	579	215	59	3	Moderate-term on-the-job training
Network systems and data communications analysts	186	292	106	57	1	Bachelor's degree
Physician assistants	63	94	31	49	1	Bachelor's degree
Social and human service assistants	305	454	149	49	3	Moderate-term on-the-job training
Home health aides	580	859	279	48	4	Short-term on-the-job training
Medical records and health information technicians	147	216	69	47	3	Associate degree
Physical therapist aides	37	54	17	46	3	Short-term on-the-job training
Computer software engineers, applications	394	573	179	46	1	Bachelor's degree
Computer software engineers, systems software	281	409	128	45	1	Bachelor's degree
Physical therapist assistants	50	73	22	45	2	Associate degree
Fitness trainers and aerobics instructors	183	264	81	44	3	Postsecondary vocational award
Database administrators	110	159	49	44	1	Bachelor's degree
Veterinary technologists and technicians	53	76	23	44	3	Associate degree
Hazardous materials removal workers	38	54	16	43	2	Moderate-term on-the-job training
Dental hygienists	148	212	64	43	1	Associate degree
Occupational therapist aides	8	12	4	43	3	Short-term on-the-job training
Dental assistants	266	379	113	42	3	Moderate-term on-the-job training
Personal and home care aides	608	854	246	40	4	Short-term on-the-job training
Self-enrichment education teachers	200	281	80	40	2	Work experience in a related occupation
Computer systems analysts	468	653	184	39	1	Bachelor's degree
Occupational therapist assistants	18	26	7	39	2	Associate degree
Environmental engineers	47	65	18	38	1	Bachelor's degree
Postsecondary teachers	1,581	2,184	603	38	1	Doctoral degree
Network and computer systems administrators	251	345	94	37	1	Bachelor's degree
Environmental science and protection technicians, including health	28	38	10	37	2	Associate degree
Preschool teachers, except special education	424	577	153	36	4	Postsecondary vocational award
Computer and information systems managers	234	387	103	36	1	Bachelor's or higher degree, plus work experience
Physical therapists	137	185	48	35	1	Master's degree
Occupational therapists	82	110	29	35	1	Bachelor's degree
Respiratory therapists	86	116	30	35	2	Associate degree

[a]The quartile rankings of Occupational Employment Statistics annual earnings data are presented in the following categories: 1 = very high ($41,820 and over), 2 = high ($27,500 to $41,780), 3 = low ($19,710 to $27,380), and 4 = very low (up to $19,600). The rankings were based on quartiles using one-fourth of total employment to define each quartile. Earnings are for wage and salary workers.

Note: Add three zeros to employment numbers.

Source: D. E. Hecker (2004, February), Occupational employment projections to 2012, *Monthly Labor Review,* p. 100.

Table 2-4 Occupations with the Largest Job Growth, 2002–2012 (numbers in thousands of jobs)

	Employment		Change		Quartile Rank by 2002 Median Annual Earnings[a]	Most Significant Source of Postsecondary Education or Training
	2002	2012	Number	Percentage		
Registered nurses	2,284	2,908	623	27	1	Associate degree
Postsecondary teachers	1,581	2,184	603	38	1	Doctoral degree
Retail salespersons	4,076	4,672	596	15	4	Short-term on-the-job training
Customer service representatives	1,894	2,354	460	24	3	Moderate-term on-the-job training
Combined food preparation and serving workers, including fast food	1,990	2,444	454	23	4	Short-term on-the-job training
Cashiers, except gaming	3,432	3,886	454	13	4	Short-term on-the-job training
Janitors and cleaners, except maids and housekeeping cleaners	2,267	2,681	414	18	4	Short-term on-the-job training
General and operations managers	2,049	2,425	376	18	1	Bachelor's or higher degree, plus work experience
Waiters and waitresses	2,097	2,464	367	18	4	Short-term on-the-job training
Nursing aides, orderlies, and attendants	1,375	1,718	343	25	3	Short-term on-the-job training
Truck drivers, heavy and tractor-trailer	1,767	2,104	337	19	2	Moderate-term on-the-job training
Receptionists and information clerks	1,100	1,425	325	29	3	Short-term on-the-job training
Security guards	995	1,313	317	32	4	Short-term on-the-job training
Office clerks, general	2,991	3,301	310	10	3	Short-term on-the-job training
Teacher assistants	1277	1,571	294	23	4	Short-term on-the-job training
Sales representatives, wholesale and manufacturing, except technical and scientific products	1,459	1,738	279	19	1	Moderate-term on-the-job training
Home health aides	580	859	279	48	4	Short-term on-the-job training
Personal and home care aides	608	854	246	40	4	Short-term on-the-job training
Truck drivers, light or delivery services	1,022	1,259	237	23	3	Short-term on-the-job training
Landscaping and groundskeeping workers	1,074	1,311	237	22	3	Short-term on-the-job training
Elementary school teachers, except special education	1,467	1,690	223	15	2	Bachelor's degree
Medical assistants	365	579	215	59	3	Moderate-term on-the-job training
Maintenance and repair workers, general	1,266	1,472	207	16	2	Moderate-term on-the-job training
Accountants and auditors	1,055	1,261	205	19	1	Bachelor's degree
Computer systems analysts	468	653	184	39	1	Bachelor's degree
Secondary school teachers, except special and vocational education	988	1,167	180	18	1	Bachelor's degree
Computer software engineers, applications	394	573	179	46	1	Bachelor's degree
Management analysts	577	753	176	30	1	Bachelor's or higher degree, plus work experience
Food preparation workers	850	1,022	172	20	4	Short-term on-the-job training
First-line supervisors/managers of retail sales workers	1,798	1,962	163	9	2	Work experience in a related occupation

[a]The quartile rankings of Occupational Employment Statistics annual earnings data are presented in the following categories: 1 = very high ($41,820 and over), 2 = high ($27,500 to $41,780), 3 = low ($19,710 to $27,380), and 4 = very low (up to $19,600). The rankings were based on quartiles using one-fourth of total employment to define each quartile. Earnings are for wage and salary workers.

Note: Add three zeros to employment numbers.

Source: D. E. Hecker (2004, February), Occupational employment projections to 2012, *Monthly Labor Review*, p. 101.

Table 2-5 Occupations with the Largest Job Decline, 2002–2012 (numbers in thousands of jobs)

	Employment		Change		Quartile Rank by 2002 Median Annual Earnings[a]	Most Significant Source of Postsecondary Education or Training
	2002	2012	Number	Percentage		
Farmers and ranchers	1,158	920	−238	−21	3	Long-term on-the-job training
Sewing machine operators	315	216	−99	−31	4	Moderate-term on-the-job training
Word processors and typists	241	148	−93	−39	3	Moderate-term on-the-job training
Stock clerks and order fillers	1,628	1,560	−68	−4	4	Short-term on-the-job training
Secretaries, except legal, medical, and executive	1,975	1,918	−57	−3	3	Moderate-term on-the-job training
Electrical and electronic equipment assemblers	281	230	−51	−18	3	Short-term on-the-job training
Computer operators	182	151	−30	−17	2	Moderate-term on-the-job training
Telephone operators	50	22	−28	−56	2	Short-term on-the-job training
Postal service mail sorters, processors, and processing machine operators	253	226	−26	−10	2	Short-term on-the-job training
Loan interviewers and clerks	170	146	−24	−14	2	Short-term on-the-job training
Data entry keyers	392	371	−21	−5	3	Moderate-term on-the-job training
Telemarketers	428	406	−21	−5	4	Short-term on-the-job training
Textile knitting and weaving machine setters, operators, and tenders	53	33	−20	−39	3	Long-term on-the-job training
Textile winding, twisting, and drawing out machine setters, operators, and tenders	66	46	−20	−30	3	Moderate-term on-the-job training
Team assemblers	1,174	1,155	−19	−2	3	Moderate-term on-the-job training
Order clerks	330	311	−19	−6	3	Short-term on-the-job training
Door-to-door sales workers, news and street vendors, and related workers	155	137	−18	−12	3	Short-term on-the-job training
Travel agents	118	102	−16	−14	3	Postsecondary vocational award
Brokerage clerks	78	67	−11	−15	2	Moderate-term on-the-job training
Eligibility interviewers, government programs	94	83	−1t	−12	2	Moderate-term on-the-job training
Prepress technicians and workers	91	81	−10	−11	2	Long-term on-the-job training
Fishers and related fishing workers	36	27	−10	−27	3	Moderate-term on-the-job training
Sewers, hand	36	29	−8	−21	4	Short-term on-the-job training
Textile cutting machine setters, operators, and tenders	34	26	−8	−23	3	Moderate-term on-the-job training
Textile bleaching and dyeing machine operators and tenders	27	19	−8	−29	3	Moderate-term on-the-job training
Announcers	76	68	−8	−10	3	Long-term on-the-job training
Meter readers, utilities	54	46	−8	−14	2	Short-term on-the-job training
Chemical plant and system operators	58	51	−7	−12	1	Long-term on-the-job training
Mixing and blending machine setters, operators, and tenders	106	99	−7	−7	2	Moderate-term on-the-job training
Credit authorizers, checkers, and clerks	80	74	−5	−7	3	Short-term on-the-job training

[a]The quartile rankings of Occupational Employment Statistics annual earnings data are presented in the following categories: 1 = very high ($41,820 and over), 2 = high ($27,500 to $41,780), 3 = low ($19,710 to $27,380), and 4 = very low (up to $19,600). The rankings were based on quartiles using one-fourth of total employment to define each quartile. Earnings are for wage and salary workers.

Note: Add three zeros to employment numbers.

Source: D. E. Hecker (2004, February), Occupational employment projections to 2012, *Monthly Labor Review*, p. 103.

Table 2-6 Fastest-Growing Employment in Selected Industries, Projected 2000–2010 (numbers by percentage)

Industry	Projected Employment Growth by Percent, Projected 2000–2010
Computer and data processing services	86%
Home healthcare services	68
Social services, residential care facilities	64
Cable and pay TV services	51
Personnel supply services	49
Offices of health practitioners, except dentists and physicians	47%
Public warehousing and storage	45
Water supply and sanitary service	45
Offices of physicians, including osteopaths	44
Veterinary services	44
Landscape and horticultural services	43%
Miscellaneous equipment rental and leasing	42
Management and public relations	42
Social services, child day care	42
Wood buildings and mobile homes	40
Local and suburban transportation	40%
Freight transportation arrangement	39
Research and testing services	38
Nonstore retailers	35
School buses	34
Total, wage and salary employment growth	16%

Source: U.S. Department of Labor, (2001–2002, Winter), Industry employment, *Occupational Outlook Quarterly,* p. 28.

(Text continued from page 66)

(A change to a new occupational classification system delayed this report, scheduled for November 2003, to February 2004.) As of February 2004, the projection for the average employment growth of all occupations in the United States between 2002 and 2012 dropped slightly from 16 to 14.8 percent. The bureau summarizes the same employment trends in the *Occupational Outlook Quarterly*. One article from the *Quarterly* you should examine is "The Job Outlook in Brief." It usually appears in the spring issue of even-numbered years, and is a valuable resource for any career planner.

"The Job Outlook in Brief" provides short summaries of employment information for each occupation in the current edition of the *Occupational Outlook Handbook* (published every two years). For all occupations, you will find the estimated employment at the beginning of a 10-year span and the change in employment, by percentage and number projected for that time period. A concise description of employment prospects for the occupation concludes its section. For example, in the spring 2002 issue of the *Occupational Outlook Quarterly*, you can read the following figures for accountants and auditors: year 2000 estimated employment, 976,000; percentage change in employment, 2000–2010, 19 percent projected increase; numeric change, 2000–2010, 181,000 increase; and then a brief summary of job prospects for accountants and auditors. The format in the "Brief" allows you to compare employment outlooks in many different occupations. The next section in this chapter gives an abbreviated version of the "Job Outlook in Brief" for 2000–2010. A later edition may be available by the time you read this book.

Table 2-7 Employment Growth or Decline in Selected Industries, Projected 2000–2010 (numbers in thousands)

Industries Gaining the Most Jobs	Projected Employment Growth, 2000–2010	Industries Losing the Most Jobs	Projected Employment Decline, 2000–2010
Personnel supply services	1,913	Private households	−226
Computer and data processing services	1,805	Federal government, except postal service	−145
Education services, public and private	1,603	Apparel	−103
Eating and drinking places	1,486	Railroad transportation	−61
Offices of physicians, including osteopaths	864	Blast furnaces and basic steel products	−49
Local government, except education and hospitals	563	Commercial banks, savings institutions, and credit unions	−38
Social services, residential care facilities	512	Weaving, finishing, yarn and thread mills	−34
Hospitals, public and private	488	Electric services	−33
Management and public relations	460	Life insurance	−30
Home health-care services	437	Crude petroleum, natural gas, and gas liquids	−29
Nursing and personal care facilities	394	Preserved fruits and vegetables	−25
Legal services	340	Dairy products	−24
Local and long-distance trucking and terminals	313	Plastics materials and synthetics	−24
Engineering and architectural services	313	Electrical industrial apparatus	−23
Social services, child day care	298	Coal mining	−23
All other social services, except job training	295	Pulp, paper, and paperboard mills	−23
State government, except education and hospitals	293	Beverages	−22
Air carriers	288	Clothing and accessories stores	−22
Hotels and motels	255	Petroleum refining	−20
Research and testing services	244	Household appliances	−19

Note: Remember to add three zeros to these numbers.
Source: U.S. Department of Labor (2001–2002, Winter), Industry employment, *Occupational Outlook Quarterly,* pp. 27, 29.

Another resource is "Matching Yourself with the World of Work," published and updated every few years in the *Occupational Outlook Quarterly.* "Matching" enables you to go beyond employment trends for given occupations. Occupations are matched with a list of characteristics, including education required, data, people, things, and working conditions. "Matching Yourself with the World of Work" appears in the *Occupational Outlook Quarterly* and is available from the Bureau of Labor Statistics of the U.S. Department of Labor.

TRENDS IN SPECIFIC OCCUPATIONS WITHIN OCCUPATIONAL GROUPS

The Bureau of Labor Statistics in the U.S. Department of Labor groups occupations into 11 major categories in its *Occupational Outlook Handbook* (Moncarz and Reaser, 2002). These are (1) management and business and financial; (2) professional and related; (3) service; (4) sales and related; (5) office and administrative support; (6) farming, fishing, and forestry; (7) construction trades and related; (8) installation, maintenance, and repair, (9) production; (10) transportation and material moving; and (11) military occupations. In the occupational projections that you find in this section, consider the time lag and the uncertainty of unforeseen events that come with all forecasts. The information you read here, as well as elsewhere, may have changed somewhat between the time it was written and the time you read it.

An Abbreviated Bureau of Labor Statistics Job Outlook in Brief for 2000–2010

Occupation/Group	Employment in 2000	Employment Change, Projected 2000–2010		Employment Prospects
		Percentage	Number	
A. Management and business and financial operations				
Accountants and auditors	976,000	19	181,000	Avg-Gr
Administrative services managers	362,000	20	74,000	Avg-Gr*
Advertising, marketing, public relations, and sales managers	707,000	32	229,000	Fast-Gr*
Budget analysts	70,000	15	10,000	Avg-Gr*
Claims adjusters, appraisers, examiners, and investigators	207,000	15	31,000	Avg-Gr
Computer and information systems managers	313,000	48	150,000	Mfast-Gr+
Construction managers	308,000	16	50,000	Avg-Gr
Cost estimators	211,000	17	35,000	Avg-Gr
Education administrators	453,000	13	61,000	Avg-Gr
Engineering and natural science administrators	324,000	8	26,000	Slow-Gr
Farmers, ranchers, and agricultural managers	1,462,000	–22	–318,000	Decline
Financial analysts and personal financial advisers	239,000	29	69,000	Fast-Gr
Financial managers	658,000	19	122,000	Avg-Gr
Food service managers	465,000	15	70,000	Avg-Gr
Funeral directors	39,000	2	900	No Ch
Human resources, training, and labor relations managers and specialists	709,000	16	116,000	Avg-Gr*
Industrial production managers	255,000	6	16,000	Slow-Gr
Insurance underwriters	107,000	2	2,100	No Ch
Loan counselors and officers	265,000	6	16,000	Slow-Gr
Lodging managers	68,000	9	6,400	Slow-Gr
Management analysts	501,000	29	145,000	Fast-Gr*
Medical and health services managers	250,000	32	81,000	Fast-Gr
Property, real estate, and community association managers	270,000	23	61,000	Fast-Gr
Purchasing managers, buyers, and purchasing agents	536,000	2	12,000	No Ch
Tax examiners, collectors, and revenue agents	79,000	8	6,600	Slow-Gr
Top executives	2,999,000	15	464,000	Avg-Gr*
B. Professional and related occupations				
1. *Architects, surveyors, and cartographers*				
Architects, except landscape and naval	102,000	18	19,000	Avg-Gr
Landscape architects	22,000	31	6,800	Fast-Gr
Surveyors, cartographers, photogram metrists, and surveying technicians	121,000	17	20,000	Avg-Gr
2. *Drafters and engineering technicians*				
Drafters	213,000	19	42,000	Avg-Gr
Engineering technicians	519,000	12	62,000	Avg-Gr
3. *Engineers*	1,465,000	9	138,000	Slow-Gr
Aerospace engineers	50,000	14	7,000	Avg-Gr
Agricultural engineers	2,400	15	400	Avg-Gr
Biomedical engineers	7,200	31	2,300	Fast-Gr
Chemical engineers	33,000	4	1,400	Slow-Gr
Civil engineers	232,000	10	24,000	Avg-Gr

Key to Employment Prospects Column: Mfast-Gr = much faster than average growth, 36% or more; Fast-Gr = faster-than-average growth, 21–35%; Avg-Gr = average growth, 10–20%; Slow-Gr = slower-than-average growth, 3–9%; No Ch = little or no change, 0–2%; Decline = decrease of 1% or more. An asterisk (*) means keen competition for jobs in the occupation is expected because job openings compared to the number of job seekers may be fewer. For projected total employment in 2010, add (or subtract) the projected employment change number for 2000–2010 to (from) the employment number in 2000. The + marker means opportunities in that occupation are very good or excellent because of substantial employment growth or expected high turnover rates.

Occupation/Group	Employment in 2000	Employment Change, Projected 2000–2010		Employment Prospects
		Percentage	Number	
Computer hardware engineers	60,000	25	15,000	Fast-Gr
Electrical and electronics engineers	288,000	11	31,000	Avg-Gr
Environmental engineers	52,000	26	14,000	Fast-Gr
Industrial engineers, including health and safety	198,000	6	12,000	Slow-Gr
Materials engineers	33,000	5	1,800	Slow-Gr
Mechanical engineers	221,000	13	29,000	Avg-Gr
Mining and geological engineers, including mining safety engineers	6,500	–1	–100	Decline
Nuclear engineers	14,000	2	300	No Ch
Petroleum engineers	9,000	–7	–600	Decline
4. *Art and design*				
Artists and related workers	147,000	20	29,000	Avg-Gr*
Designers	492,000	21	104,000	Fast-Gr
5. *Entertainers and performers, sports, and related*				
Actors, producers, and directors	158,000	27	42,000	Fast-Gr*
Athletes, coaches, umpires, and related workers	129,000	19	24,000	Avg-Gr*
Dancers and choreographers	26,000	16	4,300	Avg-Gr
Musicians, singers, and related workers	240,000	19	45,000	Avg-Gr*
6. *Media and communication-related*				
Announcers, radio and television	71,000	–6	–4,000	Decline*
Broadcast and sound engineering technicians and radio operators	87,000	14	12,000	Avg-Gr
News analysts, reporters, and correspondents	78,000	3	2,200	Slow-Gr
Photographers	131,000	17	22,000	Avg-Gr*
Public relations specialists	137,000	36	49,000	Mfast-Gr*
Television, video, and motion picture camera operators and editors	43,000	26	11,000	Fast-Gr*
Writers and editors	305,000	26	80,000	Fast-Gr
7. *Community and social services*				
Counselors, school, job, rehabilitation	465,000	26	120,000	Fast-Gr
Probation officers and correctional treatment specialists	84,000	24	20,000	Fast-Gr+
Social and human service assistants	271,000	54	147,000	Mfast-Gr+
Social workers	468,000	30	141,000	Fast-Gr
Clergy (data not available)				
8. *Computer and mathematical*				
Actuaries	14,000	5	800	Slow-Gr
Computer programmers	585,000	16	95,000	Avg-Gr*
Computer software engineers	697,000	95	664,000	Mfast-Gr+
Computer support specialists and systems administrators	734,000	92	677,000	Mfast-Gr+
Mathematicians	3,600	–2	–100	Decline
Operations research analysts	47,000	8	3,800	Slow-Gr
Statisticians	19,000	2	500	No Ch
Systems analysts, computer scientists, and database administrators	887,000	62	554,000	Mfast-Gr+
9. *Education, training, library, and museum*				
Archivists, curators, and museum technicians	21,000	12	2,600	Avg-Gr*
Instructional coordinators	81,000	25	20,000	Mfast-Gr
Librarians	149,000	7	10,000	Slow-Gr
Library technicians	109,000	19	21,000	Avg-Gr
Teacher assistants	1,262,000	24	301,000	Fast-Gr+
Teachers: adult literacy and remedial and self-enrichment education	252,000	19	47,000	Avg-Gr+
Teachers: postsecondary	1,344,000	23	315,000	Fast-Gr+

An Abbreviated Bureau of Labor Statistics Job Outlook in Brief for 2000–2010 *(continued)*

Occupation/Group	Employment in 2000	Employment Change, Projected 2000–2010		Employment Prospects
		Percentage	Number	
Teachers: preschool, kindergarten, elementary, middle, and secondary	3,831,000	15	571,000	Avg-Gr +
Teachers: special education	453,000	31	140,000	Fast-Gr+
10. *Legal*				
Court reporters	18,000	16	3,000	Avg-Gr
Judges, magistrates, and other judicial workers	43,000	4	1,600	Slow-Gr
Lawyers	681,000	18	123,000	Avg-Gr*
Paralegals and legal assistants	188,000	33	62,000	Fast-Gr*
11. *Life scientists*				
Agricultural and food scientists	17,000	9	1,500	Slow-Gr
Biological and medical scientists	138,000	21	30,000	Fast-Gr
Conservation scientists and foresters	29,000	8	2,200	Slow-Gr
12. *Physical scientists*				
Atmospheric scientists	6,900	17	1,200	Avg-Gr
Chemists and materials scientists	92,000	19	18,000	Avg-Gr
Environmental scientists and geoscientists	97,000	21	21,000	Fast-Gr
Physicists and astronomers	10,000	11	1,000	Avg-Gr
13. *Science technicians*	198,000	17	34,000	Avg-Gr
14. *Social scientists and related*				
Economists, and market and survey researchers	134,000	25	34,000	Fast-Gr
Psychologists	182,000	18	33,000	Avg-Gr
Urban and regional planners	30,000	16	4,900	Avg-Gr
Social scientists, other	15,000	17	2,600	Avg-Gr
15. *Health diagnosing and treating practitioners*				
Chiropractors	50,000	23	12,000	Fast-Gr
Dentists	152,000	6	8,800	Slow-Gr
Dietitians and nutritionists	49,000	15	7,400	Avg-Gr
Occupational therapists	78,000	34	27,000	Fast-Gr
Optometrists	31,000	19	5,900	Avg-Gr
Pharmacists	217,000	24	53,000	Fast-Gr
Physical therapists	132,000	33	44,000	Fast-Gr
Physician assistants	58,000	53	31,000	Mfast-Gr+
Physicians and surgeons	598,000	18	107,000	Avg-Gr
Podiatrists	18,000	14	2,500	Avg-Gr
Recreational therapists	29,000	9	2,500	Slow-Gr
Registered nurses	2,194,000	26	516,000	Fast-Gr+
Respiratory therapists	110,000	35	38,000	Fast-Gr
Speech-language pathologists and audiologists	101,000	40	40,000	Mfast-Gr+
Veterinarians	59,000	32	19,000	Fast-Gr
16. *Health technologists and technicians*				
Cardiovascular technologists/technicians	39,000	35	14,000	Fast-Gr
Clinical laboratory technologists and technicians	295,000	18	53,000	Avg-Gr
Dental hygienists	147,000	37	54,000	Mfast-Gr+
Diagnostic medical sonographers	33,000	26	8,600	Fast-Gr
Emergency medical technicians and paramedics	172,000	31	54,000	Fast-Gr
Licensed practical nurses and licensed vocational nurses	700,000	20	142,000	Avg-Gr
Medical records and health information technicians	136,000	49	66,000	Mfast-Gr+
Nuclear medicine technologists	18,000	22	4,100	Fast-Gr
Occupational health and safety specialists and technicians	35,000	15	5,200	Avg-Gr
Opticians, dispensing	68,000	19	13,000	Avg-Gr
Pharmacy technicians	190,000	36	69,000	Mfast-Gr+
Radiologic technologists/technicians	167,000	23	39,000	Fast-Gr
Surgical technologists	71,000	35	25,000	Fast-Gr

Occupation/Group	Employment in 2000	Employment Change, Projected 2000–2010		Employment Prospects
		Percentage	Number	
C. Service occupations				
1. *Building and grounds cleaning and maintenance*				
Building cleaning workers	4,200,000	10	431,000	Avg-Gr+
Grounds maintenance workers	1,132,000	27	304,000	Fast-Gr+
Pest control workers	58,000	22	13,000	Fast-Gr
2. *Food preparation and serving related*				
Chefs, cooks, food preparation workers	2,847,000	12	345,000	Avg-Gr+
Food and beverage serving workers	6,500,000	18	1,156,000	Avg-Gr*+
3. *Health care support*				
Dental assistants	247,000	37	92,000	Mfast-Gr+
Medical assistants	329,000	57	187,000	Mfast-Gr+
Medical transcriptionists	102,000	30	30,000	Fast-Gr
Nursing, psychiatric; home health aides	2,053,000	30	623,000	Fast-Gr+
Occupational therapist assistants/aides	25,000	42	10,000	Mfast-Gr+
Pharmacy aides	57,000	19	11,000	Avg-Gr
Physical therapist assistants and aides	80,000	45	36,000	Mfast-Gr+
4. *Personal care and service*				
Animal care and service workers	145,000	21	31,000	Fast-Gr+
Barbers, cosmetologists, and other personal appearance workers	790,000	11	90,000	Avg-Gr
Childcare workers	1,193,000	11	127,000	Avg-Gr
Flight attendants	124,000	18	23,000	Avg-Gr
Gaming service occupations	167,000	26	44,000	Fast-Gr
Personal and home care aides	414,000	62	258,000	Mfast-Gr+
Recreation and fitness workers	427,000	28	118,000	Fast-Gr*
5. *Protective services*				
Correctional officers	457,000	32	145,000	Fast-Gr+
Firefighting occupations	332,000	9	29,000	Slow-Gr*
Police and detectives	834,000	21	174,000	Fast-Gr
Private detectives and investigators	39,000	24	9,200	Slow-Gr*
Security guards and gaming surveillance	1,117,000	35	393,000	Fast-Gr+
D. Sales and related				
Cashiers	3,363,000	15	488,000	Avg-Gr+
Counter and rental clerks	423,000	19	82,000	Avg-Gr
Demonstrators, product promoters, and models	121,000	25	30,000	Fast-Gr*
Insurance sales agents	378,000	3	13,000	Slow-Gr
Real estate brokers and sales agents	432,000	9	41,000	Slow-Gr
Retail salespeople	4,109,000	12	510,000	Avg-Gr+
Sales engineers	85,000	18	15,000	Avg-Gr
Sales representatives, wholesale and manufacturing	1,821,000	6	111,000	Slow-Gr
Sales worker supervisors	2,504,000	8	193,000	Slow-Gr
Securities, commodities, and financial services sales agents	367,000	22	82,000	Fast-Gr
Travel agents	135,000	3	4,300	Slow-Gr
E. Office and administrative support				
1. *Communications equipment operators*	339,000	−19	−65,000	Decline
2. *Computer operators*	194,000	−17	−33,000	Decline
3. *Data entry, information processing*	806,000	−4	−32,000	Decline
4. *Desktop publishers*	38,000	67	25,000	Mfast-Gr+
5. *Financial clerks*	3,696,000	3	126,000	Slow-Gr
Bill and account collectors	400,000	25	101,000	Fast-Gr
Billing and posting clerks and machine operators	506,000	9	43,000	Slow-Gr
Bookkeeping, accounting, and auditing clerks	1,991,000	2	39,000	No Ch
Gaming cage clerks	22,000	25	5,500	Fast-Gr

An Abbreviated Bureau of Labor Statistics Job Outlook in Brief for 2000–2010 *(continued)*

Occupation/Group	Employment in 2000	Employment Change, Projected 2000–2010		Employment Prospects
		Percentage	Number	
Payroll and timekeeping clerks	201,000	2	4,600	No Ch
Procurement clerks	76,000	–12	–9,300	Decline
Tellers	499,000	–12	–59,000	Decline
6. *Information and record clerks*	5,099,000	20	1,000,000	Avg-Gr+
Brokerage clerks	70,000	–1	–1,000	Decline
Credit authorizers, checkers, and clerks	86,000	4	3,600	Slow-Gr
Customer service representatives	1,946,000	32	631,000	Fast-Gr+
File clerks	288,000	9	26,000	Slow-Gr
Hotel, motel, and resort desk clerks	177,000	33	59,000	Fast-Gr
Human resources assistants	177,000	19	34,000	Avg-Gr
Interviewers	410,000	1	2,300	No Ch
Library assistants, clerical	98,000	20	19,000	Avg-Gr
Order clerks	348,000	–20	–71,000	Decline
Receptionists and information clerks	1,078,000	24	256,000	Fast-Gr+
Reservation and transportation ticket agent and travel clerks	191,000	15	28,000	Avg-Gr
7. *Material recording, scheduling, dispatching, and distributing occupations except postal workers*	3,550,000	10	346,000	Avg-Gr+
Cargo and freight agents	60,000	8	5,000	Slow-Gr
Couriers and messengers	141,000	–4	–5,500	Decline
Dispatchers	254,000	20	50,000	Avg-Gr
Meter readers, utilities	49,000	–26	–13,000	Decline
Production, planning, and expediting clerks	332,000	18	60,000	Avg-Gr
Shipping, receiving, and traffic clerks	890,000	9	83,000	Slow-Gr
Stock clerks and order fillers	1,679,000	8	142,000	Slow-Gr
Weighers, measurers, checkers, and samplers, recordkeeping	83,000	18	15,000	Avg-Gr
8. *Office and administrative support worker supervisors and managers*	1,392,000	9	130,000	Slow-Gr
9. *Office clerks, general*	2,705,000	16	430,000	Avg-Gr+
10. *Postal Service workers*	688,000	–1	–4,500	Decline
11. *Secretaries and administrative assistants*	3,902,000	7	265,000	Slow-Gr+
F. Farming, fishing, and forestry				
Agricultural workers	987,000	4	37,000	Slow-Gr+
Fishers and fishing vessel operators	53,000	–12	–6,400	Decline
Forest, conservation, and logging workers	90,000	–2	–1,600	Decline
G. Construction trades and related				
Boilermakers	27,000	2	600	No Ch
Brickmasons, blockmasons, and stonemasons	158,000	13	21,000	Avg-Gr
Carpenters	1,204,000	8	98,000	Slow-Gr+
Carpet, floor, and tile installers and finishers	167,000	13	22,000	Avg-Gr
Cement masons, concrete finishers, segmental pavers, terrazzo workers	166,000	3	5,000	Slow-Gr
Construction and building inspectors	75,000	15	11,000	Avg-Gr
Construction equipment operators	416,000	8	34,000	Slow-Gr
Construction laborers	791,000	17	135,000	Avg-Gr
Drywall installers, ceiling tile installers, and tapers	188,000	9	17,000	Slow-Gr+
Electricians	698,000	17	120,000	Avg-Gr+
Elevator installers and repairers	23,000	17	4,000	Avg-Gr
Glaziers	49,000	15	7,200	Avg-Gr+
Hazardous materials removal workers	37,000	33	12,000	Fast-Gr+
Insulation workers	53,000	14	7,200	Avg-Gr+
Painters and paperhangers	518,000	19	99,000	Avg-Gr

Occupation/Group	Employment in 2000	Employment Change, Projected 2000–2010		Employment Prospects
		Percentage	Number	
Pipelayers, plumbers, pipefitters, and steamfitters	568,000	10	59,000	Avg-Gr+
Plasterers and stucco masons	54,000	12	6,400	Avg-Gr
Roofers	158,000	19	31,000	Avg-Gr+
Sheet metal workers	224,000	23	51,000	Fast-Gr+
Structural and reinforcing iron and metal workers	111,000	18	20,000	Avg-G
H. Installation, maintenance, and repair				
1. *Computer, automated teller, and office machine repairers*	172,000	14	24,000	Avg-Gr
2. *Electrical and electronics installers and repairers*	171,000	9	15,000	Slow-Gr
3. *Electronic home entertainment equipment installers and repairers*	37,000	−18	−6,600	Decline
4. *Radio and telecommunications equipment installers and repairers*	196,000	−4	−7,500	Decline
5. *Vehicle and mobile equipment mechanics, installers, and repairers*				
Aircraft and avionics equipment mechanics and service technicians	173,000	16	28,000	Avg-Gr
Automotive body and related repairers	221,000	10	23,000	Avg-Gr
Automotive service technicians and mechanics	840,000	18	151,000	Avg-Gr
Diesel service technicians and mechanics	285,000	14	40,000	Avg-Gr
Heavy vehicle and mobile equipment service technicians and mechanics	185,000	9	17,000	Slow-Gr
Small engine mechanics	73,000	9	6,200	Slow-Gr
6. *Other installation, maintenance, and repair*				
Coin, vending, and amusement machine servicers and repairers	37,000	18	6,800	Avg-Gr
Heating, air conditioning, and refrigeration mechanics and installers	243,000	22	54,000	Fast-Gr+
Home appliance repairers	43,000	6	2,700	Slow-Gr
Industrial machinery installation, repair, and maintenance workers	1,636,000	5	75,000	Slow-Gr
Line installers and repairers	263,000	21	54,000	Fast-Gr
Precision instrument and equipment repairers	63,000	10	6,100	Avg-Gr
I. Production occupations				
1. *Assemblers and fabricators*	2,653,000	6	171,000	Slow-Gr
2. *Food processing occupations*	760,000	3	23,000	Slow-Gr
3. *Metal workers and plastic workers*				
Computer control programmers and operators	186,000	19	36,000	Avg-Gr+
Machinists	430,000	9	39,000	Slow-Gr+
Machine setters, operators, and tenders	1,641,000	5	74,000	Slow-Gr
Tool and die makers	130,000	2	2,800	No Ch+
Welding, soldering, and brazing workers	521,000	19	97,000	Avg-Gr+
4. *Power and system operators*				
Power plant operators, distributors, and dispatchers	55,000	0	−200	No Ch*
Stationary engineers and boiler operators	57,000	−1	−800	Decline*
Water and liquid waste treatment plant and system operators	88,000	18	16,000	Avg-Gr
5. *Printing occupations*				
Bookbinders and bindery workers	115,000	7	8,500	Slow-Gr
Prepress technicians and workers	162,000	−8	−13,000	Decline
Printing machine operators	222,000	5	12,000	Slow-Gr*
6. *Textile, apparel, and furnishings occupations*	1,317,000	−2	−32,000	Decline
7. *Woodworkers*	409,000	9	37,000	Slow-Gr
8. *Other production occupations*				
Dental laboratory technicians	43,000	6	2,700	Slow-Gr

An Abbreviated Bureau of Labor Statistics Job Outlook in Brief for 2000–2010 *(continued)*

Occupation/Group	Employment in 2000	Employment Change, Projected 2000–2010 Percentage	Number	Employment Prospects
Inspectors, testers, sorters, samplers, and weighers	602,000	–2	–11,000	Decline
Jewelers; precious stone workers	43,000	1	600	No Ch
Ophthalmic laboratory technicians	32,000	6	1,800	Slow-Gr
Painting and coating workers	195,000	14	28,000	Avg-Gr
Photographic process workers and processing machine operators	76,000	2	1,600	No Ch
Semiconductor processors	52,000	32	17,000	Fast-Gr
J. Transportation and material moving				
1. *Air transportation*				
Aircraft pilots and flight engineers	117,000	10	11,000	*Avg-Gr
Air traffic controllers	27,000	7	1,900	*Slow-Gr
2. *Material-moving occupations*	4,986,000	14	710,000	Avg-Gr+
3. *Motor vehicle operators*				
Bus drivers	666,000	13	88,000	Avg-Gr
Taxi drivers and chauffeurs	176,000	24	43,000	Fast-Gr
Truck drivers and driver/sales workers	3,268,000	18	589,000	Avg-Gr
4. *Rail transportation occupations*	115,000	–19	–21,000	Decline
5. *Water transportation occupations*	70,000	4	3,100	*Slow-Gr
K. U.S Armed Forces	1,500,000	(projections not available)		

EXERCISE 2-1   FACTORY SHUTDOWN EXERCISE

Let's say a plant shuts down or lays off much of its workforce, and the unemployment figures in the community soar. Unless workers can sell their homes and find jobs elsewhere, they may become unemployed or be forced to take a job at much less than the pay they once earned. Scapegoats abound. Some people accuse business leaders of greed, thinking only of profits and ignoring the social costs of their actions. Others blame government because of taxes or too much regulation of business. Unions are criticized for demanding high wages. Some people point to the workers themselves, saying they have turned away from the work ethic—the idea that hard work, self-discipline, thrift, and deferred gratification lead to economic progress. If unemployed workers are to be retrained, who will pay for it? The government, the companies that lay them off, the community, or the workers themselves? This exercise will give you a quick entry into the perplexing interaction of economic problems and the availability of jobs and occupations. Focusing on a threatened factory shutdown, the activity allows you to take roles as some of the players in an economic drama. The exercise can be done individually, but the group dynamics are interesting too.

The Situation: The XYZ Affair

The XYZ Manufacturing Company is facing competition from other states and from foreign imports. To remain afloat, the company is seeking tax reductions from local government and wage reductions from its workers. The company argues that it must remain competitive with other companies in its industry, both in the United States and abroad. XYZ has considered moving its plant from your hometown to another state where taxes and labor costs are lower. Because of changeable economic conditions, XYZ cannot guarantee how long it will stay in your community, regardless of the outcome of its requests to lower taxes and wages. You will be asked to take a role in a group of four people and attempt to reach a decision about this situation. First, however, you will meet with those who are playing the same role as you and plan strategy. After that, you will meet with representatives of the other groups affected by the forthcoming decision.

Roles

1. *Representative from the XYZ Manufacturing Company.* Your problem is high taxes and high labor costs. You come to the decision-making committee stating that the cost of doing business is too high in this community. You request a tax break for your company and lower wages from the union. Without the tax break and wage concessions, you estimate that 500 employees will be laid off within a month and that the entire workforce of 2,000 will be out of work in two years.

2. *Representative from the local government.* Your problem is not only the loss of money from lowered taxes, but also the loss of jobs and the subsequent loss of people who would move. The size of the tax base would be reduced. You would need to increase the tax rate just to stay even with the revenues generated now. Local taxes have risen steadily over the past 10 years, partly to cover the needs of the XYZ factory (water supply, pollution control). The money you now take in is barely adequate to pay for services such as clean water, sewage disposal, road construction and maintenance, police and fire protection, and school costs. Lowering taxes for XYZ would mean cuts in these services. But if XYZ leaves town, taxes will have to be raised to offset the loss of tax revenues from the company, or services will have to be reduced.

3. *Representative from the union and its workers.* Your problem is the threat of lower wages and loss of jobs. Lack of job security and possible layoffs have made your task as a union representative much more difficult. Wages have not kept up with inflation for the past five years, and two years ago the union and its members reluctantly accepted a wage freeze to protect jobs. Despite these grim circumstances, your wages are still higher than elsewhere in the same industry. If XYZ moves out, most of your members will lose the demand for their skills. If they lose their jobs and suffer economic losses, they will also be susceptible to psychological stress, emotional disorders, and mental depression.

4. *Representative from the community.* Your concern is for other businesses and residents in the community. Many local businesses will be affected because they are suppliers for the XYZ Company. The community would feel a ripple effect if XYZ left: Gas stations, coffee shops, stores, restaurants, bars, and other businesses would lose customers. The community would lose the income XYZ employees normally spend there. Charities would suffer because XYZ is very active in local fund drives.

Questions to Consider

- Who should make the greatest concessions: The XYZ Manufacturing Company? Local government? The workers? The community? What should the concessions be? Why?
- Which of the remaining groups should make the second greatest number of concessions? What should they be? Why?
- Of the two remaining groups, who should make the most concessions? What would they be? Why?
- Who should make the fewest concessions? Is there any group who should not make any concessions? Why?

Other Questions

- Is it ethical for a company to pull out and leave workers behind for a community to train for other jobs?
- Can local government offer tax breaks to a large company such as XYZ without making the same offer to all businesses, no matter how small they are?
- Should a union press for higher wages when it knows, if it is successful, that the company will be forced to lay off workers?
- Should the community ask for something from the manufacturing company in return for lower wages and tax breaks? For example, should the manufacturing company be forced to make guarantees on the number of jobs and its length of stay in the community? Why? If so, how many jobs, and how long a commitment to stay?

SUMMARY

1. Study forecasts of future events in the world of work as part of your career planning, but not to the exclusion of other considerations in choosing an occupation. Some people mistakenly rush into an occupation that is predicted to experience extraordinary growth, without considering their own interests and abilities.

2. Many economic forces and labor trends affect occupations and job openings. The high rate of growth in the U.S. labor force between 1950 and 2000 will become much lower in the next 50 years. The proportion of women in the workforce will level off at about 48 percent. Minorities and foreign-born will play a larger role in the labor force; the white share dropping to 53 percent by 2050. Mid-life career changes and two-income families will become common. Job opportunities will flourish in white-collar work, knowledge-based and service industries, and in small companies. Large companies aren't going away, but they will be smaller and still attractive to many workers. Creativity is becoming the driving force in the U.S. economy. Replacement needs provide more job vacancies than growth needs.

3. New work values will change the meaning of work for many people. Money is no longer the only reason many people go to work. Free agents and independent contractors have replaced the "organization man." Alternative work styles featuring temporary and part-time work and entrepreneurial self-employment are increasing. A skills gap exists between people and available jobs. Workers' skills will need continual upgrading. A college education is needed for many of the fastest-growing occupations, but on-the-job training provides the basic preparation for a majority of jobs. The U.S. foreign-trade deficit in the global economy, corporate and national debt, deregulation, automation, and company restructuring are economic forces that influence the availability of many jobs.

4. More work will be done at home; the computer is the main reason for this. The percentage of multiple jobholders or "moonlighters" in the labor force has increased since 1975, but the rate is now expected to decline slightly. Hours on the job have increased even with a reaction against longer hours at work. The "social contract" of loyalty to the work organization in exchange for job security has crumbled. "Vertical" loyalty has diminished, but "horizontal" loyalty to colleagues, teams, professions, customers, family, and friends still exists. Unemployment is more of a problem than officially recognized. Underemployment will remain a potential problem for some college graduates. Signs of a turbulent economy are revealed with higher turnover rates.

5. The gap between high-income "haves" and low-income "have-nots" is widening. Union membership is declining; in some ways, labor unions are a victim of their own success. Families seek ways to blend work and family. Working harder and smarter in this economy does not always guarantee a raise in pay.

6. Some occupations die, but new ones come along to replace them. New jobs are created as employers need workers to do tasks never done before—stemming

from advances in technology, changes in consumer needs and tastes, new research, higher levels of education, and so on. Not only are there occupations that are new, they are constantly emerging and evolving. New occupations are exciting and challenging, but they have their share of difficulties as well.

7. Job openings vary greatly among occupations. The fastest-growing and -declining occupations and industries are reported every couple of years.

8. Important trends in a number of occupational groups serve as markers of change, including managerial, professional, service, sales, office and administrative support, agriculture, construction, installation and maintenance and repair, production, and transportation.

REFERENCES

Amirault, T. 1996–1997, Winter. Multiple jobholders: What else do I want to do when I grow up? *Occupational Outlook Quarterly,* 40(4), 43–46.

Armas, G. C. 2003, May 27. Senior employees: More older Americans are staying in the workforce, Census says. Jackson, MI: *Jackson Citizen Patriot,* C5.

Associated Press. 2003, May 15. Personal bankruptcies rise 7.4 percent. *Yahoo! News.* Available online at www.yahoo.com. Accessed on May 15, 2003.

Baba, M. L. 2003, March. United States lags behind in helping workers balance their lives. *The Dean's Update.* East Lansing: College of Social Science, Michigan State University.

Baker, S. 2002, August 26. The coming battle for immigrants. *Business Week,* 3796, 138–140.

Berman, J. M. 2001, November. Industry output and employment projections to 2010. *Monthly Labor Review,* 124(11), 39–56.

Berman, J. M. 2004. Industry output and employment projections to 2012. *Monthly Labor Review,* 127(2), 58–79.

Bernstein, J. 2002, November 4. It's full employment, stupid. *The American Prospect,* 13(20), 28–29.

Birch, D. L. 1987. *Job creation in America: How our smallest companies put the most people to work.* New York: Free Press.

Bix, A. S. 2000. *Inventing ourselves out of jobs?: America's debate over technological unemployment, 1929–1981.* Baltimore: Johns Hopkins University Press.

Bluestone, B., and Harrison, B. 1982. *The deindustrialization of America: Plant closings, community abandonment, and the dismantling of basic industry.* New York: Basic Books.

Bogus bucks, presidents. 2002, December 9. *U.S. News & World Report,* 134(21), 18.

Botstein, L. 1997. *Jefferson's children: Education and the promise of the American culture.* New York: Doubleday.

Boyett, J. H., and Boyett, J. T. 1995. *Beyond workplace 2000: Essential strategies for the new American corporation.* New York: Dutton.

Brady, D. 2002, August 26. Rethinking the rat race. *Business Week,* 3796, 142–143.

Bridges, W. 1994. *Job shift: How to prosper in a workplace without jobs.* Reading, MA: Addison-Wesley.

Buchholz, T. G. 1996. *From here to economy: A shortcut to economic literacy.* New York: Plume/Penguin.

Calvert, R. 2002, October. "Soft skills" a key to employment today. *Career Opportunities News,* 20(2), 1, 6.

Cetron, M. J. 1984. *Jobs of the future: The 500 best jobs—where they'll be and how to get them.* New York: McGraw-Hill.

Cetron, M. J., and Davies, O. 2003, March–April. Trends shaping the future: Technological, workplace, management, and institutional trends. *The Futurist,* 37(2), 30–43.

Challenger, J. A. 2002, November–December. Blurring the line between home and work. *The Futurist,* 36(6), 10–11.

Cosgrave, G. 1973. *Career planning: Search for a future* (rev. ed.). Toronto: Guidance Centre, Faculty of Education, University of Toronto.

Crosby, O. 2002, Fall. New and emerging occupations. *Occupational Outlook Quarterly,* 46(3), 16–25.

Curry, A. 2003, March 3. The history of work in America over the past century. *U.S. News & World Report,* 134(6), 50–56.

Delehanty, H. 2000, July–August. Follow the money. *Modern Maturity,* p. 6.

Dembo, D., and Morehouse, W. 1997. *The underbelly of the U.S. economy: Joblessness and the pauperization of work in America.* New York: Apex Press.

DiNatale, M. 2001, March. Characteristics of and preference for alternative work arrangements, 1999. *Monthly Labor Review,* 124(3), 28–49.

Donald, D. H. 1995. *Lincoln.* New York: Simon and Schuster.

Downs, A. 1995. *Corporate executions: The ugly truth about layoffs—how corporate greed is shattering lives, companies, and communities.* New York: AMACOM.

Drucker, P. F. 1985. *Innovation and entrepreneurship: Principles and practices.* New York: Harper & Row.

Drucker, P. F. 1986, Spring. The changed world economy. *Foreign Affairs,* 65(2), 768–791.

Drucker, P. F. 1993. *Post-capitalist society.* New York: HarperCollins.

Drucker, P. F. 2002. *Managing in the next society.* New York: Truman Talley, St. Martin's.

Dukcevich, D. 2003, February 20. U.S. trade deficit balloons. *Forbes.com.* Available on the Web at www.forbes.com. Retrieved April 25, 2003.

Dunlap, A. J., with Andelman, B. 1996. *Mean business: How I save bad companies and make good companies great.* New York: Times Books.

Florida, R. 2002. *The rise of the creative class: And how it's transforming work, leisure, community, and everyday life.* New York: Basic Books.

Folks, M. 2003, April 28. Franchise business option with lot of growth potential. *Nashville Business Journal Online.* Available on the Web at www.bizjournals.com/nashville. Retrieved June 1, 2003.

Franchise News Briefs, 2003, June 1. *Fast facts.* New York: International Franchise Association.

Franklin, J. C. 1997, November. Industry output and employment projections to 2006. *Monthly Labor Review,* 120(11), 39–57.

Frenkel, S. J., Korczynski, M., Shire, K. A., and Tam, M. 1999. *On the front line: Organization of work in the information economy.* Ithaca, NY: Cornell University Press.

Friedman, E. M. 1997, May 29. The new economy almanac: A statistical and informational snapshot of the business world today. *Inc.,* 19(6), 108–121.

Fullerton, H. N., and Toossi, M. 2001, November. Labor force projections to 2010: Steady growth and changing composition. *Monthly Labor Review,* 124(11), 21–38.

Goodman, B., and Steadman, R. April 2002. Services: Business demand rivals consumer demand in driving job growth. *Monthly Labor Review,* 125(4), 3–9.

Griswold, D. T. 1998. *The causes and consequences of the U.S. trade deficit.* Washington, DC: Cato Institute.

Halal, W. E. 1996, November–December. The rise of the knowledge entrepreneur. *The Futurist,* 30(6), 13–16.

Handy, C. 2002. *The elephant and the flea: Reflections of a reluctant capitalist.* Cambridge, MA: Harvard Business School Press.

Harris, S. 2002, November 24. Work at-home scams. *Jackson Citizen Patriot* (Jackson, MI), B2.

Harrison, B. 1994. *Lean and mean: The changing landscape of corporate power in the age of flexibility.* New York: Basic Books.

Harrison, B., and Bluestone, B. 1988. *The great U-turn: Corporate restructuring and the polarizing of America.* New York: Basic Books.

Hecker, D. E. 2001, November. Occupational employment projections to 2010. *Monthly Labor Review,* 124(11), 57–78.

Hecker, D. E. 2004, February. Occupational employment projections to 2012. *Monthly Labor Review,* 127(2), 80–105.

Herman, R. E., Olivo, T., and Gioia, J. L. 2003. *Impending crisis: Too many jobs, too few people.* Winchester, VA: Oakhill Press.

Herr, E. L., and Cramer, S. H. (1996). *Career guidance and counseling through the life span: Systematic approaches,* 5th ed. New York: HarperCollins.

Hipple, S., and Kosanovich, K. 2003, February. Computer and Internet use at work in 2001. *Monthly Labor Review,* 126(2), 26–35.

Hochschild, A. R. 1997. *The time bind: When work becomes home and home becomes work.* New York: Metropolitan Books (Henry Holt).

Hopkins, M. 1997, May 20. Help wanted. *Inc.,* 19(5), 35–42.

Howkins, J. 2001. *The creative economy: How people make money from ideas.* New York: Allen Lane, Penguin Press.

Huang, L., Pergamit, M., and Shkolnik, J. 2001, August. Youth initiation into the labor market. *Monthly Labor Review,* 124(8), 18–24.

Hughes, P. M. 2002, September–October. The dilemmas of terrorism. *The Futurist,* 36(5), 28–29.

Johnson, H. 2002. *The best of times: The boom and bust years of America before and after everything changed.* San Diego, CA: Harvest/Harcourt.

Judy, R., and D'Amico, C. 1997. *Workforce 2020: Work and workers in the 21st century.* Indianapolis, IN: Hudson Institute.

Kalleberg, A. L., Rasell, E., Cassier, N., Reskin, B. F., Hudson, K., Webster, D., Appelbaum, E., and Spalter-Roth, R. M. 1997. *Nonstandard work, substandard jobs: Flexible work arrangements in the U.S.* Washington, DC: Economic Policy Institute.

Kimmel, J. 1995, Spring. Moonlighting in the United States. *Upjohn Institute Employment Research,* 4–6.

Kuttner, B. 1983, July. The declining middle. *Atlantic Monthly*, 108(1), 60–72.

Lee, S. 1987. *Susan Lee's ABZs of economics*. New York: Pocket Books.

Levitan, S. A. 1987, November–December. Beyond "trendy" forecasts: The next 10 years for work. *The Futurist*, 21(6), 28–32.

Lexington. 2003, January 11. Democratic hopefuls. *The Economist*, 366(8304), 25.

Litan, R. E., and Rivlin, A. M. 2001. Beyond the dot.coms. Washington, DC: Brookings Institute.

McDaniels, C. 1989. *The changing workplace: Career counseling strategies for the 1990s and beyond*. San Francisco: Jossey-Bass.

Miller, A. 1949. *Death of a salesman*. New York: Viking Press.

Mishel, L., Bernstein, J., and Schmitt, J. 1999. *The state of working America, 1998–99*. Washington, DC: Economic Policy Institute.

Mittlehauser, M. 1998, Summer. The outlook for college graduates, 1996–2006: Prepare yourself. *Occupational Outlook Quarterly*, 42(2), 2–9.

Moncarz, R., and Reaser, A. 2002, Spring. The 2000–10 job outlook in brief. *Occupational Outlook Quarterly*, 46(1), 2–47.

Mosisa, A. T. 2002, May. The role of foreign-born workers in the U.S. economy. *Monthly Labor Review*, 125(5), 3–14.

Naisbitt, J. 1982. *Megatrends: Ten new directions transforming our lives*. New York: Warner.

Nocera, J. 1996, April 1. Living with layoffs. *Fortune*, 133(6), 70–71

Nussbaum, B. 2002, August 26. Why the world needs new thinking. *Business Week*, 3796, 66–67.

Pink, D. 2001. *Free agent nation*. New York: Warner.

Reich, R. B. 2000. *The future of success*. New York: Knopf.

Reinhold, R. 2000, Winter. Union membership in 2000: Numbers decline during record economic expansion. *Illinois Labor Monthly Review*, 6(4).

Richman, T. 1997, May 20. Creators of the new economy. *Inc.*, 19(5), 44–48.

Rifkin, J. 1995. *The end of work: The decline of the global labor force and the dawn of the post-market era*. New York: Tarcher/Putnam.

Rones, P. L., Ilg, R. E., and Gardner, J. M. 1997, April. Trends in the hours of work since the mid-1970s. *Monthly Labor Review*, 120(4), 3–14.

Rukeyser, L. 1988. *Louis Rukeyser's business almanac*. New York: Simon & Schuster.

Saltzman, A. 1997, October 27. When less is more. *U.S. News & World Report*, 124(14), 78–84.

Schor, J. B. 1993. *The overworked American: The unexpected decline of leisure*. New York: Basic Books.

Schumpeter, J. A. 1962. *Capitalism, socialism, and democracy*. New York: Harper Torchbooks.

Scott, R. E. 1999. *The U.S. trade deficit: Are we trading away our future?* Washington, DC: Economic Policy Institute.

Scott. R. E. 2000, March. *Issue brief: The facts about trade and job creation*. Washington, DC: Economic Policy Institute.

Scott, R. E. , and Rothstein, J. 1998. *American jobs and the Asian crises: The employment impact of the coming rise in the U.S. trade deficit*. Washington, DC: Economic Policy Institute.

Silvestri, G. T. 1999, Summer. Considering self-employment: What to think about before starting a business. *Occupational Outlook Quarterly*, 43(2), 15–23.

Thurow, L. C. 1996. *The future of capitalism: How today's economic forces shape tomorrow's world*. New York: Penguin Books.

Toffler, A. 1981. *The third wave*. New York: Bantam.

Toffler, A. 1983. *Previews and premises*. New York: Bantam.

Toossi, M. 2002, May. A century of change: The U.S. labor force, 1950–2050. *Monthly Labor Review*, 125(5), 15–28.

U.S. Bureau of Labor Statistics. 2001. Contingent and alternative employment arrangements, February 2001. News release. Washington, DC: U.S. Department of Labor.

U.S. Bureau of Labor Statistics. 2002a. *Career guide to industries, 2002–2003 edition*. Washington, DC: U.S. Government Printing Office.

U.S. Bureau of Labor Statistics. 2002b. Work at home in 2001. *News release*. Washington, DC: U.S. Department of Labor.

U.S. Bureau of Labor Statistics. 2003a, February. Volunteer work measured. *Monthly Labor Review*, 126(2), 2.

U.S. Bureau of Labor Statistics. 2003b, March. Students at work. *Monthly Labor Review*, 126(3), 2.

U.S. Bureau of Labor Statistics. 2004. BLS releases 2002–12 employment projections. *News*. Washington, DC: U.S. Department of Labor.

U.S. Bureau of the Census. 2003. *Household shares of aggregate income by fifths of the income distribution: 1967 to 2001 (Table IE-3)* and *Mean income received by each fifth and top 5 percent of households (All Races): 1967 to 2001*. Washington, DC: U.S. Department of Commerce.

U.S. Department of Labor. 2000, Summer. Futurework: Trends and challenges for work in the 21st century. *Occupational Outlook Quarterly*, 44(2), 31–37.

U.S. Department of Labor. 2002. Multiple jobholding in states, 2001. *Monthly Labor Review,* 125(11), 39–40.

U.S. Department of Labor. 2003, March. Union membership rate declines. *Monthly Labor Review,* 126(3), 2.

Van Horn, C. 2002. *Heldrich work trends study.* New Brunswick, NJ: Center for Workforce Development.

Wegmann, R. G., Chapman, R., and Johnson, M. 1989. *Work in the new economy: Careers and job seeking into the 21st century,* rev. ed. Indianapolis, IN: JIST Works, Inc., and Alexandria, VA: American Association for Counseling and Development.

White, J. 2001, February 26. Union membership in US at lowest level in 60 years. *WSWS: News & Analysis: North America* (World Socialist Web Site). Available on the Web at www.wsws.org. Retrieved May 3, 2003.

Whyte, W. H., Jr. 1956. *The organization man.* Garden City, NJ: Doubleday Anchor.

Wilson, W. J. 1996. *When work disappears: The world of the new urban poor.* New York: Knopf.

Wolfe, A. 1997, September–October. The moral meanings of work. *The American Prospect,* 8, 82–90.

Wolfe, A. 1998. *One nation, after all.* New York: Viking.

Chapter 3

Your Preferences in the World of Work

"I had no idea how deep and bewildering career planning could get," exclaimed a typical student who had taken a couple of psychological inventories and was beginning to examine the "Who am I?" question. "I thought looking at economic forces, labor trends, and what's going on in the world outside was complex enough. Now that I'm starting to look inside myself and trying to figure out what I'm all about, I can see things are getting even more complicated. Where does it all end?"

The study of our world and our inner selves never stops. When you study your inner self—your personality—you begin to discover what interests you, what motivates and energizes you, what your strengths and weaknesses are, and what is really most important to you—the subjects of this and later chapters. This chapter focuses on your preferences and interests— activities you like (or dislike) and subjects that arouse your attention. One way to learn about your inner self and your career interests is to take one or more personality and vocational interest inventories. They can help you find out where your career preferences lie.

Psychological inventories that measure vocational interests suggest occupations for you to consider. From the suggestions of these inventories and the guides that go with them, you can start to generate a list of *occupational prospects*—kinds of work that interest you enough to explore and study as you go through the career-planning process. In addition to vocational interest inventories, you can use a variety of other methods to generate occupational prospects. These methods are addressed in the exercises that complete this chapter. The assumption right now is that you have absolutely no idea what occupation you would like to enter. There's no reason to panic! Later, your problem is more likely to be too many occupations from which to choose. Right now, you need to discover what they are.

OCCUPATIONAL INTERESTS

In career planning, one kind of interest predominates—occupational interests. It's pretty hard to draw boundaries for these interests. As soon as you mention nonwork interests, such as recreational, school, or home interests, you realize that almost all interests have some connection with the work people do.

There are many kinds of occupational interests, and they are used to classify the world of work. Classifying occupations is a huge task, but it is necessary for understanding the universe of occupations. Fortunately, you won't have to do the classification; several recognized occupational classification systems are already available.

To acquaint yourself with titles of groups of occupational interests, look at Table 3-1. Mark the interest categories that most appeal to you now.

Table 3-1 Groups of Occupational Interests and Their Descriptions

Group	Description
Agricultural interests	You like to sow seeds, cultivate soil, watch plants grow, and harvest crops; you like to raise livestock and poultry.
Artistic interests	You like to use paint, clay, fabrics, furniture, clothing, and so on, for the expression of beauty and for color coordination.
Athletic interests	You enjoy physical activities—running, jumping, playing team sports, staying in good shape through exercise, and watching others perform in athletic events.
Business/economic interests	You like to participate in commercial activities that involve buying, selling, and trading products and services; you would like to own, manage, and work in a business enterprise; you want to be involved in financial affairs and watch the workings of the economy.
Clerical/office interests	You like keeping business records, filing materials, typing letters and reports, preparing data for processing in computers, serving customers, and performing any activity that requires detail, accuracy, and neatness.

(continued)

Table 3-1 (continued)

Group	Description
Communication interests	You prefer activities that allow you to express ideas or knowledge in written, spoken, or symbolic form; you like to relate news and information to other people.
Electronic interests	You like to work with electricity in doing electrical wiring, taking apart a radio or television set, constructing or repairing a computer, and the like.
Engineering interests	You would like to design plans for the manufacture of such things as engines, machines, buildings, bridges, and chemical plants.
Homemaking interests	You like to perform domestic activities, such as keeping an attractive and clean home, caring for children, preparing food, maintaining clothes, and managing a household.
Literary interests	You like to read and write stories, poems, essays, and articles; you read many books and magazines and discuss the ideas you find in them.
Management interests	You like to plan things for yourself and others, organize functions, and supervise people.
Mechanical interests	You like to work with machines and tools, repair broken things, and take shop courses in school.
Medical/health interests	You like activities where you can heal people or animals, diagnose and treat diseases, and preserve good health.
Musical interests	You like to play a musical instrument, and you prefer to occupy yourself in musical activities, such as going to concerts, singing, and teaching music to others.
Numerical interests	You have a preference for working with numbers; you like mathematics, algebra, geometry, calculus, and statistics classes.
Organizational interests	You like to be part of a team or group of people and are willing to sacrifice some of your personal interests so that your company, agency, or department can progress or continue.
Outdoor/nature interests	You want to be outside most of the time; you enjoy camping and outdoor recreational activities; you like to raise pets and plants.
Performing interests	You like to be in front of other people, entertaining them at parties, acting in plays, or giving dramatic speeches.
Political interests	You like to follow campaigns and elections; you would want to be in a position of authority, making decisions and determining policies that affect other people as well as yourself.
Religious interests	You want to promote your religious and spiritual beliefs; you admire religious leaders, work to advance your place of worship, and worship God.
Scientific interests	You like to study and investigate the natural world; you enjoy taking classes in biology, chemistry, geology, astronomy, and physics; you wish to discover truth using a rational, scientific method.
Skilled trades interests	You like to install or operate machinery, equipment, and tools and make things with wood or metal; you like to drive cars, trucks, and heavy equipment; you would like being a carpenter, machine repairer, plumber, auto mechanic, welder, or tool and die maker.
Social interaction interests	You prefer working with people, caring for their welfare, helping them with their problems, teaching them skills, and providing them with services (protective, health, transportation).
Technician interests	You prefer working for another person (such as an engineer) who is in charge and has responsibility; you want to work on technical projects in the automotive, electrical, industrial, and manufacturing industries; typical occupations include drafter, surveyor, and electronic technician.

USING INVENTORIES

Some of the most widely used inventories are based on the psychological type theories of John Holland and Carl Jung. According to John Holland's theory, discussed briefly in Chapter 1, there is a strong relationship between your personality and your choice of occupation. Holland has identified six basic personalities and given them the following labels: Realistic, Investigative, Artistic, Social, Enterprising, and Conventional. Each type has a set of traits. No person is exclusively one type; everyone is a combination of all six types, arranged in a hierarchy from the highest to the lowest for each individual. This hierarchy, called the *personality pattern*, can be discovered by using an inventory based on Holland's theory. Work environments and occupations can be described in the same way. They, too, have a collective personality pattern, using the same six labels. Holland proposes that your satisfaction at work is largely dependent on knowing your true personality pattern and finding work in an occupational environment that agrees with it.

Another inventory, one grounded in Swiss psychologist Carl Jung's psychological types, is the *Myers-Briggs Type Indicator* (MBTI). This inventory measures 16 types of human personality. The MBTI suggests that choosing a career is more successful if you know your own preferences in obtaining information, making decisions, and forming attitudes about the world that surrounds you. Several other inventories are also covered in this chapter. You can use results from inventories to generate occupational prospects. Your teacher or counselor can help you select an appropriate inventory.

One type of interest inventory is self-administered, self-scored, and self-interpreted. Another kind of inventory is given by a test administrator, scored by a machine, and interpreted by a counselor. To get meaningful results from an inventory, you are asked about how much you like or dislike certain activities, such as school subjects, hobbies, leisure pursuits, and occupations. Your responses are grouped into categories similar to the divisions of the occupational world and are then compiled into a total score for each category. Your scores may be compared with the scores of other people to give you an indication of how strong or weak your preferences are in the occupational groups that the inventory measures.

To receive valid results, be honest when you complete an inventory. Interest inventory items are usually somewhat transparent and could easily be falsified. When responding to the activities on an inventory, give your first impression and then go immediately to the next item. This usually produces the most honest reaction and saves time in taking the inventory.

The most important characteristic of an interest inventory is that it measures interest, not ability. An *interest* is whatever arouses your attention, curiosity, or involvement; something you are attracted to instead of to other things. An *ability* is something you can do well. It may or may not be something in which you are interested. Descriptions of interest inventory results may include the words *high* or *low*. These words are not interpreted as measures of your abilities. You are receiving information about your pattern of likes and dislikes, not about things you can or cannot do well. Your future success is based on more than a score on an interest inventory. Being identified and classified as a certain personality type does not mean you need not study yourself further. Also, career assessment instruments have their limitations; they are not models of perfection (Mastie, 1994).

THE SIX HOLLAND PERSONALITY/ENVIRONMENT TYPES

If you take one or two vocational inventories, you are likely to encounter John Holland's classification of personality types and work environments. *Personality* describes a pattern of values, attitudes, and behaviors that represent distinctive ways people think and act. *Personality types* are groups of traits that describe the similar characteristics of whole groups of people.

People with similar traits are classified into categories; it is easier to study a few groups than to compare yourself with thousands of separate individuals. Work environments are studied and classified in the same way; Holland assigns the same labels to work environments as to personality types.

Holland's theory is useful in career planning if you accept the assumption that occupational choice is an expression of personality and that personality type can be measured by an inventory. The characteristics that make up your personality began to form when you were very young. You have gradually acquired ideas about your own personality, as well as impressions of others in your environment. As you get to know people and their occupations, you develop useful, if sometimes inaccurate, ideas about them. Holland maintains your perceptions of people and occupations have validity, as do the ideas you have of yourself. You use your perceptions of self, others, and occupations when you respond to the activities on inventories.

In Holland's scheme, each occupation attracts people with similar personalities. As people with similar personalities respond to many events of life in similar ways, they create characteristic environments, including those at work. Holland proposes that, all else being equal, *congruence*—or agreement—between person and work environment leads to job satisfaction, career path stability, and occupational achievement. Conversely, a mismatch between the person and the job environment leads to job dissatisfaction, career path instability, and poor performance (Holland, 1996).

Four fundamental assumptions form the basis of Holland's theory of careers. (1) The personality traits of most people can be organized into six types: Realistic, Investigative, Artistic, Social, Enterprising, and Conventional. (2) There are six models of work environments, which have the same labels and descriptions as the six personality types. (3) People search for compatible work environments by trying to find an occupation where they can use their skills, express their values, and adopt agreeable roles. For example, a "Realistic person" tries to find employment in a "Realistic work environment"—and the same matching process follows for the other types. (4) Behavior is determined by interactions between personality and environment. Knowing your personality pattern and the pattern of your environment allows predictions to be made about your occupational choice, job changes, vocational achievement, personal competence, and educational and social behavior (Holland, 1997).

Personality Types

As you read the description of each Holland personality type, remember that these sets of traits are ideal or "pure" versions of each type. No one description will fit anyone exactly. When you code yourself with the Holland types, expect to find that you share many, but not all, of the traits of the personality type on which you score highest. As you descend in the order of your Holland types, the traits should become less similar; when you reach the lowest type in your hierarchy, the traits mentioned should be quite different from your own.

Realistic. People who score high on the *Realistic* scale show a preference for working with their hands and using tools to build and repair things, according to Holland. They like to work with material things rather than with ideas or people. Realistic people often prefer to work outside or with a machine rather than at a desk in an office. They see themselves as practical, physically strong, rugged, stable, and mechanically and physically skilled. They are likely to seek such occupations as construction, fish and wildlife management, skilled trades, mechanics, farming, technology, forestry, and certain engineering specialties and military jobs. Sometimes Realistic people have difficulty expressing themselves in words or telling other people about their feelings. As with each of the six types, no single word can be used to describe this type of person, but *realistic* has been chosen as the best word to characterize this particular pattern of traits.

Investigative. The *Investigative* individual likes research activities that involve ideas in mathematics and the physical, biological, and social sciences. Such people enjoy working on abstract problems that require analytical thinking. Investigative people often perceive themselves as intellectual, curious, scholarly, original, critical, and talented in mathematics and science. They like working independently, although they are often part of a research team. Such occupations as research laboratory worker, biologist, chemist, social scientist, design engineer, physicist, medical technologist, and programmer are Investigative.

Artistic. People who have high scores on the *Artistic* scale like opportunities for self-expression and artistic creation in writing, music, art, and theater. Artistic people often try to avoid highly structured situations. They like to involve themselves totally in projects of their own making. They look on themselves as expressive, intuitive, imaginative, creative, artistically talented (acting, writing, composing, speaking), and aesthetically oriented. Occupational choices include author, artist, musician, poet, cartoonist, actor or actress, drama coach, composer, orchestra conductor, and interior designer.

Social. The *Social* type is best illustrated by people who like to work cooperatively with other people, have strong concern for the welfare of others, like to train or inform others, and want to help others solve their personal problems. Social people like situations that involve establishing relationships with others, being with groups of people, getting along well with others, and resolving problems and difficulties by talking things out. Social people describe themselves as cooperative, friendly, humanistic, sociable, tactful, and understanding of others. They prefer occupations in such areas as teaching, social work, religion, counseling, and recreation.

Enterprising. People who score high on the *Enterprising* scale like activities where they can lead, control, or persuade other people to reach a personal or organizational goal. They often seek a higher-than-average income, enjoy the use of power, are concerned about status, and want to accomplish things. Enterprising people seem to gravitate toward business and politics. They see themselves as energetic, ambitious, enthusiastic, self-confident, adventurous, in control of situations, skilled in leadership and speaking, and oriented toward political and economic achievement. Representative occupations for the Enterprising type are business executive, lawyer, political campaigner, salesperson, marketing or sales manager, sports promoter, buyer, realtor, television producer, and insurance agent.

Conventional. Individuals who score high on the *Conventional* scale prefer structured jobs and activities. They want to know exactly what is expected of them and what they are supposed to do. They like everything neatly in its place. Conventional people can be somewhat uncomfortable in leadership positions; they would prefer to follow directions and are often content with a subordinate position in a large organization. They describe themselves as careful, obedient, dependable, orderly, systematic, persistent, efficient, oriented toward business accomplishment, and skilled in clerical and numerical tasks. Typical occupations include accountant, bank teller, bookkeeper, secretary, file clerk, tax expert, and computer operator (Holland, 1997, 2000).

Work Environments

Holland proposes six environmental models and gives them the same labels as the personality types. A work environment is an atmosphere created by the people who dominate a given setting; it can be viewed as having a distinctive personality or pattern of values, attitudes, and behaviors. Environments and occupations have varying degrees of all six types, with two or three types tending to predominate in the pattern. "People flourish in their work environment when there is a good fit between their personality type and the characteristics of the environment" (Holland, 1996, p, 397). The interaction of your personality pattern with a compatible work environment (for example, a Social personality type in a Social environment) should bring such desirable results as job satisfaction, achievement, and vocational stability. The six environmental models that follow are paraphrased from Holland's descriptions (Holland, 1997).

The *Realistic* work environment is characterized by the manipulation of objects, tools, machines, and animals. Workers in a Realistic environment have Realistic personalities, are encouraged to see themselves as practical and mechanical, are rewarded for having traditional values, cope with situations in a simple and direct way, and use their mechanical and technical abilities to produce things.

The *Investigative* work environment calls for research and exploration of physical, biological, or cultural knowledge. Workers in an Investigative environment have Investigative personalities, are encouraged to see themselves as scholarly and intellectual, are rewarded for demonstrating scientific values, cope with situations through rational and analytical thinking, and are encouraged to view the world in complex and abstract ways.

The *Artistic* work environment is characterized by the creation of artistic, literary, musical, and dramatic works or products. Workers in an Artistic environment have Artistic personalities; are encouraged to see themselves as expressive, original, intuitive, nonconforming, and independent; are rewarded for exhibiting artistic values; cope with others in emotional and expressive ways; and are encouraged to view the world in complex and unconventional ways.

The *Social* work environment calls for interaction with other people in order to inform, train, develop, cure, or enlighten. Workers in a Social environment have Social personalities, are encouraged to see themselves as helpful and cooperative, are rewarded for displaying social values, cope with others by being friendly and cooperative, and are encouraged to be understanding of other people and to be flexible and sociable.

The *Enterprising* work environment calls for the manipulation of others to attain personal and organizational goals. Workers in an Enterprising environment have Enterprising personalities. They are encouraged to see themselves as skilled in leadership and speaking; are rewarded for demonstrating the enterprising values of money, power, and status; cope with a situation by trying to dominate it; and are encouraged to view the world in terms of power, status, and responsibility.

The *Conventional* work environment is characterized by the detailed, ordered, systematic manipulation of data, such as keeping records, filing materials, organizing information, and operating business machines. Workers in a Conventional environment have Conventional personalities, are encouraged to see themselves as orderly and skilled at clerical tasks, are rewarded for conforming and being dependable, cope with situations in a careful and practical manner, and are encouraged to view the world in conventional and dependent ways.

The environment of a given workplace can be measured by classifying the occupations, the training, or the educational or vocational preferences of the people who work there. For example, a school could consist of people creating the following environmental pattern: 40 percent Social, 25 percent Investigative, 15 percent Artistic, 10 percent Conventional, 6 percent Realistic, and 4 percent Enterprising. The environmental pattern for the school would be described with the code SIACRE. Several assumptions could be made about that school's environment—for example, that the atmosphere is likely to be more cooperative than competitive, more liberal than conservative, and more flexible than inflexible. A business firm might be described with the following pattern: 45 percent Conventional, 25 percent Enterprising, 15 percent Realistic, 8 percent Social, 4 percent Investigative, and 3 percent Artistic—or CERSIA. Such a company might be more concerned with money and status, more conservative in political and economic beliefs, and more structured and dependable in its organizational behavior. The six-letter code or hierarchy of types offers a brief set of assumptions as to what a particular work environment might be like.

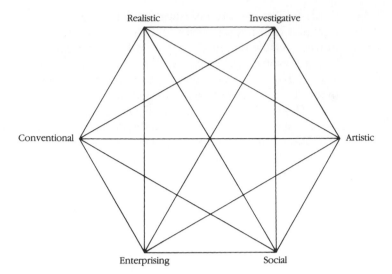

Figure 3-1   A hexagonal model for defining the psychological resemblances among types and environments and their interactions. *Source:* Holland (1997, p. 35). Reproduced by special permission of the Publisher, Psychological Assessment Resources, Inc., from *Making Vocational Choices, Third Edition,* © copyright 1973, 1985, 1992, 1997 by Psychological Assessment Resources, Inc. All rights reserved.

Occupations can be described with the same six-letter hierarchy of types, although the three-letter codes are more practical to use. For example, the AIR code letters for architects mean that architects resemble the Artistic type most of all, the Investigative type somewhat less, and the Realistic type still less. This code also implies that architects least resemble the Social, Enterprising, and Conventional types. Automotive engineers' RIE code letters indicate that they correspond most to the Realistic type and somewhat less to the Investigative and Enterprising types. In this way, occupations can be summarized by showing their degrees of resemblance to three occupational groups (Holland, 2000). Some three-letter code combinations describe only a few occupations or none at all. In such cases, Holland suggests using the first two letters of your own summary code rather than a three-letter code and exploring all the occupations that contain those letters in their code.

Relationships among the Six Holland Types

Holland uses a hexagonal model to explain the relationships among the six types and environments (see Figure 3-1). The rule of thumb is this: The shorter the distance between any two types, the greater their similarity or psychological resemblance (Holland, 1997). For example, Enterprising and Social are next to each other on the model, so they resemble each other closely.

The hexagonal model shows the degree of *consistency* in your personality pattern. Adjacent types—those next to each other on the hexagon—make up the most consistent patterns. As you can see on the hexagonal model, the most consistent patterns are Realistic–Investigative–Conventional, Social–Enterprising–Artistic, Enterprising–Conventional–Social, and so on. Personality patterns composed of opposite types (Realistic–Social, Enterprising–Investigative, and so on) are the least consistent in that they include many opposing traits. For example, Conventional–Artistic is inconsistent, because the two types have opposite traits, such as conformity and originality or control and expressiveness (Holland, 1997).

The hexagonal model can help you assess the degree of *congruence,* or agreement, between you as a person and a work environment. For example, a person whose dominant type is Social would feel most comfortable in a Social environment and would be most uneasy or discontented in a Realistic environment, because Social and Realistic are opposite types. Holland's concept of congruence supports his theory that the dominant type in your personality pattern points to the primary direction of your choice of occupation and work environment.

Holland also suggests that you note the *differentiation* in your personality pattern. Consider the scores that form a three-letter code taken from Holland's *Self-Directed Search,* an inventory that measures the six personality types. Scores of 30, 20, and 10 for the first three types of a code differ from scores of 21, 20, and 18. The first combination of scores (30-20-10) represents a "differentiated" or more stable pattern; the second example (21-20-18) is *not* well differentiated. When scores are close together, as in the second example, the first three code letters and their six possible combinations should be studied about equally, because the three types are not well differentiated. When the first two code letters are close with the third scale score distant (27-25-7, for example), study all combinations with the first two code letters, including those that appear in first and third places and second and third places in the three-letter summary codes.

From his formulation of the six types, Holland (1997, pp. 37–39) proposes several hypotheses, suggesting that (all other things being equal) the following behavior will occur:

1. *High vocational aspiration* will be positively associated with the types in the following order: Enterprising, Social, Artistic, Investigative, Conventional, Realistic. (This order is also hypothesized for *achievement* in one's occupational life.)
2. The likelihood of *creative performance* increases the more a personality pattern resembles the following order: Artistic, Investigative, Social, Enterprising, Realistic, Conventional.
3. *Effective coping with job changes and unemployment* goes with the following personality pattern order: Social, Enterprising, Artistic, Investigative, Conventional, Realistic. The closer a person's pattern resembles this one, the greater the competence.
4. *High educational aspirations* go with the following personality pattern order: Investigative, Social, Artistic, Conventional, Enterprising, Realistic. (This order is also hypothesized for *educational achievement.*)
5. *Competence in interpersonal relations* increases the more a personality pattern resembles the following order: Social, Enterprising, Artistic, Investigative, Conventional, Realistic.

GENERATING OCCUPATIONAL PROSPECTS WITH THE HOLLAND CODES

Inventories that use the six Holland personality and environmental types include the *Self-Directed Search* (SDS), the *Vocational Preference Inventory* (VPI), the *Strong Interest Inventory* (SII), and the *Career Assessment Inventory* (CAI). When you obtain the results of any of these inventories, remember that no person is entirely one type. Actually, you are a combination of all six. The six types are arranged in order from most dominant to least dominant. Practical considerations limit the use of the hierarchy of Holland types to your highest or strongest three. An example would be the Realistic–Investigative–Enterprising combination (RIE, to use the code letter abbreviations). A person coded RIE would resemble the Realistic type most of all, the Investigative type somewhat less, and the Enterprising type still less. The other three types are not mentioned, because their characteristics are the least influential in describing the personality pattern. Work environments and occupations are classified with the same six labels, and they receive similar descriptions.

Some inventories other than the SDS, VPI, SII, and CAI are similar to, or can be adapted to, the six Holland types. (See Table 3-2.)

Table 3-2 Relationship of Holland Types to Four Other Interest Inventories

Holland Types	Campbell Interest and Skill Survey (CISS)	Harrington/O'Shea Career Decision-Making (CDM) System	Kuder Occupational Interest Survey (KOIS)—Form DD	Career Development Inventory (CDI)
Realistic	Producing, Adventuring	Crafts	Outdoor, Mechanical	Technical/Mechanical/ Skilled
Investigative	Analyzing	Scientific	Scientific	Scientific/Theoretical
Artistic	Creating	The Arts	Artistic, Literary, Musical	Artistic/Literary/ Musical
Social	Helping	Social	Social Service	Social Service/Personal Service
Enterprising	Influencing	Business	Persuasive	Persuasive/Managerial
Conventional	Organizing	Office Operations	Clerical, Computational	Clerical/Computational

Finally, if you do not have access to an interest inventory that will provide you with a three-letter Holland summary code, use the Holland Personality Pattern Word List, reproduced on page 96. You can get a rough measure of the Holland types and environments from this exercise.

After you have obtained your three-letter summary code (for example, RCE, SEC, or ESR), use the *Occupations Finder* (Holland, 2000) or the *Dictionary of Holland Occupational Codes* (Gottfredson and Holland, 1996) to generate occupational prospects. Consider combinations other than your original three-letter code; the number of occupations suggested by some three-letter codes is very small or nonexistent. Your three-letter code will form six possible combinations. For example, if your code is SAI, also look up occupations suggested under SIA, ASI, AIS, ISA, and IAS. If the number of occupational prospects suggested is too small, use the first two letters of your summary code, particularly if they are well differentiated from the third letter, and consider the occupations generated with those two letters. For example, if your code is SAI, study the occupations listed under any three-letter codes that have both *S* and *A* letters in them.

The *Occupations Finder* lists more than 1,300 of the most common occupations. Each occupation listed in the *Occupations Finder* has a nine-digit *Dictionary of Occupational Titles* (DOT) code, which helps you locate the description of the occupation in the DOT. The same DOT occupations are also listed alphabetically and matched with their Holland codes in *The Alphabetized Occupations Finder*. A single-digit number gives you an idea of the general educational level required by the occupation. The third edition of the *Dictionary of Holland Occupational Codes* (Gottfredson and Holland, 1996) applies the three-letter Holland codes to 12,860 DOT occupations. In addition, the Holland codes are used to access six other occupational classification systems.

The first edition of the Holland dictionary (Gottfredson, Holland, and Ogawa, 1982) gives data on the number of occupations that appear under the labels of the six Holland types. Table 3-3 reveals that of 12,099 occupations listed, 66.7 percent are classified as Realistic, 13.4 percent as Conventional, and 11.1 percent as Enterprising when using a *one-letter* Holland code. Undoubtedly, changes have taken place since these data were collected. For example, Realistic and Conventional workers are in a shrinking labor market. Their work environments have encouraged following the rules; now, they must find work in more unsystematic, ambiguous work environments (Holland, 1996). Table 3-3 also gives the number of occupations among the 12,099 with each of the six Holland types appearing somewhere in the *first three letters* of the Holland code. Realistic (R) and Enterprising (E) appear most frequently,

Table 3-3 Percentage Distribution of One-Letter Holland Codes and Number of Occupations with Each Code Letter Appearing Somewhere in the First Three Letters

Occupational Group/Code	Percentage of One-Letter Holland Codes	Number of Occupations in First Three Letters
Realistic (R)	66.7	10,708
Investigative (I)	3.0	2,551
Artistic (A)	1.2	570
Social (S)	4.6	6,064
Enterprising (E)	11.1	10,405
Conventional (C)	13.4	5,999

Source: Gottfredson, Holland, and Ogawa (1982).

whereas Artistic (A) appears least frequently. RES, RCE, and REC are the most common three-letter combinations. Some three-letter codes describe only a few occupations or none at all; these tend to be the inconsistent combinations. Again, consider all six possible combinations of a three-letter code.

Another strategy with the three-letter Holland code is to calculate a "summary occupational daydream code." (The *Self-Directed Search Assessment Booklet* provides a page to record the names of occupations you can remember from daydreams with occupational content.) A form is provided for you next. In the first column, print the names of the occupations from your daydreams. List 10 or more occupations. Each occupation has a three-letter code. Use the *Occupations Finder* or the *Dictionary of Holland Occupational Codes* to find the name of the occupation and the three-letter code that goes with that occupation. Each of the remaining six columns has a letter of the Holland RIASEC code: R = Realistic, I = Investigative, A = Artistic, S = Social, E = Enterprising, and C = Conventional. For the letter in the first position in the code, record a 3 under that letter in the columns. Give a 2 for each letter in the second position, and a 1 for each letter in the third position. Then add down each of the six RIASEC columns to obtain a *summary occupational daydream code.* Compare this code with your summary code for the entire *Self-Directed Search* (Rayman, 1998).

Name of Occupation (in the daydream)	Code:	R	I	A	S	E	C
Total Points							
		R	I	A	S	E	C

Holland Personality Pattern Word List

Circle all words that you believe describe you as a person. A few words will appear twice. Use a dictionary if you don't understand any word. Read the scoring directions *after* you have completed the exercise.

Group I—Realistic	Group II—Investigative	Group III—Artistic
1. athletic	16. analytical	31. artistic
2. conforming	17. creative	32. creative
3. frank	18. critical	33. disorderly
4. materialistic	19. curious	34. emotional
5. mechanical	20. independent	35. expressive
6. outdoor-type	21. intellectual	36. idealistic
7. persistent	22. logical	37. impractical
8. practical	23. mathematical	38. independent
9. realistic	24. methodical	39. innovative
10. rugged	25. precise	40. insightful
11. shy	26. questioning	41. intuitive
12. stable	27. rational	42. original
13. strong	28. reserved	43. perceptive
14. technical	29. scientific	44. reflective
15. thrifty	30. studious	45. sensitive
R _____	I _____	A _____

Group IV—Social	Group V—Enterprising	Group VI—Conventional
46. accepting	61. acquisitive	76. conforming
47. altruistic	62. adventurous	77. conventional
48. caring	63. ambitious	78. dependable
49. cooperative	64. articulate	79. efficient
50. empathetic	65. assertive	80. methodical
51. friendly	66. confident	81. obedient
52. generous	67. determined	82. orderly
53. helpful	68. dominant	83. organized
54. humanitarian	69. energetic	84. persistent
55. idealistic	70. enthusiastic	85. practical
56. kind	71. influential	86. precise
57. persuasive	72. persuasive	87. reliable
58. responsible	73. political	88. systematic
59. sociable	74. productive	89. traditional
60. understanding	75. resourceful	90. well-controlled
S _____	E _____	C _____

Score each circled or checked item as one point. Enter the total in the space below each column.

Check the consistency of your responses. Items 2 and 76, 7 and 84, 17 and 32, 20 and 38, 24 and 80, 25 and 86, 36 and 55, and 57 and 72 were the same words. Give yourself one point where you responded to each pair of words the same way. At least six of the eight pairs of words should have been answered in the same way to be consistent.

THE STRONG INTEREST INVENTORY (SII) AND THE CAREER ASSESSMENT INVENTORY (CAI)

The *Self-Directed Search* (SDS) and the *Vocational Preference Inventory* (VPI) provide you with the three-letter code for Holland personality types. In the *Strong Interest Inventory* (SII) and the *Career Assessment Inventory* (CAI), the general themes are labeled with the six Holland types and are combined with two other sets of scores: basic interest scales and specific occupational scales. The SII also has a series of personal style measures.

Table 3-4 Relationship of Basic Interest Scales on the SII and CAI to the Holland Types

Strong Interest Inventory

Realistic	*Artistic*	*Enterprising*
Agriculture	Music/Dramatics	Public Speaking
Nature	Art	Law/Politics
Military Activities	Applied Arts	Merchandising
Athletics	Writing	Sales
Mechanical Activities	Culinary Arts	Organizational Management
Investigative	*Social*	*Conventional*
Science	Teaching	Data Management
Mathematics	Social Service	Computer Activities
Medical Science	Medical Service	Office Services
	Religious Activities	

Career Assessment Inventory: Enhanced Version

Realistic	*Artistic*	*Enterprising*
Animal Service	Creative Arts	Law/Politics
Athletics/Sports	Performing/Entertaining	Management/Supervision
Carpentry	Writing	Public Speaking
Electronics		Sales
Manual/Skilled Trades		
Mechanical/Fixing		
Nature/Outdoors		
Protective Services		
Investigative	*Social*	*Conventional*
Mathematics	Community Service	Clerical/Clerking
Medical Science	Educating	Food Services
Scientific Research/	Medical Service	Office Practices
Development	Religious Activities	

Source: Based on Harmon, Hansen, Borgen, and Hammer (1994), and Johansson (1993).

There are two forms of the CAI: an Enhanced Version for occupations needing various types of postsecondary education and a Vocational Version for occupations requiring two years or less of postsecondary training. Recent research on the SII has found the general occupational themes (the six Holland types) for college-educated satisfied workers to be very similar among African American, Asian American, Caucasian American, Hispanic American, and Native American groups (Zunker & Osborne, 2002).

Basic Interest Scales

The *basic interest scales* on the SII and CAI represent a middle range of interest inventory scores. The basic interest scales are more specific than the six Holland types and environments (called *general occupational themes* on the SII and *general themes* on the CAI) and are more general than single occupational scales (called *occupational scales* on the SII and the CAI). The *Strong Interest Inventory* and the *Career Assessment Inventory-Enhanced Version* have 25 basic interest scales. The CAI-Vocational Version has 22 basic interest scales. Each basic interest scale is more closely related to one Holland type than to any of the other Holland types. Table 3-4 summarizes this relationship.

Specific Occupational Scales

The SII and the CAI include a third set of scales, the occupational scales. This is the most specific set of scales on these two inventories. There are currently 211 occupational scales on the SII (Harmon, Hansen, Borgen, and Hammer, 1994), 111 on the CAI-Enhanced Version, and 91 on the CAI-Vocational Version (Johansson, 1993).

When you use the basic interest scales and the occupational themes on the SII and the CAI, your scores are compared with those of people in general, representing the occupational population of the United States. On the specific occupational scales, however, your scores are compared only with workers in certain selected occupations. For the SII, the characteristics of people tested within each specific occupation are that they (1) enjoy and are satisfied with their work in the occupation, (2) have at least three years of experience in the occupation, (3) perform the job in a typical manner, and (4) are generally between the ages of 25 and 60 (Harmon et al., 1994).

Whenever these people (just described) express a preference on a given item much more or much less frequently than do people in general, that preference is used in making the occupational scale for that particular occupation. When you indicate a preference ("like," "indifferent," or "dislike") that is the same as the preference of a significant number within a certain occupation, this mark adds to your score on the corresponding occupational scale. For example, suppose computer programmers choose "like" on an item in the inventory much more frequently than people in general. If you choose "like" for the item, your score on the computer programmer occupational scale will increase slightly. If you respond again and again in the same way as the computer programmers did, your final score on this occupational scale will be high, and placed in the "similar interests" part of the scale. In other words, you have interests, preferences, and attitudes similar to those of people in computer programming.

Thus a high score (designated as "similar interest") on an occupational scale means that you share preferences with people in that occupational group. A high score represents an assumption that you are likely to be compatible with other people working within that occupation, interested in the same things that they are, and accepted by them as well as enjoy the nature of the work, achieve, and be successful in the occupation.

However, a high score on an occupational scale does not necessarily mean that you *should* choose that occupation for your life's work. For the moment, it is simply an option to consider as an occupational prospect. Also investigate the ability level the occupation requires—something that interest inventories do not measure. You would definitely want to know whether the jobs within that occupation express many of your important work values and would help you meet your most essential needs. Explore these concerns after an interest inventory has suggested a prospective occupation.

It is possible for a person to have a high score on a basic interest scale, such as mathematics, yet have a low score on a similar type of occupational scale, such as mathematician. In that case, a person may show a general preference for mathematical subjects without expressing a liking for a wider range of interests and activities that describe people in the mathematics profession. Low scores on basic interest scales and high scores on similar occupational scales can also occur—for example, between art and fine artist, agriculture and farmer, or military activities and military officer.

Although most interest inventory profiles have a number of high scores, some profiles have very few specific occupational scales in a high range. If this is true of your results, focus on the basic interest scales and the general occupational themes (using the *Occupations Finder*) to discover your occupational prospects.

Your pattern of responses ("like," "indifferent," "dislike") influences the High–Average–Low results reported on your SII or CAI profile. A high percentage of "like" responses tends to raise scores and put them into the High or Similar columns. A high percentage of "dislike" responses tends to lower scores and put them in the Low or Dissimilar columns. This pattern is particularly true of the occupational themes and the basic interest scales. For example, if five or all six of the theme scores are high or very high, this may indicate a very positive outlook on many things. This perspective may or may not be realistic, and should perhaps be explored in a counseling session. If five or all six of the theme scores are low or very low, you may show a general negative orientation to the items selected from the inventory. If five or all six of the theme scores are average, balancing likes and dislikes, you prefer certain parts of each theme. Checking the basic interest scales very carefully will show where these interests are. High "indifferent" responses may cause inconsistencies to appear among the scales, perhaps reflecting indifference toward the inventory, lack of knowledge about the world of work, chronic indecision, or an unwillingness to make commitments.

Personal Style Scales

There are four personal style measures in the *Strong Interest Inventory.* (1) The *Work Style* scale indicates how much contact you want with people in your work or how much preference you have for working with data, things, or ideas. (2) The *Learning Environment* scale shows the kind of educational setting you prefer: a practical learning situation that emphasizes short-term training, hands-on activities, and training to achieve a specific goal or an academic atmosphere that emphasizes long-term education, lectures, books, and seeking knowledge for its own sake. (3) The *Leadership Style* scale reveals the kind of leader you prefer to be: leading by example rather than taking charge of others directly, or leading by initiating action and persuading or directing others to do a task. (4) The *Risk-Taking/Adventure* scale tells whether you like bold, daring, risky activities or prefer to play it safe and avoid danger (Harmon et al., 1994).

THE MYERS-BRIGGS TYPE INDICATOR

As you live your life, you direct your attention outward to the world around you (*extraversion*) and inward to the world within you (*introversion*). You gather information about the world by *sensing* (using your five senses) and by *intuition* (going beyond what your eyes, ears, and other senses tell you). You use information to make decisions and judgments about the world through *thinking* in a logical way and *feeling* on the basis of your personal values. You act in the world by *judging* when you reason from thinking and feeling to control your environment in a planned, orderly way and by *perceiving* when you sense and intuit in a spontaneous, adaptive way. These four dimensions—extraversion or introversion, sensing or intuition, thinking or feeling, and judging or perceiving—are pairs of orientations and attitudes we have toward people, careers, and life in general. They constitute important parts of the conscious side of one's personality.

The dimensions just named are measured by the *Myers-Briggs Type Indicator* (MBTI). The MBTI is based on Carl Jung's ideas about perception, judgment, and attitude in human personality, as expressed in his book *Psychological Types* (Jung, 1921/1971). Although the main purpose of occupational inventories is to provide you with specific occupations to explore, one strength of the MBTI is that it shows you *why* certain occupations may be of greater interest than others (Myers and McCaulley, 1985). The MBTI develops four scales from the eight attitudes and functions already mentioned.

The Extraversion–Introversion (EI) Scale. *Extraversion* means directing your attention and energy to the outer world of people and objects. *Introversion* means focusing primarily on the inner world of ideas and concepts. According to Jung, the differences between these attitudes create a tension that provides energy for the personality (Hall and Lindzey, 1957). Extraverts are outgoing and seek group interaction with others. Introverts are quiet and reserved and prefer to be alone or in one-to-one relationships. When an extravert and an introvert are together, they can have a difficult time understanding each other (Baron, 1998).

The Sensing–Intuition (SN) Scale. The sensing and intuition functions are ways in which you perceive the world as you take in information. *Sensing* means using your five senses directly to become aware of concrete facts and realities of the environment. Sensors are practical, want precise information, and are focused on the present. *Intuition* means perceiving the meanings, symbols, and potential of information by way of imagination, unconscious processes, and going beyond knowledge gained from the senses. Intuitives prefer insights and abstract information and are more future-oriented. (The letter "*N*" is used for *iNtuition* because "*I*" has already been used.)

The Thinking–Feeling (TF) Scale. Thinking and feeling are ways in which you make judgments and decisions from information you have acquired. *Thinking* means making choices and drawing conclusions logically and objectively by analyzing data and weighing the evidence. *Feeling* means making decisions on the basis of value judgments, giving information a personal, subjective appraisal. ("Feeling" in this context is not the same as "emotion"; it is a reasoned process of making judgments.) Thinkers are direct and analytical; they want to decide things with their head. Feelers are more convinced by their values and decide with their heart.

The Judgment–Perception (JP) Scale. The judgment and perception attitudes concern what you do with decisions and how you act in and relate to the external environment. *Judgment*, or a judging attitude, means using thinking and feeling to organize, plan, and control your life. ("Judging," as the term is used here, does not mean "judgmental." The authors of the MBTI emphasize that any personality type may be judgmental.) *Perception*, or a perceiving attitude, means using sensing and intuition to orient yourself to the outer world in a manner that is adaptable, flexible, and open-minded. Judgers like to structure things and prefer a more orderly lifestyle; when they make a decision, they are likely to make definite plans for implementing that decision and close out other options. Perceivers like to have things more spontaneously developed and adapt as they go, preferring to keep their options open.

Thus the MBTI measures eight personality characteristics, along four dimensions or scales. How you respond to the items on the inventory determines the preferences that make up your four-letter type. A *preference* is "an inborn tendency to be, act, or think in a certain way" (Baron, 1998, p. 9). No one preference is better or worse than its opposite. The preferences appear in this order: E or I, S or N, T or F, and J or P. For example, an ESFP is the code for an extravert (E) who would rather obtain information by sensing (S), prefers to use feeling (F) in making decisions, and takes primarily a perceiving (P) attitude toward the outside world. An INTJ is an introvert (I) who prefers using intuition (N) in perceiving the world, thinking (T) for making judgments, and takes a judging (J) attitude toward the external world (Myers, 1987).

Your scores on the MBTI indicate the consistency with which you choose one attitude or function over the other. High scores—scores further away from the other alternative on the scale—usually mean a clear preference. Low scores, or scores that are closer to the other alternative, mean your preference is not clear for some reason. Your scores do not show how well you use a preference or how well developed it is (Myers, 1987).

The dominant preference in your four-letter code does not mean you exclude the less dominant preference. For example, extraverts sometimes want to be alone, and introverts can be sociable. The dominant preference is merely the one with which a person is most comfortable.

The four preferences in your MBTI code indicate 1 of 16 possible types. Table 3-5 lists descriptive words that help explain each type. Of course, humans are more varied than these 16 types. Results of the MBTI give only partial descriptions of people (Myers and McCaulley, 1985). Before you receive your MBTI results, try to predict your type results. When you get your four-letter code, ask yourself whether you agree that it is accurate.

The MBTI by no means tells you what you are; it simply reports the choices you made when you responded to the items on the inventory.

The combinations of the perception and judgment functions, the second and third letters of the MBTI code, are considered the most important grouping of the types where career choices are concerned. Either kind of perception (sensing or intuition) can join with either kind of judgment (thinking or feeling) to form four possible

Table 3-5 Brief Descriptors of the 16 MBTI Types

ISTJ	ISFJ	INFJ	INTJ
dependable	accommodating	compassionate	analytical
exacting	detailed	conceptual	autonomous
factual	devoted	creative	determined
logical	loyal	deep	firm
organized	meticulous	determined	global
practical	organized	idealistic	independent
realistic	patient	intense	organized
reliable	practical	intimate	original
reserved	protective	loyal	private
sensible	quiet	methodical	systems-minded
steadfast	responsible	reflective	theoretical
thorough	traditional	sensitive	visionary

ISTP	ISFP	INFP	INTP
adaptable	adaptable	adaptable	autonomous
adventurous	caring	committed	cognitive
applied	cooperative	curious	detached
expedient	gentle	deep	independent
factual	harmonious	devoted	logical
independent	loyal	empathetic	original
logical	modest	gentle	precise
practical	observant	idealistic	self-determined
realistic	sensitive	imaginative	skeptical
resourceful	spontaneous	intimate	speculative
self-determined	trusting	loyal	spontaneous
spontaneous	understanding	reticent	theoretical

ESTP	ESFP	ENFP	ENTP
activity-oriented	adaptable	creative	adaptive
adaptable	casual	curious	analytical
adventurous	cooperative	energetic	challenging
alert	easygoing	enthusiastic	clever
easygoing	enthusiastic	expressive	enterprising
energetic	friendly	friendly	independent
outgoing	outgoing	imaginative	original
persuasive	playful	independent	outspoken
pragmatic	practical	original	questioning
quick	sociable	restless	resourceful
spontaneous	talkative	spontaneous	strategic
versatile	tolerant	versatile	theoretical

ESTJ	ESFJ	ENFJ	ENTJ
decisive	conscientious	appreciative	challenging
direct	cooperative	congenial	controlled
efficient	harmonious	diplomatic	decisive
gregarious	loyal	energetic	energetic
logical	personable	enthusiastic	logical
objective	planful	expressive	methodical
organized	responsible	idealistic	objective
practical	responsive	loyal	opinionated
responsible	sociable	organized	planful
structured	sympathetic	personable	straightforward
systematic	careful	responsible	strategic
task-focused	traditional	supportive	tough-minded

The underlined letter in each personality type indicates the dominant function or process.

Source: Hirsh and Kummerow (1990). Modified and reproduced by special permission of the Publisher, Consulting Psychologists Press, Inc., Palo Alto, CA 94303 from *Introduction to Type in Organizations, Second Edition* by Sandra Krebs Hirsh and Jean M. Kummerow. Copyright 1990 by Consulting Psychologists Press, Inc. All rights reserved. Further reproduction is prohibited without the Publisher's written consent.

combinations. ST (sensing plus thinking) people are practical, matter-of-fact types. Their best chance of success and satisfaction may be found in occupations that require impersonal analysis of concrete facts, such as economics, law, surgery, business, accounting, production, and handling machines and materials. SF (sensing plus feeling) people are sympathetic and friendly types. They may be inclined to work where their personal warmth can be used, such as selling material products, teaching young children, and providing direct health care. NF (intuition plus feeling) people have the same personal warmth, along with enthusiasm and insight for meeting human needs. They may be drawn particularly to high school and college teaching, selling services, counseling, writing, and research. NT (intuition plus thinking) people tend to be logical and original in solving problems within their special fields of interest. They may do well in areas such as scientific research, electronic computing, mathematics, finance, or developing innovations in technical or administrative occupations (Myers and McCaulley, 1985).

Dominant and auxiliary functions, or processes, are indicated by the middle two letters of your type, S or N and T or F. *Dominant* in this case means your favorite process; *auxiliary* means the secondary process. In other words, one process takes the lead while the second one helps out. The other functions, even though they do not appear in the four-letter MBTI code, are still used, but not as often as are the dominant and auxiliary functions.

If you are an extravert, your judgment–perception (JP) scale points to the dominant and auxiliary processes because JP reflects only the process used in dealing with the outer world. For the extravert whose type ends with J, the dominant process is a judging one—either T or F. If the extravert's type ends with P, the dominant process is a perceptive one—either S or N.

For introverts, the reverse is true because their orientation is toward their inner world, not the outer one. The J or P in their type reflects the auxiliary rather than the dominant process. If the introvert's type ends in J, the dominant process is a perceptive one, either S or N. If it ends in P, the dominant process is a judging one, either T or F (Myers with Myers, 1980). The dominant process is more obvious with extraverts, but is often hidden by introverts, who use it mainly in connection with their inner world. Introverts often show only their auxiliary function to the outside world. Because of this tendency, the strengths and attributes of introverts are usually more difficult to recognize. The letter underscored in each MBTI code on Table 3-5 shows the dominant process for each personality type.

Consider the ESFJ type. This type would be called "Extraverted Feeling with Sensing." Feeling, the dominant process, is used primarily in relation to the outer world because this person is an extravert whose strength is in judging between things in the external world using person-centered values. The auxiliary function, sensing, is centered mostly on this person's inner world and can provide facts to help make a decision (Hirsh and Kummerow, 1990).

If we change to an ISFJ type, the dominant function becomes sensing because this person is an introvert whose strength is perceiving things in the external world with careful observation of details. The auxiliary function, feeling, is focused on a sympathetic concern in caring for people.

The preferences among the MBTI types help explain the different ways people use their minds, especially the way perception is used in gathering information and the way decisions are made after that information has been assembled. Perception and judgment are processes that make up much of your mental activity and subsequent outward behavior. Perception has a lot to do with how you view circumstances and events in life, and judgment influences what you decide to do about those circumstances and events (Myers with Myers, 1980).

Brief descriptions of the 16 types appear on the *Report Form for the Myers-Briggs Type Indicator* (Myers and Myers, 1993). More complete descriptions of the types and explanations of the theory and applications of the MBTI can be found in *Introduction to Type* (Myers, 1993) and in *Gifts Differing* (Myers with Myers, 1980). *What Type Am I?*

(Baron, 1998) provides clear descriptions of the eight preferences among the four MBTI scales, and characterizations of the 16 types with lists of occupations appropriate to each one. Also, this book has a connection of the Myers-Briggs types with a device known as the "enneagram," a system of nine personality types based on strategies developed in childhood to deal with the outer world. *Introduction to Type in Organizations*, second edition (Hirsh and Kummerow, 1990), and *The Character of Organizations* (Bridges, 1992) may provide you with many insights into organizational behavior. For more information about type and the MBTI, contact the Center for Applications of Psychological Type (CAPT), 2720 NW Sixth Street, Gainesville, Florida 32602. Table 3-6 gives the order of functions or processes, provides examples of possible occupational interests, and gives several words or phrases about the preferred work environment of each of the 16 MBTI types.

Table 3-6 Order of Functions, Possible Occupational Interests, and Preferred Work Environments of the 16 MBTI Types

Type	Order of Functions	Examples of Possible Occupational Interests*	Preferred Work Environment
ISTJ	Sensing Thinking Feeling Intuition	Accounting/office work Engineering Police work/law Production work Construction jobs Health occupations	Focus is on facts and results Provides security, structure, order Rewards a steady pace Hard-working, task-oriented people Allows privacy for uninterrupted work
ISTP	Thinking Sensing Intuition Feeling	Scientific research Mechanics and repairers Farming Engineering and science technicians	Focus is on immediate solutions to problems Project-oriented; action-oriented Unconstrained by rules Allows for hands-on experience
ESTP	Sensing Thinking Feeling Intuition	Marketing and sales Engineering/technical Credit investigation Health technologies Construction/Production Recreation	Focus is on firsthand experience Lively, results-oriented people Provides for flexibility in working Allows time for fun/unbureaucratic Responsive to needs of the moment Technically oriented
ESTJ	Thinking Sensing Intuition Feeling	Business management Banking, finance Construction/production Teaching: technical Service work	Focus is on getting the job done correctly and efficiently Task-oriented; structured, organized Provides stability and predictability Rewards meeting goals
ISFJ	Sensing Feeling Thinking Intuition	Health professions Teaching/library work Office work Personal service Clerical supervision	Focus is on well-structured tasks Provides security and privacy Clearly structured; efficient Conscientious, calm, quiet people Service-oriented
ISFP	Feeling Sensing Intuition Thinking	Mechanics and repairers Factory operatives Food services Office work Household work	Cooperative people enjoying their work Allows for private space Flexible; aesthetically appealing Includes courteous coworkers People-oriented
ESFP	Sensing Feeling Thinking Intuition	Health services Sales work/design Transportation jobs Supervisory work Machine operation Office work	Focus is on present realities Action-oriented; lively, energetic people Includes people who are adaptable Harmonious; people-based Attractive work setting

(continued)

Table 3-6   (continued)

Type	Order of Functions	Examples of Possible Occupational Interests*	Preferred Work Environment
ESFJ	Feeling Sensing Intuition Thinking	Health services Receptionist Sales work Child care Household work	Focus is on helping others Goal-oriented people and systems Organized; friendly atmosphere Appreciative, conscientious people Operates on facts
INFJ	Intuition Feeling Thinking Sensing	Religious work Teaching/library work Media specialist Social service Research and development	Focused on ideas and human well-being Opportunities for creativity Harmonious, quiet, organized Has a personal "feel" Allows time and space for reflection
INFP	Feeling Intuition Sensing Thinking	Counseling Teaching: literature, art, drama, science Psychology Writing, journalism	Focus is on values of importance to others Cooperative atmosphere Allows privacy and time for reflection Flexible, calm, quiet, unbureaucratic
ENFP	Intuition Feeling Thinking Sensing	Teaching Counseling Religious work Advertising, sales Art, drama, music	Focus is on human possibilities Colorful; participative atmosphere Lively, unconstrained Offers variety and challenge Idea-oriented
ENFJ	Feeling Intuition Sensing Thinking	Sales Artists and entertainers Religious work Counseling Teaching: health	Focus in on changing things for the betterment of others Supportive, social, harmonious People-oriented; settled and orderly Encourages the expression of self
INTJ	Intuition Thinking Feeling Sensing	Science Engineering Politics/law Philosophy Computer specialist	Focus is on implementing long-range visions Efficient, task-focused Allows privacy for reflection Supports creativity and independence Includes effective, productive people
INTP	Thinking Intuition Sensing Feeling	Science, research Engineering Social science Computer programming Psychology/law	Focus is on solving complex problems Encourages independence, privacy Flexible, unstructured, quiet Rewards self-determination
ENTP	Intuition Thinking Feeling Sensing	Photography, art Marketing Selling, promoting Computer analyst Entertainment	Has independent people working on models to solve complex problems Flexible, challenging, unbureaucratic Change-oriented Rewards risk-taking
ENTJ	Thinking Intuition Sensing Feeling	Administration Operations and systems analysts Sales managers Marketing Personnel relations	Results-oriented, independent people focus on solving complex problems Goal-oriented; rewards decisiveness Efficient systems and people Challenging; structured Includes tough-minded people

*A complete list of occupations by type can be found in Appendix D of the MBTI *Manual*. Occupations on the list have individuals from all 16 types, but each occupation attracts some types more than others.

OTHER INVENTORIES

You may encounter occupational interest and personality inventories other than the *Myers-Briggs Type Indicator*, the *Self-Directed Search*, the *Vocational Preference Inventory*, the *Strong Interest Inventory*, or the *Career Assessment Inventory*. Two of them are the *Harrington/O'Shea Career Decision-Making System* (CDM) and the *Career Occupational Preference System* (COPS). Following these two, brief descriptions are given of the *Campbell Interest and Skill Survey* (CISS), the *Kuder Occupational Interest Survey-Form DD* (KOIS), the *Career Development Inventory* (CDI), the *Hall Occupational Orientation Inventory*, the *Jackson Vocational Interest Inventory*, and the *College Major Interest Inventory*.

The Harrington/O'Shea Career Decision-Making (CDM) System—Level 2

The CDM measures six career interest areas derived from the Holland model of six personality/environment types: (1) Crafts (Realistic), (2) Scientific (Investigative), (3) The Arts (Artistic), (4) Social (Social), (5) Business (Enterprising), and (6) Office Operations (Conventional) (Harrington and O'Shea, 1993). A two-scale code is obtained from the two highest scores from the interest inventory. This two-scale code suggests 3 or 4 of 18 career clusters for exploration. Each career cluster lists a number of typical jobs, related school subjects, job values, and abilities (in an interpretation folder used with the CDM) and relates to the work groups of the *Guide for Occupational Exploration* (explained in the next chapter). Each occupation mentioned gives the first three digits of the *Dictionary of Occupational Titles* or DOT code (also explained in the next chapter), the U.S. Department of Labor estimate of national growth and competition for job openings in the occupation, and the minimum education and training requirements for the occupation. The following six career interest areas and 18 career clusters with their representative occupations are adapted from the *CDM Interpretative Folder* (Harrington and O'Shea, 1992, 2000):

I. Crafts

1. Manual—bricklayer, construction equipment operator, construction laborer, farmhand, fire fighter, machine-tool operator, miner, truck driver
2. Skilled crafts—auto mechanic, carpenter, cook, electrician, electronic assembler, farmer, jeweler, plumber, tailor, TV/VCR repairer, welder
3. Technical—air traffic controller, airline pilot, drafter, electronic technician, forester aide, quality-control technician, surveyor

II. Scientific

4. Math/science—architect, astronomer, biologist, chemist, computer programmer, engineer, forester, geologist, mathematician, pharmacist, physicist, soil conservationist, statistician, surgeon, systems analyst
5. Medical/dental—audiologist, cardiologist, chiropractor, dentist, optometrist, podiatrist, psychiatrist, radiologist, speech pathologist, veterinarian

III. The Arts

6. Literary—copywriter, editor, news writer, novelist, playwright, poet, reporter, script writer, technical writer, translator
7. Art—art teacher, clothes designer, commercial artist, floral designer, industrial designer, interior designer, painter, photographer, set designer
8. Music—composer, conductor, dancer, music arranger, music teacher, musician, singer
9. Entertainment—actor/actress, comedian, disc jockey, drama teacher, model, public relations specialist, radio/TV announcer

IV. Social

10. Customer service—barber, beautician, bus driver, flight attendant, food counter worker, gas station attendant, hairstylist, messenger, park ranger, parking lot attendant, security guard, taxi driver, waiter/waitress

11. Personal service—athlete, child care attendant, coach, emergency medical technician, home health aide, homemaker, nursing aide, occupational therapy aide, physical therapy aide, recreation leader
12. Social service—clergy, counselor, dental assistant, dental hygienist, economist, historian, occupational therapist, political scientist, probation officer, registered nurse, social worker, sociologist
13. Education—college admissions director, college professor, elementary school teacher, financial aid officer, high school teacher, librarian, school administrator, teacher's aide

V. Business

14. Sales—automobile sales representative, buyer, dispensing optician, insurance sales representative, manufacturer's representative, purchasing agent, retail sales worker, real estate sales representative, travel agent
15. Management—bank manager, contractor, farm manager, government administrator, hotel/motel manager, legislative assistant, personnel manager, production manager, sales/marketing manager, store manager
16. Legal—claims adjuster, detective, FBI agent, fire chief, food and drug inspector, judge, lawyer, paralegal assistant, police chief

VI. Office operations

17. Clerical—bank teller, cashier, file clerk, hotel/motel clerk, mail carrier, receptionist, secretary, typist/word processor
18. Data analysis—accountant, auditor, bank clerk, bookkeeper, computer operator, insurance underwriter, market research analyst, payroll clerk

The Career Occupational Preference System (COPS)

COPS provides scores for 14 occupational clusters; it reflects the structure of occupations proposed by Anne Roe in which occupations are classified by group and level. COPS uses two levels—professional and skilled—for the science, technology, business, arts, and service categories. The other four groups (consumer economics, outdoor, clerical, and communication) are not divided into professional and skilled levels. Professional occupations usually require college training and, in some cases, advanced degrees. Skilled occupations often require vocational or business school or on-the-job training. Illustrations of the 14 COPS occupational clusters are adapted from descriptions in the *COP System Technical Manual* (Knapp, Knapp, and Knapp-Lee, 1990).

1. *Science, professional*—planning and conducting research and gathering knowledge in mathematics and in the medical, life, and physical sciences
2. *Science, skilled*—observing and classifying facts, assisting in laboratory research, and applying information from medicine and the life and physical sciences
3. *Technology, professional*—designing and engineering the manufacture, construction, or transportation of products or utilities
4. *Technology, skilled*—working with your hands in a skilled trade that constructs, manufactures, installs, or repairs products in the related fields of construction, electronics, and mechanics
5. *Consumer economics*—preparation and packaging of foods and the production, care, and repair of clothing and textile products
6. *Outdoor*—growing and tending of plants and animals and the cultivation and gathering of crops and natural resources in agriculture, forestry, park service, fishing, and mining
7. *Business, professional*—responsibility for the organization, administration, and efficient functioning of businesses and governmental bureaus; involves finance, accounting, management, and business promotion
8. *Business, skilled*—sales, promotion, and the related financial and organizational activities of businesses

9. *Clerical*—recording, posting, and filing of business records requiring attention to detail, accuracy, neatness, orderliness, and speed in office work and contact with customers

10. *Communication*—use of language skills in the creation or interpretation of literature or in the written and oral communication of knowledge and ideas

11. *Arts, professional*—expression of creative or musical talent and ability in the fields of design, fine arts, and performing arts

12. *Arts, skilled*—applying artistic skill in the fields of graphic arts and design

13. *Service, professional*—responsibility involving interpersonal relations in caring for the personal needs and welfare of others in the fields of social service, health, and education

14. *Service, skilled*—providing services to people and attending to the tastes, desires, and welfare of others in the fields of personal, social, and health-related service, protection, and transportation

Brief Descriptions of Six More Inventories

Campbell Interest and Skill Survey (CISS). The CISS is a survey of self-reported interests and skills (Campbell, Hyne, and Nilsen, 1992). One difference the CISS has from many interest inventories is a focus on self-estimates of skill based on experiences from doing similar tasks and learning new things. Implied in the development of the CISS is the belief that interests and abilities are closely related; people tend to perform well in activities they find interesting. The report you receive from the CISS contains 7 orientation scales, 29 basic interest and skill scales, and 60 occupational scales. The last two sets of scales are grouped within the 7 orientation scales. The orientation scales resemble the Holland RIASEC model (see Table 3-2, earlier in this chapter).

Kuder Occupational Interest Survey, Form DD (KOIS). The KOIS is "intended for use in . . . career exploration to enhance self-knowledge and understanding, reduce possibilities to a manageable few, and suggest new alternatives" (Kuder and Zytowski, 1991, p. 10). Vocational interest estimates are provided in 10 groups: outdoor, mechanical, computational, scientific, persuasive, artistic, literary, musical, social service, and clerical. These groups can be related to the Holland RIASEC model (see Table 3-2, earlier in this chapter). Your responses on the KOIS are compared with people in 40 college majors and in 109 occupational groups who have been employed in the occupation at least three years and are satisfied with their occupation.

Career Development Inventory (CDI). The CDI is an interest inventory with a broader scope of assessing career development and vocational maturity. Part One consists of four basic scales: career planning, career exploration, decision making, and world of work. The total of these four scales provides a measure of Super's concept of career or vocational maturity discussed in Chapter 1 of this book. Part Two measures a "knowledge of preferred occupational group" scale. It also uses your career planning and career exploration scores to form a "career development–attitudes" scale, and combines the decision-making and world-of-work scores for a "career development–knowledge and skills" scale.

Hall Occupational Orientation Inventory. The Hall inventory is described as a self-administered, self-scored, and self-interpreted occupational survey, a self-guided examination of career and lifestyle goals. The 35 occupational and personality characteristics are grouped into five self-examination scales: career interest, ability, needs and values, job characteristics, and choice style scales. The career interest and ability scales have measurements of six characteristics: "people-social-accommodating," "data-information," "things-physical," "people-business-influencing," "ideas-scientific," and "aesthetic-arts" (Hall, 2001).

Jackson Vocational Interest Inventory. Scores on this inventory are reported for 10 general occupational themes and 34 basic interest scales. The Jackson inventory compares your scores with college student groups in 13 academic majors such as education, engineering, and liberal arts.

College Major Interest Inventory (CMII). The CMII compares your educational interests with those of successful students who have completed degrees in various academic majors in colleges and universities.

Keep a record on page 109 of your results on the interest and personality inventories you take. Indicate the date (month, year) you were given the inventory, and save your scores for future reference.

EXERCISES FOR GENERATING OCCUPATIONAL PROSPECTS

An *occupational prospect* is a potential occupation that attracts you enough to spend some time researching the occupation. This section presents methods for creating occupational prospects. Your teacher or counselor may suggest certain exercises, or you may pick and choose a number of them to complete. Use those exercises you believe will be the most productive for you. When you have worked through an exercise, write the names of the suggested occupations in the spaces provided.

Don't be too critical in your thinking at this point; your aim is to produce as many occupational prospects as you can. This isn't the time to ask whether you have the skill to perform the tasks required for an occupation, whether you have the preparation needed, or whether the occupation is in harmony with your values. These concerns will be considered at a more appropriate time. All you are doing now is identifying prospective occupations that you believe merit your attention and investigation.

EXERCISE 3-1 REMEMBERING

Write down all the occupations or jobs that have interested you at one time or another (Chapman, 1976). Include any occupation that interests you now. Concentrate on this exercise for 15 or 20 minutes when you are alone. Try it several times during the next week or month. Close your eyes and let your mind wander backward in time, covering all the stages of your life. Think of any kind of job that ever attracted you earlier in your life, no matter how fantastic or ridiculous it may seem now, as well as any occupation that appeals to you at the present time. Write these occupational titles in the spaces provided.

_____   _____

_____   _____

_____   _____

_____   _____

_____   _____

_____   _____

EXERCISE 3-2 ASKING

Ask one, two, or several people who know you well to suggest occupations in which they could imagine you working. Sometimes another person can uncover a career suggestion for you that you cannot imagine for yourself. Also, others may know about

INTEREST AND PERSONALITY INVENTORY RECORD

Holland Types from the *Self-Directed Search* (SDS), *Vocational Preference Inventory* (VPI), *Strong Interest Inventory* (SII), or *Career Assessment Inventory* (CAI)

Date: _____	Raw Score	Standard Score	Percentile Rank
Realistic	_____	_____	_____
Investigative	_____	_____	_____
Artistic	_____	_____	_____
Social	_____	_____	_____
Enterprising	_____	_____	_____
Conventional	_____	_____	_____

Harrington/O'Shea Career Decision-Making System—Revised (CDM-R)

Date: _____	Raw Score
Crafts	_____
Scientific	_____
The Arts	_____
Social	_____
Business	_____
Office Operations	_____

Three career clusters suggested for exploration:

_____

_____

_____

Kuder General Interest Survey, Form E (KGIS)

Date: _____	Raw Score	Percentile Rank
Outdoor	_____	_____
Mechanical	_____	_____
Computational	_____	_____
Scientific	_____	_____
Persuasive	_____	_____
Artistic	_____	_____
Literary	_____	_____
Musical	_____	_____
Social Service	_____	_____
Clerical	_____	_____

Myers-Briggs Type Indicator (MBTI)

Date: _____ _____

	Scale Score		Scale Score
Extraversion (E)	_____	Introversion (I)	_____
Sensing (S)	_____	Intuition (N)	_____
Thinking (T)	_____	Feeling (F)	_____
Judging (J)	_____	Perceiving (P)	_____

Career Occupational Preference System (COPS)

Date: _____	Total (Raw) Score	Percentile Rank
Science, professional	_____	_____
Science, skilled	_____	_____
Technology, professional	_____	_____
Technology, skilled	_____	_____
Consumer Economics	_____	_____
Outdoor	_____	_____
Business, professional	_____	_____
Business, skilled	_____	_____
Clerical	_____	_____
Communication	_____	_____
Arts, professional	_____	_____
Arts, skilled	_____	_____
Service, professional	_____	_____
Service, skilled	_____	_____

Other (name)

Date: _____ Name of Scale	Raw Score	Standard Score	Percentile Rank
_____	_____	_____	_____
_____	_____	_____	_____
_____	_____	_____	_____
_____	_____	_____	_____
_____	_____	_____	_____
_____	_____	_____	_____
_____	_____	_____	_____
_____	_____	_____	_____
_____	_____	_____	_____

occupations of which you are completely unaware (Chapman, 1976). Of course, you can and should evaluate their recommendations. You may want to eliminate some of their ideas, but other prospects may be retained and investigated. Write them in the spaces provided.

_____   _____

_____   _____

_____   _____

EXERCISE 3-3 OCCUPATIONAL DAYDREAMING

Can you think of several times recently when you've had daydreams? Did they have any occupational content? If so, list the occupations involved in the space provided. Fantasy is a part of any person's healthy development. Daydreams play a central role in career planning (Morgan and Skovholt, 1977). Include occupational prospects from daydreams, no matter how fanciful they may seem. Your subconscious may be trying to tell you something important. Studs Terkel, in his classic book *Working* (1972), talks to a stonemason who dreams of stone. "I daydream all the time, most times it's on stone . . . all my dreams, it seems like it's got to have a piece of rock mixed in them."

_____   _____

_____   _____

_____   _____

_____   _____

EXERCISE 3-4 WISHING

Write down seven activities that make you happy or proud of yourself and that you wish you could do more often. You can also list activities you have *not* done but wish you could do. Come up with 15, 20, or 25 things on a separate sheet of paper if you can. For each activity you mention, ask, "Is it related to a job or an occupation?" If so, write the name of the occupation after the activity (adapted from Simon, Howe, and Kirschenbaum, 1995).

Seven Things or Activities That Make You Happy or Proud	Job-Related?	Name of Job or Occupation
1. _____	_____	_____
2. _____	_____	_____
3. _____	_____	_____
4. _____	_____	_____
5. _____	_____	_____
6. _____	_____	_____
7. _____	_____	_____

EXERCISE 3-5 BROWSING

Look at the occupational literature in a career resource center or in a library. Look at pamphlets, booklets, and monographs in the file drawers. Check the index for the location of a specific occupation. Many free handouts are kept in racks. Thumb through the encyclopedic books such as *Occupational Outlook Handbook, Dictionary of Occupational Titles,* and *Guide for Occupational Exploration.* With a computer, use search engines that let you access Internet sites by typing in the word "career" or "occupation" or "job." The next chapter (Chapter 4) has a section listing many sites on the World Wide Web. Sometimes you just happen to come across an occupation that pops out at you and grabs your attention. The idea of browsing is to widen your perspective of the world of work. Write any prospects you uncover this way in the spaces provided.

_____   _____

_____   _____

_____   _____

_____   _____

EXERCISE 3-6 WHAT NEEDS TO BE DONE?

"We are here to do, and through doing to learn; and through learning to know; and through knowing to experience wonder; and through wonder to attain wisdom; and through wisdom to find simplicity; and through simplicity to give attention; and through attention—to see what needs to be done."

—Ben Hei Hei (quoted in Shapiro, 1995).

The human community faces a vast array of issues and problems; an actual 10,233 global challenges were listed (Hansen, 1997). The more we know about the world, the more questions are raised. You could react with dismay to all of the world's problems. Instead, think of them as invitations that provide opportunities for new jobs or unusual occupations. Ask, "What needs to be done?" Try to think of occupations or organizations, those already in existence or new ones, that could deal with the problem. Circle the problems that concern or interest you, and name the occupation(s) that would address them in the spaces provided. Here is a short list of problems and issues to which you can add others you know about. What needs to be done about them?

Problems	Occupation(s)	Problems	Occupation(s)
Abortion	_____	Debt	_____
Accidents	_____	Deforestation	_____
Acid rain	_____	Digital divide	_____
Aging	_____	Disease	_____
AIDS	_____	Disease/epidemics	_____
Air/water pollution	_____	Divorce	_____
Alcoholism	_____	Drug addiction	_____
Care of terminally ill	_____	Drug trade	_____
Child abuse	_____	Economic decline	_____
Citizen indifference	_____	Endangered species	_____
Climate/weather	_____	Energy shortages	_____
Conflict in marriage	_____	Energy waste	_____
Crime	_____	Ethnic prejudice	_____
Cruelty to animals	_____	Fair distribution of wealth, resources	_____
Crumbling roads	_____		

Problems	Occupation(s)	Problems	Occupation(s)
Global warming	_____	Overconsumption	_____
Health costs	_____	Political repression	_____
Homelessness	_____	Population explosion	_____
Homophobia	_____	Poverty	_____
Hunger/starvation	_____	Race discrimination	_____
Illegal weapons	_____	Rape	_____
Illiteracy	_____	Rehabilitation of criminals	_____
Inadequate health care	_____	Reinventing taxation	_____
Inadequate shelter	_____	Soil erosion	_____
Infectious diseases	_____	Spiritual emptiness	_____
Inferior education	_____	Spouse abuse	_____
Inflation	_____	Suicide	_____
Inner-city restoration	_____	Terrorism	_____
Job stress	_____	Unemployed workers	_____
Loneliness	_____	Unfair labor practices	_____
Low productivity	_____	Unsafe products	_____
Low-paid jobs	_____	Unwanted babies	_____
Malnutrition	_____	Urban congestion	_____
Managing change	_____	Violence	_____
Mental illness	_____	Waste disposal	_____
Migrants	_____	Wildlife preservation	_____
Militarism	_____	Work absenteeism	_____
Missing children	_____	Work injuries	_____
Noise/hearing loss	_____		

Other problems (write in)   Occupation(s) (write in)

_____   _____

_____   _____

_____   _____

_____   _____

_____   _____

EXERCISE 3-7 CAREER KITS AND GAMES

Occupational kits and career games provide activities that can give you more occupational alternatives and allow you to explore a variety of occupations. Examples are the *Occupational View-Deck*, which helps students relate occupations to temperaments, interests, and educational plans (Chronicle Guidance Publications); *Career Opportunity*

Boxes (Houghton Mifflin); *Career Awareness Laboratory* (Singer Career Systems); *Occupations Scanner* (Science Research Associates); and *Desk Top Career Kit* (Careers, Inc.). Write prospects generated by kits and games in the spaces provided.

_____   _____

_____   _____

_____   _____

_____   _____

_____   _____

EXERCISE 3-8 CARD SORTS

Card sorts are decks of cards where each card gives the title and a short description of an occupation or an occupational group. Usually the directions go something like this: Scan each card. Discard those that carry a description of an occupation or a work activity you would dislike. Then eliminate any card showing an occupation or work activity toward which you are indifferent or uninterested. You are left with occupations and work activities that stimulate your interest. You can subdivide these occupations further according to the reasons you chose them. If you have more than 10 or 12 cards left, put them in order from the highest to the lowest. Consider the highest 10 or 12 as occupational prospects. Write these occupations in the following spaces.

Card sorts are part of the *Vocational Exploration and Insight Kit* (Holland, 1980). Also available are the *Occupational Interests Kit* (Knowdell, 2002), *Occ-U-Sort* cards (Jones, 1981), the *Worker Trait Keysort Deck, Career Values Card Sort*, and the *Missouri Occupational Card Sort*. Some teachers and counselors have developed their own card sorts.

_____   _____

_____   _____

_____   _____

_____   _____

_____   _____

EXERCISE 3-9 COMPUTER-BASED CAREER GUIDANCE SYSTEMS

Several computerized career-guidance programs are described in the next chapter. These include the *System of Interactive Guidance and Information* (SIGI Plus), *Discover, Choices,* and *Career Information System* (CIS). All these systems contain units or sections that develop lists of occupations for you to explore. The lists can be short or long, depending on the specifications you program into the system. Write the names of the occupational prospects generated in the spaces provided.

_____   _____

_____   _____

_____   _____

_____   _____

_____   _____

EXERCISE 3-10 LOCAL OR STATE CAREER SYSTEMS

Many local, state, or regional career information delivery systems exist. Check in your area; local guidance committees and state vocational education services may have created instruments to generate occupational prospects. For example, the Michigan Occupational Information System has an inventory that instructs you to choose among three broad types of work (data, people, or things), six areas of work, kinds of physical strength you prefer to use, five physical capabilities, inside or outside working conditions, ten levels of education, and ten kinds of adjustments made on the job. The information is coded on a worksheet, which you compare to characteristics of occupations on a "scan sheet." When a match occurs, you have another occupational prospect. Use a local or state career information delivery system. Write the prospects it generates in the spaces provided.

_____   _____

_____   _____

_____   _____

_____   _____

_____   _____

_____   _____

EXERCISE 3-11 SPECIAL FAMILY

Pretend you could make up your own special family. Choose any four or five people in the world, from all of history and literature. Select people for whom you have a special feeling and whose ideas and activities you admire. Pick out people who, because of their experiences in life, would be understanding and compassionate toward you, would encourage you to analyze and try out your talents, and would support you when things weren't going so well (Sher, 1979). Write the names of these people in the space provided.

_____   _____

_____   _____

_____   _____

Then respond to these questions: What have these people done in their lives that appeals to you? What would they say to you and tell you to do? (Have them "talk" to you on paper.) Could any occupations come from their activities or statements? If so, write them in the spaces provided.

_____   _____

_____   _____

_____   _____

EXERCISE 3-12 FANTASIZING

Have someone read you the following fantasy. It should be read slowly and softly, with pauses where they are indicated in the text. Close your eyes, take a few deep breaths, and relax. Now begin.

"Imagine you are starting a typical day about five years from now. It's a workday. You're trying to decide what to wear. Look over your clothes. What do you finally decide to wear? (*Pause*) Imagine you are making yourself look nice in front of a mirror. How do you feel as you think ahead to your day at work? Calm? Excited? Bored? Afraid? (*Pause*) You are eating breakfast now. Is there anyone with you, or are you eating alone? (*Pause*) You're ready to head for work. Do you stay at home? If not, how do you get to work? How far is it? (*Pause*)

"You are entering your workplace now. Stop for a moment and try to get a mental picture of your workplace. Where is it? What does it look like? (*Pause*) What people are there? How many do you work with? What are they doing? (*Pause*) Complete your morning's work right up to lunchtime. Form an image of the things you do on your job. Think about what you are actually doing. Are you working with ideas or adding figures? Are you working with people, talking with them, helping them in some way? Are you using tools or running a machine? Do you work mostly by yourself or with lots of people? Are you mostly inside or outdoors? (*Pause*)

"Now it's lunchtime. Where do you go? Who are the people you eat with? What are they like? What are you talking about? (*Pause*) Return to work now and finish the workday. Is anything different from the morning's work? What is the last thing you do before you quit for the day? (*Pause*) Your workday is coming to an end. Has it been mostly a satisfying day or a frustrating day? What has made it so? (*Pause*) Open your eyes when you are ready and just sit quietly for a moment." (*Source:* Based on Morgan and Skovholt, 1977.)

Now go back over the fantasy. Write any occupational roles that occur to you in the spaces provided. Titles aren't necessary, but use them if you can think of them.

_____   _____

_____   _____

_____   _____

_____   _____

EXERCISE 3-13 FAMILY TREE

Identify the occupations, where they apply, held by members of your immediate family, extended family, neighborhood, and circle of friends. Circle the occupations in which you believe you have an interest.

Relationship	What Occupation(s) Do They Have (or Have They Had)?
Father	_____
Mother	_____
Sister(s)	_____
Brother(s)	_____
Uncle(s)	_____
Aunt(s)	_____
Grandmother(s)	_____
Grandfather(s)	_____
Cousin(s)	_____
Neighbor(s)	_____
Friend(s)	_____
Other(s)	_____

EXERCISE 3-14 INTEREST INVENTORIES AND CODING SYSTEMS

Part A: Interest Inventories

All occupational interest inventories suggest either groups of occupations or specific occupations to explore. Most inventories can be completed in less than an hour's time. Several well-known interest inventories are the *Strong Interest Inventory* (SII), the *Self-Directed Search* (SDS), the *Career Assessment Inventory* (CAI), the *Myers-Briggs Type Indicator* (MBTI), the *Career Occupational Preference System* (COPS), the *Harrington/O'Shea Career Decision-Making System* (CDM), the *Hall Occupational Orientation Inventory*, the *Kuder General Interest Survey—Form E*, the *Kuder Occupational Interest Survey—Form DD*, the *Campbell Interest and Skill Survey* (CISS), and the *Jackson Vocational Interest Inventory*. Use any of these inventories or others not mentioned. Transfer the names of any prospects from the inventory to the following spaces.

Name of Inventory: _____   Name of Inventory: _____

Occupational Prospects Generated: Occupational Prospects Generated:

_____   _____

_____   _____

_____   _____

_____   _____

_____   _____

_____   _____

_____   _____

Part B: Coding Systems

The best-known occupational coding system is the one developed by John Holland. You identify the three highest personality types from the Realistic, Investigative, Artistic, Social, Enterprising, and Conventional types. The three-letter code can be obtained from Holland's *Self-Directed Search* or *Vocational Preference Inventory* and general occupational themes of the *Strong Interest Inventory* or the *Career Assessment Inventory*. The three-letter codes provide descriptions of occupations as well as of people. Occupations are grouped under codes they most resemble in Holland's *Occupations Finder*, which classifies more than 1,300 of the most common occupations, or the *Dictionary of Holland Occupational Codes*, which classifies 12,756 occupations (Gottfredson and Holland, 1996).

The *Myers-Briggs Type Indicator* (MBTI) identifies 16 personality types. Each type is drawn more to certain occupations than to others. When you determine your MBTI code, several MBTI booklets, such as *Introduction to Type and Careers* (Hammer, 1994), can help you generate a number of occupational prospects to consider. List these prospects in the following spaces.

_____   _____

_____   _____

_____   _____

_____   _____

_____   _____

_____   _____
_____   _____
_____   _____
_____   _____

_____

EXERCISE 3-15 OCCUPATIONAL CLASSIFICATION SYSTEMS

In the next chapter, you will find classification systems in the new *Occupational Information Network* or *O*Net* with its electronic database and in the "big books" of occupational information: the *Occupational Outlook Handbook* (11 clusters), the *Dictionary of Occupational Titles* (82 two-digit groups), and the *Guide for Occupational Exploration* (133 work groups and subgroups). We have even included the Canadian *National Occupational Classification* system in Appendix C: *The National Occupational Classification (NOC) of Canada*, which is available to students in the United States via the Internet as well as to Canadians. In any of these systems or in commercially produced encyclopedias of occupations, identify three, four, or five groups of occupations that are the most attractive to you. Come back to these pages and write down the names of the occupations in each group or cluster that are of greatest interest to you.

Name of System: Name of System: Name of System:
_____   _____   _____

Occupational Prospects   Occupational Prospects   Occupational Prospects
Generated: Generated: Generated:

_____   _____   _____
_____   _____   _____
_____   _____   _____
_____   _____   _____
_____   _____   _____
_____   _____   _____
_____   _____   _____
_____   _____   _____

SUMMARY

1. Occupational inventories ask you for likes and dislikes about school subjects, occupations, leisure-time pursuits, and various other activities. Your responses are then organized into a set of scores based on a division of the world of work created by the inventory.

2. The ideas of John Holland are very influential in identifying personality types of people and the work environments these types create. Personalities and environments are classified into six types: Realistic, Investigative, Artistic, Social, Enterprising, and Conventional. Holland's theory suggests that people try to find work in occupations that have environments compatible with their personalities.

3. Inventories based on the Holland model yield results measuring the strength of the six types and establishing a hierarchy of those types within your

personality. The same hierarchy of types can be extended to work environments and occupations. Inventories that directly measure the Holland personality types are the *Self-Directed Search* and the *Vocational Preference Inventory*, as well as the general occupational themes of the *Strong Interest Inventory* and the *Career Assessment Inventory*.

4. The relationships among the six Holland types can be explained by use of a hexagonal figure. The shorter the distance between two types, the more similar those two types become. Holland's concepts of consistency among two- and three-type combinations, congruence between people and their work environments, and the degree of differentiation in personality patterns were discussed. Several hypotheses exist about the hierarchy of types in personality patterns and vocational aspirations and achievement, creative performance, coping with job changes, educational aspirations and achievement, and competence in interpersonal relations.

5. Holland's three-letter summary codes can be used to generate occupational prospects. Use of the *Occupations Finder* and the *Dictionary of Holland Occupational Codes* is especially helpful in producing occupational prospects to explore.

6. The basic interest scales and the specific occupational scales on the *Strong Interest Inventory* and the *Career Assessment Inventory* are further extensions of those inventories, although these scales still have definite relationships with the six basic Holland types.

7. The *Myers-Briggs Type Indicator* (MBTI), based on C. G. Jung's psychological types, measures preferences on 4 scales that yield 16 personality types. The scales are extraversion–introversion (EI), sensing–intuition (SN), thinking–feeling (TF), and judgment–perception (JP). The middle two letters of the four-letter MBTI code indicate dominant and auxiliary processes.

8. Other interest inventories are the *Harrington/O'Shea Career Decision-Making System* (CDM), the *Career Occupational Preference System* (COPS), the *Campbell Interests and Skills Survey* (CISS), the *Kuder Occupational Interest Survey—Form DD* (KOIS), the *Career Development Inventory* (CDI), the *Hall Occupational Orientation Inventory*, the *Jackson Vocational Interest Inventory*, and the *College Major Interest Inventory* (CMII). The CDM reflects the Holland classification, whereas the COPS reflects Roe's classification of occupations.

9. Fifteen exercises were suggested as methods to generate occupational prospects that reflect your preferences in the world of work. From your list of prospects come occupations that could be explored as a part of your career planning.

REFERENCES

Baron, R. 1998. *What type am I?: Discover who you really are.* New York: Penguin.

Bridges, W. 1992. *The character of organizations: Using Jungian type in organizational development.* Palo Alto, CA: Consulting Psychologists Press.

Campbell, D. P., Hyne, S. A., and Nilsen, D. 1992. *Manual for the Campbell Interest and Skill Survey.* Minneapolis, MN: National Computer Systems.

Chapman, E. 1976. *Career search: A personal pursuit.* Chicago: Science Research Associates.

Gottfredson, G. D., and Holland, J. L. 1996. *Dictionary of Holland occupational codes*, 3rd ed. Odessa, FL: Psychological Assessment Resources.

Gottfredson, G. D., Holland, J. L., and Ogawa, D. 1982. *Dictionary of Holland occupational codes.* Palo Alto, CA: Consulting Psychologists Press.

Hall, C. S., and Lindzey, G. 1957. *Theories of personality.* New York: Wiley.

Hall, L. G. 2001. *Hall occupational orientation inventory: Young adult/college/adult form,* 4th ed. Bensenville, IL: Scholastic Testing Service.

Hammer, A. L. 1994. *Introduction to type and careers.* Palo Alto, CA: Consulting Psychologists Press.

Hansen, L. S. 1997. *Integrative life planning: Critical tasks for career development and changing life patterns.* San Francisco: Jossey-Bass.

Harmon, L. W., Hansen, J. C., Borgen, F. H., and Hammer, A. L. 1994. *Strong Interest Inventory: Applications and technical guide.* Palo Alto, CA: Consulting Psychologists Press.

Harrington, T., and O'Shea, A. 1992, 2000. *CDM interpretative folder.* Circle Pines, MN: American Guidance Service.

Harrington, T., and O'Shea, A. 1993. *CDM—revised manual.* Circle Pines, MN: American Guidance Service.

Hirsh, S. K., and Kummerow, J. M. 1990. *Introduction to type in organizations,* 2nd ed. Palo Alto, CA: Consulting Psychologists Press.

Holland, J. L. 1980. *Vocational exploration and insight kit.* Palo Alto, CA: Consulting Psychologists Press.

Holland, J. L. 1996. Exploring careers with a typology: What we have learned and some new directions. *American Psychologist,* 51, 397–406.

Holland, J. L. 1997. *Making vocational choices: A theory of vocational personalities and work environments,* 3rd ed. Odessa, FL: Psychological Assessment Resources.

Holland, J. L. 2000. *Occupations finder,* rev. ed. Odessa, FL: Psychological Assessment Resources.

Johansson, C. B. 1993. *Career assessment inventory: The enhanced version.* Minneapolis: NCS Pearson.

Jones, L. K. 1981. *Occ-U-Sort.* Monterey, CA: CTB Macmillan, McGraw-Hill.

Jung, C. G. 1971. *Psychological types.* H. G. Baynes, trans.; revised by R. F. C. Hull. In *The collected works of C. G. Jung.* Vol. 6. Princeton, NJ: Princeton University Press. (Original work published 1921.)

Knapp, R. R., Knapp, L., and Knapp-Lee, L. 1990. *COPSystem technical manual.* San Diego: Ed-ITS/Educational and Industrial Testing Service.

Knowdell, R. L. 2002. *Occupational interests kit.* San Jose, CA: Career Research & Testing.

Kuder, F., and Zytowski, D. G. 1991. *Kuder occupational interest survey general manual.* Monterey, CA: Macmillan/McGraw-Hill.

Mastie, M. M. 1994. Using assessment instruments in career counseling: Career assessment as compass, credential, process and empowerment. In J. T. Kapes, M. M. Mastie, and E. A. Whitfield, eds., *A counselor's guide to career assessment instruments,* 3rd ed., pp. 31–40. Alexandria, VA: National Career Development Association.

Morgan, J. I., and Skovholt, T. M. 1977. Using inner experience: Fantasy and daydreams in career counseling. *Journal of Counseling Psychology,* 24, 391–397.

Myers, I. B. 1987. *Report form for the Myers-Briggs Type Indicator.* Palo Alto, CA: Consulting Psychologists Press.

Myers, I. B. 1993. *Introduction to type.* Palo Alto, CA: Consulting Psychologists Press.

Myers, I. B., and McCaulley, M. H. 1985. *Manual: A guide to the development and use of the Myers-Briggs Type Indicator.* Palo Alto, CA: Consulting Psychologists Press.

Myers, I. B., with Myers, P. B. 1980. *Gifts differing.* Palo Alto, CA: Consulting Psychologists Press.

Myers, P. B., and Myers, K. D. 1993. *Report form for the Myers-Briggs Type Indicator.* Palo Alto, CA: Consulting Psychologists Press.

Rayman, J. R. 1998. Interpreting Ellenore Flood's self-directed search. *The Career Development Quarterly,* 46, 330–337.

Shapiro, R. M., Rabbi. 1995. *Wisdom of the Jewish sages.* New York: Bell Tower.

Sher, B. 1979. *Wishcraft: How to get what you really want.* New York: Ballantine.

Simon, S., Howe, L., and Kirschenbaum, H. 1995. *Values clarification: A practical, action-directed workbook.* New York: Warner.

Terkel, S. 1972. *Working: People talk about what they do all day and how they feel about what they do.* New York: Pantheon.

Zunker, V. G., and Osborn, D. S. 2002. *Using assessment results for career development,* 6th ed. Pacific Grove, CA: Brooks/Cole-Wadsworth-Thomson Learning.

Chapter 4

Gathering Information about Your Occupational Prospects

Gathering information about occupations that interest you is at the heart of the career-planning process. Career decisions are only as good as the information you bring to them. We live in an information society, and occupational information is plentiful. There is really no reason to be uninformed about prospective occupations.

Occupational information is virtually everywhere. You might have found a local newspaper article about an insect control officer; it sounds like a worthwhile job performing a valuable public service. Before taking the job, however, it just might be a good idea to get some information about this occupation. What's behind that occupational title? Fortunately, the news article gave the necessary information. From April through October, the insect control officer operates as a mosquito counter. You go to almost 40 checkpoints each day, stand with legs uncovered and your bare arms extended, and wait patiently for mosquitoes. When you have averaged five or more mosquito bites per minute, your job is to call for the area to be sprayed with insect repellent. You might also want to know how one treats hundreds of mosquito bites and how long the typical worker stays in this kind of work. At least, you have some information by which you can decide whether or not to take this job. (Maybe you could arrange to get hired in November and plan to quit before next April, but that requires information ahead of time.)

Imagine you are a student considering working as a supervisor in the meat products industry. In a meat-packing plant where you would like to work, you would be an entry-level meat cutter and advance to a supervisory position as you gain experience. One of your relatives works there; it's in a nearby town and you've observed the assembly line, watching workers with clean garments drop sausages into cardboard cartons and slide hams into plastic bags. This is the picture you have of the meat industry, and it looks fine to you. In a management class at school, you have a report on labor relations to prepare. You begin scanning a copy of *No Retreat, No Surrender* (Haga and Klauda, 1989), a book about a strike at a meat-packing plant. As you read the book, you inadvertently receive occupational information. You discover there are many occupations involved in converting a live hog into ham, bacon, sausage, and other meat products. The authors of the book write several pages to describe that process—and it is rather "picturesque." Checking the *Dictionary of Occupational Titles* for the authors' accuracy, you discover the work stunners, shacklers, stickers, shavers, gamblers, skinners, carcass splitters, offal separators, eviscerators, trimmers, and about 30 other types of workers actually do in the meat industry. Now, you are in a better position to determine whether you would want to become a supervisor or manager in a meat-packing plant. If nothing else, you will have gained insight into where your hot dogs, hams, and pepperoni come from.

To judge whether an occupation is going to have the qualities you want to find in your work, you need to know the tasks an average worker does on the job, wages you can earn, skills and training required, working conditions, typical work environment, advancement opportunities, and so on. What people do at work provides the basis for a formal set of roles, functions, or activities on which occupational titles are hung. You study those roles by gathering information about them. Acquiring occupational information from a variety of sources will take work and some time on your part, but this information is absolutely essential for making good career decisions.

The world of work is so huge that you could not possibly learn about all the occupations in it. The only way to make sense out of a subject this big is to divide it into manageable parts. Fortunately, that job has been done for you. Just as a biologist classifies the plant and animal world, labor experts and researchers have classified the world of work. Classification lets you impose some order and logic on your career search. No one occupational classification system is commonly agreed on, but several "crosswalks" connect one classification to another. Four occupational classification systems are presented in this chapter: those used in the *Occupational Outlook Handbook* (OOH), the *Occupational Information Network* or *O*Net* (which is gradually replacing the *Dictionary of Occupational Titles*, or DOT, although we have included the DOT because people are still using it), and the *Guide for Occupational Exploration*

(GOE)—plus a fifth system developed by Dr. Anne Roe. The OOH, DOT, and GOE are encyclopedic books, covering enormous numbers of occupations. The O*Net is not a book; it is an electronic database. Moving through the entire OOH, O*Net, DOT, or GOE would be a gigantic undertaking, more than is necessary for your career planning. In this chapter, Exercises 4-1 through 4-5 can help you identify the occupational groups that interest you the most. Then you can use these resources selectively, turning to only the parts of them that you need. More occupational prospects can be generated this way and you will have discovered where to obtain important career information about them. Even if these resources are not available to you in book form, information from the OOH and O*Net can be located on the Internet, and you can do a lot of your research on your occupational prospects electronically.

Exercise 4-6 enables you to combine all your occupational prospects into one list and select the most attractive occupations for exploration and research. It is easier to deal with a combined list of prospective occupations than with the several shorter lists created in Chapter 3. Exercise 4-6 contains a matrix to help you select the most likely occupations to consider.

You can then begin to explore any occupation you believe merits your serious investigation. This can involve reading in career resource centers and libraries, talking to people about occupations, working through a computer-based occupational program, accessing career information using the Internet and the World Wide Web, and more. In this chapter you will start applying the knowledge you have gained about occupations. Exercise 4-7 and the accompanying worksheet will give you ideas about the kinds of information to obtain. When you make decisions in your career planning, you need to be well informed about your career choices. You will want to know that the decisions you make about prospective occupations are based on solid information. However, it does take time and effort to get this information.

OCCUPATIONAL INFORMATION

What do you need to know about an occupation? Here are some items to consider: (1) nature of the work; (2) education, training, or experience; (3) personal qualifications; (4) pay; (5) working conditions; (6) location of employment; (7) personality characteristics of people working in the occupation; (8) employment and advancement outlook; (9) personal satisfaction from the work; (10) advantages and disadvantages for you; (11) perceptions of people with whom you talk; and (12) related occupations. There is a saying, "You are only as good as your information." If that is true, then where do you get the information?

The Range of Occupational Information

Sources of occupational information range from publications to actual work experience. One system lists the ways you can acquire information about occupations (Isaacson and Brown, 1997):

1. Publications (books, monographs, articles, and so on)
2. Audiovisual aids (films, tapes, slides, and the like)
3. Programmed instructional materials (books, workbooks, and so forth)
4. Computer-based systems (electronic storage and retrieval systems)
5. Interviews with experts (direct questioning of occupational representatives)
6. Simulated situations (role playing, taking on various work roles)
7. Occupational laboratories (imitations or models of work settings)
8. Direct observation (visits to work sites, job shadowing)
9. Directed exploratory experiences (work samples)
10. On-the-job tryouts (internships, part-time work)

This list can be divided into three broad groups. The sources of information in numbers 1–3 are passive, and are usually found in a library or a career resource center. Numbers 4–6 require interacting with other people or with equipment in a classroom or career center. Numbers 7–10 require interactive, hands-on involvement with tools, equipment, and workers in a laboratory or in actual work environments. Several of these sources of information are included in the following sections.

Government Sources of Occupational Information

Printed and electronic sources of occupational information are numerous, and those of the U.S. Department of Labor are especially noteworthy. Career planners can be helped with three major sources: the *Occupational Outlook Handbook* (OOH), the *Occupational Information Network* (the O*Net) or the *Dictionary of Occupational Titles* (DOT), and the *Guide for Occupational Exploration* (GOE). The DOT is being replaced by the O*Net, but you can still use it as a basic source of job information.

A new edition of the *Occupational Outlook Handbook* is published every two years by the Bureau of Labor Statistics of the U.S. Department of Labor. The OOH covers the most popular occupations in the United States, based on numbers of workers. If you wanted to investigate a specific occupation, you would use the index at the back of the OOH. Descriptions of occupations in the OOH will give you the following information: (1) nature of the work; (2) working conditions; (3) employment numbers; (4) training, other qualifications, and advancement; (5) job outlook; (6) earnings; (7) related occupations; and (8) sources of additional information. The OOH occupations are arranged into 11 clusters, or groups of related occupations, and are listed in the table of contents. A somewhat different approach to career information is offered by the Bureau of Labor Statistics in its *Career Guide to Industries*. This guide gives information on occupations by industry. Descriptions of 42 industry groups include the nature of the industry, working conditions, employment, occupations in the industry, training and advancement, earnings and benefits, employment outlook, and sources of additional information.

The O*Net, the Occupational Information Network, is a comprehensive database system accessible from any Web browser. The O*Net gives information about occupational characteristics and requirements, worker characteristics and requirements, and experience needed. Currently, it includes information for over 950 occupations. Each occupation is coded by the Standard Occupational Classification (SOC) system. The *Dictionary of Occupational Titles* (DOT), 4th edition revised, is the "parent" of the O*Net. The "child" (O*Net) will soon take over from its parent, and the DOT will "fade away into the sunset." (A touching story, to be sure, but when you lift the DOT, you'll discover there are advantages to electronic communication.) The DOT contains 12,741 occupational definitions. For each occupation, the DOT gives an assigned nine-digit code number, a title, an industry designation, an alternate (or similar) title, and the body of the definition—what the worker does, equipment and tools used, and so on. The current (fourth) edition of the DOT uses three methods for locating an occupational title: (1) an Occupational Group Arrangement, a classification system; (2) an alphabetical index; and (3) an arrangement by industry designation. To find an occupation in the DOT, refer to the section called "How to Find an Occupational Title Code," located in the front of the book. Although the DOT does not give you as much information on a specific occupation as does the OOH, its coverage extends to many more kinds of jobs.

The *Guide for Occupational Exploration* (GOE) is in its third edition. It begins with Table A, which lists 14 broad job interest areas, each of which is divided into 2 to 10 work groups for a total of 83 work groups. Table B records nearly 1,000 job titles described in the GOE. Part 1 covers broad interest area and more specific group descriptions, kinds of work done in the occupations within the groups, things about you that would point to this work, skills and abilities needed to do the work, and specific job titles associated with the work. Also included are the educational courses and training options that lead to the occupations in the work group. Part 2 contains descriptions from the O*Net for the nearly 1,000 occupations listed in Part 1. Part 3 has "crosswalks," or cross-references, connecting occupations to work values, leisure and home activities, school subjects, work settings, skills, abilities, and knowledges. An alphabetical index at the end of the book helps you locate the occupations, work groups, and interest areas in the GOE.

Other Printed Sources of Occupational Information

Commercial publishers print comprehensive volumes on occupations. One such set of books is the four-volume *Encyclopedia of Careers and Vocational Guidance*, 12th edition (Morkes, 2002). Volume 1 profiles 93 industries from accounting to the wood industry and includes two appendixes, one containing resources and associations for people with disabilities and the second covering internships, apprenticeships, and training programs. Among the indexes in Volume 1 are commonly used government classifications in the United States and Canada: the *Dictionary of Occupational Titles*, the *Guide for Occupational Exploration*, the *National Occupational Classification System* (Canada's classification of occupations), and the O*Net-SOC (Standard Occupational Classification). Volumes 2 through 4 contain 709 career articles, ranging from accountant/auditor to zoologist. Each occupation is described according to the following outline: summary of important facts, definition, history, job description, requirements, ways to explore the field, employers who hire in the occupation, where to look for employment, advancement, earnings, work environment, outlook, and sources of additional information. Within many broader occupational categories, specific or specialized occupations are briefly described in the "nature of the work" section and are highlighted by italics.

Another comprehensive set of books is the 13-volume *Career Information Center*, 8th edition (Kestler and Ciaston, 2002). It is organized by occupational interest area so that people who do not know exactly the occupational title they want can read about several related occupations. There are 12 occupational clusters: agribusiness, environment, and natural resources; communication and the arts; communication, business, and office; construction; consumer, homemaking, and personal services; engineering, science, and technology; health; hospitality and recreation; manufacturing; marketing and distribution; public and community services; and transportation. Each occupation contains information on the following: definition and nature of the work, education and training requirements, getting the job (job search methods), advancement possibilities and employment outlook, working conditions, earnings and benefits, and where to go for more information (names, addresses, telephone numbers, and Web sites of organizations).

There are hundreds of books published on careers. Some are one-volume books; others have a number of volumes like the two sets just mentioned. Publishers offer series of career books; each one in the series covers an occupation or a group of occupations and is updated every few years. The *Opportunities In* series contains nearly 100 books. The *Careers for You* series has catchy names for about 50 titles, such as *Animal Lovers, Color Connoisseurs, History Buffs, Introverts, Mystery Buffs, Number Crunchers, Puzzle Solvers, Sports Nuts,* and *Talkative Types.* The *Great Jobs* series answers the question, "What can I do with a degree in . . . ?" About 25 college majors are covered, ranging from degrees in accounting to theater. Libraries and career resource centers keep career books and pamphlets on shelves and in file cabinets. Other sources of printed occupational information include professional associations; labor unions; industrial organizations; private companies; educational institutions; national magazines such as the *Occupational Outlook Quarterly, U.S. News & World Report,* and various business magazines; as well as the business and employment sections of newspapers. For example, *U.S. News & World Report* publishes an annual career guide issue. In the March 8, 2004, edition, the article "Jobs with Staying Power" provides examples of occupations that are currently "in" and others that are on the way "out" (Pethokoukis et al., 2004). Your instructor, counselor, librarian, or career resource specialist can help you locate information.

Talking to People about Their Jobs

Writer Studs Terkel became famous by talking to people. For his book *Working: People Talk about What They Do All Day and How They Feel about What They Do* (1972), he talked with people about their jobs, recorded the conversations, and edited what they said for publication. The book became one of America's greatest best-sellers. As Terkel found out, it isn't hard to get people talking about their work.

Interviewing people for information about their occupation doesn't have to be formal and nerve wracking; it can simply be a casual conversation. You can start with someone you know well—a relative, neighbor, or even one of your parents. You may feel hesitant about approaching someone you don't know or know only slightly, such as a teacher or a counselor. The chances are good that this person will be happy to talk with you, because (1) people feel complimented when someone asks them for advice, and (2) most people love to talk about their jobs, even if they don't like them. (Have you ever gone to a party where people said, "Now, we're not going to talk shop tonight," and you realized that 90 percent of the conversation dealt with things going on at work?)

There are advantages to getting some of your career information this way. By talking with people at their workplace, you can get direct information about the job and its work environment that simply isn't obtainable any other way. You can check on the accuracy of information previously gathered from other sources. You can learn how workers feel about their occupations, which you won't find in most career literature. You can ask questions you couldn't find answers to in printed sources. You can add a personal contact, a person who may help you later in your job search.

Job-shadowing programs offer the opportunity to explore an occupation by going to a work site and observing a worker in an occupation that interests you. Your school's career center may sponsor a shadowing program. When you register for the program, the career center starts with an orientation to job shadowing and arrange your visit, matching you with someone working in a prospective occupation. The duration of the visit may vary, but it is usually for a few hours. It gives you the opportunity to get acquainted, watch, ask questions, make contacts, and see for yourself what life is like on the job (Mariani, 1998). You don't have to wait for your school to schedule a job visit. You can set up shadowing experiences yourself—with a parent, relative, or friend of the family.

Bad examples of job shadowing

As you acquire occupational prospects, try to talk with people who work in occupations high on your list. If no one doing that job lives in your area, talk with a teacher in your school or with a person in a related occupation. For example, if your prospective occupation is social work, talk with a counselor or a teacher in psychology, sociology, or human services. For engineering, talk with a teacher in engineering, physics, or math. A business instructor or school administrator could talk with you about careers in management or marketing. A biology teacher could give you information about occupations relating to the environment and conservation. A machine shop teacher may be able to give you some facts about work as a tool and die maker. And talk with your mother. After all, she may hold or have held the positions of cook, dietitian, laundress, housekeeper, school subject tutor, landscaper, gardener, interior decorator, wardrobe manager, social secretary, seamstress, hostess, raising children, labor negotiator, diplomat, and no doubt a few more jobs.

When you talk with people about their occupations, verify the information they give you by consulting other sources. It is possible the person with whom you are talking is not typical or representative of those working in an occupation. Also, your informant's more personalized data are subjective; they could be more biased than information from other sources.

What questions could you ask? Use the following questions as a guide, and add others of your own. Write down ahead of time the information you want to obtain. That way you won't waste anyone's time during the conversation.

- How did you decide on this occupation? How did you prepare for it?
- What skills do you need for this work? If you were hiring a person for your job, what qualifications would you look for?
- What are your major responsibilities on the job? How are you evaluated?
- What do you enjoy about your occupation? What personal rewards are there?
- What is a typical day like in your work (or on your job)?
- What are working conditions like on your job? (This item could include hours, work environment, type of work associates, supervisory practices, dress requirements, possible hazards, and how work decisions are made.)
- What are the starting and average pay scales for people in the occupation? (Don't ask what the person you are interviewing earns, just the average pay.)
- What fringe benefits are usually made available?
- What kind of future do you see for your occupation (and company)?
- What other occupations are closely related to this one? What part-time work experiences could help me get acquainted with this occupation?
- With whom else could I talk about work in this occupation?

Computer-Assisted Career Guidance Systems

Computer technology has become an integral part of life, from banking to space exploration; it has also been applied to career planning. Computers will not solve all the problems in career decision making, but they can save you time, labor, and money. Computer-stored information can provide up-to-date local, state, or regional data that may differ from the national scene. Computer-assisted career guidance systems usually involve four kinds of activities: (1) learning about one's self in terms of interests, abilities, and values; (2) learning about occupations in the world of work; (3) expanding occupational alternatives, narrowing choices, and making decisions; and (4) making plans that deal with education and job search methods (Isaacson and Brown, 1997).

When you first log in to a computer-assisted career guidance system, by typing a code word or a set of numbers you tell the software on the computer that you are a valid user. You receive specific directions from the software system, and you respond and give commands to it. If the system is interactive, it will ask you questions, give you an array of possible responses, and respond according to the answer you give. Information you receive is shown on your computer screen. Usually you can print out information you want to keep.

Information retrieved from a computer data bank is often quite general. For example, occupations may be listed in their broadest terms, such as engineer or teacher, without their subgroups. Follow up your computer sessions by referring to sources such as the *Occupational Outlook Handbook,* the O*Net, and the *Guide for Occupational Exploration;* they give more specific data.

The following paragraphs summarize four of the most widely used computer-assisted career guidance systems at the present time: Discover, Choices, Career Information System, and System of Interactive Guidance and Information. Computer technology in career development is evolving so rapidly that what you read here is accurate at the time of writing, but changes may have occurred between that time and the time you read this material.

Discover is a comprehensive system that consists of four "halls," or units. Figure 4.1 shows the structure of Discover.

> *Hall 1: Learn about self and career.* The self assessment part of this section includes taking one or more interest, abilities, or work-related values inventories. These inventories result in a Holland code. This code is converted into regions and job families on a "World-of-Work Map." A second part of Hall 1 connects you to material about the Life-Career Rainbow (Super, 1990), a combination of life roles that a person plays at any given time in that person's life. These roles are as son or daughter, learner, worker, spouse or friend, homemaker, parent, leisurite, and citizen.

> *Hall 2: Choose occupations.* The Discover database contains information about more than 500 occupations, updated each year. It can be accessed by inventories taken in Hall 1, by the World-of-Work Map, by job characteristics, and by quick lookup methods. Occupations from the Discover database can be selected by indicating educational entry levels or other important criteria. When you have created a personal list of occupations, you can obtain information about them by clicking on tabs printed across the top of the screen. Information is also provided on educational majors related to the occupation, schools that offer the major, and financial aid programs associated with the major.

> *Hall 3: Plan my education.* This section helps you find educational majors from occupations, by the World-of-Work Map, and by lookup methods. Schools can be located by choosing among 13 characteristics and by various lookup methods. Hall 3 describes financial aid programs. It can also calculate an expected family contribution for one year's attendance at college, and allows you to search through Discover's database of over 1,800 sources of financial aid.

> *Hall 4: Plan for work.* The first part of Hall 4 offers information about apprenticeships, military service, and internships. If you have completed the Myers-Briggs Type Indicator, those results can be used to help you in the job search process. Another activity is to describe an ideal job through a questionnaire. Important aspects of the job search are covered: learning about ways to find sources of job leads, completing a job application and a cover letter, developing a résumé and receiving instruction about job interviewing.

Choices is a comprehensive career exploration and information system that has databases of occupations, post-secondary and graduate schools, and sources of financial aid. It guides career planners through a career research process and relates interests, skills, and work experiences to occupational and educational options. Computerized links connecting occupations, majors, and schools are provided. This computer-assisted career guidance system operates in Canada with a version tailored to that country. It can be used on an elementary school, a middle school, a high school, or a college level. The Choices system contains several units:

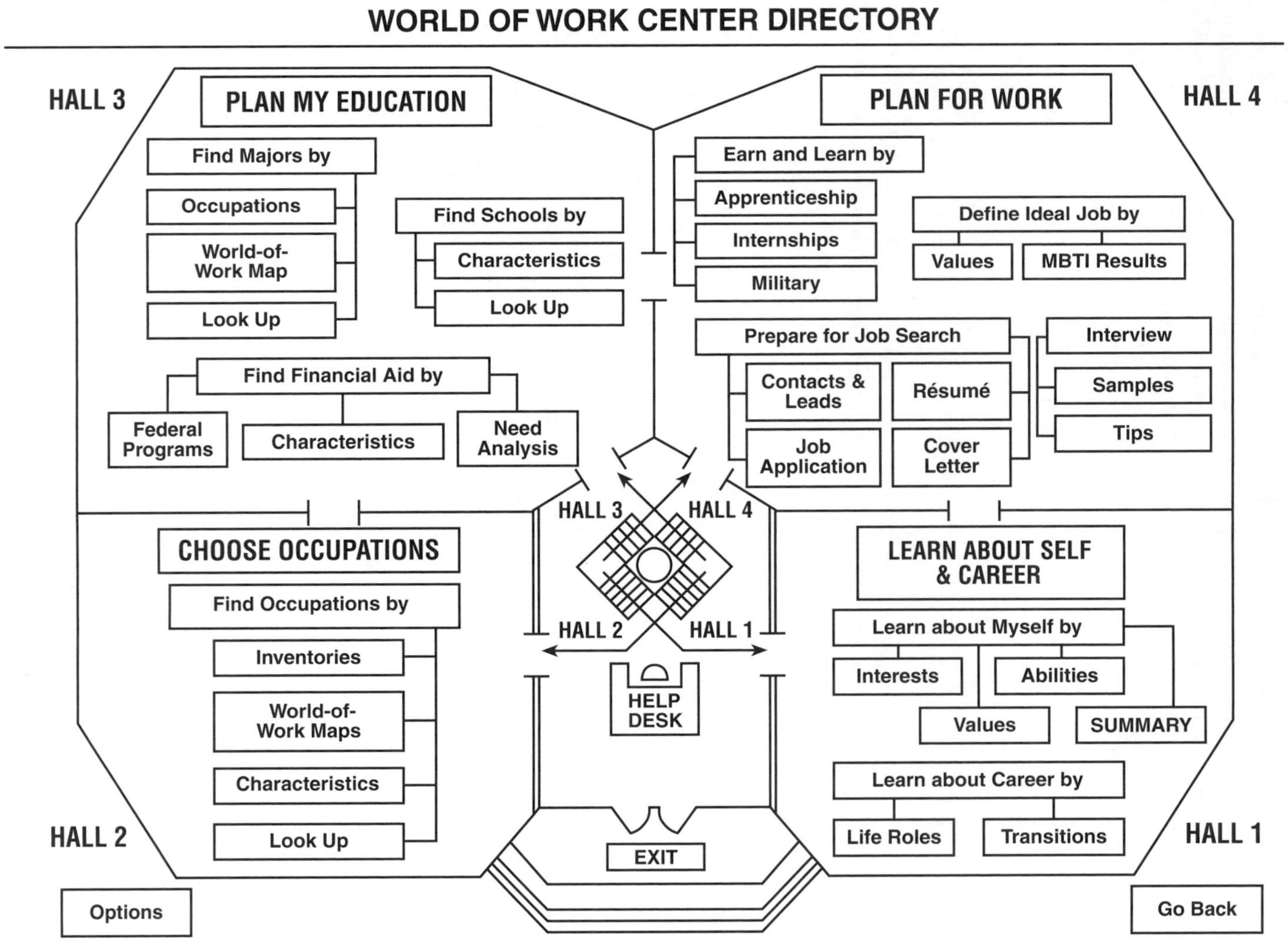

128

WORLD OF WORK CENTER DIRECTORY

Figure 4-1 The four "halls" or units of Discover. *Source:* Harris-Bowlsbey, J. (1998). *Using DISCOVER to its fullest: A workshop offered by the ACT Center for the enhancement of educational practices.* Iowa City, IA: ACT.

1. *Learn about your interests.* This module uses the O*Net Interest Profiler, which measures the six Holland personality types (Realistic, Investigative, Artistic, Social, Enterprising, and Conventional) to identify your most influential types and occupations of greatest interest.

2. *Learn about work values.* The O*Net Work Importance Locator and Profiler is used to measure six types of work values (Achievement, Independence, Recognition, Relationships, Support, and Working Conditions). Career planners can identify appropriate occupations based on the similarity between their work values and the characteristics of the occupations.

3. *Get information about jobs.* Search selected occupational prospects from more than 650 occupations, compare two occupational profiles in side-by-side columns, and connect to America's Job Bank, a network that connects the local offices of state employment services.

4. *Career decision making based on interests, education, and earnings.* Bring up a list of suggested occupations that match your selection of topics—interests, education, training and work experiences, and earnings.

5. *Get information about schools.* Find connections between occupations, majors, and schools. Choices can help you locate schools that offer a particular program or major by state or geographic location. Explore educational options with information about 7,000 or more colleges, technical schools, and graduate schools in the United States and Canada.

6. *Identify transferable skills.* These are skills from any aspect of life that you can transfer to a job. You can go through a Skills Checklist that contains 25 clusters of work content skills. You can choose any skill cluster you believe you have. A list of Suggested Occupations that match at least one of your transferable work content skills will appear on your computer screen.

7. *Find a new job.* By selecting previous jobs you have held in your work history and the skills you have used in them, you can develop a list of occupations that interest you.

8. *Get started with the Choices Planner.* This section helps you organize information about the world of work, from which you can develop a personal and educational career plan. Choices users can record personal information that can be printed later as part of a career portfolio, make educational and occupational plans, demonstrate skills for the job, and carry out job search activities.

9. *Learn about colleges and student loans.* You can obtain advice concerning the amount of money you will need for college and where to find it, apply to multiple colleges without having to re-create your application each time, and get online help for the ACT (American College Test), SAT (Scholastic Aptitude Test), and other entrance exams.

10. *Professional tools.* Choices has designed this particular module for the counselor, teacher, or manager at your school or agency to customize the system to meet the needs of students and other users at the site you are using.

The *Career Information System* (CIS) has both desktop and Internet versions. CIS operates on a national basis as well as creating localized versions with state agencies and universities in 12 states: Alaska, Georgia, Idaho, Illinois, Indiana, Massachusetts, Minnesota, Montana, Nebraska, Nevada, Ohio, and Oregon. In the national CIS, a survey asks you to estimate your physical limitations, geographic preferences, expected level of education, aptitudes, interests, and desired beginning wage. Given those responses, you receive a list of occupations to explore. Scores from other inventories and tests can be entered into the system. These include the *Career Assessment Inventory* (CAI), the Harrington/O'Shea *Career Decision-Making System* (CDM), the *Career Occupational Preference System* (COPS), the *Differential Aptitude Tests* (DAT), The *O*NET Interest Profiler* (IP), the *Self-Directed Search* (SDS), and the *Strong Interest Inventory* (SII). Nearly 500 occupations are described in the CIS file. The descriptions cover duties performed, required aptitudes, nature of the work setting, outlook for employment, wages, and local labor market information. All accredited two-year, four-year, and graduate schools are referenced. A School file contains information on schools and colleges beyond high school in your area, a local Financial Aid file gives state and local sources, and a Job Search file includes applying for job positions, developing a résumé, and interviewing for a job.

The *System of Interactive Guidance and Information* (called *SIGI Plus*) is based on the idea that you need to identify your values before you can make effective career decisions. Rewards and risks connected with each prospective occupation are assessed. SIGI Plus is composed of nine separate sections. The sections are interrelated, but each one can stand separately.

1. *Introduction:* Provides an overview and a recommended guide through SIGI Plus.
2. *Self-Assessment:* Inventory your work-related values, interests, and skills; a "values game" helps you to explore your work-related values in greater depth.
3. *Search:* Construct a list of occupational alternatives, based on the specifications you indicate from your work-related values, interests, skills, and level of education; occupations with characteristics you want to avoid can be removed from your list.
4. *Information:* Ask up to 27 questions about one or two occupations at a time.
5. *Skills:* Rate yourself on specific skills required by any occupation in the SIGI data bank.
6. *Preparing:* Typical training or education patterns and your estimate of the likelihood of completing the preparation for any occupation in SIGI Plus.
7. *Coping:* Suggestions for taking action related to time management, financing an education, common worries about school, finding day care facilities, working at home, job relocation, and earning credit for previous learning.
8. *Deciding:* Strategies for dealing with the risks and rewards of three occupations at a time.
9. *Next Steps:* Planning short-term goals for more education, developing new skills, proving you can do the work, building a network of contacts, writing a résumé, and overcoming obstacles.

Occupational Information Using the Internet and the World Wide Web

The Internet is a connection of computer networks that enables millions of people all over the world to communicate with each other. Your computer is linked to other computers by telephone lines or other cable systems, all using a common set of rules (called "protocols") that let computers communicate with each other. You can connect to the Internet through an Internet service provider (ISP), a subscription service that charges a monthly fee. College students may be able to register for a free Internet account, probably the same one available to the faculty. After you move through your ISP's gateway, you are free to explore the Internet (Bounds and Karl, 1996).

Occupational information is becoming increasingly available on the World Wide Web, the most popular branch of the Internet. The Web is a network of electronic sites linked together to form a global system for transmitting information. The Web has grown exponentially. Hundreds of new Web sites are created and added each day (Miller, 1998). Some resources can be accessed in ways other than the Web—Gopher or Telnet, for example—but the Web is the primary route.

The system of communication on the World Wide Web is HTTP (short for *hypertext transfer protocol*). When you are Web browsing (or "surfing the Net"), either you click on a hypertext link (which contains a Web address in HTML, or *hypertext markup language*), or you type in a Web address (or URL, which stands for *uniform resource locator*). Some of the better known browsers are Netscape Navigator, Mosaic, Internet Explorer, and the browsers provided by online services such as America Online and CompuServe. The browser allows you to view documents in a file of information from a Web site, an organization's electronic collection on the World Wide Web. If you find a Web site that is particularly helpful, you can "bookmark" it for future reference. In Netscape, for example, go to the navigation bar at the top of the screen and click on "Bookmarks." When the menu drops down, click on "Add Bookmark." To go to a bookmarked URL, click on "Bookmarks," then scroll down for the site you want to view and you are on your way.

Search engines provide a way to obtain information on the Web. These online programs let you find information stored in databases. When you log on to the Web with your Internet service provider, type in the URL to a search engine site. Then type in the word(s) that describe the information you are trying to find. Some of the best known and most popular search engines are *Google* (www.google.com), *Yahoo!* (www.yahoo.com), *MSN Search* (Microsoft) (http://search.msn.com), *AltaVista* (www.altavista.com), *Lycos* (www.lycos.com), *HotBot* (www.hotbot.com), *Web Crawler* (http://webcrawler.com), and *Northern Light* (www.northernlight.com). *MetaCrawler* (www.metacrawler.com) employs several search engines in a single search. (Do not enter the parentheses when typing the electronic address.) Most career sites on the Internet are concerned with job postings, résumés, and company research—aspects of the job search, the subject of the second book in this *Career Planning Guide* series. However, some online sites give you occupational information. Here is a list of a number of them.

- *The Occupational Outlook Handbook* (www.bls.gov/oco). The OOH is online as well as in hard copy. A more detailed description of the *Handbook* is given later in this chapter.
- *Occupational Outlook Quarterly* (www.bls.gov/opub/ooq/ooqhome.htm). The OOQ supplements the *Handbook* four times a year with topics about careers.
- *Career Guide to Industries* (www.bls.gov/oco/cg). This is the online version of the U.S. Department of Labor's book *Career Guide to Industries*. The site gives information on careers by industry and the employment needs of the industries it covers.
- *The Occupational Information Network, or O*Net* (www.onetcenter.org), which is in the process of replacing the *Dictionary of Occupational Titles*.
- *America's Career InfoNet (www.acinet.org)* has links to the following sources of occupational information: general outlook, wages and trends, employers, state profiles, and career exploration.
- *Wages, Earnings, and Benefits* (www.bls.gov). Click on this title when you reach the Bureau of Labor Statistics home page. Information is presented on the following: wages by area and occupation, earnings by industry, employee benefits, employment costs, state and county wages, national compensation data, collective bargaining, and a wage calculator.
- *State-based career information delivery systems.* All states provide information about occupations and educational programs within that state. Click on "State Info" on the America's Career InfoNet home page (www.acinet.org), then scroll to the state you want.
- *National Occupational Classification (Canada)* (www23.hrdc-drhc.gc.ca) When you reach this site, click on "Occupational Descriptions." The index of occupations in Canada's system is printed in Appendix C: *The National Occupational Classification (NOC) of Canada,* in this book.
- *Canada Workinfonet* (www.workinfonet.ca) is a bilingual (English and French) career directory on the Internet; it links to hundreds of other sites in Canada that offer career-planning information among many other services.
- *Career Planning Process* (www.bgsu.edu/offices/sa/career/students/planning_process.html) from Bowling Green State University in Ohio. The first step in the process is self-assessment. The next step is academic/career options through investigating the world of work. This is followed by relevant/practical experience, job search/graduate school preparation, and career change steps.

- *Career Development Manual, University of Waterloo, Canada* (www.cdm.uwaterloo.ca). This site also has *The Scholarly Societies Project*, covered later in this list. Click on "subject guides" and go to the major(s) of interest to you; these are listed in seven broad categories.
- *Workopolis.com* (www.workopolis.com) is primarily a site that covers all of Canada, receiving résumés and posting job listings. However, a variety of career services is offered such as connecting to a number of Canadian newspapers that give career advice.
- *JobWeb* (www.jobweb.com/Career_Development/choice.htm) is an occupational information program of the National Association of Colleges and Employers. After you reach the Web site, among the options you can click on are Career Choices, Career Resources, Explore Careers Library, Colleges and Universities, and Graduate and Professional Schools.
- *Exploring Occupations*, Student Counselling and Career Centre, University of Manitoba (www.umanitoba.ca/counselling/careers.html). Each occupational title links you to sites that give information on the occupation you select, majors that are connected to the occupation, labor market information, and related professional associations.
- *Career Cruising*, SUNY-Delhi College of Technology (www.academicservices.delhi.edu/Career/Career.htm). After you reach the site, click on "Career Cruising" for an interest assessment, occupational profiles, and a college and university database.
- *Career Journal* (www.careerjournal.com). This site comes from the *Wall Street Journal.* The Salary and Hiring Info section gives information on current salaries and hiring trends. Articles cover changing careers, using the Internet, résumé and cover letters, and interviewing.
- *CareerStorm* (www.careerstorm.com). CareerStorm provides online tools for career development using its Storm Navigator. Available in English, Spanish, French, Italian, German, Dutch, Danish, and Finnish, the Storm Navigator Map charts the course of your career by locating your current position or situation and by setting your destination (career goals). The Storm Navigator Compass identifies your style of working, skills you enjoy using, your subjects of interest, and your career values.
- *U.S. News & World Report* (www.usnews.com/usnews/edu/eduhome.htm). Career information often appears in news magazines as well as newspapers. *U.S. News* conducts rankings of colleges by major fields; these rankings are sometimes controversial.
- *Career Consulting Corner* (www.careercc.com/careerexp.shtml). Career exploration links provide access to information in 18 groups of occupations.
- *College Board Career Browser* (www.collegeboard.com/apps/careers/index). Descriptions of hundreds of occupations, educational requirements, salaries, and a questionnaire to help select career choices.
- *Job Hunters Bible* (www.jobhuntersbible.com/library/hunters/library.shtml). This site developed by Richard Bolles complements his annual *What Color Is Your Parachute?* book. A number of articles, written by Bolles, cover life/work planning.
- *Career & Educational Guidance Library* (www.uhs.berkeley.edu/students/careerlibrary). Produced by the University of California at Berkeley, this site has many sources of career and industry information.
- *Careers for Physicists*, American Institute of Physics (www.aip.org/careersrc/). Informs students about various careers in the physical sciences.
- *NextSteps.org*, Calgary Youth Employment Center (www.nextsteps.org). This Web site is supported by the city of Calgary in Canada. It provides a guide to career planning, career exploration, and decision making through a series of interactive tools.

- *The Scholarly Societies Project*, University of Waterloo, Canada (www. scholarly-societies.org). Information on academic majors throughout the world by subject (currently 77), by country, and by language.
- *Major Resource Kit*, University of Delaware (www.udel.edu/CSC/mrk.html). Descriptions of academic subjects and majors are linked to bachelor's degree/entry level and further education/experience, ways to enhance your employability, a list of some (but not all) employers, and other sources of information.
- *Military Career Guide Online*, U.S. Government Defense Manpower Data Center (www.militarycareers.com). This source gives information about 152 enlisted and officer occupations, most of which are comparable to one or more civilian occupations. Each of the major armed services has a Web site: U.S. Army (www.army.mil), U.S. Navy (www.navyjobs.com), U.S. Air Force (www.airforce.com), U.S. Marine Corps (www.usmc.mil), U.S. Coast Guard (www.uscg.mil/jobs/).

There are, no doubt, other worthy sites that have been missed, or that have been developed since the time of this printing, but this list will get you started.

Using Literature and the Media as Sources of Occupational Information

Writers of career information have an obligation to be accurate and objective. Because of those qualities, some people regard reading about occupations as dry and dull. The media, from novels to television, can glamorize an occupation to make the material more interesting to readers and viewers. Truth may get lost when the facts are not allowed to get in the way of a good story. A police or detective story usually focuses on danger and action; it may leave out routine aspects of the work, such as painstaking investigation and writing reports. In addition, the professions tend to be overemphasized in novels and nonfiction, and skilled, semiskilled, clerical, and service occupations are almost nonexistent in popular literature (Norris, Hatch, Engelkes, and Winborn, 1979). Literature and the media can be included among your sources of occupational information, but they should not be your only sources.

Despite these cautionary notes, you can still gain useful impressions about occupations from the media and literature. Many biographies have been written about the careers of famous artists, composers, inventors, politicians, and scientists. Every decade brings new books on Rembrandt, Goya, Mozart, Beethoven, Edison, Bell, Jefferson, Lincoln, Curie, Austen, O'Keeffe, and Pasteur.

Occupations that have appeared in recent biographies are journalist (Daniel Schorr), political science professor (Condoleeza Rice), lawyer (Archibald Cox), physicist (Richard Feynman), spiritual leader (Billy Graham), musician (Leonard Bernstein), architect (Philip Johnson), writer and poet (Maya Angelou), novelist (Edith Wharton), mathematician (John Nash), psychoanalyst (Karen Horney), spy (Allen Dulles), news reporter (Jim Lehrer), diplomat (Averell Harriman), playwright (Tennessee Williams), politician (Harry Truman and all other presidents), publisher (Katharine Graham), singer (Billie Holiday), professional athlete (Wayne Gretzky), labor organizer (Walter Reuther), and naturalist (Edward Wilson).

Occupations that have taken a central role in selected recent novels and nonfiction literature are music composer (*Listening Out Loud*), hospital careers (*Life and Death*), automobile designer (*Car*), teacher (*Small Victories*), coroner (*Natural Death: Confessions of a Medical Examiner*), the helping professions (*The Call of Service*), the military (*Sacred Honor*), retail trade (*Made in America*), politician (*Turning Point*), fire fighting (*Blacker than a Thousand Midnights*), country doctor (*A Measure of My Days*), neurosurgeon (*Judith's Pavilion*), television newscaster (*A Reporter's Life*), coach (*They Call Me Sparky*), environmentalist (*The House of Life*), detective (*An Unsuitable Job for a Woman*), and public administrator (*Locked in the Cabinet*). In the last book, Robert Reich wrote about situations where he wanted to say something truthful about his job as

U.S. secretary of labor—but couldn't. One incident occurred on the *Tonight* show with Jay Leno. Secretary Reich is nervous. Leno senses it and throws out an easy question: "So, what's it like to be in the President's cabinet? (What Reich wants to say: "It sucks. I'm working all the time, don't see enough of my family, and I'm haunted by the fear of failure, that I won't accomplish what I came to Washington to do because the President decided he had to make huge cuts in the deficit and use up every remaining ounce of political capital on a monster health care plan, which is going nowhere.") Instead, he said, "It's exciting, Jay." Leno: "What happens at a cabinet meeting, anyway?" (What Reich wanted to say: "Nothing. We rarely have them. And when we do, they're complete bores.") Instead: "For example, Jay, at the last one, which was a luncheon, we were talking about a major issue of national security when the President leaned over to me and quietly asked, in complete confidence, 'Are you done with that?' It was thrilling" (Reich, 1998, pp. 174–175). When you read honest insights like these, they can tell you something about the job you are not likely to read in a career monograph.

Publishers of career books have developed series of biographies that tell the stories of famous people and where their careers have taken them. For example, included in the *Career Biography* series (Ferguson Publishing Company) are Tiger Woods (professional golfer), Rachel Carson (biologist), Martin Luther King, Jr. (minister, civil rights activist), Colin Powell (army general, secretary of state), Carl Sagan (astronomer), Laura Ingalls Wilder (teacher, author), and two people mentioned earlier in other biographies: Maya Angelou (author), and Leonard Bernstein (composer, conductor).

You may think that famous people are not true representatives of most workers. However, many books also deal with occupations such as homemaker, farmer, teacher, social worker, conservationist, fisher, nurse, miner, photographer, and religious worker. The possibilities for learning about occupations from literature and the media are restricted only by the limits of one's imagination. Years ago, Kathryn Haebich listed 1,070 books in her annotated *Vocations in Biography and Fiction* (1962). Many more books depicting various occupations have been written since then.

Information on Local Employment Opportunities

Most printed material about opportunities in selected occupations is nationwide in scope. But it is also important to obtain information about local occupational situations. For example, getting a job in teaching may be more competitive in Michigan because of the greater number of teacher training institutions and higher salaries for teachers in that state. Here are some suggestions for locating information about local employment opportunities:

- Community surveys made by a local college, chamber of commerce, service club, or governmental agency.
- Statewide occupational information systems usually have local or regional employment data. Every state has a *State Occupational Information Coordinating Committee (SOICC),* which is linked to the National Occupational Information Coordinating Committee (NOICC). Together, they have the job of developing and improving career information delivery systems, reducing the overlap and preventing gaps in the availability of career materials, and improving the quality of occupational information (Isaacson and Brown, 1997).
- Branch offices of your state employment service make local job information available. State employment services publish a monthly newsletter on labor market information for many local or regional areas. (The title of this newsletter may vary.) The branch office can also furnish you with a current list of local job openings. Some labor market information needs to be translated by employment counselors. For example, a counselor who knows the occupations or types of industries you are considering can obtain an industry code and title from the Standard Industrial Classification (SIC) and locate it on an

industry–occupation matrix. You and the counselor then have access to local staffing patterns in a given area.

- Follow-up studies of college career services offices could give you ideas about where former students found jobs after graduation.
- *County Business Patterns* is published annually by the Bureau of the Census of the U.S. Department of Commerce and should be available at the state employment service office. It's also available online (www.census.gov/eped/cbp/view/cbpview.html). *County Business Patterns* is a comprehensive source of industry employment data on a countywide basis. It also identifies the number of business establishments in each industry and gives the distribution of these businesses by employee class size (McKee and Froeschle, 1985).
- *State and County QuickFacts* (http://quickfacts.census.gov/qfd). QuickFacts gives data on *people* (population, ethnic and racial education, housing, household and earnings data), *business* (private establishments and employment, manufacturing, retail sales, minority- and female-owned firms, housing units, federal grants, and local government employment), and *geography* (land area and people per square mile) in all states and counties in the United States.
- *Area and Occupation Wage Surveys* (www.bls.gov/bls/blswage.htm). The U.S. Bureau of Labor Statistics provides wage information by national, regional, state, and metropolitan area for occupations, groups of occupations, and over 400 industries.
- Directories of manufacturers and businesses are usually published nationwide or statewide but are broken down into counties, cities, and even villages. Names of companies, addresses, telephone numbers, names of officers, products made or services provided, occupations employed, and numbers of employees are generally included. Business directories can be found in local city or college libraries and in career resource centers.
- Newspaper "help wanted" advertising can yield some information on the visible job market for a local area. The "hidden" job market, however, is usually larger.

Printed sources of information aside, your personal contacts and informational interviews with people willing to talk with you can furnish data that are not always found in published sources. *Job Search*, the second book in this series, contains material on establishing personal contacts and interviewing for information.

Visiting a Career Resource Center

A career resource center is a place where you can (1) read, listen to, and view occupational information and job search material in books, computer-based programs, and video presentations; (2) generate occupational prospects through a variety of materials, games, kits, inventories, and computer programs; (3) take interest inventories, aptitude tests, and other psychological inventories; and (4) receive career counseling. Most career resource centers provide the following materials and services.

- File cabinets that contain folders labeled with the names of occupations or occupational groups. An index is available to help you find the occupations in the file. Each folder contains pamphlets, monographs, briefs, and bulletins.
- A career library that includes books, encyclopedias, and handbooks, including the *Occupational Outlook Handbook,* the *Guide for Occupational Exploration,* and many books on specific occupations, groups of careers, and job-hunting strategies.
- Computer-based career guidance programs such as SIGI Plus, CIS, Choices, or Discover, which provide self-study surveys, lists of occupational prospects, occupational information, educational planning, and decision-making strategies.

- Computers for accessing career information found electronically, such as the O*Net.
- Audiovisual presentations of occupational information on videotape.
- Career games and kits, instruments designed to generate occupational prospects keyed to a set of occupational briefs.
- College catalogs and directories to use for educational planning.
- A "company" file containing booklets on employment opportunities and annual reports published by businesses and employers. A job seeker should know the occupations a company employs as well as the products it manufactures or services it performs.
- Magazines and reprints with articles on career planning and occupations. For example, the *Occupational Outlook Quarterly* updates the *Occupational Outlook Handbook* four times a year.
- Handouts placed in racks or open files.
- Psychological and educational testing. Ask for a current list of tests and inventories. The results are used for counseling purposes only and are kept confidential. Some testing is administered and scored electronically.
- Career counseling and general assistance. Some career centers have professional counselors who can assist you in your career search. Technicians and secretaries can help you locate occupational information.

Evaluating Occupational Information

You would not buy a car without first considering its quality, performance, price, style, color, and size. Likewise, you need to assure yourself that the occupational information you receive is accurate, current, objective, comprehensive, readable, and properly credited (Baer and Roeber, 1964; Hoppock, 1976; Isaacson, 1977; Shertzer, 1985). Ask yourself the following questions:

- Is the information *accurate*? It should be real, valid, genuine, authentic, and factual. The material should truly represent typical workers in the occupation.
- Is the information *current*? Occupational information should be up-to-date, reflecting changes in today's fast-paced society. Some occupations change very slowly, but it is hard to keep up with others. Look at the date of publication. Material over five years old should be viewed with caution unless you know that the characteristics of an occupation are relatively constant.
- Is the information *objective*? The material should be free from racial, religious, ethnic, sexual, and social bias, and it should not present self-serving promotion (Norris, Hatch, Engelkes, and Winborn, 1979). Some career information files may contain material sponsored by a company or industry, possibly stacking the deck in favor of the sponsor. Occupational information should be objective in the sense that it neither encourages nor discourages entering the occupation.
- Is the information *comprehensive*? Occupational materials should contain information about the nature of the work, education and preparation required, skills needed, pay, working conditions, location of employment, personal traits of typical people in the occupation, employment and advancement opportunities, values expressed in the work, related occupations, and so on. Some occupational literature emphasizes pay and economic factors to the near exclusion of psychological satisfaction and social aspects of the work.
- Is the information *readable*? Pay attention to the author's writing style and the reading difficulty of the material. Occupational literature should be attractive and easy to read. Because of the factual nature of occupational information, the style can be dull at times. An author who can breathe life into precise writing of facts has a great gift indeed.

- Is the information *credited*? Credits should include the author, publisher, references, consultants, and sponsors (or who is paying for the material). Occupational literature should also lead you to additional sources of information.

Robert Hoppock (1976), a career information expert, suggests that you ask when, where, who, why, and how. *When* was the information written? *Where* does it apply—one city, one state, or the whole country? *Who* wrote it? *Why* was it written? *How* were the facts collected and presented? Keeping these questions in mind can help make reading occupational information a more rewarding experience.

MAKING SENSE OF THE WORLD OF WORK: CLASSIFYING OCCUPATIONS INTO GROUPS

One way to get a handle on the gigantic world of work is to classify the thousands of occupations found in it. Many books on occupations and occupational interest inventories divide the occupational world into groups or clusters. By taking the time to identify the occupational groups on which you want to concentrate, you will save yourself time in the long run. You may become aware of occupations that have previously escaped your attention in the occupational groups that interest you most. Observing that some occupational prospects in one cluster are similar to other occupations in the same cluster is another way to expand your list of prospects.

Classification of Occupations in the Occupational Outlook Handbook

How can the *Occupational Outlook Handbook* help you? First, the OOH provides a classification system that groups occupations into several (currently 11) clusters of related occupations. You can use the OOH Occupational Cluster Checklist (Exercise 4-1) to identify your major fields of interest in the OOH. Second, the OOH gives you relatively current information on more than 250 broad kinds of occupations, covering nearly 90 percent of all jobs in the economy (U.S. Department of Labor, 2002). The OOH is published every two years by the Department of Labor and is available on the Internet, wherever career materials and books are found, or from the Superintendent of Documents, U.S. Government Printing Office, Washington, DC 20402. Each description of an occupation in the OOH follows a standard procedure:

> Numbers appear just below the title of most occupational descriptions; these are from the *Dictionary of Occupational Titles*, an encyclopedic book covered in the next section of this chapter. Then two or three significant points highlight the most important current characteristics of the occupation. The first section deals with the *nature of the work* and can help you determine whether the work activities appeal to you. You discover the tasks typical workers do on the job, the skills they need, the kinds of tools and equipment they use, how much independence or close supervision they have, how much variety there is on the job, and the responsibilities they may have. Job duties may differ by employer or industry. Workers in larger companies tend to have more specialized jobs; in smaller firms there may be a wider variety of jobs (U.S. Department of Labor, 2002).
>
> The second section deals with *working conditions*. Would you want to work in the evening, or at night, or avoid those hours? Bartenders, security guards, some factory workers, nurses, and police officers may work those hours. Would you like a split-shift arrangement—working, as bus drivers may do, during morning and evening rush hours with time off in the middle of the day? Work settings differ greatly. Would you prefer a quiet, air-conditioned office, or would you like the noise and clang of machinery in a factory? Some workers must be outdoors much or all of the time. Being a mail carrier, construction worker, fire fighter, or forester means much of your work is outside.

Are you willing to risk the hazards of cuts, scratches, bumps, nicks, falls, or burns that can occur in some workplaces? Some jobs require protective clothing or specially designed equipment. Other jobs call for lots of standing, crouching in awkward positions, or heavy lifting that requires physical strength and endurance.

The *employment* section gives the number of jobs or workers in the occupation. Occupations with large numbers of workers, even those growing slowly, offer more job openings than occupations with small numbers, even those growing more rapidly. Occupations with large numbers of workers include accountant, computer software engineer, teacher, administrative assistant and secretary, registered nurse, waiter and waitress, retail sales clerk, cashier, landscaper and groundskeeper, building custodian, security guard, and truck driver. Do you have a certain industry or geographic area in mind? Most aircraft mechanics work near large cities, at the airlines' main stops. Actors are concentrated in a few major centers. Secretaries and typists, however, work throughout the country in almost every industry. Information on part-time work, included in the employment section, could be valuable to a student, homemaker, or retired person. Do you want to be self-employed? About 8 percent of the workforce was in 2000. They are concentrated in a small number of occupations, such as farmers and ranchers, child care workers, lawyers, health practitioners, and the construction trades (U.S. Department of Labor, 2002).

The next section of the OOH occupational descriptions involves *training, other qualifications,* and *advancement.* You can prepare for an occupation in many different ways. Programs of various lengths of time lead to degrees or certificates in colleges, vocational schools, home study courses, the armed forces, apprenticeships, and so on. The OOH gives the preferred training or education for each occupation. The amount of education you have often determines the level at which you enter an occupation and the rate at which you can advance in it. Construction laborer, dishwasher, typist, freight handler, and store clerk are types of entry-level occupations that need little or no work experience, but some kinds of work are not open to beginners. Occupations such as physician, teacher, nurse, barber, cosmetologist, electrician, and plumber require a certificate or license. Each state sets its own certification requirements.

The *job outlook* section gives the *Occupational Outlook Handbook* its title. Demand for workers in a given occupation depends on a number of factors, including educational background, skill level, personal qualities, professional credentials, and previous experience. The job outlook of an occupation usually begins with a sentence about the expected change in employment. You should consider the size of an occupation as well as its growth rate. Some occupations that have slower-than-average growth rates really are unfavorable prospects because the jobs are being automated or reduced by the introduction of labor-saving technologies. However, other slow-growing occupations, such as general manager, secretary, bookkeeper, and building custodian, have a large number of job openings because of the sheer size of the occupation and the constant need to replace workers. Generally, the larger the occupation, the more job openings are created by replacement needs—people leaving a job through retirement, death, promotion, advancement, and the like. If an occupation you are exploring is expected to have relatively few job openings, consider this information but do not let it prevent you from pursuing that career, particularly if you are confident about your ability to do the job and are motivated to reach your goal. Keep in mind that no one can forecast future job trends with perfect accuracy. Also, job prospects in your local community may not be the same as those described in the OOH. Check with state and local employment agencies about local employment projections.

The next section of the OOH is *earnings*. Will the occupation pay enough to maintain the lifestyle you want? Salary or wages, benefits, commissions, tips, and payment in kind are the most common methods by which people are paid. Pay scales may differ widely within an occupation, mostly because of differences in experience, level of responsibility, geographic location, presence or absence of unions, seniority, performance, and differences between companies. Earnings are generally higher in cities than in rural areas, but a higher wage may be canceled out by a higher cost of living.

The *related occupations* section should be carefully read by all who want to expand their list of occupational prospects. Related occupations generally involve similar aptitudes, interests, and education. Finally, the OOH provides *sources of additional information* with mailing addresses, toll-free telephone numbers, Internet home page addresses, fax numbers, and electronic mail addresses. Information from associations, unions, companies, government agencies, and other organizations may be mentioned and available in libraries and school career centers.

Before delving into the OOH, read through the OOH Occupational Cluster Checklist (Exercise 4-1). Determine which cluster of occupational groups you should investigate most carefully in the handbook. A more detailed survey of the OOH, the *Occupational Cluster Survey*, can be found in Appendix B: *Occupational Cluster Survey (for the Occupational Outlook Handbook)*, at the back of this book. The detailed survey will give you a quick look at the entire world of work.

You don't need to read every page of the OOH. It is best used as a reference. Instead, concentrate your attention on the groups that mean the most to you. As soon as you have identified two or three groups of interest in the OOH, find their page numbers in the table of contents. Focus on these pages; if you come across any new occupational prospects by reading the OOH, write their titles in the spaces provided at the end of the OOH Occupational Cluster Checklist. Employment numbers and changes from 2002 to 2012 for the occupational groups in the checklist or survey, with the exception of the military group, are shown in Table 4-1.

Table 4-1 Employment by Major Occupational Group, 2002, and Projected 2012 (Numbers in thousands of jobs; add three zeros)

Occupational Group	Employment				Change	
	Number		Percent distribution			
	2002	2012	2002	2012	Number	Percentage
Total, all occupations	144,014	165,319	100.0	100.0	21,305	14.8
Management, business, and financial occupations	15,501	17,883	10.8	10.8	2,382	15.4
Professional and related occupations	27,687	34,147	19.2	20.7	6,459	23.3
Service occupations	26,569	31,905	18.4	19.3	5,336	20.1
Sales and related occupations	15,260	17,231	10.6	10.4	1,971	12.9
Office and administrative support occupations	23,851	25,464	16.6	15.4	1,613	6.8
Farming, fishing, and forestry occupations	1,072	1,107	.7	.7	35	3.3
Construction and extraction occupations	7,292	8,388	5.1	5.1	1,096	15.0
Installation, maintenance, and repair occupations	5,696	6,472	4.0	3.9	776	13.6
Production occupations	11,258	11,612	7.8	7.0	354	3.1
Transportation and material moving occupations	9,828	11,111	6.8	6.7	1,282	13.0

Note: Detail may not equal total or 100 percent due to rounding.

Source: Hecker, D. E. (2004, February), Occupational employment projections to 2012. *Monthly Labor Review,* 127(2), p. 51.

EXERCISE 4-1 OOH OCCUPATIONAL CLUSTER CHECKLIST

The OOH Occupational Cluster Checklist lists 11 categories of occupational groups from the *Occupational Outlook Handbook*. Four categories (professional specialty, service, office and administrative support, and production occupations) are subdivided for this exercise. Check or mark the occupational groups you believe you should explore because they interest you most; try to identify at least three such groups. Then look in the table of contents of the *Occupational Outlook Handbook* to find the page numbers for the groups you have checked.

Instead of this checklist exercise, you may prefer to complete a second exercise for the OOH, the Occupational Cluster Survey, which is found in Appendix B: *Occupational Cluster Survey (for the Occupational Outlook Handbook)* and is more detailed than this list of occupational groups. Although this exercise takes more time to complete, it is more valid in locating OOH groups of occupations to explore.

Check the occupational groups of greatest interest to you:

____ Group A: Management and business and financial operations occupations (accountant, financial manager, human resources manager, purchaser, top executive, etc.)

Group B: Professional specialty occupations (divided into nine subgroups)

____ Group B-1: Architects, engineers, drafters, surveyors, etc.

____ Group B-2: Art, design, entertainment, media and communications occupations

____ Group B-3: Community and social service occupations (clergy, counselor, social work, etc.)

____ Group B-4: Computer and mathematical occupations

____ Group B-5: Education, training, library, and museum occupations

____ Group B-6: Social science and legal occupations (economist, lawyer, paralegal, psychologist, etc.)

____ Group B-7: Life science, physical science, and science technicians (biologist, chemist, geologist, physicist, etc.)

____ Group B-8: Health diagnosing and treating occupations (chiropractor, dentist, pharmacist, physician, nurse, etc.)

____ Group B-9: Health technologists and technicians (clinical laboratory technician, dental hygienist, emergency medical technician, licensed practical nurse, radiologic technician

Group C: Service occupations (divided into four subgroups)

____ Group C-1: Food preparation and serving related occupations (baker, chef, waiter, etc.)

____ Group C-2: Health care support occupations (dental assistant, medical assistant, nursing aide, occupational therapy assistant, physical therapy assistant, etc.)

____ Group C-3: Personal care and service (animal care worker, barber/cosmetologist, child care worker, home care aide, recreation and fitness worker, etc.)

____ Group C-4: Protective and building service occupations (corrections officer, fire fighter, police officer, security guard, etc.)

___ Group D: Sales and related occupations (cashier, insurance agent, real estate, retail salesperson, sales representative, etc.)

Group E: Office and administrative support occupations (divided into four subgroups)

___ Group E-1: Financial clerks (bill collector, billing clerk, payroll clerk, bank teller, etc.)

___ Group E-2: Information and record clerk (customer service representative, file clerk, order clerk, receptionist, etc.)

___ Group E-3: Material recording, scheduling, dispatching, and distributing (messenger, dispatcher, production and planning clerk, shipping and receiving, stock clerk, etc.)

___ Group E-4: Other office and administrative support (computer operator, data entry and information processing, general office clerk, postal service, secretary, etc.)

___ Group F: Farming, fishing, and forestry occupations (farmer, rancher, fishing boat captain, forester, conservation scientist, logging equipment operator, etc.)

___ Group G: Construction trades and related workers (brickmason, carpenter, electrician, painter, plasterer, plumber, pipefitter, etc.)

___ Group H: Installation, maintenance, and repair occupations (automotive body repairer, automotive service technician and mechanic, computer and office machine repairer, home appliance repairer, industrial machinery installer and repairer, etc.)

Group I: Production occupations (divided into two subgroups)

___ Group I-1: Production occupations, except metal, plastics, and wood workers (assembler, food processor, inspector, printing machine operator, water treatment plant operator, etc.)

___ Group I-2: Metal, plastic, and wood workers (machinist, machine setter, tool and die maker, welder, wood worker, etc.)

___ Group J: Transportation and material moving occupations (airline pilot, bus driver, locomotive engineer, taxi driver, truck driver, etc.)

___ Group K: Armed forces/military service (over 360 basic and advanced military occupational specialties, with 75 percent having civilian counterparts)

(Over 100 additional occupations are covered at the back of the *Occupational Outlook Handbook*. Employment projections are developed for these occupations; however, detailed information about them is not included.)

Now copy the names of the occupational groups you marked as being of the greatest interest to you, and go to the table of contents in the *Occupational Outlook Handbook* for their page numbers.

Highest Occupational Clusters in OOH	Page Numbers in OOH
1. _____	_____
2. _____	_____
3. _____	_____
4. _____	_____

List the occupational prospects you generate from your exploration of the *Occupational Outlook Handbook* in the spaces provided for Exercise 3-15 (Chapter 3) and/or in the following spaces.

_____	_____
_____	_____
_____	_____
_____	_____
_____	_____
_____	_____
_____	_____

Occupational Group Arrangement in the DOT, the O*Net, and the Canadian NOC

Before we start with the *Dictionary of Occupational Titles* (DOT) and the new Occupational Information Network (O*Net), let us mention the National Occupational Classification (NOC) system of Canada. The NOC is the authoritative resource on occupational information in Canada, and thousands of people use it daily. The NOC has an Internet address, www.23.hrdc-drhc.gc.ca, which makes it accessible to students in the United States (and the whole world, for that matter). Some career explorers have said they like the Canadian system better than the U.S. one, but we'll let you be the judge of that! The government of Canada encourages career counselors and students to use its *Career Handbook* in combination with the NOC.

The National Occupational Classification of Canada is divided into 10 broad, one-digit groups as follows:

0   Management occupations
1   Business, finance, and administration occupations
2   Natural and applied sciences and related occupations
3   Health occupations
4   Occupations in social science, education, government service, and religion
5   Occupations in art, culture, recreation, and sport
6   Sales and service occupations
7   Trades, transport and equipment operators, and related occupations
8   Occupations unique to primary industry
9   Occupations unique to processing, manufacturing, and utilities

Major groups are designated with two digits, and their subgroups have three digits. All occupational descriptions are reached by a four-digit code. An index of titles allows you to go directly to an occupational description, using the four-digit numeric code. To look at the occupational groups, subgroups, and individual occupations in the NOC, go to Appendix C: *The National Occupational Classification (NOC) of Canada*, located at the back of this book.

The Dictionary of Occupational Titles (DOT)

The revised fourth edition of the *Dictionary of Occupational Titles* (DOT), published in 1991, contains 12,741 definitions of occupations. It also includes thousands of related occupational titles that are not defined. The computerized Occupational Information Network, or O*Net, is in the process of replacing the DOT as the primary source of occupational information in the United States. The O*Net is not a book; it is a comprehensive database that identifies and describes worker skills and training requirements for all occupations (Ettinger, 1996). Because the DOT will continue to be used in career-planning classes, career resource centers, and career counselors' offices during the transition to the O*Net, we will continue to pay attention to the *Dictionary of Occupational Titles*. After a look at the DOT, we'll come back to the O*Net.

Each occupational definition in the DOT is presented in the following sequence (see Figure 4-2): (1) the nine-digit *occupational code number* (explained later in more detail); (2) the *occupational title* or *"base title"* in uppercase boldface letters; (3) the *industry designation*, which can give the location of the occupation, types of duties associated with the occupation, products manufactured, processes used, and raw material used (if an occupation is found in many industries, the words "any industry" will be used); (4) *alternate titles* (if any) for this occupation; (5) the *body of the definition*; (6) *undefined related titles* (if any), which are variations or specializations of the base occupation; and (7) a *definition trailer*.

The *body of the definition* consists of two or three parts: (1) a *lead statement* summarizing the overall purpose of the job; (2) *task element statements*, indicating functions or specific tasks workers perform on the job; and, in many but not all definitions, (3) *"may" items*—one or more sentences beginning with the word "may" that describe duties required of workers in some work organizations but not in others. ("May" items should not be confused with "May be designated . . ." sentences that introduce undefined related titles.)

The *definition trailer* includes coded information in this sequence: a *Guide for Occupational Exploration* (earlier than third edition) six-digit code; a physical *strength* rating (S = Sedentary, L = Light, M = Medium, H = Heavy, V = Very heavy); the level of *general educational development* (GED) in terms of *reasoning* (R), *math* (M), and *language* (L) on a six-point scale, with 6 representing the highest level; the amount of *specific vocational preparation* (SVP) needed on a nine-point scale, ranging from a short demonstration to more than 10 years preparation; and the date of the last update (DLU).

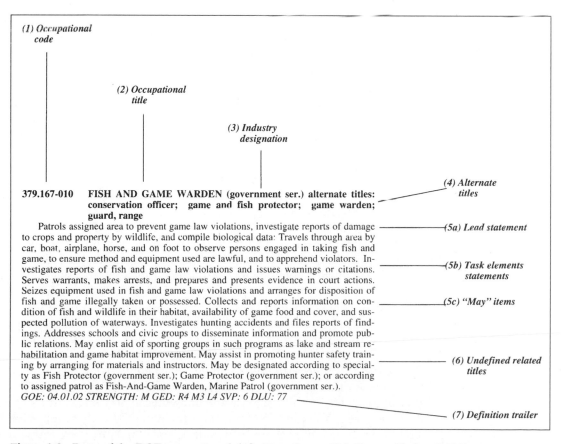

Figure 4-2 Parts of the DOT occupational definition. *Source:* U.S. Dept. of Labor (1991).

Each occupation in the *Dictionary of Occupational Titles* has a nine-digit code number. The first three digits identify a particular occupational group. The first digit places each occupation into one of nine broad categories.

0/1 *Professional, technical, and managerial occupations.* Fields such as architecture, engineering, mathematics, physical and social sciences, medicine and health, education, law, theology, the arts, administrative specialties, and management.

2 *Clerical and sales occupations.* Clerical jobs involve preparing, transcribing, systematizing, and preserving written communications and records, distributing information, and collecting accounts; sales jobs involve influencing customers in favor of a commodity or service.

3 *Service occupations.* Jobs concerned with providing domestic services in private households; preparing and serving food and drink; providing lodging; providing grooming, cosmetic, and other personal- and health-care services; maintaining and cleaning clothing; protecting people and their property; recreation services; and cleaning and maintaining buildings.

4 *Agricultural, fishery, forestry, and related occupations.* Jobs concerned with growing, caring for, and gathering plant and animal life and products.

5 *Processing occupations.* Jobs concerned with refining, mixing, compounding, and chemical or heat treatment of various materials and products.

6 *Machine trades occupations.* Jobs concerned with machine operations on such materials as metals, wood, plastics, and stone; disassembly, repair, reassembly, installation, and maintenance of machines and mechanical equipment.

7 *Bench-work occupations.* Jobs concerned with the use of body members, hand tools, and bench machines to fabricate (construct), inspect, or repair relatively small products such as jewelry, light bulbs, musical instruments, tires, footwear, pottery, and garments.

8 *Structural work occupations.* Jobs concerned with fabricating, erecting, installing, paving, painting, and repairing structures and structural parts such as bridges, buildings, roads, motor vehicles, cables, internal combustion engines, girders, plates, and frames.

9 *Miscellaneous occupations.* Jobs concerned with transporting people and cargo, packaging and warehousing materials, mining, utilities, modeling, motion pictures, radio and television, and graphic arts.

These 9 categories are divided into 83 two-digit divisions, which in turn are subdivided into 564 distinctive three-digit occupational groups.

The middle three digits of the DOT occupational code represent work functions according to the primary tasks performed in the occupation (see Table 4-2). Every job requires a worker to function to some degree in relation to data, people, and things. The fourth digit of the DOT code represents *data*, the fifth digit *people*, and the sixth digit *things*. Worker functions having more complex responsibility are given lower numbers; those involving less complicated functions are assigned higher numbers. For example, "synthesizing" and "coordinating" data are more complex tasks than "copying" data. The numbers assigned to the middle three digits in the DOT code identify the highest appropriate worker function for each occupation.

The DOT gives each work function a specific definition, which has been shortened and summarized later in this book; consult the DOT for the complete definition (Fine, 1973; U.S. Department of Labor, 1991). Familiarize yourself with the meanings of the work functions in the data, people, and things categories. Then circle or identify in each category the highest function you can honestly claim and would feel comfortable doing. You can compare your estimated DOT code number for data, people, and things functions with those of your occupational prospects found in the DOT. Do any occupations on your list have higher or more complex worker functions than

Table 4-2 Work Functions in Relation to Data, People, and Things

Data (fourth digit)	People (fifth digit)	Things (sixth digit)
0 Synthesizing	0 Mentoring	0 Setting up
1 Coordinating	1 Negotiating	1 Precision working
2 Analyzing	2 Instructing	2 Operating/controlling
3 Compiling	3 Supervising	3 Driving/operating
4 Computing	4 Diverting	4 Manipulating
5 Copying	5 Persuading	5 Tending
6 Comparing	6 Speaking/signaling	6 Feeding/offbearing
	7 Serving	7 Handling
	8 Taking instructions/helping	

Source: U.S. Department of Labor (1991).

you have now or could learn in the future? Are the abilities required by your occupational prospects too far above your own ability levels? Chapters 6 and 8 address these concerns.

Data. Working with data means working with facts, information, and ideas made from observations, research, and interpretations. Data are presented as numbers, words, symbols, and statistics and appear as information and specifications.

0   *Synthesizing.* Collecting and combining data from different sources to make a coherent, related system in order to discover facts or develop new ideas.
1   *Coordinating.* Putting information together from an analysis of the data so those who use it can do so in an organized, harmonious way.
2   *Analyzing.* Examining the nature and relationship of various parts of data for evaluation and the development of alternative courses of action.
3   *Compiling.* Collecting, arranging, and classifying information.
4   *Computing.* Calculating numbers and reporting them or carrying out an action in relation to them.
5   *Copying.* Transcribing, entering, and posting data.
6   *Comparing.* Examining data to discover similarities to or differences from known standards or models.

People. This category refers to working with human beings, as well as with animals as if the animals were human.

0   *Mentoring.* Advising, counseling, and guiding people in terms of their total personalities.
1   *Negotiating.* Exchanging ideas with others to form policies and programs or to arrive jointly at decisions or solutions.
2   *Instructing.* Teaching subject matter to others through explanation, demonstration, and supervised practice.
3   *Supervising.* Assigning duties for workers, keeping good relations among them, and promoting efficiency.
4   *Diverting.* Amusing or entertaining others, usually through stage presentations, movies, television, or radio.
5   *Persuading.* Influencing others in favor of a product, service, or point of view.
6   *Speaking/signaling.* Talking or giving signals to give or exchange information; giving directions to helpers or assistants.
7   *Serving.* Attending to the needs, requests, and wishes of people.
8   *Taking instructions/helping.* Paying attention to work assignments and following the directions of a supervisor.

Things. Working with things means working with inanimate objects such as machines, tools, equipment, and products. Things are tangible in that they have form, shape, and substance.

0   *Setting up.* Preparing machines and equipment to perform their functions and restoring their proper functioning if they need repair.

1   *Precision working.* Using judgment in the selection and adjustment of tools and guiding them in order to attain correct standards.

2   *Operating/controlling.* Starting, stopping, controlling, and adjusting machines, gauges, valves, and other equipment.

3   *Driving/operating.* Steering or guiding one or more machines to move people or make things.

4   *Manipulating.* Moving, guiding, and placing several objects or materials, using some individual judgment.

5   *Tending.* Observing the functioning of machines.

6   *Feeding/offbearing.* Inserting, throwing, dumping, or placing materials in or removing them from machines that are automatic or tended by other workers.

7   *Handling.* Moving and carrying objects and materials.

The last three digits of the DOT code are used to separate occupational titles with the same first six digits. A number of occupations can have the same first six digits, but no two occupations can have the same nine digits. The full nine digits give each occupation listed in the DOT a distinctive, unique code number.

For example, DOT code number 090.227-010 describes a teacher or faculty member at a college. The first digit tells you that the occupation is in a professional, technical, and managerial category. The first two digits (09) locate the occupation in education, and the first three digits (090) subdivide education into college and university education. The middle three digits (fourth, fifth, and sixth digits) give you the number of the highest worker functions for this occupation. College teachers analyze data, instruct people, and handle things. They do other tasks on their jobs, but these are their highest functions. The last three digits separate college teachers from any other occupation that is similar and has the same first six digits.

The *Dictionary of Occupational Titles* is one of the "big books" used in career planning. You won't want to read the whole book (you'll understand why we say that when you see it), so you'll want to focus on the parts of the DOT that interest you most. Exercise 4-2 (Survey of Two-Digit DOT Divisions), or a survey of three-digit groups in Appendix D: *Dictionary of Occupational Titles (DOT)*, at the back of this book will help you locate your most attractive occupations in the *Dictionary of Occupational Titles*.

EXERCISE 4-2 SURVEY OF TWO-DIGIT DOT DIVISIONS

All the two-digit occupational divisions found in the DOT are listed next. Three-digit groups appear in Appendix D: *Dictionary of Occupational Titles (DOT)*. Circle the number of any two-digit division you would like to explore further. Then get hold of a copy of the *Dictionary of Occupational Titles* (from your counselor, teacher, library, or career resource center) and locate the two-digit occupational divisions you have circled. (They are found in the same numeric order as listed in the exercise.) Read the short description or definition of each occupation in the circled divisions. Write the names of any occupations you want to put on your occupational prospect list in the spaces provided at the end of this exercise and/or in Exercise 3-15 of the previous chapter. (The letters "n.e.c." in a division stands for "not elsewhere classified.")

Professional, Technical, and Managerial Occupations
01 Architecture, engineering, drafting, and surveying
02 Mathematics and physical sciences (astronomers, chemists, geologists)
03 Computer-related occupations (systems analysts, programmers)
04 Life sciences (agricultural sciences, biology, psychology)
05 Social sciences (economics, political science, history, sociology)
07 Medicine and health (physicians, dentists, veterinarians, nurses)

09 Education (college, secondary, primary, handicapped, vocational)
10 Museum, library, and archival sciences
11 Law and jurisprudence (lawyers, judges)
12 Religion and theology
13 Writing (writers, editors, interpreters, translators)
14 Art (commercial artists, designers, photographers, fine artists)
15 Entertainment and recreation (dramatics, dancing, music, sports)
16 Administrative specializations (accountants, management, advertising)
18 Managers and officials, n.e.c. (not elsewhere classified)
19 Miscellaneous professional, technical, and managerial occupations, n.e.c.

Clerical and Sales Occupations

20 Stenography, typing, and filing (secretaries, typists, file clerks)
21 Computing and account recording (bookkeepers, data processors)
22 Production, stock clerks (production, shipping, receiving)
23 Information, message distribution (telephone operators, receptionists)
24 Miscellaneous clerical occupations (government service, medical service)
25 Sales and services (real estate, finance, transportation)
26 Sales, consumable commodities (food products, textiles, drugs)
27 Sales, commodities (home furnishings, farm and industrial equipment)
29 Miscellaneous sales occupations (salesclerks, vendors, delivery sales)

Service Occupations

30 Domestic service (household work, launderers, domestic cooks)
31 Food and beverage preparation and service (waiters, bartenders, chefs)
32 Lodging and related service (boardinghouse keepers, hotel cleaners)
33 Barbering, cosmetology, and related service (barbers, hairdressers)
34 Amusement and recreation service (attendants, ushers)
35 Miscellaneous personal service (guides, checkroom attendants)
36 Apparel and furnishings service (laundering, dry cleaning, pressing)
37 Protective service (security guards, firefighters, police officers)
38 Building and related service (porters, janitors, elevator operators)

Agricultural, Fishery, Forestry, and Related Occupations

40 Plant farming (grain, vegetable, fruit, field crop, groundskeeping)
41 Animal farming (domestic animals, game farming, animal service)
42 Miscellaneous agricultural and related occupations (general farming)
44 Fishery and related occupations (net and line fishers, aquatic life)
45 Forestry (tree farming, forest conservation, forest products, logging)
46 Hunting, trapping, and related occupations

Processing Occupations

50 Processing of metal (electroplating, melting, heat treating, coating)
51 Ore refining and foundry occupations (mixing, separating, melting)
52 Processing of food, tobacco, and related products
53 Processing of paper and related materials
54 Processing of petroleum, coal, gas, and related products
55 Processing of chemicals, plastics, rubber, paint, and related products
56 Processing of wood and wood products (mixing, preserving, drying)
57 Processing of stone, clay, glass, and related products
58 Processing of leather, textiles, and related products (shaping, felting)
59 Processing occupations, n.e.c.

Machine-Trades Occupations

60 Metal machining (machinists, toolmakers, turning, milling, boring, sawing)
61 Metalworking occupations, n.e.c. (forging, sheet rolling, fabricating)
62/63 Mechanics and machinery repairers (auto, aircraft, rail equipment, marine, farm, engine, metalworking machinery, printing)
64 Paperworking (cutting, winding, folding, creasing, gluing)

65 Printing (typesetters, composers, printing press, bookbinding)
66 Wood machining (cabinetmakers, patternmakers, sanding, sawing)
67 Machining stone, clay, glass, and related materials
68 Textile occupations (spinning, weaving, knitting, forming)
69 Machine trades occupations, n.e.c. (plastics, rubber, leather, wire)

Bench-Work Occupations
70 Fabrication, assembly, and repair of metal products, n.e.c.
71 Fabrication and repair of scientific, medical, photographic, optical, horological, and related products
72 Assembly and repair of electrical equipment (radio, TV, motors)
73 Fabrication and repair of products made from assorted materials (musical instruments, games and toys, sporting goods, office materials, jewelry)
74 Painting, decorating, and related occupations (brush and spray painters)
75 Fabrication and repair of plastics, synthetics, rubber, and related products
76 Fabrication and repair of wood products (cutting, shaping, sanding)
77 Fabrication and repair of sand, stone, clay, and glass products (jewelry, glass blowing, pottery, porcelain, asbestos, abrasives)
78 Fabrication and repair of textile, leather, and related products (furniture, hand sewing, fur and leather working, hats, gloves, tailoring)
79 Bench-work occupations, n.e.c. (food, tobacco, paper products)

Structural Work Occupations
80 Metal fabricating, n.e.c. (riveters, tinsmiths, boilermakers)
81 Welders, cutters, and related occupations
82 Electrical assembling, installing, and repairing (power plant equipment, transmission lines and circuits, signaling equipment, lighting equipment)
84 Painting, plastering, waterproofing, cementing, and related occupations
85 Excavating, grading, paving, and related occupations
86 Construction (carpenters, brick and stone masons, plumbers, glaziers)
89 Structural work, n.e.c. (structural maintenance)

Miscellaneous Occupations
90 Motor freight (truck drivers: concrete-mixing truck, dump truck, trailer truck)
91 Transportation (railroad, water, air, passenger, parking lots)
92 Packaging and materials handling (packaging, conveying, moving, storing)
93 Extraction of minerals (earth boring, blasting, loading, crushing)
95 Production and distribution of utilities (stationary engineers, firers)
96 Amusement, recreation, motion picture, radio, television occupations
97 Graphic art work (artwork, photoengraving, lithography, electrotype)

Now you can go to the *Dictionary of Occupational Titles* and investigate the two-digit divisions you have circled. Search these groups for occupational prospects. Also, examine the middle three digits of the nine-digit DOT code of the occupations you want to consider as prospects. Remind yourself that the fourth digit represents data; the fifth, people; and the sixth, things. Identify your highest function for data, people, and things in Table 4-2. If you haven't already done so, do it now. The same, or approximately the same, numbers as yours in the occupational codes for data, people, and things functions should help you identify occupational prospects. Write them in the following spaces, or in Exercise 3-15 of Chapter 3.

_____   _____

_____   _____

_____   _____

_____   _____

_____   _____

_____   _____

_____   _____

_____   _____

_____   _____

_____   _____

The Occupational Information Network—the O*Net

The *O*Net*, the *Occupational Information Network,* is a skills-based system for assembling and organizing information about occupations and worker characteristics. It uses over 400 variables, describing the content and context of work (Mariani, 2001). The O*Net is replacing the *Dictionary of Occupational Titles* (DOT) as it becomes increasingly accessible to the public. Crosswalks (bridges or cross-references) connect O*Net occupations to other occupational classification systems, including the DOT. The information you can get from O*Net is shown graphically in Figure 4-3 and is organized into six categories or "domains."

1. *Worker characteristics* are given in the form of 52 abilities, 6 interests, and 21 work values. *Abilities* are grouped into *cognitive* (verbal, numerical, perceptual, spatial), *psychomotor* (arm–hand steadiness, manual and finger dexterity), *physical* (strength, endurance, flexibility, balance, and coordination), and *sensory* abilities (visual, auditory, and speech). *Interests* cover the six Holland types: the *Realistic, Investigative, Artistic, Social, Enterprising*, and *Conventional* patterns that were described in Chapter 3 of this book. *Work values* take in values such

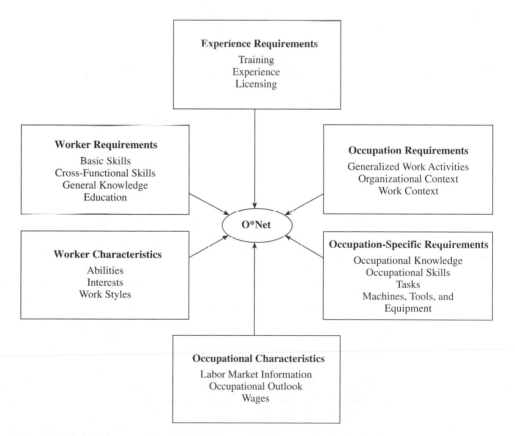

Figure 4-3 Information put into the O*Net database. *Source:* U.S. Department of Labor, Employment and Training Administration.

as *achievement, altruism, autonomy, comfort, safety*, and *social status*. Occupational profiles developed by O*Net contain numeric ratings for its job and worker characteristics. For abilities, one rating indicates on a scale of 1 to 100 the level of ability, and another rating gauges the importance of the ability in performing the work. Occupations have special ratings for interests and work values.

2. *Worker requirements* are given in the form of 46 basic and cross-functional skills, 33 knowledge descriptors, and 11 levels of education. *Basic skills* are divided into *content* skills (reading comprehension, active listening, writing, speaking, mathematics, and science) and *process* skills (critical thinking, active learning, learning strategies, and monitoring). *Cross-functional skills* consist of *social* (persuasion, negotiation, instructing, and so on), *problem solving* (problem identification, information gathering, solution appraisal, and so on), *technical* (installing, testing, maintenance, repairing, and so on), *systems* (visioning, judgment, decision making, and so on), and *resource management* skills (time management, financial resources, and so on). *Knowledge requirements* are organized sets of principles and facts about various kinds of subjects such as business and management, manufacturing and production, engineering and technology, mathematics and science, arts and humanities, and communication. *Education requirements* deal with level of education and instructional program in a specific subject.

3. *Experience requirements* cover *specific preparation* and/or *past work* experience required for entry into a job and *licenses, certificates,* or *registrations* used to identify levels of skill or performance needed to enter an occupation. O*Net assigns to each occupation one of five *job zones. Zone 1* means *little or no preparation* is needed. *Zone 2* signifies *some preparation* is necessary. *Zone 3* indicates a *medium amount of preparation* is needed; previous work-related skill, knowledge, or experience is required. A *Zone 4* designation tells you *considerable preparation* is necessary; at least two to four years of work-related skill, knowledge, or experience. *Zone 5* means *extensive preparation* is needed; at least five or more years are essential.

4. *Occupation requirements* are given in the form of 42 general work activities, organizational context, and work context. *Generalized work activities* occurring on a number of jobs in an occupation include getting information needed to do the job, processing and evaluating information, making decisions, solving problems, thinking creatively, performing physical and technical work activities, and interacting with others (communicating and coordinating with others and developing, managing, advising, and administering others). *Organizational context* is a grouping of characteristics of organizations that influence the way people do their work. Among many circumstances are the amount of control workers have in making decisions; job characteristics such as variety of skills used, significance of the work, autonomy, and feedback; human resources systems and practices (recruitment and selection of employees, training and development, and pay and benefits); social processes (work goals and roles and organizational values); and the role of supervisors. *Work context* involves social and physical factors that influence how people do their work. It involves methods of communication, job interactions, work setting, environmental conditions, job hazards, physical demands, clothing worn on the job, routine or challenging nature of the work, and pace and scheduling of work.

5. *Labor market characteristics* include information about the occupation's industry, its *current numbers of workers, employment projections,* and *earnings.* Employment projections come from the Bureau of Labor Statistics. Wage data are gathered by two surveys: the Occupational Employment Survey and the Current Population Survey.

6. *Occupation-specific information* describes the characteristics that pertain to a specific occupation in terms of five types of information: *knowledge; skills; tasks; duties;* and *machines, tools, and equipment* (Mariani, 1999).

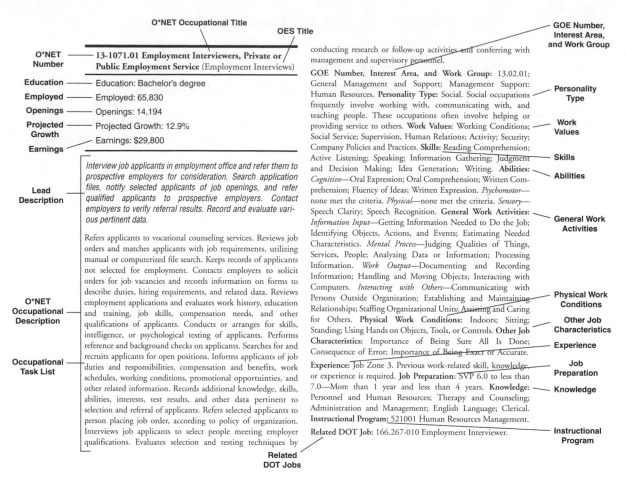

Students can access the O*Net online. You need a computer with Internet access. A printer is helpful, to print the reams of information you are likely to obtain. The O*Net Internet address is http://online.onetcenter.org. Over 950 occupations are on file. You can find out which jobs fit your interests, skills, abilities, and work values. O*Net's career profiles use the latest labor market information. For each occupation in the O*Net database, you can get details on tasks, knowledge needed, skills and abilities that are important, work activities on the job, work conditions, education and training needed, interests, work values and needs, related occupations, and wages and employment information in your state. All that information on one occupation may be presented to you on an average of 10 to 12 pages. You may limit the amount of O*Net printed material by choosing a summary report. Another alternative is to "customize" your report by indicating you want only the data on the most important ratings in the O*Net occupational descriptions. For example, you can ask the "Custom Report" to display only those items where you scored 50 on a 1-to-100 rating scale of importance for knowledge, skills, abilities, and work activities and 50 on the occupational interest scale and the extent scales for work values and work needs.

O*Net gives you information on occupations related to the one you are concentrating on, and it provides a "crosswalk" (a connection or bridge) to another occupational classification system such as the *Dictionary of Occupational Titles* and the *Guide for Occupational Exploration*. The O*Net system provides links connecting you with state and local information about wages and employment prospects on the occupations you are exploring.

To locate the occupations that interest you the most on the O*Net, go through the following list of occupational groups. Then turn to Appendix E: *O*Net Search for Occupations (Exercise 4-3 in Chapter 4),* in the back of the book to discover the specific occupations under the group titles. You can add those occupations to your occupational prospect list in Chapter 3. Also, obtain a summary, customized, or detailed report from your computer, the Internet, and printer by tapping into the O*Net database. Again, the Web address for O*Net is http://online.onetcenter.org.

The O*Net team at the U.S. Department of Labor has created a set of career exploration instruments to help people consider career options and transitions. The O*Net *Interest Profiler* gives results based on the Holland RIASEC codes, covered in Chapter 3 of this book. The *Ability Profiler* is a new version of the General Aptitude Test Battery (covered in Chapter 6 of this text); it measures nine job-related abilities. The O*Net *Work Importance Locator* and *Work Importance Profiler* are a paper-and-pencil inventory that includes a card sort activity; it helps people identify occupations consistent with six types of work values (Mariani, 2001).

EXERCISE 4-3 O*NET SEARCH FOR OCCUPATIONS

Check the occupational groups of greatest interest to you, and then go to Appendix E: *O*Net Search for Occupations (Exercise 4-3 in Chapter 4).* The numbers are from the *Standard Occupational Classification* system. (Gaps in the numbers are deliberate; new occupations are being created constantly and may be added to the O*Net at a future time.) The number after the name of the occupational group refers to the number of occupations described by the O*Net in that group.

Management occupations (11-0000)

____ 11-1000 Top executives (5)

____ 11-2000 Advertising, marketing, promotions, public relations, and sales managers (4)

____ 11-3000 Operations specialties managers (14)

____ 11-9000 Other management occupations (21)

Business and financial operations occupations (13-0000)

___ 13-1000 Business operations specialists (27)

___ 13-2000 Financial specialists (17)

Computer and mathematical occupations (15-0000)

___ 15-1000 Computer specialists (11)

___ 15-2000 Mathematical science occupations (6)

Architectural and engineering occupations (17-0000)

___ 17-1000 Architects, surveyors, and cartographers (4)

___ 17-2000 Engineers (23)

___ 17-3000 Drafters, engineering, and mapping occupations (22)

Life, physical, and social science occupations (19-0000)

___ 19-1000 Life scientists (20)

___ 19-2000 Physical scientists (10)

___ 19-3000 Social scientists and related workers (18)

___ 19-4000 Life, physical, and social science technicians (17)

Community and social service occupations (21-0000)

___ 21-1000 Counselors, social workers, and other community and social service specialists (14)

___ 21-2000 Religious workers (3)

Legal occupations (23-0000)

___ 23-1000 Lawyers, judges, and related workers (4)

___ 23-2000 Legal support workers (7)

Education, training, and library occupations (25-0000)

___ 25-1000 Postsecondary teachers (38)

___ 25-2000 Primary, secondary, and special education school teachers (10)

___ 25-3000 Other teachers and instructors (3)

___ 25-4000 Librarians, curators, and archivists (5)

___ 25-9000 Other education, training, and library occupations (5)

Arts, design, entertainment, sports, and media occupations (27-0000)

___ 27-1000 Art and design workers (19)

___ 27-2000 Entertainers and performers, sports and related workers (20)

___ 27-3000 Media and communication workers (14)

___ 27-4000 Media and communication equipment workers (10)

Health care practitioners and technical occupations (29-0000)

___ 29-1000 Health diagnosing and treating practitioners (30)

___ 29-2000 Health technologists and technicians (21)

___ 29-9000 Other health care practitioners and technical occupations (4)

Health care support occupations (31-0000)

___ 31-1000 Nursing, psychiatric and home health aides (3)

___ 31-2000 Occupational and physical therapist assistants and aides (4)

___ 31-9000 Other health care support occupations (8)

Protective service occupations (33-0000)

___ 33-1000 First-line supervisors/managers, protective service workers (6)

___ 33-2000 Fire fighting and prevention workers (7)

___ 33-3000 Law enforcement workers (15)

___ 33-9000 Other protective service workers (7)

Food preparation– and serving–related occupations (35-0000)

___ 35-1000 Supervisors, food preparation and serving workers (2)

___ 35-2000 Cooks and food preparation workers (7)

___ 35-3000 Food and beverage serving workers (5)

___ 35-9000 Other food preparation and serving-related workers (4)

Building and grounds cleaning and maintenance occupations (37-0000)

___ 37-1000 Supervisors, building and grounds cleaning and maintenance workers (6)

___ 37-2000 Building cleaning and pest control workers (4)

___ 37-3000 Grounds maintenance workers (4)

Personal care and service occupations (39-0000)

___ 39-1000 Supervisors, personal care and service workers (3)

___ 39-2000 Animal care and service workers (2)

___ 39-3000 Entertainment attendants and related workers (9)

___ 39-4000 Funeral service workers (2)

___ 39-5000 Personal appearance workers (6)

___ 39-6000 Transportation, tourism, and lodging attendants (6)

___ 39-9000 Other personal care and service workers (6)

Sales and related occupations (41-0000)

___ 41-1000 Supervisors, sales workers (2)

___ 41-2000 Retail sales workers (5)

___ 41-3000 Sales representatives, services (7)

___ 41-4000 Sales representatives, wholesale and manufacturing (8)

___ 41-9000 Other sales and related workers (8)

Office and administrative support occupations (43-0000)

___ 43-1000 Supervisors, office and administrative support workers (3)

___ 43-2000 Communications equipment operators (5)

___ 43-3000 Financial clerks (10)

___ 43-4000 Information and record clerks (28)

___ 43-5000 Material recording, scheduling, dispatching, and distributing workers (16)

___ 43-6000 Secretaries and administrative assistants (4)

___ 43-9000 Other office and administrative support workers (16)

Farming, fishing, and forestry occupations (45-0000)

___ 45-1000 Supervisors, farming, fishing, and forestry workers (8)

___ 45-2000 Agricultural workers (9)

___ 45-3000 Fishing and hunting workers (2)

___ 45-4000 Forest, conservation, and logging workers (6)

Construction and extraction occupations (47-0000)

___ 47-1000 Supervisors, construction and extraction workers (3)

___ 47-2000 Construction trades workers (42)

___ 47-3000 Helpers, construction trades (7)

___ 47-4000 Other construction and related workers (10)

___ 47-5000 Extraction workers (15)

Installation, maintenance, and repair occupations (49-0000)

___ 49-1000 Supervisors of installation, maintenance, and repair workers (1)

___ 49-2000 Electrical and electronic equipment mechanics, installers, and repairers (25)

___ 49-3000 Vehicle and mobile equipment mechanics, installers, and repairers (19)

___ 49-9000 Other installation, maintenance, and repair occupations (36)

Production occupations (51-0000)

___ 51-1000 Supervisors, production workers (1)

___ 51-2000 Assemblers and fabricators (15)

___ 51-3000 Food-processing workers (9)

___ 51-4000 Metal workers and plastic workers (56)

___ 51-5000 Printing workers (29)

___ 51-6000 Textile, apparel, and furnishings workers (26)

___ 51-7000 Woodworkers (11)

___ 51-8000 Plant and system operators (18)

___ 51-9000 Other production occupations (72)

Transportation and material-moving occupations (53-0000)

___ 53-1000 Supervisors, transportation and material-moving workers (3)

___ 53-2000 Air transportation workers (4)

___ 53-3000 Motor vehicle operators (10)

___ 53-4000 Rail transportation workers (9)

___ 53-5000 Water transportation workers (9)

___ 53-6000 Other transportation workers (12)

___ 53-7000 Material-moving workers (26)

Military specific occupations (55-0000)

___ 55-1000 Military officer special and tactical operations leaders/managers (8)

___ 55-2000 First-line enlisted military supervisor/managers (3)

___ 55-3000 Military enlisted tactical operations and air/weapons specialists and crew members (9)

Having completed Exercise 4-3, now you can go to Appendix E: *O*Net Search for Occupations (Exercise 4-3 in Chapter 4)* in the back of this book and consider the titles of the occupations within the groups you have checked as the most interesting to you. Then you can look at descriptions of those occupations in the *O*Net Dictionary of Occupational Titles* (Farr and Ludden, 2002) or go online to the O*Net Center (http:// onetcenter.org) and get a summary, customized, or detailed report on the occupations you have selected. Table 4-3 gives employment and wage information about the major occupational groups you have just surveyed.

Although the O*Net is a computerized database, the book, *O*Net Dictionary of Occupational Titles*, second edition (Farr and Ludden, 2002), is available. The second edition contains the new numbering sequence organized under the Standard Occupational Classification (SOC) system.

Information about occupations in *The O*Net Dictionary of Occupational Titles* is organized as shown in Figure 4-4. A short illustration of each element of an *O*Net DOT* occupational description follows:

- *O*Net Number*—Each occupation is assigned a unique number based on the Standard Occupational Classification (SOC); every occupational description in the book is in numeric order.

Table 4-3 National Cross-Industry Estimates of Employment and Mean Annual Wage for SOC Major Occupational Groups, 2001

Major Occupational Group	Estimated Employment	Estimated Average Annual Wage
Management	7,212,130	$ 70,800
Business and Financial Operations	4,676,690	$ 50,580
Computer and Mathematical	2,825,820	$ 60,350
Architecture and Engineering	2,489,040	$ 56,330
Life, Physical, and Social Sciences	1,067,750	$ 49,710
Community and Social Services	1,523,940	$ 34,190
Legal	909,360	$ 69,030
Education, Training, and Library	7,658,800	$ 39,130
Arts, Design, Entertainment, Sports, and Media	1,508,730	$ 39,770
Health Care Practitioners and Technical	6,118,880	$ 49,930
Health Care Support	3,123,160	$ 21,900
Protective Service	2,958,050	$ 32,530
Food Preparation and Serving	9,917,790	$ 16,720
Building and Grounds Cleaning and Maintenance	4,275,660	$ 20,380
Personal Care and Service	2,801,640	$ 21,010
Sales and Related	13,418,770	$ 28,920
Office and Administrative Support	22,798,460	$ 27,230
Farming, Fishing, and Forestry	453,010	$ 19,630
Construction and Extraction	6,239,250	$ 35,460
Installation, Maintenance, and Repair	5,322,980	$ 34,960
Production	11,270,180	$ 27,600
Transportation and Material Moving	9,410,340	$ 26,570

Source: Occupational Employment Statistics, U.S. Department of Labor (2003). (Military data not available.)

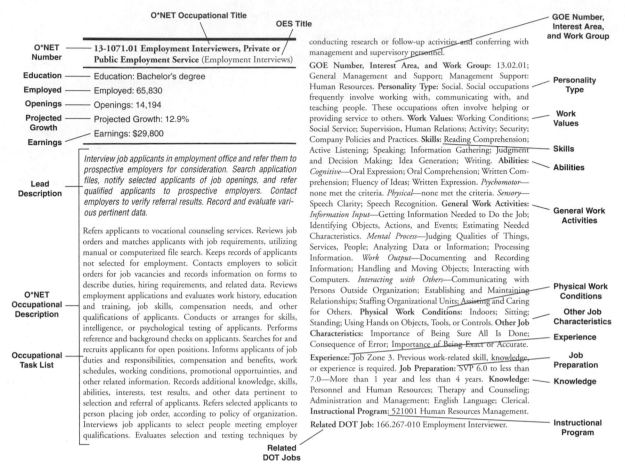

Figure 4-4 Sample of an O*Net job description. *Source:* Reproduced by permission from Farr, J. M. and Ludden, L. L. with Shatkin, L., *The O*Net dictionary of occupational titles,* 2nd edition. Indianapolis, IN: JIST Works, 2001, p. 3.

- *O*Net Occupational Title*—In boldface type, this is the name given for the occupation by the U.S. Department of Labor.
- *OES Title*—The job title used in the Occupational Employment Survey (OES) system most closely related to the O*Net job title.
- *Education*—The education or training typically required for entry into a job in the occupation; the Department of Labor uses 11 levels of education from short-term OJT (on-the-job training) to professional degree.
- *Employed*—The most current number of people employed in the occupation.
- *Openings*—The number of openings anticipated to be available each year.
- *Projected growth*—The percentage of projected new jobs over a 10-year period.
- *Earnings*—The median earnings (half above and half below) for all people in the job; remember that new entrants earn less and pay rates vary in different regions of the country.
- *Lead description and O*Net Occupational Description*—The lead description appears in italics followed by additional statements written in "résumé style"—that is, every sentence starts with a verb; otherwise, the descriptions would start with "Workers" or "Employees" every time, which would soon become tiresome. (Use this method of expressing yourself when writing your own résumé.)
- *Occupational task list*—A list of occupational tasks performed by workers in the occupation.
- *GOE Number, Interest Area, and Work Group*—numbers and names of groups in the *Guide for Occupational Exploration* (GOE) are cross-referenced (the GOE is discussed next in this chapter).

- *Personality type*—One of the six Holland types of personality and work environment.
- *Work values*—The highest ratings of the 21 work values used by O*Net; helps you identify occupations that match your personal values.
- *Skills*—The highest of the 46 skills used by O*Net to measure the level of performance required in the occupation.
- *Abilities*—Higher-than-average abilities needed according to the job description; abilities are organized into four subgroups: cognitive (21 abilities), psychomotor (10), physical (9), and sensory (12).
- *General work activities*—Three to five of the most important activities performed on the job; there are four subgroups: information input (10 activities), mental process (10), work output (10), and interacting with others (17).
- *Physical work conditions*—Three to five work conditions (out of 26) that are the most important; this characteristic involves a variety of work environments and working conditions such as physical setting, environmental conditions, job hazards, body positioning, and work clothing.
- *Other job characteristics*—Three to five characteristics you may find helpful to know.
- *Experience*—This is one of the five "job zones" that explain the experience needed for entry into the occupation.
- *Job preparation*—The "Standard Vocation Preparation" system is used to assign one of five levels of training or education for a job in the occupation.
- *Knowledge*—The highest 5 of 33 O*Net knowledge descriptors, knowledge gained from school, training programs, self-employment, military, volunteer work, and other life experiences.
- *Instructional program*—The Classification of Instructional Programs (CIP) is a system of naming and grouping educational and training programs developed by the U.S. Department of Education.
- *Related DOT jobs*—gives the nine-digit numeric DOT code and title for all related DOT jobs.

Each of the occupational information elements briefly described in the preceding list are explained in greater detail in the Introduction of the *O*Net Dictionary of Occupational Titles*, developed under the direction of J. Michael Farr and LaVerne Ludden with database work by Laurence Shatkin (2002).

In the following spaces or in Exercise 3-15 of Chapter 3, list any occupational prospects you have uncovered through your use of the O*Net, either through the book or online.

_____	_____
_____	_____
_____	_____
_____	_____
_____	_____
_____	_____
_____	_____

Arrangement of Occupations in the Guide for Occupational Exploration

Occupations in the third edition of the *Guide for Occupational Exploration* (GOE) are classified into 14 broad interest areas, which are divided into 83 work groups. Adding subgroups to the work groups makes a total of 133 groups in the third edition of the GOE. The first two digits identify one of the 14 interest areas, the first four-digit code helps you locate the work group, and all six digits designate the subgroup. In Part 1 of the GOE, each work group has a description about the work you would do in it, things about you that would point to this kind of work, skills and knowledge you would need, other considerations about the work, and how you can prepare for this kind of work through specialized training.

Here are the definitions for the 14 interest areas given by the authors of the *Guide for Occupational Exploration*, third edition (Farr, Ludden, and Shatkin, 2001). In the spaces provided, indicate the two or three interest areas you believe would be the most attractive to you.

___   01 *Arts, Entertainment, and Media.* An interest in creatively expressing feelings or ideas, in communicating news or information, or in performing.

___   02 *Science, Math, and Engineering.* An interest in discovering, collecting, and analyzing information about the natural world; in applying scientific research findings to problems in medicine, the life sciences, and the natural sciences; in imagining numerical data; and in applying technology to economic activities.

___   03 *Plants and Animals.* An interest in working with plants and animals, usually outdoors.

___   04 *Law, Law Enforcement, and Public Safety.* An interest in upholding people's rights, or in protecting people and property by using authority, inspecting, or monitoring.

___   05 *Mechanics, Installers, and Repairers.* An interest in applying mechanical, electrical and electronic principles to practical situations by use of machines or hand tools.

___   06 *Construction, Mining, and Drilling.* An interest in assembling components of buildings and other structures, or in using mechanical devices to drill or excavate.

___   07 *Transportation.* An interest in operations that move people or materials.

___   08 *Industrial Production.* An interest in repetitive, concrete, organized activities most often done in a factory setting.

___   09 *Business Detail.* An interest in organized, clearly defined activities requiring accuracy and attention to details, primarily in an office setting.

___   10 *Sales and Marketing.* An interest in bringing others to a particular point of view by personal persuasion, using sales and promotional techniques.

___   11 *Recreation, Travel, and Other Personal Services.* An interest in catering to the wishes and needs of others, so they may enjoy cleanliness, good food and drink, comfortable lodging away from home, and enjoyable recreation.

___   12 *Education and Social Service.* An interest in teaching people or improving their social and spiritual well-being.

___   13 *General Management and Support.* An interest in leading and influencing people, and in making an organization run smoothly.

___   14 *Medical and Health Services.* An interest in helping people to be healthy.

Exercise 4-4 is a checklist of the 83 work groups in the GOE. You can focus on the two or three interest areas you just indicated as being the most attractive to you. Of course, you can go through the entire checklist just to make sure you have thoroughly covered the complete contents of the *Guide for Occupational Exploration*. The work groups have a four-digit number within a two-digit interest area. The work groups are listed by title only; they do not have a definition attached to them as did the preceding interest areas, but the titles give a good indication of the kinds of occupations in the work group. The numbers after some work groups indicate the number of subgroups in the work group. (For a more thorough coverage of the GOE, go to Appendix F: *GOE Group Checklist*, in the back of this book. There, you can move through an entire checklist of 133 work groups *and subgroups* of occupations in the GOE.)

EXERCISE 4-4 GOE WORK GROUP CHECKLIST

01 Arts, Entertainment, and Media

___ 01.01 Managerial work in arts, entertainment, and media

___ 01.02 Writing and editing

___ 01.03 News, broadcasting, and public relations

___ 01.04 Visual arts (2)

___ 01.05 Performing arts (3)

___ 01.06 Craft arts

___ 01.07 Graphic arts

___ 01.08 Media technology

___ 01.09 Modeling and personal appearance

___ 01.10 Sports: Coaching, instructing, officiating, and performing

02 Science, Math, and Engineering

___ 02.01 Managerial work in science, math, and engineering

___ 02.02 Physical sciences

___ 02.03 Life sciences (4)

___ 02.04 Social sciences (2)

___ 02.05 Laboratory technology (2)

___ 02.06 Mathematics and computers (2)

___ 02.07 Engineering (4)

___ 02.08 Engineering technology (4)

03 Plants and Animals

___ 03.01 Managerial work in plants and animals (2)

___ 03.02 Animal care and training

___ 03.03 Hands-on work in plants and animals (4)

04 Law, Law Enforcement, and Public Safety

___ 04.01 Managerial work in law, law enforcement, and public safety

___ 04.02 Law (2)

___ 04.03 Law enforcement (3)

___ 04.04 Public safety (2)

___ 04.05 Military (5)

05 Mechanics, Installers, and Repairers

___ 05.01 Managerial work in mechanics, installers, and repairers

___ 05.02 Electrical and electronic systems (2)

___ 05.03 Mechanical work (4)

___ 05.04 Hands-on work in mechanics, installers, and repairers

06 Construction, Mining, and Drilling

___ 06.01 Managerial work in construction, mining, and drilling

___ 06.02 Construction (3)

___ 06.03 Mining and drilling

___ 06.04 Hands-on work in construction, mining, and drilling

07 Transportation

___ 07.01 Managerial work in transportation

___ 07.02 Vehicle expediting and coordinating

___ 07.03 Air vehicle operation

___ 07.04 Water vehicle operation

___ 07.05 Truck driving

___ 07.06 Rail vehicle operation

___ 07.07 Other services requiring driving

___ 07.08 Support work in transportation

08 Industrial Production

___ 08.01 Managerial work in industrial production

___ 08.02 Production technology (3)

___ 08.03 Production work (6)

___ 08.04 Metal and plastics machining technology

___ 08.05 Woodworking technology

___ 08.06 Systems operation (2)

___ 08.07 Hands-on work: loading, moving, hoisting, and conveying

09 Business Detail

___ 09.01 Managerial work in business detail

___ 09.02 Administrative detail (3)

___ 09.03 Bookkeeping, auditing, and accounting

___ 09.04 Material control

___ 09.05 Customer service

___ 09.06 Communications

___ 09.07 Records processing (2)

___ 09.08 Records and materials processing

___ 09.09 Clerical machine operation

10 Sales and Marketing

___ 10.01 Managerial work in sales and marketing

___ 10.02 Sales technology (2)

___ 10.03 General sales

___ 10.04 Personal soliciting

11 Recreation, Travel, and Other Personal Services

___ 11.01 Managerial work in recreation, travel, and other personal services

___ 11.02 Recreational services

___ 11.03 Transportation and lodging services

___ 11.04 Barber and beauty services

___ 11.05 Food and beverage services (2)

___ 11.06 Apparel, shoes, leather, and fabric care

___ 11.07 Cleaning and building services

___ 11.08 Other personal services

12 Education and Social Service

___ 12.01 Managerial work in education and social service

___ 12.02 Social services (2)

___ 12.03 Educational services (4)

13 General Management and Support

___ 13.01 General management work and management of support functions

___ 13.02 Management support (4)

14 Medical and Health Services

___ 14.01 Managerial work in medical and health services

___ 14.02 Medicine and surgery

___ 14.03 Dentistry

___ 14.04 Health specialties

___ 14.05 Medical technology

___ 14.06 Medical therapy

___ 14.07 Patient care and assistance

___ 14.08 Health protection and promotion

Descriptions of the 83 work groups are in Part 1 of the *Guide for Occupational Exploration,* third edition. In each work group, there are illustrations of the kind of work you would do, things about you that point to the kind of work in the occupations of the group, the skills and content knowledge you would need, and various other things to consider about the work. You can find out the preparation necessary for jobs in the occupations of the work group, the specialized training you would need for the work, and where that training is obtained.

Job descriptions for specific occupations are in Part 2 of the GOE. These descriptions start with the O*Net number and job title and include information on the things people do in the occupation, education needed, Holland personality type, average salary, projected growth or decline of workers, occupational values, skills and abilities required, interactions with other people on the job, and physical work conditions. The five "job zones" of the O*Net are also covered, indicating how much experience, education, and training is needed. Figure 4-5 gives an illustration of a GOE job description.

A "Crosswalks to Careers" section is found in Part 3 of the GOE. A *crosswalk* is a bridge that connects you to other occupational classification systems or with work

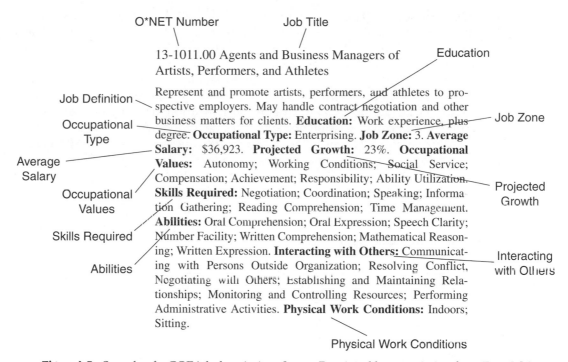

O*NET Number   Job Title

13-1011.00 Agents and Business Managers of   Education
Artists, Performers, and Athletes

Job Definition

Occupational Type

Average Salary

Occupational Values

Skills Required

Abilities

Represent and promote artists, performers, and athletes to prospective employers. May handle contract negotiation and other business matters for clients. **Education:** Work experience, plus degree. **Occupational Type:** Enterprising. **Job Zone:** 3. **Average Salary:** $36,923. **Projected Growth:** 23%. **Occupational Values:** Autonomy; Working Conditions; Social Service; Compensation; Achievement; Responsibility; Ability Utilization. **Skills Required:** Negotiation; Coordination; Speaking; Information Gathering; Reading Comprehension; Time Management. **Abilities:** Oral Comprehension; Oral Expression; Speech Clarity; Number Facility; Written Comprehension; Mathematical Reasoning; Written Expression. **Interacting with Others:** Communicating with Persons Outside Organization; Resolving Conflict, Negotiating with Others; Establishing and Maintaining Relationships; Monitoring and Controlling Resources; Performing Administrative Activities. **Physical Work Conditions:** Indoors; Sitting.

Job Zone

Projected Growth

Interacting with Others

Physical Work Conditions

Figure 4-5 Sample of a GOE job description. *Source:* Reprinted by permission from Farr, J. M., Ludden, L. L., and Shatkin, L. *Guide for occupational exploration,* 3rd edition. Indianapolis, IN: JIST Works, 2002, p. 13.

groups. The GOE identifies the work groups that match work values, leisure activities, home activities, school subjects, work settings, skills, abilities, and certain kinds of knowledge. By using the crosswalks, you could discover new occupational prospects that might otherwise be overlooked. An alphabetical index at the end of the GOE helps you locate occupations and their descriptions.

Be sure to list the occupational prospects you have obtained from the *Guide for Occupational Exploration* in the following spaces and/or in Exercise 3-15 of Chapter 3.

If you are using one of the older editions of the Guide for Occupational Exploration, consider updating your information from the latest edition. The first and second editions of the GOE were published in the late 1970s and mid-1980s. A revised version of the GOE called *Complete Guide for Occupational Exploration* (Maze and Mayall, 1993) was cross-referenced with the 12,741 occupations in the last edition of the *Dictionary of Occupational Titles* in 1991. The *Enhanced Guide for Occupational Exploration* (Farr, 1995) was organized in the same manner as the earlier editions of the

GOE, providing DOT descriptions of 2,800 occupations, a scaled-down number that still covered more than 95 percent of the labor force. These older editions had 12 interest areas instead of the current 14 in the third edition. The older GOEs are mentioned in case you are reading them in a library or career resource center.

The Enhanced GOE of 1995 codes information for various characteristics of each occupation: general educational development (GED); specific vocational preparation (SVP); academic demands (degree, certification, or diploma required and the amount of English usage skill needed); work field codes (specific skills used in the occupation); materials, products, subject matter, and services (MPSMS) used in the work; temperament (personality traits needed by the worker); aptitude (one of five levels used with the aptitudes in the General Aptitude Test Battery, described in Exercise 6-7 in Chapter 6 of this book); physical demands required of the worker in the occupation; work environment (noise level, exposure to weather, hazards on the job); salary (five salary ranges are coded); and outlook (length of time usually needed to find a job in the occupation).

EXERCISE 4-5 ROE CLASSIFICATION OF OCCUPATIONS

Dr. Anne Roe (1956) created a widely used classification of occupations in her book *The Psychology of Occupations;* this exercise will help you understand it.

A. Read the following eight definitions, each of which describes an occupational group. Then look at the eight labels or titles in the box that follows the eight definitions. Your job is to match the titles with the definitions. Write the appropriate title in the blank space to the left of each definition.*

_____   I. These occupations are primarily concerned with serving and attending to the personal tastes, needs, and welfare of other people.

_____   II. These occupations are primarily concerned with the face-to-face sales of commodities, investments, real estate, and services.

_____   III. These are the managerial and white-collar jobs in business, industry, and government: the occupations concerned primarily with the organization and efficient functioning of commercial enterprises and of government activities.

_____   IV. This group includes occupations concerned with the production, maintenance, and transportation of commodities and utilities.

_____   V. This group includes agricultural, fishery, forestry, mining, and related occupations: the occupations primarily concerned with the cultivation, preservation, and gathering of crops, of marine or inland water resources, of mineral resources, of forest products, and of other natural resources, and with animal husbandry.

_____   VI. These are the occupations primarily concerned with scientific theory and its application under specified circumstances, other than technology.

_____   VII. These occupations are primarily concerned with the preservation and transmission of the general cultural heritage.

_____   VIII. These occupations include those primarily concerned with the use of special skills in the creative arts and in entertainment.

Organization	Outdoor	Technology	General Cultural
Arts and Entertainment	Service	Business Contact	Science

*Based on Loughary and Ripley (1974).

B. Put each of the following occupations into one of the eight occupational groups shown in the chart.

Accountant	Laborer	School administrator
Athlete	Law clerk	Social worker
Auctioneer	Lumberjack	Stagehand
Barber	Mechanic	Store owner
Cashier	Newspaper editor	Taxi driver
Designer	Photographer	Teacher
Electrician	Police officer	Technical assistant
Engineer	Public relations adviser	Typist
Farm owner	Racing car driver	U.S. president
Forest ranger	Radio announcer	Veterinarian
Gardener	Research scientist	Waiter/Waitress
Inventive genius	Salesperson	X-ray technician

These eight occupational groups classified by Anne Roe can be linked to the Holland personality/work environment types you studied in Chapter 3 (see Table 4-4).

Service	Business Contact	Organization	Technology
Outdoor	Science	General Cultural	Arts and Entertainment

Table 4-4   Connecting Roe's Classification of Occupational Groups to Holland's Personality/Work Environment Types

Roe's Classification of Occupational Groups	Holland's Personality/Work Environment Types
Service	Social, Realistic
Business contact	Enterprising
Organization	Enterprising, Conventional
Technology	Realistic, Investigative
Outdoor	Realistic, Investigative
Science	Investigative, Realistic
General cultural	Artistic
Arts and entertainment	Artistic

Source: Adapted from R. S. Sharf (2002), p. 471.

C. Dr. Roe adds another dimension to the classification: level of work. It is based on degrees of responsibility and ability called for in the occupation. Roe (1956) identifies the following six levels:

Level 1—*Professional and Managerial: Independent Responsibility*. This level includes innovators, creators, and top managers and administrators. These people make policy or rules for others to follow. They have independent responsibility in important matters. For occupations at this level, there is usually no higher authority except society itself.

Level 2—*Professional and Managerial: 2*. The distinction between this level and Level 1 is primarily one of degree. Some independence is necessary, but there is narrower or less significant responsibility than in Level 1.

Level 3—*Semiprofessional and Small Business*. Several characteristics are suggested here: (a) low-level responsibility for others, (b) application of policy made by others or determination for self only (as in managing a small business), (c) high school education needed, plus technical school or the equivalent.

Level 4—*Skilled*. Skilled occupations require apprenticeship or other special training or experience.

Level 5—*Semiskilled*. Semiskilled occupations require some training and experience but markedly less than the occupations in Level 4. Also, much less independence and initiative are permitted.

Level 6—*Unskilled*. These occupations require no special training or education and not much more ability than is needed to follow simple directions and engage in simple repetitive actions.

After reading these descriptions of the six levels of work, return to the chart in Part B. Assign a level of work to each occupation you put into the groups. Write the appropriate level number after each occupation. (Answers can be found in the Answer Key, placed upside down so you can play fair!) You may have identified a group and level for yourself in Table 1-1 of Chapter 1. Check it now.

Answer Key for Exercise 4-5

VIII. *Arts and Entertainment*	VII. *General Cultural*	VI. *Science*	V. *Outdoor*
Athlete—2	Law clerk—4	Research scientist—1	Farm owner—3
Designer—2	Newspaper editor—2	Technical assistant—4	Forest ranger—3
Photographer—4	Radio announcer—3	X-ray technician—3	Gardener—5
Racing car driver—4	School administrator—1	Veterinarian—2	Lumberjack—6
Stagehand—5	Teacher—2		

IV. *Technology*	III. *Organization*	II. *Business Contact*	I. *Service*
Electrician—4	Accountant—3	Auctioneer—4	Barber—4
Engineer—2	Cashier—4	Public relations adviser—2	Police officer—3
Inventive genius—1	Typist—5	Salesperson—3	Social worker—2
Mechanic—4	U.S. president—1	Store owner—3	Taxi driver—5
Laborer—6			Waiter/Waitress—5

Source: Based on Roe (1956).

EXERCISE 4-6 SELECTING OCCUPATIONAL PROSPECTS TO RESEARCH

By now you may have generated as many as 50 or 100 occupational prospects. Which ones should you most seriously consider for exploration? This exercise presents a way to identify the top 10 or 15 occupations on your prospect list. Four

	Selecting Occupational Prospects to Research	Names of Methods Used to Generate Occupational Prospects												
Titles of Occupational Prospects	*Directions*: Place a check mark for each occupation suggested as a prospect by each method you used.	Remembering	Asking Others	Daydream Analysis	Card Sort	SDS/Occupations Finder	Mich. Occup. Info. Sys.	Career/Occ. Pref. Sys.	OOH	DOT	GOE	SIGI Plus	Occup. View-Deck	Total Number of Check Marks
Science Teacher						✓		✓	✓	✓	✓			5
Veterinarian		✓				✓	✓	✓	✓	✓		✓	✓	8
Veterinarian Assistant		✓	✓	✓	✓									4
Forester				✓				✓	✓	✓	✓			5
Conservation Technician		✓	✓		✓	✓	✓	✓		✓	✓	✓		9
Biologist							✓	✓		✓	✓	✓	✓	6
Farm Manager		✓	✓	✓		✓				✓	✓	✓		7
Biological Photographer			✓				✓	✓		✓	✓			5
Biophysicist							✓			✓	✓			3
Career Counselor							✓							1
Electrical Engineer							✓	✓	✓		✓	✓	✓	6
Clergy/Religious Worker			✓			✓	✓	✓		✓	✓	✓	✓	8
Zoologist					✓			✓	✓	✓		✓	✓	6
Mathematician						✓		✓	✓	✓	✓		✓	6
Computer Applications Engineer			✓				✓	✓		✓	✓			5
Police Detective						✓		✓	✓	✓	✓			5
Engineering Analyst										✓	✓			2
Art Historian								✓		✓	✓			3
Dairy Scientist				✓		✓				✓	✓			4
Travel Agent		✓					✓	✓	✓	✓	✓			6
Occupational Therapist							✓	✓	✓					3
Food Technologist								✓		✓	✓	✓		4
Microbiologist									✓	✓	✓			3
Political Leader		✓	✓	✓	✓	✓				✓	✓	✓	✓	9
Soil Conservationist						✓		✓	✓	✓	✓	✓		6
Agricultural Engineer										✓		✓		2
Tool and Die Maker										✓				1

Figure 4-6   Completed example of Exercise 4-6.

blank forms are provided for your use. Photocopy the forms to make additional copies as needed. A completed example is shown in Figure 4-6.

1. Return to each method in Chapter 3 you used to produce occupational prospects. On the left side of the chart provided in Exercise 4-6, record the titles of all occupations suggested as prospects.
2. At the top of the chart on the right side, fill in the names of all the methods you used to generate occupational prospects. To do this, turn the page and print the names of the methods sideways. Use a short title for each method used, as follows (see Figure 4-6):

    *   Remembering (occupations that attracted you at any time of your life)
    *   Asking others (people who know you well)
    *   Daydream analysis (for occupational content)
    *   Wishing (to do activities related to occupations)
    *   Browsing (through books, files, and pamphlets about occupations)
    *   What needs to be done? (solving social problems)
    *   Career kits and games (record their names)
    *   Card sorts
    *   Computer-based occupational guidance system (record its name, using initials)
    *   Local or state career system (record its name, using initials)
    *   Special family (occupational ideas that come from these special people)
    *   Fantasizing (a typical workday in the future)
    *   Family tree (occupations your family or neighbors have that interest you)
    *   Interest inventories (record their names, using initials) and/or a coding system (such as the Holland codes in the *Occupations Finder*)
    *   OOH *(Occupational Outlook Handbook)*
    *   DOT *(Dictionary of Occupational Titles)*
    *   The O*Net (Occupational Information Network)
    *   GOE *(Guide for Occupational Exploration)*
    *   Other (name):

    _____

3. Take each method you used to generate occupational prospects, and go down the list of occupational prospects. When you come to the title of an occupation suggested by the method, place a check mark in the space where that occupation and that method intersect. Otherwise, leave the space blank to indicate that the occupation was not suggested by the method.
4. Total the number of check marks for each occupational prospect, and write that number in the last column to the right. The more often an occupational prospect has appeared, the more seriously you should consider that occupation. Let's say you have tried 10 methods of generating occupational prospects, and an occupation has appeared 7 times. That occupation certainly merits attention. (This is not meant to imply that an occupational prospect that has appeared only once or twice after using 10 different methods should necessarily be ignored or dropped from your list. It could turn out to be a valid choice for you.)

The average number of occupational prospects generated by over 3,000 of the author's students during a 25-year span has been from 50 to 60 occupations, using an average of 10 methods. If you need to generate more occupational prospects, return to the exercises in Chapter 3; try them again, or try some you may have missed the first time.

Selecting Occupational Prospects to Research

List the titles of all the occupational prospects you have generated in the column on the left. Indicate the methods you used to generate prospects across the top of the chart. Place a check mark for each occupation suggested as a prospect by that method in the appropriate box. Total the number of check marks for each occupational prospect and put that number in the last column. Refer to Figure 4-6 for an example of a completed chart.

Selecting Occupational Prospects to Research	Names of Methods Used to Generate Occupational Prospects											Total Number of Check Marks
Directions: Place a check mark for each occupation suggested as a prospect by each method you used. Titles of Occupational Prospects												

Selecting Occupational Prospects to Research

List the titles of all the occupational prospects you have generated in the column on the left. Indicate the methods you used to generate prospects across the top of the chart. Place a check mark for each occupation suggested as a prospect by that method in the appropriate box. Total the number of check marks for each occupational prospect and put that number in the last column. Refer to Figure 4-6 for an example of a completed chart.

Selecting Occupational Prospects to Research	Names of Methods Used to Generate Occupational Prospects											Total Number of Check Marks
Directions: Place a check mark for each occupation suggested as a prospect by each method you used. Titles of Occupational Prospects												

Selecting Occupational Prospects to Research

List the titles of all the occupational prospects you have generated in the column on the left. Indicate the methods you used to generate prospects across the top of the chart. Place a check mark for each occupation suggested as a prospect by that method in the appropriate box. Total the number of check marks for each occupational prospect and put that number in the last column. Refer to Figure 4-6 for an example of a completed chart.

Selecting Occupational Prospects to Research	Names of Methods Used to Generate Occupational Prospects	Total Number of Check Marks
Directions: Place a check mark for each occupation suggested as a prospect by each method you used. Titles of Occupational Prospects		

Selecting Occupational Prospects to Research

List the titles of all the occupational prospects you have generated in the column on the left. Indicate the methods you used to generate prospects across the top of the chart. Place a check mark for each occupation suggested as a prospect by that method in the appropriate box. Total the number of check marks for each occupational prospect and put that number in the last column. Refer to Figure 4-6 for an example of a completed chart.

Selecting Occupational Prospects to Research	Names of Methods Used to Generate Occupational Prospects												Total Number of Check Marks
Directions: Place a check mark for each occupation suggested as a prospect by each method you used. Titles of Occupational Prospects													

Photocopy this page before writing on it if you need more space.

EXERCISE 4-7 AN OCCUPATIONAL SEARCH REQUIRES OCCUPATIONAL RESEARCH

What do you need to know about your prospective occupations, now that you are aware of them? Listed next are things to consider as you do your research. Notice that the suggested topics for research are the same ones to which you responded on your ideal job description (Exercise 1-1). Compare the real job you research to the ideal job you described back in Chapter 1. Which occupations come closest to your ideal job description?

Nature of the Work
- Why the job exists, needs the occupation serves, purpose of this work
- Job functions performed, major duties and responsibilities involved
- Products made or services provided by this occupation
- Specializations within the occupation
- Equipment, tools, machines, or work aids used in the occupation
- Definition of the occupation (for example, from the DOT)

Education, Training, or Experience Needed
- College or school courses required (or helpful) in preparation
- Previous work experience needed to enter the occupation
- Location of education, training, or work experience
- Length of time and financial costs to obtain the necessary training
- On-the-job training provided by employers

Personal Qualifications, Skills, and Abilities Required
- Abilities, skills, or aptitudes a person should have to enter the occupation
- Physical strength required (lift heavy objects, stand for long periods of time)
- Other physical demands (good vision or hearing, no color blindness, climbing, kneeling, stooping, carrying objects)
- Personal interests (work with data, people, things)
- Special qualities or temperaments (ability to work under pressure, with accuracy, take risks, use logic, do repetitive tasks)
- Standards required (must be able to type 60 words a minute)
- Licensing, certification, or other legal requirements
- Special requirements necessary or helpful (know a foreign language)

Earnings, Salary Range, and Benefits
- Money earned (beginning, average, and top earnings; differences from region to region or city to city)
- Benefits typically offered (pensions, insurance, vacations, sick leave)

Working Conditions
- Physical conditions and hazards (office, factory, outdoors, noise, temperature)
- Work schedule (hours, time of day or night, overtime, seasonal work)
- Opportunities for initiative, creativity, self-management, recognition
- Equipment, supplies, tools to be furnished by the worker
- Union or association membership required as a condition of employment
- Type of supervision or management associated with the occupation
- Dress requirements or clothing preferences of employers
- Travel requirements
- Possible discriminatory practices experienced by workers in the occupation

Location of Employment
- Type of work organizations (companies, institutions, agencies, businesses, industries that employ people in this occupation; self-employment opportunities)
- Geographic areas where the occupation is found (throughout the nation, or in certain regions or cities)

Personality Characteristics of Typical People Working in the Occupation

- Personal traits of people who dominate the environment of the occupation or comprise a significant population in the occupation
- Age range, percentage of males and females, numbers of minority workers

Employment and Advancement Outlook

- Normal methods of entry into the occupation
- Employment trends on the local, state, and national levels
- Advancement or promotion opportunities, career ladder (where do you start and what can you move up to?)
- Average time to become employed after training or education is completed
- Average time to get a promotion or advance to a higher position
- Stability of employment in the occupation

Personal Satisfaction

- Values expressed in or by the occupation (high income, achievement, security, independence, creativity, time for leisure or family, variety, helping others, prestige, recognition). Which of these work values match your values?
- Status of the occupation as seen by others and the community: What do they like and dislike about the occupation?

Advantages and Disadvantages

- Positive features of the occupation: What do you like about it (uses skills that you possess, expresses values that are important to you)?
- Negative features of the occupation: What do you dislike about it? What does the occupation have in it that you would rather avoid?

Related Occupations

- What other occupations are similar to this one?

Sources of Occupational Information

- Where did you obtain information about the occupation? Was it accurate, objective, up-to-date, complete?
- Where can you obtain more information about the occupation?
- Where can you observe this occupation directly?
- Where can you get part-time, co-op, work/study, or temporary employment leading to a job in the occupation?

Worksheet for Occupational Information
Make photocopies for each occupational prospect. Record whatever information you need.

Name of Occupation _____

DOT or SOC Number* _____

Definition of occupation, nature of work, job functions performed

Education, training, experience needed

Personal qualifications, skills, abilities required

Earnings (salary range, benefits)

Working conditions, hours

Location of employment

    a. Work organizations

    b. Geographic areas

Personality characteristics of people in the occupation

Employment and advancement outlook

Personal satisfaction from this work

Advantages and disadvantages of this work

Related occupations

Sources of information

*SOC Number means the number used by the O*Net (SOC = Standard Occupational Classification).

Go to Appendix I: *Worksheets for Occupational Information* to locate more worksheets for occupational information.

SUMMARY

1. Information about occupations is essential in career planning. Ways to get occupational information range from publications (a relatively passive approach) to on-the-job tryouts (an active approach).

2. Government sources of occupational information are the *Occupational Outlook Handbook,* the Occupational Information Network or O*Net, the *Dictionary of Occupational Titles* (scheduled to be replaced by the O*Net), and the *Guide for Occupational Exploration.* Other printed sources include government and commercial books, pamphlets, and audiovisual materials. This material is usually factual and objective.

3. You encounter emotional and subjective information about occupations as you talk to people about their jobs. These important aspects of working are difficult to learn any other way. Talking with people ranges from formal interviews to casual conversations.

4. Several computer-assisted career guidance programs such as Discover and SIGI Plus are available. Nowadays, you are more and more likely to use computer technology as a method of obtaining occupational information.

5. Occupational information is increasingly found by way of the Internet and the World Wide Web.

6. Novels, biographies, and nonfiction books can give you interesting, but sometimes subjective, accounts of various aspects of occupations.

7. Information on local employment opportunities can come from community surveys, computer-based guidance systems, branch offices of your state employment service, college follow-up studies, *County Business Patterns,* area wage surveys, business directories, help-wanted ads in newspapers, personal contacts, and informational interviews.

8. Career resource centers contain a wealth of materials and services. Plan to use career centers and libraries often in your career planning.

9. As you read, hear, and view occupational information, keep in mind several considerations about the material: its accuracy, timeliness, objectivity, completeness, and readability.

10. The only way to understand the immense world of work is to classify it. Classification systems divide the world of work into groups of related occupations. The big books of occupational information—the *Occupational Outlook Handbook* (OOH), the *Dictionary of Occupational Titles* (DOT), the *O*Net DOT,* and the *Guide for Occupational Exploration* (GOE)—are organized according to their own classification systems. Another occupational classification system, one originated by Dr. Anne Roe, was discussed in this chapter.

11. Exercises can help you identify and use the parts of the OOH, DOT, O*Net, and GOE that interest you most. The exercises give you a glimpse of the immense complexity of the world of work while allowing you to focus on the parts to explore for occupational prospects and information.

12. After finding a number of occupational prospects, consolidate all your prospects into one list and select the most attractive occupations to research. For your exploration of these occupations, gather and analyze information on a number of topics pertinent to each occupational prospect, using the worksheet provided in this chapter.

REFERENCES

Baer, M. F., and Roeber, E. 1964. *Occupational information: The dynamics of its nature and use.* Chicago: Science Research Associates.

Bounds, S., and Karl, A. 1996. *How to get your dream job using the Internet.* Scottsdale, AZ: Coriolis Group Books.

Ettinger, J. M., ed. 1996. *Improved career decision making in a changing world,* 2nd ed. Garrett Park, MD: Garrett Park Press.

Farr, J. M., ed. 1993. *Complete guide for occupational exploration.* Indianapolis: JIST Works.

Farr, J. M., Ludden, L. L., and Shatkin, L. 2001. *The guide for occupational exploration,* 3rd ed. Indianapolis: JIST Works.

Farr, J. M., and Ludden, L. L., with Shatkin L. 2002. *The O*Net Dictionary of Occupational Titles,* 2nd ed. Indianapolis: JIST Works.

Fine, S. 1973. *Functional job analysis scales: A desk aid.* Kalamazoo, MI: W.E. Upjohn Institute for Employment Research.

Haebich, K. A. 1962. *Vocations in biography and fiction.* Chicago: American Library Association.

Haga, D., and Klauda, P. 1989. *No retreat, no surrender: Labor's war at Hormel.* New York: Morrow.

Harrington, T., and O'Shea, A., eds. 1984. *Guide for occupational exploration,* 2nd ed. Circle Pines, MN: American Guidance Service.

Harris-Bowlsbey, J. 1998. *Using DISCOVER to its fullest: A workshop offered by the ACT Center for the enhancement of educational practices.* Iowa City, IA: ACT.

Hecker, D. E. 2004, February. Occupational projections to 2012. *Monthly Labor Review,* 127(2), 51.

Hoppock, R. 1976. *Occupational information,* 4th ed. New York: McGraw-Hill.

Isaacson, L. E. 1977. *Career information in counseling and teaching,* 3rd ed. Boston: Allyn and Bacon.

Isaacson, L. E., and Brown, D. 1997. *Career information, career counseling, and career development,* 6th ed. Boston: Allyn and Bacon.

Kestler, D., and Ciaston, C. J., eds. 2002. *Career information center,* 8th ed. New York: Macmillan.

Loughary, J., and Ripley, T. 1974. *This isn't quite what I had in mind.* Eugene, OR: United Learning Corporation.

Mariani, M. 1998, Summer. Job shadowing for college students. *Occupational Outlook Quarterly,* 42(2), 46–49.

Mariani, M. 1999, Spring. Replace with a database: O*Net replaces the Dictionary of Occupational Titles. *Occupational Outlook Quarterly,* 43(1), 2–9.

Mariani, M. 2001, Fall. O*Net update. *Occupational Outlook Quarterly,* 45(3), 26–27.

Maze, M., and Mayall, D. 1995. *Enhanced guide for occupational exploration,* 2nd ed. Indianapolis: JIST Works.

McKee, W. L., and Froeschle, R. C. 1985. *Where the jobs are: Identification and analysis of local employment opportunities.* Kalamazoo, MI: W.E. Upjohn Institute for Employment Research.

Miller, E. B. 1998. *The Internet resource directory for K–12 teachers and librarians.* Englewood, CO: Libraries Unlimited.

Morkes, A., ed. 2002. *Encyclopedia of careers and vocational guidance,* 12th ed. Chicago: J. G. Ferguson.

Norris, W., Hatch, R., Engelkes, J., and Winborn, B. 1979. *The career information service,* 4th ed. Chicago: Rand McNally.

Pethokoukis, J. M., Marek, A. C., Perry, J., Barnett, M., Andrews, P., Clark, K., and Loftus, M. 2004. Jobs with staying power . . . and those with far less promise. *U.S. News & World Report,* 136(8), 66–72.

Reich, R. B. 1998. *Locked in the cabinet.* New York: Vintage Books.

Roe, A. 1956. *The psychology of occupations.* New York: Wiley.

Sharf, R. S. 2002. *Applying career development theory to counseling.* Pacific Grove, CA: Brooks/Cole.

Shertzer, B. 1985. *Career planning: Freedom to choose.* Boston: Houghton Mifflin.

Super, D. E. 1990. A life span, life space approach to career development. In D. Brown, L. Brooks, and Associates, *Career choice and development,* 2nd ed., pp. 197–261. San Francisco: Jossey-Bass.

Terkel, S. 1972. *Working: People talk about what they do all day and how they feel about what they do.* New York: Pantheon.

U.S. Department of Labor. 1979. *Guide for occupational exploration.* Washington, DC: U.S. Government Printing Office.

U.S. Department of Labor. 1991. *Dictionary of occupational titles,* 4th ed., rev. Washington, DC: U.S. Government Printing Office.

U.S. Department of Labor. 2002. *Occupational outlook handbook, 2002–03.* Washington, DC: U.S. Government Printing Office.

Chapter 5

Motivation and Achievement

The subject of this chapter—motivation and achievement—is one that could be easily slighted or ignored. However, whenever you think about it, motivation is important. *Without motivation, not much, if anything, gets done*—unless you are forcibly driven to do an activity by someone or something *outside* of yourself. The best motivation is an *inner desire* to achieve goals and purposes you have set for yourself. Thinking about your achievements and what you want to accomplish is key to the enthusiasms that make life worth living. The "germs" of your enthusiasms are infectious; they provide the energy by which you achieve your goals.

Until now, you have focused on your interests, using them to discover sectors in the world of work that attract you and to develop occupational prospects to explore. At this point, you begin to examine your needs—specifically, your need to achieve. Achievement involves setting goals and producing the energy to accomplish them. In the chapters to follow, you will investigate more deeply the nature of your abilities and work values, subjects that are at the heart of the career decision-making process. Interests, goals, motivation, achievements, abilities, and values are clues to a career "mystery" that you are trying to solve. Your "detective work" now concentrates on motives and achievements.

This chapter starts with setting goals. First, learn how to conceive of a goal in your mind and write it in words on paper. Next, you can practice setting and attempting to achieve a short-term goal. Later, you can transfer what you have learned to a longer-term career goal, which will give purpose and direction to your studies in school or college. More people give up on higher education because they don't have a clear goal than for any other reason.

A career goal by itself, however, means little if there isn't the energy, the drive, and the persistence—the motivation—to move toward your goal. You are likely to set a challenging goal, and you will need to strengthen the motive to achieve it. This chapter can teach you achievement thoughts you can use to consciously increase your achievement motivation, and this is absolutely necessary for completing any goal you set for yourself.

Success stories abound. If you read some of them, you will discover that high achievers know the anguish of defeat and failure as well as the thrill of victory and success. When they fail, achievers don't give up; they keep coming back, setting new goals and reaching deep for the energy and the motivation to achieve them (read Bill Lundberg's achievement story in this chapter). But the important thing is eventually to write your own achievement story—the accomplishment of your own career goal.

Achievement is not only about the future. You've had plenty of achievements already, probably hundreds of them. To get as far as you have come in life, you have had to achieve. There are a few exercises for you to do in this chapter. One is to identify as many achievements as possible, large and small, in all parts of your life; a second exercise may help you identify more achievements. Another exercise involves collecting documents, papers, and objects that support your claims of achievement and putting them in a file called a *portfolio*, which can be a great help when you apply for a job, a scholarship, or admission to a college. Knowing your achievements (this chapter) and your abilities (the subject of the next chapter) will become increasingly important as you use them to make career decisions, to convince employers of your worth, and to build your self-esteem.

GOALS, MOTIVES, AND NEEDS

Think back to a time when you really exerted yourself to get something done. You stayed up most of the night to complete a project or were so involved in an activity that you never noticed the hours ticking by. Recall the inner drive that pushed you to complete your objective. Remember the satisfaction you felt when you finished; you were tired, but you had a good feeling of accomplishment. You may even have experienced a sense of relaxation, knowing that your hard work was over for the time being and that you had done something of real worth.

While this memory is fresh, get a piece of paper and write about that experience. Describe the thoughts you had and the actions you took at the time. Did you receive praise or recognition from others, overcome obstacles, risk failure, seek help, or anticipate success? Put all these details into your story. Transform the memory of your experience into words; it will be valuable to you later.

Goals

This chapter is about goals and the drive to achieve them. A goal is any achievement toward which you direct your efforts. You set all kinds of goals in life, consciously or unconsciously. Some goals are long term, involving the broad expanse of life; career goals can fall into this category. Short-term goals usually cover a few days to a month. Intermediate goals often last from a month to a year. Short-term and intermediate goals often mark stages in a long-term career goal. Mini-goals are objectives you set for a particular day or part of a day, such as working through a list of things you want to accomplish. Mini-goals are important as small steps toward a larger goal. As an old adage says, "A journey of a thousand miles begins with a single step."

Some people never seem to get started with those first steps—perhaps because they do not have a goal in mind. *Why* do you go to college? To achieve something worthwhile? To live a more meaningful life? To get a better job? To discover the truth? To develop new skills? To make new friends? Some students are not sure why they are in college. They may not know what else to do, they attend to please someone else, or they don't quite feel up to the rigors of the working world. These are the students who most need a goal to strive toward. The most common cause of failure in college is not lack of ability, it is the failure to establish a purpose for being there. Your objective in career planning is to reach a decision (even if only a tentative one) about a career goal, which can help you determine your educational goal. Your success on the job, in school, and in much of life depends on your ability to set goals. However, frustration can set in if you do not have the energy and the drive to reach your goals. Something is necessary to get started toward accomplishing a goal. That "something" is motivation.

Motives

Motivation is an internal process that compels you to act in a purposeful way. The word comes from a Latin root meaning "movement." Motives move you to action and drive you toward a goal.

Because motives are inner drives, you can't see them. You can only make an inference that motives cause certain kinds of behavior. When you see a person eating, you may assume the motive behind the action is a need to reduce hunger. Behavior is not that simple, however—the motive that causes a person to eat could be compensation for loneliness or escape from boredom. When you consider more complicated actions such as searching for a career, assessing motives is even more difficult.

There is a relationship between motivation and goals. Your motivation is likely to be stronger when you have a goal. Think of a time when you had to get something done, perhaps something you didn't particularly want to do. You accomplished the task because you had a goal to achieve. Your motivation increases when you focus your energies.

Needs

Motives develop from needs. Needs are requirements for your survival or growth; they have a lot to do with your physical and psychological health. Having your needs satisfied prevents and cures illnesses, and inability to satisfy your needs can produce illness. A famous psychologist, Abraham Maslow, has suggested that everything you do in life is for the purpose of satisfying your needs. Maslow proposed, based on his research, five basic need levels that are common to all human beings. Needs on the lowest level must be mostly filled before you can move on to the next higher level of needs.

Level 1: Physiological Needs. The most basic human needs are for food, water, sleep, air, warmth, elimination, physical activity, sex, sensory stimulation, and so on. The purpose of these first-level needs is to enable you to survive physically. The survival-oriented person is chronically unfulfilled in trying to satisfy the physiological needs. If you are constantly hungry, thirsty, or deprived of sleep, most of your behavior will be directed toward satisfying Level 1 needs. A baby is at Level 1 in Maslow's hierarchy, complaining loudly whenever the physiological needs are not met. The poor often battle to survive at a physiological level.

Level 2: Safety Needs. Next, people need to live in an environment that is secure, orderly, consistent, dependable, predictable, protected, and free from fear and anxiety. The purpose of these second-level needs is to obtain physical and psychological security. The Level 2 individual is a security-oriented person who is relatively well satisfied physiologically, but unfulfilled in terms of the safety needs. If you are at Level 2, most of your behavior is concerned with law and order, feeling secure in a structured environment, developing financial security, and the like. (Think of the large number of occupations that respond to Level 1 and 2 needs. Agriculture, the food distribution industry, and restaurants depend on the need for food. The hotel and motel business relies on the need for sleep. Police and fire departments and the defense establishment depend on safety needs.)

Level 3: Relationship Needs. Maslow calls them *love and belongingness needs:* the needs to receive acceptance and affection from others and to give love and affection to others. The purpose of these third-level needs is to develop social relationships with other people. The Level 3 individual is an affiliation-oriented person. Having satisfied many of the physiological and safety needs, a Level 3 person directs much attention toward companionship and social interaction because of feeling unfulfilled in terms of these social needs.

Level 4: Esteem Needs. At the fourth level, people have a need for respect from others in the form of attention, appreciation, recognition, or status, and for self-respect based on feelings of competence, achievement, mastery, and independence. Satisfaction of Level 4 needs builds self-esteem and a sense of self-worth. An achievement-oriented person is reasonably well satisfied as to physiological, safety, and affiliation needs, so he or she directs much attention toward achieving goals, becoming proficient and skillful, seeking recognition, getting good grades in school or advancing in an occupation, and becoming independent and self-directed. This is the level with which we are most concerned in career planning.

Level 5: Self-Actualization Needs. At the top of Maslow's hierarchy are the needs to develop your highest potential, to realize your talents and abilities, to fulfill your mission in life, and to achieve unity and integration within your own personality. Only when you are reasonably well satisfied in meeting your needs on the first four levels can you function in a self-actualizing manner. Maslow describes the self-actualizing person as having a superior perception of reality; a greater acceptance of self, others, and nature; spontaneity; the ability to focus on problems outside of self; increased detachment and desire for privacy; a high degree of autonomy; greater freshness of appreciation and richness of emotional expression; a higher number of "peak" or mystical experiences; charitable feelings toward all humankind; close relationships with a few friends or loved ones; a democratic character structure; a strong ethical sense; an unhostile sense of humor and creativeness; and an objective attitude toward his or her own culture (Maslow, 1970).

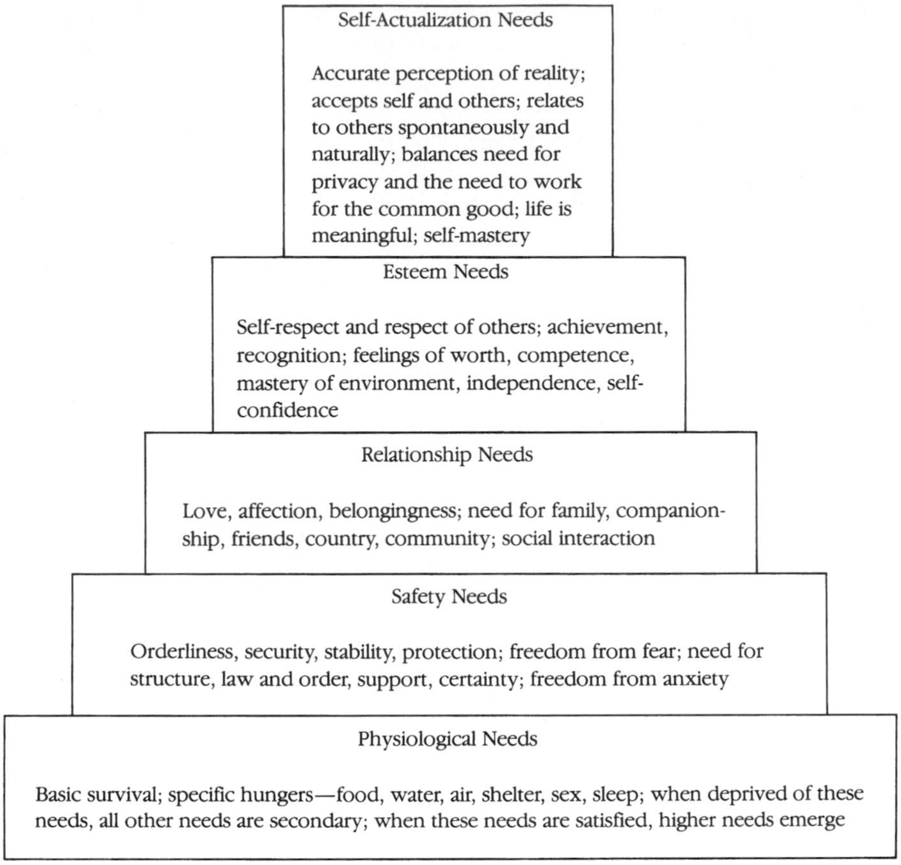

```
Self-Actualization Needs

Accurate perception of reality;
accepts self and others; relates
to others spontaneously and
naturally; balances need for
privacy and the need to work
for the common good; life is
meaningful; self-mastery
```

```
Esteem Needs

Self-respect and respect of others; achievement,
recognition; feelings of worth, competence,
mastery of environment, independence, self-
confidence
```

```
Relationship Needs

Love, affection, belongingness; need for family, companion-
ship, friends, country, community; social interaction
```

```
Safety Needs

Orderliness, security, stability, protection; freedom from fear; need for
structure, law and order, support, certainty; freedom from anxiety
```

```
Physiological Needs

Basic survival; specific hungers—food, water, air, shelter, sex, sleep; when deprived of these
needs, all other needs are secondary; when these needs are satisfied, higher needs emerge
```

Figure 5-1 Maslow's hierarchy of needs

Personal growth, as Maslow sees it, is progressive satisfaction of the needs in the hierarchy and movement toward self-actualization (see Figure 5-1). As more needs at a given level are fulfilled, the next need level begins to emerge, and you are motivated to seek satisfaction of those needs. Other need levels may press into awareness at any given time, but one need level tends to predominate. Movement through the needs hierarchy is not steady or automatic; you can move back to a lower level. Maslow has developed a powerful set of concepts with which to explain behavior. One question you can ask yourself right now is this: *At which level am I directing much of my current behavior?* Go back through the descriptions of the need levels you have just read. Assess how much of your conscious attention you give to each of these levels. For example, a Level 4 person could divide consciousness this way: Level 1, 5 percent; Level 2, 10 percent; Level 3, 15 percent; Level 4, 65 percent; Level 5, 5 percent (see Figure 5-2).

Teachers assume their students are operating primarily on Maslow's Level 4 (the esteem level). This level has the most to do with achievement and gaining competence and mastery in school subjects. However, this assumption may not be well founded. You may have had an argument with a loved one, so that your attention is directed toward your relationship needs and away from achievement in school. If you are ravenously hungry, you are not likely to concentrate on your studies. When your physical, safety, and relationship needs are relatively well satisfied, you are more likely to direct your attention to your studies.

Another list of needs comes from Allen Edwards, who constructed the Edwards Personal Preference Schedule (EPPS). By taking and scoring the EPPS, you can obtain a measure of the strength of 15 social needs or motives in your own personality. The *EPPS Manual* (Edwards, 1959) describes these 15 needs:

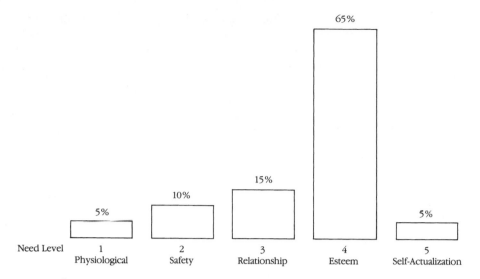

Figure 5-2   Appearance of need levels in a person at Level 4

1. Achievement (to do one's best and be successful)
2. Deference (to defer to the judgment and leadership of others)
3. Order (to have things neat and organized)
4. Exhibition (to have attention focused on you)
5. Autonomy (to be free and independent)
6. Affiliation (to have friendships)
7. Intraception (to analyze and understand the motives and feelings of oneself and others)
8. Succorance (to receive help when needed)
9. Dominance (to persuade and influence others)
10. Abasement (to feel guilty and depressed when things go wrong)
11. Nurturance (to help others when they need it)
12. Change (to do new and different things in the daily routine)
13. Endurance (to keep at a job or activity until completed)
14. Heterosexuality (to engage in social activities with the opposite sex)
15. Aggression (to attack contrary points of view or blame others when things go wrong)

Do any of these needs explain your behavior? In career planning, an assessment of needs can reveal your motives for entering a particular occupation.

SETTING GOALS

The first exercise directs you to practice setting goals by establishing a short-term goal for yourself. Before doing the exercise, read the following eight guidelines, called the "ABCs of Goal Setting" (adapted from Peterson, 1972). Your goal must be achievable (*A*), believable (*B*), controllable (*C*), definable (*D*), explicit (*E*), for yourself (*F*), growth-facilitating (*G*), and quantifiable (*Q*).

A. *Achievable* (or *attainable*) means that you can realistically accomplish the goal, considering the nature of your abilities and aptitudes. If you are 50 years old, weigh 200 pounds, lead a sedentary life, and set a goal of running a four-minute mile after two weeks of training, this goal is simply not achievable.

B. *Believable* suggests that you truly believe you can accomplish the goal and have confidence in your ability to reach it within the time you have allotted. High achievers push themselves by setting challenging goals, but their goals are never so difficult that they lose their self-confidence or the "believability" of their goals.

C. *Controllable* refers to your ability to control the factors that affect and influence the outcome of your goal. The way you express your goal is particularly important here. You might say, "My goal is to land a job at the XYZ Company." However, stating your goal this way violates the guideline of controllability; it does not recognize the possibility of your being turned down. "My goal is to apply for a position at the XYZ Company by next Wednesday" is an acceptable goal statement because you can control the factors involved. Depending on other people to help you achieve your goal runs the risk of ignoring the "controllability" principle of goal setting. If your goal involves other people, you need to enlist their cooperation by asking them to be involved in it.

D. *Definable* means that your goal is expressed in language, spoken or written, that can be understood by everyone. A long-term goal must be carefully worded so you can divide it into a series of steps, or short-term goals. Sometimes you will have difficulty expressing a goal because it requires translating a vague feeling into a specific, clear statement.

E. *Explicit* means that you state a specific goal and concentrate on one goal at a time. Again, this guideline requires the careful use of language. You might, for example, state a goal of "decorating a room." That's fine, but what does "decorating" mean—painting, repairing, rearranging, buying new furniture, wallpapering, cleaning, all of these, one of these, something else? The danger in not concentrating on one goal at a time is that you are likely to establish alternatives, then approach your deadline without having done any of them.

F. *For yourself* indicates that your goal is something *you* really want to do; it is not imposed on you by someone else. Of course, some things in life you must do whether you want to or not, but there should be substantial portions of your life where you choose to do the things you want to do. If a teacher has assigned you 50 pages in a textbook, you cannot claim it as your own goal unless reading the 50 pages is an activity you would consciously choose for yourself whether the teacher assigned it or not.

G. *Growth facilitating* means that your goal is not injurious or destructive to yourself or anyone else. A person could set a goal of smashing 10 store windows by 1 A.M. and meet all the criteria of goal setting except this one. Adolf Hitler had goals and successfully reached many of them in the 1930s and early 1940s, but few of them were growth facilitating.

Q. *Quantifiable* means that your goal is expressed in such a way that it can be measured—in numeric terms, if possible, rather than in broad, general, vague, or abstract terms. It is not enough to say, "I'll work harder on my tennis game" or "My goal is to use time better." How can you measure "harder" and "better"? You need to express your goal in measurable terms, such as "My goal is to write seven pages of my report by 11 P.M. next Tuesday." When next Tuesday night comes, you will know whether you have achieved your goal, because you have used measurable units—time and quantity—in setting your goal. You need a measurable standard of success or failure to evaluate your goal properly. Then you can keep the goal for another time, change a part of it, or replace it completely if necessary.

Stating your goal in measurable terms allows you to keep a behavioral count of your progress toward a goal. For example, in order to "become a more outgoing person" you might set a goal of starting at least three 2-minute conversations with people you don't know on each of the next 10 days. You could keep a record of your goal this way:

Number of Two-Minute Conversations

Day 1	Day 2	Day 3	Day 4	Day 5	Day 6	Day 7	Day 8	Day 9	Day 10
___	___	___	___	___	___	___	___	___	___

Some goals seem hard to quantify. Take the goal of being a better parent or student. The goal is expressed in words that are too vague. Think of specific actions you can perform to achieve your broad, general goal. One specific action might be similar to the goal mentioned in the previous paragraph: having at least three 2-minute conversations or activities with your child on each of the next 10 days, or getting help from a teacher or a tutor at least three times over a 10-day period. Notice that target dates are set in these examples. A target date not only helps you to make goals specific and measurable, it increases your motivation and commitment to the goal as well. More examples are given in the box.

Setting Measurable Goals

Too vague:

My goal is to . . .

. . . work harder on my homework.

. . . get more exercise every day.

. . . sell more magazine subscriptions.

. . . do better in my tennis game.

. . . lose some weight.

Much better:

My goal is to . . .

. . . read at least 12 pages per day in my history book to total at least 60 pages by next Sunday at 10 P.M.

. . . walk a three-mile distance within 45 minutes each day for the next two weeks.

. . . sell 30 magazine subscriptions by this time next week.

. . . place 40 or 50 practice serves into correct service zone on the tennis court each day for the next week.

. . . lose 5 pounds by _____. (date)

Now set your own short-term goal in Exercise 5-1.

EXERCISE 5-1 SHORT-TERM GOAL-SETTING EXERCISE

State a short-term goal that you would like to achieve within the next two weeks. Use the goal-setting guidelines in conceiving your goal.

_____

_____

_____

Give the exact date by which you plan to achieve your goal: _____

On a separate sheet of paper, explain why and how your goal is achievable, believable, controllable, explicit, for yourself, growth facilitating, and quantifiable.

After the date you set for achieving this goal, answer the following questions: Did you achieve your goal? Why or why not? Explain, using the goal-setting guidelines.

_____

_____

_____

An Example of an Experience with the Short-Term Goal-Setting Exercise

I gave myself two weeks to accomplish a short-term goal, which was to increase my children's self-esteem by showing approval of the good things they do. My career-planning teacher said my goal was a nice idea, but how could I measure it? So, it was back to the drawing board! Then, my goal became praising each child for an accomplishment at least once a day for the next 14 days. Since I would be with my children during that time, this goal was achievable. Furthermore, I truly believed I could reach the goal because there is always something positive to focus on, even if it's a bad day. I can control my thoughts and speech. I am putting the goal into words, so it's definable. I explicitly made it a point to talk with each child at lunch or dinner or just before bed and focus on some thought or action of theirs that was praiseworthy. While compliments are rewards I can give them, this goal was definitely for me. My actions were certainly growth facilitating—no question about it. To make my goal measurable, I kept a tally sheet of my actions. I listed each day I worked on my goal with the names of my children at the top of the page. There was a space to tally where dates and names intersected.

Did I achieve my goal? No—although I came close. Most of the eight guidelines were followed, but I found there were some things that were not controllable. For example, I missed a couple of days when the grandparents invited the kids for a visit over a weekend and I didn't want to deprive them of that. Another time, I was simply too tired and forgot; by the time I remembered, the children were asleep. Despite these lapses, I believe my overall goal of increased self-esteem within each child is a step closer to being achieved. Maybe my short-term goal of giving praise each day was not really achievable. Perhaps I should be more realistic and change my goal to expressing praise for 10 of the next 14 days. (Adapted with permission from Sharon Ficek)

Although Sharon did not achieve her specific, measurable short-term goal, she is closer to achieving it than if she had not set the goal in the first place. Failure to reach a goal is often a greater learning experience than success, and there is no reason why we cannot use that experience to change our original goals and make them more realistic.

ACHIEVEMENT MOTIVATION

To reach any goal, you must have achievement motivation—the need to accomplish that goal. Achievement motivation is perhaps the most thoroughly researched of all the social motives. It is defined by David C. McClelland, a well-known researcher in this field, as performance in terms of a standard of excellence, or a desire to be successful. McClelland's idea is that achievement motivation can be learned and used to improve one's performance (McClelland, 1961). People with a strong need to achieve are energized individuals, learn certain tasks and solve problems faster than others, are well aware of achievement opportunities, seek out challenging and moderately difficult tasks, want feedback in order to know how well they are doing, want control over situations, don't like to gamble or rely solely on luck, and take personal responsibility for outcomes, even for failure (McClelland, 1972). How strong is your need to achieve? How could you measure the strength of your achievement motivation? One method devised by McClelland and his associates is to flash pictures on a screen and ask people to write a story about them guided by several questions. The story is then scored for achievement content.

J. W. Atkinson, another psychologist who has done extensive studies of achievement motivation, gives an example of a story that reveals a strong achievement theme. The picture shows a young boy with an indistinct scene of an operating room in the background.

This young boy is dreaming of the day he will have completed his training and become a great and famous doctor. Perhaps this portrays someone already famous for research. He has been asked by his father or relative what he wants to do when he grows up, and he is trying to tell them the mental picture that he has in his mind of himself in thirty years. The boy is thinking of the great thrill that must be experienced by a doctor when he performs a delicate operation saving someone's life. The boy will go on through college and eventually become a world-famous doctor. (Atkinson, 1958)

The story is judged for the number of achievement themes in it. In this case, the writer expresses a strong need to achieve. The story is a fantasy, but it expresses an inner need. When asked directly about achievement, a person might deny a need to achieve, yet reveal that need in fantasy. Other stories might emphasize ideas that do not involve achievement, such as fear of a medical operation or guilt feelings about the person who was injured.

People who have a high need to achieve learn and perform better than those with low achievement motivation. However, don't take it for granted that high achievers will do better on everything they try. They are not likely to do well on a task where there is no challenge. Achievement motivation has been described as a

> . . . restless, driving energy aimed at attaining excellence, getting ahead, improving on past records, beating competitors, doing things faster, better, more efficiently, and finding unique solutions to difficult problems. People with strong achievement motivation generally are self-confident individuals who are at their best taking personal responsibility in situations where they can control what happens to them. They set challenging goals demanding maximum effort, but goals which are possible to attain; they are not satisfied with automatic success that comes from easy goals, nor do they try to do the impossible. Time rushes by them and causes mild anxiety that there won't be enough hours to get things done. As a result, they make more accurate long-range plans than people with less achievement motivation. They like to get regular, concrete feedback on how well they are doing so that their plans can be modified accordingly. They take pride in their accomplishments and get pleasure from striving for the challenging goals of excellence they set. (Alshuler, Tabor, and McIntyre, 1971, p. 6)

McClelland believes that achievement motivation characterizes entrepreneurs—the organizers, risk takers, and economic builders of a country. The idea that entrepreneurs are motivated only by profit runs counter to McClelland's theory; the entrepreneur puts money back into the business for research, improvement, and expansion. This idea was expressed by Ray Kroc, the millionaire who turned the original McDonald's one-spot hamburger stand into a worldwide business: "I have never worshiped money and I have never worked for money. I worked for pride and accomplishment. Money can become a nuisance. It's a hell of a lot more fun chasin' it than gettin' it. The fun is in the race" (Halberstam, 1994, p. 172). Achievement motivation doesn't operate only in competitive, capitalist economies; managers in countries where the economy is controlled by the government score as high on McClelland's tests for achievement motivation as their counterparts in free enterprise countries. Entrepreneurs are motivated primarily by an inner drive to get things done. Income and productivity may serve as symbols of competence and success, but they are external reflections of an inner need for achievement, a motive to succeed because of the nature of the activity. *The most important rewards are in the work itself.*

You can appreciate the importance of achievement motivation for career planning. If you do not have the need to achieve in some degree, you are not going to accomplish your career goals. The achievement motive energizes you; it provides you with the power to reach your goals. For career planning, then, achievement motivation can be described as *the power, drive, and energy needed to accomplish a career goal once it has been established.* Establishing a career goal is the subject of this book; providing the necessary energy to achieve that goal is within your control. Your job now is to strengthen your own need to achieve. That strengthening will come if you can clearly perceive the achievement motive in your mind. The next exercise can help you strengthen achievement motivation within yourself. Your teacher or counselor may suggest other exercises for you.

EXERCISE 5-2 EXERCISES IN IMAGINATION

In this exercise, you will look at a picture, then make up and write a brief, imaginative story. The idea is to use your imagination and show how you can create ideas and situations by yourself. There is no "right" or "wrong" story. Any kind of story is all right, as long as it truly reflects what you think about the picture.

To help you cover all the parts of a story, consider these questions: (1) What is happening? Who are the people? (2) What has led up to this situation—that is, what has happened in the past? (3) What will happen? What will be done? (4) What is being thought? What is wanted? By whom? These questions are only guides for your thinking and writing; you need not answer each question specifically. Your story should be continuous, not just a set of answers to these questions. Make your story interesting and dramatic. Instead of just describing the illustration, write a vivid story about it.

Now look at the illustration shown here, and write the story that the picture suggests to you. Do not be concerned that the situation is not well defined; simply write about whatever you think is happening, has happened, and is going to happen in this situation. Do not read further until you have written your story.

_____

_____

_____

_____

_____

Scoring Your Story

Next you are going to score your story. This may surprise you, because you weren't given any instructions on how to write the story. The idea was to let you establish a base rate of your usual way of thinking. The standards you will use to score your story are 10 achievement thoughts. After you have learned to recognize these, you will use them in other stories you will be asked to write about other pictures.

Were there any achievement thoughts in the story you have just written? Look for phrases that express achievement, and check off any of the following achievement thoughts you find.

_____ *Achievement imagery (AIm)*. Did your story contain achievement imagery? It did if achievement was the central theme of the story, not just a secondary or minor part of your narrative. Did any of your characters try to accomplish something at a high level of excellence? Did anyone talk about doing well, improving, getting better, winning, or setting a record? A story has achievement imagery whenever it shows people competing with others (CO), in competition with a self-made standard or with their own past performance (CS), trying for a unique accomplishment (UA), or developing their skills through some long-term involvement (LTI). Each of these four types of AIm reflects the goal of striving for excellence (Alshuler, Tabor, and McIntyre, 1971). AIm is the most important of the 10 achievement thoughts, because without achievement imagery there is no achievement motivation.

_____ *Need (N)*. Did anyone in your story deeply want to achieve something? ("He wants to be an engineer.")

_____ *Action (ACT)*. Did any of your characters make any plans or take any action toward achieving a goal with a high degree of excellence? ("She studied for five hours and then did very well on her test.")

_____ *Hope of success (HOS)*. Did any character expect success before a goal could be reached, thinking about what success would be like when a goal was achieved? ("He anticipates that his invention will make him famous.")

_____ *Fear of failure (FOF)*. Did anyone express worry about failing before it could happen, thinking about what failure to reach a goal would be like? ("She was afraid she would fail despite her hard work.")

_____ *Success feelings (SF)*. Did anyone in your story express good feelings of happiness and elation after succeeding at something? ("She feels elated that she won.")

_____ *Failure feelings (FF)*. Did anyone express bad or critical feelings after failing to reach a goal? ("He blamed himself for the mistake.")

_____ *World obstacle (WO)*. Did some environmental obstacle interfere with the possible success of any of your characters? ("He doesn't have the right tools to do the job.")

_____ *Personal obstacle (PO).* Did an internal barrier or a personal, physical, or mental shortcoming keep any of your characters from succeeding? ("She didn't have the ability to do it.")

_____ *Help (H).* Did anyone in your story seek help from an expert in order to achieve successfully? ("The instructor gave her advice on how to do a better job.")

Now give yourself one point for each type of achievement thought found in your story, for a maximum of 10 points. How many points did you score? _____

A little reflection may help you understand why these elements are achievement thoughts. You may wonder why fear of failure (FOF) is an achievement thought. Unless the fear is so severe that it paralyzes you, worrying about failure can motivate you just as much as anticipating success (HOS), maybe even more so. Remembering the bad feelings (FF) you had after failing to reach a goal can make you more determined not to fail again. Recognizing both internal and external obstacles (PO, WO) that can get in the way of success will motivate you to overcome them. Getting help (H) from someone who knows more about a subject than you do is typical behavior for high achievers. Those with low achievement motivation often feel too embarrassed to ask for help.

The following is a model of an imaginative story with a high score in achievement motivation. Notice how you can use abbreviations to represent the 10 achievement thoughts. Compare the story you have just written to the model, which was created in response to the picture presented to you.

> The people are trainees. Their goal is to complete a one-year training program and compete successfully in the job world after that. [AIm] They want to be the very best they can be in their work. [N] They have dropped out of school in the past and have been unable to obtain good jobs because of their lack of training and skills. [PO] They have run into prejudices by employers when trying to get well-paid jobs. [WO] They know what it is like to fail, because they have experienced failure on several occasions. [FF] Sometimes they are afraid they are going to fail in the new program also. [FOF] The instructor is interested in the students, encourages them, and supports them in their efforts. [H] They are listening to the instructor very closely, asking questions, and trying very hard to understand every detail of the teaching. [ACT] The trainees are starting to feel proud about learning some new skills. [SF] They often imagine what it will feel like to complete the training program successfully. [HOS] Because of their efforts, these students will complete the program, become highly skilled in their work, and serve as examples for others like them. [AIm]*

Unless you naturally think in terms of achievement, your story (like that of the author when he first wrote one) probably scored quite a bit lower than this one. From now on, consciously insert as many achievement thoughts into your stories as you can. You can compose more achievement stories for the pictures in this chapter and use pictures you find in newspapers, magazines, and billboards. You can even create stories to reflect images that appear in your mind or on videos and television. If writing achievement stories takes too much time, practice thinking the achievement thoughts as you make up a story. You can also dictate a story into a tape recorder and then go back to label the achievement thoughts. As you practice composing these stories using the achievement thoughts, your need to achieve will strengthen. At first, creating achievement stories and using the 10 thoughts may seem artificial, but before long, thinking in achieving terms will become more natural, a regular part of your life.

Source: Story and picture based on an achievement motivation workshop conducted by John Waidley of Eastern Michigan University.

Mental Imagery in Athletics and in Life

If you are skeptical about how well imagining achievement and success can work for you, keep in mind that many athletes do imagery exercises before competing. They visualize a successful activity as vividly as possible before they actually perform it. They feel the same positive emotions that they will experience when they achieve the actual success. Paul Westhead, coach of several college and professional basketball teams, writes, "In basketball keep your eye on the rim and expect the ball to go in. (Make a mental picture of the ball swishing through the hoop as you are in the act of shooting.) The key to mental imagery in picturing the ball going in is you do not allow any interference to alter your shot process . . . The quality of the process is your goal. The end result . . . will take care of itself" (Westhead, 1994, p. 130). To improve their free throws, his players shoot five for physical practice, picture five for mental practice, close their eyes and picture five (more mental practice), close their eyes and shoot five (combined mental and physical practice), and then open their eyes and shoot five for physical practice. His players even made three or four of every five shots with their eyes closed, demonstrating the power of mental imagery. "Practice makes perfect" is only half true, *mental* practice makes perfect.

Imagine yourself in a basketball game in front of thousands of screaming fans, waving anything hoping to distract you from making a crucial free throw. You are on the foul line, time has just expired, and your team is two points behind. Saying to yourself, "We lose if I miss this free throw" is not going to help. Thinking about the crowd, the clock, the score, or your teammates expecting you to perform turns your mind into an obstacle or a barrier to achievement. When many athletes say they "choked," they speak of not being "in the zone" or not "going with the flow" (Tolson, 2000). You are far more likely to perform well by imagining achievement learned in a mental, emotional, and physical ritual you've repeated thousands of times. However, acquiring a new mental strength you can tap into at will requires a long-term involvement. The correct physical mechanics of shooting a free throw (breathing, eyes focused on the rim, fingertip control releasing the ball, follow-through, and so on) become habitual responses through shooting in hundreds of practice sessions. The free throw is the only shot in basketball that is the same every time, but you repeat it over and over again so you can be successful at the foul line without thinking about it. Mastering the mental mechanics takes time as well. Eventually you can learn how to transport your consciousness out of the moment, mentally picture the ball going into the basket, and actually hear the satisfying swish of the net. Your sole focus is concentrating your entire mental, emotional, and physical being on making the successful shot. Mind and body become one whole, coordinated mechanism. Experience will teach you when to use imagery and when not to.

The same mental process is taught and used in many sports. For example, high jumpers close their eyes before a jump to mentally picture themselves going over the crossbar, and golfers rehearse a putt in their minds before actually striking the ball (LeUnes and Nation, 1989). Tennis players, gymnasts, skiers, swimmers, runners, and many other kinds of athletes go through their mental exercises, living the intense excitement of successful performances of their inner experience. Sports psychology focuses on concentration, stress management, visualization, self-regulation, goal setting, and relaxation.

You can use the same techniques as you approach work, family, and spiritual life because mental conditioning works the same way in any situation. Julio Bocca, a world-acclaimed ballet dancer from Argentina, worried that he would decline as he approached his 30s. Mental focus enhanced his performance. He describes his solo ballet presentations as moments when the only thing in his mind is the character he is portraying. He has been doing this for so many years that he doesn't have to think about what to do with his body, as in "Now I pirouette, now I jump" (Tolson, 2000). Skilled actors will tell you that when they lose the focus on their character they are in trouble. They must forget how they look in front of the audience and put their mind solely on the performance.

Imagery is a skill that can be learned. Watching another person model desired behavior is helpful, but seeing yourself perform a skill successfully in your own mind is even more valuable. *Your nervous system cannot tell the difference between an imagined experience and a real one.* That explains the value of role-playing. Use the role of a successful person, and rehearse that role in your imagination (Westhead, 1994). You can imagine yourself in various problem situations and solve those problems in your mind until you know what to say and do whenever that situation comes up in life. Mental imagery can be a powerful tool as you perform the tasks needed to determine a career goal and to carry out job-hunting activities such as getting ready for a job interview.

Arnold Lazarus, a psychologist who develops achievement imagery programs, says, "If you have difficulty imagining yourself achieving something, it is unlikely that you will manage to accomplish it in reality. In other words, we usually need to see ourselves performing something in our imaginations before we are able to perform this act in real life situations" (Lazarus, 1982). McClelland and his associates have succeeded in improving the performance of small-business people in a number of countries around the world (McClelland and Winter, 1969).

Write More Achievement Stories to Strengthen Your Achievement Motivation

Now that you have composed and scored one imaginative story to establish a base rate of your usual thinking, write more stories to strengthen your achievement motivation. Use the illustrations on these pages, pictures in magazines and newspapers, or images that appear in your mind or on videos and television (preferably with the sound off). Look briefly at the picture or drawing, or visualize a picture in your mind, then make up a dramatic story suggested by what you see. *This time, however, write in as many achievement thoughts as you can.* Psychologists, beginning with Sigmund Freud, have documented how fantasy reflects motivational states. The imaginative stories you fantasize will induce a greater need to achieve, as long as you keep rein-

forcing your achievement thinking. Remember the programs of athletes just described; they go through their mental exercises hundreds and thousands of times before the imagery becomes a natural part of their thinking. One of the author's students remarked, "I didn't believe you at first, but now that I've been at it for a month, I'm beginning to realize these achievement thoughts are becoming a normal way of thinking." Use the Chart for Scoring Achievement Motivation in Imaginative Stories on page 192 to evaluate your first few stories. Put a check mark next to those achievement thoughts that appear in your stories. Give yourself one point for each type of achievement thought, even if it appears more than once in each story.

Chart for Scoring Achievement Motivation in Imaginative Stories

Achievement Thought	Story 1	Story 2	Story 3	Story 4	Story 5	Story 6	Story 7	Story 8	Story 9
Achievement Imagery	AIm ___	AIm ___	AIm ___	AIm___	AIm___	AIm ___	AIm ___	AIm ___	AIm ___
Need	N ___	N ___	N ___	N ___	N ___	N ___	N ___	N ___	N ___
Action	ACT __	ACT __	ACT __	ACT __	ACT __	ACT __	ACT __	ACT __	ACT __
Hope of Success	HOS __	HOS __	HOS __	HOS __	HOS __	HOS __	HOS __	HOS __	HOS __
Fear of Failure	FOF __	FOF __	FOF __	FOF __	FOF __	FOF __	FOF __	FOF __	FOF __
Success Feelings	SF __	SF __	SF __	SF __	SF __	SF __	SF __	SF __	SF __
Failure Feelings	FF __	FF __	FF __	FF __	FF __	FF __	FF __	FF __	FF __
World Obstacle	WO __	WO __	WO __	WO __	WO __	WO __	WO __	WO __	WO __
Personal Obstacle	PO __	PO __	PO __	PO __	PO __	PO __	PO __	PO __	PO __
Help	H __	H __	H __	H __	H __	H __	H __	H __	H __
Total Points for Story	_____	_____	_____	_____	_____	_____	_____	_____	_____

One Person's Real-Life Achievement Story

Athletics reflects life in many ways and provides illustrations of the 10 achievement thoughts in practice. The following true story illustrates how those thoughts work in actual situations.

When Bill Lundberg entered community college, he had an athletic goal as well as an educational goal in mind. Bill was a runner. He had a sign in his gym locker that reminded him of his goal every day: "I want to be a national champion" (N). His events were the one- and two-mile distances. Bill hadn't participated in track until his junior year of high school, and even then his coach had to talk him into running (PO). Bill wasn't sure he would amount to anything in track; his skinny body might not be able to endure the rigors of distance running (FOF). Sure enough, a leg injury in the second meet kept him out of competition for the rest of his junior year (FF). Despite the setback, he sensed that he might gain some recognition from track (HOS). Next year he wanted to compete in the mile (N), but there was already an established miler on the team (WO). Bill accepted his coach's suggestion that the team could better use him as a half-miler, so his first goal was to be best on the team in that event (AIm–UA). This goal was accomplished quickly (SF), and his next goal was to become best in the city (AIm–UA). Soon the goal was to become best in the region. To accomplish these goals, Bill asked the coach for a training program (H). In addition to regular practice, Bill ran before school and ended practice sessions with extra sprints (ACT). Bill won his regional half-mile, experiencing for the first time the thrill of running the distance in under two minutes (SF). Now the goal was to be best in the state (AIm–UA), but there he came in a disappointing eighth (FF) against tougher competition (AIm–CO). Bill later achieved this goal in the state Jaycee meet (SF), which qualified him to run in the national meet (HOS), where he had the personal satisfaction of reaching his best half-mile time (SF, AIm–CS). Although this time was only good enough for fifth place, he had accomplished a lot in his first full year of track competition (SF).

Because of his late start in running (PO), Bill was not recruited by the major senior (four-year) colleges (WO). The local community college was convenient and affordable. His coaches created a training program for Bill, and his family and friends followed him to meets to cheer him on (H). Getting up early to run 9 miles to school and running from 3 to 10 miles with the track team, Bill intensified the discipline he had started in high school (ACT). Bill often ran more than 100 miles per week, a practice he continued for years (AIm–LTI). Bill set all kinds of personal short-term goals, and his locker door reminded him daily of the long-term goal: "I want to be a national champion" (AIm–UA). Bill soon found he was better in the longer distances, so the mile and 2-mile races became his events. New school records and first-place finishes became commonplace for him (SF), and he began to anticipate and worry about the competition at the National Junior College Track championships (HOS, FOF). The big moment came in Bill's second college year, when he broke the indoor 2-mile record and won national championships in the mile and 2-mile. In the 2-mile run, 20 yards beyond the finish line, Bill realized that he had achieved his long-term goal. Tears of joy ran down his face as he kept thinking, "Can this be happening to me? It's like a dream come true." All the imagined and envisioned success had indeed come true (AIm–UA). Now he was a national champion, with All-American status (SF). He would later be named to the National Junior College Hall of Fame (AIm–UA). In three years, Bill had come a long way by establishing achievable goals and setting his sights higher and higher as he reached one goal after another (SF, AIm–LTI).

The story doesn't stop there; Bill developed new goals. Now he was recognized. He accepted an offer from the University of Kansas after being recruited by Jim Ryun, one of the greatest distance runners in American sports. At Kansas, Bill could pursue his career plans in art education (N) and be challenged by new goals, taking on ever-stiffer competition (AIm–CO). The imagery of working harder and succeeding (N, HOS) was translated into a strenuous training program worked out by Bill and his coach (ACT, H). Bill was to score many victories for Kansas in the 5-mile cross-country run and in the mile, 2-mile, and 5000-meter track events. He also took on the challenge of a new event, the 3000-meter steeplechase, which requires not only endurance, but also jumping ability and motor coordination.

Like many track-and-field events, the steeplechase has a history, having started in Europe with races from one church steeple to another. Steeplechase is rather like running cross-country on an oval track; there are 35 obstacles, consisting of 28 barriers and 7 water jumps (WO). The water jumps can be intimidating (PO); the runner must step onto the hurdle, then push off and land in the water pit before continuing the race. Getting over the hurdle is hard enough, but slogging through water is even worse (FOF). Through practice, Bill conquered his fears (ACT). Eventually, he became Conference steeplechase champion (SF) and All-American, finishing sixth in the national meet after setting a National Collegiate Athletic Association record in the qualifying heats (AIm–UA).

The record earned Bill a shot at qualifying for the Olympic team. He was the youngest runner in the steeplechase finals, which was amazing because he had spent only 14 months in that event. Some competitors shook his confidence by questioning whether a runner so young and inexperienced should even be in the race (FOF, WO). Bill moved quickly into the lead (HOS). Maybe the fast pace added pressure (PO). After leading the pack of 13 runners, Bill slipped back to seventh and lost contact with the leaders. He could have quit there, rationalizing that his hopes of making the team were gone, but giving up was something he didn't want on his mind for four more years (FOF). So Bill blasted his way past two runners and finished fifth, proving to his competitors that he belonged with them (SF). His emotions were mixed, however—the Olympic team took only the first three runners, and Bill didn't qualify (FF).

After his two years of running track and cross-country at Kansas, Bill stayed on to finish his degree in art education and to work for the Lawrence schools as a traveling art teacher in elementary schools. Perhaps it was there that Bill conceived the idea of being a teacher and a coach (N, AIm–LTI). He thought, "Now that I'm on the other side of the desk, it's a chance to give rather than just receive." The achievement motive combined with other motives, such as the need to serve others.

Bill was running for the University of Chicago Track Club when he established a record in the 1000-yard event, running the mile in 4:01.9, and bringing his two-mile time down to 8:40.4 (SF). Track enthusiasts encouraged Bill to postpone a coaching career and enter international competition (H). At the U.S. Track and Field Federation championships, he placed second in the steeplechase. Then, Bill got a job offer from his old community college to teach and coach there. It was too attractive to turn down. He had attained his teaching and coaching goal after only five and a half years of being involved in the sport (SF), but a time of harsh testing was still ahead.

Bill spent four years as head track coach, attracting many athletes and a hometown following with his enthusiasm, sincerity, and character. He worked at building a solid track program (AIm–LTI), perhaps not devoting as much time as he should have to training for the next Olympics (WO). As a coach-athlete, he won the steeplechase at the Kansas Relays (SF). Among those who prepared for Olympic competition, Bill had one of the best times of all the steeplechase competitors (HOS). About a week before the qualifying races for the Olympic team, Bill noticed some tenderness in his right heel (PO) but felt he could work through it (HOS).

As the race started, Bill felt fine. With two-thirds of the race over, he was in first place, never having been less than third. As Bill went into the pit of the fifth water jump, his knee gave way. He staggered for four or five more strides and then went down, lying flat on the track (FF). As runner after runner went by, images of hometown and family shot through his mind, followed by this thought: "I've got to get up. I've come this far and I must finish" (HOS). Bill got up and tried to run again. When he stepped off his right foot, the whole earth seemed to go out from under him.

Bill's Achilles tendon had ruptured and been severed. Surgery tied the tendon back together. A scar that goes halfway up his leg remains to this day, a painful reminder of the years of training that were erased in one blinding flash (FF). Bill's first impulse was to cry out, "Why me?" His religious faith was severely tested.

Then a new spirit took hold, and Bill began to see new opportunities in his disappointment. His foot would heal; he would be able to run again, whereas some people couldn't even walk. He became more sensitive to the plight of the handicapped. Bill thought of larger things. He wrote about the race of life: "Lord, I've just begun to run! The end isn't in sight. How many laps yet to go? Help me look past the finish line to what is beyond" (H). Bill resumed his running, completing a seven-mile run (on crutches!) and eventually running the mile in 4:18. As Bill took charge of his life, more trials followed.

Bill's father died a few months later (WO). In the middle of an indoor season in which his team was to finish fourth in the nation (SF), Bill was left with the emotions of career success mixed with the trauma of great personal loss and a reminder of his own mortality (WO). Another devastating blow soon followed. The community college eliminated its entire program of intercollegiate athletics, and the track program went first (WO). In his loyalty to his team and school, Bill had turned down opportunities to go elsewhere; now he was laid off and left with nothing. Letters and editorials of protest appeared in the local newspaper, and Bill's colleagues appealed to the school administration—but to no avail. Interviews for jobs at other colleges netted nothing (FF).

Refusing to let events crush him, Bill decided to invest his savings in a new goal: a master's degree from the University of Michigan (N, HOS). He needed 20 more credits for a master's degree in physical education (WO). Bill worked in the university's track program as an unpaid assistant, but his savings dwindled fast (FOF). Volunteering at Michigan paid off, however, when nearby Eastern Michigan University offered him a paid graduate-assistant position (SF). Now he could teach physical education, work as a substitute teacher at a local high school, complete his master's degree at Eastern, and help out with the track program (AIm–LTI). At this time, Bill met Sharon, his future wife. After two years as a teaching assistant, Bill became assistant track coach at Eastern Michigan, a track power in its own right, where he worked with future Olympic athletes.

Although Bill was grateful for the opportunity at Eastern, he still hoped to achieve his goal of college teaching as a head track coach (HOS). His chance came when a head coaching position in track and cross-country opened at Michigan's Hillsdale College. Bill was the college's first choice (SF). He had reached another goal. New goals have continued to emerge (N). His men's track and cross-country teams have dominated league competition (AIm-CO), and he has coached over 100 Academic and Athletic All-Americans and 13 national champions since coming to Hillsdale (SF). Achievement motivation has been thoroughly implanted into Bill Lundberg's makeup. He is now doing the job he set out to do—teaching and coaching a sport that has given him so much and required so much of him (AIm–LTI).

You can put achievement thoughts to work for you as Bill did. It takes some imagination and concentrated effort, but you can do it. Go for it! Bill writes about his achievement thoughts this way. *Need* is the decision you make to "go for it," whatever the dream or the goal may be. *Personal obstacles* are the injuries and setbacks you have in life, and *world obstacles* are hurdles to overcome, as in a steeplechase race. *Help* is something given by other people, such as coaches or mentors. Rigorous training is the *action* step; that's the part people see in your behavior. *Fear of failure* comes from tough competition, and it drives you to be better than you are now. Defeat brings *failure feelings*, which often result in learning experiences more meaningful than successes. *Hope of success* stems from the decision to win, and *success feelings* occur after victories. There is *achievement imagery* in attaining the prized goal. Perhaps Glenn Cunningham, who was physically handicapped in his youth but went on to set world records in running the mile, expressed the essence of achievement motivation when he wrote,

> People can't understand why a man runs. They don't see any sport in it and argue that it lacks the sight and thrill of body contact. Yet, the conflict is there, more raw and challenging that any man-against-man competition. In running, it is man against himself [AIm–CS], the cruelest of opponents. The other runners are not the real enemies. His adversary lies within him, in his ability, with brain and heart, to control and master himself and his emotions.

Challenge yourself. Set your own goals. Compete with yourself. You may set goals that are too high at first, but with new knowledge about your performance you can set new goals. You may set goals that are too easy, but if you think about them, you'll learn to establish new ones that challenge the best within you. Your awareness of the need to achieve will make a difference for the rest of your life. Develop the habits of goal setting and achievement thinking, which can be done only with your dedication and your own decision to "go for it."

High-Achiever Strategies

In a group or classroom, games can be used to increase awareness of achievement motivation and of the characteristics of high achievers. For example, you could be involved in a business game in which you construct a product (see Appendix G: *Origami: An Achievement Motivation Game*). You set a preliminary goal by estimating how many products you can make in a given time. After a time trial, you set a final goal. To set these goals, you need to assess information about the costs of materials, the selling prices of acceptable products made, and the penalties for changing goals. After the production period, you calculate your profit or loss. Another game is ring toss, with points for each ringer. Points increase as the distance of the toss increases. Before each toss, players announce their distance from the peg to a scorekeeper, who needs to know how many points to award if a ringer is made. You can play as an individual or as part of a team (Alshuler, Tabor, and McIntyre, 1971).

Such competitive games can teach you a number of strategies of high achievers. One well-established trait of people with high achievement motivation is that they are *moderate risk takers*. They set goals that challenge them but are still realistic; in other words, they avoid goals that are either too easy or impossible. In a ring toss game, for example, this means standing a moderate distance from the peg. There is a chance of failure, which provides the challenge; a goal that ensures automatic success gives no feeling of accomplishment. An impossibly long toss, which can succeed only through luck, doesn't attract the high achiever, either. You can easily translate the principle of moderate risk taking from game situations into setting career goals. The same principle applies whether you make decisions in a game or a career choice.

People with achievement motivation *compete with a standard of excellence,* whether that standard is performing better than others (CO) or competing with themselves, trying to improve on an earlier performance (CS).

High achievers *take personal responsibility* for the outcomes of their goal setting. Attributing success to our own skill and effort is natural and easy, but high achievers also take the blame for failure rather than accusing others, or fate. Taking personal responsibility is ultimately more productive. You can correct your personal mistakes more easily than you can change others or the environment.

High achievers learn to *use feedback from previous performances* to modify future goals and make them more realistic. In a business game, if high achievers set a goal of making 10 products in five minutes but find it takes them 45 seconds to make one product in a time trial, they will lower the goal to seven products, even if there is a penalty for changing goals. Making the change is more realistic and helps them avoid failure. In a ring toss game, after high achievers score a ringer they move farther away from the peg to increase the challenge; after a miss, they move closer.

High achievers also *research the environment in an alert, curious, active, energetic, and purposeful manner* when they set goals. In a game, they take the initiative by sizing up the situation, checking out the playing materials, learning the rules, figuring out the obstacles, and often inventing new ways of doing things in order to reach their goals (Alshuler, Tabor, and McIntyre, 1971).

Concluding Thoughts about Achievement Motivation

David McClelland's major research hypothesis was that the economic growth or decline of nations depends, to a considerable extent, on the degree of achievement motivation prevalent in the populations of those nations. He tested his hypothesis using some of the methods described in this chapter to measure and strengthen the need to achieve. McClelland also counted the number of achievement themes that appeared in the popular literature of a nation's culture (McClelland, 1961). What does this research into a nation's achievement motivation mean to you as an individual? You can make a logical deduction. Because McClelland has provided much evidence for his achievement motivation thesis, you can say that your own degree of achievement motivation will go a long way in determining your success in achieving your career goals. It seems reasonable to assume that your economic growth or decline depends, to a considerable extent, on your own need to achieve.

High achievement and success in reaching your career goals appear to be related to several factors that you can identify and use:

1. Generating an interest in life and the environment around you
2. Developing independence and self-reliance early in life
3. Setting moderate goals that are realistic yet challenging
4. Delaying satisfaction for a larger reward in the future
5. Using information gained from earlier performances to change goals if necessary
6. Taking personal responsibility for the outcomes of decisions
7. Having the persistence to complete goals and the good sense to revise them if they are too difficult or too easy
8. Imagining success or learning to anticipate it through fantasy

I suppose you *could* say I'm an overachiever . . .

9. Developing a positive self-concept and a sense of self-worth
10. Setting goals for yourself, not allowing goals to be imposed on you
11. Having the desire to achieve for the sake of achievement, or to work because you are interested in whatever you are working on, not for rewards like money or good grades

Achievement motivation is essential to success, but it can be carried to excess. Having high achievement motivation doesn't by itself make you a better person; it must be balanced by other needs such as relationship and affiliation motives. The quality of your values and goals is important, too. Competing with others—one element of achievement motivation—can involve the risk of creating jealousy and bitterness, which are hardly growth facilitating. An extreme drive for achievement can make a person so obsessed with success that he or she neglects family, friends, and even good health. It is harmful to subscribe to the values of others in order to win approval or recognition if it is done at the expense of your own values. The resulting loss of self-esteem, revealing itself through anxiety, depression, feelings of emptiness, or reliance on drugs, makes all your efforts toward achievement self-defeating and hollow. The need for achievement needs to be harmonized with other motives, because there are other important things in life besides achievement.

IDENTIFYING YOUR ACHIEVEMENTS

Thus far, you have looked at achievement from the inner perspective of motivation. Now it is time to study achievement in its outward expression: performance—the observable results of your inner need to achieve. It is important to ask, "What have I successfully achieved in my life up to this point?" A typical response is "Nothing, really, of importance." This cannot be true; you must have accomplished hundreds of things to get where you are in life now. Some self-disrespect may come from people who try to help you learn by pointing out what you have done wrong. Instead, why not concentrate on what you have done right? To illustrate this point, Bernard Haldane (1975) composed an imaginary conversation between Alice and the Mad Hatter from Lewis Carroll's *Alice in Wonderland*.

Alice: Where I come from, people study what they are NOT good at in order to be able to do what they ARE good at.

Mad Hatter: We only go around in circles here in Wonderland, but we always end up where we started. Would you mind explaining yourself?

Alice: Well, grown-ups tell us to find out what we did wrong, and never to do it again.

Mad Hatter: That's odd! It seems to me that in order to find out about something you would have to study it. And when you study it, you should become better at it. Why should you want to become better at something and then never do it again? But please continue.

Alice: Nobody ever tells us to study the right things we do. We're only supposed to learn from the wrong things. But we are permitted to study the right things OTHER people do. And sometimes we're even told to copy them.

Mad Hatter: That's cheating!

Alice: You're quite right, Mr. Hatter. I do live in a topsy-turvy world. It seems like I have to do something wrong first, in order to learn from that what not to do. And then, by not doing what I'm not supposed to do, perhaps I'll be right. But I'd rather be right the first time, wouldn't you? (Haldane, 1975, pp. 13–14)

So look at what you've done right. The following two exercises will help you identify your past achievements. You will benefit from remembering the times when you were motivated to achieve something and felt good about what you did.

EXERCISE 5-3 REMEMBERING PAST ACHIEVEMENTS

In this exercise, use your memory to identify achievements in your life—things you have done well and felt good about, whether or not anyone else noticed. Of course, you want to note accomplishments from full-time and part-time work experiences and achievements in school. However, accomplishments away from work or school may have as much—or more—significance for your career planning. Achievements at school can include extracurricular activities such as drama, sports, music, publications, clubs, and the like. Outside school, achievements can involve hobbies, leadership roles, travel, family activities, things done around the home, and so on. Your achievements may involve actions such as the following:

- Writing or telling a story
- Organizing people to work together
- Persuading a person or a group
- Growing flowers or vegetables
- Planning a meeting or a party
- Repairing an appliance
- Building something
- Solving a problem
- Researching new information
- Being dependable and responsible
- Decorating a house or a room

EXERCISE 6-8 PRIORITIZING MATRIX FOR RANKING WORK ABILITIES

To use the prioritizing matrix, list the 10 or more work abilities you have identified on the diagonal lines. Each work ability is designated by a number. For each number pair in the matrix, ask yourself, "Which ability do I prefer, or enjoy using the most?" Circle the number of that choice. When you finish circling, record the total number of times you chose each ability and indicate the final rank in the bottom two rows of the matrix. To break ties, go back to the place in the matrix where the two tying numbers were paired and note the one that is circled. (Figure 6-2 shows an example of a completed matrix.)

In this example, 11 work abilities were identified from achievements and aptitude test scores. Each work ability was assigned a temporary number. For each number pair in the matrix, a choice was made as to which ability of the two was preferred, and its number was circled. (For example, teaching outdoor education was preferred over writing biology reports, so 2 is circled in the 1–2 number pair.) The circled numbers were counted and ranked. Now these 11 abilities can be rearranged in a new order of priority. If you have more than 12 abilities to rank by priority, add new rows on a blank sheet of paper and place the paper under the last row of the matrix.

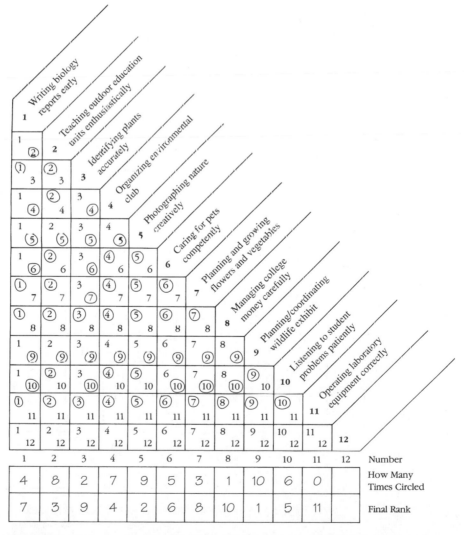

Figure 6-2 Example of a completed prioritizing matrix ranking abilities. *Source:* From the *National Career Development Project Four-Day Workshop,* by Richard N. Bolles, copyright © 1981. Used by permission.

Prioritizing Matrix for Exercise 6-8   *Source:* From the *National Career Development Project Four-Day Workshop*, by Richard N. Bolles, copyright © 1981. Used by permission.

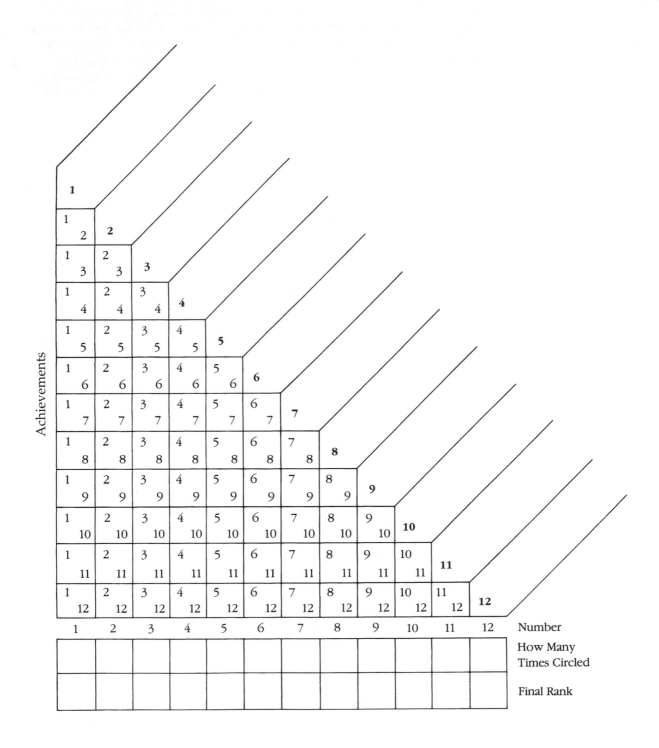

EXERCISE 6-9 MY PRIORITIZED, DOCUMENTED LIST OF WORK ABILITIES

On the form that follows, write your new list of prioritized work abilities in the spaces provided. Start with your favorite work ability, and move down to your least favorite ability. Keep writing your skills properly, combining a functional skill with a work-content or special-knowledge skill and an adaptive skill. To the right of each one, *give evidence that you possess that ability by naming the achievement in which the ability or skill was used or by noting a high score on an aptitude test.*

My Prioritized, Documented List of Work Abilities

Work Ability	Example of Use/Evidence
1. _____	_____
2. _____	_____
3. _____	_____
4. _____	_____
5. _____	_____
6. _____	_____
7. _____	_____
8. _____	_____
9. _____	_____
10. _____	_____
11. _____	_____
12. _____	_____

SUMMARY

1. Abilities, skills, and aptitudes represent the "can do" of career planning. Some career-planning experts believe discovering what you can do well is so important that skills and abilities become the most necessary ingredients in your career decision.

2. Three types of skills are functional (or transferable), work content (or special-knowledge), and adaptive (or self-management). Functional skills are things you do in order to function in life. To describe them, you use action verbs such as *communicated, organized, designed, assembled, repaired, researched,* and *operated.* Functional skills are highly valued because they are transferable to many jobs.

3. Work-content or special-knowledge skills are the things you know that help you do a job. They involve learning subject matter, such as the parts of a machine, the language required by a certain computer, or the names of people within a particular department. Although these skills are needed to perform on a job, they are not as easily transferred to other jobs as are the functional and adaptive skills.

4. Adaptive skills are those qualities that characterize you as a person. You have probably thought of them as traits that make up your personality, but in another sense they are skills that you definitely need to get and keep a job. For example, being courteous, effective, careful, honest, tactful, prudent, responsible, punctual, and imaginative are qualities greatly prized and appreciated by employers and coworkers. Adaptive skills are all skills that can be learned and improved on.

5. In communicating your skills to others, connect functional skills with work content and adaptive skills in order to provide a clear, sharp description of what you can do and how you do it.

6. Use the descriptions of your previous achievements and your high or above-average aptitude test scores to identify and document your work abilities. After you construct a list of your confirmed work abilities, arrange your favorite ones in order of priority so you will know exactly what you want to do in your occupation.

REFERENCES

Allen, M., Hummel, T, Koenig, C., Lewis, B., Maire, J., and McKay, D. 2003. *The General Aptitude Test Battery (GATB).* Clear Lake, TX: The University of Houston at Clear Lake. Available online at http://port.inst.cl.uh.edu/portfolio/MAIREJO/GATB.pdf. Accessed April 23, 2003.

Appalachia Educational Laboratory. 1978. *Exploring career decision-making.* Bloomington, IL: McKnight.

ASVAB Career Exploration Program. 2002. *ASVAB educator and counselor guide.* Seaside, CA: Defense Manpower Data Center, Department of Defense Center, Monterey Bay.

Bennett, G. K., Seashore, H. G., and Wesman, A. G. 1996. *Administrator's handbook for the Differential Aptitude Tests, Forms V and W.* San Antonio, TX: The Psychological Corporation, Harcourt Brace Jovanovich.

Bolles, R. N. 1975. *The quick job-hunting map, advanced version.* Berkeley, CA: Ten Speed Press.

Bolles, R. N. 1978. *The three boxes of life and how to get out of them: An introduction to life/work planning.* Berkeley, CA: Ten Speed Press.

Bolles, R. N. 1985. *The new quick job-hunting map.* Berkeley, CA: Ten Speed Press.

Bolles, R. N. 1989. *How to create a picture of your ideal job or next career.* Berkeley, CA: Ten Speed Press.

Bolles, R. N. 1998, revised annually. *What color is your parachute?* Berkeley, CA: Ten Speed Press.

Bugbee, B., Cousins, D., and Hybels, B. 1994. *Network: The right people . . . in the right places . . . for the right reasons.* Grand Rapids, MI: Zondervan.

Fine, S. A., and Wiley, W. W. 1971. *An introduction to functional job analysis: A scaling of selected tasks from the social welfare field.* Kalamazoo, MI: W.E. Upjohn Institute for Employment Research.

Henkel, D. 1994. The reason privatization will be the ruin of your school district. *MEA Voice,* 72(3), A10.

Knapp, L., Knapp, R. R., and Knapp-Lee, L. 1992. *CAPS technical manual.* San Diego: EdITS/Educational and Industrial Testing Service.

Lyman, H. B. 1963. *Test scores and what they mean.* Englewood Cliffs, NJ: Prentice Hall.

McMahon, F. B. 1977. *Psychology: The hybrid science.* Englewood Cliffs, NJ: Prentice Hall.

U.S. Department of Labor. 2002. *O*Net Ability Profiler administration manual.* Washington, DC: Employment and Training Administration.

Chapter 7

Cultural, Personal, and Work Values

"I could not have forgiven myself if I had walked away." Those words were said by an Iranian student working as an intern at the Bank of New York on Wall Street, as he told about his memories of the two hijacked planes slamming into the twin towers of the World Trade Center on September 11, 2001.

Shahran Hashemi could not believe what he saw that morning. He watched people jumping from windows. People ran over each other as they ran for their lives. However, some people ran in the opposite direction—toward the Trade Center, firefighters, and police officers. "They knew that it might be the end of their lives, but they went."

Shahran went, too, back into the inferno, into the chaos, into the terror to do anything he could to help. He noticed many women covered by dust and frozen in fear. One by one, he led them safely into the lobby of the Bank of New York. Next trip out, a fireman spotted the young man and handed Shahran a protective jacket to shield him from the roaring flames. Shahran asked, "Is there anything I can do?"

"Yes," came the reply, "We lost a lot of people back there. We need all the help we can get."

Darkness and fire were everywhere. Shahran told the fireman, "I don't have anyone here. My name is Shahran Hashemi, and just in case anything happens to me, let my family in Tehran know." The fireman said he would, then embraced the young man and made the sign of the cross, saying, "Christ protect you."

Thinking back to that unforgettable moment, Shahran Hashemi, a Muslim, wept. He doesn't know if the fireman survived; he never saw him again.

Shahran and other civilians were formed into teams and sent to Ground Zero, where they put out fires and searched for survivors. Soon, they heard a rumbling sound—the second tower was about to come down. Everyone began to run. Shahran found refuge in the American Express Building, waited, and then emerged once more into almost complete darkness. Fires burned out of control around him. Hashemi and the other volunteers rejoined the firefighters. Most of all, they tried to extinguish fires burning cars, extremely dangerous because of the possibility of further explosions.

As more help came, Shahran's job changed to taking buckets of water to quench the thirst of the firefighters. Hours later, as a 47-story building collapsed in ruins near him, Hashemi became disoriented and trapped in the wreckage and rubble. He was noticed by a mobile triage unit and given first aid and oxygen. He noticed all the doctors were Jewish. They sent him to a hospital on Staten Island for a night to recuperate.

"The way I see it," he said later to a reporter from an Amnesty International magazine, "I was blessed by three religions that day. It was my Islamic faith that motivated me to go back and help. That is what Islam taught me to do: to help others, to sacrifice my life in order to bring peace. I was blessed in the name of Jesus at the most dangerous moment of my life and then I was helped by Jewish doctors" (adapted from Lajoie, 2001–2002, pp. 12–13).

What better way is there to begin a chapter on values than to show how our values can propel us into motion, even at the risk of our own lives? The values that Shahran Hashemi had adopted from his religious faith and his culture compelled him to take action, instinctively sending him on a mission to help other people save their lives. So, too, the values we all carry within our personal being cause us to act on those values. It is part of our human nature to do so.

One of the most important activities in our lives, of course, is work. We seek the kind of work that will satisfy our values. Deciding on what we will do in our work will most assuredly involve our values. The thought may have occurred to you in the last chapter, on abilities, that career planning seems rather one-sided. Everything appears to be for the employer and the skills you can *give to* your work. "Fair enough," perhaps you thought, "but what I can *take from* my work? We need some sort of balance here."

If those were your thoughts, then this chapter is for you. It involves the satisfactions and payments you can gain from working in your chosen occupation. We call these reward *values,* and in this chapter, we distinguish three types of values: cultural, personal, and work values.

A study of your work values is central to understanding why you are drawn to some occupations and not to others. Employers are typically more interested in your abilities than in your values, because they want people who can perform and produce on the job. As a career decision maker and job seeker, your major concern is more likely to be the reward and personal fulfillment you can derive from an occupation. Abilities are the skills and aptitudes you give to your career; values have more to do with the reward and satisfaction you receive. However, abilities and values are not mutually exclusive. If you receive important reward from an occupation, you are likely to give more of yourself and your talents to it.

The study of values in this chapter starts with the immense cultural diversity that exists in the United States and a brief overview of the cultural values you encounter in that environment. These values are communicated to you in a variety of ways—some direct, some subtle and indirect. They come from a variety of sources, beginning with your parents, and become the core of the personal values by which you live. You can probably state several personal values, but some of them may be vaguely felt sentiments that can be expressed only after much thought and self-examination. Studying your personal values is a worthwhile activity, because it helps you appreciate yourself as a unique, individual personality.

The main focus of this chapter is on identifying and prioritizing your work values, just as you identified and prioritized your work abilities in the last chapter. Work values define the reward, satisfaction, and desirable qualities you seek in the occupational prospects you are considering. Many work values are discussed here; you need to designate those that are important to you and put them in order of priority. There is a list of work values you can evaluate; you can measure 15 work values by taking the Work Values Inventory or assess 21 values from the Values Scale; and you can take a Review of Work Values to measure the strength of 30 work values in your thinking. From these exercises, you should be able to identify 10 or 12 work values you believe would be significant to you in choosing your occupation. The final step is to prioritize your personal list of work values—that is, put them in order from the most important to the least important. Your prioritized list of work values will be an essential part of the foundation for the career decision you are building.

VALUES

Like every person, you have a value system that is uniquely your own. As you seek self-knowledge in order to make a career decision, you need to determine which values operate most strongly within your own personality.

A *value* is anything to which a person gives worth, merit, or usefulness. It is a quality that makes something desirable. Whenever you say that something is important to you or has significance for you, you are stating a value. Think of things you have or would like to have, such as new clothes in your closet, food on the table, a car in the garage, or a stereo in your room. Things have qualities about them that humans value. Think of characteristics you admire in people—for example, courage, decisiveness, imagination, love, self-control, or ethical behavior. Think of conditions of life you desire such as peace, friendship, beauty, good health, security, and personal influence. These and hundreds of other qualities express your values, features of life that are important to you.

Values are related to needs, but they are not the same as needs; technically, a need is a lack of something desirable. Values are not behavior traits that can be observed outwardly; they are internal. Values are not the same as attitudes; rather, they are standards by which attitudes are formed (Peterson, 1972).

You express values in your thinking, speech, and behavior, whether or not you are aware of them. The more you become aware of your values and how they affect the countless decisions you make in life, the more you know about yourself. You cannot ignore your values if you want to know who you are and why you act as you do.

You acquire your values beginning in early childhood, through contact with your surroundings and your experiences in it. You absorb values into your developing personality through relationships with your parents, brothers, sisters, relatives, neighbors, friends, teachers, institutions, and all parts of the community and society in which you live. You also take in values from what you read in books, newspapers, and magazines and from what you see or hear on television, in movies, on the radio, and in art.

As you encounter the names of hundreds of values in this chapter, you will be asked to identify those that are important to you. Louis Raths, a pioneer in the study of the valuing process, suggests that if you can answer yes to the following seven questions about a given value, you can be certain it is important to you.

1. Am I *proud* of (or do I prize and cherish) this value?
2. Would I *publicly affirm* this value—that is, defend it openly before others?
3. Have I chosen this value after *considering* other *alternatives*?
4. Have I *thought* about the *consequences* of expressing this value?
5. Have I chosen this value *freely*—that is, not had it imposed on me by anyone or anything else?
6. Have I *acted* on this value?
7. Have I acted with *repetition* or *consistency* or repeated a pattern of behavior regarding this value?

Thus the valuing process consists of choosing freely, choosing from among alternatives, choosing after thoughtful consideration of the consequences of each alternative, prizing and cherishing, affirming, acting on choices, and repeating or acting with consistency (Raths, Harmin, and Simon, 1966).

A study of values can give a greater sense of direction to your life. If you have no direction, life becomes aimless and deadening, without commitment or meaning. A lack of purpose, worth, meaning, or value in living leads to dispiritedness, despair, or a mental illness that psychoanalyst Viktor Frankl calls *noogenic neurosis* (Jourard, 1974). It is not my intent to detail the conditions that lead to meaninglessness, apathy, indifference, and cynicism in everyday life, only to note that identifying and clarifying your values can help you avoid or move away from these unhappy modes of existence.

Even when you try to learn about your values, you can become confused. In contrast to an earlier era, it may be more difficult to develop clear values today. Changing ways of life have weakened family ties. Value conflicts have increased separation, divorce, and broken homes. Ever-proliferating channels of communication, ranging from radio, movies, and television to comic books and music, have brought increasing competition among values. Different value orientations enter the living room with the evening news. People now have more access to communication and transportation and thus are exposed to a greater number of new ideas, lifestyles, novelties, customs, practices, and beliefs. Higher sophistication, heightened stimulation, greater diversity, and a knowledge explosion have their price: difficulty and confusion in comprehending one's own values in a complex world.

Learning to understand your values is a lifelong process. If you haven't already started, it's time to begin now. Granted, the study of values is complex, ever changing, and difficult, but you must make the attempt. Your concern in career planning is to construct a set of work values—qualities that will help you choose a career and give your work purpose and meaning. Work values are part of a larger framework of life values. Knowing these values can help you answer three vital questions: Who am I? What work will I do? What does my life stand for?

CULTURAL DIVERSITY AND CULTURAL VALUES

As you read through this section on diverse cultural values, notice that cultural differences in eye contact, communication, and body language can help or sabotage your efforts in dealing with others. Whether in a job interview, contract negotiation, making a sale, getting along with coworkers, or establishing a relationship for the future, an awareness of these different values can be vital.

All of us are members of a culture. Sociologists define *culture* as the sum total of ways of thinking and living built up by a group of human beings and transmitted from one generation to another. We are also members of a subculture. A *subculture* is a group that has social, economic, ethnic, and other characteristics distinctive enough to set the group apart from others within the same culture. Thus, we live in an American culture, and within it are white American, African American, Hispanic or Latino American, Asian American, and Native American subcultures. Within those subcultures are further identifiable groups. For example, within the Asian American subculture are Chinese Americans, Japanese Americans, Korean Americans, Filipino Americans, Vietnamese Americans, and so on. Within the white American subculture are ethnic subdivisions, each with its own identifying set of characteristics. Although the white subculture has been a majority culture in the United States since it was established, by 2059 at the latest the groups labeled "minorities" will collectively outnumber white Americans, according to the U.S. Census Bureau. Already, in America's most integrated city (Sacramento, California), everyone is a minority; 41 percent are non-Hispanic white, 15.5 percent are African American, 22 percent are Hispanic, and 17.5 percent are Asian/Pacific Islander (Stodghill and Bower, 2002). Throughout the world today, people of color are a majority (Sharf, 2002).

Although there are vast differences among people within subcultures, sociologists and others have attributed *cultural tendencies* to many of these groups. The word *tendencies* is used deliberately, to get away from *stereotypes*. A group tendency is a characteristic that is shared by many people within a subculture but certainly not all of them. Stereotyping exists when a trait displayed by some members of a group is said to be characteristic of all. To say or believe that "Men are better than women in math and science" creates an expectation that is not necessarily valid when applied to individuals (Cochrane, 1997).

A stereotypical view of young people deeply embedded in the minds of many adults is the picture that teenagers as a group are drugged-out, lazy, self-absorbed, or violent. The media often portray youth in the context of crime, trivial pursuits, and accidents. One poll revealed that only 16 percent of adult Americans believe young people share most of their moral and ethical values. If the adult public believes teens have disgusting values, it becomes very difficult to get support for youth programs but easy to pass harsh, punitive laws for youthful offenders. Most young people are not trampling the social values of adults, but the difficult task is one of reframing adults' mental picture of the young (Mooney, 2003).

To assign stereotypes to all members of a group as a generalization denies the existence of individual traits among any of them. Stereotypes exaggerate group tendencies and often have a negative impact. "Gender, ethnicity, national origin, religion, age, sexual orientation, and disability are seen as inaccurate and unreliable bases for estimating the skills, abilities, needs, values, personality styles, and adjustment style of a particular person" (Dawis, 1994, p. 41). Misunderstandings result whenever all members of subculture groups are perceived as the same, or homogeneous. The reality is that they are very diverse; not only are there the unique characteristics of individuals, but also within groups such as African Americans you find differences based on education, occupation, religion, generation, gender, region, sexual orientation, and place of residence (Hogan-Garcia, 1997). When all is considered about group identities, a focus on the individual characteristics of each person separately is more realistic and honest. However, our individuality is conditioned by the culture in which we live. All of us learn a culture and many subcultures. Once learned, they become a part of our identity (who we are) and are a driving force in our lives. A person can be identified as Mexican American, female, a physical therapist, a Southern Baptist Christian, an environmentalist, a Republican or socialist and belong to the middle class, live in the Midwest, and more—all at the same time (Naylor, 1998).

Some of the tendencies that characterize various groups are discussed here, and these tendencies inevitably involve values found in many people within a subculture. Moreover, those distinguishing traits that strongly identify a first generation of a subculture will quite likely be modified the longer a group lives in the United States. The following, necessarily short descriptions of the varied subcultures of the United States introduce the topic of cultural diversity. The history, communication patterns, and behaviors of the people within these groups reveal many cultural and personal values they often express. As you read through this section, remember that it has been frequently said that 90 percent of career development issues are the same for all individuals, but many people have specific issues needing attention (Ettinger, 1996). A study involving over 1000 white, Asian, and Hispanic high school students in California found that, regardless of sex and ethnicity, occupations with high pay and supportive supervisor feedback were rated more attractive, whereas occupations with low pay and critical supervisor feedback were uniformly rated unattractive (Krumboltz et al., 1994).

African Americans. The feature that has set African Americans apart from other groups is color visibility and the negative perception of African Americans as a group by many in the dominant white culture. Whereas some nonwhite Asian and Latino immigrants have found acceptance in the United States, the barrier of color has been more difficult for African Americans to overcome. Despite an increasing number of black people in positions of power in the workplace, most African Americans expect to meet obstacles and difficulties in the world of work. All cultural specialists acknowledge the devastating effects of racism and that blacks have had to overcome incredible odds to survive and succeed in the workplace (Blank and Slipp, 1994).

African Americans are more likely to show emotional intensity, be spontaneous, express themselves in a direct manner, and use physical touch than many other subcultural groups. Eye contact is often quite direct when speaking, less so in the case of listening—the opposite of white cultural patterns, where the speaker tends to look away from a listener and the listener looks directly at the speaker (Elliott, 1999). The values of mutual help, education, and equal opportunity can be found in the major institutions of African American life: family, church, school, community service, and political organizations (Hogan-Garcia, 1997). African Americans are more group oriented, sensitive to interpersonal relationships, and value cooperation in contrast to the white American values of individuality, uniqueness, and competition (Sue and Sue, 1990).

The most obvious shared characteristic among African Americans is color. Many African American workers say that "[we] can never get away from color as an identifier; [we] are always seen as blacks, not as human beings" (Blank and Slipp, 1994, p. 16). In front of members of other groups, they often feel they are expected to represent all black people, feeling they are constantly on display. They aren't seen as a person with individual characteristics; their behavior is always related to being black. African Americans believe they are stereotyped and lose much of their identity as individuals, yet in numerous interpersonal exchanges with whites, they are expected to conform to the patterns of white culture. African Americans struggle with unemployment, over twice as high as for white Americans, and with poverty, three times higher than for white families (Gonzalez, 1993).

Hispanics/Latinos/Chicanos. Hispanics, or Latinos as most people from Latin America would rather be called, or Chicanos as many Mexican Americans prefer (Cross, 2000; Mitchell and Salsbury, 1999) share the common bond of the Spanish language, although many speak English or various Native American languages first and Spanish second. The word "Latina" or "Chicana" is used to describe a woman. Cultural conflicts and differences between Hispanics and Latinos in the United States and Latin America can be quite sharp. There are 37 million Latinos, Chicanos, and Hispanics in the United States, the fastest-growing minority and accounting for 13 percent of the nation's population (Streisand, 2003). They are a very diverse group, having come from more than 20 nations in Central and South America, the Caribbean, Puerto Rico, Portugal, and Spain. They are white, black, Native American, or more likely, a mixture of these groups. Language brings them together, along with an emphasis on family and communal ties.

In the Hispanic-Latino-Chicano culture, a person's identity is often closely associated with the family and its status in the community, lasting over a lifetime. (For mainstream white Americans, individual identity is usually more significant.) Decisions are often made by Latinos, Hispanics, and Chicanos in terms of perceived obligations to the family. One's own desires take second place. Social identity is concentrated on interpersonal relationships, even at work, whereas white Americans usually separate social and work relationships (Blank and Slipp, 1994). Certain transitions in life are celebrated with the group. For example, a Latina comes of age on her 15th birthday with a Quinceanera, a celebration of the day she becomes a young woman. Most Hispanics, Latinos, and Chicanos are Catholic; therefore, the celebration usually begins with a church service in which a priest presents the new woman to the parish. Next comes a reception where people dance, eat good food, and give presents.

Hispanics, Latinos, and Chicanos may converse quite directly and more closely in terms of space; however, this is usually done in a quiet and respectful manner. (White Americans prefer their interpersonal space to be at arm's length, about 2 feet, but this strikes many Chicanos, Hispanics, and Latinos as unfriendly or cold, or as a way to show superiority.) Direct eye contact is often seen as disrespectful; Hispanics, Latinos, and Chicanos may look down or away as a mark of respect, especially if the speaker is older or in a position of authority.

Asian Americans. Originating from a wide geographic area with 57 percent of today's world population, Asian Americans come from many nationalities and range from those who have been in the United States for many years to the surge of immigrants who have recently arrived. Limitations of space allow us to focus primarily on the cultural tendencies of Asian people from East and Southeast Asia (China, Japan, Korea, Vietnam, and so on); these collectively number the largest groups of people identified as Asian American. Their religious heritage is animist, Confucian, and Buddhist in its various forms. Filipinos are Christian because of the Spanish influence in their history. Indian Americans and Pakistani Americans share some characteristics with other Asians; however, there are some important differences in religion—Hindu, Muslim, and Sikh.

Asian Americans have a strong loyalty to family and community. They display a modest reserve and avoid confrontation; one "loses face" with a show of strong emotion. A solid work ethic describes most Asian Americans. They work hard, obey authority, give respect to their elders, and are reluctant to complain. Asian Americans speak in a quiet tone of voice and are less likely to touch another person or use gestures while talking. Personal identity and status are closely connected to that of the family. Many Asian Americans believe they are often combined together in one group; they would prefer to be identified by their national origin (Chinese American, Japanese American, Korean American, and so on).

Native Americans. Native Americans do not compose one monolithic culture; they are in a category that is made up of 10 to 16 million people coming from a wide variety of subcultural groups. There were more than 600 tribes at the time the United States was "discovered." Without the help of these tribes, many of the early European settlers would not have survived. Each tribe had its own culture, sovereignty, territory, government, religion, and language and each was recognized as an independent nation. As the number of European immigrants increased, the demand for more Native American land became irrepressible and conflict soon resulted. Through treaties, purchases, and wars, land was eventually transferred to the ownership of the ever-increasing number of European Americans. Native Americans lost their status as separate nations, and the U.S. government began to force assimilation of Indians into American society. Indian children were to be "civilized" by removal from their homes and sent far away to boarding schools. There they were forbidden to speak their tribal language, being taught that their native language was vulgar and the only proper one was English. Nevertheless, much of their original culture has survived even today (Naylor, 1998).

Perhaps their history explains why Native Americans often speak dispassionately about things that are very meaningful to them. Communication is usually indirect, giving others the opportunity to refuse a request without directly saying no or to avoid a subject another person does not want to discuss. Elders with high status can be very direct with people younger than themselves. Gestures are restrained, and eye contact passes swiftly. Direct, steady looks at an elder or very respected person are considered a rude violation of personal space. In formal group experiences where everyone speaks, turns are taken by all present, and no one speaks until the previous speaker is completely finished and a period of silence has been observed. In two-person conversations, a side-by-side arrangement is preferred. When speaking with a person they do not know well, Native Americans may be more comfortable with more than an arm's length between them (Elliott, 1999).

White or European Americans. The dominant strain in American culture has been white and Anglo (English), although it is important to note that other ethnic groups have left their mark on regions of the United States—the Spanish in the Southwest and the French, German, and Scandinavian in the Midwest, for example. Many groups from Europe came to further their economic status, escape persecution, find religious freedom, start a new life, and practice the values of their culture. The primary values were and still are freedom and individualism. These ideas are directly related to many values European Americans hold, such as self-reliance, equal opportunity, independence, privacy, free speech, free enterprise, achievement, progress, success through hard work, a free press, and a separation of church and state in religion. In a subject like career planning, white Americans are more likely to put more value on self-exploration and individual decision making, but some ethnic and racial group members will place a higher value on family and group decisions (Fouad, 1993).

Americans tend to put a high value on material things (related to one's status), technology (what works is what counts), and an optimistic view of change (the future can be better). Diversity is another value; it is a theme of long standing in the United States, and yet one responsible for constant conflict in American society. Americans are competitive; they have a high regard for winners and low regard for those not successful. Winning at any cost is acceptable to many; this notion has led to ethical problems in business and sports. Communication is usually direct; you "lay your cards on the table," but certain topics are avoided in polite company, such as religion and politics. More attention is given to facts (particularly numbers) rather than metaphor or emotion. Like other people in the world, Americans believe their actions are "natural"—only "others" have "customs" (Naylor, 1998).

European Americans prefer an appearance of easygoing friendliness even when there are strong differences of opinion, believing that intensely emotional expressions may lead to a loss of self-control. Eye contact with a speaker should be steady. A medium number of gestures should be employed while speaking, but not as frequently as by Arabs or southern Italians.

White Americans are more likely to take a rational, logical, linear approach to problem solving and decision making. The concept of time is also linear; it is not to be wasted. This leads to an emphasis on efficiency and being task oriented. There is an adherence to time schedules and commitments. People must be punctual. Attention is focused on one thing or one person at a time. European Americans are not likely to touch others in public. These last several features strike members of other cultures as coldness and as not showing much interest in personal relationships and building trust (Elliott, 1999).

As in all cultures, there are contradictions and inconsistencies in the American culture. Most Americans have noticed them when they have thought about it. The value of *equal opportunity* suggests that everyone will have the same opportunity to achieve the "American Dream" of a decent job, happy family life, home ownership, nice furniture and appliances, a good-looking car, a better future, and so on. The existence of prejudice, poverty, racism, and discrimination contradicts this ideal. There are wide differences between people in terms of education, occupation, money, and possessions. Regarding material aspects of the Dream, for many people there is never enough. Appearances are often more important than reality. Some people buy a home plainly beyond their ability to maintain it. Or they may buy an expensive automobile they can't afford, to give the appearance they have successfully "made it." Others donate to charities, political parties, and churches or join the expensive country club because it suggests success to others. The wealthy have advantages in the economic, legal, and political systems that do not exist for the poor. Most Americans are simply unaware of the poor and starving in their own communities (Naylor, 1998). Religion teaches to "love one's neighbor," but this gets contradicted in the fiercely competitive business world. Americans view themselves as generous humanitarians. In many ways they are, but there has been steadily growing opposition to foreign aid programs since World War II and the Marshall Plan's assistance to a beleaguered Europe. Thus there is a discrepancy between the ideal of equality for all and the growing unwillingness to share.

Not only are people within a nationality distinguished on the basis of ethnicity and race, they are also identified according to disablement, gender, sexual orientation, age, occupation, socioeconomic status, region, and religion. Value orientations of some (but not all) of these groups are briefly discussed next.

People with Disabilities. Workers with disabilities encounter all kinds of attitudes. They comment that they are pitied, seen as helplessly dependent, and treated like children on one hand or unnecessarily considered brave and courageous on the other. The most frequent objection is that workers with disabilities are defined by their disability rather than seen as whole people. They are often called "handicapped," a word that comes from "cap in hand"—many people once thought (and some still do) all that disabled people could do was take handouts (Gunn, 2003). Most disabilities are acquired. Actually, all people are disabled in some way, some more obviously than others. Disabilities are a normal part of the human experience.

Because of the 1990 Americans with Disabilities Act (ADA), people with disabilities have increasingly entered the work force. The law prohibits discrimination against the disabled person who can perform the essential functions of the job. Employers are expected to offer reasonable accommodations for disabled workers to perform those functions on the job. The definition of disability has expanded beyond a condition clearly visible such as blindness or use of a wheelchair. The ADA defines any person with a physical, mental, or emotional impairment as disabled. Included in this definition is anyone with epilepsy, diabetes, cancer, HIV infection, AIDS, paralysis, hearing impairment, speech disorders, mental retardation, emotional illness, and those recovering from alcohol or drug abuse (Blank and Slipp, 1994).

Gender. One writer notes that

Although there are differences in the values of men and women within various professions and occupations, the differences in the career values of men and women appear to be decreasing, with both males and females valuing accomplishment, salary, security, and so on. Although differences in abilities, achievements, personality, interests, and values between men and women do exist, they are often rather small. The differences between workers within occupational groups are often much greater than those between men and women in general. (Sharf, 2002, p. 58)

On the six Holland personality types you may have measured in Chapter 3, men are more likely to have higher scores on the Realistic, Investigative, and Enterprising scales, whereas women score higher on the Artistic, Social, and Conventional scales (Holland, 1997). Women in college are more likely to seek ways of combining work with family roles than to make a choice between them (Hallett and Gilbert, 1997). They also rate people-related and intrinsic values higher than do college men (Lips, 1992).

Despite legislation mandating equal pay for the same work, the pay gap between men and women certainly does exist. Women earn 76 cents for every dollar earned by men, and that figure has not changed much over the past quarter-century. Women are promoted less often; in some cases they hit the "glass ceiling"—an invisible barrier to top executive positions, an unseen but real line beyond which they cannot go. Although 43 percent of first-line supervisors and middle managers are women, at the next higher level females make up only 3 percent of the ranks of corporate executives. Of the 4,000 highest paid executives in the country, only 0.5 percent are women (Blank and Slipp, 1994). Perhaps this helps explain why so many women have left jobs to form their own companies.

Pregnancy and childbirth can mean being downgraded on the job or even losing a job. Child care arrangements can pose a problem, too. An overwhelming majority of preschool and school-age children have mothers in the labor force. Some men believe that a woman's performance in leadership roles is less competent than a man's. Sexual harassment affects far more women than men (see Chapter 9 in *Job Search*, book 2 of this series, for a discussion of sexual harassment). Some women have encountered male prejudices, such as unfair accusations of using sex as a means of advancement in their careers.

White males have always had advantages in the workplace, but this is changing because of increasing numbers of minorities and women in the labor force and because of legislation that prohibits discrimination in the hiring practices of employers. Many males have been brought up believing that only men can perform jobs requiring physical strength, and some women believe this, too. White men are brought up to be competitive, strong, aggressive, and dominant and to keep their emotions under control. Some white men complain that minorities and women assume all of them are racist or sexist. And some blue-collar male workers say their manhood is being taken away from them when women enter the workplace to do the same work.

Gay, Lesbian, and Bisexual People.   Two issues disturb gay, lesbian, and bisexual (GLB) people greatly: social disapproval and lack of protective legislation. As a result, most GLB people chose not to "come out" and reveal their sexual orientation openly in the workplace. They remain invisible, or "closeted," in their status, and heterosexual people do not realize their existence. Many people don't realize there is no federal legislation and little state and municipal legislation offering legal protection against widespread discrimination based on sexual orientation.

Those who do come out face two other issues of great importance: workplace discrimination and the denial of benefits to long-term domestic partners. Many gay, lesbian, and bisexual people believe they are seen only in terms of their sex life, not as whole persons who have many kinds of other interests in life. Sexual orientation does not invalidate the great range of personalities, races, religions, professions, and interests; there is as much diversity among the GLB community as in all other groups. To be gay, lesbian, or bisexual is only one part of a person's entire life (Blank and Slipp, 1994).

In dealing with potential employment discrimination, there are three vocational choice strategies for gay, lesbian, and bisexual people: self-employment, job tracking, and risk taking. *Self-employment* means working independently or as an employer. The obvious advantage of self-employment is that it eliminates the threat of being fired for one's sexual orientation. The term *job tracking* refers to working in places owned by GLB people, or where large numbers of GLB people are employed, or working in industries that serve the GLB community or that are affirmative to GLB people. Self-employment and job tracking provide relatively safe working environments; however, these strategies do not completely rule out the possibility of discrimination. With self-employment, GLB people may encounter discrimination from business partners and customers. Job tracking does not eliminate the possibility of informal discrimination when there are homophobic coworkers. Self-employment and job tracking may not always be workable strategies; being one's own boss may not be possible for some, and job tracking may limit career alternatives too much. Also, other factors such as an occupational interest or one's work values may be considered more important than sexual orientation in making career decisions. A third strategy is *risk taking*—choosing a job in work environments with varying degrees of tolerance for GLB people. These workplaces can range from those with nondiscriminatory policies to those known to be homophobic and discriminatory (Chung, 2001).

Younger and Older Workers. Age diversity is a feature of the workplace more than ever before. Work teams in many organizations are composed of people whose ages vary widely, so it is essential to understand different perspectives based on age. Perhaps the greatest difference between younger and older workers is in how they view the world. The older workers' view of the world is often quite clear. Rules and regulations are followed; this creates stability in the workplace. In the past, you knew where you stood. The work environment was secure. For the most part, employers and workers were loyal to each other. The employee was happy to have work; the job occupied a central place in one's life and respect for work and the organization was solid.

A lot of younger workers look at the world differently. The work environment is seen as insecure and full of risk. Rules and regulations are open to examination and questions. Often employers seem indifferent to the needs of workers; so why should employees be loyal in return? Many younger workers believe work has no intrinsic value in itself; it has meaning only if it provides self-fulfillment and/or money (Blank and Slipp, 1994). Clearly, two such divergent views of the workplace can lead to misunderstandings.

Identifying the Values of Your Culture and Subculture

Among the following cultural and subcultural value statements, check the ones that are important to you personally. Leave the space blank for the values that are not important to you, and write a question mark next to the values you believe are not significant in your culture. (The numbers at the left refer to sets of values; they are explained later.)

1. ___ Success is the most important thing, even if it comes at a cost.

   ___ Success is desirable, but the most important thing is how it is attained.

2. ___ The needs of others (family, community, and so on) comes before one's own goals.

   ___ Obligations we have toward one's self come before the needs of others.

3. ___ Be free and be all you are meant to become.

   ___ All people are created equal.

4. ___ Explore new ways, be innovative; seek change for the better.

   ___ Hold fast to tradition and respect your heritage.

5. ___ Follow the dictates of your own conscience.

   ___ Be a loyal member of the organization, team, or family.

6. ___ My major career goal should be to acquire personal wealth and possessions.

___ My major career goal should be one of service to others and the community.

7. ___ The highest loyalty is to your ethnic, racial, religious group, and so on.

___ The highest loyalty is to the country and its government.

8. ___ The purpose of an education is to get a better job.

___ The purpose of an education is to learn wisdom and truth.

9. ___ Be creative and inventive in a natural, spontaneous way.

___ Be neat, systematic, organized, and methodical in your work.

10. ___ Be true to yourself and make your own way in life.

___ Develop contacts and get to know the "right" people.

11. ___ Have confidence in your own ability to make good decisions.

___ Give responsibility on complex matters to knowledgeable experts.

12. ___ It is better to be polite and reserved, avoiding confrontation with others.

___ A person should be direct and honest, saying whatever is on one's mind.

13. ___ A listener should look at the speaker squarely in the eye.

___ When listening, looking steadily at the speaker is rude and impolite.

14. ___ Being touched by a person with whom I am talking shows warmth and friendliness.

___ Being touched by a person with whom I am talking is a violation of my personal space.

15. ___ Play to win; get ahead; be smarter, faster, and more productive than others.

___ The highest satisfaction is working together with others toward a common goal.

16. ___ There is men's work and there is women's work, and the two shouldn't mix.

___ There is no such thing as men's work and women's work; there is simply work.

17. ___ Be religious, believe in God, attend church, synagogue, or mosque.

___ Be skeptical toward things that cannot be empirically proven.

18. ___ Have the courage of your own convictions.

___ Blend in and get along with others to be popular and avoid criticism.

19. ___ The main concern in making career decisions are my family responsibilities.

___ The main concern in making career decisions is my need for self-expression.

20. ___ Some occupations are better than others.

___ All work has worth and dignity.

Can you think of other cultural values not listed here? Which cultural values do you share personally that could be important in your choice of occupation? (Circle them for future reference.)

_____   _____   _____

Where did you get these values? Circle your most influential sources in the following list: *parents; spouse; relatives; teachers; friends; boyfriend/girlfriend; religious leader; writer; political figure; TV or movie star; historical figure; books; authors; ethnic or racial group; nationality; other.*

Write the individuals' names here:

_____

_____

_____

_____

Conflicting Values in the Culture

Notice the number that marks each pair of cultural values in the previous section. The first value in each set conflicts in some way with the second. The value conflicts in each case are as follows:

1. Ends versus means
2. Altruism versus self-assertion
3. Liberty versus equality
4. Change versus stability
5. "Inner" direction versus "other" direction
6. Materialism versus idealism
7. Focus on group interest versus focus on national interest
8. Practical knowledge versus liberal arts education
9. Creativity versus discipline
10. Self-reliance versus reliance on others
11. Self-confidence versus respect for authority
12. Deference versus assertiveness
13. Direct eye contact versus indirect eye contact
14. Close, intimate contact versus open, formal contact
15. Competitiveness versus cooperation
16. Separate gender roles versus unisex work roles
17. Religious belief versus secular skepticism
18. Independence versus conformity
19. Consideration for others versus individualism
20. Status versus equal respect for all work

If everyone in society believed in one set of values and ranked them in the same order, discussion of values would be easy, and the formation of your values would be a simple, straightforward process. Some people may yearn for such a state—but then the society would probably be totalitarian. As long as people are free to think, they will hold diverse beliefs and values that will often conflict with one another. As bothersome as these conflicts can be, it is a sign of freedom. Value conflicts often develop today as values become blurred and indistinct. Parents and teachers are an important influence on value formation, yet these authority figures are in conflict with some of society's values. Your own values are likely to change over a period of time as you react to your culture and because of contradictions within your personality. No wonder the study of values can be complicated and people often have problems identifying and ranking their own values and beliefs.

Take the last value conflict in the previous list as an example: "Some occupations are better than others" versus "All work has worth and dignity." Are some occupations better than others? Society says yes and goes on to rank the status of occupations, giving some higher prestige ratings than others. Everyone participates in this rating game, using values to judge the status of occupations. Exercise 7-1 invites you to rank a list of 18 occupations, first by your own set of values and then by the values you believe operate strongly in society. When you finish, consider the values that helped produce your ranking of these occupations. Reflect also on the relation of your own values to those of your culture.

EXERCISE 7-1 OCCUPATIONAL PRESTIGE EXERCISE

The *prestige* of an occupation refers to the respect, esteem, significance, and importance bestowed on it by the general population. A particular occupation's position among all occupations is usually based on the personal values of individuals and on the shared values in society such as money earned, amount of education required, working conditions, and nature of the work.

In this exercise, use the column at the left titled "My Personal Rank Order" to rank the 18 occupations according to the prestige you give them. Write the number 1 in the space for the occupation you believe has the highest prestige, number 2 in the space for the next highest, and continue to number 18, which in your estimation has the least prestige in this group of 18 occupations.

Next, in the column at the right titled "My Perception of Society's Ranking," rank the same 18 occupations according to the prestige you believe society as a whole attaches to them. Is there any difference between your personal rank order of the 18 occupations and your perceptions of society's rank order?

My Personal Rank Order	Occupation	My Perception of Society's Ranking
_____	Accountant	_____
_____	Auto mechanic	_____
_____	Barber/beautician	_____
_____	Doctor	_____
_____	Drafter/designer	_____
_____	Engineer	_____
_____	Farmer	_____
_____	Machine operator	_____
_____	Plumber	_____
_____	Police officer	_____
_____	Professional athlete	_____
_____	Salesperson	_____
_____	Secretary	_____
_____	Social welfare caseworker	_____
_____	Store manager	_____
_____	Teacher	_____
_____	Truck driver	_____
_____	Waiter/waitress	_____

Table 7-1   Prestige Ranking of 18 Occupations

My Personal Rank Order				My Perception of Society's Ranking			
Rank	Occupation	Mean	Median	Rank	Occupation	Mean	Median
1	Doctor	2.17	1.77	1	Doctor	1.50	1.46
2	Engineer	4.29	3.85	2	Engineer	4.15	3.82
3	Accountant	5.39	4.90	3	Accountant	4.82	4.78
4	Police officer	5.54	5.50	4	Police officer	5.64	5.52
5	Drafter/designer	6.02	6.04	5	Drafter/designer	5.96	5.58
6	Teacher	7.03	7.16	6	Professional athlete	6.92	6.15
7	Social welfare caseworker	8.58	8.41	7	Teacher	7.73	7.25
8	Professional athlete	9.36	8.77	8	Social welfare caseworker	9.64	9.63
9	Secretary	10.30	10.74	9	Store manager	9.86	9.73
10	Store manager	10.36	11.00	10	Secretary	10.72	11.00
11	Farmer	10.63	10.57	11	Farmer	11.22	12.13
12	Auto mechanic	11.55	12.41	12	Auto mechanic	12.06	13.08
13	Salesperson	11.92	12.86	13	Plumber	12.24	12.89
14	Plumber	12.89	13.49	14	Machine operator	12.46	13.17
15	Machine operator	12.91	13.59	15	Salesperson	12.46	13.40
16	Barber/beautician	13.23	14.13	16	Barber/beautician	13.48	14.12
17	Truck driver	13.24	14.93	17	Truck driver	14.25	15.46
18	Waiter/waitress	15.59	17.11	18	Waiter/waitress	16.24	17.66

Note: N = 180 psychology and career-planning students at Jackson Community College (Michigan), October 1985. The median age of JCC students is 29 years.

What value criteria did you use to rank the 18 occupations in your personal rank order and in order of your perception of society's ranking? Possible factors could include the amount of money earned, the level of education required, the type of clothing worn on the job, the work environment, and the recognition received from other people. Factors proposed by Caplow (1954) as elements in occupational prestige were extent of responsibility in the work, nature of the work, amount of formal education required, authority, social class attributes of the occupation, income (both amount and certainty), and behavior control. Less apparent reasons may involve more subtle psychological factors, such as independence, job security, service to others, advancement, creativity, type of people with the occupation, leisure time, and so on. Table 7-1 lets you compare your occupational prestige rankings with those of 180 college students ranging in age from late teens to their 50s.

Occupational status has remained relatively stable over time in the United States (Isaacson and Brown (1997). Kanzaki (1976) and others discovered little change in the social status of occupations over a period of 50 years. In Kanzaki's study, 25 occupations were ranked, with physician ranking first and civil engineer placing second. A later study involving college students in mainland China, Taiwan, and the United States produced similar results and placed physician first, lawyer (not in this book's list of 18 occupations) second, and civil engineer third (Fredrickson, Lin, and Xing, 1992).

PERSONAL VALUES

This section includes exercises involving incomplete value sentences and a list of personal values. Before you do those exercises, consider the following six basic value orientations. They come from a long-standing, widely used values inventory designed by Gordon Allport, Philip Vernon, and Gardner Lindzey (1960).

1. *Theoretical.* The theoretical person is characterized by a dominant interest in the discovery of truth; in the pursuit of this goal, he or she takes an empirical, critical, rational, intellectual approach. This person seeks basically to observe, reason, and order or systematize knowledge, not to make judgments about the beauty or utility of things.

2. *Economic.* The economic person emphasizes what is useful and practical, embracing the values of the business world: production, marketing, and consumption of goods and accumulation of tangible wealth. This type wants education to be useful, regards unapplied knowledge as waste, and is more interested in surpassing other people in wealth than in dominating them (political attitude) or in serving them (social attitude).

3. *Aesthetic.* The aesthetic person places high value on form and harmony and judges each experience from the standpoint of grace, symmetry, or fitness. Life is viewed as a progression of events and impressions, each enjoyed for its own sake; this attitude is characteristic of an aesthetic person, whether the person is a creative artist or not.

4. *Social.* The social person is described as altruistic or philanthropic, regarding love and caring for others as the only proper or suitable form of human relationship. This type of person often finds theoretical, economic, and aesthetic attitudes cold and inhuman and tends to approach closely to the religious attitude.

5. *Political.* The political person is primarily interested in power, influence, and fame. This person's activities are not necessarily limited to the field of politics; they can apply to any vocation. Leaders in any field generally have high power value. Because competition and struggle are a large part of all life, many philosophers have seen power as the most universal and most fundamental of motives.

6. *Religious.* The religious person is concerned with the unity of all experience, is mystical, and seeks to comprehend the cosmos as a whole, relating one's self to an all-embracing totality. Some people of this type find their religious experience in an active participation in and affirmation of life, whereas others seek it through withdrawal from life, self-denial, and meditation.

Religion is a great source of human values. It upholds moral principles of righteousness, as in Buddhism's Eightfold Path of right knowledge, right aspiration, right speech, right conduct, right occupation, right effort, right mindfulness, and right contemplation. Islam emphasizes the oneness of God, prayer, pilgrimage, and submission to God. The prophets of Judaism have proclaimed the need for social justice, and Christianity teaches the virtues of faith, hope, and love. The religions of the world contribute significantly to the search for value and meaning in life.

EXERCISE 7-2 INCOMPLETE VALUE SENTENCES

As one of the strategies for value clarification, Sidney Simon, Leland Howe, and Howard Kirschenbaum (1995) suggest a sentence completion activity. Using an adaptation of that idea, complete each of the following sentences with the first thing that comes to your mind.

___ 1. If I had a million dollars, I would . . . _____

___ 2. The best idea I ever heard or read is . . . _____

___ 3. One thing I would change in the world is . . ._____

___ 4. What I want most in life is . . . _____

___ 5. I do best when . . . _____

___ 6. I am most concerned about . . ._____

___ 7. I daydream most about . . . _____

Source: Adapted from Howe and Howe (1975).

___ 8. I think my parents would like me to . . . _____

___ 9. The greatest joy in my life is . . . _____

___ 10. I am . . . _____

___ 11. People who know me well think I am . . . _____

___ 12. I believe . . . _____

___ 13. If I had 24 hours to live, I would . . . _____

___ 14. The kind of music I like best is . . . _____

___ 15. The people I work with best are . . . _____

___ 16. My job must give me . . . _____

___ 17. Advice I would give my children would be . . . _____

___ 18. The best programs on television are . . . _____

___ 19. I secretly wish . . . _____

___ 20. In school I do (did) best when . . . _____

___ 21. If I could save only one thing in a fire, it would be . . . _____

___ 22. If I could change one thing about myself, it would be . . . _____

Now analyze the endings to these sentences. What values are suggested? Code your statements in one or more of the following ways (Simon, Howe, and Kirschenbaum, 1995).

Write *P* next to statements about which you are most *proud*.

Write *PA* next to statements that you would *publicly affirm*.

Write *CA* next to statements for which you have *considered alternatives*.

Write *TC* next to statements in which you *thought* about the *consequences*.

Write *F* next to statements you know you have chosen *freely*.

Write *A* next to statements on which you have actually *acted*.

Write *R* next to statements on which you have acted with *repetition*.

EXERCISE 7-3 RANK ORDERING OF 21 PERSONAL VALUES

Arrange the following 21 values in the order of their importance to you. If you have time, print the names of the values on small cards, and then arrange the 21 "values cards" in order of priority. On the following list, write the number 1 next to the value that is the most important to you. Next, place the number 2 next to the value that is second in its importance to you. Continue until you have ranked all 21 values, with the number 21 by the value that is least important to you. Circle the highest three or four values for future reference.

_____ *Achievement:* accomplishment; a result brought about by resolve, persistence, or endeavor. The word *achieve* is defined as "to bring to a successful conclusion; to attain a desired goal."

_____ *Aesthetics:* the appreciation and enjoyment of beauty for beauty's sake.

_____ *Altruism:* regard for or devotion to the interests of others.

_____ *Autonomy:* the ability to be a self-determining individual.

Source: Peterson (1972).

_____ *Creativity:* the creating of new and innovative ideas and designs.

_____ *Emotional well-being:* freedom from overwhelming anxieties and barriers to effective functioning; peace of mind; inner security.

_____ *Health:* the condition of being sound in body; freedom from physical disease or pain; the general condition of the body.

_____ *Honesty:* fairness or straightforwardness of conduct; integrity; uprightness of character or action.

_____ *Justice:* the quality of being impartial or fair; righteousness; conformity to truth, fact, or reason; fair treatment of others.

_____ *Knowledge:* the seeking of truth, information, or principles for the satisfaction of curiosity, for use, or for the power of knowing.

_____ *Love:* affection based on admiration or benevolence; warm attachment, enthusiasm, or devotion; unselfish devotion that freely accepts another in loyalty and seeks that person's good.

_____ *Loyalty:* maintaining allegiance to a person, group, institution, or political unit.

_____ *Morality:* the belief in and keeping of ethical standards.

_____ *Physical appearance:* concern for the beauty of one's own body.

_____ *Pleasure:* the agreeable emotion accompanying the possession or expectation of what is good or greatly desired. Pleasure stresses satisfaction or gratification rather than visible happiness.

_____ *Power:* possession of control, authority, or influence over others.

_____ *Recognition:* being made to feel significant and important; being given special notice or attention.

_____ *Religious faith:* communion with, obedience to, and activity in behalf of a supreme being.

_____ *Skill:* the ability to use one's knowledge effectively and readily in execution or performance; technical expertise.

_____ *Wealth:* abundance of valuable material possessions; affluence.

_____ *Wisdom:* the ability to discern inner qualities and relationships; insight, good sense, judgment.

Table 7-2 presents a group ranking of these values.

Table 7-2 Group Ranking of 21 Values in Exercise 7-3

Value	Mean	Rank	Value	Mean	Rank	Value	Mean	Rank
Achievement	9.55	7	Honesty	6.57	3	Pleasure	12.15	13
Aesthetics	15.65	20	Justice	10.14	8	Power	16.63	21
Altruism	13.99	18	Knowledge	7.82	5	Recognition	13.96	17
Autonomy	11.69	11	Love	5.90	2	Religious faith	12.79	14
Creativity	13.13	16	Loyalty	10.44	10	Skill	10.17	9
Emotional well-being	6.99	4	Morality	11.82	12	Wealth	14.77	19
Health	5.33	1	Physical appearance	13.04	15	Wisdom	8.47	6
						(*Group mean*	11.00	11)

Note: Respondents were Jackson Community College students and CETA trainees. *N* = 329

WORK VALUES

A study of work values is fundamental to career planning. If your values are expressed in your occupational life, then your work takes on meaning and purpose; your job becomes a joy rather than a curse. If your work does not provide personal satisfaction, life itself grows stale, flat, and boring.

Many lists of work values have been proposed. Table 7-3 lists 16 basic values expressed in work developed for the *System of Interactive Guidance and Information* (SIGI PLUS) computer-based career decision-making program. The 16 values are presented in adapted form. Can you arrange the 16 values in order, from the most important to the least important to you? Work values are often linked closely with

Table 7-3   SIGI PLUS® Work-Related Values

The computerized career guidance and planning software SIGI PLUS lists two kinds of work-related values: *occupation-related* values, those generally associated with an occupation as a whole, and *job-related* values, those that depend on the specific job a person might hold. Following are the eight occupation-related values and the eight job-related values in SIGI PLUS.

Occupation-Related Values	Job-Related Values
Contribution to society Almost all work contributes to the functioning of society, but you want your work to be devoted mainly to the improvement of the health, education, or welfare of society as a whole.	*Advancement* You want a chance to be promoted in predictable steps or to move directly to a higher-level job. You want to avoid a dead-end job.
High income You want an occupation in which the median income is high compared with other occupations. (The median is the point at which half earn more, half less.)	*Challenge* You want to use your abilities to solve difficult problems. The work won't be easy, but it can give you a feeling of accomplishment.
Independence You want to be your own boss, make your own decisions, or work without close supervision, rather than be required to follow daily instructions to the letter.	*Easy commute* You want your work to be close to home, so getting there and back takes little time. You may want convenient public transportation, carpooling, or vanpooling to be available.
Leadership You want to guide others, to tell them what to do, to get them to work together, and to be responsible for their performance. You're willing to accept the blame when things go wrong.	*Flexible hours* You want a flexible work schedule, so that you can adjust on-the-job hours as long as you put in the required total time.
Leisure You want short hours or long vacations. You feel that the satisfactions you get off the job are so important that work must not interfere with them.	*Fringe benefits* You want work that offers many "extras" besides pay—such as health benefits, tuition aid, and child care.
Prestige You want an occupation that will lead people to look up to you, to listen to your opinions, or to seek your help in community affairs.	*On-the-job learning* You want to learn new skills and ideas, so that you can learn the job as you go or prepare for a higher-level job. You may simply enjoy learning for its own sake.
Security You want work that is not sensitive to recession, abrupt changes in technology, government spending, or public taste. You want to avoid seasonal ups and downs.	*Pleasant coworkers* You want to work with people who are agreeable, who share your interests and attitudes, and who are easy to get along with.
Variety You want different activities and problems, people, or locations, rather than a fixed routine.	*Staying put* You want work that will not require a move to another geographic area.

Source: Adapted from *SIGI PLUS® Counselor's Manual* (1998) by permission of Educational Testing Service, the copyright owner.

certain occupations and can be the basis of a good match between you and your job. For example, suppose creativity is an important work value to you. Architects, designers, advertising workers, engineers, and performing artists work in occupations where creativity is a significant job characteristic (Rosenthal, 1989). The work values of journalists have been described as independence, variety, travel, recognition, and influence (Fallows, 1996). A mismatch can occur when certain values important to you are missing in an occupation.

EXERCISE 7-4 WORK VALUES AUCTION

In this group exercise, each of the items listed in the Work Values Auction chart will be auctioned off to the highest bidder.

You have $1000 to spend at this auction. Before the auction begins, budget the amount you plan to spend on any given item. You can spend the entire $1000 on one item or divide it between two items or among as many items as you wish, as long as your total budget does not exceed $1000. Write the amount of money you plan to budget for each item you desire in the first column of the Work Values Auction chart.

Here are the directions for bidding. You are not restricted to the amount in bidding you budgeted for an item. If you decide to spend more than you budgeted for an item, you may do so as long as the total amount does not exceed $1000.

When you have bought an item, the amount of your bid is subtracted from your total of $1000. If you bid and do not get the item, the money budgeted for that item can be used on another item of your choice.

Keep a record of what happened during the auction. Enter the highest amount you bid for any item in the second column (whether you won or lost the item). In the third column, check any items that you won.

Finally, all bids must start at no less than $5 and must increase by amounts of at least $5. Of course, bids can be much higher than that. The first bid of $1000 (the highest possible bid) on any item stops the bidding, and the item is automatically sold to the bidder.

The items will be auctioned off at random. They will be drawn from an envelope, *not* by starting with number 1 at the top and going numerically down the list of items. An item can appear at any time.

Work Values Auction

Occupations for Sale	Amount You Budgeted	Highest Amount You Bid	Items You Won	Values Associated with Item
An occupation that lets me . . .				
1. Be attractive and well-liked by everyone I know.	_____	_____	____	_____
2. Have good health—a long life without illness.	_____	_____	____	_____
3. Attain self-understanding—that is, know for certain who I am.	_____	_____	____	_____
4. Earn more than a million dollars per year.	_____	_____	____	_____
5. Become the most influential person in a company or a community.	_____	_____	____	_____
6. Have time for a rewarding, happy, fulfilling family life.	_____	_____	____	_____

Sources: Adapted from McHolland and Trueblood (1972) and from Peterson, Sharp, Hall, and Thomas (1972).

Work Values Auction

Occupations for Sale	Amount You Budgeted	Highest Amount You Bid	Items You Won	Values Associated with Item
An occupation that lets me . . .				
7. Contribute toward the beliefs of my religious faith.	_____	_____	_____	_____
8. Attend social events—concerts, plays, ballets, or athletic games.	_____	_____	_____	_____
9. Work toward a world free of prejudice, unfairness, and cheating.	_____	_____	_____	_____
10. Give outstanding service to the poor and the sick.	_____	_____	_____	_____
11. Do whatever I like to do whenever I want to do it.	_____	_____	_____	_____
12. Have a job and an income for as long as I want.	_____	_____	_____	_____
13. Discover truth and know the meaning of life.	_____	_____	_____	_____
14. Achieve mastery and success in all that I do.	_____	_____	_____	_____
15. Acquire a learning center with all the books, computers, and aids I need.	_____	_____	_____	_____
16. Create an atmosphere where people give and receive love freely.	_____	_____	_____	_____
17. Take risks, meet challenges, and have an exciting life.	_____	_____	_____	_____
18. Originate new ideas and create new ways of doing things.	_____	_____	_____	_____
19. Set my own working conditions, hours, location, clothing worn, and so on.	_____	_____	_____	_____
20. Make attractive things and contribute beauty to the world.	_____	_____	_____	_____
21. Gain national or international fame and popularity.	_____	_____	_____	_____
22. Go on long vacations where I have nothing to do but enjoy myself.	_____	_____	_____	_____

After the auction, consider the items you selected. Then reflect on what value was really in your mind when you selected each item. Several values may be represented by one item; some possibilities are suggested in Table 7-4.

Consider each item in terms of the values it represents. If a person's highest bid was $600 or even $1000 for the opportunity to direct the destiny of the nation or of an organization, perhaps power, altruism, or national security are important and active values in that person's life.

Were your feelings different when you were engaged in a real contest with someone else for the same item? Did you stay close to the amount you budgeted for each item, or did your emotional involvement upset your rational plans during the auction?

EXERCISE 7-5 EVALUATING A LIST OF WORK VALUES

Hundreds of possible work values exist. This exercise gives you an opportunity to review some values that could be important to you in your work. As you go through the list of values, a word or phrase used in the definition may appeal to you more than

Table 7-4 Values Associated with Items on the Work Values Auction Chart

Occupations for Sale	Values Associated with Item*
An occupation that lets me . . .	
1. be attractive and well-liked.	Physical appearance, recognition
2. have good health.	Health, emotional well-being
3. know for certain who I am.	Wisdom, self-knowledge, inner harmony
4. earn over $1 million per year.	Wealth, high income, money, profit
5. be the most influential.	Power, leadership, advancement
6. have a rewarding family life.	Family relationships, lifestyle
7. practice my religious faith.	Moral/religious concerns, salvation
8. attend social events.	Aesthetics, leisure, excitement
9. be free of prejudice.	Fairness, justice, honesty, morality
10. give service to the poor and sick.	Altruism, helping others, friendship
11. do whatever I like to do.	Autonomy, independence, way of life
12. have job/income as wanted.	Job security, stability, steady work
13. know the meaning of life.	Wisdom, truth, personal growth
14. achieve mastery and success.	Achievement, skill, recognition
15. acquire a learning center.	Knowledge, intellectual stimulation
16. give and receive love.	Affection, love, friendship
17. take risks, meet challenges.	Adventure, excitement, competition
18. originate new ideas.	Creativity, variety, change
19. set my own working conditions.	Freedom, independence, personal power
20. contribute beauty to the world.	Aesthetics, artistic creativity
21. gain fame and popularity.	Recognition, exhibition, prestige
22. go on long vacations.	Leisure time, relaxation, health

*Values mentioned here are not the only values that could be associated with the item. This list of values is merely suggestive, and many other values could be added.

the one used to label that work value. Circle or mark that word or phrase so you will notice it when you list your most important work values in later exercises.

Using the following rating scale, write the appropriate letter next to each item on the list that follows. Where the work value is or may be related as much or more to work organizations than to occupations, it is marked with an asterisk (*).

Rating Scale

A = Very important to me in my work
B = Above average in importance to me in my work
C = Of average importance to me in my work
D = Of little or no importance to me in my work

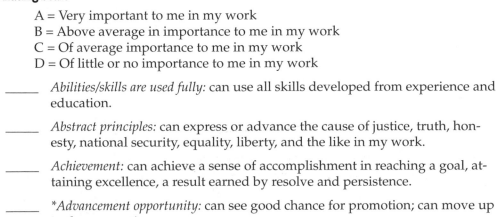

_____ *Abilities/skills are used fully:* can use all skills developed from experience and education.

_____ *Abstract principles:* can express or advance the cause of justice, truth, honesty, national security, equality, liberty, and the like in my work.

_____ *Achievement:* can achieve a sense of accomplishment in reaching a goal, attaining excellence, a result earned by resolve and persistence.

_____ *Advancement opportunity:* can see good chance for promotion; can move up in the occupation.

Rating Scale

A = Very important to me in my work
B = Above average in importance to me in my work
C = Of average importance to me in my work
D = Of little or no importance to me in my work

_____ *Adventure:* can engage in action, excitement, risk taking, and possible hazards are part of the work.

_____ *Altruism/service:* can be helpful to others, express concern for people and society, social welfare interest, empathy.

_____ *Animal work:* can be around and take care of animals.

_____ *Artistic creativity:* can engage in expressive activity such as artwork, music, entertainment, drama, and writing.

_____ *Authority:* can give instructions and directions to others on the job.

_____ *Beauty/aesthetics:* can express a sense of balance and harmony, exercise artistry, contribute beauty to the environment and world.

_____ **Casual dress:* can do work that allows me to dress informally and not have to wear business suits or tailored clothes.

_____ **Challenge:* can enter into activities that test me (even when there is a chance I might fail); demanding work, struggle, risk, pressure.

_____ *Cleanliness:* can do work that allows me to stay clean and neat on the job; can avoid dirty work.

_____ **Comfortable surroundings:* working conditions that have pleasantness and ease; appropriate temperature, quietness, proper lighting.

_____ *Community/social concern:* can get involved with and make contributions to local problem areas and public affairs; civic-mindedness.

_____ *Competence (sense of):* can do work I know I can perform well; opportunity to use my skills; feel I can meet work requirements.

_____ *Competition:* can do work that involves struggle, rivalry, and a contest with others for honors and recognition.

_____ *Continuous activity:* I can be busy all the time at work in an occupation.

_____ *Creativity:* can originate new ideas, experiments, research, and new ways of doing things.

_____ *Demand for my skills:* people are needed in my occupation; undersupply of workers in my field; little or no competition for jobs.

_____ *Detailed work:* can work with specific details or do work that requires precision, such as accounting or watch repair.

_____ *Discovery of truth:* can enter into activities (study, research) where I can bring to light the actual state of affairs or knowledge.

_____ **Dress well on the job:* can be well dressed and make a good physical appearance on the job.

_____ *Early entry:* can enter an occupation with little or no additional training or education beyond what I have now.

_____ *Enterprise:* can enter into activities that allow me to work hard; opportunity to make plans for projects and participate in those projects.

Rating Scale

A = Very important to me in my work
B = Above average in importance to me in my work
C = Of average importance to me in my work
D = Of little or no importance to me in my work

_____ *Exhibition/fame:* can do work in which I get noticed or achieve a widespread reputation.

_____ **Fair supervision:* can work for supervisors or bosses who are fair and honorable and with whom I can get along.

_____ **Family relationships:* can do work that allows me to have and maintain good, active relationships with my family; can take time with family.

_____ **Flexible work hours:* can do work that allows me to set my own hours on the job

_____ *Follow directions:* can do work that requires me to be directed by other people, where I don't have to make a lot of decisions on my own.

_____ **Friendship:* can be in work that gives fellowship with work associates and creates companionship with them; needs for affiliation are satisfied.

_____ **Fringe benefits:* can have work that pays much or all of my medical expenses; has life insurance, pension plans, accident insurance, paid vacations.

_____ **Health:* can do work that promotes good health and physical well-being; little or no risk of injury or disease; manageable stress factors.

_____ *Heavy work/physical strength:* can do work that involves the use of muscles, standing on feet, physical endurance, heavy lifting.

_____ *High income:* can earn good money, high pay, adequate salary, wealth, good commissions.

_____ *Independence/autonomy/freedom:* can work in my own way, structure my own time.

_____ *Inner harmony:* can have peace of mind or emotional well-being.

_____ *Knowledge:* can use and increase my intelligence, logic, analytical skill, or learning on the job.

_____ **Large work organization:* can work in large companies or work organizations that offer more opportunities to express my values.

_____ *Leadership/management:* can plan and administer programs or activities, direct others, make decisions, lay out work for others to do.

_____ **Leisure time:* can have time for recreation, family activities, vacations, social events; can do the things besides work that I want to do.

_____ *Light physical labor:* can avoid heavy lifting, walking long distances, lots of standing, or frequent stooping.

_____ **Location of work:* can work in jobs that are located in a geographic area where I want to live.

_____ *Mathematics:* can use mathematics (arithmetic, algebra, geometry, trigonometry, calculus, statistics) on the job.

_____ *Mechanical opportunities:* can use and be around machines, tools, and mechanical equipment on the job.

Rating Scale

A = Very important to me in my work
B = Above average in importance to me in my work
C = Of average importance to me in my work
D = Of little or no importance to me in my work

_____ *Moral/ethical/religious commitment:* can avoid violating my principles; devotion to ideals; personal integrity.

_____ *Observable results:* can have the satisfaction of seeing what I have accomplished.

_____ *Older people:* can be in contact and work with elderly people.

_____ *Optimal levels of stress:* can avoid the stresses of life-threatening situations, deadlines, and the like.

_____ *Outdoor work:* can be outside all or most of the time I am on the job.

_____ *People contact:* can work with many people (whether they are friends or not), have a good chance of meeting new people.

_____ *Personal growth/education/enlightenment:* can be in work that lets me develop into a more mature, knowledgeable person; can keep learning new things.

_____ *Personal influence/power:* can dominate situations, influence others, exercise authority, control others.

_____ *Persuasion:* can persuade or sell others on my ideas or products that I can offer.

_____ *Physical work:* can engage in manual labor, use my athletic skills, use fingers and hands in making things.

_____ *Pleasure/fun:* can have a good time and have a chance to play.

_____ *Prestige/status:* can work at a job that is important in the minds of other people; high social position goes with the occupation.

_____ *Problem solving:* can decide what needs to be done in finding a solution to a problem.

_____ *Profit:* can have opportunities for financial gain through investment of my own money, time, and energy.

_____ *Rapid work/fast pace:* can operate at a fast pace, where quickness and liveliness are major factors.

_____ *Reading:* can read a lot of books, newspapers, magazines, technical reports, essays, drama scripts, poetry, novels, nonfiction.

_____ *Recognition/appreciation:* can get attention or acknowledgment of what I do on the job; public honor, social approval, fame, tribute.

_____ *Repetition:* can do the work over and over again after learning it; lets me do things that don't change much day after day.

_____ *Responsibility:* can be in charge of and accountable for my own work and the work of others; can show my dependability and trustworthiness.

_____ *Safety:* can work in a safe environment; avoid potentially hazardous situations such as high places, explosives, or dangerous machinery.

_____ *Security (job security):* can have work that is steady and available even in hard times; not likely to be laid off.

Rating Scale

A = Very important to me in my work
B = Above average in importance to me in my work
C = Of average importance to me in my work
D = Of little or no importance to me in my work

_____ *Self-employment:* can establish my own business and be my own boss (with all the risk this involves).

_____ *Small work organization:* can work mostly in small companies or organizations where I feel I can contribute more.

_____ *Social poise/civility:* can work in an atmosphere of courtesy, discipline, dignity, sensitivity, patience, self-control.

_____ *Stability:* can have job duties that are predictable and that are not likely to change over a long period of time.

_____ *Teamwork:* can be part of a team or group of people in getting a job done.

_____ *Tradition/heritage:* can be loyal to customs of those who have preceded me in this work; can do a job that my father or mother did.

_____ *Travel (on the job):* can go from one place to another by various forms of transportation while working; can be on the move constantly.

_____ *Understanding/wisdom:* can work on a job that lets me better understand myself, other people, and the world around me.

_____ *Utility/usefulness:* can do work that is valuable to others and produces material results; occupations that emphasize the practical side of things.

_____ *Variety/change:* can do many different kinds of activities in the same occupation; diverse job functions.

_____ *Way of life:* can express a lifestyle or live the kind of life I want.

_____ *Work alone:* can work by myself without much contact with others; allows solitude, contemplation, anonymity, detachment.

_____ *Work associates:* can work with people who have similar personalities; can be with people who are very much like I am.

_____ *Young children:* can be in contact with young children.

Now go back through the list of work values that you rated "A," and circle or check those values that are (or would be) essential or indispensable to you in your occupational life. Do this so the circled values can be noticed and used in later exercises.

The Work Values Inventory

The Work Values Inventory (WVI) was developed by Donald E. Super to measure values—both in and outside of work—and to assess the goals that motivate people to work. The WVI measures 15 work values by having you rate statements on their degree of importance to you. The WVI was recently revised to measure 12 of the 15 original values. Both original and revised versions are currently in use. In the revised edition, three values (altruism, aesthetic, and management) have been deleted and six have the same names as in the original. The other six values have been renamed in the revised edition, and these are indicated in parenthesis. The following descriptions of the work values are summarized from the WVI manual (Super, 1970). Circle three to five of the most important values. If you take the WVI, record your scores in the spaces next to each work value and circle three to five of the highest values.

_____ *Altruism*—work that allows you to contribute to the welfare of other people, a social service interest.

_____ *Aesthetic*—work that permits you to make beautiful things and contribute beauty to the environment.

_____ *Creativity*—work that enables you to invent new things, design new products, or develop new ideas.

_____ *Intellectual stimulation (mental challenge)*—work that provides opportunities for independent thinking and for learning how and why things operate or function.

_____ *Achievement*—work that gives you a feeling of accomplishment in doing a job well. People who value achievement like work that gives visible, tangible results.

_____ *Independence*—work that allows you to work in your own way, as fast or as slowly as you wish.

_____ *Prestige*—work that gives you standing or esteem in the eyes of others and evokes respect.

_____ *Management*—work that permits you to plan and lay out work for others to do.

_____ *Economic returns (income)*—work that pays well and enables you to have the things you want.

_____ *Security*—work that gives you a high probability of having a job, even in hard times.

_____ *Surroundings (work environment)*—work that is carried out under pleasant conditions (not too hot or cold, not too noisy or dirty). Surroundings, or the physical environment in which the work is done, are important to people with interests not specifically in the work itself but more in accompanying conditions of work on the job.

_____ *Supervisory relations (supervision)*—work that is carried out under a supervisor who is fair and with whom you can get along; getting along with the boss.

_____ *Associates (coworkers)*—work that brings you into contact with coworkers whom you like. For some people, the social life on the job is more important than the nature of the work itself.

_____ *Way of life (lifestyle)*—work that lets you live the kind of life you choose and be the type of person you wish to be.

_____ *Variety*—work that provides an opportunity to do many different kinds of functions on the same job.

The Values Scale

The *Values Scale* (VS), developed by Donald Super and Dorothy Nevill (1985), extends the range of values covered in the *Work Values Inventory* (WVI) by including other values that emerged through research. The VS, like the WVI, asks you to rate the importance of statements of values. The scale for each value consists of five items. At least two of these items relate to work values, and at least two relate to values in general, except for the Working Conditions Scale, where all five items are related to work values (Nevill and Super, 1989). Following are descriptions of the 21 values, adapted from the Values Scale (Super and Nevill, 1985). Circle the values that are the highest in importance to you. If you take the Values Scale, record your score for each value and circle several of the highest values. (The range of raw scores for each value is 5 to 20.)

_____ 1. *Ability utilization:* being able to use my skill and knowledge

_____ 2. *Achievement:* having accomplishments that show I have done well

_____ 3. *Advancement:* opportunities to move ahead; getting promotions

_____ 4. *Aesthetics:* making life more beautiful and being appreciated for it

_____ 5. *Altruism:* being involved in activities that help people; improving life for others

_____ 6. *Authority:* leading and managing other people in what they do

_____ 7. *Autonomy:* making decisions for myself; being on my own

_____ 8. *Creativity:* discovering, inventing, or designing new ideas and things

_____ 9. *Economic reward:* being well-paid; having a high standard of living

_____ 10. *Lifestyle:* planning life and work according to my own ideas

_____ 11. *Personal development:* growing and advancing as a person and finding satisfaction in life as a result

_____ 12. *Physical activity:* getting a lot of exercise and being physically active

_____ 13. *Prestige:* being recognized for work done; being held in high esteem

_____ 14. *Risk:* being challenged by activities that involve danger when there is something to gain

_____ 15. *Social interaction:* doing things in a group of people rather than by myself

_____ 16. *Social relations:* being with friends and/or people like myself

_____ 17. *Variety:* doing different things each day; changing activities frequently

_____ 18. *Working conditions:* having a comfortable place to work: clean facilities, protection from bad weather, and so on

_____ 19. *Cultural identity:* being accepted as a member of my race or ethnic group; working with people of my own background

_____ 20. *Physical prowess:* using strength; moving things that are heavy; operating powerful machines

_____ 21. *Economic security:* having regular employment in a secure position

For the reader who cannot take the Work Values Inventory or the Values Scale, Exercise 7-6 offers the *Review of Work Values* (ROWV).

EXERCISE 7-6 REVIEW OF WORK VALUES INVENTORY

Using the same format as the WVI and VS, this inventory measures 30 values and uses 4 statements for each scale. After you have finished rating 120 statements, you will be given directions for scoring the inventory and identifying your highest work values. The best way to take the ROWV is to respond to the statement with your first impression and go right on to the next statement. Most people can complete the inventory in 25 or 30 minutes.

The statements in this inventory reflect values that have degrees of importance to people and can bring them satisfaction in their occupations. Read each sentence and indicate its importance to you by ranking it according to the following number key:

4 means the statement is *very important* to me.

3 means the statement is *important* to me.

2 means the statement is of *average importance* to me.

1 means the statement is of *little importance* to me.

0 means the statement is of *no importance* to me.

I need work in which I . . .

_____ 1. feel I have accomplished something with excellence

_____ 2. will be promoted regularly for work well done

_____ 3. experience feelings of excitement and action

_____ 4. study and appreciate beauty and beautiful things

_____ 5. help other people solve their problems

_____ 6. compete with others either by myself or on a team

_____ 7. use my imagination to create something new

_____ 8. start a new job right away or in a short time

_____ 9. gain the attention of other people

_____ 10. know that the policies of my workplace are reasonable

_____ 11. make many new friends among my work associates

_____ 12. am not subjected to an excessive amount of strain and stress

_____ 13. have more than enough money to live on

_____ 14. can be at home more with my family

_____ 15. can do my job in the way I want

_____ 16. have a job in my main field of interest

_____ 17. manage and direct the work of other people

_____ 18. live the kind of life I want to live

_____ 19. can get a job where I live now or in a nearby area

_____ 20. use my hands and body in performing tasks on the job

_____ 21. express my religious beliefs

_____ 22. am outside more than indoors

_____ 23. meet lots of people as a result of what I do on the job

_____ 24. wear nice clothes on the job

_____ 25. follow established procedures and customs

_____ 26. know other people are aware that I have done a good job

_____ 27. will have a job even in hard times

_____ 28. am respected and looked up to

_____ 29. have many changes of duties and assignments

_____ 30. do the job under pleasant working conditions

_____ 31. know I have achieved the goal I have set for myself

_____ 32. advance to higher positions in a reasonable time frame

4 means the statement is *very important* to me.

3 means the statement is *important* to me.

2 means the statement is of *average importance* to me.

1 means the statement is of *little importance* to me.

0 means the statement is of *no importance* to me.

I need work in which I . . .

_____ 33. take risks in getting a job completed

_____ 34. use my artistic, musical, or literary ability

_____ 35. instruct other people to do things for their own benefit

_____ 36. must come out ahead of others in order to move forward

_____ 37. design new or different things, products, or ideas

_____ 38. need little or no further education or training

_____ 39. show my skills and talents in front of people

_____ 40. have a boss who is fair and treats everyone alike

_____ 41. meet people that I like and enjoy

_____ 42. can stay in sound physical and mental condition

_____ 43. make money to buy things beyond the necessities of life

_____ 44. spend more time taking care of family and loved ones

_____ 45. have freedom to make my own decisions

_____ 46. am challenged by new problems to solve

_____ 47. have the power to make decisions that affect other people

_____ 48. have a way of life I like and enjoy

_____ 49. am employed in a workplace that is accessible to me

_____ 50. operate machines, tools, or other equipment

_____ 51. can live up to an ethical code of behavior

_____ 52. do not have to be indoors very often

_____ 53. perform direct services for other people

_____ 54. dress any way I want to

_____ 55. have job duties that are predictable and won't change

_____ 56. obtain public attention and approval

_____ 57. know the job will last for a long time

_____ 58. am aware that other people see my job as important

_____ 59. have many different kinds of functions on the same job

_____ 60. have an attractive place at which to do my job

_____ 61. see the results of a job well done

_____ 62. move up rapidly in my work organization

_____ 63. take on daring assignments that call for courage

4 means the statement is *very important* to me.

3 means the statement is *important* to me.

2 means the statement is of *average importance* to me.

1 means the statement is of *little importance* to me.

0 means the statement is of *no importance* to me.

I need work in which I . . .

_____ 64. contribute beauty and harmony to the world

_____ 65. care for people who are poor or sick

_____ 66. contend with others who are rivals for the same reward

_____ 67. bring into being a new product or way of doing something

_____ 68. begin a job without much delay from school or preparation

_____ 69. have my personal achievements noticed by other people

_____ 70. know my supervisors and coworkers are honest and truthful

_____ 71. cooperate closely with fellow employees

_____ 72. won't burn out or get run-down

_____ 73. earn extra income for luxuries and additional possessions

_____ 74. have longer vacations than most workers

_____ 75. control my own area of responsibility

_____ 76. get so involved that I don't notice the passing of time

_____ 77. am responsible for the work that other people do

_____ 78. am the kind of person I want to be

_____ 79. have no transportation problems getting to the job

_____ 80. rely on my physical strength and muscular coordination

_____ 81. am not required to do things I consider morally wrong

_____ 82. must be outdoors most of the time

_____ 83. deal with people more than ideas or things

_____ 84. look physically attractive on the job

_____ 85. act in accordance with instructions set down by other people

_____ 86. am praised and esteemed by others

_____ 87. can be sure of keeping the job

_____ 88. gain higher status than most other workers

_____ 89. face new problems, people, and situations frequently

_____ 90. am employed in a clean, well-lighted place

_____ 91. have been rewarded for an assignment I have completed

_____ 92. know I am progressing toward more responsibility and pay

_____ 93. gamble and take a chance on the outcome

_____ 94. make attractive things for others to see, read, or hear

4 means the statement is *very important* to me.

3 means the statement is *important* to me.

2 means the statement is of *average importance* to me.

1 means the statement is of *little importance* to me.

0 means the statement is of *no importance* to me.

I need work in which I . . .

_____ 95. teach students to improve their education, health, or welfare

_____ 96. compete with other people for honors, prizes, or bonuses

_____ 97. express new ideas in art, science, music, and literature

_____ 98. don't have to complete years of costly education

_____ 99. am at the center of attention

_____ 100. am in a job where everyone plays by the rules

_____ 101. share things with friends I have on the job

_____ 102. avoid hazardous and unsafe situations

_____ 103. make a lot of money to keep well ahead of the cost of living

_____ 104. can take time off from the job

_____ 105. do my job without supervision

_____ 106. think about job-related things even off the job

_____ 107. administer programs and organize activities of other people

_____ 108. choose the way I want to spend my time and money

_____ 109. have a job in or near my home

_____ 110. use my hands and fingers to make things

_____ 111. am able to achieve inner harmony and peace of mind

_____ 112. am not confined to a desk inside a building

_____ 113. am primarily involved with people, such as customers

_____ 114. dress in professional clothing

_____ 115. follow routines established by other people

_____ 116. am rewarded with extra pay and promotion

_____ 117. know I will be employed even if my company folds

_____ 118. am listened to and have my opinions valued

_____ 119. will not have to do the same thing over and over again

_____ 120. do the job in comfortable surroundings

After you have responded to every statement on the Review of Work Values, transfer your ratings for each of the 120 statements to the Summary Score Sheet. Then add the four responses *across* each row for a total score (between 0 and 16). Percentile ranks and median scores can be found in Tables 7-5 and 7-6.

Summary Score Sheet

Total Score

1. _____	31. _____	61. _____	91. _____	ACH	_____
2. _____	32. _____	62. _____	92. _____	AVA	_____
3. _____	33. _____	63. _____	93. _____	AVE	_____
4. _____	34. _____	64. _____	94. _____	AES	_____
5. _____	35. _____	65. _____	95. _____	ALT	_____
6. _____	36. _____	66. _____	96. _____	COM	_____
7. _____	37. _____	67. _____	97. _____	CRE	_____
8. _____	38. _____	68. _____	98. _____	EAN	_____
9. _____	39. _____	69. _____	99. _____	EXH	_____
10._____	40. _____	70. _____	100._____	FAI	_____
11. _____	41. _____	71. _____	101. _____	FRI	_____
12. _____	42. _____	72. _____	102. _____	HEA	_____
13. _____	43. _____	73. _____	103. _____	HIN	_____
14. _____	44. _____	74. _____	104. _____	HLL	_____
15. _____	45. _____	75. _____	105. _____	IND	_____
16. _____	46. _____	76. _____	106. _____	INT	_____
17. _____	47. _____	77. _____	107. _____	LEA	_____
18. _____	48. _____	78. _____	108. _____	LIF	_____
19. _____	49. _____	79. _____	109. _____	LOC	_____
20. _____	50. _____	80. _____	110. _____	MPA	_____
21. _____	51. _____	81. _____	111. _____	MRC	_____
22. _____	52. _____	82. _____	112. _____	OUT	_____
23. _____	53. _____	83. _____	113. _____	PEC	_____
24. _____	54. _____	84. _____	114. _____	PHA	_____
25. _____	55. _____	85. _____	115. _____	PRE	_____
26. _____	56. _____	86. _____	116. _____	REC	_____
27. _____	57. _____	87. _____	117. _____	SEC	_____
28. _____	58. _____	88. _____	118. _____	STP	_____
29. _____	59. _____	89. _____	119. _____	VAR	_____
30. _____	60. _____	90. _____	120. _____	WEN	_____

Total Score	Descriptions of Work Values on the Review of Work Values

_____ ACH = *Achievement:* work in which I can accomplish something

_____ AVA = *Advancement:* work in which I can rise to a higher position

_____ AVE = *Adventure:* work that involves excitement and risk taking

_____ AES = *Aesthetics:* work that expresses beauty and artistry

_____ ALT = *Altruism:* work that expresses a concern for others

_____ COM = *Competition:* work that has a rivalry for honors or prizes

_____ CRE = *Creativity:* work that brings into being something original

_____ EAN = *Early entry:* work in which I can enter an occupation with little or no further training

_____ EXH = *Exhibition:* work in which I am at the center of attention

_____ FAI = *Fairness:* work in which people are treated equally

_____ FRI = *Friendships at work:* work in which I can make friends and have a social life because of the job

_____ HEA = *Health:* work in which I can maintain good health

_____ HIN = *High income:* work that pays me more than is needed for basic expenses

_____ HLL = *Home and leisure life:* work that allows more than average time off the job to be with the family or to pursue personal interests

_____ IND = *Independence:* work in which I can do a job in my own way

_____ INT = *Interesting work:* work that is challenging, absorbing, and in my major field of interest

_____ LEA = *Leadership:* work that allows me to be in charge of and responsible for others

_____ LIF = *Life-style:* work that lets me live the way I want to live and be the person I want to be

_____ LOC = *Location of work:* work in a convenient, easy-to-reach place

_____ MPA = *Mechanical and physical activity:* work in which I can use machines and tools or use physical and athletic skills

_____ MRC = *Moral and religious concerns:* work that expresses ideals and ethical and religious values

_____ OUT = *Outdoor work:* work that is done outside most of the time

_____ PEC = *People contact:* work in which I can deal with many people

_____ PHA = *Physical appearance:* work in which I can dress as I please

_____ PRE = *Predictable work:* work that is routine, where I know beforehand what the job is like

_____ REC = *Recognition:* work where I receive attention and approval

_____ SEC = *Security:* work in which there is little fear of losing the job

_____ STP = *Status/prestige:* work that brings a high position in society

_____ VAR = *Variety:* work in which I can do many kinds of activities

_____ WEN = *Work environment:* work that is done in attractive surroundings and under pleasant conditions

Table 7-5 Review of Work Values: Percentile Ranks and Median Scores

Raw Score	ACH	AVA	AVE	AES	ALT	COM	CRE	EAN	EXH	FAI	FRI	HEA	HIN	HLL	IND	Raw Score
16	95	96	99	99	98	99	98	99	99	96	95	96	87	97	95	16
15	82	87	97	96	94	98	95	99	97	87	85	87	70	91	85	15
14	68	77	93	94	89	96	91	98	94	73	74	74	62	83	76	14
13	51	64	89	90	83	94	86	96	90	57	61	60	54	74	61	13
12	31	52	83	85	77	91	81	92	84	40	45	44	44	64	45	12
11	17	39	74	79	69	86	74	87	77	27	31	30	34	51	29	11
10	9	27	63	70	59	79	67	79	68	17	21	20	24	37	17	10
9	4	16	52	60	47	70	59	70	58	9	12	11	17	26	10	9
8	2	9	40	51	35	59	50	62	47	5	7	6	11	16	5	8
7	2	5	29	41	26	48	40	50	37	3	5	3	7	8	3	7
6	1	3	20	32	19	37	31	38	27	2	3	1	5	5	2	6
5		2	13	25	13	28	22	28	17	1	2		3	2	1	5
4		1	8	19	8	20	14	20	11		2		3	1		4
3			4	14	5	13	10	12	6		1		1			3
2			2	10	3	9	6	7	3							2
1			1	6	1	6	4	4	1							1
0				2		2	2	1								0
Median	12.9	11.9	8.8	7.9	9.2	7.2	8.0	7.0	8.2	12.6	12.3	12.4	12.5	10.9	12.3	Median
Place*	3	10	21	25	20	27	24	28	23	4	9	6	5	14	8	Place*

Raw Score	INT	LEA	LIF	LOC	MPA	MRC	OUT	PEC	PHA	PRE	REC	SEC	STP	VAR	WEN	Raw Score
16	98	99	86	98	99	99	99	98	96	99	98	86	96	98	93	16
15	93	97	62	92	99	96	98	94	91	98	94	63	89	94	83	15
14	85	95	44	85	97	92	97	89	86	97	89	50	83	88	73	14
13	72	91	28	77	96	85	96	83	79	95	82	38	72	80	60	13
12	56	86	17	64	92	74	94	75	72	89	73	25	57	70	45	12
11	39	77	9	49	87	60	89	63	61	83	61	18	42	56	34	11
10	25	67	4	35	80	44	83	51	49	75	48	11	29	41	25	10
9	12	56	1	25	71	32	77	41	38	64	35	7	18	29	17	9
8	6	43		16	61	23	70	33	28	51	22	4	11	19	13	8
7	2	31		10	51	13	61	24	19	37	13	2	6	10	8	7
6	1	23		7	40	6	52	17	13	24	9	1	4	6	4	6
5		17		4	31	3	42	11	9	17	6		2	3	2	5
4		11		3	23	1	33	6	5	11	4		1	2	2	4
3		7		1	15		26	3	3	7	2			1	1	3
2		4			9		17	1	2	5	1					2
1		2			5		10		1	3						1
0		1			2		3			1						0
Median	11.7	8.4	14.3	11.1	6.9	10.4	5.8	9.9	10.1	7.9	10.1	14.0	11.5	10.7	12.3	Median
Place*	11	22	1	13	29	16	30	19	18	26	17	2	12	15	7	Place*

*Place among the 30 work values for all 335 respondents at Jackson Community College (Michigan), 1985–1989.

Table 7-6 Group Median Scores and Rankings for 30 Work Values on the Review of Work Values

Rank	Work Value	Median Score
1	Lifestyle (LIF)	14.3
2	Security (SEC)	14.0
3	Achievement (ACH)	12.9
4	Fairness (FAI)	12.6
5	High income (HIN)	12.5
6	Health (HEA)	12.4
7	Work environment (WEN)	12.347
8	Independence (IND)	12.30
9	Friendships at work (FRI)	12.29
10	Advancement (AVA)	11.9
11	Interesting work (INT)	11.7
12	Status/prestige (STP)	11.5
13	Location of work (LOC)	11.1
14	Home and leisure life (HLL)	10.9
15	Variety (VAR)	10.7
16	Moral and religious concerns (MRC)	10.4
17	Recognition (REC)	10.14
18	Physical appearance (PHA)	10.09
19	People contact (PEC)	9.9
20	Altruism (ALT)	9.2
21	Adventure (AVE)	8.8
22	Leadership (LEA)	8.4
23	Exhibition (EXH)	8.2
24	Creativity (CRE)	8.0
25	Aesthetics (AES)	7.92
26	Predictable work (PRE)	7.898
27	Competition (COM)	7.2
28	Early entry (EAN)	7.0
29	Mechanical and physical activity (MPA)	6.9
30	Outdoor work (OUT)	5.8

Note: N = 335. The 335 respondents are from Jackson Community College (Michigan), 1985–1989.

EXERCISE 7-7 EXPERIENCES WITH WORK VALUES

In the column at the side of the matrix, print 10 activities in which you have done something you would describe as work. *Work* is defined here as any expenditure of energy, so you can list recreation, sports, hobbies, volunteer work, school activities, and things done around the home, as well as full-time, part-time, or temporary work experiences. (Lots of people put forth more energy in play than in work!) Across the top of the matrix, print (sideways) the name of 12 work values you have studied and think are important to you. Be sure that you know the meaning of each work value and that it is distinct from the others you have listed. (You can return to the names of work values and their definitions presented earlier in this chapter.)

Ten activities I have done in which I have expended energy (work):														Total
1.														
2.														
3.														
4.														
5.														
6.														
7.														
8.														
9.														
10.														
Total														

For each work activity at the left, consider each work value you have listed at the top. If the value is expressed in the activity, put a check mark (or an X) where the value and the activity intersect on the matrix. When you finish with all of your 10 work activities, total the check marks for each work value and for each activity.

Which work values were expressed the most often in your 10 work activities? If you have trouble coming up with enough work activities, here are some examples from other career-planning students. Perhaps their ideas will stimulate your thinking.

Gardening/planting seeds   Doing laundry

Playing basketball   Sewing/making clothes

Doing research in the library   Cutting wood

Acting in a play   Cleaning the garage

Mopping floors	Teaching Sunday school
Babysitting	Using a computer
Typing a research paper	Studying for tests
Washing/repairing the car	Practicing music
Planning a party	Painting a room (or house)
Dancing	Remodeling a kitchen
Jogging, running	Teaching swimming
Taking pictures	Selling things to people
Raising funds	Taking care of a pet animal
Busing tables	Playing softball
Mowing the lawn	Clipping bushes and shrubs
Raising kids	Repairing a bike
Preparing meals	Washing dishes
Shoveling snow	Cleaning the cat's litter box

One thing you can learn from this exercise is that values differ from interests. Even though you may not like some of the work activities you listed, they are likely to contain something of value, or else you wouldn't have engaged in the activity. Unpleasant activities are done despite their unpleasantness because they express important qualities. Cleaning the cat's litter box isn't most people's idea of fun, but it does have a certain aesthetic value.

PRIORITIZE YOUR WORK VALUES

Just as you arranged your favorite abilities in order of priority at the end of Chapter 6, Exercise 7-8 can enable you to do the same with your major work values. First, review the value-identifying exercises you have completed in this chapter and come up with 10 or 12 work values you want expressed in your occupation.

You may be able to intuitively organize your work values in an order from the most to the least important, but most people prefer to use the prioritizing matrix in Exercise 7-8. A ranked list of work values will be very helpful when you are evaluating your occupational prospects in career decision making.

Prioritizing your work values will not be easy, because there are some agonizing judgments to make as you pair each value with each of the others and decide which one is more important. All the values you select for Exercise 7-8 are certain to be worthy or admirable in some way; choosing between two desirable values can bring about a mental struggle. To choose one over the other, as you do in this exercise, often means gaining or keeping something desirable by giving up something else almost equally desirable. It's like a child who is told, "Here are two delicious desserts from which to choose—a luscious piece of cake and a yummy ice cream sundae—but you can have just one." The child, torn by conflict, cannot decide and bursts into tears. Prioritizing values is a more serious business; the choices you make when you prioritize your work values require you to think deeply about matters of meaning and importance in your life.

EXERCISE 7-8 PRIORITIZING MATRIX FOR RANKING WORK VALUES

On the numbered *diagonal* lines of the blank matrix, list 10 or 12 major work values you identified as qualities you would want expressed in your occupation. Consider the meaning of each work value; be sure it is distinct from the other values you list.

Each work value is now designated by a number. For each number pair in the matrix, ask yourself, "Which work value is more important to me?" Circle the number of that choice. When you finish circling, record the total number of times each value was chosen and indicate the final rank in the bottom two rows of the matrix. To break ties, go back to the place in the matrix where the two numbers were paired and note the one that is circled. If you have more than 12 work values to prioritize, add new rows on a blank sheet of paper and place the paper under the last row of the matrix.

For an example of a completed matrix, see Figure 7-1. In this example, 12 work values were identified from exercises and values inventories. Each work value was assigned a temporary number. For each number pair in the matrix, a choice was made according to which value of the two was considered to be the more important, and its number was circled. (In Figure 7-1, independence was chosen over home and family life, so 1 was circled in the 1–2 number pair.) The circled numbers were counted and ranked. Now these 12 values can be rearranged in a new order of priority.

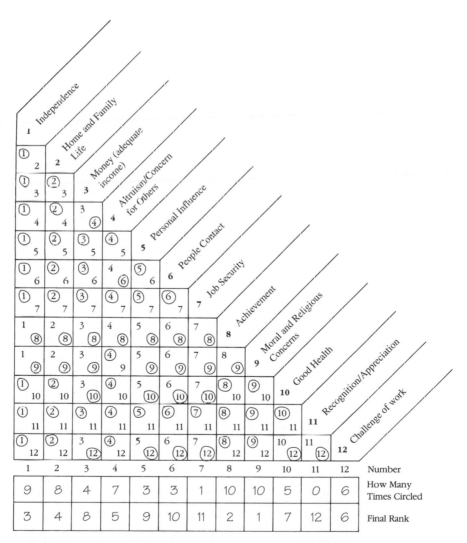

Figure 7-1 Example of a completed prioritizing matrix ranking work values. *Source:* From the *National Career Development Project Four-Day Workshop*, by Richard N. Bolles, copyright © 1981. Used by permission.

Prioritizing Matrix for Exercise 7-8   *Source:* From the *National Career Development Project Four-Day Workshop*, by Richard N. Bolles, copyright © 1981. Used by permission.

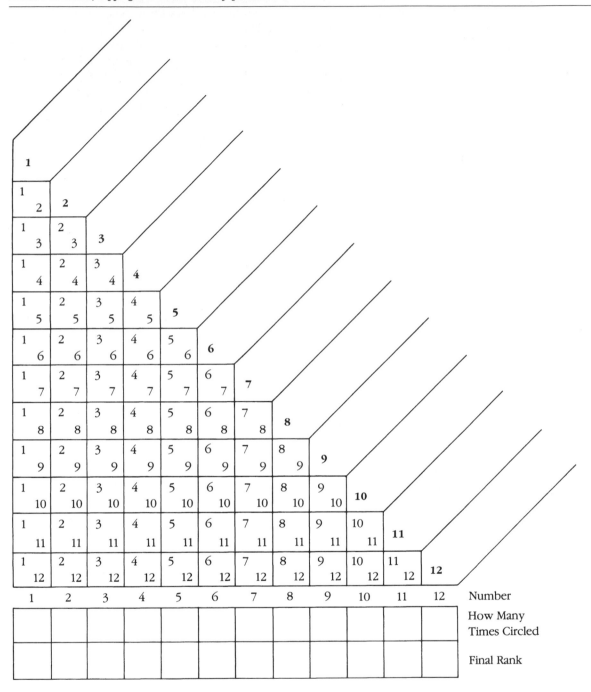

1	2	3	4	5	6	7	8	9	10	11	12	Number
												How Many Times Circled
												Final Rank

EXERCISE 7-9 MY PRIORITIZED LIST OF WORK VALUES

Write your new list of prioritized work values in the spaces provided. Start with your highest or most important work value and move down to the least important one on your list. To the right of each one, define the meaning of the work value, making sure that it is distinct from the others on the list.

Name of Work Value	Meaning of the Work Value
1. _____	_____
2. _____	_____
3. _____	_____
4. _____	_____
5. _____	_____
6. _____	_____
7. _____	_____
8. _____	_____
9. _____	_____
10. _____	_____
11. _____	_____
12. _____	_____

SUMMARY

1. Values—those things or qualities to which you ascribe worth or usefulness—are learned through your experiences with people and interaction with your environment. Most values are not taught consciously or deliberately but are adopted subtly and indirectly.

2. Contemplating your values will add meaning and commitment to your life. Giving your life purpose and direction is one of the best things you can do for yourself. Meaninglessness and aimlessness usually result in frustration, indifference, and depression—experiences you would rather avoid.

3. Within our diverse and complex society, many cultural subgroups exist that are based on ethnicity, race, religion, gender, sexual orientation, age, disability, region, or occupation. People within these subgroups share certain *cultural tendencies*. Ascribing a set of characteristics that are applied to all members of the group is to *stereotype* them and deny their unique individuality. With this caution, it is possible to say that some cultural tendencies are expressed by many (but not all) people within a subgroup. The major subcultural groups are African Americans, Hispanics/Latinos/Chicanos, Asian Americans, Native Americans, white or European Americans, people with disabilities, males and females (gender), gays and lesbians, and age groups.

4. You receive mixed messages from your culture because of modern society's complexity and diversity, as contrasted with a simpler age when fewer avenues of communication and travel existed. Value conflicts are common today; for example, all work is said to have worth and dignity, yet some occupations are widely considered better than others. Thus occupations can be ranked according to their prestige. The factors you use to judge the prestige of an occupation are values—both those of your own and those of society.

5. Your work values reflect your personal values. A study of your personal values should come before a study of your work values. Six value orientations are measured by the Allport, Vernon, and Lindzey Study of Values. This chapter includes a list of 21 personal values from which you can select several values of significance to you. Completing unfinished sentences can help you uncover important personal values.

6. Work values are an integral part of developing a career decision. Recognizing values that operate most strongly in your thinking is a first step in understanding the qualities that can give you satisfaction in your work.

7. A Work Values Auction gives you an opportunity to assess the relative worth of values and to learn how these values might change under the pressures of competing with other people.

8. An extensive list of work values and their definitions is included for your consideration and evaluation. The 15 work values in Super's Work Values Inventory (WVI) and the 21 values in the Values Scale (VS) by Super and Nevill are explained. In addition, the Review of Work Values (ROWV) provides you with the opportunity to measure 30 different work values.

9. Values differ from attitudes, needs, and interests. Some activities that may be regarded as unpleasant are completed because there is value in doing so.

10. This chapter can help you select 10 to 12 of your most significant work values and then prioritize them. Later, you can use these work values to judge your occupational prospects in a career decision-making exercise.

REFERENCES

Allport, G. W., Vernon, P. E., and Lindzey, G. 1960. *Study of values manual.* Boston: Houghton Mifflin.

Blank, R., and Slipp, S. 1994. *Voices of diversity: Real people talk about problems and solutions in a workplace where everyone is not alike.* New York: ANACOM, A Division of American Management Association.

Caplow, T. 1954. *The sociology of work.* Minneapolis: University of Minnesota Press.

Chung, Y. B. 2001, September. Work discrimination and coping strategies: Conceptual frameworks for counseling lesbian, gay, and bisexual clients. *The Career Development Quarterly*, 50, 33–44.

Cochrane, L. 1997. *Career counseling: A narrative approach.* Newbury Park, CA: Sage.

Cross, E. Y. 2000. *Managing diversity—the courage to lead.* Westport, CT: Quorum Books.

Dawis, R. V. 1994. The theory of work adjustment as convergent theory. In M. L. Savickas and R. W. Lent, eds., *Convergence in career development theories*, pp. 33–44. Palo Alto, CA: Consulting Psychologists Press.

Elliott, C. E. 1999. Cross-cultural communication styles. In C. E. Elliott, R. J. Adams, and S. Sockalingam, *Multicultural toolkit (Toolkit for cross-cultural collaboration).* Available online at www.awesomelibrary.org/multiculturaltoolkit.html. Accessed March 14, 2003.

Ettinger, J. M. 1996. Meeting the career development needs of individuals with disabilities. In R. Feller and G. Walz, eds., *Career transitions in turbulent times: Exploring work, learning, and careers*, pp. 239–244. Greensboro, NC: ERIC/CASS Publications.

Fallows, J. 1996. *Breaking the news: How the media undermine American democracy.* New York: Vintage.

Fouad, N. A. 1993. Cross-cultural vocational assessment. *The Career Development Quarterly*, 42, 4–13.

Fredrickson, R. H., Lin, J. G., and Xing, S. 1992. Social status ranking of occupations in the People's Republic of China, Taiwan, and the United States. *The Career Development Quarterly*, 40, 351–360.

Gonzalez, J. L. 1993. *Racial and ethnic groups in America.* Dubuque, IA: Kendall/Hunt.

Gunn, H. 2003, April. Disabling the attitudes around disability awareness. *The Record* (Episcopal Diocese of Michigan), 14(4).

Hallett, M. B., and Gilbert, L. A. 1997. Variables differentiating university women considering role-sharing and conventional dual-career marriages. *Journal of Vocational Behavior*, 50, 308–322.

Hogan-Garcia, M. 1997. African-Americans as a cultural group. In L. L. Naylor, ed., *Cultural diversity in the United States.* Westport, CT: Bergin & Garvey.

Holland, J. L. 1997. *Making vocational choices: A theory of vocational personalities and work environments*, 3rd ed. Odessa, FL: Psychological Assessment Resources.

Howe, L. W., and Howe, M. M. 1975. *Personalizing education: Values clarification and beyond.* New York: Hart.

Isaacson, L. E., and Brown, D. 1997. *Career information, career counseling, and career development*, 6th ed. Boston: Allyn and Bacon.

Jourard, S. M. 1974. *Healthy personality: An approach from the viewpoint of humanistic psychology.* New York: Macmillan.

Kanzaki, G. A. 1976. Fifty years (1925–1975) of stability in the social status of occupations. *Vocational Guidance Quarterly, 25*, 101–105.

Krumboltz, J. D., Blando, J. A., Kim, H., and Reikowski, D. J. 1994, September–October. Embedding work values in stories. *Journal of Counseling and Development, 73*, 57–62.

Lajoie, R. 2001–2002, Winter. Courage of the morning. *Amnesty Now, 12*–13.

Lips, H. M. 1992. Gender and science-related attitudes as predictors of college students' academic choices. *Journal of Vocational Behavior, 40*, 62–81.

McHolland, J. D., and Trueblood, R. W. 1972. *Human potential seminars: Participants handbook.* Evanston, IL: Kendall College Press.

Mitchell, B. M., and Salsbury, R. E. 1999. *Encyclopedia of multicultural education.* Westport, CT: Greenwood Press.

Mooney, C. April, 2003. Breaking the frame. *The American Prospect, 14*(4), 38–41.

Naylor, L. L. 1998. *American culture: Myth and reality of a culture of diversity.* Westport, CT: Bergin & Garvey.

Nevill, D. D., and Super, D. E. 1989. *The values scale: Theory, application and research,* 2nd ed. Palo Alto, CA: Consulting Psychologists Press.

Peterson, A. J., with the cooperation of Sharp, B. B., Hall, L., and Thomas, W. J. 1972. *Leader's guide: Motivation advance program.* Chicago: W. Clement and Jessie Stone Foundation.

Raths, L. E., Harmin, M., and Simon, S. B. 1966. *Values and teaching: Working with values in the classroom.* Columbus, OH: Charles E. Merrill.

Rosenthal, N. H. 1989, December. More than wages at issue in job quality debate. *Monthly Labor Review, 112*(12), 4–8.

Sharf, R. S. 2002. *Applying career development theory to counseling.* Pacific Grove, CA: Brooks/Cole.

SIGI PLUS Counselor's Manual. 1994. Princeton, NJ: Educational Testing Service.

Simon, S. B., Howe, L. W., and Kirschenbaum, H. 1995. *Values clarification: A practical, action-directed workbook.* New York: Warner.

Stodghill, R., and Bower, A. 2002, September 2. Where everyone is a minority. *Time, 160*(9), 26–30.

Streisand, B. 2003, March 17. Latin power: Big media tune in to the nation's largest minority. *U.S. News & World Report, 134*(8), 34–36.

Sue, D. W., and Sue, D. 1990. *Counseling the culturally different: Theory and practice.* New York: Wiley.

Super, D. E. 1970. *Work values inventory manual.* Boston: Houghton Mifflin.

Super, D. E., and Nevill, D. D. 1985. *The values scale.* Palo Alto, CA: Consulting Psychologists Press.

Focusing on Your Career Decision

The first two parts of this book have dealt primarily with self-assessment and occupational exploration. Now we are ready to begin a third part of the process—making career decisions. First we look at the nature of decision making and types of career decision makers that seem to exist.

The remainder of this chapter is intended for career planners who have created an extensive list of occupational prospects, perhaps numbering 25, 50, 100, 200, or more. Now comes the time to reduce that list to a few occupations that can be described as "best fit" or "apparently appropriate," from which tentative choices can be made (Isaacson, 1985). If you have a list of between 5 and 15 occupations, keep them as they are. If you have only two or three prospects, go back to Chapter 3 and use the methods described there to generate more.

The chapter presents five methods for reducing the number of occupations on your prospect list. You can use any one method, a combination of methods, or all of them. One method is to take the information you have collected about your occupational prospects, compare it with your Ideal Job Description from Chapter 1, and remove those occupations that differ widely from the characteristics you have described for your ideal job. A second technique is to remove any occupations that appeared only once or twice in the occupation-generating methods used in Chapter 3. Three other methods (adapted from Chapman, 1976) are removing occupations that (1) you know are far above or below your own ability level, (2) express none or very few of your most important work values, or (3) require education beyond your means in terms of time, money, and locations available.

When you narrow down your list of prospective occupations, you must act from a base of information about your own personal characteristics (abilities and work values in particular) and your occupational prospects. Avoid discarding occupations by guesswork. Keep any prospect about which you know nothing. If you have any doubt about removing an occupation, keep it on your list until you obtain further information that indicates it should be eliminated. Remove an occupational prospect only when it is obviously right to do so; that way, you have no second thoughts about it.

THE NATURE OF DECISION MAKING

As a human being, you engage in decision making, one of the most specifically human acts there is. Beyond humans, how much of the animal kingdom engages in conscious, deliberate thinking is unknown. To humans, animals seem to be programmed by environmental and inner forces, relying on instinct and automatic stimulus–response reactions. Superior development of language, thinking, and problem solving seems to distinguish humans from all other forms of life (Silverman, 1971). However, even with humans, there are questions about how much decision making is done on a rational, conscious level and how much is done by mental processes outside conscious awareness (Krieshok, 1998).

In real life, you cannot avoid making decisions. Even when you do not decide, that is a decision in itself. You have chosen not to decide. Having to decide among alternative courses of action is a price of freedom. Free people are "condemned" to choose. Being truly free to choose is desirable, but sometimes you are depressed about it because of the responsibility involved. Some people in totalitarian dictatorships believe they have more freedom because the dictator has relieved them of the burden to make decisions for themselves. Sometimes a person may think it is easier to give up one's freedom of choice in order to blame someone else if the consequences of a decision become unpleasant. In career planning, a great number of options among occupations make the relationship between freedom and decision making even more complicated.

Decision making goes on all the time. From the moment you wake up in the morning to the time you fall asleep at night, you are constantly deciding among many choices about arranging your day, the clothing to wear, the food you eat, the road to take, and so on. Others may make some of these choices for you, but your life is filled with hundreds of daily decisions you make for yourself. Generally, the more important a decision is to you, the harder it is to make. Selecting a pair of shoes is easier than choosing an occupation or deciding whether to make a career change. Thus decision making is an unavoidable, constantly recurring, and often-difficult human activity.

To gain an appreciation of the relative importance of decisions, rate the following decisions according to the degree of importance you place on them. Use this key:

0 = The decision is not under your control; it is made by others or by circumstance.

1 = The decision is automatic or **routine**; you never think about it; it is habitual.

2 = You occasionally think about the decision before you choose.

3 = You think about the decision, but you don't study or investigate it.

4 = You study about the decision a little; you think about it and ask others about it before you choose.

5 = You study and think about the decision a lot; you ask questions and read about it before you choose.

In each of the following spaces, write the number (0, 1, 2, 3, 4, or 5) that indicates the relative importance of each decision to you.

_____ 1. To get up in the morning	_____ 12. Whom to vote for
_____ 2. What to wear to school	_____ 13. Where to go on vacation
_____ 3. What food to eat	_____ 14. To drive beyond the speed limit
_____ 4. To tell the truth	_____ 15. Which TV show to watch
_____ 5. To drink beer or liquor	_____ 16. To criticize a friend
_____ 6. To take a summer job	_____ 17. To choose an educational major
_____ 7. What book to read	_____ 18. Where to dispose of waste paper
_____ 8. To stop at stop signs	_____ 19. Where to attend college
_____ 9. To believe in God	_____ 20. To disagree with parents
_____ 10. What movie to see	_____ 21. To choose an occupation or career
_____ 11. Whom to marry	_____ 22. To take a job with more responsibility

Source: Based on Gelatt, Varenhorst, Carey, and Miller, 1973.

The Career Decision-Making Process Revisited

Chapter 1 identified eight parts in a career decision-making process:

1. *Becoming aware and committed:* recognizing there is a problem concerning career choices and engaging in a decision-making effort to resolve that problem.
2. *Studying your environment:* examining information about the social, economic, political, and geographic setting in which you live.
3. *Studying yourself:* analyzing personal information about your interests, motivations, abilities, and work values.
4. *Generating alternatives:* developing a number of occupational prospects to choose from in the career decision-making process.
5. *Gathering information:* collecting data about your occupational alternatives.
6. *Making the decision:* determining your career goal from judgments based on your knowledge of your own characteristics and those of your career alternatives.

7. *Implementing the decision:* putting the career decision into practice by acquiring the necessary education or training and using the job search techniques of finding job leads, writing résumés, interviewing, and so on.

8. *Getting feedback:* evaluating how well the career decision is working. Too much negative feedback starts the career decision-making process in motion again.

Probably you developed a lengthy list of occupational prospects from the exercises in Chapters 3 and 4. You may have dropped some occupations off your list as you explored them and obtained information about them. At the end of this chapter, you are encouraged to complete some exercises designed to reduce the number of occupational prospects to a manageable number—say, anywhere from 5 to 15 occupations. Chapter 9 presents career decision-making exercises that arrange your occupational prospects in an order of desirability. The occupation that emerges as your number one choice represents your occupational goal; however, don't lose sight of the other occupations that score below it. Any one of those occupations has the potential to become your number one career goal at a later time. Having a plan B and a plan C is valuable in anyone's career planning.

Types of Career Decision Makers According to Degrees of Decidedness

Career researchers are constantly coming up with names for collections of characteristics that describe how people face the task of making career decisions. An article in *The Career Development Quarterly* about career decision making organizes the results of 15 studies based on level of decision status. Three general categories of *decided*-type people and four groups of *undecided* types emerged from the research literature: *very decided, somewhat decided, unstable decided, tentatively undecided, developmentally undecided, seriously undecided,* and *chronically indecisive* (Gordon, 1998). While you are reading through brief descriptions of each type, ask yourself which one applies most to you and to your career decision-making situation.

You are a *very decided* type if you believe you have personal control over your life and can make good decisions, and you picture your future career as important to you (Wanberg and Muchinsky, 1992). You are considered confident, knowledgeable, and clear about your decision making (Multon, Heppner, and Lapan, 1995). However, some *very decided* people may make career decisions prematurely and not be aware of their lack of information (Gordon, 1998).

You are a *somewhat decided* type if you have some doubts about your career decisions, perhaps having made them under pressure from parents, friends, or school requirements (Newman, Fuqua, and Minger, 1990). The doubts that somewhat decided people have may actually be helpful, because these types are aware of their need for additional occupational information. Whatever anxiety you may have experienced may be reduced in time, when you receive support from a career counselor or class and when solid information serves to confirm an original career choice or identify a new alternative (Gordon, 1998).

You are an *unstable decided* type if you feel insecure, unsteady, or changeable about your career goals and values. A distinguishing characteristic of this type is a higher level of anxiety than the previous two groups and a lack of confidence in the ability to make decisions (Gordon, 1998). Van Matre and Cooper (1984) found unstable decideds susceptible to long-lasting worry and anxiety, feelings of being controlled by others, and low degrees of satisfaction with their career decisions. Unstable decided people may often feel they have really chosen a career direction, but this certainty can prevent them from seeking help when they really need it (Gordon, 1998).

You are a *tentatively undecided* type if you are not ready to commit yourself to a career choice and need to engage in further career exploration to specify what that choice might be (Savickas and Jorjoura, 1991). Tentatively undecided people are described as relatively well adjusted, close to deciding, intuitive as decision makers, and confident that a decision will be right when it is made. The characteristic separating these people from the next group (the developmentally undecided) is their greater closeness to making a decision (Lucas and Epperson, 1988) and vocational maturity (Chartrand et al., 1994). Tentatively undecideds may have a fear of commitment, which could mean regular behavior that tends to avoid issues such as career decision making (Serling and Betz, 1990).

You are a *developmentally undecided* type if you have mature career attitudes but a high level of indecision (Rojewski, 1994). This is a normal transition for many people who are developing skills to accomplish the tasks required to commit to a career choice. This group, along with the previous one, is largely uninformed about career decision making and needs help in the form of a career-planning class or career counseling that includes self-study about interests, abilities, and values and occupational-educational information to improve their career decision-making skills. Developmentally undecided individuals need to identify career alternatives and information to narrow and verify their choices—essentially, the subject of this book. Usually they are interested in many occupational fields and competent to succeed in most of them (Gordon, 1998).

You are a *seriously undecided* type if you experience such anxiety over the career (or any other) choice process that the indecisiveness is severe and debilitating and leads to feeling exhausted, worn out, and deprived of strength (Goodstein, 1965). Seriously undecided people often suffer from low self-esteem, low levels of knowledge about career and academic alternatives, and a belief that their lives are controlled by powerful others or by chance (Wanberg and Muchinsky, 1992). Some are apt to look for an authority that will tell them the "right choice." Some may be perfectionists seeking the perfect choice. Others are frustrated in that they want to make a choice but something blocks them from it (Savickas and Jorjoura, 1991). More intensive counseling may be needed for seriously undecided people, because personal concerns must be addressed before the usual career exploration activities can take place. The distinction between this group and the next one, the chronically indecisive, is in the level of anxiety. Both groups have similar degrees of career indecision and feelings of being controlled externally, but the seriously undecided group's level of anxiety is moderate whereas the chronically indecisive group's anxiety level is excessive (Gordon, 1998).

You are a *chronically indecisive* type if a great amount of anxiety describes your life (Crites, 1981; Fuqua, Newman, and Seaworth, 1988; Hartman and Fuqua, 1983) and you experience considerable concern and discouragement over trying to identify possible career alternatives (Rojewski, 1994). Other words and phrases researchers have used to describe chronically indecisive people are *pervasive aimlessness and uncertainty* (Salamone, 1982), *lacking motivation to become more clear about values and goals* (Multon, Heppner, and Lapan, 1995), *fearing commitment* (Leong and Chervinko, 1996), and *bearing a sense of inferiority* (Cohen, Chartrand, and Jowdy, 1995). Until long-term counseling intervenes with the core personality problems of the chronically indecisive person, the efforts of a career-planning class or a career counselor will not be effective and career decisions will not be made (Gordon, 1998).

Decisions in general—and career decisions in particular—involve many factors; one of the most frequently cited is anxiety. The next chapter discusses five patterns of coping with the tensions of making decisions. In the section you have just read anxiety is presented in a rather negative way. We need to remind ourselves that there is an optimal level of stress and anxiety for good performance. It is one that is moderate, not so low that we lapse into apathy and indifference nor so high that we become paralyzed or disabled and run the risk of making *any* decision, however harmful it may be, just to get rid of the tension.

EXPANSION AND CONTRACTION OF OCCUPATIONAL PROSPECTS

You may feel able to determine intuitively several occupations on your list that can be eliminated. Resist the temptation to do so unless you have specific knowledge of the occupation or information about your own interests, abilities, motives, and

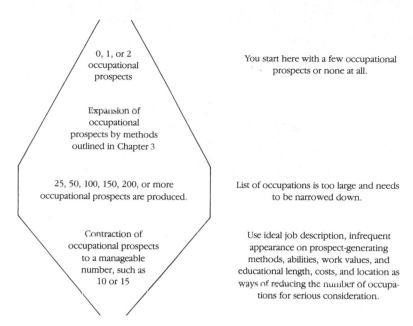

Figure 8-1   Expansion and contraction of occupational prospects

work values. An occupational title gives you some data, but the title can be misleading. For example, a "belly builder" (730.684-018) (from the fourth edition of the *Dictionary of Occupational Titles,* or DOT) sounds like a person who eats a lot of food, but actually it is someone who fits and assembles a wood soundboard, a metal plate, and wood bridges to a wooden frame in order to make the back panel of a piano. A "frog shaker" (521.687-110) may seem bent on rattling the nerves of frogs, but actually is someone who shakes leaves of cured tobacco to separate, straighten, and expose them to air and remove dirt. A tooth polisher (715.682-026) and a crown attacher (715.684-070) might appear to be occupations in the dental field, but actually they are positions in the clock and watch industry, according to the *Dictionary of Occupational Titles* (U.S. Department of Labor, 1991). Only when you have gathered information about the occupation can you realistically decide whether to keep or eliminate it. Anything else is sheer guesswork.

Even when you have gathered sufficient data about an occupation, eliminate it as a prospect only when the evidence makes the decision an obvious one. If you are in doubt about it, keep the occupation on your list. When in doubt, the best way to clear up the confusion is to gather more information about the occupation and about yourself. Most people using this career-planning program have been able to produce a list of at least 50 occupational prospects. You may not have reached that number yet, but you will probably keep on generating more occupational prospects. New occupations enter the world of work constantly, and you are likely to discover existing ones you haven't encountered yet. Expanding your career options is an ongoing process, but reducing the number of occupational prospects occurs regularly, too. You may have already eliminated some prospects by thinking to yourself, "I might like that occupation, but I don't think I have the ability to do the work in it" or "Getting the amount of education required for that is going to be too difficult." As long as you have solid information to support your decision to eliminate an occupational prospect, this procedure is perfectly valid. Occupational decision making is a process of gradual exclusion of unacceptable career alternatives (Crites, 1969). The process of expansion and contraction of occupational prospects in career planning looks somewhat like the illustration in Figure 8-1.

Do You Know Your Occupations?

How well do you know your occupational prospects? You have a start on knowing them if you have consulted books such as the fourth edition of the *Dictionary of Occupational Titles* (DOT). Try to figure out the work functions and specific tasks of the occupations on the following list. Use the nine-digit code to find the occupations in the DOT and discover what these workers really do on the job. If you are in a career-planning class, divide into teams and compete with one another.

Blow-up Operator (529.485-014)
Bobbin Disker (734.687-022)
Bottom Polisher (603.685-034)
Butt Maker (529.685-042)
Car Whacker (910.687-014)
Chaser (704.381-010) (921.667-014)
Cripple Worker (788.684-042)
Crook Operator (609.682-018)
Dope-House Operator Helper
  (559.685-046)
Dropper (522.685-054)
Floor Winder (681.685-050)
Foot Straightener (715.687-030)
Girdler (770.261-014)

Governor Assembler (721.381-018)
Grizzly Worker (933.687-010)
Hog Tender (564.685-018)
Hot-Car Operator (519.663-014)
Kiss Setter (529.687-122)
Mother Repairer (705.684-042)
Scratcher Tender (555.685-050)
Slubber (680.685-098)
Smash Hand (683.684-026)
Spider Assembler (721.684-026)
Stripper (556.686-018)
Thrill Performer (159.347-018)
Throw-out Clerk (241.367-030)
Toe Puncher (689.685-162)

For any occupation dropped off your prospect list, you should have a reason to explain why it isn't worth pursuing any further. It could be that the occupation: (1) doesn't come close to your conception of the ideal job in Exercise 1-1, (2) was generated by only one or two of the several occupational-prospect–producing methods (Exercises 3-1 to 3-15) you used, (3) requires abilities too far above or below your own ability level in Exercise 6-8 or 6-9, (4) doesn't express work values from Exercises 7-8 or 7-9 that you consider essential or important in your career, or (5) requires education for which the time, money, or location isn't available to you. Each of these reasons can be used to challenge your current occupational prospects.

METHODS OF CHALLENGING CURRENT OCCUPATIONAL PROSPECTS

You can use each of the five reasons just listed as a method for challenging a prospect, and each reason is presented in the form of an exercise in this chapter. Remember, if you decide to remove a prospective occupation on the basis of the challenge method you are using, your decision must be an obvious one. Otherwise, keep the occupation on your list. It is important to note that at no time should you narrow your list down to fewer than five or six prospective occupations. You should have at least five or six occupations for the career decision-making exercise in the next chapter. (Most people average 10 to 12 prospects for that exercise.)

EXERCISE 8-1 CHALLENGE YOUR OCCUPATIONAL PROSPECTS WITH YOUR IDEAL JOB DESCRIPTION

At the end of Chapter 1, you worked on an exercise in which you used your imagination to write your Ideal Job Description. The job description had 10 parts:

1. *Nature of the work:* work activities that would seem like play to you and in which you could lose yourself completely
2. *Education/training:* preferred major, type of school, length of program, degree (if any)

3. *Skills/abilities:* those you have that you would most enjoy using on the job
4. *Pay/fringe benefits:* ideal beginning, average, and top salary or hourly wage; characteristics of preferred lifestyle
5. *Working conditions:* model physical environment, hours, time of day, clothing worn on the job, management style
6. *Location:* ideal type of organization or workplace and preferred geographic area
7. *Personality characteristics of work associates:* kinds of people you would want to work with
8. *Employment and advancement outlook:* degree of competition desired for the job and at work, and how far up the career ladder you want to go
9. *Personal satisfactions expected:* values you want to express or have expressed in your work
10. *Advantages and disadvantages:* other positive qualities you want in your work and negative features you want to avoid

Place your Ideal Job Description alongside the worksheets for occupational information (or computer-generated occupation information) you have gathered about the real occupations on your prospect list. The worksheets, outlined and detailed at the end of Chapter 4, include the same components as those in your Ideal Job Description. How close does the real job description come to the ideal job? If it misses by a wide margin, this occupational prospect becomes a candidate for elimination. No mathematical formula exists to measure whether you should keep or drop an occupation; you must rely mainly on intuition. After comparing the real occupation with the various parts of the Ideal Job Description, you must be absolutely certain that the occupation is not for you in order to take it off your list. If you have any hesitation about removing it as a prospect, keep it on your list. When you decide to reject occupations by this method, write them in the following spaces provided in case you want to retrieve some of them later.

Occupations Eliminated by Comparing Prospects with Your Ideal Job Description

_____	_____
_____	_____
_____	_____
_____	_____
_____	_____
_____	_____
_____	_____

EXERCISE 8-2 CHALLENGE OCCUPATIONAL PROSPECTS GENERATED ONLY ONCE OR TWICE

This exercise is a variation of Exercise 4-5 in Chapter 4, which was actually an earlier version of narrowing or reducing the number of occupational prospects. The idea then was to choose several occupations that had appeared most often as a result of the methods you used to generate occupational prospects in order to more thoroughly explore those occupations. In Chapter 3, you used several of the following methods to produce a list of occupational prospects: remembering, asking others, daydream analysis, the "wishing" exercise, browsing, thinking about what needs to be done, occupational kits and career games, card sorts, computer-based programs, state or local systems, the "special family" exercise, fantasizing a typical workday, the "family tree" exercise, occupational handbooks—the *Occupational Outlook Handbook, O*Net Dictionary of Occupational Titles,* and *Guide for Occupational Exploration*—and one or more interest inventories. Suppose you used 10 of these methods and produced 50 occupational prospects. Of the 50, however, 25 were generated only once, whereas 8 occupations were suggested five or more times. You would keep the eight occupational prospects, of course, but you could drop some or all of the 25 occupations from your list on the grounds they had come up only once. There is no mathematical formula to determine whether you keep or drop a prospect. If you have any doubt about removing an occupation, keep it on your list.

Write the names of any rejected occupations in the following spaces so you can retrieve them again if you need to.

Occupations Eliminated Because They Were Suggested by Too Few Prospect-Generating Methods

Name of Occupation	Number of Methods That Suggested the Occupation	Name of Occupation	Number of Methods That Suggested the Occupation

EXERCISE 8-3 CHALLENGE OCCUPATIONAL PROSPECTS ON THE BASIS OF YOUR WORK ABILITIES

For this exercise, you will need to consult Chapter 6, in which you explored your abilities, skills, and aptitudes. You also need to know the levels of the abilities required to qualify you for each of your occupational prospects. Knowledge of your abilities and of the skills and aptitudes required for an occupation is information you must have to determine whether you keep or eliminate the occupation.

The essence of this exercise is to consider removing any occupational prospect that is far above or far below your own ability level (Chapman, 1976). Entering an occupation that greatly exceeds your own ability level leads to feelings of frustration and incompetence. Similarly, entering an occupation where the required ability level is far below your own level quickly leads to boredom because the occupation does not challenge you. Both are extreme situations to avoid. One situation involves overwhelming risks; your success depends on luck, and the results might be disastrous to those for whom you are responsible. The other situation has no risk at all as far as ability is concerned, but lack of challenge can bring lack of motivation, which involves its own type of risk. You are looking for occupational goals that pose moderate risks—occupations that are realistic but still challenging. Recall that high achievers favor such a career choice strategy.

Your job in this exercise is to determine where your range of ability lies and, on the basis of your knowledge of the levels of abilities required by your occupational prospects, to eliminate any occupations that require abilities far above or far below your own. Consult the skill and aptitude analysis you made in Chapter 6, previous school grades, aptitude test results, performance evaluations of your work, and any other objective appraisal of your abilities you can obtain. Avoid overestimating your abilities. Some people regularly overstate their qualifications, but effort, drive, and motivation cannot always make up for the lack of some kinds of abilities. Be honest enough with yourself to admit that certain occupations are beyond your mental capacities.

However, be careful not to underestimate your ability and potential. Some people grow up in an environment that does not encourage self-confidence; therefore, they downgrade their potential. If you need further help determining your abilities, skills, and aptitudes, return to Chapter 6 and check with your instructor or counselor. If you need further information about the abilities required for entrance into any of your occupational prospects, obtain the data from your career information sources.

Occupational Prospects Eliminated on the Basis of Ability Levels

_____   _____

_____   _____

_____   _____

_____   _____

_____   _____

_____   _____

_____   _____

EXERCISE 8-4 CHALLENGE OCCUPATIONAL PROSPECTS ON THE BASIS OF YOUR WORK VALUES

Return first to Chapter 7 to review your major work values. Then go to Exercise 4-7 in Chapter 4 for the information you collected on your worksheets for each occupational prospect. The most direct indication of work values on the worksheets is in section 9 of Exercise 4-7: personal satisfaction from the work in the occupation. Actually, an examination of all information sections could reveal values. The sections on nature of work activities, type of education needed, abilities used, pay, working conditions, location of employment, personality characteristics of people typically found in the occupation, and employment and advancement outlook are likely to contain words, phrases, and even numbers that directly or indirectly indicate work values.

You are looking for occupations on your prospect list that are _not_ in harmony with your values. Go back to your final ranked list of work values at the end of Chapter 7. Have the research worksheets with you if they are available. Ask yourself whether each occupational prospect remaining on your list expresses all or most of your major work values. Occupations that do not express at least half of your values become candidates for removal. Be conservative when rejecting an occupational prospect; if you have any doubt, leave the occupation on your prospect list. No formula can be given for removing an occupation. Some of you may feel that an occupation must express all your work values to stay on your list. The problem here is that you will often face value conflicts; you must sacrifice one important value to gain another. For example, in a certain attractive occupational alternative, you may have to give up independence in order to obtain job security. Of course, you can drop that occupation and look for ones that contain both values, but sometimes this is impossible. One reason you prioritize your values is to resolve value conflicts by giving up a less important value for the sake of a more important one.

You are trying to eliminate those occupations that are inconsistent with many of your major work values. Suppose one of your occupational prospects is librarian, and one of your important values is to be outdoors much of the time. Unless you know of any outdoor libraries, there is a conflict. If, however, being around books is a more important work value, the conflict can be resolved and librarian kept on your list. More inconsistencies between librarian and other values might indicate that the occupation should be removed from your list of prospects.

**Occupational Prospects Eliminated Because the Occupation
Did Not Express Enough Important Work Values**

_____	_____
_____	_____
_____	_____
_____	_____
_____	_____
_____	_____
_____	_____
_____	_____

EXERCISE 8-5 CHALLENGE OCCUPATIONAL PROSPECTS BY LENGTH, COST, AND LOCATION OF EDUCATION

The fifth and last challenge to your occupational prospects involves time, money, and location for obtaining the education or training the occupation requires (Chapman, 1976). Your fundamental question is "Am I willing to take the time, pay the price, and travel to the place in order to prepare and qualify myself for the occupation I am considering?"

First, determine whether or not the occupational prospect requires further education on your part. If it doesn't, the occupation can stay on your list of prospects. If the occupation requires further education, ask yourself these questions:

1. How much time will I need to complete the education required by the occupation?
2. How much money will I need to obtain the education necessary to enter the occupation?
3. Where is the education for the occupation located?

Answers to these basic questions can probably be found in Exercise 4-7, section 2, on your worksheet of researched information on the occupational prospect. You can also consult college catalogs, educational directories, and sources of occupational information in career resource centers, counseling offices, and libraries.

Once you have obtained information about the educational requirements of the occupational prospect, ask yourself about the time, money, and location required.

1. Do I have enough *time* to obtain the education or training required?
2. Do I have sufficient *financial resources* to pay for the education or training?
3. Is the education or training at a *location* I can reach?

These are questions that only you can answer, but answering no to any one of these factors effectively eliminates the occupational prospect.

Therefore, before you definitely answer no to any of these questions, check all possibilities to keep an occupation that otherwise interests you. Could time priorities be rearranged to allow for the length of an educational program? Would going to school part time over a longer period be an option? Is financial aid available to help you with the costs of your program? (Practically every school has a financial aid office.) Are you willing to invest some of your personal savings, or is your family able to pay part of your educational expense? Could you earn some money from working part time or summers to help finance your education? Is the location of a training program really impossible for you, or can you make some sacrifices or use creative thinking in order to attend a school that has the program you need? Explore all ideas of possible support before you give up on an occupation that really interests you.

Occupational Prospects Eliminated Because of Length, Cost, or Location of Education

_____ _____

_____ _____

_____ _____

_____ _____

_____ _____

_____ _____

_____ _____

SUMMARY

1. Exercising freedom of choice is the most human thing we do. Decision making cannot be avoided; even choosing *not* to decide is a decision. You make hundreds of decisions daily, most of which are automatic or intuitive and require little thought. The more important a decision is to you, the harder it is to make, and career decisions are among the most difficult decisions you face in life.

2. Several types of decision makers according to degrees of decidedness have been identified in the research literature on forming career decisions. These are *very decided, somewhat decided, unstable decided, tentatively undecided, developmentally undecided, seriously undecided,* and *chronically indecisive* (Gordon, 1998).

3. A career decision-making process starts by building a list of occupational prospects, expanding the number of prospects, and then, if necessary, reducing that number to a more manageable size. If you have generated a lengthy list of occupations to consider, you will probably want to reduce the number to around 10 or 15 prospects. In any case, do not consider fewer than five or six occupational prospects.

4. Before you eliminate an occupational prospect, gather enough information about its requirements and rewards, and about your own abilities and work values, to make an informed judgment. Remove an occupation from your prospect list only when the evidence proves it an obvious choice for elimination. If you have any doubts, keep the occupation.

5. Removing an occupational prospect may be appropriate when: (a) information gathered about it deviates widely from your Ideal Job Description, (b) it appears only once or twice among several methods used to generate prospects, (c) the ability level of the occupation is too far above or too far below your own ability level, (d) none, few, or less than half of your work values are expressed by the occupation, or (e) the occupation requires education or training that is too lengthy, expensive, or inconveniently located for your particular circumstances.

REFERENCES

Chapman, E. N. 1976. *Career search: A personal pursuit.* Chicago: Science Research Associates.

Chartrand, J. M., Martin, W. E., Robbins, S. B., McAuliffe, G. J., Pickering, J. W., and Calliotte, J. 1994. Testing a level versus an interactional view of career indecision. *Journal of Career Assessment*, 2, 55–69.

Cohen, C. R., Chartrand, J. M., and Jowdy, D. P. 1995. Relationships between career indecision subtypes and ego identity development. *Journal of Counseling Psychology*, 42, 440–447.

Crites, J. O. 1969. *Vocational psychology.* New York: McGraw-Hill.

Crites, J. O. 1981. *Career counseling: Models, methods, and materials.* New York: McGraw-Hill.

Fuqua, D. R., Newman, J. L., and Seaworth, T. B. 1988. Relation of state and trait anxiety to different components of career indecision. *Journal of Counseling Psychology*, 35(2), 154–158.

Gelatt, H. B., Varenhorst, B., Carey, R., and Miller, G. P. 1973. *Decisions and outcomes.* New York: College Entrance Examination Board.

Goodstein, L. D. 1965. Behavioral theoretical views of counseling. In B. Stefflre, ed., *Theories of counseling*, pp. 140–192. New York: McGraw-Hill.

Gordon, V. N. 1998. Career decidedness types: A literature review. *The Career Development Quarterly*, 46, 386–403.

Hartman, B. W., and Fuqua, D. R. 1983. Career indecision from a multidimensional perspective: A reply to Crites. *School Counselor*, 30, 340–349.

Isaacson, L. E. 1985. *Basics of career counseling.* Boston: Allyn and Bacon.

Krieshok, T. S. 1998. An anti-introspectivist view of career decision making. *The Career Development Quarterly*, 46, 210–229.

Leong, F. T. L., and Chervinko, S. 1996. Construct validity of career indecision: Negative personality traits as predictors of career indecision. *Journal of Career Assessment*, 4, 315–329.

Lucas, M. S., and Epperson, D. L. 1988. Personality types in vocationally undecided students. *Journal of College Student Development*, 29, 460–466.

Multon, K. D., Heppner, M. J., and Lapan, R. T. 1995. An empirical derivation of career decision subtypes in a high school sample. *Journal of Vocational Behavior*, 47, 76–92.

Newman, J. L., Fuqua, D. R., and Minger, C. 1990. Further evidence for the use of career subtypes in defining career status. *The Career Development Quarterly*, 39, 178–188.

Rojewski, J. W. 1994. Career indecision types for rural adolescents from disadvantaged and nondisadvantaged backgrounds. *Journal of Counseling Psychology*, 41, 356–363.

Salamone, P. R. 1982. Difficult cases in career counseling II: The indecisive client. *The Personnel and Guidance Journal*, 60, 496–499.

Savickas, M. L., and Jorjoura, D. 1991. The Career Decision Scale as a type indicator. *Journal of Counseling Psychology*, 38, 85–90.

Serling, D. A., and Betz, N. E. 1990. Development and evaluation of a measure of commitment. *Journal of Counseling Psychology*, 37, 91–97.

Silverman, R. E. 1971. *Psychology.* New York: Appleton-Century-Crofts.

U.S. Department of Labor. 1991. *Dictionary of occupational titles*, 4th ed., rev. Washington, DC: U.S. Government Printing Office.

Van Matre, G., and Cooper, S. 1984. Concurrent evaluation of career indecision and indecisiveness. *Personnel and Guidance Journal*, 62, 637–639.

Wanberg, C. R., and Muchinsky, P. M. 1992. A typology of career decision status: Validity extension of the Vocational Decision Status Model. *Journal of Counseling Psychology*, 39, 71–80.

Chapter 9

Making Career Decisions: Putting It All Together

"Whenever it's time to make a tough decision, I sidestep it until tomorrow. When tomorrow comes, I wait until the next day. By then, maybe it will go away. No decision is so difficult that it can't be put off for another day." The fallacy of this line of reasoning is that a decision has actually been made; the decision has been made to make no decision.

Some people choose to steer clear of decision making, hoping a perfect decision will somehow present itself, one with no risk or effort involved. Thinking this way, you can think forever but nothing gets done.

"But if I make a decision," you may be thinking, "then I'm stuck with it forever. What happens if I make the wrong decision?" In real life, there aren't many decisions that are unchangeable if a bad choice has been made. With careers, there is always the opportunity to end a course of action, go into another cycle of career decision making, select a new occupation, and get moving again. This situation may be forced on you in the future; you should be prepared for it anyway.

Many people lack the confidence to make decisions for themselves. They believe they're not competent or will make too many mistakes to be successful. Gaining the competence and the confidence to make good career decisions is one reason you are using this book. You have generated a number of occupational prospects, gathered information about your alternatives, worked on strengthening your motivation, identified and prioritized your work abilities and values, and—if needed—reduced your occupational alternatives to a more reasonable number. That took commitment and ability on your part. You have already built the foundation for your career decision. Now comes the payoff.

In this chapter, you will encounter a decision-making matrix that will enable you to put your remaining occupational prospects into an order of priority. Of course, it is possible to make decisions without using a matrix, but this exercise requires you to think carefully about the occupational alternatives that remain on your prospect list—something you might not otherwise do. You can then emerge from your career decision-making exercise with a number one occupational choice, a number two choice, and so on. More important, you will be able to answer questions about your selection of an occupation. Suppose you are asked to give reasons for choosing a certain career. Your answers are already factored into the decision-making matrix. From the information you have about yourself and your occupational prospects, you will have ranked and coded all the factors that influenced your decision. Others may question the judgments you make about your values and abilities and the extent to which they are expressed in an occupation, but at least you can give reasons why you made the choice.

It isn't easy to go through a rational process of career decision making that asks you to produce occupational prospects, explore career options, and study your personal characteristics so you can explain your career choices to yourself and others. Most people don't want to work that hard to make a decision. Recall the survey in Chapter 1 that revealed 68 percent of all workers had no career plan when they began their first full-time job. Before that study, another national survey discovered 64 percent had no career plan (Lester and Hoyt, 1994). Consider that, for both high school dropouts and graduates, the average length of time spent on the first job is less than one year. College academic advisers and counselors say that anywhere from 20 to 60 percent of the students in their first-year classes are undecided about a major (Hayes, 1997), a majority do not have clearly defined career goals, and 50 percent do not graduate. Among those who do graduate, many do not seriously think about their options beyond college until the last few months of school. Five years after graduation, most are in occupations not directly related to their college major (Jarvis, 1990). Overall, vast numbers of people eventually end up in some kind of occupation, not because they truly like it, but because they have family responsibilities, rent or mortgage obligations, and car payments. They must adjust and make the best of it. They engage in a process known as "satisficing"—trying to make do with conditions where job satisfactions are limited by sacrifices that barely suffice to make work bearable—not the most inspiring scenario for a future.

The career decision-making exercises in this chapter give you some distinct benefits. First, you can establish a career goal. That goal can give your life purpose, meaning, and direction, perhaps the most valuable assets you can possess. Being clear in your own mind about your career direction is the most essential factor in searching for a job. Employers are more impressed by job seekers who know what they want than by those who do not. Second, prioritizing your prospective occupations gives you more than one plan in case your first plan doesn't work out. Circumstances could prevent you from carrying out your first choice. You could be driven to go with your second or a lower choice, at least temporarily. Also, your ideas about your number one occupation could change; an occupation currently second or third on your prospect list could become your primary occupational choice in time.

After looking at ways people struggle and cope with situations calling for decisions, the quality of your decisions, and the strategies and risks involved in making decisions, you can either start with a practice exercise concerning a choice of colleges or go directly into your career decision-making exercise. To do the exercise, you must have completed gathering information about yourself and the occupational prospects you are seriously considering. Your decision is only as good as the information you put into it.

COPING WITH THE RISKS AND STRESS OF DECISION MAKING

From all reports, stress—or mental or emotional strain and anxiety—is a condition afflicting more and more people in modern life. Stress almost always accompanies what is important to us, whether it be achieving something worthwhile or establishing and maintaining good relationships with other people whose love and friendship we value. We experience stress from anything that disturbs our normal functioning as a human being. Making a decision that launches us into an unpredictable future easily turns into a stressful situation. Career decisions are like that; they involve risks and unknown outcomes. How people deal with these uncertainties is a topic to which we now turn.

Coping Patterns in Decision Making

There is no question that people feel psychological stress and inner conflict when an important decision must be made. How do you manage the pressure that arises when you think of the commitment, costs, and risks involved in an important choice, regardless of the course of action you choose? Janis and Mann (1977) have identified five styles of coping with the need to make decisions: (1) rigid attachment to a choice despite negative feedback and warnings of trouble, (2) quickly changing goals without thought, (3) evasion and avoidance of responsibility, (4) delaying until a deadline creates a pressured decision made under extreme tension, and (5) making effective decisions in an alert, informed, observant, and prudent manner. The work of Janis and Mann relates to decision-making styles in general, and their findings can be applied to making career decisions. Each pattern is briefly explained in the following paragraphs. Ask yourself which pattern fits you best at the present time.

1. *Unconflicted adherence* is a pattern of decision making that sticks to an occupational choice already made, no matter what happens. The person stays on one course of action despite signals that it could be disastrous. This approach is like saying, "My mind is made up; don't bother me with the facts." Some people enter a career-planning program with an occupation already chosen and never honestly challenge it with any serious consideration of other occupational prospects. Apathy, indifference, complacency, and lack of attention to danger signals often characterize this pattern. This type of decision maker denies any risk about the chosen occupation and exhibits a low degree of stress and anxiety about career decisions in general.

2. *Unconflicted change* is a pattern of constantly shifting occupational goals, without much thought given to the changes in direction. The person is attracted by one occupation for a while but switches to another, then another, and so on. Alternatives are not thoroughly investigated, and the information that is obtained is not adequately processed. You could call this approach "Don't look before you leap." The decision maker detects many risks in a current course of action but doesn't see any unfavorable outcomes from a new course of action. As with unconflicted adherence to a previous decision, unconflicted change is marked frequently by indifference and a low degree of stress and anxiety.

3. *Defensive avoidance* involves evading any serious discussion of making a decision and denying there is any problem. Denial helps the person reduce the inner conflict of knowing that a decision must be made. The person lessens the tension by delaying, shifting responsibility onto someone else, or propping up a choice through overstating its positive aspects and minimizing its negative consequences. Procrastination and transferring responsibility are easy to understand as ways to avoid the obligations of decision making. Janis and Mann have observed several methods of bolstering an occupational choice and avoiding issues that might question its appropriateness. Among these methods are exaggerating favorable qualities of an occupation, dismissing possible unfavorable outcomes, denying hesitant feelings about a choice, assuming that nothing needs to be done about a decision for a long time, and believing that it will not matter whether the decision maker lives up to the commitment or not. Defensive avoidance is much like saying, "Don't disturb me now, I'll cross that bridge later." Because there are risks in any course of action, the person is easily persuaded to do nothing; a good solution cannot be found.

4. *Hypervigilance is* the word Janis and Mann use to describe the stressful condition of being overwhelmed by the need to make a decision but having little time in which to choose from many possible courses of action. The person may be threatened with serious loss if he or she fails to make a decision. As the deadline for a decision draws closer, panic may take hold as a result of high levels of stress and anxiety. The person's thought processes are virtually paralyzed, and effective decisions are unlikely to be made. For example, a student may have reached the last days of school without a plan about what to do after graduation; the pressure builds to select an occupation and get a job. There is not enough time to create alternative courses of action and make a careful search for information on which to base a decision. The student becomes agitated, tense, high-strung, and excessively nervous from the pressure of the situation. Extreme emotional reactions crowd out the careful thinking needed in this situation; a good decision is much less likely to be the result. Another example could be a person who is forced to change occupations because layoffs in his or her current occupation make jobs scarce. If the new career decision is delayed by defensive avoidance, unemployment compensation and savings begin to run out. The person urgently needs income from a new occupation, and hypervigilance sets in. Under these circumstances the decision maker is less likely to make an appropriate occupational choice.

5. *Vigilance* is the term Janis and Mann use to identify the most effective decision-making style. A vigilant decision maker is attentive, watchful, observant, open, alert, flexible, sincere, committed, careful, and prudent. A vigilant career decision maker

   - Produces a wide range of occupational alternatives and sincerely explores many of them
   - Makes a commitment to gather and study information about each occupation under serious consideration and to survey personal goals and values associated with those occupations

- Carefully evaluates costs, risks, and both positive and negative consequences of each occupational prospect
- Searches for new information in order to conduct further evaluations of each alternative
- Assimilates and takes into account new information or expert judgment, even when it does not support preferred occupational choices
- Re-examines the positive and negative consequences of all remaining alternatives before making a final career choice
- Makes detailed plans to implement the career choice once it has been chosen, with supplemental plans that could be used if the first choice develops risks that are too great (*Source:* List based on Janis and Mann, 1977).

Vigilant decision makers go through a process similar to the career decision-making process used in this book. They become aware of the challenge created by problems such as personal job dissatisfaction and the need to choose a new occupation. Finding the risks more serious if no change is made from current behavior, they survey and weigh alternatives and obtain new information about their options. Vigilant decision makers commit themselves at some point to a new course of action and remain faithful to it despite some negative feedback. They stay with their decision at least until they encounter a challenge so powerful that it provokes dissatisfaction (Janis and Mann, 1977). The vigilant decision maker feels a moderate degree of stress and anxiety, contrasted with the strong tensions of hypervigilance and the low pressures of unconflicted adherence or unconflicted change. Effective decision making seems to involve some intermediate level of stress—not so high that it causes the decision maker to become inefficient, nor so low that no problem is perceived when there actually is one.

Janis and Mann believe that decision makers pose questions to themselves when they experience a need to make a decision. The first question is "Are there risks involved if I do not change from what I am doing now?" Answering no does not involve stress and conflict, and the result is *unconflicted adherence*. For example, if you are transferred from one job to another in a lateral move that makes very little difference in your life, you are unlikely to experience stress and conflict. The second question for a decision maker is "Are the risks serious if I do change?" If the answer is no, the result is *unconflicted change*. If you leave school to join the family business and are also not committed to any other occupational alternative (a requirement of unconflicted change), this situation will not cause much stress and conflict, because commitment produces its own tensions and strains (Brown, 1990).

Where conflict and stress is great, the third question a decision maker asks is "Can I find a realistic solution?" If you answer no to this question, this may bring about *defensive avoidance* in the form of delaying thought and action (procrastination), becoming dependent on others, or rationalizing (bolstering) a particular choice by minimizing its risks of loss or exaggerating its hoped-for gains. If the answer is yes to the third question, a fourth appears: "Is there enough time to search for reasonable options?" Responding no to this question results in *hypervigilance*. Here decision making occurs under the pressures of emergency situations and lack of adequate time to properly gather information and consider alternative solutions. If you have lost a job you enjoy, you might easily adopt a defensive avoidance position. On top of this, if you have financial concerns that are overwhelming and immediate, the result can develop into hypervigilance. *Vigilance*, to use Janis and Mann's term, is of course the preferred decision-making mode: generating alternatives, collecting data about your options, analyzing yourself, and weighing information about the decision objectively (Brown, 1990).

Which decision-making style best describes you? Keep in mind that no one style is permanent. With effort and motivation, you can change from a pattern of defensive avoidance to a vigilant pattern. And conversely, a vigilant decision maker may become hypervigilant if the deadline for a decision is rapidly approaching.

The Quality of Your Decisions

The seven features of vigilant decision making listed in the previous section can serve as criteria for judging the quality of your decision making. If any one of these seven criteria is not met, it is reasonable to conclude that your decision making is deficient in some way. The more deficiencies there are in your decision-making style, the greater the possibility of disappointment. Applying the ideas of Janis and Mann to career decision making, ask yourself honestly whether you have adequately met their seven criteria. If you cannot honestly answer yes to these questions (especially the first three), you have reason to be skeptical of the quality of your decision.

1. Have you used a number of methods (6 or more) to generate a wide range of occupational prospects (15 or more)?   Yes___ No___

2. Have you carefully researched and studied your narrowed list of occupational alternatives (five or more), including the values they represent and the abilities they require?   Yes___ No___

3. Have you thoughtfully weighed both positive and negative consequences or outcomes of each occupational prospect?   Yes___ No___

4. Have you searched intensively for new information that would help you judge and evaluate your occupational alternatives?   Yes___ No___

5. Have you honestly taken into account and incorporated new information or expert judgment about your occupational alternatives, even when the information or judgment has not supported an occupation you might prefer?   Yes___ No___

6. Have you re-examined the positive and negative consequences of your occupational prospects, including those you thought might be unacceptable to you, before making a final choice?   Yes___ No___

7. Have you made detailed plans to implement your major occupational choice (getting the required education, job searching) and additional plans to substitute a new career goal in the event that your first choice develops risks that are too costly?   Yes___ No___

Strategies and Risks in Decision Making

Because most decisions are made under some degree of risk and uncertainty, people develop strategies to make a choice among alternatives. A strategy is a plan for making a decision that uses your values and abilities, the data you have gathered about your alternatives, and information about the risks involved.

Gelatt, Varenhorst, Carey, and Miller (1973) have suggested four decision-making strategies, designated the *wish, safe, escape,* and *combination* strategies. Before you read the description of each strategy, answer the question about which course of action you would take in each of the following three situations.

Situation 1

Suppose you are at a horse race and have $100 to bet on the last race. Only three horses are entered, and you must pick the winner. If your horse doesn't win, you will lose the $100. Which alternative would you choose?

_____   Option A. Old Gray Mare at 100-to-1 odds. If you win, you get $10,000.

_____   Option B. Speed Demon at 2-to-1 odds. If you win, you get $200.

_____   Option C. You decide not to bet anything. You keep the $100.

_____   Option D. Black Beauty at 4-to-1 odds. If you win, you get $400.

Situation 2

Assume you have $1000 to invest in one of three stocks. Which one, if any, would you be most likely to buy?

_____ Option A. This stock pays extremely high dividends but is so unstable that you run a high risk of losing your investment.

_____ Option B. This stock pays very low dividends, but it is very unlikely that you will lose money on it.

_____ Option C. You decide not to invest your money in any stock option because you fear any loss of it.

_____ Option D. Another stock pays moderate dividends and is more reliable than Option A but less reliable than Option B.

Situation 3

You are looking for high income and success in your career choice. Imagine you have three job offers. Which one, if any, would you pick?

_____ Option A. This job has an excellent chance of earning a very large income, but you have only a slim chance of succeeding in it.

_____ Option B. This job pays a modest income, but it is one in which you have an extremely good chance of success.

_____ Option C. You decide to make no choice among the three job offers, hoping that you will find another job that pays well and has very little risk of failure.

_____ Option D. This job generally pays an average-sized income and has some chance of paying a fairly large income; you have a rather good chance of succeeding in it.

In all three situations, Option A represents the _wish_ strategy, Option B is the _safe_ strategy, Option C typifies the _escape_ strategy, and Option D expresses the _combination_ strategy. The four decision-making strategies are described as follows:

1. The wish strategy leads you to choose the alternative that gives you whatever you desire the most. Risks and probabilities are ignored. You select the most desirable outcome, regardless of cost or probability of failure. This strategy is fairly easy to apply; all you need to do is produce a list of alternatives and pick the one you value most. In the horse race, you would bet on the long shot. Assuming you value earning money, a wish strategy would dictate choosing the stock that could pay the highest dividends or the job in which you could earn the highest income. Note, however, that risks and chances of success are disregarded.

2. The safe strategy suggests that you select the course of action most likely to succeed. You must be able to estimate the chances for success in each of your alternatives so you can select the option with the highest probability of succeeding. You would bet on the favorite in a horse race. The stock option that offers the least chance of losing your money and the job you are almost certain to keep are the safest choices.

3. The escape strategy leads you to choose the option that avoids the worst possible outcome. You try to escape disaster or misfortune by predicting the outcomes of your alternatives and determining what the worst result could be. If loss of money is the worst possible outcome, you won't bet any money in the horse race, nor will you invest in any stock. In the job choice situation, delaying (avoiding a decision) is the mechanism of escape. Escape and delay are rational strategies in some circumstances—for example, when no alternative is tolerable or rewarding.

4. The combination strategy requires you to bring together the wish and safe strategies to choose an option that combines the most desirable outcome with the highest probability of success. Your goal is modified because of the values expressed in your alternative options and their probabilities of success. The combination strategy is the most logical one to use, but it is also the most difficult to apply. It requires knowing your values and abilities, assessing your chances of success in each alternative, predicting possible outcomes, stating your goals clearly, and ranking the desirability or designating the relative value of your alternatives (Gelatt, Varenhorst, Carey, and Miller, 1973). Despite its difficulties, the combination strategy holds the greatest hope for effective decision making and personal satisfaction with the outcome. As noted in Chapter 5, high achievers prefer moderate risks when they decide on a course of action.

A PRACTICE DECISION-MAKING EXERCISE: CHOOSING A COLLEGE

In this exercise, adapted from Oxhandler (1975), imagine that you must decide among five college choices: Hallowed Halls College, Mid-State University, Robotron Technical Institute, Homeville Community College, or no college at all. You are not sure about your future career or college major. Engineering technology, art, computer science, and drafting have crossed your mind. A basic liberal arts program also sounds good.

You have never been away from home for any great length of time. You could easily commute to the local community college. Your brother went to Robotron Tech, but he knew before he went that he wanted to major in electronics engineering technology. Your mother believes the teachers at Mid-State are among the finest in the land, and you are attracted by the idea of going to a prestigious state university with a big sports program. Dad has told you about his student days at old Hallowed Halls, and you sense he would be very proud if you went there. Money is a little tight now, and Homeville Community College would be less expensive than anywhere else. No one has ever suggested not going to college, but that, of course, is another option.

At this point, ask yourself, "Can I make a choice now?" If you can choose, is the choice easy to make? What information is missing, and what would be helpful to know? If the decision turns out badly, who is responsible?

Intuitive Decision Making

You could make a decision now, relying mostly on intuition. *Intuition* is a kind of awareness of truth—knowledge without any conscious reasoning. We make many decisions intuitively, but intuition works best when it is combined with rational planning, logical thinking, and information analysis. It is possible to make a decision in the situation described, but you really don't know how good it will be without more information to back it up.

A Rational, Systematic Approach to Decision Making

A rational, logical approach to making decisions operates from a base of information. Intuition is a form of data, but often it isn't enough. Let's collect more information about your alternatives in choosing a college.

Hallowed Halls College (HHC) is a private liberal arts college with about 800 students, located in a small community about 100 miles from where you live. HHC is strong in academic subjects but doesn't offer much in technical training and occupational programs. Its liberal arts courses give the school an excellent reputation, and it always attracts more applicants than it can admit. Hallowed Halls is very selective in its admissions policies. Your Scholastic Aptitude Test scores are somewhat below the average of those who are admitted to HHC, making it a fairly high risk in terms of academic success. Dormitory living is pleasant, the rooms are comfortable and uncrowded, and the food service is good. Buildings and grounds are attractively maintained. Social activities off campus are somewhat restricted, and social life on campus tends to revolve around sororities and fraternities. School policy encourages students to join the school's small drama club, the staff of a weekly campus newspaper, the college band, or one of several sports programs. Faculty members are interested in their students, and most classes are small. HHC has a religious orientation; all students are urged to attend chapel. Most graduates go directly into graduate school for professional training. Tuition and fees at Hallowed Halls are high.

Mid-State University (MSU) is a large public university with many separate departments and nearly 40,000 students. It is centered in an urban area about 40 miles from your home. It is well known throughout the country and around the world. Educational programs of either an intellectual or a practical nature are available. There is always something to do at Mid-State; social, cultural, athletic, and other extracurricular events take place daily. MSU has an excellent drama department. The music program and daily newspaper are highly rated but difficult to join. Social and political clubs proliferate. Highly recruited athletes make up most of the intercollegiate sports teams, but an intramural sports program attracts many participants. You could easily get lost at Mid-State, but an active counseling and academic advising program, along with a decentralized administrative structure, aims to preserve a small-school atmosphere in the midst of the large university. Admissions are somewhat selective. There is great diversity in the requirements of the many academic programs. For you, some educational majors would involve a high risk of failure; others would represent a moderate or low risk of failing to finish the program. There are almost no social restrictions at Mid-State. Dorms are modern, but crowded conditions can make studying difficult. Your friends tell you the food service is acceptable, but institutional. The professors are friendly, but many are absorbed in their research. Many classes take place in large lecture halls with television monitors and hundreds of students. If you need help in your studies, you must seek it yourself. Many ethnic, racial, religious, and cultural groups comprise the student body. Several departments are nationally ranked, and there are about 5000 students in the graduate schools. Tuition is moderate.

Robotron Technical Institute (RTI) is a relatively new technical school that has developed good programs in electronics engineering technology, robotics, computer science, drafting, industrial technology, information processing, and automotive technology. RTI has also developed many apprenticeship programs in the skilled trades. All students take math and English courses. RTI is located in a medium-sized city about 60 miles from your hometown; you feel that the distance is too great for you to commute. You would have to find an apartment nearby, which would mean buying and preparing your own food. Few social activities exist at Tech; the school concentrates on offering quality technical instruction. You haven't been able to find any information about extracurricular activities. A total of 500 students currently attend Robotron—400 of them male—and most come from within a 30-mile radius of the school. Enrollment has doubled in the past five years; RTI expects to continue growing rapidly. Teachers take a personal interest in their students, but many of them are hard to contact outside class because they have full-time jobs elsewhere. Counseling is not well established, because the administration believes most students are already committed to an occupational education program leading to a technical career. So far, you haven't been able to find much data on the scholastic aptitude of Tech students. You sense, however, that most students have a range of abilities quite similar to your own. The school accepts most applicants. You have heard that the average student at Tech is highly motivated. Funding comes from private foundations and corporations, tuition is moderate, and a strong financial-aid program helps many students.

Homeville Community College (HCC) counts about 2000 people as full-time students, with another 4000 enrolled part time. The school is in the same urban area as your hometown, and all students commute to the campus. HCC is convenient to the population center. Almost all the full-time students work at part-time jobs to help pay their college expenses. The typical community college student lives at home. Homeville offers the first two years of a four-year college liberal arts program, as well as an occupational division program that leads to a two-year associate degree. Teachers concentrate on teaching and are readily available to give individual help to students. Some social and cultural activities exist, but college events are not very well attended. School athletic teams have given way to physical fitness programs. There is no band, and a school newspaper is an on-and-off proposition; currently, it is "on." A struggling drama department produces excellent performances. HCC accepts all applicants. Practical training tends to be emphasized somewhat more than intellectual experiences. Your aptitude test scores will probably qualify you for almost any program at Homeville. A strong counseling program helps students who need career guidance and academic advice. Tuition is low.

You have thought about your personal characteristics. Recent results on the Scholastic Aptitude Test are consistent with your other aptitude scores. Your verbal score was in the 60th- to 78th-percentile band, and your mathematics score was in the 45th- to 65th-percentile band, as compared with other college applicants throughout the nation. Your school grades are shown here:

10th Grade	Semester 1st	2nd	11th Grade	Semester 1st	2nd	12th Grade	Semester 1st
English	C+	B	Literature	B−	B	College English	B+
Geometry	D	B	Algebra-Trigonometry	B	C+	Computer Science	B
Biology	B	B	Chemistry	B	C	Physics	C
World History	B	B−	U.S. History	B	B	American Government	A
Latin II	C	C+	Technical Drafting	A	A−	Journalism	A
Physical Education	A	B+	Band	B	A	Band	A

Your school counselor is helping you with your choice of college and major. An educational interest inventory suggested business, engineering technology, and several social sciences as educational majors of greatest attraction, but you want to explore your educational prospects further. For now, your thoughts are to pursue a general liberal arts program for the first year of college. That curriculum can meet the graduation requirements of almost any college and give you time to narrow your range of educational options and decide on a college major.

Among your achievements outside the classroom are winning first prize in a photography contest, being elected president of the drama club, performing a lead role in a play, writing articles and taking pictures for your school newspaper, and playing on the basketball team. You have held a part-time job in a camera store and wondered what it would be like to go into the photography business.

Obviously, you now have more data on which to base a decision. By intuition, you can probably begin to detect a narrowing or focusing process occurring. A clear choice may even be emerging. However, one problem with relying only on intuition is that there is a strong element of mystery about it. Mysteries are fun and exciting, but career detectives must be able to explain their solutions logically. A rational decision-making method allows you to place all the parts of the decision in front of you for comparison and analysis. You can examine the factors in a decision by constructing a decision-making matrix; Janis and Mann (1977) call it a *decisional balance sheet.*

Procedures in Using the Decision-Making Matrix

Follow these steps for using a decision-making matrix. Use a pencil to allow for changes. Look at Tables 9-1 and 9-2 for examples of the method. (Note that a simplified method is offered in steps 4, 5, and 7 and can be used if you prefer.)

1. List your alternatives (in this case, names of colleges) horizontally across the top of the matrix.
2. List the values you want expressed and the abilities you want to use in your college choice vertically down the left side of the matrix. (Refer to Chapter 7 if you need help identifying your educational values; return to Chapter 6 for the abilities you enjoy using.)
3. Give each value and each ability a weight number. The higher the number of a value or ability, the greater its importance. You have a choice of weighting systems; however, the same system should be used for both your values and your abilities.

   a. *The rank-order system.* Prioritize your educational values (as you did for work values in Chapter 7), and then prioritize your educational abilities (as you did in Chapter 6). Count the number of values or abilities, use that number as the weight of your most important value, and number consecutively down to 1. For example, suppose you have 10 values (as in Table 9-1). The most important value receives the number 10, the next most important receives a 9, and so on down to 1. Thus the values are weighted 10–9–8–7–6–5–4–3–2–1. Rank your abilities in the same way.

      Suppose you think that your top value is not 10 times as important as the one you placed at the bottom of your list, or that two or three values

Table 9-1 Decision-Making Matrix Using a Rank-Order Weighting System

	Weights	Hallowed Halls College	Mid-State University	Robotron Technical Institute	Homeville Community College
Educational Values					
Academic quality	(10)	++ (20)	+ (10)	+ (10)	+ (10)
Good counseling	(9)	0 (0)	++ (18)	– (–9)	++ (18)
Low tuition/expense	(8)	– (–8)	– (–8)	+ (8)	++ (16)
Location of school	(7)	+ (7)	+ (7)	+ (7)	++ (14)
Good chance for academic success	(6)	– (–6)	+ (6)	0 (0)	+ (6)
Personal attention	(5)	++ (10)	– (–5)	– (–5)	++ (10)
Educational programs	(4)	+ (4)	++ (8)	+ (4)	+ (4)
Living accommodations	(3)	+ (3)	+ (3)	– (–3)	+ (3)
Prestige of school	(2)	+ (2)	++ (4)	++ (4)	– (–2)
Social life	(1)	– (–1)	++ (2)	– (–1)	– (–1)
Educational Abilities					
Taking photographs	(9)	++ (18)	+ (9)	0 (0)	++ (18)
Promoting drama club	(8)	+ (8)	++ (16)	0 (0)	+ (8)
Verbal reasoning	(7)	+ (7)	+ (7)	+ (7)	+ (7)
Drawing blueprints	(6)	– (–6)	0 (0)	++ (12)	+ (6)
Writing news stories	(5)	++ (10)	+ (5)	0 (0)	+ (5)
Studying politics/history	(4)	++ (8)	+ (4)	0 (0)	+ (4)
Computer skills	(3)	+ (3)	+ (3)	++ (6)	+ (3)
Spatial aptitude	(2)	0 (0)	0 (0)	++ (4)	+ (2)
Playing in band	(1)	+ (1)	+ (1)	0 (0)	– (–1)
Total score	100	80	90	44	130
Sum of weights (× 2)* =	× 2	3rd	2nd	4th	1st
*Total Ideal Score**	200	40%	45%	22%	65%

* Multiply by 2 if the ++ code is used.

should be weighted the same in importance. In that case, the rank-order system doesn't truly reflect the strength of your values, so you need to use another weighting system.

b. *The scale system.* You can list your values and abilities in the same order, then assign weights on a scale from 1 to 10, with 10 as the highest possible weight (as shown in Table 9-2). If you prefer smaller numbers, you could use a 1-to-7 scale or a 1-to-5 scale. Attach a descriptive term to each number in your scale to indicate the importance of the value or ability in relation to the others you have listed, as follows:

1-to-10 Scale	1-to-7 Scale	1-to-5 Scale
10 = Essential		
9 = Very high	7 = Very high	
8 = High	6 = High	5 = High
7 = Above average	5 = Above average	4 = Above average
6 = Slightly above average		
5 = Average	4 = Average	3 = Average
4 = Slightly below average		
3 = Below average	3 = Below average	2 = Below average
2 = Low	2 = Low	1 = Low
1 = Very low (least in importance)	1 = Very low	

Table 9-2   Decision-Making Matrix Using a 1-to-10 Scale Weighting System

	Weights	Hallowed Halls College	Mid-State University	Robotron Technical Institute	Homeville Community College
Educational Values					
Academic quality	(8)	++ (16)	+ (8)	+ (8)	+ (8)
Good counseling	(8)	0 (0)	++ (16)	− (−8)	++ (16)
Low tuition/expense	(8)	− (−8)	− (−8)	+ (8)	++ (16)
Location of school	(7)	+ (7)	+ (7)	+ (7)	++ (14)
Good chance for academic success	(7)	− (−7)	+ (7)	0 (0)	+ (7)
Personal attention	(5)	++ (10)	− (−5)	− (−5)	++ (10)
Educational programs	(5)	+ (5)	++ (10)	+ (5)	+ (5)
Living accommodations	(4)	+ (4)	+ (4)	− (−4)	+ (4)
Prestige of school	(3)	+ (3)	++ (6)	++ (6)	− (−3)
Social life	(3)	− (−3)	++ (6)	− (−3)	− (−3)
Educational Abilities					
Taking photographs	(9)	++ (18)	+ (9)	0 (0)	++ (18)
Promoting drama club	(8)	+ (8)	++ (16)	0 (0)	+ (8)
Verbal reasoning	(6)	+ (6)	+ (6)	+ (6)	+ (6)
Drawing blueprints	(6)	− (−6)	0 (0)	++ (12)	+ (6)
Writing news stories	(6)	++ (12)	+ (6)	0 (0)	+ (6)
Studying politics/history	(5)	++ (10)	+ (5)	0 (0)	+ (5)
Computer skills	(5)	+ (5)	+ (5)	++ (10)	+ (5)
Spatial aptitude	(4)	0 (0)	0 (0)	++ (8)	+ (4)
Playing in band	(1)	+ (1)	+ (1)	0 (0)	− (−1)
Total score	108	81	99	50	131
Sum of weights (× 2)* =	× 2*	3rd	2nd	4th	1st
*Total Ideal Score**	216	38%	46%	23%	61%

* Multiply by 2 if the ++ code is used.

Table 9-3   List of Educational Values with One Value Outweighing All Others Combined

Educational Values	Weights
Location of school	20
Low tuition and expense	5
Academic quality	3
Good counseling	2
Educational programs	2
Personal attention	1
Active social life	1
Prestige of school	1
Chance to play sports	1

$5 + 3 + 2 + 2 + 1 + 1 + 1 + 1 = 16$ (which does not outweigh 20)

If you have a value or ability that is clearly more important to you than all the others combined, your number weight for it should be extended beyond the upper limits of the scale to reflect this condition. Table 9-3 provides an example in which location of school outweighs all other values combined.

Accurate self-knowledge is the key to competence in weighting your values and abilities. (*Note:* Be sure to use the same weighting system for your abilities that you used for your values.)

4. Match each college with each value and ability, using the following codes: *very positive* (++), *positive* (+), *neutral* (0), or *negative* (–). Friel and Carkhuff (1974) call these codes *favorability scales.*

> + + = Educational value is *strongly expressed* in the college.
> + + = Ability is *used very much* in the college.
>   + = Educational value is *expressed somewhat* in the college.
>   + = Ability is *used somewhat* in the college.
>   0 = *Don't know / can't determine* whether the value is expressed
>   0 = *Don't know / can't determine* whether the ability is used in the college.
>   – = Educational value is *not expressed* in the college.
>   – = Ability is *not used* in the college.

Here, accurate knowledge about your alternatives is necessary. Place the code you believe to be the most accurate, according to your information, under the appropriate college and across from the value or ability being considered.

> *Simplified method.* Eliminate the ++ code, and use the following three codes:
> + = Value is expressed; ability is used.
> 0 = Don't know / can't determine.
> – = Value is not expressed; ability is not used.

5. Multiply the weight number by the code you have given to each value and ability; use +2 for ++, +1 for +, 0 for 0, and –1 for –. Write the product in the parentheses to the right of each code mark. For example, a weight of 10 multiplied by the ++ code (+2), equals 20; multiplied by the + code (+1), it is 10. Any number multiplied by 0 equals 0.

Any number multiplied by –1 becomes negative (9 times –1 equals –9; be sure to include the minus sign inside the parentheses). Review the examples in Tables 9-1 and 9-2.

> *Simplified method.* Multiply by plus one (+1), zero (0), or minus one (–1).

6. Obtain a total score for each alternative by adding all the numbers in parentheses in each column (subtracting when a number is negative). Compare total scores to determine the place of each college among the alternatives.
7. To obtain your total ideal score, add the column of value weights and ability weights and multiply by 2. This is the score that would be obtained if every value and ability were coded ++.

> *Simplified method.* Because the ++ code is not used, simply add the weights column; do not multiply by 2.

Divide the total score for each alternative by the ideal score to find out what percentage of the ideal is reached by each alternative choice (Friel and Carkhuff, 1974).

EXERCISE 9-1   CHOOSING A COLLEGE

List two to six schools at the top of the blank matrix titled "Decision-Making Matrix for Choosing a College." The schools may be actual ones, if you are facing such a decision, or they may be the fictitious ones already described in this chapter. Then list your own educational values and abilities, assign a numeric weight to them, and give them positive, neutral, or negative codes to show their relationship to each school. Follow the directions outlined in steps 1 through 7 in the previous section.

Discussion

As long as you use information to form judgments for the matrix, you are relying on a rational method of decision making. Of course, intuition is a part of assessing the weights you give your values and abilities and the codes you assign to each alternative. All data are filtered through your emotional system of feelings and perceptions, but when you are pressed to present evidence justifying your decision, you must rely on information. The quality of your decision depends on the quality of your information and the wisdom of your judgments. The decision-making matrix is a logical culmination of all that this book has taught you to do: Generate alternatives, gather information about them, and study and prioritize your values and abilities in order to base your decision on a solid foundation of information.

After you make a decision, the next step is to implement it. If you actually used the decision-making matrix in Exercise 9-1 to choose a school, you can take action to put that decision into practice. This means applying for admission, checking financial aid resources, learning graduation requirements, developing a list of courses for the first semester, considering educational programs of study, arranging for housing and meals, and so forth. A decision involves a commitment to action.

THE CAREER DECISION

In making decisions, Janis and Mann (1977) propose a balance sheet that involves 16 steps. All steps require assigning "importance ratings" to each factor on a +5 to –5 scale. Included in the steps are these factors: generating career alternatives, listing useful (advantageous) gains for one's self with each alternative, giving useful (beneficial) gains with each alternative for others, listing sources of social approval and social disapproval for each alternative, and listing types and sources of self-approval and self-disapproval for each alternative. The final step is to compute the value of each alternative by summing the positive and negative weights (Brown, 1990). In the college choice decision of Exercise 9-1 in this chapter and in the career decision-making activity of Exercises 9-2, 9-3, and 9-4 that lie ahead, we use a modified form of Janis and Mann's decisional balance sheet model.

Decision-Making Matrix for Choosing a College

Weighting system used:

____ Rank order

____ Scale: 1 to ____

Code system used:

____ Regular (++, +, 0, −)

____ Simplified (+, 0,)

Educational Values	Weights	Name of College Code (W × C)	Name of College Code (W × C)	Name of College Code (W × C)	Name of College Code (W × C)	Name of College Code (W × C)	Name of College Code (W × C)
_____	___	___ (___)	___ (___)	___ (___)	___ (___)	___ (___)	___ (___)
_____	___	___ (___)	___ (___)	___ (___)	___ (___)	___ (___)	___ (___)
_____	___	___ (___)	___ (___)	___ (___)	___ (___)	___ (___)	___ (___)
_____	___	___ (___)	___ (___)	___ (___)	___ (___)	___ (___)	___ (___)
_____	___	___ (___)	___ (___)	___ (___)	___ (___)	___ (___)	___ (___)
_____	___	___ (___)	___ (___)	___ (___)	___ (___)	___ (___)	___ (___)
_____	___	___ (___)	___ (___)	___ (___)	___ (___)	___ (___)	___ (___)
_____	___	___ (___)	___ (___)	___ (___)	___ (___)	___ (___)	___ (___)
_____	___	___ (___)	___ (___)	___ (___)	___ (___)	___ (___)	___ (___)
_____	___	___ (___)	___ (___)	___ (___)	___ (___)	___ (___)	___ (___)
_____	___	___ (___)	___ (___)	___ (___)	___ (___)	___ (___)	___ (___)
_____	___	___ (___)	___ (___)	___ (___)	___ (___)	___ (___)	___ (___)

Educational Abilities	Weights	Code (W × C)	Code (W × C)	Code (W × C)	Code (W × C)	Code (W × C)	Code (W × C)
_____	___	___ (___)	___ (___)	___ (___)	___ (___)	___ (___)	___ (___)
_____	___	___ (___)	___ (___)	___ (___)	___ (___)	___ (___)	___ (___)
_____	___	___ (___)	___ (___)	___ (___)	___ (___)	___ (___)	___ (___)
_____	___	___ (___)	___ (___)	___ (___)	___ (___)	___ (___)	___ (___)
_____	___	___ (___)	___ (___)	___ (___)	___ (___)	___ (___)	___ (___)
_____	___	___ (___)	___ (___)	___ (___)	___ (___)	___ (___)	___ (___)
_____	___	___ (___)	___ (___)	___ (___)	___ (___)	___ (___)	___ (___)
_____	___	___ (___)	___ (___)	___ (___)	___ (___)	___ (___)	___ (___)
_____	___	___ (___)	___ (___)	___ (___)	___ (___)	___ (___)	___ (___)
_____	___	___ (___)	___ (___)	___ (___)	___ (___)	___ (___)	___ (___)
_____	___	___ (___)	___ (___)	___ (___)	___ (___)	___ (___)	___ (___)
_____	___	___ (___)	___ (___)	___ (___)	___ (___)	___ (___)	___ (___)

Total ideal score:

Sum of weights (× 2)* = _____

	Total ___	Total ___	Total ___	Total ___	Total ___	Total ___
	Place ___	Place ___	Place ___	Place ___	Place ___	Place ___
	% ___	% ___	% ___	% ___	% ___	% ___

*Multiply by 2 if the ++ code is used

Source: Adapted from Friel and Carkhuff (1974).

Photocopy this page if more matrices are needed.

You can now apply the decision-making skills you have been learning to choose a career direction. You are in complete control of this choice. Exercise 9-2 brings together all the factors you have developed to form your career decision. These factors are the occupational prospects that remain on your list and the information you have accumulated on them, your prioritized list of work values, and the prioritized list of abilities and aptitudes you want to use in your occupation. Exercise 9-3 is the actual career decision-making exercise.

EXERCISE 9-2   SUMMARY LIST OF OCCUPATIONAL PROSPECTS, WORK VALUES, AND WORK ABILITIES

1. *Name your occupational prospects*—the alternatives that have survived your challenges and stayed on your list. Refer to Exercise 4-5 and your completed occupational research worksheets. You should be able to name at least 8 to 12 occupational prospects for this exercise. If you have eliminated any occupation(s) from those you have researched, draw a line through the name of the occupation and give the reason(s) for doing so, but save at least 5 or 6 occupational prospects for the decision-making exercise. Chapter 8 covers reasons to eliminate an occupation: too wide a gap from your ideal job description, ability level too far above or below your own, not enough of your work values expressed, or the education and training is not accessible to you. Reject an occupation only when there is an obvious reason to do so; if in doubt, keep the occupation on your prospect list.

2. *Name your work values in order of priority*—the desirable qualities important to you in making a career choice. Refer to Exercise 7-9 at the end of Chapter 7. Be certain about the meaning of your work values; each one should be distinct from all the others. Try to use 10 to 12 work values for this exercise. After you have listed your work values, ask yourself, "Where would I place each value on a 1-to-10 scale, with 10 representing the highest weight and 1 the lowest?"

3. *Name your work abilities in order of priority*—skills and aptitudes you would enjoy using in your occupation and can legitimately claim. Refer to Exercise 6-9 at the end of Chapter 6. Connect functional and work content skills, adding adaptive skills if possible. You can also use high or above-average aptitudes. Try to come up with 10 to 12 work abilities. After you have listed your work abilities, ask yourself, "Where would I place each ability on a 1-to-10 scale, with 10 representing the highest weight and 1 the lowest?"

Occupational Prospects	Work Values	Work Abilities

Occupation(s) Eliminated   Reason(s) for Doing So

_____   _____

_____   _____

_____   _____

_____   _____

Next comes Exercise 9-3, the career decision-making exercise itself, on pages 328–329. List your occupational prospects across the top of the matrix; each page has room for six occupations. Two matrices are presented to allow room for up to 12 occupations; photocopy a blank matrix if you are considering more than 12 occupations. *Use a pencil* so you can change number weights and judgments, if necessary, when you obtain new information. On the left side of the matrix, enter your work values and abilities in the same prioritized order in which you arranged them in Chapters 6 and 7. Then assign a number weight to your work values and abilities and give them a positive, neutral, or negative code according to the degree to which they are expressed in the occupation. Now the hard part—the judgment part—is over. Only the human brain can do what you have done up to this point. You have now programmed your decision; the rest of the exercise is an arithmetic problem. Multiply the weight numbers by the codes, and add the products to obtain a sum total for each occupation. When you finish, you will have constructed a ranked or prioritized list of occupations, starting with your number one choice, followed by number two, and going on through however many occupations from your prospect list you want to use. Note that the simplified method available in steps 4, 5, and 7 can be used if you prefer.

As you read the directions for the career decision-making exercise, look at the examples provided by Tables 9-4, 9-5, and 9-6. Inventing some fanciful occupational titles from literature (such as Button-Molder, from Ibsen's *Peer Gynt*), I settled for (1) Political Leader, like Machiavelli's *The Prince* or Willie Stark in Warren's *All the King's Men;* (2) Clergy, from Goldsmith's *Vicar of Wakefield;* (3) Tour Guide, taking people to a place no one really wants to go—Dante's *Inferno;* (4) Farm Manager, like Scarlett O'Hara in Mitchell's *Gone With the Wind;* and (5) Detective, like Doyle's Sherlock Holmes.

Literature and the media can give you information and impressions about occupations, though the information and impressions are often outdated or stereotyped. Can you think of some more occupations represented in great works of literature?

Table 9-4 Career Decision-Making Matrix Using a Rank-Order Weighting System

Weighting system used:

✓ Rank order

___ Scale: 1 to ___

Code system used:

✓ Regular (++, +, 0, –)

___ Simplified (+, 0, –)

	Weights	Political Leader		Clergy		Tour Guide		Farm Manager		Detective	
Work Values											
Independence	(10)	+	(10)	+	(10)	0	(0)	+	(10)	+	(10)
Achievement	(9)	++	(18)	+	(9)	+	(9)	+	(9)	+	(9)
Altruism/helping others	(8)	+	(8)	++	(16)	+	(8)	0	(0)	+	(8)
Money/salary	(7)	++	(14)	–	(–7)	0	(0)	+	(7)	–	(–7)
Leisure/home/family	(6)	–	(–6)	+	(6)	–	(–6)	+	(6)	–	(–6)
Opportunity for travel	(5)	++	(10)	+	(5)	++	(10)	–	(–5)	+	(5)
Job security	(4)	–	(–4)	0	(0)	+	(4)	+	(4)	–	(–4)
Moral/ethical concerns	(3)	+	(3)	++	(6)	0	(0)	0	(0)	0	(0)
Prestige/status	(2)	–	(–2)	+	(2)	+	(2)	+	(2)	++	(4)
Personal power	(1)	++	(2)	+	(1)	0	(0)	+	(1)	+	(1)
Work Abilities											
Counseling/advising people	(10)	+	(10)	++	(20)	+	(10)	0	(0)	0	(0)
Verbal reasoning	(9)	++	(18)	++	(18)	+	(9)	+	(9)	+	(9)
Computing numbers	(8)	+	(8)	+	(8)	+	(8)	++	(16)	+	(8)
Leading/supervising people	(7)	++	(14)	+	(7)	+	(7)	++	(14)	0	(0)
Growing plants	(6)	–	(–6)	–	(–6)	–	(–6)	++	(12)	–	(–6)
Researching information	(5)	++	(10)	+	(5)	+	(5)	+	(5)	++	(10)
Analyzing data logically	(4)	++	(8)	+	(4)	+	(4)	+	(4)	++	(8)
Inspiring people	(3)	++	(6)	++	(6)	0	(0)	–	(–3)	–	(–3)
Budgeting money	(2)	++	(4)	+	(2)	+	(2)	++	(4)	0	(0)
Operating machinery	(1)	–	(–1)	–	(–1)	–	(–1)	++	(2)	0	(0)
Total score	110		124		111		65		97		46
Sum of weights (× 2)* =	× 2*		1st		2nd		4th		3rd		5th
Total Ideal Score*	220		56%		50%		30%		44%		21%

* Multiply by 2 if the ++ code is used.

EXERCISE 9-3   CAREER DECISION-MAKING EXERCISE

Follow the basic steps for using a decision-making matrix. Use a pencil to allow for changes.

1. Across the top of the blank matrix titled Career Decision-Making Matrix, list the occupational prospects you have researched. Obtain these occupational prospects from Exercise 9-2.

2. Down the left side of the matrix, list 10 to 12 work values you want expressed and 10 to 12 abilities you want to use in your occupation. List them in their prioritized order from Exercise 9-2.

3. Give a weight number to each work value and work ability. Choose one of two weighting systems, but use the same system for both abilities and work values.

   a. *The rank-order system.* Count the number of work values, use the highest number as the weight for the most important value, and number consecutively down to 1. If you list 10 work values, for example, the values are weighted 10–9–8–7–6–5–4–3–2–1. Assign numbers to work abilities in the same way. (See the example in Table 9-4.) If the rank-order weighting

Table 9-5   Career Decision-Making Matrix Using a 1-to-10 Scale Weighting System

Weighting system used:

____ Rank order

✓ Scale: 1 to 10

Code system used:

✓ Regular (++, +, 0, –)

____ Simplified (+, 0, –)

	Weights	Political Leader		Clergy		Tour Guide		Farm Manager		Detective	
Work Values											
Independence	(10)	+	(10)	+	(10)	0	(0)	+	(10)	I	(10)
Achievement	(8)	++	(16)	+	(8)	+	(8)	+	(8)	+	(8)
Altruism/helping others	(8)	+	(8)	++	(16)	+	(8)	0	(0)	+	(8)
Money/salary	(7)	++	(14)	–	(–7)	0	(0)	+	(7)	–	(–7)
Leisure/home/family	(7)	–	(–7)	+	(7)	–	(–7)	+	(7)	–	(–7)
Opportunity for travel	(6)	++	(12)	+	(6)	++	(12)	–	(–6)	+	(6)
Job security	(5)	–	(–5)	0	(0)	+	(5)	+	(5)	–	(–5)
Moral/ethical concerns	(5)	+	(5)	++	(10)	0	(0)	0	(0)	0	(0)
Prestige/status	(3)	–	(–3)	+	(3)	+	(3)	+	(3)	++	(6)
Personal power	(2)	++	(4)	+	(2)	0	(0)	+	(2)	+	(2)
Work Abilities											
Counseling/advising people	(9)	+	(9)	++	(18)	+	(9)	0	(0)	0	(0)
Verbal reasoning	(7)	++	(14)	++	(14)	+	(7)	+	(7)	+	(7)
Computing numbers	(6)	+	(6)	+	(6)	+	(6)	++	(12)	+	(6)
Leading/supervising people	(6)	++	(12)	+	(6)	+	(6)	++	(12)	0	(0)
Growing plants	(6)	–	(–6)	–	(–6)	–	(–6)	++	(12)	–	(–6)
Researching information	(6)	++	(12)	+	(6)	+	(6)	+	(6)	++	(12)
Analyzing data logically	(5)	++	(10)	+	(5)	+	(5)	+	(5)	++	(10)
Inspiring people	(5)	++	(10)	++	(10)	0	(0)	–	(–5)	–	(–5)
Budgeting money	(4)	++	(8)	+	(4)	+	(4)	++	(8)	0	(0)
Operating machinery	(2)	–	(–2)	–	(–2)	–	(–2)	++	(4)	0	(0)
Total score	117		127		116		64		97		45
Sum of weights (× 2)* =	× 2*		1st		2nd		4th		3rd		5th
Total Ideal Score*	234		54%		50%		27%		41%		19%

* Multiply by 2 if the ++ code is used.

Source: This exercise, excluding tables, was adapted from Friel and Carkhuff (1974).

system does not truly reflect your thinking about work values, use a scale weighting system instead.

b. *The scale system.* Assign weights on a scale from 1 to 10, with 10 as the highest possible weight. (See Table 9-5 for an example.) Use a 1-to-7 or a 1-to-5 scale if you prefer. Attach a descriptive term to each number on your scale to indicate the importance of the work value or ability in relation to the other values or abilities you have listed. Be sure to use the same scale for work abilities that you use for work values. That is, if you use a 1-to-7 scale for work values, use a 1-to-7 scale for abilities also. For example,

1-to-10 Scale	1-to-7 Scale	1-to-5 Scale
10 = Essential		
9 = Very high	7 = Very high	
8 = High	6 = High	5 = High
7 = Above average	5 = Above average	4 = Above average
6 = Slightly above average		
5 = Average	4 = Average	3 = Average
4 = Slightly below average		
3 = Below average	3 = Below average	2 = Below average
2 = Low	2 = Low	1 = Low
1 = Very low (least in importance)	1 = Very low	

If you have a work value or ability that is definitely more important to you than all the others combined, your number weight for it must be extended above the upper limits of your scale to represent its value to you. In Table 9-6, for example, money/salary is a work value that outweighs all other values combined.

Table 9-6 List of Work Values with One Value Outweighing All Others Combined

Work Values	Weights
Money/salary	20
Advancement	4
Achievement	3
Independence	3
Recognition	2
Friendships at work	1
Location of work	1
Health	1
Comfortable surroundings	1
Security	1

4 + 3 + 3 + 2 + 1 + 1 + 1 + 1 + 1 = 17 (which does not outweigh 20)

4. Use a code showing whether each of your occupational prospects is *very positive* (++), *positive* (+), *neutral* (0), or *negative* (–) in relation to each work value or ability listed.

> ++ = Work value is *strongly expressed* in the occupation.
> ++ = Work ability is *used greatly* in the occupation.
>
> + = Work value is *expressed somewhat* in the occupation.
> + = Work ability is *used somewhat* in the occupation.
>
> 0 = *Don't know / can't determine* whether the work value is expressed.
> 0 = *Don't know / can't determine* whether the ability is used in the occupation.
>
> – = Work value is *not expressed* in the occupation.
> – = Work ability is *not used* in the occupation.

Consult your occupational research worksheets (Exercise 4-7) for information on which to base your judgments. (Work values are either explicitly stated or implied throughout the worksheet. Abilities are likely to be concentrated in items 2 and 3, which cover education and personal qualifications.) Place the code on the line just to the left of the parentheses, as shown in Tables 9-4 and 9-5.

> *Simplified method.* Eliminate the ++ code, and use the following three codes:
>
> + = Value is expressed; ability is used.
> 0 = Don't know / can't determine.
> – = Not expressed; ability is not used.

5. Multiply the weight number of the work value or ability by +2 (for ++), +1 (+), 0 (0), or –1 (–). Write the product of your multiplication inside the parentheses to the right of each code mark (the $W \times C$ column). Write minus signs inside the parentheses so you will know when to subtract instead of add in totaling each column. Remember to multiply by +2 when you encounter a ++ code and that anything multiplied by 0 is 0. See the examples in Tables 9-4 and 9-5.

> *Simplified method.* Multiply by plus one (+1), zero (0), or minus one (–1).

6. Obtain a total score by totaling the products for each occupation. Add the numbers of each column, subtracting where you have placed a minus sign. Compare total scores to determine the place of each occupation among your alternative prospects. You have now ranked your choices in order of priority.
7. To obtain a total ideal score, add all numbers in the weights column (values and abilities) and multiply by 2. The ideal score is the highest possible score you could obtain for any occupation.

> *Simplified method.* Because the ++ code is not used, simply add the weights column; do not multiply by 2.

Compare each occupational prospect with the total ideal score by dividing the total number of points for each occupation by the total ideal score to obtain a percentage (Friel and Carkhuff, 1974). The percentage figure can range from +100% (+1.00) to –50% (–0.50) with the regular codes and from +100% (+1.00) to –100% (–1.00) using the simplified system.

Career Decision-Making Matrix

Weighting system used: Code system used:

_____ Rank order   _____ Regular (++, +, 0, –)

_____ Scale: 1 to ___   _____ Simplified (+, 0, –)

		Title of Occupation	Title of Occupation	Title of Occupation	Title of Occupation	Title of Occupation	Title of Occupation
Work Values	Weights	Code (W × C)	Code (W × C)	Code (W × C)	Code (W × C)	Code (W × C)	Code (W × C)
_____	___	___ (___)	___ (___)	___ (___)	___ (___)	___ (___)	___ (___)
_____	___	___ (___)	___ (___)	___ (___)	___ (___)	___ (___)	___ (___)
_____	___	___ (___)	___ (___)	___ (___)	___ (___)	___ (___)	___ (___)
_____	___	___ (___)	___ (___)	___ (___)	___ (___)	___ (___)	___ (___)
_____	___	___ (___)	___ (___)	___ (___)	___ (___)	___ (___)	___ (___)
_____	___	___ (___)	___ (___)	___ (___)	___ (___)	___ (___)	___ (___)
_____	___	___ (___)	___ (___)	___ (___)	___ (___)	___ (___)	___ (___)
_____	___	___ (___)	___ (___)	___ (___)	___ (___)	___ (___)	___ (___)
_____	___	___ (___)	___ (___)	___ (___)	___ (___)	___ (___)	___ (___)
_____	___	___ (___)	___ (___)	___ (___)	___ (___)	___ (___)	___ (___)
_____	___	___ (___)	___ (___)	___ (___)	___ (___)	___ (___)	___ (___)
_____	___	___ (___)	___ (___)	___ (___)	___ (___)	___ (___)	___ (___)
Work Abilities	Weights	Code (W × C)	Code (W × C)	Code (W × C)	Code (W × C)	Code (W × C)	Code (W × C)
_____	___	___ (___)	___ (___)	___ (___)	___ (___)	___ (___)	___ (___)
_____	___	___ (___)	___ (___)	___ (___)	___ (___)	___ (___)	___ (___)
_____	___	___ (___)	___ (___)	___ (___)	___ (___)	___ (___)	___ (___)
_____	___	___ (___)	___ (___)	___ (___)	___ (___)	___ (___)	___ (___)
_____	___	___ (___)	___ (___)	___ (___)	___ (___)	___ (___)	___ (___)
_____	___	___ (___)	___ (___)	___ (___)	___ (___)	___ (___)	___ (___)
_____	___	___ (___)	___ (___)	___ (___)	___ (___)	___ (___)	___ (___)
_____	___	___ (___)	___ (___)	___ (___)	___ (___)	___ (___)	___ (___)
_____	___	___ (___)	___ (___)	___ (___)	___ (___)	___ (___)	___ (___)
_____	___	___ (___)	___ (___)	___ (___)	___ (___)	___ (___)	___ (___)
_____	___	___ (___)	___ (___)	___ (___)	___ (___)	___ (___)	___ (___)
_____	___	___ (___)	___ (___)	___ (___)	___ (___)	___ (___)	___ (___)
Total ideal score:		Total ___	Total ___	Total ___	Total ___	Total ___	Total ___
Sum of weights (× 2)* = _____		Place ___	Place ___	Place ___	Place ___	Place ___	Place ___
		% _____	% _____	% _____	% _____	% _____	% _____

*Multiply by 2 if the ++ code is used

Source: Adapted from Friel and Carkhuff (1974).

Career Decision-Making Matrix

Weighting system used: | Code system used:

____ Rank order | ____ Regular (++, +, 0, –)

____ Scale: 1 to ____ | ____ Simplified (+, 0, –)

		Title of Occupation	Title of Occupation	Title of Occupation	Title of Occupation	Title of Occupation	Title of Occupation
Work Values	Weights	Code (W × C)	Code (W × C)	Code (W × C)	Code (W × C)	Code (W × C)	Code (W × C)
_____	___	__ (__)	__ (__)	__ (__)	__ (__)	__ (__)	__ (__)
_____	___	__ (__)	__ (__)	__ (__)	__ (__)	__ (__)	__ (__)
_____	___	__ (__)	__ (__)	__ (__)	__ (__)	__ (__)	__ (__)
_____	___	__ (__)	__ (__)	__ (__)	__ (__)	__ (__)	__ (__)
_____	___	__ (__)	__ (__)	__ (__)	__ (__)	__ (__)	__ (__)
_____	___	__ (__)	__ (__)	__ (__)	__ (__)	__ (__)	__ (__)
_____	___	__ (__)	__ (__)	__ (__)	__ (__)	__ (__)	__ (__)
_____	___	__ (__)	__ (__)	__ (__)	__ (__)	__ (__)	__ (__)
_____	___	__ (__)	__ (__)	__ (__)	__ (__)	__ (__)	__ (__)
_____	___	__ (__)	__ (__)	__ (__)	__ (__)	__ (__)	__ (__)
_____	___	__ (__)	__ (__)	__ (__)	__ (__)	__ (__)	__ (__)
_____	___	__ (__)	__ (__)	__ (__)	__ (__)	__ (__)	__ (__)
Work Abilities	Weights	Code (W × C)	Code (W × C)	Code (W × C)	Code (W × C)	Code (W × C)	Code (W × C)
_____	___	__ (__)	__ (__)	__ (__)	__ (__)	__ (__)	__ (__)
_____	___	__ (__)	__ (__)	__ (__)	__ (__)	__ (__)	__ (__)
_____	___	__ (__)	__ (__)	__ (__)	__ (__)	__ (__)	__ (__)
_____	___	__ (__)	__ (__)	__ (__)	__ (__)	__ (__)	__ (__)
_____	___	__ (__)	__ (__)	__ (__)	__ (__)	__ (__)	__ (__)
_____	___	__ (__)	__ (__)	__ (__)	__ (__)	__ (__)	__ (__)
_____	___	__ (__)	__ (__)	__ (__)	__ (__)	__ (__)	__ (__)
_____	___	__ (__)	__ (__)	__ (__)	__ (__)	__ (__)	__ (__)
_____	___	__ (__)	__ (__)	__ (__)	__ (__)	__ (__)	__ (__)
_____	___	__ (__)	__ (__)	__ (__)	__ (__)	__ (__)	__ (__)
_____	___	__ (__)	__ (__)	__ (__)	__ (__)	__ (__)	__ (__)
_____	___	__ (__)	__ (__)	__ (__)	__ (__)	__ (__)	__ (__)
Total ideal score:		Total ____	Total ____	Total ____	Total ____	Total ____	Total ____
Sum of weights (× 2)* = _____		Place ____	Place ____	Place ____	Place ____	Place ____	Place ____
		% _____	% _____	% _____	% _____	% _____	% _____

*Multiply by 2 if the ++ code is used

Source: Adapted from Friel and Carkhuff (1974).

EXERCISE 9-4   FINAL, PRIORITIZED LIST OF OCCUPATIONAL PROSPECTS

Place and Name of Occupational Prospects	Total Points	Percentage of Ideal Score
1. _____	_____	_____ %
2. _____	_____	_____ %
3. _____	_____	_____ %
4. _____	_____	_____ %
5. _____	_____	_____ %
6. _____	_____	_____ %
7. _____	_____	_____ %
8. _____	_____	_____ %
9. _____	_____	_____ %
10. _____	_____	_____ %
11. _____	_____	_____ %
12. _____	_____	_____ %
_____	_____	_____ %
_____	_____	_____ %
_____	_____	_____ %
_____	_____	_____ %
_____	_____	_____ %
_____	_____	_____ %
_____	_____	_____ %
_____	_____	_____ %
_____	_____	_____ %

The career decision-making matrix you have completed is only a device to let you lay out as many factors for your consideration and to encourage as much thinking and self-examination in a career decision as possible. The anatomy of a decision is there in front of you. The reason you chose your number one occupational prospect is something you can now explain rationally to others and, most importantly, to yourself. You may be surprised or even dismayed that a particular occupation came in ahead of one you thought would come out the highest, but now you have an answer as to why that happened. You may have reinforced a career decision you already had in mind, and now you feel more certain of it because it survived a challenge from other occupational prospects. Or, if you were completely undecided before you started this book and its activities and exercises, you can feel much better now having made a decision, even if it is still a tentative one.

Keep your completed career decision-making matrix for future reference. You may want to change parts of it (in pencil!) as you learn new information about yourself and the world of work. Re-examine the judgments you have made, and continue doing so—we'll start doing that in the last chapter of this book. You will always have choices and the freedom to change them, so this process that is now yours will come to your aid over and over again.

SUMMARY

1. Important decisions often create stress and psychological tension. When you struggle with important decisions, you develop a coping pattern or style of decision making. Janis and Mann (1977) have identified five such patterns. Four of them have serious defects: (1) "Unconflicted adherence" indicates staying rigidly on a chosen course even though there are extremely high risks and warnings of disaster ahead. (2) "Unconflicted change" involves a continual shifting of goals without thought or purpose. (3) "Defensive avoidance" is a way of evading serious thought about a necessary decision (by delaying or shifting responsibility) or bolstering a decision already made (by overemphasizing its positive characteristics and minimizing its negative consequences). (4) "Hypervigilance" means becoming virtually paralyzed from extreme anxiety and overwhelmed by stress and tension as the deadline approaches for a decision.

2. Vigilance is logically the most effective decision-making style, as described by Janis and Mann (1977). It involves a process similar to the one used in this book: producing alternatives, collecting and studying information about them, evaluating risks and consequences, searching for and assimilating new information, re-examining alternatives, implementing the decision, and having contingency plans in case the first choice develops risks that are too great.

3. You should examine the quality of your decision making when you make such important choices as selecting a career. Ask seven questions based on the characteristics of a vigilant decision maker. Failure to answer yes to most of them should cause you to question the wisdom of your career decision.

4. Every decision involves risk. Four strategies for dealing with risk have been identified by Gelatt, Varenhorst, Carey, and Miller (1973). The *wish* strategy is to choose the most desired outcome regardless of risk. The *safe* strategy is to decide the course of action most likely to succeed without considering your values. The *escape* strategy is to choose to avoid the worst possible outcome. The *combination* strategy brings together the wish and safe strategies by choosing the most desirable outcome consistent with the highest probability of success. The combination strategy is the most logical of the four, but it is also the most difficult to use. Nevertheless, it holds the greatest promise for personal satisfaction.

5. The practice decision-making matrix lets you make a choice among four fictitious colleges; you can substitute the names of real schools if you want. The decision-making process can be intuitive or rational. The rational method relies on information and a system for evaluating your decision.

6. The career decision-making exercise can be the culmination of all your efforts in selecting an occupation. First you list the occupational alternatives that remain on your prospect list. Next you list your work values and work abilities and weight them in rank order or on a scale of your choosing. Then you enter data that tell whether or not each occupational prospect expresses your work values and favorite work abilities. Finally, you multiply the value and ability weights by your coded judgments and add the products to obtain a total score for each occupation. The number of points you award each occupational alternative indicates its relative standing on your prospect list.

7. Your number one occupational choice should represent your preferred career at the present time. If it doesn't, you should re-examine your career decision-making matrix to discover the reason.

REFERENCES

Brown, D. 1990. Models of career decision making. In D. Brown, L. Brooks, and Associates, *Career choice and development*, 2nd ed., pp. 395–421. San Francisco: Jossey-Bass.

Friel, T. W., and Carkhuff, R. R. 1974. *The art of developing a career*. Amherst, MA: Human Resource Development Press.

Gelatt, H. B., Varenhorst, B., Carey, R., and Miller, G. P. 1973. *Decisions and outcomes: A leader's guide.* New York: College Entrance Examination Board.

Hayes, L. 1997, October. The undecided college student. *Counseling Today Online.* Alexandria, VA: American Counseling Association.

Janis, I. L., and Mann, L. 1977. *Decision making: A psychological analysis of conflict, choice, and commitment.* New York: Free Press (Macmillan).

Jarvis, P. S. 1990, Spring. A nation at risk: The economic consequences of neglecting career development. *Journal of Career Development,* 16(3), 157–171.

Lester, J. N., and Hoyt, K. B. 1994. *Learning to work: The NCDA Gallup survey.* Alexandria, VA: National Career Development Association.

Oxhandler, R. 1975. *Post-secondary career guidance project: Instructional manual for Foundations 100—Career decision-making.* Kalamazoo, MI: Kalamazoo Valley Community College.

Chapter 10

Reality-Testing Your Career Choice

When you have made a definite career decision, the next step is to implement it. (What good is a decision if you don't act on it?) One of the first actions you are likely to take is to seek any further education the chosen occupation may require. You can use Exercise 9-1 in the previous chapter to assist you in choosing a school or college. In planning for an education, it is important to think about the purposes of education and to know about different types of educational institutions, programs, costs, and financial aid. First, obtain information from advisers, printed material, and the Internet. You can then establish a semester-by-semester or term-by-term plan to accomplish your educational goals.

Reality-testing takes place after you make the career decision. If your decision is realistic, you might be living with it for a long time. An unworkable decision will need to be changed at some point, unless you are the kind of person who adheres to any decision, come what may. This chapter includes a set of reality-testing exercises designed to help you assess the appropriateness of your career choice.

The ultimate reality test of your occupational choice is acquiring and holding a job within that occupation. The job search is an action phase of career planning and is the subject of a second book in the *Career Planning Guide* series. Beyond this final chapter in this first book on career decision making, Appendix A: *Implementing Your Career Decision—The Job Search* has a number of brief summaries that outline the contents of the second book, *Job Search*. Included are approaches to and principles of job hunting; sources of job leads, résumés, and cover letters; job application forms; investigating workplaces; interviewing for information and for jobs; evaluating job offers; keeping a job; and dealing with the problems of work.

EDUCATIONAL DECISIONS

After you select a career direction, implementing the decision usually brings up a question: Does my occupational choice involve further planning for education or training? In 2001, 2.5 million students graduated from U.S. high schools; 1.6 million, or 61.7 percent, were enrolled in college by the following October. Of the young women high school graduates, 63.6 percent chose this course of action, compared with 59.8 percent for young men. A large majority of these high school graduates were in college on a full-time basis. Of the full-time college students, 42.9 percent were *employed or looking for work* in October 2001, compared with 87.5 percent of the part-time students. Students attending two-year schools were more likely to *participate in the labor force* than were students in four-year schools, by a 71.6 to 35.3 percent margin. Students in two-year colleges were more likely to be enrolled on a part-time basis than were students enrolled in four-year colleges; here the margin was 31.3 to 11.3 percent (U.S. Department of Labor, 2002).

Although the labor market now wants workers with higher-level skills than it has demanded in the past, most jobs do not require the skills obtained only from a college education. Of course, high school graduates who immediately enter the labor force can choose to enroll in college at a later time. Indeed, in some cases, delaying college by choosing work first may improve a person's chances of benefiting from the college experience later (Rosenbaum, 2001). U.S. Census Bureau data show that the proportion of the labor force with college degrees grew from 25 percent in 1992 to 28 percent in 2000. Among workers 25 to 34 years old, the proportion rose from 26 to 33 percent (Dohm and Wyatt, 2002).

For those who choose to further their education, whether immediately after high school graduation or after some work experience, what is the kind of education wanted? If you want specific occupational training, trade and technical schools or adult education courses or apprenticeships may be appropriate choices of educational institutions. Broader educational programs that combine liberal arts and academic courses with preparation for a career are more likely to be found in colleges, universities, and community colleges.

Table 10-1 Median Weekly Earnings of Workers Aged 25 to 64 in Year 2000 by Highest Level of Educational Attainment; Proportions of Those Workers Who Earned Less Than the Median for High School Graduates in Year 2000; and Estimated Work-Life Earnings throughout 40 Years of Year-Round Full Employment, by Highest Level of Education

Education Level	Median Weekly Earnings in Year 2000	Percentage Who Earned Less than the Median for High School Graduates	Estimated Work-Life Earnings (in 1999 dollars) of Full Employment for 40 Years
High school diploma or equivalent	$ 507	—	$ 1,200,000
Bachelor's degree	834	17%	$ 2,100,000
Master's degree	983	10	$ 2,500,000
Professional degree	1,174	9	$ 4,400,000
Doctoral degree	1,214	6	$ 3,400,000

Source: Dohm and Wyatt (2002), pp. 3–15.

What is a college education for? Career-minded students want courses related to their occupational goal; they believe the fundamental purpose of school is preparation for a job. A college education allows you to compete more effectively in the career game. College graduates have greater career options, more job opportunities, better chances for job promotions, higher salaries, and lower rates of unemployment than their non–college-educated counterparts. There are a number of occupations in which only a person with a college degree can qualify. Many occupations are classified as "college preferred"—in other words, a college degree is helpful, but not required. As for pay, a college education can mean substantially higher earnings. For workers 25 to 64 years of age, those with a bachelor's degree earned $834 for their median weekly pay, compared with $507 for workers whose highest level of education was a high school diploma or its equivalent. A college degree does not automatically guarantee you will earn more than all high school graduates, as Table 10-1 shows (Dohm and Wyatt, 2002). However, we can say that people are more likely to average higher earnings the more educated they are; this is particularly true when you add pay for all 40 years of a work life (see last column of Table 10-1).

Educational degrees alone do not determine a person's earnings potential over an entire work life. These averages assume year-round full-time employment over a normal work life of 40 years; circumstances could alter a work-life income estimate based on highest college degree level. These other variables or changeable factors could be economic cycles, periods of unemployment, sickness or injury, location of work, field of study, work experience, pay rates for the occupation, and so on.

College graduates tend to stay longer with their occupational choice than do any other group of workers. They are more likely to be found in professional specialty and executive, administrative, and managerial occupations. These two groups account for two-thirds of college-level employment. Professional specialty occupations include engineer, registered nurse, lawyer, teacher, physician, and social worker, and these occupations provide the most jobs for college graduates. The occupations having the most jobs in the executive, administrative, and managerial group are accountant and auditor; marketing, advertising, and public relations manager; medical and health manager; and administrators and officials in public administration (Mittelhauser, 1998).

If you earn a degree that has an obvious relationship to an occupational title, you are less likely to be underemployed. In other words, an engineering degree leads to a job in engineering and an accounting degree leads to a job in accounting, but what a history or an English degree prepares you for is not as obvious. Many college majors are designed for academic purposes rather than for career training, and this explains why the connection between many college majors and specific career fields is often unclear (Taylor, 2003).

So, then, why study the liberal arts, those basic arts and science courses that colleges and universities usually require for graduation? Beyond a deep interest in the subject matter itself, three primary reasons can be mentioned here:

1. Remember the list of functional/transferable skills you studied in Chapter 6. Many of those skills come from liberal arts courses and are carried over to a wide variety of jobs. These skills are called *functional* because they enable you to perform productively on the job as well as in the activities of life.
2. Liberal arts courses are more likely to provide a lifelong foundation for learning and living, whereas the technical specialty that seems so important today may become outmoded tomorrow.
3. On the job, as well as off, you constantly deal with situations where a knowledge of literature, language, history, politics, art, religion, science, mathematics, and music can give you an advantage over those who have confined themselves to a narrower, specialized kind of training.

Attending college in order to get a better job is a worthwhile goal as long as you do not place such heavy emphasis on your own career needs that you ignore the larger social and political concerns of the community, nation, and world in which you live. Liberal arts subjects reach beyond your immediate career interests and into the very essence of life itself. The true student searches for truth both in the rich imagination of the arts and in the painstaking investigations of science. A real education is a struggle to discover the meaning of nature, humanity, and God. One might call these matters high-minded and noble, but they are also very practical, because they touch the very fundamentals of life and existence.

Colleges and Occupations

Educational programs that require four years of undergraduate education for a bachelor's degree, or graduate school leading to a master's degree or a doctorate, are found at colleges and universities. Many programs of study at both the graduate and undergraduate levels lead to specific jobs, an approach rewarded by many employers. Other employers are favorably impressed by a degree in liberal arts, emphasizing academic and intellectual values. Some colleges offer cooperative programs (especially in business and engineering), where students alternate a semester of classroom studies with a semester of paid work in their major field of study. Tuition costs vary; private schools are more expensive than state-supported colleges. Among those who receive their training at colleges and universities are engineers, social workers, teachers, chemists, accountants, business administrators, ministers, foresters, biologists, and home economists. Occupations such as doctor, lawyer, clinical psychologist, and college teacher require additional education in a graduate or professional school after completion of a four-year undergraduate degree program.

It is not difficult to get printed or electronic information about colleges. All colleges publish a catalog of programs and courses; they may be available in your counselor's office or a career resource center. If you want your own copy, colleges will send you one free or for a modest price. Many college directories are published annually and can be found in counseling offices, libraries, and bookstores. These handbooks contain descriptions of every college and university that functions in all states of the United States and the provinces of Canada. A few of these directories are *The College Board College Handbook*, Barron's *Profile of American Colleges*, Lovejoy's *College Guide*, Princeton Review's *Complete Book of Four-Year Colleges* (including Canadian colleges), and the *Fiske Guide to Colleges*. Profiles of individual colleges in directories typically cover characteristics of the student body, housing, activities, sports, provisions for disabled students, services offered (career counseling, for example), programs of study, requirements for graduation, admission and transfer procedures, financial aid, number of graduates, and a name to contact in the admission department. For Canadian students there is *The Complete Guide to Canadian Colleges*. Most Canadian colleges are less than 100 miles from the U.S. border, and interested students in the United States can consult *College in Canada for American Students*. These books are in local bookstores or on the Internet.

The National Center for Education Statistics in the U.S. Department of Education maintains direct links to nearly 7,000 colleges and universities in the United States. This program is called *IPEDS College Opportunities On-Line,* and it includes large universities, small liberal-arts colleges, specialized schools, community colleges, career or technical colleges, and trade schools. Contact the National Center for Education Statistics, Institute of Education Sciences, U.S. Department of Education, 1990 K Street NW, Washington, DC 20006, or phone 1-202-502-7300, or use the Internet address: http://nces.ed.gov/ipeds/cool/Search.asp. Internet addresses to college and university Web sites and community college Web sites can also be accessed from the University of Texas at Austin (www.utexas.edu/world/univ/). Schools are listed alphabetically and by state.

What happens to college students after they graduate? Do they find work that puts their college degrees to use? The class of 1993 is under study by the National Center for Education Statistics of the U.S. Department of Education. A representative sample   11,190 of the nearly 1.2 million bachelor's degrees awarded to graduates in 1993—was surveyed in 1997, the second and most recent of a series of follow-up studies that will continue over a 12-year period. The purpose of the study is to provide information on academic enrollment, degree completion, employment, and the relationship between academic performance and success in the job market (Stringer, 2000–2001).

Four years after receiving their bachelor's degrees, employment rates for the graduates of the class of 1993 were high. Table 10-2 divides the college graduates into two categories: professional fields and arts and sciences. Five undergraduate majors are in the occupation-related professional fields of business and management, education, engineering, health professions, and public affairs and social services—93 percent of those graduates were employed full time or part time four years later. An 83 percent employment rate was recorded for the six undergraduate majors in the arts

Table 10-2 Class of 1993: Employment Status, 1997, and Full-Time Enrollment in Education beyond the Bachelor's Degree, 1994 and 1997 (all figures are percentages)

| | Employment Status | | | | Full-Time Enrollment in Education beyond the Bachelor's Degree | |
| | Working | | Not Working | | | |
	Full-Time	Part-Time	Unemployed	Not in Labor Force	1994	1997
All graduates	**81%**	**8%**	**3%**	**8%**	**26%**	**22%**
Professional fields (total)	**85**	**8**	**2**	**6**	**9**	**5**
Business and management	89	4	2	5	5	4
Education	81	10	2	7	11	7
Engineering	92	3	1	5	15	7
Health professions	77	13	3	8	11	8
Public affairs and social services	85	8	2	5	9	4
Arts and sciences (total)	**73**	**10**	**4**	**13**	**18**	**17**
Biological sciences	57	10	5	28	27	38
History	78	7	4	11	18	15
Humanities	71	14	4	11	14	12
Mathematics, computer sciences, and physical sciences	81	8	2	10	21	14
Psychology	72	11	4	13	18	19
Social sciences	80	9	3	9	14	13

Figures for employment status may not sum to 100 percent due to rounding.

Source: Adapted from Stringer (2000–2001), pp. 18, 19.

and sciences: biological sciences; history; humanities; mathematics, computer sciences, and physical sciences; psychology; and social sciences. The main reason for a higher employment rate in the professional fields is that more arts and sciences graduates continue their education on a full-time basis than do graduates in the occupation-related majors of the professional fields, also shown in Table 10-2. The highest percentages of graduates continuing their education were in the biological sciences (38 percent). Engineering had the highest full-time employment rate (92 percent) and the lowest unemployment rate (1 percent).

In Tables 10-2 through 10-4, biological science includes majors in zoology, botany, biochemistry, and biophysics. Health professions include allied health majors such as dental or medical technician, community or mental health, and nurse assisting; physical education or recreation; and other areas of health, such as audiology, dentistry, medicine, nursing, health or hospital administration, and dietetics. The humanities field includes foreign languages, philosophy, theology, and the arts. Public affairs and social services include the protective services, social work, and public administration. The social sciences include anthropology, archaeology, economics, sociology, political science, and international relations (Barkume, 1998).

The graduates of the class of 1993 were asked whether they believed their current jobs required a bachelor's degree, were related to their undergraduate major, and had career potential. The average salaries of the graduates who were employed full time were also surveyed. Table 10-3 summarizes these data. Among the 11 groups surveyed, health professions and education graduates rated highest in believing their jobs were related directly to their college major. Health professions and engineering graduates were the highest in believing a bachelor's degree was required for their jobs. Engineers, mathematicians and computer and physical scientists, and business and management graduates were the largest groups reporting they believed their job had career potential. Engineering, health professions, business and management, and mathematics and computer and physical sciences graduates reported the highest salaries.

Table 10-3 Relationship of Current Job to Undergraduate Major and Average Salaries of College Graduates by Major and with Bachelor's Degree Four Years after Graduation, 1997 (figures in percentages, except for average salaries)

	Relationship of Current Job to Major, Degree Requirement, and Career Potential			Average Salary of 1993 Graduates Employed Full-Time, by Undergraduate Major
	Attributes of Current Job			
	Bachelor's Degree Required	Related to Major	Career Potential	
All graduates	62	55	55	$32,500
Professional fields (total)	68	65	55	
Business and management	57	57	60	$36,500
Education	69	67	50	$24,900
Engineering	79	60	64	$43,800
Health professions	80	82	55	$37,300
Public affairs and social services	55	58	47	$29,900
Arts and sciences (total)	60	45	51	
Biological sciences	63	51	45	$26,700
History	57	34	52	$27,000
Humanities	50	40	50	$28,100
Mathematics, computer sciences, and physical sciences	71	63	62	$36,400
Psychology	64	48	48	$26,300
Social sciences	57	33	53	$32,800

Source: Adapted from Stringer (2000–2001), pp. 19, 23.

Table 10-4   Occupations of Employed Graduates of Class of 1993, by Major, Four Years after Graduation (in 1997)

Field of study (in **bold** type) is followed by occupation and percentages of those employed.

Biological sciences: health professions (22%), teaching (17%); other professions (16%); administrative and clerical support (11%); business and management (9%); noncomputer technician (8%); mechanic, operator, and laborer (7%); sales (4%); services (3%); computer science and programming (3%)

Business and management: business and management (39%); administrative and clerical support (19%); sales (13%); other professions (12%); mechanic, operator, and laborer (6%); computer science and programming (5%); services (3%); teaching (3%)

Education: teaching (64%), other professions (11%), administrative and clerical support (8%), business and management (6%), health professions (5%), sales (3%), services (3%)

Engineering: engineering (49%); other professions (17%); computer science and programming (11%); sales (8%); business and management (7%); mechanic, operator, and laborer (5%); administrative and clerical support (3%)

Health professions: health professions (61%), business and management (15%), other professions (9%), teaching (7%), engineering (4%), administrative and clerical support (4%)

History: teaching (34%); business and management (15%); other professions (14%); administrative and clerical support (11%); sales (10%); mechanic, operator, and laborer (5%); health professions (4%); services (4%); computer science and programming (3%)

Humanities: other professions (23%); teaching (20%); administrative and clerical support (18%); business and management (16%); sales (6%); services (5%); mechanic, operator, and laborer (5%); computer science and programming (4%); health professions (3%)

Mathematics, computer sciences, and physical sciences: computer science and programming (24%); teaching (16%); business and management (12%); administrative and clerical support (12%); other professions (12%); engineering (7%); mechanic, operator, and laborer (7%); health professions (4%); noncomputer technician (3%); sales (3%)

Psychology: other professions (30%); business and management (18%); teaching (17%); administrative and clerical support (15%); health professions (8%); sales (5%); services (4%); mechanic, operator, and laborer (3%)

Public affairs and social services: other professions (28%); military and protective services (19%); administrative and clerical support (18%); business and management (11%); teaching (6%); health professions (5%); sales (5%); mechanic, operator, and laborer (4%); service (4%)

Social sciences: business and management (24%); administrative and clerical support (19%); other professions (19%); teaching (11%); sales (8%); mechanic, operator, and laborer (6%); health professions (5%); services (5%); military and protective services (3%)

Source: Stringer (2000–2001), pp. 24–29.

The figures in Table 10-4 show that the proportion of employed college graduates holding jobs in an occupation related to their major field of study was higher for occupation-related majors such as education (64 percent), health professions (61 percent), engineering (49 percent), and business and management (39 percent) than for those with degrees in the social sciences, psychology, humanities, history, and the biological sciences. Although the percentages of employed graduates in jobs related to their major were lower for those in the arts and sciences in this and earlier surveys, keep in mind an advanced degree is required in many occupations that employ liberal arts graduates (Stringer, 2000–2001).

"Once upon a time"—that is, in the 1950s and early 1960s—a college degree was a passport to a well-paid job in the occupation of a student's choice. Times have changed. The college student of today needs to know that a college degree by itself will not guarantee high pay and a "college-level" job. About 5.6 million or 16.6 percent of all college graduates in 1996 were *underemployed*—some by choice, but many because they could not find jobs in their chosen occupation. Underemployment figures were not as bad in 2000, with the economy creating jobs at a record clip. Using projections for the 2000–2010 period, the U.S. economy is expected each year to create 1.28 million jobs that require a college education. (This figure may be rather optimistic, because of the recession that began in 2001.) An annual average of 1.37 million college graduates are projected to be chasing those 1.28 million jobs, for a yearly oversupply of about 90,000 college-graduated job seekers (Fleetwood and Shelley, 2000). Whenever the number of college graduates is larger than the number of openings for college-level jobs, some will settle for jobs that do not require a college degree. This, in turn, puts more pressure on people with less education.

The prospect of vigorous competition for college-level jobs, an estimate of up to 10 or 15 percent of college graduates underemployed per year, and knowing there are even a few college graduates currently unemployed is unpleasant news indeed, but this picture should be balanced with additional information. It is important to remember that a substantial majority of all college graduates will enter occupations requiring a college degree. The unemployment rate for college graduates in 2000 was 1.8 percent for those with a bachelor's degree, 1.6 percent for master's degree holders, and 0.9 percent for graduates with a professional or doctoral degree, half to a quarter of the 3.5 percent rate for high school graduates (Dohm and Wyatt, 2002). The number of college graduates in non–college-level jobs or unemployed goes down after five years in the labor market. And whereas a college degree does not automatically mean high income, the earnings of college graduates have risen sharply in recent years in relation to the pay of high school graduates. In the first quarter of 2003, the median annual income earned by all college graduates was $49,961 compared to $28,548 for high school graduates age 25 and over—a difference of 75 percent (U.S. Department of Labor, 2003a). Although their income amounts have risen slightly, real wages (adjusted for inflation) have remained stagnant or dropped for high school graduates and those with less than a high school diploma since the 1970s.

Many high school students see a college degree as the golden ticket to higher wages, but there are wide variations in income for the college educated. Certain majors lead to higher earnings than other majors, as Table 10-3 has indicated. Some of the reasons for these differences are reflected in the nature of the labor market. Skills acquired in some majors are in short supply, and this usually results in almost all these graduates entering well-paid, college-level jobs. Other majors where skills are in surplus may find some of their graduates forced into lower-paying work. Moreover, some majors are generally perceived to be more difficult, enhancing the value employers may put on graduates in those fields. There can be differences in the values held by people. Some majors attract students who place high income as their highest priority. Other college graduates could have high-paying jobs but choose lower-earning ones, such as education, social work, and theology, preferring their payoff in satisfactions other than higher wages. Other reasons influencing pay differences among college graduates may reflect distinctions made regarding the quality of the college and variations in grade point averages (Hecker, 1996).

Not surprisingly, college graduates predominate in the professional specialty and the executive, administrative, and managerial occupational groups. Table 10-5 shows the proportion of 25- to 34-year-old college graduates with bachelor's or advanced degrees within major occupational groups and selected occupations that had significant educational upgrading between 1992 and 2000 or are considered key occupations in a group. Percentages in Table 10-5 may be slightly underestimated, particularly the proportion of workers with advanced degrees. The reason for this is only 11 percent of college undergraduates are over 35 years old, whereas 33 percent of people attending graduate school are over age 35 (Dohm and Wyatt, 2002).

All things considered, a college education gives substantial benefits to graduates working in occupations requiring a college degree. Competition for many of those jobs is intense. People who choose a full college-baccalaureate program need to assess their career goals realistically and acquire the most appropriate academic preparation for their chosen occupation.

Table 10-5 Proportion of College Graduates, Ages 25 to 34, in Major Occupational Group and Selected Occupations, 1992 and 2000 (numbers are percentages)

Occupational Group/Occupation	Workers Ages 25 to 34 with Bachelor's or Higher Degree		Workers Ages 25 to 34 with Advanced Degree	
	1992	2000	1992	2000
Total, all workers	26	33	6	8
Executive, administrative, and managerial	49	57	9	12
Professional specialty occupations	76	82	29	30
Engineer, architect, and surveyor	83	84	23	23
Mathematical and computer scientist	74	76	20	18
Natural scientist	90	94	45	44
Health diagnosing occupations	97	99	95	97
Health assessment and treating occupations	62	71	14	20
Registered nurse	55	63	8	7
Therapist	73	82	28	48
Teacher, college and university	94	98	66	72
Teacher, except college and university	82	87	22	27
Social scientist and urban planner	81	91	42	46
Writer, artist, entertainer, and athlete	56	69	10	9
Technicians and related support occupations	32	36	6	5
Sales occupations	31	37	3	4
Sales representative, finance and business services	54	60	7	6
Sales representative, mining, manufacturing, and wholesale	48	54	4	5
Sales worker, retail and personal services	17	20	2	3
Administrative support, including clerical	16	17	—	—
Private household occupations	9	7	2	2
Service workers, except private household	9	11	—	—
Protective service occupations	14	21	—	—
Firefighting and fire prevention occupations	13	23	1	2
Police and detective	15	24	—	—
Farming, forestry, and fishing occupations	7	9	—	—
Farm operator and manager	13	21	—	—
Precision production, craft, and repair occupations	6	7	—	—
Mechanic and repairer	5	8	—	—
Construction trades	5	5	—	—
Machine operators, assemblers, and inspectors	4	4	—	—
Transportation and material-moving occupations	4	5	—	—
Handlers, equipment cleaners, helpers, and laborers	3	5	—	—

— Indicates that less than 2 percent of workers have a degree.

Source: Dohm and Wyatt (2002), p. 14.

Community Colleges and Occupations

These postsecondary schools offer a wide variety of educational programs, ranging from business and technical subjects to preprofessional and liberal arts studies. Some vocationally oriented or technical community college courses of study require from a month or two up to a year of training, with specialized certificates awarded on successful completion. Most programs, however, take two years on a full-time schedule (longer on a part-time basis) and lead either directly to employment or transfer to a four-year college. The degree given on successfully finishing a two-year program is called an *associate degree.* Table 10-6 shows the 15 most popular fields of study for which associate degrees were conferred and the 15 most popular types of certificates that were

Table 10-6 Associate Degrees and Certificates Conferred by Public Two-Year Community Colleges by Field, 1999–2000

Associate Degrees, 1999–2000 School Year		Certificates, 1999–2000 School Year	
Liberal/general studies and humanities	168,530	Health professions and related sciences	54,819
Health professions and related sciences	61,243	Business management and administrative services	27,214
Business management and administrative services	60,034	Mechanics and repairers	16,410
Engineering-related technologies	14,662	Protective services	12,321
Protective services	13,965	Precision production trades	10,910
Multidisciplinary studies	11,254	Vocational home economics	8,724
Computer and information sciences	9,970	Personal and miscellaneous services	7,916
Mechanics and repairers	7,474	Transportation and material-moving workers	7,841
Vocational home economics	6,696	Engineering-related technologies	6,680
Education	6,658	Construction trades	6,578
Visual and performing arts	6,368	Computer and information services	5,817
Precision production trades	6,185	Marketing operations/marketing and distribution	3,380
Social science and history	4,692	Agricultural business and production	2,816
Law and legal studies	3,771	Liberal/general studies and humanities	2,216
Agricultural business and production	3,548	Visual and performing arts	1,501

Source: National Center for Education Statistics. Adapted from Kasper (2002–2003), p. 18.

awarded by U.S. community colleges in the 1999–2000 academic year. The sum total of associate degrees outnumbered the certificates by a better than 2-to-1 margin in that year.

The great advantage of the community or junior college is its lower cost, open-door admissions policy, convenient location, and comprehensive course offerings. Tuition and fees for in-state students for the 2000–2001 academic year averaged $1,359 at public two-year community colleges, compared with $3,506 at public four-year colleges, saving over $2,000 per year at the community college. Admission to a community college is usually simpler, less time consuming, and less expensive than at a four-year school. Many community college students live at home, saving the costs of room and board that would be incurred if travel was necessary to attend the four-year college. With the technical and occupational emphasis found in the same institution with the arts and sciences programs of liberal education, the argument is made that community colleges offer a more extensive range of educational programs than any other postsecondary school.

Added to the advantages already mentioned is the idea that community college instructors give students more personal attention because of smaller class sizes in most associate-degree programs. Perhaps the reason for this opinion is that community college instructors spend more time in teaching, generally being spared the pressures of research and publishing experienced by four-year college faculty. Over 80 percent of community colleges give remedial help to students, preparing them for college-level study. There are walk-in centers for help in writing and mathematics (Crosby, 2002–2003).

Future nurses, auto mechanics, dental hygienists, computer programmers, medical assistants, engineering technologists, and drafters receive their training at a community college. Some bachelor's-degree graduates, finding it difficult to land a job in the occupation of their choice, have come back to a community college to obtain the associate degree they believe will make them more employable. Enrollment surged in community colleges from about 1.0 million students nationwide in 1965 to 5.3 million in 1999, increasing five times over, whereas four-year college enrollment doubled in that same time period. As of the 2000–2001 academic year, there were 1,076 community colleges in the United States. No other part of postsecondary education has been more responsive to its community's workforce needs (Kasper, 2002–2003).

Community college students can transfer their credits to meet bachelor's-degree requirements at four-year baccalaureate colleges and universities under agreements between these two types of postsecondary educational institutions. By completing the first two years of courses at a community college, students can reduce the cost of earning a four-year bachelor's degree. Under special arrangements, a number of high school students take courses at local community colleges. Students have benefited from alliances that have been created between employers and community colleges. These alliances not only serve students by offering new and innovative courses and programs, but they also help local businesses and attract new employers to their area.

Women now make up 55 percent of all community college students, becoming a majority in the late 1970s. Of all students, 64 percent attend part time, meaning they take less than 12 credits of classes in a given semester. Most courses carry 2, 3, or 4 credits. Many part-timers are older students who attend one or two classes at night and on weekends.

Crosby (2002–2003) lists some of the career areas available to workers with an associate degree: agriculture and landscaping, arts and design, business administration, communications, computer studies, construction and metal trades, drafting, education for teacher aides and child care, electronics, engineering technicians, health care, human services, law enforcement and fire safety, legal assistants, library science, precision production, natural and physical science technicians, and veterinary technicians.

Associate degrees are generally one of two types: (1) occupationally focused degrees, which prepare students for work immediately after graduation, and (2) transfer degrees that prepare students to advance into bachelor's-degree studies. Associate-degree programs typically require students to complete 60 to 63 credits, which takes a transfer student about halfway toward a bachelor's degree. About 20 courses in all are usually taken for the associate degree. If a student in a transfer program receives an associate in arts or an associate in science degree, many two-year community colleges have agreements with four-year colleges and universities, acknowledging that the associate degree fulfills the general education requirements of a bachelor's degree.

Employers value the occupation-related, specialized career training that associate degree graduates have. Many career services offices in community colleges conduct follow-up studies of their graduates and issue reports on what happens to them after they leave school. You might want to discover where the school's graduates are employed, how long it took them to find their jobs, and the names of their employers. People who have an associate degree receive higher pay than those having a high school diploma as their highest level of educational attainment (Crosby, 2002–2003). Table 10-7 shows the occupations of the highest-earning associate-degree holders in 2001 and the projected job openings between 2000 and 2010 in 14 occupations typically held by workers with an associate degree.

To find out about the specific details of associate-degree and certificate programs at community colleges, request information from the schools that offer them. Addresses can be obtained from career resource centers, counselors, and directories such as *Peterson's Annual Guide to Two-Year Colleges*. Nearly every community college will supply you with a free catalog that describes the programs and courses they have. Many schools maintain Web sites to answer your questions. There is no doubt in the fact that education beyond high school increases earnings for those who go on to get degrees from community colleges, four-year colleges, and universities. Table 10-8 furnishes information about the weekly earnings of full-time workers over age 16 by highest level of educational attainment in the year 2001.

Table 10-7 Highest-Earning Occupations, 2001, and Job Openings in Occupations, Projected 2000–2010, Commonly Held by Workers with an Associate Degree

Highest-Earning Occupations, Associate Degree, 2001		Projected Job Openings, Associate Degree, 2000–2010	
Occupation	Median Weekly Earnings of Workers with an Associate Degree	Occupation	Job Openings for Workers New to the Occupation
Heating, air-conditioning, and refrigeration mechanic	$942	Registered nurse	1,000,000
Electrician	$852	Computer support specialist	510,000
Telephone installer and repairer	$790	Supervisors, administrative support	400,000
Electrical and electronic equipment repairer	$785	Licensed practical nurse	320,000
Data processing equipment repairer	$782	Electrician	250,000
Registered nurse	$767	Hairdresser and cosmetologist	240,000
Police and detective	$757	Electrical and electronic equipment repairer	180,000
Dental hygienist	$745	Engineering and related technologist and technician	170,000
Radiologic technician	$736	Designer	150,000
Electrical and electronic technician	$731	Dental assistant	140,000
Designer	$725	Clinical laboratory technologist and technician	120,000
Manager, medicine and health	$719	Drafting occupations	110,000
Engineering and related technologist and technician	$709	Medical records and health information technician	90,000
Drafting occupations	$659	Dental hygienist	80,000

Source: Adapted from Crosby (2002–2003), pp. 7, 9.

Table 10-8 Average Weekly Earnings of Full-Time Workers Age 16 and Older in Selected Occupations by Highest Level of Educational Attainment, 2001

Occupation	High School Graduate or Equivalent	Some College, No Degree	Associate Degree	Bachelor's or Higher Degree	All Workers
All occupations	**$ 497**	**$ 568**	**$ 625**	**$ 832**	**$ 597**
Accountants and auditors	522	612	629	849	777
Assemblers	462	484	442	504	433
Automobile mechanics	571	610	634	—	815
Carpenters	599	666	701	605	572
Clinical laboratory technologists and technicians	474	544	646	786	609
Computer equipment operators	505	584	598	—	549
Computer programmers	741	845	773	1024	960
Computer systems analysts and scientists	891	871	846	1139	1096
Construction trades	624	712	762	777	611
Designers	520	719	725	830	
Electrical and electronic engineers	1021	947	898	1206	1166
Electrical and electronic equipment repairers	728	736	785	783	748
Electricians	685	787	852	—	730
Engineering technologists and technicians	681	710	709	776	713
Engineers	975	959	922	1154	1140
Farm operators and managers	448	542	531	582	499
Guards	424	423	536	708	424
Information clerks	406	419	451	532	420
Insurance sales occupations	586	582	632	914	681
Investigators and adjusters, except insurance	484	491	502	578	498
Janitors and cleaners	387	405	414	411	363
Legal assistants	536	646	621	710	646
Machine operators and tenders, except precision	483	518	522	562	450
Machine operators, assorted materials	488	528	511	596	465
Machinists	690	706	726	—	679

Table 10-8 (continued)

Occupation	High School Graduate or Equivalent	Some College, No Degree	Associate Degree	Bachelor's or Higher Degree	All Workers
Mail and message-distributing occupations	623	698	671	671	652
Managers, food serving and lodging establishments	505	594	680	762	593
Managers, health and medicine	615	667	719	947	783
Managers, marketing, advertising, and public relations	705	924	1028	1239	1119
Managers, properties and real estate	588	664	710	973	697
Mechanics and repairers	648	705	739	776	653
Motor vehicle operators	592	610	639	624	577
Nursing aides, orderlies, and attendants	362	391	417	393	361
Officials and administrators, public administration	625	706	749	970	886
Personnel, training, and labor relations specialists	637	644	645	791	715
Police and detectives	594	692	757	789	687
Receptionists	394	404	414	489	400
Registered nurses	698	690	767	859	823
Sales workers, retail and personal services	340	378	377	613	362
Supervisors, administrative support occupations	557	580	653	773	618
Supervisors, production occupations	675	758	796	923	710
Teachers, except college and university	380	429	505	684	733
Truck drivers	608	627	664	728	595
Waiters and waitresses	331	334	401	451	325

Source: Adapted from Crosby (2002–2003), pp. 10–13.

Apprenticeships and Occupations

Four standards are necessary for an occupation to be registered as *apprenticeable*: (1) The occupation must be clearly defined. (2) It is typically learned on the job. (3) The occupation requires manual, mechanical, or technical skill. (4) It requires at least 2,000 hours of work experience and at least 144 hours of related classroom instruction. As of 2002, the number of occupations meeting those standards stood at 858. As employers propose and register them, the U.S. Department of Labor's Bureau of Apprenticeship and Training adds more apprenticeable occupations. Several computer occupations are under consideration. Internet-working technician, youth development practitioner, and plastic molds designer were recent additions. The most common apprenticed occupations are listed in Table 10-9 (Crosby, 2002).

Employers and employee groups sponsor and manage apprenticeship programs, select applicants, develop training standards, and pay wages and other expenses. A

Table 10-9 Apprenticeships: The 25 Most Popular, 2001

According to the U.S. Department of Labor apprenticeship database, the occupations listed below had the highest numbers of apprentices in 2001. These findings are approximate because the database includes only about 70 percent of the registered apprenticeship programs, none of the unregistered ones.

Boilermaker	Electrician (maintenance)	Pipefitter (construction)
Bricklayer (construction)	Electronics mechanic	Plumber
Carpenter	Firefighter	Power plant operator
Construction craft worker	Machinist	Roofer
Cook (any industry)	Maintenance mechanic	Sheet metal worker
Cook (hotel and restaurant)	(any industry)	Structural-steel worker
Correction officer	Millwright	Telecommunications technician
Electrician	Operating engineer	Tool and die maker
Electrician (aircraft)	Painter (construction)	

Source: Crosby (2002), p. 5.

person who desires to become an apprentice signs an agreement with the sponsor(s). This contract specifies the skills the apprentice will learn on the job, the related instruction the apprentice will receive, the wages to be earned, and the time the program will take. Registered apprenticeship training is more structured and planned than most on-the-job training experiences. Apprentices begin by learning simpler tasks at work and gradually move on to more complex assignments. A journey worker closely supervises the apprentice in the beginning stages. In time, the apprentice progresses toward greater independence, with the journey worker available to answer questions and demonstrate new skills.

The period of training varies by occupation from one to six years (shown later in Table 10-12). Classroom attendance varies by occupation. Many apprentices are in class at a vocational school or community college one or two evenings per week. Some programs may train apprentices on a full-time basis for a few weeks at certain times each year. Other programs might use the Internet or require correspondence study through the mail. A joint apprenticeship committee, composed of representatives from labor and management, establishes the training program. Teaching covers the techniques of the occupation and the theory that supports those techniques. There are apprenticeship training classes that count toward college or certificate programs. Some schools and colleges offer apprentices dual enrollment, providing an opportunity to earn a degree.

Apprentices must be paid at least at the rate of the current minimum wage, but they usually earn more. Pay normally starts at about half the earnings of an experienced worker and increases progressively through the training program. Apprentices increase their value by learning more skills and by becoming more proficient in the skills they have acquired. After an apprentice has become licensed as a journey worker in an occupation, the median annual earnings for a number of apprenticed occupations are quite high, as shown in Table 10-10. The wages apprentices receive vary from one program to another, usually because of geographic location and an employer's situation. Where there are labor shortages, apprentice wages may increase. Benefits also vary from offering no benefits at all to a full range of health, dental, and retirement benefits. Some programs pay for the time apprentices spend in class.

To get started in an apprenticeship program, you must obtain an application form at a sponsor's office or job site. You can ask to have an application sent to you.

Table 10-10 Commonly Apprenticed Occupations with the Highest Earnings

Occupation	Median Annual Earnings, 2000
Power distributor and dispatcher	$ 48,570
Electrical and electronics repairer, powerhouse, substation, and relay	$ 48,540
Ship engineer	$ 47,530
Elevator installer and repairer	$ 47,380
Power plant operator	$ 46,090
Electrical power-line installer and repairer	$ 45,780
Petroleum pump system operator, refinery operator, and gauger	$ 45,180
Gas plant operator	$ 44,730
Telecommunications equipment installer and repairer, except line installer	$ 44,030
Avionics technician	$ 41,300
Tool and die maker	$ 41,110
Aircraft structure, surfaces, rigging, and systems assembler	$ 40,850
Chemical plant and system operator	$ 40,750
Aircraft mechanic and service technician	$ 40,550
Stationary engineer and boiler operator	$ 40,420

Note: Includes apprenticeable occupations for which long-term on-the-job training or a postsecondary vocational award is the most common form of training, according to the Bureau of Labor Statistics.

Source: Crosby (2002), p. 6.

Most apprenticeship programs require applicants to have a high school diploma or a passing score on an equivalency test and to be at least 18 years of age (although the minimum age is 16). You may be asked to complete certain classes related to the occupation. Classes in English, math, and science are common requirements. Courses in drafting and industrial arts are helpful for applicants applying for apprenticeships in mechanical, manufacturing, and construction occupations. You may be asked to take a set of aptitude tests. Apprenticeship programs that involve physical skills may require a doctor's examination.

An interview is usually scheduled for those who meet the basic qualifications of the apprenticeship program. Applicants meet with the employer or several people from the organization sponsoring the program. Treat an apprenticeship interview like any job interview. In other words, dress neatly, arrive on time, shake hands firmly, keep eye contact with any speaker, and be prepared to demonstrate your qualifications and work habits. Research the organization, and ask questions of the people interviewing you. After the interview, write and send a thank-you note. These subjects are covered in the chapters on interviewing in the second book of this series, *Job Search*. Some apprenticeship programs offer "preapprenticeship" programs such as job shadowing, job site visits, assessment tests, practice interviews, and mentoring. Some schools sponsor school-to-apprenticeship programs, allowing high school students to start their apprenticeships as juniors and seniors. Gaining entrance to some apprenticeable occupations is quite challenging, depending on the demands of the local area. (One of my career-planning class students remarked, "It's easier to get into Harvard Law School than to become a plumber!") Table 10-11 has a list of commonly apprenticed occupations expected to have the most job openings from the year 2000 to 2010.

To find an apprenticeship program in the United States, contact the nearest U.S. Department of Labor Bureau of Apprenticeship Training (BAT) office. The BAT registers apprenticeship programs and qualified apprentices in 23 states and oversees State Apprenticeship Councils, which maintain apprenticeship programs in 27 states.

Table 10-11 Commonly Apprenticed Occupations Expected to Have the Most Job Openings, Projected 2000 to 2010

Occupation	Total Job Openings for Workers New to the Occupation, Projected 2000–2010
Cook, restaurant, and cafeteria	502,435
Automotive service and technician and mechanic	349,049
Licensed practical nurse and licensed vocational nurse	321,841
Carpenter	301,791
Police and sheriff's patrol officer	268,745
Electrician	251,152
Hairdresser, hairstylist, and cosmetologist	237,720
Maintenance and repair worker, general	221,172
Welder, cutter, solderer, and brazer	211,365
Plumber, pipefitter, and steamfitter	134,007
Machinist	127,139
Bus and truck mechanic and diesel engine specialist	113,581
Emergency medical technician and paramedic	97,499
Firefighter	89,574
Computer-controlled machine tool operator, metal and plastic	89,390
Heating, air-conditioning, and refrigeration mechanic and installer	79,485
Telecommunications line installer and repairer	76,170
Automotive body and related repairer	69,430
Cabinet maker and bench carpenter	66,263

Note: Includes apprenticeable occupations for which long-term on-the-job training or a postsecondary vocational award is the most common form of training, according to the Bureau of Labor Statistics.

Source: Crosby (2002), p. 7.

Your state's Apprenticeship Council Office is usually listed in the blue pages of the local telephone directory, or click on its Web site at www.doleta.gov/atels_bat/stateoffices.asp. The major national contact office in the United States is at Office of Apprenticeship Training, Employer, and Labor Services; Bureau of Apprenticeship and Training; Frances Perkins Building; 200 Constitution Avenue NW; Washington, DC 20210. Its Internet address is www.doleta.gov/atels_bat/national.asp. The Employment and Training Administration of the U.S. Department of Labor gives apprenticeship information on its Web site: www.doleta.gov/atels_bat. More information on apprenticeships can be obtained by writing or calling the Office of Apprenticeship Training, Employer and Labor Services, U.S. Department of Labor, 200 Constitution Avenue NW, Washington, DC 20210; telephone (202) 693-3812. The Department of Labor has a toll-free telephone number: 1-866-487-2365. Regional offices of the BAT may be reached in Boston, New York, Philadelphia, Atlanta, Dallas, Denver, Chicago, Kansas City, San Francisco, and Seattle. Locally, you can contact employers and unions who sponsor apprenticeship programs.

Canadian workers must have a Certificate of Qualification to be a journeyperson, meaning they have passed a provincial qualification test measuring their knowledge of their occupation. Under the terms of the Canadian Constitution, provinces and territories are responsible for their own apprenticeship training. These programs are generally administered by departments that have charge of education, labor, and training in their province or territory. Each has its own Web site address; these can be reached through the Inter-Provincial Standards Program or "Red Seal program" (www.hrdc-drhc.gc.ca/hrib/hrp/prh/redseal/english/websites_e.shtml). The Red Seal program maintains standards among provinces and provides greater continuity and mobility for skilled workers across Canada. For more information about apprenticeship in Canada, contact the local Ministry of Training, Colleges, and Universities Apprenticeship office; for example, the Web site address of the office for Ontario is www.edu.gov.on.ca/eng/training/apprentices/offices.html ("on" is for Ontario; use "eng" for English and "fre" for French).

For all its benefits, apprenticeship takes time and commitment. When an apprentice finishes the training program, he or she becomes a licensed journeyperson, or journey worker. (The term *journeyman* is no longer used; women have equal access to apprenticeship programs.) When apprentices complete their programs, they are licensed to work in the occupation for which they trained. That license or certificate is good anywhere in the nation.

When choosing an apprenticeship program, carefully consider each training program's characteristics. Different programs exist for the same occupation in a number of cases. The training program should be registered with the U.S. Department of Labor (or the provincial or territorial labor and training department in Canada). Employers generally have greater trust in registered programs than in the training offered by unregistered ones. Registered programs give their graduates journey worker status and are likely to increase their job choices. Because national training guidelines have been established for many occupations, employers know exactly the skills that have been taught to the graduates of registered programs.

All apprenticeships require at least 2,000 hours of work experience, and some programs take up to 12,000 hours. Most programs have a range of one to six years, the average being four years on the job (Crosby, 2002). Table 10-12 shows the approximate number of years required to train for each apprenticeable occupation.

Other Educational Alternatives

Although colleges, universities, community colleges, and apprenticeships provide a majority of educational programs, other institutions and alternative modes of instruction offer learning experiences that can lead to occupations. There is something

(continued on page 355)

Table 10-12   Apprenticeable Occupations Officially Recognized by the U.S. Department of Labor, Bureau of Apprenticeship and Training

As of 2002, 858 occupations have met the standards to be considered apprenticeable. In 2002, 518 of these occupations had apprentices working in them. The number of occupations available for apprenticeship varies from state to state; however, in most states a person can choose from among hundreds of occupations. The number after the occupation refers to the approximate number of years required to train for each apprenticeable occupation. An asterisk (*) indicates a skills-based apprenticeship; no number of years is given.

ARTS

Actor	2
Audio operator	2
Bank-note designer	5
Camera operator	3
Cartoonist, motion pictures	3
Cloth designer	4
Commercial designer	4
Decorator	4
Director, television	2
Display designer	4
Displayer, merchandise	1
Electronic prepress system operator (desktop publisher)	5
Field engineer, radio and television	4
Film or videotape editor	4
Floral designer	1
Fur designer	4
Furniture designer	4
Graphic designer	1.5
Illustrator	4
Industrial designer	4
Interior designer	2
Light technician	4
Mailer	4
Painter	1
Painter, hand (any industry)	3
Photographer, lithographic	5
Photographer, photoengraving	6
Photographer, still	3
Program assistant	3
Radio station operator	4
Recording engineer	2
Script supervisor	1
Sound mixer	4
Stage technician	3
Stained glass artist	4
Taxidermist	3
Transportation clerk	1.5
Wardrobe supervisor	2
See also: printing	

BUSINESS AND ADMINISTRATIVE SUPPORT

Alarm operator	1
Dispatcher, service	2
Funeral director	2
Hotel associate	2
Legal secretary	1
Manager, retail store	3
Material coordinator	2
Medical secretary	1
Office manager/administrative services	2
Paralegal	3
Photocomposing-perforating-machine operator	2
Post-office clerk	2
Purchasing agent	4
Salesperson, parts	2
Supercargo	2
Telecommunicator (police, fire, and ambulance dispatcher)	4
Telegraphic-typewriter operator	3

CONSTRUCTION AND MINING

Acoustical carpenter	4
Architectual coatings finisher	3
Asphalt-paving-machine operator	3
Assembler, metal building	2
Boatbuilder, wood	4
Boilerhouse mechanic	3
Boilermaker fitter	4
Boilermaker I	3
Boilermaker II	3
Bricklayer, brick and tile	4
Bricklayer, construction	3
Bricklayer, firebrick and refractory tile	4
Carpenter	4
Carpenter, interior systems	4
Carpenter, maintenance	4
Carpenter, mold	6
Carpenter, piledriver	4
Carpenter, rough	4
Carpenter, ship	4
Carpet layer	3
Casket assembler	3
Cement mason	2
Chimney repairer	1
Construction craft laborer	2
Construction driver	4
Coppersmith (ship and boat)	4
Cork insulator, refrigeration	4
Drilling-machine operator	3
Dry-wall applicator	2
Electrician	4
Electrician, ship and boat	4
Elevating-grader operator	2
Elevator constructor	4
Elevator repairer	4
Fence erector	3
Floor layer	3
Floor-covering layer	3

Form builder, construction	2
Gas-main fitter	4
Gauger	2
Glazier	3
Glazier, stained glass	4
Hazardous-waste-material technician	2
Inspector, building	3
Insulation worker	4
Joiner, ship and boat	4
Lather	3
Marble finisher	2
Marble setter	3
Mine inspector (government) coal	4
Mine inspector (government) metal and nonmetal	4
Miner I (mine and quarry)	1
Monument setter	4
Mosaic worker	3
Motor-grader operator	3
Multi-story window installer or builder	3
Neon-sign servicer	4
Operating engineer	3
Ornamental-iron worker	3
Painter, construction	3
Painter, shipyard	3
Paperhanger	2
Pavement striper	2
Pipe coverer and insulator	4
Pipefitter (construction)	4
Pipefitter (ship and boat)	4
Plasterer	2
Plumber	4
Prop maker	4
Prospecting driller	2
Protective-signal installer	4
Protective-signal repairer	3
Reinforcing-metal worker	3
Residential carpenter	2
Residential wireperson	2.4
Roofer	2
Sheet-metal worker	4
Shipwright	4
Sign erector I	3
Soft-tile setter	3
Steam service inspector	4
Stonemason	3
Street-light servicer	4
Structural-steel worker	3
Tank setter (petroleum)	2
Taper	2

(continued)

Table 10-12 (Continued)

Terrazzo finisher	2	Meteorological equipment		Pump erector (construction)	2
Terrazzo worker	3	repairer	4	Pump servicer	3
Tile finisher	2	Power-transformer repairer	4	Repairer I, chemical industry	4
Tile setter	3	Propulsion-motor-and-generator		Repairer, welding equipment	2
Tuckpointer, cleaner, caulker	3	repairer	4	Repairer, welding systems	
Well-drill operator	4	Radio repairer	4	and equipment	3
		Relay technician	2	Rubberizing mechanic	4
INSTALLATION, MAINTENANCE, AND		Repairer, hand tools	3	Scale mechanic	4
REPAIR, INCLUDING TELECOMMUNICA-		Tape-recorder repairer	4	Sewing-machine repairer	3
TIONS AND POWER PLANT OPERATION		Television-and-radio repairer	4	Stoker erector and servicer	4
Communications equipment		Transformer repairer	4	Treatment-plant mechanic	3
Automatic-equipment technician	4				
Central-office installer	4	**Industrial machinery**		**Line installers**	
Central-office repairer	4	Automated equipment engineer-		Cable installer-repairer	3
Electrician, radio	4	technician	4	Cable splicer	4
Equipment installer		Automotive-maintenance-		Cable television installer	1
(telecommunications)	4	equipment servicer	4	Line erector	3
Maintenance mechanic,		Aviation support equipment		Line installer-repairer	4
telephone	3	repairer	4	Line maintainer	4
Private-branch-exchange installer	4	Bakery-machine mechanic	3	Line repairer	3
Private-branch-exchange repairer	4	Canal-equipment mechanic	2	Trouble shooter II	3
Radio mechanic	3	Composing-room machinist	6		
Sound technician	3	Conveyor-maintenance mechanic	2	**Precision equipment**	
Station installer and repairer	4	Cooling tower technician	2	Aircraft-armament mechanic	4
Submarine cable equipment		Electronic-production-line-		Aircraft-photographic-equipment	4
technician	2	maintenance	1	Aircraft mechanic, armament	4
Telecommunications technician	4	Forge-shop-machine repairer	3	Biomedical equipment technician	4
		Fuel-system-maintenance		Camera repairer	2
Electronic equipment		worker	2	Dental-equipment installer	
Aircraft mechanic, electrical	4	Hydraulic repairer	4	and servicer	3
Audio-video repairer	2	Hydraulic-press servicer	2	Electromedical-equipment	
Automotive-generator-and-		Hydroelectric-machinery		repairer	2
starter repairer	2	mechanic	3	Fretted-instrument repairer	3
Avionics technician	4	Industrial engine technician	4	Instrument mechanic, any	
Battery repairer	2	Industrial machine systems		industry	4
Control equipment electric-		technician	2	Instrument mechanic, weapon	
technician	5	Laundry-machine mechanic	3	systems	4
Corrosion-control fitter	4	Machine erector	4	Instrument repairer	4
Electrical instrument repairer	3	Machine fixer (carpet and rug)	4	Machinist, motion-picture	
Electrical-appliance repairer	3	Machine fixer (textile)	3	equipment	2
Electrical-appliance servicer	3	Machine repairer, maintenance	4	Photographic equipment	
Electrician, aircraft	4	Machinist, linotype	4	technician	3
Electrician, automotive	2	Maintenance mechanic, any		Photographic-equipment-	
Electrician, locomotive	4	industry	4	maintenance technician	3
Electrician, maintenance	4	Maintenance mechanic,		Piano technician	4
Electrician, powerhouse	4	compressed gas	4	Piano tuner	3
Electrician, substation	3	Maintenance mechanic, grain		Pipe-organ tuner and repairer	4
Electric-meter installer I	4	and feed	2	Watch repairer	4
Electric-meter repairer	4	Maintenance repairer, building	2	Wind-instrument repairer	4
Electric-motor repairer	4	Maintenance repairer, industrial	4		
Electric-tool repairer	4	Marine-services technician	3	**Vehicles**	
Electric-track-switch maintainer	4	Millwright	4	Aircraft mechanic, plumbing	
Electronic systems technician	4	Overhauler (textile)	2	and hydraulics	4
Electronic-organ technician	2	Pinsetter adjuster, automated	3	Airframe-and-power-plant	
Electronics mechanic	4	Pinsetter mechanic, automatic	2	mechanic	4
Electronic-sales-and-service		Pneumatic-tool repairer	4	Automobile air-conditioning	
technician	4	Pneumatic-tube repairer	2	mechanic	1
Field service engineer	2	Powerhouse mechanic	4	Automobile body repairer	4

Table 10-12 (Continued)

Automobile glass installer	2	Farm-equipment mechanic I	3	Precision assembler	3
Automobile mechanic	4	Farm-equipment mechanic II	4	Precision assembler, bench	2
Automobile radiator mechanic	2	Furnace installer	3	Precision lens grinder	4
Automobile-repair-service		Furnace installer and repairer	4	Production finisher	2
estimator	4	Gas-appliance servicer	3	Production technologist	*
Automobile spring repairer, hand	4	Gas-meter mechanic I	3	Rubber-stamp maker	4
Automotive cooling-system		Gas-regulator repairer	3	Ship propeller finisher	3
diagnoser	2	Heating-and-air-conditioning		Wirer, office machines	2
Automotive repairer, heavy	2	installer and servicer	3		
Aviation safety equipment		Locksmith	4	**Health**	
technician	4	Maintenance mechanic,		Artificial-glass-eye maker	5
Brake repairer	2	construction and petroleum	4	Artificial-plastic-eye maker	5
Car repairer, railroad	4	Mechanical-unit repairer	4	Blocker and cutter, contact lenses	1
Carburetor mechanic	4	Meter repairer	3	Contour wire specialist, denture	4
Construction-equipment		Office-machine servicer	3	Dental ceramist	2
mechanic	4	Oil-burner servicer and installer	2	Dental-laboratory technician	3
Diesel mechanic	4	Refrigeration mechanic	3	Finisher, denture	1
Electrician, water transportation	4	Refrigeration unit repairer	3	Shop optician, benchroom	4
Engine repairer, service	4	Rigger	3	Shop optician, surface room	4
Front-end mechanic	4	Rigger (ship and boat building)	2		
Fuel-injection servicer	4	Safe-and-vault service mechanic	4	**Inspection**	
Gas-engine repairer	4	Service planner (light, heat)	4	Airplane inspector	3
Logging-equipment mechanic	4	Signal maintainer	4	Automobile tester	4
Machinist, marine engine	4			Cable tester (telecommunications)	4
Mechanic, endless track vehicle	4	**PRODUCTION**		Calibrator (military)	2
Mechanic, industrial truck	4	**Assembly**		Complaint inspector	4
Mine-car repairer	2	Airplane coverer	4	Diesel-engine tester	4
Motorboat mechanic	3	Assembler, aircraft power plant	2	Electric-distribution checker	2
Motorcycle repairer	3	Assembler, aircraft structures	4	Electric-meter tester	4
Outboard-motor mechanic	2	Assembler, electromechanical		Electromechanical inspector	4
Repairer, recreational vehicle	4	(robotics)	4	Electronics tester	3
Rocket-engine-component		Assembler-installer, general	2	Experimental assembler	2
mechanic	4	Assembly technician	2	Grader	4
Rocket-motor mechanic	4	Canvas worker	3	Hydrometer calibrator	2
Service mechanic (automobile		Electric-motor assembler		Metal fabricating inspector	4
manufacturing)	2	and tester	4	Operational test mechanic	3
Small-engine mechanic	2	Electric-motor, general assembler	2	Outside production inspector	4
Tractor mechanic	4	Electric-motor-and-generator		Precision inspector	2
Transmission mechanic	2	assembler	2	Quality control inspector	2
Truck-body builder	4	Electric-sign assembler	4	Relay tester	4
Tune-up mechanic	2	Fabricator-assembler, metal		Rubber tester	4
Undercar specialist	2	product	4	Safety inspector and technician	3
		Fitter (machine shop)	2	Set-up and lay-out inspector	4
Other		Fitter I (any industry)	3	Testing-and-regulating technician	4
Power-saw mechanic	3	Former, hand (any industry)	2	Thermometer tester	1
Oil-field equipment mechanic	2	Glass bender	4	Trouble locator, test desk	2
Air and hydronic balancing		Glass blower	3	X-ray-equipment tester	2
technician	3	Glass blower, laboratory			
Air-conditioning installer-		apparatus	4	**Jewelry**	
servicer	3	Glass-blowing-lathe operator	4	Bench hand, jewelry	2
Cash-register servicer	3	Instrument maker	4	Bracelet and brooch maker	4
Coin-machine servicer and		Instrument maker and repairer	5	Brilliandeer-lopper (jewelry)	3
repairer	3	Machine assembler	2	Caster, jewelry	2
Dairy-equipment repairer	3	Machine builder	2	Chaser (silversmithing)	4
Dictating-transcribing-machine		Metal fabricator	4	Diamond selector (jewelry)	4
servicer	3	Optical-instrument assembler	2	Engine turner, jewelry	2
Door-closer mechanic	3	Plastics fabricator	2	Gem cutter	3
Facilities locator	2	Pottery-machine operator	3	Jeweler	2

(continued)

Table 10-12   (Continued)

Model maker II, jewelry	4	Machine setter, any industry	4	Tool-and-die maker	4
Mold maker I, jewelry	4	Machine setter, clock	4	Tool-grinder operator	4
Mold maker II, jewelry	2	Machine setter, machine shop	3	Tool-machine set-up operator	3
Pewter caster	3	Machine set-up operator	2	Turret-lathe set-up operator	4
Pewter fabricator	4	Machine try-out setter	4	Welder, arc	4
Pewter finisher	2	Machinist	4	Welder, combination	3
Pewterer	2	Machinist, automotive	4	Welder-fitter	4
Silversmith II	3	Machinist, experimental	4	Welding-machine operator, are	3
Solderer, jewelry	3	Machinist, outside (ship)	4		
Stone setter	4	Maintenance machinist	4	**Molds and models,**	
Stonecutter, hand	3	Milling-machine set-up operator	2	**except jewelry**	
		Multi-operation form machine		Cell maker	1
Metal and plastic work		setter	4	Engineering model maker	4
Blacksmith	4	Multi-operation-machine		Mock-up builder	4
Card grinder	4	operator	3	Model and mold maker (brick)	2
Caster	2	Numerical control machine		Model and mold maker, plaster	4
Coremaker	4	operator	4	Model builder, furniture	2
Cupola tender	3	Ornamental metal worker	4	Model maker pottery	
Cylinder grinder	5	Pantograph-machine set-up		and porcelain	2
Die finisher	4	operator	2	Model maker, aircraft	4
Die maker, bench, stamping	4	Patternmaker, all around	5	Model maker, auto	
Die maker, jewelry and silver	4	Patternmaker, metal	5	manufacturing	4
Die maker, paper goods	4	Patternmaker, metal, bench	5	Model maker, clock and watch	4
Die maker, stamping	3	Patternmaker, metal products	4	Model maker, firearms	4
Die maker, trim	4	Patternmaker, plastics	3	Model maker, wood	4
Die maker, wire drawing	3	Plastic fixture builder	4	Mold maker, die-casting	
Die polisher	1	Plastic process technician	4	and plastic	4
Die setter	2	Plastic tool maker	4	Mold maker, pottery	
Die sinker	4	Plater	3	and porcelain	3
Engine-lathe set-up operator	2	Roll-threader operator	1	Mold setter	1
Engine-lathe set-up operator, tool	2	Sample maker, appliances	4	Molder	4
Experimental mechanic	4	Saw filer	4	Molder, pattern (foundry)	4
Extruder operator	1	Saw maker, cutlery and tools	3	Patternmaker, plaster	3
Fastener technologist	3	Screw-machine operator,		Patternmaker, stonework	4
Fixture maker	2	multiple spindle	4	Patternmaker, wood	5
Forging-press operator	1	Screw-machine operator,		Plaster-pattern caster	5
Four-slide-machine setter	2	single spinner	3	Prototype model maker	4
Furnace operator	4	Screw-machine set-up operator	4		
Gear hobber set-up operator	4	Screw-machine set-up operator,		**Plant and system operation**	
Gear-cutting-machine set-up		single spindle	3	Boiler operator	4
operator	3	Shipfitter	4	Chemical operator, chief	3
Gear-cutting-machine set-up		Spinner, hand	3	Clarifying-plant operator, textile	1
operator, tool	3	Spring coiling machine setter	4	Electronics utility worker	4
Grinder I (clock and watch)	4	Spring maker	4	Gas utility worker	2
Grinder operator, tool	4	Spring-manufacturing set-up		Hydroelectric-station operator	3
Grinder set-up operator, jig	4	technician	4	Plant operator	3
Grinder set-up operator,		Stone polisher, machine	3	Plant operator, furnace	4
universal	4	Tap-and-die-maker technician	4	Power-plant operator	4
Gunsmith	4	Template maker	4	Refinery operator	3
Heat treater I	4	Template maker, extrusion die	4	Stationary engineer	4
Heavy forger	4	Test technician (machining)	5	Substation operator	4
Injection-molding-machine		Tool builder	4	Switchboard operator, utilities	3
operator	1	Tool grinder I	3	Turbine operator	4
Lay-out technician	4	Tool maker	4	Waste-treatment operator	2
Lay-out worker I	4	Toolmaker, bench	4	Wastewater-treatment-plant	
Lead burner	4	Tool programmer, numerical		operator	2
Machine operator I	1	control	3	Water-treatment-plant operator	3

Table 10-12   (Continued)

Printing		Reproduction technician	1	Last-model maker	4
Assistant press operator	2	Retoucher, photoengraving	5	Loft worker (ship and boat)	4
Auger press operator, manual control	2	Roller engraver, hand	2	Machine setter, woodwork	4
		Rotogravure-press operator	4	Machinist, wood	4
Ben-day artist	6	Scanner operator	2	Pipe organ builder	3
Bindery worker	4	Sign writer, hand	1	Pony edger (sawmill)	2
Bindery-machine setter	4	Sketch maker I	5	Violin maker, hand	4
Bookbinder	5	Sketch maker II	4	Wood-turning-lathe operator	1
Casing-in-line setter	4	Steel-die printer	4		
Colorist, photography	2	Stereotyper	6	**Other**	
Compositor	4	Stripper	5	Batch-and-furnace operator	4
Cylinder-press operator	4	Stripper, lithographic II	4	Chemical operator III	3
Dot etcher	5	Surface-plate finisher	2	Coating machine operator I	1
Electrotyper	5	Wallpaper printer I	4	Cutter, machine	3
Embosser	2	Web-press operator	4	Decorator (glass manufacturing)	4
Embossing-press operator	4			Electrostatic powder coating technician	4
Engraver glass	2	**Textiles and apparel**		Envelope-folding-machine adjuster	3
Engraver I	5	Alteration tailor	2		
Engraver, block	4	Automobile upholsterer	3	Fourdrinier-machine operator	3
Engraver, hand, hard metals	4	Bootmaker, hand	1	Freezer operator .	1
Engraver, hand, soft metals	4	Card cutter, jacquard	4	Gang sawyer, stone	2
Engraver, machine	4	Carpet cutter (retail trade)	1	Kiln firer	3
Engraver, pantograph I	4	Custom tailor	4	Kiln operator	3
Engraver, picture	1	Design and patternmaker, shoe	2	Liner (pottery and porcelain)	3
Engraving press operator	3	Dressmaker	4	Miller, wet process	3
Etcher, hand	5	Dry cleaner	3	Painter, sign	4
Etcher, photoengraving	4	Fur cutter	2	Painter, transportation equipment	3
Film developer	3	Fur finisher	2		
Film laboratory technician	3	Furniture upholsterer	4	Purification machine operator II	4
Film laboratory technician I	3	Furrier	4	Sandblaster, stone	3
Folding-machine operator	2	Harness maker	3	Screen printer	2
Job printer	4	Jacquard-loom weaver	4	Siderographer	5
Letterer (professional and kindred)	2	Jacquard-plate maker	1	Stencil cutter	2
		Knitter mechanic	4	Stone carver	3
Linotype operator	5	Knitting-machine fixer	4	Stone-lathe operator	3
Lithographic platemaker	4	Leather stamper	1	Tinter (paint and varnish)	2
Lithograph-press operator, tin	4	Loom fixer	3	Wire sawyer	2
Machine set-up operator, paper goods	4	Patternmaker, textiles	3		
		Saddle maker	2	SCIENCE, DRAFTING, AND COMPUTER	
Monotype-keyboard operator	3	Sample stitcher	4	Calibration laboratory technician	4
Offset-press operator I	4	Shoe repairer	3	Chemical laboratory technician	4
Paste-up artist	3	Shoemaker, custom	3	Chemical-engineering technician	4
Photoengraver	5	Shop tailor	4	Chief of the party	4
Photoengraving finisher	5	Silk-screen cutter	3	Computer operator	3
Photoengraving printer	5	Upholsterer	2	Computer programmer	2
Photoengraving proofer	5	Upholsterer, inside	3	Computer-peripheral-equipment operator	1
Photograph retoucher	3	Wire weaver, cloth	4		
Photographic-plate maker	4			Dairy technologist	4
Plate finisher	6	**Woodwork**		Design drafter, electromechanism	4
Platen-press operator	4	Accordion maker	4	Detailer	4
Press operator, heavy duty	4	Cabinetmaker	4	Die designer	4
Printer, plastic	4	Carver, hand	4	Drafter, architectural	4
Printer-slotter operator	4	Furniture finisher	3	Drafter, automotive design	4
Projection printer	4	Harpsichord maker	2	Drafter, automotive design layout	4
Proof-press operator	5	Hat-block maker (woodwork)	3		
Proofsheet corrector	4	Head sawyer	3	Drafter, cartographic	4
Recovery operator (paper)	1	Jig builder (wood contain)	2		

(continued)

Table 10-12 (Continued)

Drafter, civil	4	Weather observer	2	Health care sanitation technician	1
Drafter, commercial	4	Welding technician	4	Licensed practical nurse	1
Drafter, detail	4	Wind tunnel mechanic	4	Medical laboratory technician	2
Drafter, electrical	4			Nurse assistant	1
Drafter, electronic	4	**SERVICE AND RELATED**		Optician, dispensing	2
Drafter, heating and ventilating	4	**Buildings and grounds**		Optician, goods	4
Drafter, landscape	4	Agricultural service worker	2	Optician, goods and retail	5
Drafter, marine	4	Exterminator, termite	2	Orthodontic technician	2
Drafter, mechanical	4	Greenskeeper II	2	Orthopedic-boot-and-shoe	
Drafter, plumbing	4	Housekeeper	1	designer	5
Drafter, structural	3	Landscape gardener	4	Orthotics technician	1
Drafter, tool design	4	Landscape management		Orthotist	4
Electrical technician	4	technician	1	Paramedic	2
Electromechanical technician		Landscape technician	2	Pharmacist assistant	1
(robotics)	3	Rug cleaner, hand	1	Podiatric assistant	2
Electronics technician	4	Swimming-pool servicer	2	Prostethetist	4
Engineering assistant,		Tree surgeon	3	Prosthetics technician	4
mechanical equipment	4	Tree trimmer (line clear)	2	Tumor registrar	2
Environmental analyst	3.5				
Estimator and drafter	4	**COOKING**		**Other service**	
Foundry metallurgist	4	Baker	3	Animal trainer	2
Geodetic computator	2	Baker, hotel and restaurant	3	Barber	1
Heat-transfer technician	4	Baker, pizza	1	Childcare development specialist	2
Horticulturist	3	Bartender	1	Cosmetologist	1
Instrument technician, utilities	4	Butcher, all-round	3	Counselor	2
Instrumentation technician	4	Butcher, hotel and restaurant	3	Customer service representative	3
Internetworking technician	2.5	Candy maker	3	Direct support specialist	
Laboratory assistant	3	Cheesemaker	2	(social and human support)	1.5
Laboratory assistant, metallurgy	2	Cook, any industry	2	Embalmer	2
Laboratory technician	1	Cook, hotel and restaurant	3	Horse trainer	1
Laboratory tester	2	Cook, pastry	3	Horseshoer	2
Logistics engineer	4	Meat cutter	3	Teacher aide I	2
Materials engineer	5	Wine maker	2	Youth development	
Mechanical-engineering				practitioner	1.75
technician	4	**Protective service**			
Meteorologist	3	Arson bomb investigator	2	**OTHER**	
Mold designer (plastics industry)	2	Correction officer	1	Beekeeper	2
Nondestructive tester	1	Fire apparatus engineer	3	Buttermaker	1.2
Optomechanical technician	4	Fire captain	3	Conveyor-system operator	1
Photogrammetric technician	3	Fire engineer	1	Dragline operator	1
Programmer, engineering and		Fire inspector	4	Dredge operator	4
science	4	Fire medic	3	Farmer, general	1
Quality control technician	2	Firefighter	3	Farmworker, general I	2
Radiation monitor	4	Firefighter, crash and fire	1	Fire-control mechanic	1
Radiographer	4	Fish and game warden	2	Fish hatchery worker	2
Research mechanic, aircraft	4	Guard, security	1.5	Inspector, motor vehicles	4
Soil-conservation technician	3	Investigator, private	1	Locomotive engineer	2
Surveyor assistant, instruments	2	Police officer	2	Logger, all-round	3
Test equipment mechanic	5	Wildland firefighter specialist	1	Ordnance artificer (military)	1.5
Test-engine operator,				Pilot, ship	3
geologic samples	2	**Health**		Pumper-gauger	1
Tester, geologic samples	3	Ambulance attendant (EMT)	1	Truck driver, heavy	3
Tool design checker	4	Dental assistant	1	Truck-crane operator	3
Tool designer	4	Emergency medical technician	3		

Source: Crosby (2002), pp. 16–21.

(Text continued from page 348)

in the vast field of education to attract almost anyone who seeks to learn for whatever purpose. Beyond the institutions already mentioned, there are educational programs in distance learning, internships, business and technical schools, the military, adult education, and correspondence study.

Distance Learning. Instead of going to a classroom at a definite time period on a college campus for an academic course, many students have become "distance learners" separated from the instructor by space and time. Distance learning was once all but impossible except perhaps by correspondence study; now, the information age and the Internet have made learning "anywhere, anytime" a reality. Although most distance learning courses are given by traditional colleges and universities, other providers of this method of education are "virtual colleges" with no typical campus. They offer their courses only in cyberspace. Even complete degree programs are offered through distance learning by a number of postsecondary institutions. These courses and programs may be delivered by using the World Wide Web, email, standard mail, telephone, prerecorded video, live video, special software, or other means. However, when we say "distance learning" we usually think of Internet-based instruction, because it has grown so rapidly in recent years (Mariani, 2001). The U.S. Department of Education published results of a survey on distance learning in December 1999, stating that about one-third of all postsecondary schools offered distance learning courses and another one-fifth planned to start within three years. Eight percent of these schools designed complete college-level degree or certificate programs through distance learning. Almost 50,000 college-level courses via distance learning were offered for academic credit.

Almost all distance learning programs rely on several ways of sending information over time and space. Instructors can lecture using videocassettes, one-way video and two-way audio, and/or Web-based streaming video. Some instructors prefer not to lecture, but provide written notes on Web pages that supplement textbook reading. Teachers often post a series of topics for students to interact with each other through electronic discussion boards, email, chat rooms, the telephone, or some combination of these devices. Students and instructor can exchange ideas electronically or by first-class mail for class assignments. Students are evaluated in the same way they are in traditional on-campus courses. Regardless of how the material is delivered, instructors grade projects, give exams, and assess student participation.

Distance learning has several advantages, particularly for students who have family and work responsibilities that would make it difficult to attend class on a regular basis. If work hours are unpredictable, distance learning allows students to set most of their time schedules for course work. If some people have trouble concentrating for two or three hours at a time, they can divide the program into shorter segments. Many people prefer to set their own pace of learning. If a certain course is not offered at one's school, a student can attend classes at schools that may be far away.

Check the accreditation of a school offering distance education. Accredited schools must meet certain standards set by one of the eight regional accrediting agencies in the United States. The Distance Education and Training Council (formerly the National Home Study Council) accredits many special-focus institutions nationally, applying accreditation to specific professional programs rather than to entire educational institutions. The council's address is 1601 18th Street NW, Washington, DC 20009-2529; the telephone number is 1-202-234-5100 and the Internet address is www.detc.org. For accredited institutions and subjects taught, write to the council for its *Directory of Private Career Schools and Colleges of Technology* or use the Internet address www.detc.org/content/accred.html. If an educational institution lacks accreditation, ask about the school's standards at your state department of education, visit the school, read about the school's reputation in published distance-education directories (your local library may have one of these), or check with the Better Business

Bureau before enrolling. You can ask for opinions of the school from people in the occupational field in which you plan to work. Be aware that sometimes a disreputable school establishes its own separate accrediting organization, gives it an impressive sounding name, and says it has accredited the school.

Find out how you register for distance learning courses, buy books, use library resources, and obtain financial aid. Distance learners can increasingly register for courses and buy books online. Some schools allow you to use material from campus libraries by mail and access library resources online. To take a distance learning course or program, you need a computer and probably a television set and videocassette player. Inquire about technical support to resolve problems if they should occur. Financial aid may be more difficult for some distance learners. Federal financial aid is limited for distance learning in many cases (Mariani, 2001). Finally, be sure you are highly motivated. Distance learning calls for great self-discipline. Be sure to keep up with the schedule set by the instructor. Because you are studying with little or no supervision, it is easier to fall behind with no one pushing or reminding you. Communicating with the distant instructor and fellow classmates will take more effort on your part than if you were attending class on campus.

Internship. An internship is an agreement by a school and an employer to provide a supervised work experience with certain learning objectives over a fixed amount of time. These increasingly popular programs can be paid or unpaid, full time or part time, and with or without school credit. An internship is not a job; it is a "work experience" (Smith, 1997). Applying for an internship program is a lot like applying for a job. Employers often ask for a completed application, cover letter, résumé, transcripts, and letters of recommendation.

An intern is usually placed on the job for a period ranging from two to six months. The main benefit of an internship to students is that it gives them an experience of what it is like to work in a given occupation, in addition to any possible credits or pay that might be earned. When interns seek a job in the future, the internship program gives them an answer to the age-old question, "Do you have any experience?" Employers benefit by observing whether interns can do the job and by discovering what kind of workers they are. Many employers use internships as a way of screening people, hoping to discover potential employees with the skills, values, and attitudes they are looking for. Employers thus have the opportunity to evaluate possible future employees with little or no risk involved. Internships have much in common with cooperative work/study programs.

Internships can lead to job offers, although there is no guarantee of that. Check with your college's internship office, academic adviser, or career services office about internships available at your school. For internship opportunities outside of your school, check with your library or a bookstore for directories of internships. One book to consult about internships is *The National Directory of Internships*, published by the National Society for Experiential Education, 9001 Braddock Road, Suite 380, Springfield, VA 22151 (Internet address www.nsee.org/current.htm). Another electronic source of internship information is the National Association of Colleges and Employers' Web site on summer work and internships (www.jobweb.org/catapult/jintern.htm). Two other publications and Web sites are the *National Internship Guide*, published by Internships.com, 2020 Pennsylvania Ave. NW, PMB, Washington, DC 20006 (www.Internships.com) and the *Internship Series*, published by Internships-USA, Career Education Institutes, P.O. Box 11171, Winston-Salem, NC 27116 (www.internships-usa.com).

Business, Trade, and Technical Schools. People can be trained for such specialized jobs as secretary, computer programmer, television repair person, bookkeeper, and cosmetologist through programs at business, trade, and technical schools. Such schools often help graduates with job placement services. The programs range from six weeks to two years. Some business, trade, and technical schools are financed and operated by local and state governments, but most are proprietary schools owned and operated by private individuals.

Military Training. The various branches of the military offer training in over a thousand kinds of jobs, many of which have their counterparts in civilian life. The training varies greatly in length, and methods of teaching include classroom instruction and on-the-job training. Military trainees are paid while learning skills required for such occupations as aircraft mechanic, radio/TV repairperson, heavy-equipment operator, computer programmer, drafter, purchasing agent, and dental technician. The *Military Career Guide Online* (www.militarycareers.com) is a summary of occupational and training opportunities available in the armed services. The military has several educational assistance programs. Among these are the Reserve Officers' Training Corps (ROTC), the new G.I. Bill, and tuition assistance. Information about these programs can be obtained from local military recruiting centers or from the Internet: www.defenselink.mil/other_info/careers.html.

Adult Education. School systems, colleges, universities, and many social agencies such as the YMCA and YWCA offer a huge variety of adult education courses. Usually taught in the evenings or on Saturdays, these courses are designed to help people meet their occupational and personal needs. Adults can improve their present work skills, add new ones, or broaden their general educational background. Adult education courses are offered on almost every conceivable subject in which interest is expressed. Such courses are usually inexpensive.

Correspondence Study. A type of distance learning, correspondence study lessons are mailed to students, who complete them at home instead of in a classroom. Some students use this method to complete high school graduation requirements or build their job skills. Learning by mail may require writing answers to a series of questions on a reading assignment or preparing and submitting a project. College credit may be granted for some correspondence courses, in which case a test is often required. Many correspondence students work full time. Jobs such as accounting, radio repair, and drafting can be learned by correspondence. Go back to the section on distance learning to find resources for checking into correspondence study programs.

On-the-Job Training. Some jobs require only a short training period of weeks or months, during which an experienced worker who knows the job function teaches a trainee. The learner earns a paycheck while being trained on the job. Sales work, shoe repair, grocery checkout, and some kinds of semiskilled and unskilled work are typical examples of occupations that may be entered through on-the-job training. A local Chamber of Commerce office or manufacturer's association may be able to help you here.

Company Training Programs. In addition to the educational programs described in the preceding paragraphs, private companies frequently provide in-service training programs for both new and experienced employees. The business sector spends an estimated $50 billion per year on training. With increased emphasis on knowledge work, companies are becoming more and more involved in educational programs, believing that they pay off in the long run. Motorola, for example, believes it gains $30 for every $1 it invests in worker training (Cetron and Davies, 2003). Employers often encourage their employees to attend college classes by offering them incentives such as time off work, partial or full payment of tuition, and opportunities for advancement.

Over and above the various postsecondary institutions written about in this chapter, colleges offer numerous special programs that can be mentioned only briefly. *Accelerated programs* give opportunities to complete the requirements for a major in less time than is normally taken by carrying extra credits and attending summer school sessions. *External degree programs* allow you to earn credit through independent study, verifying personal experiences that have educational value, and proficiency exams with little or no classroom attendance required. *Honors programs* may contain combinations of advanced courses, educational enrichment, special seminars, and so on. *Study-abroad programs* or *visiting student programs* involve taking courses in foreign countries, studying the culture and language of a country. A college may operate from a campus in another nation or have a cooperative agreement with another school either from the United States or Canada or from an educational institution of another country. Colleges have experimented with many ideas to help you fit educational experiences to your needs. A career resource center, counseling office, or library is the most likely place to find college catalogs and brochures that give more detail about the offerings of each of these sources of education and training.

Educational Programs Arranged by the Holland Categories

Holland's six personality/environment categories, used for grouping occupations in Chapter 3, can also be used as a system of arranging majors, as shown in Table 10-13. A one-letter code is used here for the sake of simplicity, but every educational major or training program will have a second or third letter in their Holland code. The *Educational Opportunities Finder* (Rosen, Holmberg, and Holland, 1994) lists more than 900 majors by their three-letter summary codes and is available from Psychological Assessment Resources, Inc., 16204 N. Florida Ave., Lutz, FL 33556 (www.parinc.com).

Educational Costs and Financial Aid

In financing a college education, a student must consider the costs of tuition, fees, books, room (where you live) and board (what you eat), transportation, and personal expenses such as laundry, social activities, clothing, and recreation. Tuition is the cost of instruction and fees cover the services (library, health center, and so on) provided by the college. Costs can differ greatly from one institution to another; you need to gather information about each college under consideration. Tuition may be lower at

(continued on page 360)

Table 10-13 Educational Majors and Training Programs Classified by Holland Types

R—Realistic

Agricultural technology	Emergency medical	Moldmaker*
Agriculture	technician*	Numerical control technician
Air conditioning, heating, and re-	Engineering assistant*	Oceanography
frigeration*	Engineering mechanics	Patternmaker*
Automotive mechanics*	Fire fighting*	Petroleum engineering
Automotive technology	Forestry	Plumber/pipefitter*
Baker*	Graphic arts technology	Printing/compositor*
Butcher/meatcutter*	Industrial arts education	Radiologic technology
Carpentry*	Industrial maintenance	Robotics/automation (electro-
Climate control	mechanic*	mechanical engineering tech-
Conservation	Industrial technology	nology)
Construction trades*	Industrial truck mechanic*	Small engine repair/
Criminal justice	Machine shop	mechanic*
(security)	Machinist*	Tool and die maker*
Drafter*	Mechanical engineering	Truck driver*
Electrical/electronics	Metallurgical technology	Welding technician*
technology*	Millwright*	
Electrician*	Military science	

Table 10-13   (continued)

I—Investigative

Anthropology	Educational testing and	Microbiology
Architecture	measurement	Nuclear engineering
Astronomy	Electronics engineering	Operations research
Biochemistry/biophysics	Engineering technologies	Pharmacy
Biological sciences	Food processing	Physics
Botany	Food technology	Physiology
Chemical engineering	Geography	Respiratory therapy
Chemistry	Geology	Social sciences
Civil engineering	Horticulture*	Sociology
Computer science	Liberal arts	Statistics
Dentistry	Mathematics	Systems engineering
Earth science	Medical technology	Veterinary medicine
Economics	Metallurgical engineering	Zoology

A—Artistic

Advertising	Dance/dance education	Jewelry/metalworking*
Art/art education	Drama/theater	Landscape architecture
Art history	English/journalism	Literature
Ceramics	Fine arts	Medical illustrating
Classics	Foreign languages	Music/music education
Commercial art	Graphic arts	Printmaking
Communication arts	Industrial design	Radio/television
Creative writing	Interior design	Speech/debate

S—Social

Counseling	Hospitality services	Political science
Criminal justice (law enforce-	Human services	Psychology
ment, corrections)	International relations	Public administration
Dental hygiene	Library science	Secondary education
Elementary education	Nursing	Social work
Family/child development	Occupational therapy	Special education
Health education	Philosophy	Theology
History	Physical education/sports	
Home economics	Physical therapy	

E—Enterprising

Banking/finance	Insurance	Real estate
Business administration	Labor/industrial relations	Retailing/merchandising
Flight attendant	Law	Sales
Food distribution	Management	Small business management
Food service	Marketing	Sports administration
Hotel/motel management	Public affairs	Urban planning
Industrial engineering	Public relations	Wildlife management

C—Conventional

Accounting	Data processing	Medical secretary*
Bookkeeping	Legal secretary*	Office assistant
Business education	Medical assistant	Secretarial science
Clerk-typist	Medical records technology	Secretary, executive

*Includes apprenticeship programs.

community colleges, but because they are usually nonresidential, transportation expenses may be higher. The high price of a private college may be offset by the greater availability of financial aid. Write to each school you might attend, and request a copy of the latest catalog or information on expenses and financial aid.

Financial aid comes in three forms: (1) grants or scholarships—aid that does not have to be repaid, (2) loans—usually at low interest rates—to be repaid after the student has completed his or her education, and (3) employment—provided by the college in the form of work–study programs so the student can earn money for tuition and expenses. Help in paying for education comes from the federal and state governments, private donors, and the college you attend. College catalogs outline this information; then you can apply directly to the college for aid.

For government sources of financial aid, write for a free copy of *The Student Guide,* the *Free Application for Federal Student Aid,* and *Funding Your Education* from the U.S. Department of Education's Federal Student Aid Information Center, P.O. Box 84, Washington, DC 20044. The toll-free telephone number is 1-800-433-3243. Your school's financial aid office may have copies of these publications they can give you. They are published in English and Spanish. You can also find them online; to do this, you will need a computer (from your home, school, or local library) with access to the Internet. The Internet address that will get you to the Federal Student Aid Information Center is http://studentaid.ed.gov. (This electronic address connects you to the center; a detailed address for each publication is given next.) For *The Student Guide,* you can use this address: http://studentaid.ed.gov/students/publications/ student_guide/index.html. *The Student Guide* is a comprehensive resource from the U.S. Department of Education. Help from the department's Federal Student Aid office is through grants, loans, and work–study. For the *Free Application for Federal Student Aid,* again, write to the Federal Student Aid Information Center (P.O. Box 84, Washington, DC 20044), or use this Internet address: www.ed.gov/offices/ OSFAP/Students/apply/express.html. An online *Funding Your Education* is available at http://studentaid.ed.gov/students/publications/FYE/index.html. Another electronic source of financial aid information is the private, nonprofit College Entrance Examination Board (www.collegeboard.com), which will construct a Financial Aid Profile for you and help with your scholarship search. For access to a database of private scholarships, try www.fastWEB.com. To estimate your expected student contribution for college expenses, try the Sallie Mae site (www.salliemae.com). Another resource guide from the U.S. Department of Education is *College Is Possible,* which lists books, pamphlets, and Internet sites in English and Spanish, and is available at www.collegeispossible.org.

The U.S. Department of Education is the single most important judge of how much financial aid you receive. The financial aid programs administered by the U.S. Department of Education provide about 70 percent of all student assistance. After a student completes and submits the "Free Application for Federal Student Aid" (FAFSA), government computers process a report on how much money the student's family is expected to contribute. The FAFSA considers the family's after-tax adjusted gross income for the most recent tax year and is used to determine eligibility for the federal Pell Grants, Stafford Loans, and most state aid. The College Board charges applicants a small fee to process its Web-based College Scholarship Service profile, which is required by many private schools; the Internet address for this service is http://profileonline.collegeboard.com/index.jsp. Your college's financial aid officer uses the school's methods in calculating the amount of each award and can also allow for extenuating circumstances such as a recent job loss. Students who show the greatest need under financial guidelines and convince colleges they will bring something special to the campus will most likely receive the best offers (Clark, 2002).

Financial aid from most sources, whether federal, state, or local government, or private, is based on data provided by the student and family in applications outlining the student's financial need. *Financial need* is defined as the difference between a student's educational costs (tuition, fees, books and supplies, room and board, and miscellaneous expenses) and the amount the student and the student's family can reasonably be expected to pay toward an education. Factors in determining a student's financial need include family income, assets, family size, and other relevant information. Some scholarship grants are based on academic merit or specialized criteria such as ethnicity or place of residence. The financial aid program for an individual student often consists of a package arrangement, drawing money from all three sources (grants, loans, and employment). For example, a student needing $4,000 to help pay for a year's college costs might be offered a part-time job in a work–study program paying $1,300 over nine months, a $1,200 Stafford Loan, and a Pell Grant or a private scholarship worth $1,500 for the year.

There are many details in financial aid that require attention. Only a few can be mentioned here. Federal Pell Grants are available to undergraduate students. The amount you receive depends on your financial need, the costs to attend your school, your status as a full-time or part-time student, and whether you plan to attend school for a full academic year or less. Pell Grants can provide a foundation to which other forms of financial aid may be added. Your school will credit the Pell Grant money to your school account, pay you directly, or use a combination of these methods. If you have exceptional financial need, you may be eligible for a Federal Supplemental Educational Opportunity Grant. Being grants, these awards of money do not have to be repaid.

Of course, any loan you receive must be repaid. Here, the details are extremely important. If your school participates in the Federal Direct Loan Program, your Stafford Loan will be made through the school. The Direct Loan Program funds are lent to you directly by the U.S. government. A "subsidized" loan is made on the basis of financial need, and you will not be charged interest until you start repayments. An "unsubsidized" loan is not awarded on the basis of need, and you will be charged interest from the time the loan starts until it is paid in full. If your school does not participate in Direct Loans, the funds for your loan are lent to you from a bank, credit union, or other lender that is in the Federal Family Education Loan Program. PLUS Loans let parents with a good credit status borrow for educational expenses of dependent children. The federal Perkins Loan is a low-interest loan for undergraduate and graduate students with exceptional financial need. With any loan program, pay close attention to the promissory note, a binding legal document spelling out the conditions under which you are borrowing the money and the terms by which you agree to pay back the loan. Examine carefully the rate of interest you will be charged for the loan, and evaluate honestly your ability to repay the money.

Students can try to reduce their living expenses while attending school. Here are some suggestions. If you commute to school, use public transportation or car pool and bring your lunch rather than eat out. Avoid impulse buying, particularly when shopping for groceries and clothes. Take advantage of student discounts for necessary items. Explore entertainment opportunities offered through the school for such things as movies, theater, and other cultural events. Use free school athletic facilities instead of expensive health clubs. Try discount clothing stores before turning to a less economical department store.

Work and Time Management While Attending College

Eight out of ten students work while seeking a college degree. There are two types of working students. About a third of working undergraduates are full-time employees; these students are usually older and attend school on a part-time basis. The other two-thirds are working to meet college expenses; most are full-time students, younger, financially dependent on their parents, and work an average of 25 hours per week (King, 1998).

Research conducted by the National Center for Education Statistics has shown that working fewer than 15 hours per week can have a positive influence on whether or not students stay in college. Conversely, working more than 15 hours each week appears to have a negative effect. A conclusion drawn from this study is that academic success in terms of graduating from college is better served by borrowing (taking out loans) than by increasing the number of working hours. Working too many hours while attending school can jeopardize your chances of graduating from college and how well you perform while you are enrolled in classes. Full-time college students should work no more than 15 hours per week; anything more than that should mean a corresponding reduction in the number of credits or classes taken. I have seen all too many students who were full-time employees working 40 or more hours per week *and* enrolled for a full class load with 16 or 17 credits, only to later find them missing classes and finally dropping out of school altogether. Add study time into this equation (usually figured as twice the amount of time spent in class), and you arrive at around a 90-hour work week! Every student, sometimes with the help of a counselor, needs to find a reasonable balance between school, study, work, obligations to the family, and leisure time.

Now it's time to move into some "reality-testing" activities, to assess the practicality of your plans. Because you have just completed a section on education, the first exercise has to do with educational planning. Then you'll be asked to do some or all of the following exercises: construct a career plan, evaluate whether your career goal will express your work values and abilities, examine forces that push you toward or pull you away from your goal, answer tough questions about your career plans, and write an imaginative story about your future. That's a tall order, indeed. It is doubtful you could have done these exercises adequately before you started the career decision-making process. However, if you have read the material in this book thoughtfully and have worked carefully on the activities in the chapters before this one, you are ready to handle the challenges of the exercises ahead.

EXERCISE 10-1   EDUCATIONAL PLANNING EXERCISE

It takes time to get educational information, learn the requirements for a degree, check costs and financial aid, and make a schedule of courses over several semesters, but these steps save time in the long run. Because of failure to plan, some students take courses they don't like and don't need. A long-range educational plan is, of course, subject to unforeseen changes, but having the big picture enables you to see how each semester coordinates with your total schedule of courses. To complete this exercise, do the following:

1. Consult with an academic adviser, instructor, or school representative. Students are responsible for their own educational planning in most colleges. If you doubt the accuracy of the information you are getting from an adviser, obtain a second opinion.
2. Consult college and school catalogs, as well as directories that include all schools in the nation. Some schools list the programs and course descriptions in their catalogs; others rely on separate curriculum guide sheets.

For this exercise, if your first occupational choice does not require any further education or training, use your second choice or the next listed occupation that requires further education.

Name _____

Educational Planning Exercise

Occupational Choice _____

Education Needed
(Years and Months) _____

Name(s) of School(s)
You Plan to Attend _____

_____

Educational Major(s)
Needed for
Occupation _____

_____

Educational Minor
Needed _____

2nd Minor _____

Final Degree
to Be Earned _____

Money Needed Per Year

	First School	Second School
Tuition and Fees	$ _____	$ _____
Books and Supplies	$ _____	$ _____
Room and Board	$ _____	$ _____
Transportation	$ _____	$ _____
Personal Items	$ _____	$ _____
Total Budget	$ _____	$ _____

Name of
Academic Adviser _____

Publications
Consulted: _____
(give names
and page   _____
numbers)   _____

_____

Courses Needed

Educational Major: _____

General Education Required Subjects

Name of Subject	Credits
_____	_____
_____	_____
_____	_____
_____	_____
_____	_____
_____	_____
_____	_____
_____	_____
_____	_____
_____	_____

Educational Major Required Subjects

Name of Subject	Credits
_____	_____
_____	_____
_____	_____
_____	_____
_____	_____
_____	_____
_____	_____
_____	_____
_____	_____
_____	_____

Outline of Your Schedule of Courses

Indicate name of subjects and number of credits.

FIRST YEAR

First Semester	Second Semester	Other Terms or Sessions

SECOND YEAR

First Semester	Second Semester	Other Terms or Sessions

THIRD YEAR

First Semester	Second Semester	Other Terms or Sessions

FOURTH YEAR

First Semester	Second Semester	Other Terms or Sessions

REALITY-TESTING YOUR CAREER DECISION

In their discussion of factors that improve the quality of decision making, Janis and Mann (1977) suggest a re-examination of the consequences of a decision. The following reality-testing exercises are suggested as a way of re-examining your first occupational choice and assessing the feasibility of your goal.

EXERCISE 10-2   BASIC CAREER PLANS

Name _____

Basic Career Plan I: Long- and Short-Term Goals

Think of your career development as a series of steps in which you achieve one short-term goal after another until you accomplish the long-term career objective represented by your major occupational choice. In the form that follows, list your goals on the numbered lines. Establish and list target dates for your goals. Analyze each goal using the eight goal-setting guidelines described in Chapter 5 (A = Achievable, B = Believable, C = Controllable, D = Definable, E = Explicit, F = For yourself, G = Growth-facilitating, Q = Quantifiable or measurable). Circle the letter of any guideline you might have trouble with.

My long-term occupational goal is

_____

_____

Target date: _____   _____ Goal-setting guidelines: A B C D E F G Q

Goal-Setting

Short-Term and Intermediate Goals	Target Date	Guidelines
1. _____	_____	A B C D
_____		E F G Q
2. _____	_____	A B C D
_____		E F G Q
3. _____	_____	A B C D
_____		E F G Q
4. _____	_____	A B C D
_____		E F G Q
5. _____	_____	A B C D
_____		E F G Q
6. _____	_____	A B C D
_____		E F G Q
7. _____	_____	A B C D
_____		E F G Q
8. _____	_____	A B C D
_____		E F G Q

Short-Term and Intermediate Goals	Target Date	Guidelines
9. _____	_____	A B C D
_____		E F G Q
10. _____	_____	A B C D
_____		E F G Q

Basic Career Plan II: Time Sequence

Choose whatever time sequence seems best to you in projecting a future career plan. You need not fill in all the spaces, but try to imagine what you will be doing at six or seven points in the future. Feel free to change the time sequence so that it works for you. Think of your career development in stages; some of the vocational theories covered in Chapter 1 can help you here. Take into consideration other obligations and responsibilities, such as family obligations, that you believe are likely to influence your future career plan. (See Figure 10-1 for an example of a completed Basic Career Plan II.)

My long-range career goal can be described as

_____

_____

Right now, I am

_____

_____

In three months, I'll be

_____

_____

In six months, I'll be

_____

_____

In one year, I'll be

_____

_____

In two years, I'll be

_____

_____

In three years, I'll be

_____

_____

In five years, I'll be

_____

_____

In ten years, I'll be

_____

_____

Basic Career Plan II: Time Sequence

My long-range career goal can be described as *a manager of a dairy store selling milk, milk products, and ice cream.*

Right now, I am *a student at a community college.*

In three months, I'll be *taking courses in English, retailing, and management.*

In six months, I'll be *applying for a job (part-time) in a dairy or ice-cream store.*

In one year, I'll be *progressing toward an Associate Degree in Business Management.*

In two years, I'll be *graduating from community college with an Associate Degree.*

In three years, I'll be *working full-time in a dairy or an ice-cream store.*

In five years, I'll be *a manager of a small dairy or a branch manager of a large dairy.*

In ten years, I'll be *an owner of my own retail dairy business.*

Figure 10-1   Example of a completed Basic Career Plan II: Time Sequence

EXERCISE 10-3 OCCUPATIONAL REALITY-TESTING EXERCISE

Name _____

1. Imagine you are interviewing with an employer for a job in your number one occupational choice, which is

   _____

   _____

   _____

   _____

   Assume you have completed all the necessary education, training, and preparation.

2–3. The employer asks you to name the abilities, skills, and aptitudes you bring to the job. Then the employer asks you to give proof or evidence that you can deliver the skills you claim. What would you say? Start by going back to the career decision-making exercise in the previous chapter (Exercise 9-3), find your *number one occupational choice*, and locate the work abilities for which you gave a ++ or + code. Indicate the abilities you have or can develop that are used in the occupation, and give proof for the abilities you are claiming.

2. Name your skills
   and aptitudes.

_____

_____

_____

_____

_____

_____

_____

_____

3. Give proof or evidence you have the skill
   or aptitude.

_____

_____

_____

_____

_____

_____

_____

_____

4–5. Next, the employer asks how your own values would be satisfied by the work in this occupation. Name your important work values and explain how they would be expressed in your major occupational choice. Go back to the career decision-making exercise (Exercise 9-3), find your number one occupational choice, and locate the work values for which you gave a ++ or + code, indicating that these values are expressed in this occupation. Next, refer to the information you gathered about the occupation and explain how these work values will be expressed in the occupation.

4. Name your important
   work values.

_____

_____

_____

_____

_____

5. How will they be expressed in this
   occupation?

_____

_____

_____

_____

_____

6. Another inquiry from the employer concerns your preparation for the occupation. Give the education, training, or experience you have had that will enable you to perform with excellence in your major occupational choice.

Education, Training, and Experience You Have Had   Where?   How Long?

_____   _____   _____

_____   _____   _____

_____   _____   _____

_____   _____   _____

_____   _____   _____

Now return to the *present time* in your thinking and complete the remaining items.
    List the preparation and/or experience you still need to qualify for the job you seek. Responses can range from "No further preparation or experience needed" to specific types of formal education or experience that will require specified periods of time.

Specific Types of Preparation or Experience Still Needed   Where?   How Long?

_____   _____   _____

_____   _____   _____

_____   _____   _____

_____   _____   _____

7. On a separate sheet of paper, describe your major occupational goal, using achievement-motivation terminology.
   a. How deeply committed are you to achieving your occupational goal? (How strong is your internal need to achieve?) Explain.
   b. What specific actions are you taking or will you take to achieve your major career goal?
   c. What obstacles could prevent you from achieving your occupational goal? What actions can you take to overcome those obstacles?
   d. What kinds of help are available to you in pursuing your career goal? Who could help you?
8. For more information, give the address of one organization to which you could write or the name of one person with whom you could talk.

   a. Name of organization or person: _____

   b. Address: _____

   c. Did you follow up on this contact? Yes _____ No _____

EXERCISE 10-4   FORCE FIELD ANALYSIS

Force field analysis is a process you can use to test the feasibility of your career objective (Kirn and Kirn, 1978). It is a study of the influences that affect your thoughts, feelings, and behavior. All around and within you are forces, some of which move you toward your goal, others that move you away from it. The purpose of this exercise is to analyze the forces that influence your career goal and to become aware of actions you can take to deal with those forces. Use extra sheets of paper for this exercise if you need more space.

1. *State your number one career goal, however tentative it may be now.* The goal should be written in clear, specific terms; a goal of "happiness in a satisfying career" is too vague to be helpful. Express it more specifically: "to become a successful mechanical engineer within four years," for example. Happiness and satisfaction would seem to be the outcome of achieving such a career goal.
2. *List the forces for and against your goal. A force for* is anything that contributes something toward reaching your goal. A *force against* is anything that makes it more difficult for you to reach your goal (Kirn and Kirn, 1978). Forces may come from inside or outside of you. Examples of positive (+) forces are a skill or an aptitude, family support, availability of a course of study, strong motivation, enough time, financial assistance, and desirable attitude. Negative (–) forces could be the lack of these things, as well as other obstacles. Write down as many forces as you can; do not censor your thoughts as you make your lists. Go over the list several times with other people who could help you name additional forces. Some forces can be ambivalent—working both for and against your goal. You can indicate them in both places on your Force Field Analysis Chart. Circle those forces you believe will have the greatest impact on your career goal.
3. *Identify actions you can take to maximize positive forces and minimize or reverse negative forces.* Put a plus (+) after those positive forces that can be strengthened and after the negative forces that can be reduced or reversed into positive

forces. Be specific about the action that can be taken. Indicate who would take it, when it would be done, and what resources would be needed. If you cannot take any action to affect a force (particularly a negative one), write *NAP* (no action possible) after it.

4. *Assess the feasibility of your career goal.* Your goal is feasible if the positive forces outweigh the negative ones or if you can take action to weaken or reverse negative forces. Of course, you must follow up your listing of action steps by actually performing them. If your goal is feasible, indicate your next steps. If it is not, your next steps could include (a) making your goal more specific, (b) dividing it into two or more separate goals, (c) revising or modifying it, or (d) dropping it and choosing a different career goal, such as your second occupational choice.

See Figure 10-2 for an example of a completed Force Field Analysis Chart.

Force Field Analysis Chart

1. Career goal: _To become a registered nurse in 3 years._

2. Forces for your goal:

	Forces against your goal:
1 + (Strong need to achieve)	1 − Chemistry course.
2 + Financial assistance will pay for first semester.	2 − Family obligations.
3 + Support from family.	3 − Entrance requirements.
4 + (Learning ability.)	4 − Lack of money.
5 + Good health.	5 − Put too much pressure on myself.
6 + Study skills are better than average.	6 − Competition from others.
7 + Like to read.	7 − Have been away from school for 5 years.
8 + ("A" in physiology and anatomy.)	8 − Fear of failure.
9 + Can follow directions well.	9 − My impatience with others at times.
10 + Transportation is available.	10 −

3. Actions to maximize positive forces and minimize or reverse negative forces:

* Take Introduction to Chemistry before the required chemistry course.

* Apply for Registered Nurse program; take test for entrance requirement.

* Talk with counselor about failure fears and putting too much pressure on myself.

* Apply for financial aid at college.

* Keep talking with family for continued support and understanding.

4. Assess the feasibility of your career goal: _Yes — my career goal is realistic and involves moderate risks. Next steps: apply for registered nurse program and for financial aid._

Figure 10-2   Example of a completed Force Field Analysis Chart

Name _____

Force Field Analysis Chart

1. Career goal: _____

2. Forces for your goal:

    1 + _____

    2 + _____

    3 + _____

    4 + _____

    5 + _____

    6 + _____

    7 + _____

    8 + _____

    9 + _____

    10 + _____

   Forces against your goal:

    1 – _____

    2 – _____

    3 – _____

    4 – _____

    5 – _____

    6 – _____

    7 – _____

    8 – _____

    9 – _____

    10 – _____

3. Actions to maximize positive forces:

    _____

    _____

    _____

    _____

    _____

    _____

    _____

    _____

    _____

   Actions to minimize or reverse negative forces:

    _____

    _____

    _____

    _____

    _____

    _____

    _____

    _____

    _____

4. Assess the feasibility or realism of your career goal:

    _____

    _____

    _____

    _____

    _____

Source: Based on Kirn and Kirn (1978).

EXERCISE 10-5   THE "HOT SEAT"—A GROUP EXERCISE

When it is your turn to tell your group about your number one occupational choice, you are sitting on the proverbial "hot seat." Indicate whether your choice is a definite or tentative one and how you feel about it. Then answer questions from other group members. The questions suggested next are designed to test the feasibility of your career choice. The questions you ask of others in your group should be ones you are willing to answer yourself.

Group members have the right to pass on any question asked.

Suggested Questions

1. What have you identified as your major career field of interest? (For example, which Holland category interests you most: realistic, investigative, artistic, social, enterprising, or conventional?) Is your number one occupational choice consistent with your major field of interest? If not, could this discrepancy be a problem? (The same question could be asked of your second and third choices.)

2. What kinds of values and satisfactions do you seek in your work? Are they expressed in your number one occupational choice? (Why do you think you will be happy in your chosen occupation?) Explain.

3. What abilities, skills, and aptitudes do you need to qualify for entry into your chosen occupation? Do you have (or can you get) these qualifications? Explain.

4. What college major, business school program, technical school course of study, or type of apprenticeship leads to the kind of work in your occupational choice? What degrees, certificates, and licenses will you need? Will you be able to earn them? Explain.

5. How much money will be required for you to obtain the necessary education or training prescribed by your first occupational choice? What are the sources of your funding?

6. How much money can you earn in your occupation, in terms of beginning, average, and top pay? Will this amount of money be sufficient to support you or your family according to the lifestyle you want? Explain.

7. What kinds of people typically enter this occupation? What are their personality characteristics, typical interests, skills, and values?

8. What is the career ladder for your major occupational choice? Where do you start, and what positions do you hold as you advance in the occupation?

9. Where is the work in this occupation located? Where do you want to live? Can you be employed by this occupation in the geographic areas in which you want to live? Explain.

10. What kinds of work organizations employ people with your occupational interests and skills?

11. What are your chances of getting a job in your major occupational choice? What are the forecasts or trends in terms of supply and demand for your occupation over the next five to ten years? How will these trends affect your thinking and behavior?

12. What is the next step you are going to take in your career development?

13. Describe the usual working conditions for people employed in your chosen occupation.

14. What other types of work are closely related to your first occupational choice? What kinds of temporary or part-time employment could help you discover more information about the occupation? Have you had any of these work experiences, or do you plan to get them? Explain.

15. Write any other questions on a separate piece of paper.

EXERCISE 10-6   WRITE YOUR OWN ACHIEVEMENT STORY

In the chapter on achievement motivation (Chapter 5), the importance of mental imagery was cited as an essential factor in career success. You were encouraged to write imaginative stories with many achievement themes in order to strengthen your need to achieve the goals you set for yourself. Now you are encouraged to write an achievement story that focuses on your number one occupational goal. Use and label at least 10 of the following elements in your story. Write the story in a continuous, dramatic way, not as a set of answers to the questions. Be sure to label your achievement thoughts.

To refresh your memory, here are the original 10 achievement thoughts:

1. *Achievement Imagery (AIm).* Use any or all kinds of AIm in your story.
   a. *Competition with Others (CO).* With whom will you compete in order to reach your occupational goal?
   b. *Competition with Self (CS).* What standards will you set for yourself in striving for your goal?
   c. *Unique Accomplishment (UA).* What special accomplishment does your major occupational goal involve?
   d. *Long-Term Involvement (LTI).* Why does your goal represent long-term involvement? How long will it take to reach the goal?
2. *Need (N).* What is there about your goal that will motivate you? What values can you realize or gain if you reach your goal?
3. *Action (ACT).* What specific actions will you take to accomplish your goal?
4. *Hope of Success (HOS).* Why do you anticipate success in reaching your goal?
5. *Fear of Failure (FOF).* What worries or fears do you have when you think about working toward this career goal?
6. *Success Feelings (SF).* Describe your feelings about any past success that has brought you closer to your goal.
7. *Failure Feelings (FF).* Describe your feelings about any past failure that could reduce your chances of reaching your goal.
8. *World Obstacle (WO).* What obstacles outside yourself can block the way between you and your goal?
9. *Personal Obstacle (PO).* What obstacles inside yourself could keep you from reaching your goal?
10. *Help (H).* To whom could you turn if you needed help in reaching your career goal? Why would you do so?

Here are three more achievement thoughts that you can use when you write your story:

11. *Moderate Risk (MR).* Why is your career goal realistic but challenging? In what way is it a moderate risk, yet not too safe?
12. *Feedback (FB).* What kind of information would you expect to obtain as you strive to reach your occupational goal? How would you use these data to improve your performance or modify your goal?
13. *Goal-Setting Guidelines (GG).* How is your goal achievable, believable, controllable, definable, explicit, for yourself, growth-facilitating, and quantifiable or measurable?

The following example is from a career-planning student's achievement story:

GG	My goal is to obtain additional education to become a bank officer
GG	and then apply to several banks in the area. This goal can be achieved; I need only about 30 credits to attain the necessary educational background.
HOS	There are several banks in town. With their new and extended services, the

N GG HOS	opportunities should be good. I want to move into higher management through the loan department. As a loan officer, I will fulfill my values with regard to income, way of life, leisure time, and personal contact. Also, I will help others achieve their goals. My time frame is two years. I believe this can all happen, once I am hired, if I work accurately and diligently.
ACT SF	It is two years from now. After completing my education, I arrive at a downtown bank. I dazzle the interviewer with my financial knowledge. My recent training has given me some background and a lot of buzzwords to throw around. I hold an intelligent conversation with the bank representative.
ACT H Aim-CO	I have also done my homework on the business organization. I have a few friends within the bank who have told me something about the corporation's politics. My inside knowledge allows me to beat out 10 younger, less experienced applicants.
PO ACT WO PO H FOF PO	After I get the job, I enter the training program. I try to spend as much time on the job as possible. It is hard to get there extra early in the morning, so I stay later at night. This works well with my family, because my husband also works late. I pay very close attention to everything. Some of the accounting procedures are difficult to grasp, since that was never my strongest subject. I try to be extra accurate—this has also been one of my weak spots. Mistakes with other people's money can kill a bank officer's career. I set my mental attitude to positive. My friends, my parents, and my husband are very supportive, almost like cheerleaders on the sidelines. I know I have a lot going for me, and I don't want to disappoint them; this gives me added drive. I try to slow down so as not to make any mistakes. I also guard my opinions and sense of humor until I know how all the personalities at work will mesh with mine.
FOF WO	There is a lot of stress. I have so many things to learn, watch, keep in check, and balance with my lifestyle. Sometimes, I wonder if I can stand it. As always, there seems to be one person whose mission is to make my life difficult. This person is influential, if not powerful. I have to keep confidence in myself.
Aim-CS H FB	I work at my job, but I don't go overboard and become a workaholic. I am conscientious. I am at work on time every day. I've had excellent teachers who have given me advice, technical knowledge, and their personal evaluations of my progress. There have also been mandatory performance appraisals at the bank.
SF SF GG GG MR	My progress is slow and steady. I learn over time to enjoy my work and do it well. I find that this job as a bank officer fits well with my home life. My weekends and evenings are free, so I am home when I am needed most. Working at the bank has brought in a steady, secure income. It has allowed us some of the finer things in life: a nicely decorated home, decent transportation, and vacations. At the bank, I have been able to grow intellectually and financially. The job presents challenge as well as security.

Using your own career goal, this achievement story is the kind of story you are likely to compose in your mind many times in the future. Keep your achievement story for future reference. Add to it; change it; keep working on it. Visualizing your future can help make your career dreams come true. By constantly composing your achievement story in your mind (or on paper), you will (or at least are more likely to)

- Conceive a career goal that is achievable, believable, under control, put into words, specific, for yourself, growth oriented, and measurable.
- Strengthen within yourself the need to achieve your goal.
- Take action, instead of just think about a career goal.

- Anticipate success and the good feelings that go with it.
- Use your fears of failure to provide more energy in reaching your career goal.
- Overcome obstacles to career success, both internal and outside of yourself.
- Get help from knowledgeable people.
- Compete with a standard of excellence you set for yourself.
- Be willing to take moderate risks, ones that are realistic, yet challenging.
- Use feedback in modifying the career goal if it is too easy or becomes too difficult.
- Take personal responsibility for your decisions and actions.

A FINAL WORD ABOUT NEGATIVE FEEDBACK AND CHANGING OCCUPATIONS

As you implement your major career choice through an educational program, job hunting, and/or working in the occupation, you may experience at some point a reaction that Kennedy (1980) refers to as the killer *B*'s: blockage, boredom, and burnout. You may encounter a time when the feedback becomes so negative you must quit an occupation that once seemed so good to you it was your number one occupational choice. You have the career decision-making exercise you learned in the previous chapter to fall back on. You have a way out of the quagmire, building on a structure already in place.

Recycling your career-planning skills is something like improving a home. The basic structure is intact, but perhaps a new room needs to be added or the outside needs a fresh coat of paint. If these improvements are not enough, you will decide to move. You may look for another position within the same occupation or change occupations altogether. Make significant shifts in career direction *only* after doing a thorough job of decision making, as outlined in this book. Sometimes people decide that they entered the wrong occupation, when instead they really need to change workplaces or employers. Then again, perhaps the challenge of a once-exciting occupation has disappeared, and you really need the stimulation of a major change in career direction. These things do happen. About 10 percent of all employed people change their occupations in a given year, a figure that held steady throughout the 1970s and 1980s (Carey, 1990). Reasons for the switch include career upgrading in the form of better pay and advancement, loss of a previous job, a move to a different residence, working conditions, and so on. Therefore the chances are good that you will need to return several times to the subject of career planning. The career decision-making process doesn't stop; it is only put on hold for a while. Save the material in this book, and hold on to the exercises you have completed. You never know when you will need them again.

You have gone through a rather intense program of career development—self-appraisal, occupational exploration, planning, and decision making. Take time to relax, ponder the choices you've made, and appreciate the natural beauty in the world. Yes, there is work on your career development ahead. In this chapter, we've only begun an action phase—implementing your career decision. Also, your plans may change, calling for new decisions. Meanwhile, take time to smell the roses. We work to live, not live to work!

When you return to the career decision process, you probably will not move through it in the same way you have this time. Improvise and adapt your plans to your changing circumstances. Nevertheless, you have developed a base from which to start again. In recycling the process, you can repeat the exercises, comparing the past with the present, and analyzing the changes that have occurred. You will not necessarily have to go back to square one. Some of the work you have done now will stand the test of time. As you grow older, your interests and values will become more stable. You will add to your achievements and develop new skills. You may discover new opportunities in new directions. You are never done with career decisions, because much of career development is planning for life.

SUMMARY

1. A career decision often involves further education and training. Some considerations in this regard include the purposes of an education, types of educational institutions, classification of educational programs using Holland's six categories, educational costs, financial aid, and managing time. An educational planning exercise can help you identify courses within your major, minor (if needed), and general-education requirements and prepare a semester-by-semester plan to follow.

2. A series of reality-testing exercises can help you assess the feasibility of your major career choice. One exercise devises a basic career plan from two different angles. A second activity is simply called an *occupational reality-testing exercise*. Two other exercises are force field analysis and answering relevant questions from the "hot seat." Finally, you can create an achievement story that uses achievement thinking to overcome obstacles, anticipate success, learn from failure, strengthen the need to achieve, obtain help, take action, and form the imagery useful in accomplishing your major career goal.

3. Beyond education, the implementation of your career decision lies in obtaining and keeping a job in the occupation you have chosen, a topic briefly summarized in Appendix A: *Implementing Your Career Decision—The Job Search* of this book. Taking action on your career decision is the subject of an entire second book in the *Career Planning Guide* series, called *Job Search*. Many of the subjects condensed for Appendix A: *Implementing Your Career Decision—The Job Search* are elaborated on in *Job Search*. These topics include approaches and principles in the job search, sources of job leads, writing résumés and cover letters, completing job application forms, researching work organizations, conducting informational and job interviews, evaluating job offers, keeping a job, and coping with the problems of work.

REFERENCES

Barkume, M. 1998, Summer. The class of 1993: One year after graduation. *Occupational Outlook Quarterly*, 42(2), 10–21.

Carey, M. 1990, Summer. Occupational tenure, employer tenure, and occupational mobility. *Occupational Outlook Quarterly*, 34(2), 55–60.

Cetron, M. J., and Davies, O. 2003, March–April. Trends shaping the future: Technological, workplace, management, and institutional trends. *The Futurist*, 37(2), 30–43.

Clark, K. 2002, September 30. Who gets what? An inside look at how colleges gauge your financial need. *U.S. News & World Report*, 133(12), 88–92.

Crosby, O. 2002, Summer. Apprenticeships: Career training, credentials—and a paycheck in your pocket. *Occupational Outlook Quarterly*, 46(2), 2–21.

Crosby, O. 2002–2003, Winter. Associate degree: Two years to a career or a jump start to a bachelor's degree. *Occupational Outlook Quarterly*, 46(4), 2–13,

Dohm, A., and Wyatt, I. 2002, Fall. College at work: Outlook and earnings for college graduates, 2000–2010. *Occupational Outlook Quarterly*, 46(3), 3–15.

Fleetwood, C., and Shelley, K. 2000, Fall. The outlook for college graduates, 1998–2008: A balancing act. *Occupational Outlook Quarterly*, 44(3), 2–9.

Hecker, D. E. 1996, Summer. Earnings and major field of study of college graduates. *Occupational Outlook Quarterly*, 40(2), 10–21.

Janis, I. L., and Mann, L. 1977. *Decision-making: A psychological analysis of conflict, choice, and commitment*. New York: Free Press (Macmillan).

Kasper, H. T. 2002–2003, Winter. The changing role of community college. *Occupational Outlook Quarterly*, 46(4), 14–21.

Kennedy, M. M. 1980. *Career knockouts: How to fight back*. Chicago: Follett.

King, J. E. 1998, May 1. Too many students are holding jobs for too many hours. *Chronicle of Higher Education*, A72.

Kirn, A. G., and Kirn, M. 1978. *Life work planning*, 4th ed. New York: McGraw-Hill.

Mariani, M. 2001, Summer. Distance learning in postsecondary education: Learning whenever, wherever. *Occupational Outlook Quarterly*, 45(2), 2–10.

Mittelhauser, M. 1998, Summer. The outlook for college graduates, 1996–2006: Prepare yourself. *Occupational Outlook Quarterly*, 42(2), 2–9.

Rosen, D., Holmberg, K., and Holland, J. L. 1994. *The educational opportunities finder*. Odessa, FL: Psychological Assessment Resources, Inc.

Rosenbaum, J. E. 2001. *Beyond college for all: Career paths for the forgotten half*. New York: Russell Sage Foundation.

Shelley, K. J. 1994, Summer. More job openings—even more new entrants: The outlook for college graduates, 1992–2005. *Occupational Outlook Quarterly*, 38 (2), 4–9.

Smith, G. 1997, February. Internships: Breaking into a new career. *Career World*, 17–19.

Stringer, T. T. 2000–2001, Winter. Four years after graduation: The class of 1993. *Occupational Outlook Quarterly*, 44(4), 16–29.

Taylor, M. L. 2003. Choosing your major. *Job Web*. Bethlehem, PA: National Association of Colleges and Employers. Accessed April 10, 2003 at www.jobweb.com.

U.S. Department of Labor, Bureau of Labor Statistics. 2002, May 14. *College enrollment and work activity of 2001 high school graduates*. USDL 02-288. Washington, DC: U.S. Department of Labor.

U.S. Department of Labor, Bureau of Labor Statistics. 2003a, April 17. *Usual weekly earnings of wage and salary workers: First quarter, 2003*. USDL 03-177. Washington, DC: U.S. Department of Labor.

U.S. Department of Labor, Bureau of Labor Statistics. 2003b, January 17. *Usual weekly earnings summary*. Washington, DC: U.S. Department of Labor.

Implementing Your Career Decision—The Job Search

ACTIVATING THE JOB SEARCH

Perhaps the greatest reality-testing exercise is winning and keeping a job in the occupation you want most. Making a career decision has been the subject of this book, but it remains only a decision until you act on it. Implementing your career decision means an active job search, which is the subject of the second book in the *Career Planning Guide* series, *Job Search*. If you have coordinated your educational planning with your major occupational goal, you have already begun implementing your career choice. Appendix A of this text touches briefly on the action elements of searching for a job, a discussion that is much more fully developed in *Job Search*. The elements outlined here are approaches and basic principles of job hunting, sources of job leads, writing résumés and cover letters, completing applications, researching workplaces, interviewing for information and for jobs, evaluating job offers, practicing the art of keeping a job, and coping with problems in the working world.

AN OVERVIEW OF THE APPROACHES AND BASIC PRINCIPLES OF JOB HUNTING

The traditional approach to job hunting has been called "the numbers game" by one of its critics (Bolles, annual editions). As this name implies, it means contacting as many employers as you can. How? By sending out hundreds of copies of your résumé (posting it electronically or mailing it), making hundreds of telephone calls, applying directly to many companies, and using regular sources of job leads (newspaper help-wanted ads, employment agencies, and so on). The idea behind this approach is that when you give notice to enough people of your availability for work, sooner or later some employer will offer you a job.

A second approach turns the first one around, recommending that you start by thoroughly researching work organizations and employers who hire people with your occupational skills, goals, and values. You can then choose a few employment targets that meet the screening qualifications you have established. This approach emphasizes knowing exactly what you want in a career goal. You investigate companies or organizations by reading material and interviewing people about them and select those organizations for which you would like to work. In those companies, you identify the people or committees who have hiring authority and attract them through a demonstration of your job search skills to a point where they are willing to create a job for you. The basics of this approach are presented in Richard Bolles's popular job hunter's manual, *What Color Is Your Parachute?*

A third approach is a combination of the first two approaches, taking the elements of each that you think will work best for you and creating your own unique job search campaign. Of course, all three of these job-hunting theories involve many hours and lots of hard work. It's a full-time occupation just to get a job; it may just prove to be the hardest work you will ever do. Many prospective job hunters are not willing to face these facts. When the time comes, they just go through the motions and hope for the best or settle for whatever comes along. The job search is a subject that you can study and prepare for. This part of life, which is frightening, frustrating, and discouraging to so many people, can be turned into a challenging experience that can be faced with confidence and hope.

Some of the more important of the many principles of job hunting can be mentioned here. First and foremost, dedicate yourself to learning as much as you can about job hunting, because it is something you will do several times in your life. Read books on the subject and talk to people about it. Few subjects will have as much impact on your life and future happiness as this one. Start preparing now for your job search, even though it may be several years away. Don't think you can do it all just after graduation or when you need a job next week or next month. When the time for active job hunting comes, devote yourself to it full time, not making it just a half-hearted or once-in-a-while effort. The job search is best thought of as a continuous activity, not something that starts when you want a new job or are out of work. These days, the only real job security comes in being prepared to job hunt at any time.

The best job hunters realize it's only a minority of all job openings that are ever publicized. A majority of job vacancies exist in the hidden job market (Jackson, 1991; Lathrop, 1998). A job opening remains hidden from the time the idea for it enters an employer's mind to the time it is revealed to the public in newspapers and magazines or by personnel offices and employment agencies. Your best opportunity to learn about job openings that are hidden from public view is from your own network of personal contacts. Getting employment tips from personal contacts is especially useful for gaining jobs in small companies, where new employment has been the greatest in recent years.

The most effective job seekers understand that they have as much power and control in the job search process as the employer. Both parties need each other; the job seeker needs a job, and the employer needs the talents of workers to stay in business. Inexperienced job hunters think employers have all the power and do all the screening, but good job seekers screen and select work organizations. The best job seekers know what they want and are enthusiastic about it. They have researched their occupation, the industries it is found in, and the organizations that interest them.

Well-organized job seekers set aside space and time to do the job right. You need to make room in a desk or file cabinet to keep accurate records; you also need materials such as newspapers, stationery, envelopes, stamps, file folders, paper clips, computer access, and a telephone. You must set aside enough time to conduct an effective job search full time, 8 to 5, five days a week. If you are going to school or are working while you look for a new job, put every spare moment into service. You can use evenings, Saturdays, early mornings, lunch hours, late afternoons, personal-business days, and even vacations. Your approach to job hunting will reflect how seriously you regard it. There are many more principles of job hunting than can be covered here; they are discussed in the *Job Search* book.

SOURCES OF JOB LEADS

Sources of job openings include your school's career services office, public and private employment agencies, help-wanted advertisements in newspapers and trade magazines, electronic job banks and online services, civil service announcements, union hiring halls, job clearinghouses in professional associations, and direct contact with employers in person, by telephone, or by mail. The most productive method of uncovering job leads comes from information given by people you know or get to know. According to many job search experts, about 70 to 80 percent of all employment is obtained through a network of personal contacts. A personal contact can give you valuable inside information about potential job openings and refer you to someone in an organization with hiring authority. Personal contacts can be members of your family, friends, coworkers, neighbors, current and former employers, members of groups to which you belong, and social acquaintances. The possibilities are limited only by the boundaries of your imagination.

Do not ask a personal contact for a job. People are not likely to carry lists of job vacancies around in their pockets, and no one likes to be put on the spot about something they cannot do at that moment. Instead, ask personal contacts for their advice about the job world or their experiences in their occupations. Few people can resist a request for information about subjects they know about. You can ask them to tell you of any job openings they hear about in the future, but only if you have earned that right by listening to them courteously. Establishing a network of personal contacts is much like making friends. Do it for the motives of friendship and helpfulness to others. If you use your personal contacts only as sources of job leads, they may come to regard you as manipulative, self-serving, and interested solely in your own career. You must be sincerely interested in your personal contacts for them to want to help you. Some job seekers may consider cultivating personal contacts an activity that is beneath them, but this is the way the job world works. "It's not *what* you know, but *who* you know" is a cynical statement everyone has heard. The "who you know" does operate extensively in finding a job, but "what you know" is important, too, for it is the way in which you keep a job.

WRITING RÉSUMÉS AND COVER LETTERS

Résumés are self-designed sheets of information about yourself that briefly state your qualifications for a job. Normally, you send a résumé to an employer before the job interview is held. A résumé should contain information about your job objective, education, work experience, and anything else you want the employer to know. Some career counselors advise their clients to avoid using a résumé on the theory that employers use it mainly as a screening device. If your résumé is poorly written and contains spelling and grammatical errors, it will most certainly work against you. The résumé by itself will not get you a job; its purpose is to get you through the employer's door for an interview. If you can get an interview without a résumé, do so. However, be advised that many employers will not talk with you until you have sent them your résumé. Writing a résumé is preferable to filling out job application forms, because you can tell your story in your own way. You can emphasize your abilities, skills, and achievements—all the strengths and competencies you uncovered about yourself in Chapters 5 and 6 of this book. Your résumé can directly answer the question "Why should I hire you?" Preparing a well-designed résumé shows an employer you are serious about applying for a job; thus it can work for you in your job search campaign.

The proper writing style for a résumé is factual and concise. Start your sentences with an action verb (a functional skill from Chapter 6) and limit the use of the personal pronoun "I." Then attach a direct object to the verb (a work content or special-knowledge skill, as you learned in Chapter 6). You can also add descriptive adjectives and adverbs (adaptive skills). Refer to the worker functions in the descriptions of occupations in the O*Net or the *Dictionary of Occupational Titles* to get the idea of writing in résumé language. A job hunter seeking a position in elementary school physical education or recreation work could write about a summer job experience this way: "Managed a program of summer playground experiences competently and enthusiastically." Managing is a functional skill, summer playground program is a work content or special-knowledge skill, and competently and enthusiastically are adaptive skills, which sound like personal qualities but are skills nonetheless.

Because your résumé is very likely to be electronically scanned, especially by large and mid-sized companies, it is important to include *keywords* that match the specifications employers consider essential or desirable for the job opening they have. An "electronic" résumé usually starts with a keyword summary after the heading. A keyword or qualifications summary includes the job titles you have held, names of schools attended, names of work organizations where you have been employed, names of professional associations to which you belong, and the proven skills you possess and can put to work for the employer. Develop synonyms (equivalent words) for the keywords you have used; they can be used in the work experience and education sections or main body of your résumé. Keywords are generally nouns, and it is important to focus on them in a résumé that will be screened by a computer. Without a sufficient number of keywords that fit an employer's job description, your résumé may never be retrieved and read by a human being. A more complete description of how to write an electronic résumé is found in Chapter 3 of *Job Search.*

Correct spelling and punctuation are essential. The word order in your sentences must not be awkward. Use a dictionary if necessary. Have someone proofread your résumé before sending it to employers. Use 8½- by 11-inch paper that is of good quality. One page is generally enough; add a second page if it is made necessary by numerous work experiences and qualifications. Employers will not read long-winded résumés. Think about the physical appearance of your résumé. You want a first impression that invites the employer to read. Adequate margin space should appear on all sides of the page, and the content of your résumé should be balanced on the page. Always type or word-process your résumé and/or have it professionally printed.

Two types of résumés are *chronological* and *functional.* The chronological résumé organizes information about schools you have attended and the work experiences you have had in a reverse time order, starting with your most recent or current experience. This style may be the easiest to use; it is appropriate for job seekers with limited experience (Nutter, 1978). The functional résumé emphasizes the functions of the job positions you have held, the skills you have used, and the qualifications you have. Job hunters with a lot of work experience may find the functional style more to their liking.

The heading at the top of the résumé includes your name, street address, city, state, Zip code, and telephone number. Next comes the job objective—a clear and concise statement of the type of position you are seeking and the advancement you hope to attain. Some people suggest leaving out the job objective in order to make the résumé more versatile, but surveys indicate that employers definitely approve including a career goal in the résumé (Rogers, 1979). The employer is not left wondering what you want. Next comes a keyword summary to emphasize the education, experience, and skills the employer is hoping to find.

In the chronological résumé, names of schools and workplaces are placed in reverse chronological order, starting with the current or most recent one and working backward in time. For schools, include dates of attendance, addresses, diplomas or degrees earned, specific courses if they relate to your career objective, high grades or an outstanding grade-point average, and participation in extracurricular activities. Generally, it is not necessary to go back any further than your high school experience. Mention any honors achieved, scholarships awarded, and seminars, internships, or workshops attended. For your work experience section, indicate dates of employment, names and addresses of work organizations, job titles, descriptions of duties and responsibilities, work skills acquired, and names of supervisors (unless they are being used as references). Include military information if it is appropriate. Most personal data can be left out unless it strengthens your application. Mention hobbies, special skills, and interests, particularly if they relate to your job objective. If you list references, be sure to give their addresses and to get permission to use their names before you list them in your résumé. If you write "References available on request" in your résumé, you still need to secure the permission of the people (usually three) ahead of time.

For the functional résumé, title each part of the work experience section with the name of a work function. You can capitalize it to make it stand out more clearly. If you have had just one work experience, you may need to break it into smaller parts to create a number of work function titles. Then you can describe your achievements and skills under each title, using Chapters 5 and 6 of this book as a foundation for your writing. Still another type of formal summary of education and work experience is the *curriculum vita*. It is generally longer than the standard résumé and is used mainly for academic positions in higher education. The *Job Search* book in this series contains sample résumés; worksheets for constructing them; lists of action verbs and self-descriptive words; ideas for keywords; and examples of a cover letter, a thank-you letter, a follow-up letter, an acceptance of a job offer, and a letter declining a job offer.

A typewritten or word-processed cover letter accompanies and goes on top of the résumé. It introduces you to the employer, states your reason for writing, presents your qualifications and achievements that relate to the job position that is open, brings attention to your enclosed résumé, requests an interview, and indicates how the employer can contact you. All this is usually stated in three or four paragraphs. Like most résumés, the cover letter should be only one page long. Before you start the body of the letter, insert three items: (1) The heading, consisting of your return address and the date. (2) The inside address, which contains the same information as the address on the outside of the envelope (name and title of the person to whom you are writing and the name and address of that person's organization). (3) The salutation, the "Dear Ms. Smith" or "Dear Mr. Doe." Take time to find out the name of the person you are writing; it is better to personalize your cover letter with a person's name than to start with an impersonal "Dear Madam or Sir." The only time you cannot personalize the salutation is when you are responding to a blind ad that gives only a box number at the post office or newspaper. After the body of the letter, close with "Sincerely" or "Respectfully," leave four line spaces for your signature, and type your name. Your letter must contain no mistakes in spelling, punctuation, or sentence structure. Check the spelling of every word. Have someone proofread your cover letter before you send it. Use good-quality 8½- by 11-inch paper. Your cover letter should present a balanced appearance, leaving at least one inch of margin space on the sides of the page and as much white space at the bottom of the page as at the top.

COMPLETING JOB APPLICATION FORMS

Approach the employer's application form as you would a test, for that is exactly what it is. After completing four or five applications, some job seekers have an understandable tendency to become careless and rush through the application form too quickly. Slow down and take your time with it. If you make a mistake on the form, ask for another one rather than leave a poor impression of yourself on paper. Read the entire application form before writing anything on it. Have a résumé or some kind of personal data sheet handy so you can transfer accurate information to the application form. Use a pen, and print your responses unless otherwise directed. Answer all questions, even if you must print "not applicable" or "none" for some of them. If you are unsure of your response to a question, compose your answer on a sheet of scrap paper first. Answer all questions honestly and truthfully; if hired, your application becomes a part of your permanent record. Keep the application form clean and neat; the impression you give of yourself on the application form stays with the employer long after you have departed. Check your spelling for correctness. Obtain permission from your references before using their names. Base any requested salary figures on your research of the organization. Don't forget to sign your name in the space provided for your signature. These tips are among 25 recommendations in *Job Search* for completing an employer's application form.

Be aware that some questions on the application form (and in a job interview) could be illegal. Many of these questions involve personal information, such as birth date, marital status, height, and weight. The *Job Search* text contains a pre-employment inquiry guide to help you determine whether a question is legal or illegal. What should you do if you discover an illegal item on the application form? You probably have four options: (1) Indicate that the item is not relevant to the qualifications required by the job. (2) Answer "without answering"—for example, you are asked, "Who will take care of your children while working?" Your reply could be "I never allow personal commitments to interfere with my work." (3) Answer the question and ignore its illegal nature. (4) Inform the nearest office of your state's Civil Rights Commission or the federal Equal Employment Opportunity Commission. Try the first option, thus giving the employer a chance to comply with the law. The second option is dodging the question, and you must quickly think of a response. If the employer persists with an illegal question, your remaining choices are the third and fourth options. You may then want to reappraise whether or not you would like to work for this employer.

Some questions on application forms are difficult to answer because of special circumstances. What if you are too young or too old, are divorced or separated, have a criminal record, lack transportation, have or have had an alcohol or drug problem, have been fired, are physically handicapped, or have medical or financial problems? How do you handle these questions? Basically, you should be open and honest with employers. This is not easy to do, but the alternative is to lie or misrepresent yourself. If something comes up that is negative or a problem in the employer's mind, discuss it openly or admit you made a mistake. Indicate your desire to change and make things right, assure the employer that your problem will not become his or her problem, and ask for a chance to prove yourself on the job. Show you have taken or are taking steps to deal with the problem—a rehabilitation program, a doctor's statement of your progress, a changed attitude, a written recommendation from a probation officer, and so forth. Although this is a quick answer to a set of complex situations, more complete responses to difficult circumstances may be found in the *Job Search* book in this series.

RESEARCHING WORK ORGANIZATIONS

Most people fail to research work organizations in their job search. This is a mistake. The best job seekers are informed about a company before they make a decision as to whether or not to join it. They obtain an organizational chart to identify the department or division in which they would most likely become a member. They talk with their personal contacts who know something about the organization (or can refer them to someone who knows), so they can size up a company or department, the people who work there, and the type of group culture they create.

Company cultures develop a personality pattern just as individuals do. The reason for studying a group or company culture is that you want to have a reasonably good chance of fitting into the group of people with whom you would work. Organizational culture involves a pattern of behavior, a guiding philosophy, and a set of beliefs and assumptions shared by members of the group. Deal and Kennedy (1982) and other writers about companies identify key elements of corporate culture, including core values, company rituals and ceremonies, communications networks, and the business environment that shapes what a company does to achieve success.

Three types of company cultures identified by Margerison (1979) and Wallach (1983) are the bureaucratic, innovative, and supportive cultures. These labels were originated some time ago, but they are still viable today. Bureaucratic cultures are structured organizations—systematic, impersonal, orderly, cautious, stable, and power-oriented. Innovative cultures are creative, spirited, challenging, adventurous, competitive, enterprising, and achievement oriented. Supportive cultures emphasize harmony, trust, security, equality, warmth, sociability, and safety. These three cultures exist in all organizations in varying degrees. Different departments within a company can also create their own distinctive subcultures. The *Job Search* book suggests methods by which you can identify the cultures both of the organizations you are investigating and of the places where you have worked or are working now. You can try to match your own personality with the culture of the company and department in which you are interested. For example, a person with a strong need for power would adapt better to a bureaucratic culture, a person with a strong need to achieve would fit best into an innovative culture, and a person with a strong need for affiliation would be most comfortable in a supportive culture.

Much, if not all, of your information about organizational culture will come by word of mouth from your personal contacts and their acquaintances, both inside and outside the organization. You can, however, acquire a lot of your knowledge about a work organization from written and electronic sources. Many companies post on their Web site and/or print a hard copy of an annual report that contains sections on finances, products, and operations. Try to obtain several annual reports, covering the past few years, so you can discover trends in growth and decline of sales, assets, liabilities, net worth, working capital, and numbers of employees and stockholders.

Business magazines such as *Barron's, Business Week, Dun's Review, Financial World, Forbes, Fortune,* and *Inc.* often feature articles on companies. So do newspapers such as *The Wall Street Journal.* You can do some of your research online or in print from business directories such as Dun and Bradstreet's *Million Dollar Directory;* Hoover's *Handbook of American Business;* Moody's *Complete Corporate Index* and *Industrial Manual;* Standard and Poor's *Register of Corporations, Directors, and Executives;* and Thomas's *Register of American Manufacturers.* These resources give you names of companies, names and titles of officers, locations, products manufactured, services provided, and the financial health of the organization. Electronic sources of information about companies are readily available; most organizations of any size now have their own Web site. Two other sources are online databases and compact discs (CD-ROM).

College students should read the *Job Choices* series, published by the National Association of Colleges and Employers (62 Highland Avenue, Bethlehem, PA 18017) and found in most college career services offices. Companies included in *Job Choices* indicate the type of college majors they are interested in hiring. Books such as *The 100 Best Companies to Work for in America* by Levering, Moskowitz, and Katz (1994) are useful. Business magazines such as the ones just mentioned rate companies, often annually, according to various criteria.

What should you find out about an organization in your investigations? Definitely know the organization's products and services before you hold a job interview with them; failure to do so could be a knockout factor, according to personnel directors. Know something about the company culture and the type of people employed by the organization or department. Determine an organization's problems and whether your abilities could help solve them. Check into decision-making patterns, advancement opportunities, the wage or salary range, future prospects for the company or a department, company history and its standing or rank within its industry, staff morale, opportunities for further training, the political environment, and labor–management relations. A separate chapter on researching geographic areas appears in *Job Search;* to some people, where they live is more important than where they work.

INTERVIEWING FOR INFORMATION AND FOR JOBS

Interviewing for information and advice about jobs, occupations, and work organizations is a good way to gain knowledge and practice for the job interview. This technique allows you to control an interview and evaluate companies, but it doesn't involve being rejected, because you never ask for a job in this type of interview. Many employers like the idea that a job hunter is seeking information before deciding where to apply for a job. Such an employer may offer you a job position halfway through the informational interview. Employers can turn an informational interview into a job interview if they choose, but job seekers cannot ethically do so. It is wrong to pose as an information gatherer and then suddenly ask an employer for a job. Unfortunately, some unscrupulous job hunters have used this deception as a way to avoid the screening functions of a human resources or personnel department, thus giving informational interviewing a bad name in the minds of some employers (Bolles, 2004 and annual editions).

You should also interview people other than those who hire, for information and job advice. Staff workers, middle managers, secretaries, and custodians, for example, have knowledge of the ways an organization functions. The *Job Search* book presents a seven-step process on conducting informational interviews. Included are 27 topics to use as a guide for your questions.

In approaching a job interview, preparation is the key to controlling nervousness and anxiety. Know what the company does to keep itself in business. Learn as much as you can about the organization. Anticipate questions you are likely to be asked, such as "Why should I hire you?" or "Tell me about yourself." Rehearse answers with others in practice interviews.

Determine what you can do for the organization, and frame your answers to questions with that idea in mind. Learn the name and title of your interviewer. Take a copy of your résumé or a personal data sheet with you in case you are asked to complete an application form. Dress appropriately for the occasion.

During the interview, give an impression of optimism and energy. Be aware of nonverbal communication: sit squarely, lean slightly forward, and establish good eye contact. Avoid flat yes-or-no responses, but answer questions briefly and honestly. Ask questions about the job position and the organization; failure to do so may be interpreted as lack of interest on your part. Resist the temptation to criticize previous employers, and avoid running yourself down. When the interview is over, evaluate it as soon as you can. Write a thank-you letter to the interviewer a short time after the interview. Follow-up activities are often very important in distinguishing the serious job seeker from casual ones.

Different types of job interviews may be encountered. The initial interview is often a screening interview. There are structured and unstructured interviews, as well as combinations of the two. Responses to questions in the structured interview are directed by the question itself; in the unstructured interview, they are left open to your discretion. Other types of interviews are group, board, stress, behavioral, serial, and secondary interviews. Suggestions for handling various kinds of interviews are detailed in the *Job Search* book. The *Job Search* book also presents examples of many interview questions and ideas for your responses to them, suggested questions you can ask employers or interviewers, exercises, and an interview rating sheet you can use in practice interviews.

EXERCISE A-1 THE TWO-MINUTE SPIEL (ROLE-PLAY)

At the opening of a job interview, you are asked, "Tell me about yourself." What would you say in a two-minute time span? Role-play this exercise with one other person, the "interviewer," who instructs you, "Tell me about yourself." Suggestion: Include a description of (1) your career goal (and interests); (2) your functional, content, and adaptive skills; (3) your aptitudes; (4) your accomplishments and qualifications; (5) your work values; (6) your education (recent); and (7) your experience (if related to your goal, so much the better). You don't have to tell about yourself in this lock-step manner, but make every effort to cover all seven topics in your "spiel." Before the exercise, practice bringing your response down to no less than two minutes and no more than three minutes.

When you are done with your "spiel," ask your "interviewer" (1) Was my story interesting? (2) Was it convincing? (3) Was anything left out? (4) How could I make my response better?

EVALUATING JOB OFFERS

The *Job Search* book provides methods to evaluate one job offer or to compare two or more job offers. Among the many factors involved in weighing job offers to be rated positive, neutral, or negative are whether the job offered will fit into your career plans, express your major values, use your abilities, and meet your salary expectations.

THE WORKING WORLD

Most factors that contribute to a person's success on the job sound rather ordinary and commonplace, but failure to pay attention to them costs workers their jobs. What are these simple things? Coming to work on time. Informing your supervisor about any absence from work. Knowing company procedures. Listening to and following directions. Not taking unfair advantage of your work organization. Keeping busy at work. Being cooperative and friendly with coworkers and recognizing their contributions. Having realistic expectations about work. Avoiding mannerisms that irritate others. Being a planner and a problem solver. Emphasizing quality and excellent work. Maintaining a positive self-image. The book *Job Search* expands on all these themes. Employers have obligations, too, such as paying employees for their work, communicating exactly what is expected of workers, and complying with laws protecting the rights of workers.

Inevitably, problems arise in any job. Some problems affect certain types of workers more than they do others. For example, younger workers are more likely to express dissatisfaction with the heavy use of authority in the workplace and demand a greater voice in establishing their own working conditions. Older workers are more likely to feel ignored or devalued, and some believe they are forced into early retirement. Blue-collar workers may feel uneasy about the threat to their job security posed by advancing technology, or about the lower status accorded their work. Both blue-collar and white-collar workers bemoan downsizing practices and the lack of job security, even with increasing amounts of productivity. Minority workers still feel the effects of prejudice and must often settle for the worst jobs society has to offer. African American workers who advance in a white-dominated society may feel isolated, not fully accepted by their white colleagues and resented for their success by other African Americans. Many Latinos express concerns about immigration issues. White males sometimes complain that they are innocent victims of affirmative action programs that punish them for sins committed by others a long time ago. Working women continually encounter false myths about why they want to work, occupational gender-typing, gender stereotypes in work assignments, and sexual harassment. Sexual harassment at the workplace has been the subject of much attention. One definition of it is "deliberate and/or repeated sexual or sex-based behavior that is not welcome, not asked for, and not returned" (Webb, 1991). "Office romances" present difficulties to an organization, but try telling that to the individuals involved. Each of these problems is, in itself, worth a book; they are cited here to give you an idea of the complexity of the job world.

Burnout on the job is another major problem. It is a reaction to work stress that leaves a person feeling drained, emotionally exhausted, and inadequate (Maslach, 1982). Workers in the helping professions are particularly vulnerable, because they can often become overinvolved with clients' problems or have too many emotional demands made on them by others.

Frustrations come from being swamped with paperwork, lacking appreciation or recognition, having no opportunity to influence decisions, or being caught in a career dead end. Cynicism and indifference replace hope and idealism. The strategies you and your employer can use to counteract the effects of job dissatisfaction are discussed in the *Job Search* book.

The mysterious contradictions and paradoxes of the economy have an impact on the way you work and live. For example, why is there unemployment in a country as prosperous and productive as the United States? Underemployment—a highly trained person working in a job that does not require his or her level of training or skill—is a problem, particularly for college graduates. The problem of misplaced and displaced workers also challenges the best efforts of society. Concepts such as the work ethic, scientific management, human relations, human resources, Theory X and Theory Y, and intrinsic work motivation are covered in the *Job Search* book because they have much to do with the quality of working life today. Many ways of improving work are being tried: job enrichment, organizational democracy, profit sharing, employee ownership, self-managing work teams, job sharing, flexible time arrangements, and compressed workweeks.

Analysts try to spot broad social trends. These trends were discussed briefly in Chapter 2. Trying to understand the world and yourself will always be a large part of career planning, because this subject is rooted in your personal and social past, in what is going on now and is likely to happen in the future—as best social forces and workplace trends can be envisioned.

REFERENCES

Bolles, R. N. 2004 and annual editions. *What color is your parachute?* Berkeley, CA: Ten Speed Press.

Deal, T. E., and Kennedy, A. A. 1982. *Corporate cultures: The rites and rituals of corporate life.* Reading, MA: Addison-Wesley.

Jackson, T. 1991. *Guerrilla tactics in the new job market.* New York: Bantam Books.

Lathrop, R. 1998. *Who's hiring who: How to find that job fast*, 12th ed. Berkeley, CA: Ten Speed Press.

Levering, R., Moskowitz, M., and Katz, M. 1994. *The 100 best companies to work for in America*, rev. ed. New York: Penguin Plume Books.

Margerison, C. J. 1979. *How to assess your managerial style.* New York: AMACOM, a division of American Management Association.

Maslach, C. 1982. *Burnout—the cost of caring.* Englewood Cliffs, NJ: Prentice Hall.

Nutter, C. F. 1978. *The résumé workbook: A personal career file for job applications.* Cranston, RI: Carroll Press.

Rogers, E. 1979. Elements of effective job-hunting. *Journal of College Placement*, 40(1), 55–58.

Wallach, E. J. 1983. Individual and organization: The cultural match. *Training and Development Journal*, 37(2), 29–36.

Webb, S. L. 1991. *Step forward: Sexual harassment in the workplace: What you need to know.* New York: Mastermedia.

Occupational Cluster Survey (Detailed) for the Occupational Outlook Handbook

Read each occupational title carefully and judge your degree of interest in the occupation. Circle 0 if you have *no interest* in the occupation. Circle 1 if you have *some interest* in the occupation. Circle 2 if you are *interested* in the occupation. Circle 3 if you are *very interested* in the occupation. Circle only one number for each occupational title. Be sure to answer all items; do not skip any. There are no right or wrong answers. Just indicate your amount of interest in the work you would perform in the occupation. Do not concern yourself with other things, such as the salary, prestige, or education required. You can, if you wish, refer to Table 2-8 in Chapter 2 for information on employment prospects for all occupations covered in this exercise.

0 = No interest   1 = Some interest   2 = Interested   3 = Very interested

Group A   *Management and business and financial operations occupations*

0 1 2 3   Accountant and auditor (prepares, analyzes, and verifies financial reports)
0 1 2 3   Financial manager (supervises financial services, gives advice about money)
0 1 2 3   Human resources manager (guides employer–employee relations for companies)
0 1 2 3   Purchasing manager/agent (buys goods and materials at lowest cost for employers)
0 1 2 3   Top executive (devises strategies to achieve goals of their organizations)

_____   Total score for Group A

Group B   *Professional and related occupations (divided into nine subgroups)*

Group B-1   *Architecture, drafting, and engineering*

0 1 2 3   Architect (designs buildings, floor plans, and structural details)
0 1 2 3   Civil engineer (designs and supervises construction of buildings, roads, etc.)
0 1 2 3   Drafter (prepares drawings from specifications of engineers and architects)
0 1 2 3   Mechanical engineer (plans and designs tools, machines, and engines)
0 1 2 3   Surveyor (collects and measures data for construction sites and maps)

_____   Total score for Group B-1

Group B-2   *Art, design, entertainment, media, and communications*

0 1 2 3   Interior designer (plans space and furnishings inside homes and buildings)
0 1 2 3   Musician (plays a musical instrument; sings; composes music)
0 1 2 3   Photographer (uses cameras to picture people, places, and events)
0 1 2 3   Radio/television announcer (presents news, sports, weather; plays music)
0 1 2 3   Writer/editor (writes books, articles, scripts, poems; selects for publication)

_____   Total score for Group B-2

| 0 = No interest | 1 = Some interest | 2 = Interested | 3 = Very interested |

Group B-3   *Community and social service occupations*
0 1 2 3   Clergy: minister, priest, rabbi (leads people in the worship of God)
0 1 2 3   Counselor (assists people with personal, family, educational, and career problems)
0 1 2 3   Human service assistant (aids varied mental-health professionals serve clients)
0 1 2 3   Probation and parole officer (supervises offenders on probation or parole)
0 1 2 3   Social worker (helps people who are poor, homeless, troubled, disadvantaged, etc.)
_____   Total score for Group B-3

Group B-4   *Computer and mathematical occupations*
0 1 2 3   Computer programmer (writes, tests, and maintains instructions for computer functions
0 1 2 3   Computer software engineer (designs, develops, tests, and evaluates software)
0 1 2 3   Computer support specialist (assists and advises customers and computer networks)
0 1 2 3   Statistician (collects, analyzes, interprets, and presents numeric data)
0 1 2 3   Systems analyst (develops new and existing computer systems for organizations)
_____   Total score for Group B-4

Group B-5   *Education, training, library, and museum occupations*
0 1 2 3   Archivist and curator (acquires, preserves, and exhibits valued historical items)
0 1 2 3   Librarian (assists people in finding information, organizes book collections)
0 1 2 3   Teacher—elementary, secondary (helps students learn in various school subjects)
0 1 2 3   Teacher—postsecondary (instructs college students; conducts research)
0 1 2 3   Teacher—special education (works with students who have various disabilities)
_____   Total score for Group B-5

Group B-6   *Social science and legal occupations*
0 1 2 3   Economist (studies how scarce resources are distributed to produce goods and services)
0 1 2 3   Lawyer (represents clients in legal cases and gives advice on legal matters)
0 1 2 3   Paralegal or legal assistant (helps lawyers prepare for hearings and trials)
0 1 2 3   Psychologist (studies the human mind and behavior, counsels people with problems)
0 1 2 3   Social scientists, other (includes historians, political scientists, and sociologists)
_____   Total score for Group B-6

Group B-7   *Life science, physical science, and science technicians*
0 1 2 3   Biologist (studies animals, plants, and microscopic organisms)
0 1 2 3   Chemist (studies the chemical properties of everything in the environment)
0 1 2 3   Geoscientist (studies the composition and physical structure of Earth)
0 1 2 3   Physicist (explores the principles of matter and energy and their interactions)
0 1 2 3   Science technician (uses more practical applications of the various sciences)
_____   Total score for Group B-7

Group B-8   *Health diagnosing and treating occupations*
0 1 2 3   Chiropractor (treats patients by adjusting the body's spine and nervous system)
0 1 2 3   Dentist (diagnoses and treats problems of teeth and gums)
0 1 2 3   Pharmacist (dispenses medicines prescribed by doctors)
0 1 2 3   Physician (diagnoses illnesses, prescribes treatment for injuries or disease)
0 1 2 3   Registered nurse (administers medications, manages nursing care plans, etc.)
_____   Total score for Group B-8

0 = No interest   1 = Some interest   2 = Interested   3 = Very interested

Group B-9   *Health technologists and technicians*
0 1 2 3   Clinical laboratory technician (examines body fluids, tissues, and cells)
0 1 2 3   Dental hygienist (cleans teeth, teaches proper care of teeth, etc.)
0 1 2 3   Emergency medical technician (gives immediate care, transports the injured)
0 1 2 3   Licensed practical nurse (cares for the sick and wounded, provides bedside care)
0 1 2 3   Radiologic technician (produces x-ray films to diagnose medical problems)

_____   Total score for Group B-9

Group C   *Service occupations (divided into four subgroups)*

Group C-1   *Food preparation and serving-related occupations*
0 1 2 3   Baker (produces baked goods for restaurants, institutions, and bakeries)
0 1 2 3   Chef, cook (prepares food by measuring, mixing, and cooking ingredients)
0 1 2 3   Dining room attendant (cleans tables, removes used dishes, assists waiters)
0 1 2 3   Fast-food worker (takes orders for food at counters and drive-through windows)
0 1 2 3   Waiter/waitress (takes customers' orders, serves food, prepares checks, etc.)

_____   Total score for Group C-1

Group C-2   *Health care support occupations*
0 1 2 3   Dental assistant (performs a variety of patient care, office, and lab duties)
0 1 2 3   Medical assistant (performs routine clinical and office tasks for doctors)
0 1 2 3   Nursing aide (cares for patients under nursing and medical supervision)
0 1 2 3   Occupational therapy assistant (helps injured workers return to the labor force)
0 1 2 3   Physical therapy assistant (helps patients improve mobility, relieve pain, etc.)

_____   Total score for Group C-2

Group C-3   *Personal care and service occupations*
0 1 2 3   Animal care worker (feeds, grooms, and exercises animals; maintains their cages)
0 1 2 3   Barber/cosmetologist (cuts, trims, shampoos, and styles customers' hair)
0 1 2 3   Child care worker (nurtures and teaches children in a variety of schools and centers)
0 1 2 3   Home care aide (helps elderly, disabled, and ill in home and residential centers)
0 1 2 3   Recreation and fitness worker (plans, organizes, and directs recreational activities)

_____   Total score for Group C-3

Group C-4   *Protective and building service occupations*
0 1 2 3   Building cleaning worker (keeps offices, schools, stores, etc., in good condition)
0 1 2 3   Correctional officer (keeps order within jails and prisons; enforces rules)
0 1 2 3   Firefighter (puts out fires, operates pumps, ladders, trucks, etc.)
0 1 2 3   Police officer (enforces laws, writes reports, patrols, participates in arrests)
0 1 2 3   Security guard (protects property from theft, fire, vandalism, and illegal entry)

_____   Total score for Group C-4

Group D   *Sales and related occupations*
0 1 2 3   Cashier (totals bills, receives money, makes change, gives receipts)
0 1 2 3   Insurance agent (sells policies that protect people and businesses from losses)
0 1 2 3   Real estate broker/agent (sells and rents homes and property for and to people)
0 1 2 3   Retail salesperson (sells food, clothing, furniture, etc. to customers)
0 1 2 3   Sales representative, wholesale and manufacturing (sells products to clients)

_____   Total score for Group D

0 = No interest   1 = Some interest   2 = Interested   3 = Very interested

Group E   *Office and administrative support occupations (divided into four subgroups)*

Group E-1   *Financial clerks*
0 1 2 3   Bill and account collector (keeps track of overdue accounts and collects on them)
0 1 2 3   Billing clerk (reviews orders and records to calculate amounts due from customers)
0 1 2 3   Bookkeeping, accounting, and auditing clerk (keeps financial records for companies)
0 1 2 3   Payroll and timekeeping clerk (makes sure employees are paid accurately on time)
0 1 2 3   Teller (cashes checks, accepts deposits, and processes withdrawals in banks)
_____   Total score for Group E-1

Group E-2   *Information and record clerks*
0 1 2 3   Customer service representative (provides information about products and services)
0 1 2 3   File clerk (classifies, stores, retrieves, and updates information for organizations)
0 1 2 3   Interviewer (obtains and verifies information from people and business representatives)
0 1 2 3   Order clerk (processes incoming orders for a wide variety of goods and services)
0 1 2 3   Receptionist (greets visitors, answers telephones, routes calls, responds to inquiries)
_____   Total score for Group E-2

Group E-3   *Material recording, scheduling, dispatching, and distributing occupations*
0 1 2 3   Courier and messenger (moves and distributes documents and small packages)
0 1 2 3   Dispatcher (schedules and sends workers and vehicles to transport things or people)
0 1 2 3   Production and planning clerk (assembles records and reports on production)
0 1 2 3   Shipping and receiving clerk (keeps records of all goods shipped and received)
0 1 2 3   Stock clerk (receives, unpacks, checks, stores, and tracks merchandise and materials)
_____   Total score for Group E-3

Group E-4   *Other office and administrative support occupations*
0 1 2 3   Computer operator (sets controls on computers working from instructions)
0 1 2 3   Data entry and information processing worker (does word processing and types copies)
0 1 2 3   General office clerk (files, types, enters data; operates office equipment)
0 1 2 3   Postal service worker (carries mail, sorts incoming mail, clerks at windows, etc.)
0 1 2 3   Secretary, administrative assistant (performs and coordinates office activities)
_____   Total score for Group E-4

Group F   *Farming, fishing, and forestry occupations*
0 1 2 3   Agricultural worker (works with food crops, animals, trees, shrubs, or plants)
0 1 2 3   Farmer/rancher (manages crop, livestock, dairy, poultry, flower, etc., farms)
0 1 2 3   Fishing boat captain (plans and oversees the fishing operation)
0 1 2 3   Forester, conservation scientist (develops and protects forests and soil)
0 1 2 3   Logging equipment operator (drives tractors transporting logs from felling site)
_____   Total score for Group F

Group G   *Construction trades and related workers*
0 1 2 3   Brickmason, stonemason (builds with brick or stone and other masonry materials)
0 1 2 3   Carpenter (cuts, fits, and assembles wood framework in buildings and homes)
0 1 2 3   Electrician (installs, connects, tests, and maintains electrical systems)
0 1 2 3   Painter, plasterer (applies paint or plaster to decorate and protect surfaces)
0 1 2 3   Plumber, pipefitter (installs and repairs pipes that carry water, air, and gas)
_____   Total score for Group G

0 = No interest   1 = Some interest   2 = Interested   3 = Very interested

Group H   *Installation, maintenance, and repair occupations*
0 1 2 3   Automotive body repairer (straightens bent auto bodies, replaces crumpled parts)
0 1 2 3   Automotive service technician and mechanic (diagnoses problems and repairs cars)
0 1 2 3   Computer and office machine repairer (installs and repairs office machines)
0 1 2 3   Home appliance repairer (installs, disassembles, and repairs home appliances)
0 1 2 3   Industrial machinery installer and repairer (works with factory machinery equipment)

_____   Total score for Group H

Group I   *Production occupations (divided into two subgroups)*

Group I-1   *Production occupations, except metal, plastic, and wood workers*
0 1 2 3   Assembler, fabricator (puts together detailed parts of manufactured products)
0 1 2 3   Food processor (converts raw food products into finished goods ready for sale)
0 1 2 3   Inspector (works to guarantee quality of goods their companies produce)
0 1 2 3   Printing machine operator (prepares, operates, and maintains printing presses)
0 1 2 3   Water treatment plant operator (treats water so it is safe for people to drink)

_____   Total score for Group I-1

Group I-2   *Metal, plastic, and wood workers*
0 1 2 3   Machinist (uses machine tools to produce precision metal parts)
0 1 2 3   Machine setter, operator, and tender (sets up or tends machine for production)
0 1 2 3   Tool and die maker (produces tools and forms enabling machines to make products)
0 1 2 3   Welder (joins metal parts to form a permanent bond for construction and repair)
0 1 2 3   Wood worker (transforms logs of wood into finished products)

_____   Total score for Group I-2

Group J   *Transportation and material moving occupations*
0 1 2 3   Airline pilot, flight engineer (transports passengers and cargo on airplanes)
0 1 2 3   Bus driver (drives buses within and between cities, follows time schedules)
0 1 2 3   Locomotive engineer (operates large trains to carry passengers and goods)
0 1 2 3   Taxi driver (drives taxicab to transport people, collects fares)
0 1 2 3   Truck driver (delivers goods from factories and terminals to stores and homes)

_____   Total score for Group J

Group K   *Military occupations (most military jobs have their counterparts in civilian life)*
0 1 2 3   Administrative positions (directors, accountants, recruiters, trainers, etc.)
0 1 2 3   Combat specialties (infantry, artillery, special forces carry out combat missions)
0 1 2 3   Construction personnel (build and repair buildings, airfields, bridges, dams, etc.)
0 1 2 3   Engineering, science, and technical personnel (operate equipment, solve problems)
0 1 2 3   Human service specialists (help military personnel with their personal problems)

_____   Total score for Group K (Air Force, Army, Coast Guard, Marine Corps, Navy)

Over a hundred additional occupations are covered at the end of the *Occupational Outlook Handbook*. A short description and an employment projection is developed for each of these occupations; however, detailed information about them is not included.

Scoring: Add the number of points for each group and subgroup. The range of points is 0 to 15. List the groups with the highest scores and focus your exploration in those groups of the *Occupational Outlook Handbook* (OOH). Look at the table of contents in the front of the OOH to find the page numbers of your highest groups.

Highest Occupational Clusters in the OOH   Page Numbers in OOH

1. _____   _____

2. _____   _____

3. _____   _____

4. _____   _____

5. _____   _____

List the occupational prospects you generate from your exploration in the *Occupational Outlook Handbook*. The OOH can also be accessed online at www.bls.gov/oco.

_____   _____

_____   _____

_____   _____

_____   _____

_____   _____

_____   _____

_____   _____

_____   _____

The National Occupational Classification (NOC) of Canada

Check-mark any occupation in which you are interested, in the spaces provided.

Find an occupational description by entering its four-digit NOC code.
(Internet address: www23.hrdc-drhc.gc.ca/2001/e/groups/index.shtml)

Occupational Descriptions

0   MANAGEMENT OCCUPATIONS

1   BUSINESS, FINANCE, AND ADMINISTRATION OCCUPATIONS

2   NATURAL AND APPLIED SCIENCES AND RELATED OCCUPATIONS

3   HEALTH OCCUPATIONS

4   OCCUPATIONS IN SOCIAL SCIENCE, EDUCATION, GOVERNMENT SERVICE, AND RELIGION

5   OCCUPATIONS IN ART, CULTURE, RECREATION, AND SPORT

6   SALES AND SERVICE OCCUPATIONS

7   TRADES, TRANSPORT AND EQUIPMENT OPERATORS, AND RELATED OCCUPATIONS

8   OCCUPATIONS UNIQUE TO PRIMARY INDUSTRY

9   OCCUPATIONS UNIQUE TO PROCESSING, MANUFACTURING, AND UTILITIES

MANAGEMENT OCCUPATIONS

Major Group 00
Senior Management Occupations

001 Legislators and Senior Management

____ 0011 Legislators
____ 0012 Senior Government Managers and Officials
____ 0013 Senior Managers—Financial, Communications, and Other Business
____ 0014 Senior Managers—Health, Education, Social, and Community
____ 0015 Senior Managers—Trade, Broadcasting, and Other Services, n.e.c.*
____ 0016 Senior Managers—Goods Production, Utilities, Transportation, and Construction

Major Group 01-09
Middle and Other Management Occupations

011 Administrative Services Managers

____ 0111 Financial Managers
____ 0112 Human Resources Managers
____ 0113 Purchasing Managers
____ 0114 Other Administrative Services Managers

*n.e.c. indicates "Not Elsewhere Classified."

012 Managers in Financial and Business Services

___ 0121 Insurance, Real Estate, and Financial Brokerage Managers

___ 0122 Banking, Credit, and Other Investment Managers

___ 0123 Other Business Services Managers

013 Managers in Communication (except Broadcasting)

___ 0131 Telecommunication Carriers Managers

___ 0132 Postal and Courier Services Managers

021 Managers in Engineering, Architecture, Science and Information Systems

___ 0211 Engineering Managers

___ 0212 Architecture and Science Managers

___ 0213 Computer and Information Systems Managers

031 Managers in Health, Education, Social and Community Services

___ 0311 Managers in Health Care

___ 0312 Administrators—Postsecondary Education and Vocational

___ 0313 School Principals and Administrators of Elementary and Secondary

___ 0314 Managers in Social, Community, and Correctional Services

041 Managers in Public Administration

___ 0411 Government Managers—Health and Social Policy Development and Program Administration

___ 0412 Government Managers—Economic Analysis, Policy Development

___ 0413 Government Managers—Education Policy Development and Program Administration

___ 0414 Other Managers in Public Administration

051 Managers in Art, Culture, Recreation, and Sport

___ 0511 Library, Archive, Museum, and Art Gallery Managers

___ 0512 Managers—Publishing, Motion Pictures, Broadcasting, and Performing Arts

___ 0513 Recreation and Sports Program and Service Directors

061 Sales, Marketing, and Advertising Managers

___ 0611 Sales, Marketing, and Advertising Managers

062 Managers in Retail Trade

___ 0621 Retail Trade Managers

063 Managers in Food Service and Accommodation

___ 0631 Restaurant and Food Service Managers

___ 0632 Accommodation Service Managers

064 Managers in Protective Service

___ 0641 Commissioned Police Officers

___ 0642 Fire Chiefs and Senior Firefighting Officers

___ 0643 Commissioned Officers, Armed Forces

065 Managers in Other Services

___ 0651 Other Services Managers

071 Managers in Construction and Transportation

___ 0711 Construction Managers

___ 0712 Residential Home Builders and Renovators

___ 0713 Transportation Managers

072 Facility Operation and Maintenance Managers

___ 0721 Facility Operation and Maintenance Managers

081 Managers in Primary Production (except Agriculture)

___ 0811 Primary Production Managers (except Agriculture)

091 Managers in Manufacturing and Utilities

___ 0911 Manufacturing Managers

___ 0912 Utilities Managers

BUSINESS, FINANCE, AND ADMINISTRATION OCCUPATIONS

Major Group 11
Professional Occupations in Business and Finance

111 Auditors, Accountants, and Investment Professionals

___ 1111 Financial Auditors and Accountants

___ 1112 Financial and Investment Analysts

___ 1113 Securities Agents, Investment Dealers, and Brokers

___ 1114 Other Financial Officers

112 Human Resources and Business Service Professionals

___ 1121 Specialists in Human Resources

___ 1122 Professional Occupations in Business Services to Management

*n.e.c. indicates "Not Elsewhere Classified."

Major Group 12
Skilled Administrative and Business Occupations

121 Clerical Supervisors

____ 1211 Supervisors, General Office and Administrative Support Clerks
____ 1212 Supervisors, Finance and Insurance Clerks
____ 1213 Supervisors, Library, Correspondence, and Related Information Clerks
____ 1214 Supervisors, Mail and Message Distribution Occupations
____ 1215 Supervisors, Recording, Distributing, and Scheduling Occupations

122 Administrative and Regulatory Occupations

____ 1221 Administrative Officers
____ 1222 Executive Assistants
____ 1223 Personnel and Recruitment Officers
____ 1224 Property Administrators
____ 1225 Purchasing Agents and Officers
____ 1226 Conference and Event Planners
____ 1227 Court Officers and Justices of the Peace
____ 1228 Immigration, Employment Insurance, and Revenue Officers

123 Finance and Insurance Administrative Occupations

____ 1231 Bookkeepers
____ 1232 Loan Officers
____ 1233 Insurance Adjusters and Claims Examiners
____ 1234 Insurance Underwriters
____ 1235 Assessors, Valuators, and Appraisers
____ 1236 Customs, Ship, and Other Brokers

124 Secretaries, Recorders and Transcriptionists

____ 1241 Secretaries (except Legal and Medical)
____ 1242 Legal Secretaries
____ 1243 Medical Secretaries
____ 1244 Court Recorders and Medical Transcriptionists

Major Group 14
Clerical Occupations

141 Clerical Occupations, General Office Skills

____ 1411 General Office Clerks
____ 1413 Records Management and Filing Clerks
____ 1414 Receptionists and Switchboard Operators

142 Office Equipment Operators

____ 1422 Data Entry Clerks
____ 1423 Desktop Publishing Operators and Related Occupations
____ 1424 Telephone Operators

143 Finance and Insurance Clerks

____ 1431 Accounting and Related Clerks
____ 1432 Payroll Clerks
____ 1433 Customer Service Representatives— Financial Services
____ 1434 Banking, Insurance, and Other Financial Clerks
____ 1435 Collectors

144 Administrative Support Clerks

____ 1441 Administrative Clerks
____ 1442 Personnel Clerks
____ 1443 Court Clerks

145 Library, Correspondence, and Related Information Clerks

____ 1451 Library Clerks
____ 1452 Correspondence, Publication, and Related Clerks
____ 1453 Customer Service, Information, and Related Clerks
____ 1454 Survey Interviewers and Statistical Clerks

146 Mail and Message Distribution Occupations

____ 1461 Mail, Postal, and Related Clerks
____ 1462 Letter Carriers
____ 1463 Couriers, Messengers, and Door-to-Door Distributors

147 Recording, Scheduling, and Distributing Occupations

____ 1471 Shippers and Receivers
____ 1472 Storekeepers and Parts Clerks
____ 1473 Production Clerks
____ 1474 Purchasing and Inventory Clerks
____ 1475 Dispatchers and Radio Operators
____ 1476 Transportation Route and Crew Schedulers

NATURAL AND APPLIED SCIENCES AND RELATED OCCUPATIONS

Major Group 21
Professional Occupations in Natural and Applied Sciences

211 Physical Science Professionals

____ 2111 Physicists and Astronomers
____ 2112 Chemists
____ 2113 Geologists, Geochemists, and Geophysicists
____ 2114 Meteorologists
____ 2115 Other Professional Occupations in Physical Sciences

*n.e.c. indicates "Not Elsewhere Classified."

212 Life Science Professionals

____ 2121 Biologists and Related Scientists
____ 2122 Forestry Professionals
____ 2123 Agricultural Representatives, Consultants, and Specialists

213 Civil, Mechanical, Electrical, and Chemical Engineers

____ 2131 Civil Engineers
____ 2132 Mechanical Engineers
____ 2133 Electrical and Electronics Engineers
____ 2134 Chemical Engineers

214 Other Engineers

____ 2141 Industrial and Manufacturing Engineers
____ 2142 Metallurgical and Materials Engineers
____ 2143 Mining Engineers
____ 2144 Geological Engineers
____ 2145 Petroleum Engineers
____ 2146 Aerospace Engineers
____ 2147 Computer Engineers (except Software Engineers)
____ 2148 Other Professional Engineers, n.e.c.*

215 Architects, Urban Planners, and Land Surveyors

____ 2151 Architects
____ 2152 Landscape Architects
____ 2153 Urban and Land Use Planners
____ 2154 Land Surveyors

216 Mathematicians, Statisticians, and Actuaries

____ 2161 Mathematicians, Statisticians, and Actuaries

217 Computer and Information Systems Professionals

____ 2171 Information Systems Analysts and Consultants
____ 2172 Database Analysts and Data Administrators
____ 2173 Software Engineers
____ 2174 Computer Programmers and Interactive Media Developers
____ 2175 Web Designers and Developers

Major Group 22
Technical Occupations Related to Natural and Applied Sciences

221 Technical Occupations in Physical Sciences

____ 2211 Chemical Technologists and Technicians
____ 2212 Geological and Mineral Technologists and Technicians
____ 2213 Meteorological Technicians

222 Technical Occupations in Life Sciences

____ 2221 Biological Technologists and Technicians
____ 2222 Agricultural and Fish Products Inspectors
____ 2223 Forestry Technologists and Technicians
____ 2224 Conservation and Fishery Officers
____ 2225 Landscape and Horticultural Technicians and Specialists

223 Technical Occupations in Civil, Mechanical, and Industrial Engineering

____ 2231 Civil Engineering Technologists and Technicians
____ 2232 Mechanical Engineering Technologists and Technicians
____ 2233 Industrial Engineering and Manufacturing Technologists and Technicians
____ 2234 Construction Estimators

224 Technical Occupations in Electronics and Electrical Engineering

____ 2241 Electrical and Electronics Engineering Technologists and Technicians
____ 2242 Electronic Service Technicians (household and business)
____ 2243 Industrial Instrument Technicians and Mechanics
____ 2244 Aircraft Instrument, Electrical and Avionics Mechanics, Technicians, and Inspectors

225 Technical Occupations in Architecture, Drafting, Surveying, and Mapping

____ 2251 Architectural Technologists and Technicians
____ 2252 Industrial Designers
____ 2253 Drafting Technologists and Technicians
____ 2254 Land Survey Technologists and Technicians
____ 2255 Mapping and Related Technologists and Technicians

226 Other Technical Inspectors and Regulatory Officers

____ 2261 Nondestructive Testers and Inspectors
____ 2262 Engineering Inspectors and Regulatory Officers
____ 2263 Inspectors in Public and Environmental Health and Occupational Health and Safety
____ 2264 Construction Inspectors

*n.e.c. indicates "Not Elsewhere Classified."

227 Transportation Officers and Controllers

____ 2271 Air Pilots, Flight Engineers, and Flying Instructors
____ 2272 Air Traffic Control and Related Occupations
____ 2273 Deck Officers, Water Transport
____ 2274 Engineer Officers, Water Transport
____ 2275 Railway Traffic Controllers and Marine Traffic Regulators

228 Technical Occupations in Computer and Information Systems

____ 2281 Computer and Network Operators and Web Technicians
____ 2282 User Support Technicians
____ 2283 Systems Testing Technicians

HEALTH OCCUPATIONS

Major Group 31
Professional Occupations in Health

311 Physicians, Dentists, and Veterinarians

____ 3112 General Practitioners and Family Physicians
____ 3113 Dentists
____ 3114 Veterinarians

312 Optometrists, Chiropractors, and Other Health Diagnosing and Treating Professionals

____ 3121 Optometrists
____ 3122 Chiropractors
____ 3123 Other Professional Occupations in Health Diagnosing and Treating

313 Pharmacists, Dietitians, and Nutritionists

____ 3131 Pharmacists
____ 3132 Dietitians and Nutritionists

314 Therapy and Assessment Professionals

____ 3141 Audiologists and Speech-Language Pathologists
____ 3142 Physiotherapists
____ 3143 Occupational Therapists
____ 3144 Other Professional Occupations in Therapy and Assessment

315 Nurse Supervisors and Registered Nurses

____ 3151 Head Nurses and Supervisors
____ 3152 Registered Nurses

Major Group 32
Technical and Skilled Occupations in Health

321 Medical Technologists and Technicians (except Dental Health)

____ 3211 Medical Laboratory Technologists and Pathologists' Assistants
____ 3212 Medical Laboratory Technicians
____ 3213 Veterinary and Animal Health Technologists
____ 3214 Respiratory Therapists, Clinical Perfusionists, and Cardiopulmonary Technologists
____ 3215 Medical Radiation Technologists
____ 3216 Medical Sonographers
____ 3217 Cardiology Technologists
____ 3218 Electroencephalographic and Other Diagnostic Technologists, n.e.c.
____ 3219 Other Medical Technologists and Technicians (except Dental Health)

322 Technical Occupations in Dental Health Care

____ 3221 Denturists
____ 3222 Dental Hygienists and Dental Therapists
____ 3223 Dental Technologists, Technicians, and Laboratory

323 Other Technical Occupations in Health Care (except Dental)

____ 3231 Opticians
____ 3232 Midwives and Practitioners of Natural Healing
____ 3233 Licensed Practical Nurses
____ 3234 Ambulance Attendants and Other Paramedical Occupations
____ 3235 Other Technical Occupations in Therapy and Assessment

Major Group 34
Assisting Occupations in Support of Health Services

341 Assisting Occupations in Support of Health Services

____ 3411 Dental Assistants
____ 3413 Nurse Aides, Orderlies, and Patient Service Associates
____ 3414 Other Assisting Occupations in Support of Health Services

*n.e.c. indicates "Not Elsewhere Classified."

OCCUPATIONS IN SOCIAL SCIENCE, EDUCATION, GOVERNMENT SERVICE, AND RELIGION

Major Group 41
Professional Occupations in Social Science, Education, Government Services, and Religion

411 Judges, Lawyers, and Quebec Notaries

____ 4111 Judges
____ 4112 Lawyers and Quebec Notaries

412 University Professors and Assistants

____ 4121 University Professors
____ 4122 Postsecondary Teaching and Research Assistants

413 College and Other Vocational Instructors

____ 4131 College and Other Vocational Instructors

414 Secondary and Elementary School Teachers and Educational Counsellors

____ 4141 Secondary School Teachers
____ 4142 Elementary School and Kindergarten Teachers
____ 4143 Educational Counsellors

415 Psychologists, Social Workers, Counsellors, Clergy, and Probation Officers

____ 4151 Psychologists
____ 4152 Social Workers
____ 4153 Family, Marriage, and Other Related Counsellors
____ 4154 Ministers of Religion
____ 4155 Probation and Parole Officers and Related Occupations

416 Policy and Program Officers, Researchers, and Consultants

____ 4161 Natural and Applied Science Policy Researchers, Consultants, and Program Officers
____ 4162 Economists and Economic Policy Researchers and Analysts
____ 4163 Business Development Officers and Marketing Researchers and Consultants
____ 4164 Social Policy Researchers, Consultants, and Program Officers
____ 4165 Health Policy Researchers, Consultants, and Program Officers
____ 4166 Education Policy Researchers, Consultants, and Program Officers
____ 4167 Recreation, Sports, and Fitness Program Supervisors, Consultants
____ 4168 Program Officers Unique to Government
____ 4169 Other Professional Occupations in Social Science, n.e.c.*

Major Group 42
Paraprofessional Occupations in Law, Social Services, Education, and Religion

421 Paralegals, Social Services Workers, and Occupations in Education and Religion, n.e.c.*

____ 4211 Paralegal and Related Occupations
____ 4212 Community and Social Service Workers
____ 4213 Employment Counsellors
____ 4214 Early Childhood Educators and Assistants
____ 4215 Instructors and Teachers of Persons with Disabilities
____ 4216 Other Instructors
____ 4217 Other Religious Occupations

OCCUPATIONS IN ART, CULTURE, RECREATION, AND SPORT

Major Group 51
Professional Occupations in Art and Culture

511 Librarians, Archivists, Conservators, and Curators

____ 5111 Librarians
____ 5112 Conservators and Curators
____ 5113 Archivists

512 Writing, Translating, and Public Relations Professionals

____ 5121 Authors and Writers
____ 5122 Editors
____ 5123 Journalists
____ 5124 Professional Occupations in Public Relations and Communications
____ 5125 Translators, Terminologists, and Interpreters

513 Creative and Performing Artists

____ 5131 Producers, Directors, Choreographers, and Related Occupations
____ 5132 Conductors, Composers, and Arrangers
____ 5133 Musicians and Singers
____ 5134 Dancers
____ 5135 Actors and Comedians
____ 5136 Painters, Sculptors, and Other Visual Artists

Major Group 52
Technical and Skilled Occupations in Art, Culture, Recreation, and Sport

521 Technical Occupations in Libraries, Archives, Museums, and Art Galleries

____ 5211 Library and Archive Technicians and Assistants
____ 5212 Technical Occupations Related to Museums and Art Galleries

*n.e.c. indicates "Not Elsewhere Classified."

522 Photographers, Graphic Arts Technicians, and Technical and Coordinating Occupations in Motion Pictures, Broadcasting, and the Performing Arts

____ 5221 Photographers
____ 5222 Film and Video Camera Operators
____ 5223 Graphic Arts Technicians
____ 5224 Broadcast Technicians
____ 5225 Audio and Video Recording Technicians
____ 5226 Other Technical and Coordinating Occupations in Motion Pictures, Broadcasting
____ 5227 Support Occupations in Motion Pictures, Broadcasting, and the Performing Arts

523 Announcers and Other Performers

____ 5231 Announcers and Other Broadcasters
____ 5232 Other Performers

524 Creative Designers and Craftspeople

____ 5241 Graphic Designers and Illustrators
____ 5242 Interior Designers
____ 5243 Theatre, Fashion, Exhibit, and Other Creative Designers
____ 5244 Artisans and Craftpeople
____ 5245 Patternmakers—Textile, Leather, and Fur Products

525 Athletes, Coaches, Referees, and Related Occupations

____ 5251 Athletes
____ 5252 Coaches
____ 5253 Sports Officials and Referees
____ 5254 Program Leaders and Instructors in Recreation and Sport

SALES AND SERVICE OCCUPATIONS

Major Group 62
Skilled Sales and Service Occupations

621 Sales and Service Supervisors

____ 6211 Retail Trade Supervisors
____ 6212 Food Service Supervisors
____ 6213 Executive Housekeepers
____ 6214 Dry Cleaning and Laundry Supervisors
____ 6215 Cleaning Supervisors
____ 6216 Other Service Supervisors

622 Technical Sales Specialists, Wholesale Trade

____ 6221 Technical Sales Specialists—Wholesale Trade

623 Insurance and Real Estate Sales Occupations and Buyers

____ 6231 Insurance Agents and Brokers
____ 6232 Real Estate Agents and Salespeople
____ 6233 Retail and Wholesale Buyers
____ 6234 Grain Elevator Operators

624 Chefs and Cooks

____ 6241 Chefs
____ 6242 Cooks

625 Butchers and Bakers

____ 6251 Butchers and Meat Cutters—Retail and Wholesale
____ 6252 Bakers

626 Police Officers and Firefighters

____ 6261 Police Officers (except commissioned)
____ 6262 Firefighters

627 Technical Occupations in Personal Service

____ 6271 Hairstylists and Barbers
____ 6272 Funeral Directors and Embalmers

Major Group 64
Intermediate Sales and Service Occupations

641 Sales Representatives, Wholesale Trade

____ 6411 Sales Representatives—Wholesale Trade (Nontechnical)

642 Retail Salespeople and Sales Clerks

____ 6421 Retail Salespeople and Sales Clerks

643 Occupations in Travel and Accommodation

____ 6431 Travel Counsellors
____ 6432 Pursers and Flight Attendants
____ 6433 Airline Sales and Service Agents
____ 6434 Ticket Agents, Cargo Service Representatives, and Related Clerks (except airline)
____ 6435 Hotel Front Desk Clerks

644 Tour and Recreational Guides and Casino Occupations

____ 6441 Tour and Travel Guides
____ 6442 Outdoor Sport and Recreational Guides
____ 6443 Casino Occupations

645 Occupations in Food and Beverage Service

____ 6451 Maîtres d'hôtel and Hosts/Hostesses
____ 6452 Bartenders
____ 6453 Food and Beverage Servers

*n.e.c. indicates "Not Elsewhere Classified."

646 Other Occupations in Protective Service

____ 6461 Sheriffs and Bailiffs
____ 6462 Correctional Service Officers
____ 6463 By-law Enforcement and Other Regulatory Officers, n.e.c.*
____ 6464 Occupations Unique to the Armed Forces
____ 6465 Other Protective Service Occupations

647 Childcare and Home Support Workers

____ 6471 Visiting Homemakers, Housekeepers, and Related Occupations
____ 6472 Elementary and Secondary School Teacher Assistants
____ 6474 Babysitters, Nannies, and Parents' Helpers

648 Other Occupations in Personal Service

____ 6481 Image, Social, and Other Personal Consultants
____ 6482 Estheticians, Electrologists, and Related Occupations
____ 6483 Pet Groomers and Animal Care Workers
____ 6484 Other Personal Service Occupations

Major Group 66
Elemental Sales and Service Occupations

661 Cashiers

____ 6611 Cashiers

662 Other Sales and Related Occupations

____ 6621 Service Station Attendants
____ 6622 Grocery Clerks and Store Shelf Stockers
____ 6623 Other Elemental Sales Occupations

664 Food Counter Attendants, Kitchen Helpers, and Related Occupations

____ 6641 Food Counter Attendants, Kitchen Helpers, and Related

665 Security Guards and Related Occupations

____ 6651 Security Guards and Related Occupations

666 Cleaners

____ 6661 Light-Duty Cleaners
____ 6662 Specialized Cleaners
____ 6663 Janitors, Caretakers, and Building Superintendents

667 Other Occupations in Travel, Accommodation, Amusement, and Recreation

____ 6671 Operators and Attendants in Amusement, Recreation, and Sport
____ 6672 Other Attendants in Accommodation and Travel

668 Other Elemental Service Occupations

____ 6681 Dry Cleaning and Laundry Occupations
____ 6682 Ironing, Pressing, and Finishing Occupations
____ 6683 Other Elemental Service Occupations

TRADES, TRANSPORT AND EQUIPMENT OPERATORS AND RELATED OCCUPATIONS

Major Group 72–73
Trades and Skilled Transport and Equipment Operators

721 Contractors and Supervisors, Trades and Related Workers

____ 7211 Supervisors, Machinists, and Related Occupations
____ 7212 Contractors and Supervisors, Electrical Trades and Telecommunications
____ 7213 Contractors and Supervisors, Pipefitting Trades
____ 7214 Contractors and Supervisors, Metal Forming, Shaping, and Erecting Trades
____ 7215 Contractors and Supervisors, Carpentry Trades
____ 7216 Contractors and Supervisors, Mechanic Trades
____ 7217 Contractors and Supervisors, Heavy Construction Equipment Crews
____ 7218 Supervisors, Printing and Related Occupations
____ 7219 Contractors and Supervisors, Other Construction Trades, Installers, Repairers

722 Supervisors, Railway and Motor Transportation Occupations

____ 7221 Supervisors, Railway Transport Operations
____ 7222 Supervisors, Motor Transport and Other Ground Transit Operators

723 Machinists and Related Occupations

____ 7231 Machinists and Machining and Tooling Inspectors
____ 7232 Tool and Die Makers

724 Electrical Trades and Telecommunication Occupations

____ 7241 Electricians (except Industrial and Power System)
____ 7242 Industrial Electricians
____ 7243 Power System Electricians
____ 7244 Electrical Power Line and Cable Workers
____ 7245 Telecommunications Line and Cable Workers

*n.e.c. indicates "Not Elsewhere Classified."

____ 7246 Telecommunications Installation and Repair Workers
____ 7247 Cable Television Service and Maintenance Technicians

725 Plumbers, Pipefitters, and Gas Fitters

____ 7251 Plumbers
____ 7252 Steamfitters, Pipefitters, and Sprinkler System Installers
____ 7253 Gas Fitters

726 Metal Forming, Shaping, and Erecting Trades

____ 7261 Sheet Metal Workers
____ 7262 Boilermakers
____ 7263 Structural Metal and Platework Fabricators and Fitters
____ 7264 Ironworkers
____ 7265 Welders and Related Machine Operators
____ 7266 Blacksmiths and Die Setters

727 Carpenters and Cabinetmakers

____ 7271 Carpenters
____ 7272 Cabinetmakers

728 Masonry and Plastering Trades

____ 7281 Bricklayers
____ 7283 Tilesetters
____ 7284 Plasterers, Drywall Installers, and Finishers and Lathers

729 Other Construction Trades

____ 7291 Roofers and Shinglers
____ 7292 Glaziers
____ 7293 Insulators
____ 7294 Painters and Decorators
____ 7295 Floor Covering Installers

731 Machinery and Transportation Equipment Mechanics (except Motor Vehicle)

____ 7311 Construction Millwrights and Industrial Mechanics (except Textile)
____ 7312 Heavy-Duty Equipment Mechanics
____ 7313 Refrigeration and Air-Conditioning Mechanics
____ 7314 Railway Car Operators
____ 7315 Aircraft Mechanics and Aircraft Inspectors
____ 7316 Machine Fitters
____ 7317 Textile Machinery Mechanics and Repairers
____ 7318 Elevator Constructors and Mechanics

732 Automotive Service Technicians

____ 7321 Automotive Service Technicians, Truck Mechanics, and Mechanical Repairers
____ 7322 Motor Vehicle Body Repairers

733 Other Mechanics

____ 7331 Oil and Solid Fuel Heating Mechanics
____ 7332 Electric Appliance Servicers and Repairers
____ 7333 Electrical Mechanics
____ 7334 Motorcycle and Other Related Mechanics
____ 7335 Other Small Engine and Equipment Mechanics

734 Upholsterers, Tailors, Shoe Repairers, Jewellers, and Related Occupations

____ 7341 Upholsterers
____ 7342 Tailors, Dressmakers, Furriers, and Milliners
____ 7343 Shoe Repairers and Shoemakers
____ 7344 Jewellers, Watch Repairers, and Related Occupations

735 Stationary Engineers and Power Station and System Operators

____ 7351 Stationary Engineers and Auxiliary Equipment Operators
____ 7352 Power Systems and Power Station Operators

736 Train Crew Operating Occupations

____ 7361 Railway and Yard Locomotive Engineers
____ 7362 Railway Conductors and Brakemen/women

737 Crane Operators, Drillers, and Blasters

____ 7371 Crane Operators
____ 7372 Drillers and Blasters and Surface Mining, Quarrying, and Construction
____ 7373 Water Well Drillers

738 Printing Press Operators, Commercial Divers, and Other Trades and Related Occupations, n.e.c.*

____ 7381 Printing Press Operators
____ 7382 Commercial Divers
____ 7383 Other Trades and Related Occupations

Major Group 74
Intermediate Occupations in Transport, Equipment Operation, Installation, and Maintenance

741 Motor Vehicle and Transit Drivers

____ 7411 Truck Drivers
____ 7412 Bus Drivers and Subway and Other Transit Operators
____ 7413 Taxi and Limousine Drivers and Chauffeurs
____ 7414 Delivery and Courier Service Drivers

*n.e.c. indicates "Not Elsewhere Classified."

742 Heavy Equipment Operators

____ 7421 Heavy Equipment Operators (except Crane)
____ 7422 Public Works Maintenance Equipment Operators

743 Other Transport Equipment Operators and Related Workers

____ 7431 Railway Yard Workers
____ 7432 Railway Track Maintenance Workers
____ 7433 Deck Crew, Water Transport
____ 7434 Engine Room Crew, Water Transport
____ 7435 Lock and Cable Ferry Operators and Related Occupations
____ 7436 Boat Operators
____ 7437 Air Transport Ramp Attendants

744 Other Installers, Repairers, and Servicers

____ 7441 Residential and Commercial Installers and Servicers
____ 7442 Waterworks and Gas Maintenance Workers
____ 7443 Automotive Mechanical Installers and Servicers
____ 7444 Pest Controllers and Fumigators
____ 7445 Other Repairers and Servicers

745 Longshore Workers and Material Handlers

____ 7451 Longshore Workers
____ 7452 Material Handlers

Major Group 76
Trades Helpers, Construction Labourers, and Related Occupations

761 Trades Helpers and Labourers

____ 7611 Construction Trades Helpers and Labourers
____ 7612 Other Trades Helpers and Labourers

762 Public Works and Other Labourers, n.e.c.*

____ 7621 Public Works and Maintenance Labourers
____ 7622 Railway and Motor Transport Labourers

OCCUPATIONS UNIQUE TO PRIMARY INDUSTRY

Major Group 82
Skilled Occupations in Primary Industry

821 Supervisors, Logging and Forestry

____ 8211 Supervisors, Logging and Forestry

822 Supervisors, Mining, Oil, and Gas

____ 8221 Supervisors, Mining and Quarrying
____ 8222 Supervisors, Oil and Gas Drilling and Service

823 Underground Miners, Oil and Gas Drillers, and Related Workers

____ 8231 Underground Production and Development Miners
____ 8232 Oil and Gas Well Drillers, Servicers, Testers, and Related Workers

824 Logging Machinery Operators

____ 8241 Logging Machinery Operators

825 Contractors, Operators, and Supervisors in Agriculture, Horticulture, and Aquaculture

____ 8251 Farmers and Farm Managers
____ 8252 Agricultural and Related Service Contractors and Managers
____ 8253 Farm Supervisors and Specialized Livestock Workers
____ 8254 Nursery and Greenhouse Operators and Managers
____ 8255 Landscaping and Grounds Maintenance Contractors and Managers
____ 8256 Supervisors, Landscape and Horticulture
____ 8257 Aquaculture Operators and Managers

826 Fishing Vessel Masters and Skippers and Fishermen/women

____ 8261 Fishing Masters and Officers
____ 8262 Fishing Vessel Skippers and Fishermen/women

Major Group 84
Intermediate Occupations in Primary Industry

841 Mine Service Workers and Operators in Oil and Gas Drilling

____ 8411 Underground Mine Service and Support Workers
____ 8412 Oil and Gas Well Drilling Workers and Services Operators

842 Logging and Forestry Workers

____ 8421 Chainsaw and Skidder Operators
____ 8422 Silviculture and Forestry Workers

843 Agriculture and Horticulture Workers

____ 8431 General Farm Workers
____ 8432 Nursery and Greenhouse Workers

844 Other Fishing and Trapping Occupations

____ 8441 Fishing Vessel Deckhands
____ 8442 Trappers and Hunters

*n.e.c. indicates "Not Elsewhere Classified."

Major Group 86
Labourers in Primary Industry

861 Primary Production Labourers

8611 Harvesting Labourers
8612 Landscaping and Grounds Maintenance Labourers
8613 Aquaculture and Marine Harvest Labourers
8614 Mine Labourers
8615 Oil and Gas Drilling, Servicing and Related Labourers
8616 Logging and Forestry Labourers

OCCUPATIONS UNIQUE TO PROCESSING, MANUFACTURING, AND UTILITIES

Major Group 92
Processing, Manufacturing, and Utilities Supervisors and Skilled Operators

921 Supervisors, Processing Occupations

____ 9211 Supervisors, Mineral and Metal Processing
____ 9212 Supervisors, Petroleum, Gas, and Chemical Processing and Utilities
____ 9213 Supervisors, Food, Beverage, and Tobacco Processing
____ 9214 Supervisors, Plastic and Rubber Products Manufacturing
____ 9215 Supervisors, Forest Products Processing
____ 9216 Supervisors, Textile Processing

922 Supervisors, Assembly and Fabrication

____ 9221 Supervisors, Motor Vehicle Assembling
____ 9222 Supervisors, Electronics Manufacturing
____ 9223 Supervisors, Electrical Products Manufacturing
____ 9224 Supervisors, Furniture and Fixtures Manufacturing
____ 9225 Supervisors, Fabric, Fur, and Leather Products Manufacturing
____ 9226 Supervisors, Other Mechanical and Metal Products Manufacturing
____ 9227 Supervisors, Other Products Manufacturing and Assembly

923 Central Control and Process Operators in Manufacturing and Processing

____ 9231 Central Control and Process Operators, Mineral and Metal Processing
____ 9232 Petroleum, Gas, and Chemical Process Operators
____ 9233 Pulping Control Operators

Major Group 94–95
Processing and Manufacturing Machine Operators and Assemblers

941 Machine Operators and Related Workers in Metal and Mineral Products Processing

____ 9411 Machine Operators, Mineral and Metal Processing
____ 9412 Foundry Workers
____ 9413 Glass Forming and Finishing Machine Operators and Glass Cutters
____ 9414 Concrete, Clay, and Stone Forming Operators
____ 9415 Inspectors and Testers, Mineral and Metal Processing

942 Machine Operators and Related Workers in Chemical, Plastic, and Rubber Processing

____ 9421 Chemical Plant Machine Operators
____ 9422 Plastics Processing Machine Operators
____ 9423 Rubber Processing Machine Operators and Related Workers
____ 9424 Water and Waste Plant Operators

943 Machine Operators and Related Workers in Pulp and Paper Production and Wood Processing

____ 9431 Sawmill Machine Operators
____ 9432 Pulp Mill Machine Operators
____ 9433 Papermaking and Finishing Machine Operators
____ 9434 Other Wood Processing Machine Operators
____ 9435 Paper Converting Machine Operators
____ 9436 Lumber Graders and Other Wood Processing Inspectors and Graders

944 Machine Operators and Related Workers in Textile Processing

____ 9441 Textile Fibre and Yarn Preparation Machine Operators
____ 9442 Weavers, Knitters and Other Fabric-Making Occupations
____ 9443 Textile Dyeing and Finishing Machine Operators
____ 9444 Textile Inspectors, Graders, and Samplers

945 Machine Operators and Related Workers in Fabric, Fur, and Leather Products Manufacturing

____ 9451 Sewing Machine Operators
____ 9452 Fabric, Fur, and Leather Cutters
____ 9453 Hide and Pelt Processing Workers
____ 9454 Inspectors and Testers, Fabric, Fur, and Leather Products Manufacturing

*n.e.c. indicates "Not Elsewhere Classified."

946 Machine Operators and Related Workers in Food, Beverage, and Tobacco Processing

____ 9461 Process Control and Machine Operators, Food and Beverage Processing
____ 9462 Industrial Butchers and Meat Cutters, Poultry Preparers, and Related Workers
____ 9463 Fish Plant Workers
____ 9464 Tobacco Processing Machine Operators
____ 9465 Testers and Graders, Food and Beverage Processing

947 Printing Machine Operators and Related Occupations

____ 9471 Printing Machine Operators
____ 9472 Camera, Platemaking, and Other Pre-press Occupations
____ 9473 Binding and Finishing Machine Operators
____ 9474 Photographic and Film Processors

948 Mechanical, Electrical, and Electronics Assemblers

____ 9481 Aircraft Assemblers and Aircraft Assembly Inspectors
____ 9482 Motor Vehicle Assemblers, Inspectors, and Testers
____ 9483 Electronics Assemblers, Fabricators, Inspectors, and Testers
____ 9484 Assemblers and Inspectors, Electrical Appliance, Apparatus, and Equipment Manufacturing
____ 9485 Assemblers, Fabricators, and Inspectors, Industrial Electrical Motors and Transformers
____ 9486 Mechanical Assemblers and Inspectors
____ 9487 Machine Operators and Inspectors, Electrical Apparatus Manufacturing

949 Other Assembly and Related Occupations

____ 9491 Boat Assemblers and Inspectors
____ 9492 Furniture and Fixture Assemblers and Inspectors
____ 9493 Other Wood Products Assemblers and Inspectors
____ 9494 Furniture Finishers and Refinishers
____ 9495 Plastic Products Assemblers, Finishers and Inspectors
____ 9496 Painters and Coaters—Industrial
____ 9497 Plating, Metal Spraying, and Related Operators
____ 9498 Other Assemblers and Inspectors

951 Machining, Metalworking, Woodworking, and Related Machine Operators

____ 9511 Machining Tool Operators
____ 9512 Forging Machine Operators
____ 9513 Woodworking Machine Operators
____ 9514 Metalworking Machine Operators
____ 9516 Other Metal Products Machine Operators
____ 9517 Other Products Machine Operators

Major Group 96
Labourers in Processing, Manufacturing, and Utilities

961 Labourers in Processing, Manufacturing, and Utilities

____ 9611 Labourers in Mineral and Metal Processing
____ 9612 Labourers in Metal Fabrication
____ 9613 Labourers in Chemical Products Processing and Utilities
____ 9614 Labourers in Wood, Pulp, and Paper Processing
____ 9615 Labourers in Rubber and Plastic Products Manufacturing
____ 9616 Labourers in Textile Processing
____ 9617 Labourers in Food, Beverage, and Tobacco Processing
____ 9618 Labourers in Fish Processing
____ 9619 Other Labourers in Processing, Manufacturing, and Utilities

*n.e.c. indicates "Not Elsewhere Classified."

Dictionary of Occupational Titles (DOT)

Directions

1. Circle the three-digit groups of greatest interest to you.
2. Locate these groups in the DOT, and consider specific occupations described within each group.
3. At the end of this exercise, list the specific occupations you want to explore.

PROFESSIONAL, TECHNICAL, AND MANAGERIAL OCCUPATIONS

00/01 Occupations in architecture, engineering, and surveying
001 Architectural occupations
002 Aeronautical engineering occupations
003 Electrical/electronics engineering occupations
005 Civil engineering occupations
006 Ceramic engineering occupations
007 Mechanical engineering occupations
008 Chemical engineering occupations
010 Mining and petroleum engineering occupations
011 Metallurgy and metallurgical engineering occupations
012 Industrial engineering occupations
013 Agricultural engineering occupations
014 Marine engineering occupations
015 Nuclear engineering occupations
017 Drafters, n.e.c.
018 Surveying/cartographic occupations
019 Occupations in architecture, engineering, and surveying, n.e.c.

02 Occupations in mathematics and physical sciences
020 Occupations in mathematics
021 Occupations in astronomy
022 Occupations in chemistry
023 Occupations in physics
024 Occupations in geology
025 Occupations in meteorology
029 Occupations in mathematics and physical sciences, n.e.c.

03 Computer-related occupations
030 Occupations in systems analysis and programming
031 Occupations in data communications and networks
032 Occupations in computer systems user support
033 Occupations in computer systems technical support
039 Computer-related occupations, n.e.c.

04 Occupations in life sciences
040 Occupations in agricultural sciences
041 Occupations in biological sciences
045 Occupations in psychology
049 Occupations in life sciences, n.e.c.

05 Occupations in social sciences
050 Occupations in economics
051 Occupations in political science
052 Occupations in history
054 Occupations in sociology
055 Occupations in anthropology
059 Occupations in social sciences, n.e.c.

Note: n.e.c. means "not elsewhere classified."

Source: U.S. Department of Labor (1991).

205	Interviewing clerks
206	File clerks
207	Duplicating-machine operators and tenders
208	Mailing and miscellaneous office machine operators
209	Stenography, typing, filing, and related occupations, n.e.c.

21   Computing and account-recording occupations

210	Bookkeepers and related occupations
211	Cashiers and tellers
213	Computer and peripheral equipment operators
214	Billing and rate clerks
215	Payroll, timekeeping, and duty-roster clerks
216	Accounting and statistical clerks
217	Account-recording-machine operators, n.e.c.
219	Computing and account-recording occupations, n.e.c.

22   Production and stock clerks and related occupations

221	Production clerks
222	Shipping, receiving, stock, and related clerical occupations
229	Production and stock clerks and related occupations, n.e.c.

23   Information and message distribution occupations

230	Hand delivery and distribution occupations
235	Telephone operators
236	Telegraph operators
237	Information and reception clerks
238	Accommodation clerks and gate and ticket agents
239	Information and message distribution occupations, n.e.c.

24   Miscellaneous clerical occupations

241	Investigators, adjusters, and related occupations
243	Government service clerks, n.e.c.
245	Medical service clerks, n.e.c.
247	Advertising-service clerks, n.e.c.
248	Transportation-service clerks, n.e.c
249	Miscellaneous clerical occupations, n.e.c.

25   Sales occupations, services

250	Sales occupations, real estate, insurance, securities and financial services
251	Sales occupations, business services, except real estate, insurance, securities, and financial services
252	Sales occupations, transportation services
253	Sales occupations, utilities
254	Sales occupations, printing and advertising
259	Sales occupations, services, n.e.c.

26   Sales occupations, consumable commodities

260	Sales occupations, agricultural and food products
261	Sales occupations, textile products, apparel, and notions
262	Sales occupations, chemicals, drugs, and sundries
269	Sales occupations, miscellaneous consumable commodities, n.e.c.

27   Sales occupations, commodities, n.e.c.

270	Sales occupations, home furniture, furnishings, and appliances
271	Sales occupations, electrical goods, except home appliances
272	Sales occupations, farm and gardening equipment and supplies
273	Sales occupations, transportation equipment, parts, and supplies
274	Sales occupations, industrial and related equipment and supplies
275	Sales occupations, business and commercial equipment and supplies
276	Sales occupations, medical and scientific equipment and supplies
277	Sales occupations, sporting, hobby, stationery, and related goods
279	Sales occupations, miscellaneous commodities, n.e.c.

29   Miscellaneous sales occupations

290	Sales clerks
291	Vending and door-to-door selling occupations
292	Route sales and delivery occupations
293	Solicitors
294	Auctioneers
295	Rental clerks
296	Shoppers
297	Sales promotion occupations
298	Merchandise displayers
299	Miscellaneous sales occupations, n.e.c.

SERVICE OCCUPATIONS

30   Domestic service occupations

301	Household and related work
302	Launderers, private family
305	Cooks, domestic
309	Domestic service occupations, n.e.c.

31   Food and beverage preparation and service occupations

310	Hosts/hostesses and stewards/stewardesses, food and beverage service, except ship stewards/stewardesses
311	Waiters/waitresses, and related food service occupations
312	Bartenders
313	Chefs and cooks, hotels and restaurants

315   Miscellaneous cooks, except domestic
316   Meatcutters, except in slaughtering and packing houses
317   Miscellaneous food and beverage preparation occupations
318   Kitchen workers, n.e.c.
319   Food and beverage preparation and service occupations, n.e.c.

32   Lodging and related service occupations
320   Boarding-house and lodging-house keepers
321   Housekeepers, hotels and institutions
323   Housecleaners, hotels, restaurants, and related establishments
324   Bellhops and related occupations
329   Lodging and related service occupations, n.e.c.

33   Barbering, cosmetology, and related service occupations
330   Barbers
331   Manicurists
332   Hairdressers and cosmetologists
333   Make-up occupations
334   Masseurs and related occupations
335   Bath attendants
338   Embalmers and related occupations
339   Barbering, cosmetology, and related service occupations, n.e.c.

34   Amusement and recreation service occupations
340   Attendants, bowling alley and billiard parlor
341   Attendants, golf course, tennis court, skating rink, and related facilities
342   Amusement device and concession attendants
343   Gambling hall attendants
344   Ushers
346   Wardrobe and dressing-room attendants
349   Amusement and recreation service occupations, n.e.c.

35   Miscellaneous personal service occupations
350   Ship stewards/stewardesses and related occupations
351   Train attendants
352   Hosts/hostesses and stewards/stewardesses, n.e.c.
353   Guides
354   Unlicensed birth attendants and practical nurses
355   Attendants, hospitals, morgues, and related health services
357   Baggage handlers
358   Checkroom, locker room, and rest room attendants
359   Miscellaneous personal service occupations, n.e.c.

36   Apparel and furnishings service occupations
361   Laundering occupations
362   Dry cleaning occupations
363   Pressing occupations
364   Dyeing and related occupations
365   Shoe and luggage repairer and related occupations
366   Bootblacks and related occupations
369   Apparel and furnishings service occupations, n.e.c.

37   Protective service occupations
371   Crossing tenders and bridge operators
372   Security guards and correction officers, except crossing tenders
373   Fire fighters, fire department
375   Police officers and detectives, public service
376   Police officers and detectives, except in public service
377   Sheriffs and bailiffs
378   Armed forces enlisted personnel
379   Protective service occupations, n.e.c.

38   Building and related service occupations
381   Porters and cleaners
382   Janitors
383   Building pest control service occupations
388   Elevator operators
389   Building and related service occupations, n.e.c.

AGRICULTURAL, FISHERY, FORESTRY, AND RELATED OCCUPATIONS

40   Plant farming occupations
401   Grain farming occupations
402   Vegetable farming occupations
403   Fruit and nut farming occupations
404   Field crop farming occupations, n.e.c.
405   Horticultural specialty occupations
406   Gardening and groundskeeping occupations
407   Diversified crop farming occupations
408   Plant life and related service occupations
409   Plant farming and related occupations, n.e.c.

41   Animal farming occupations
410   Domestic animal farming occupations
411   Domestic fowl farming occupations
412   Game farming occupations
413   Lower animal farming occupations
418   Animal service occupations
419   Animal farming occupations, n.e.c.

42   Miscellaneous agricultural and related occupations
421   General farming occupations
429   Miscellaneous agricultural and related occupations, n.e.c.

44	**Fishery and related occupations**	525	Slaughtering, breaking, curing, and related occupations
441	Net, seine, and trap fishers	526	Cooking and baking occupations, n.e.c.
442	Line fishers	529	Occupations in processing of food, tobacco, and related products, n.e.c.
443	Fishers, miscellaneous equipment		
446	Aquatic life cultivation and related occupations	**53**	**Occupations in processing of paper and related materials**
447	Sponge and seaweed gatherers	530	Grinding, beating, and mixing occupations
449	Fishery and related occupations, n.e.c.	532	Cooking and drying occupations
		533	Cooling, bleaching, screening, washing, and related occupations
45	**Forestry occupations**		
451	Tree farming and related occupations	534	Calendering, sizing, coating, and related occupations
452	Forest conservation occupations	535	Forming occupations, n.e.c.
453	Occupations in harvesting forest products, except logging	539	Occupations in processing of paper and related materials, n.e.c.
454	Logging and related occupations		
455	Log grading, scaling, sorting, rafting, and related occupations	**54**	**Occupations in processing of petroleum, coal, natural and manufactured gas, and related products**
459	Forestry occupations, n.e.c.		
		540	Mixing and blending occupations
46	**Hunting, trapping, and related occupations**	541	Filtering, straining, and separating occupations
461	Hunting and trapping occupations	542	Distilling, subliming, and carbonizing occupations

PROCESSING OCCUPATIONS

		543	Drying, heating, and melting occupations
50	**Occupations in processing of metal**	544	Grinding and crushing occupations
500	Electroplating occupations	546	Reacting occupations, n.e.c.
501	Dip plating occupations	549	Occupations in processing of petroleum, coal, natural and manufactured gas, and related products, n.e.c.
502	Melting, pouring, casting, and related occupations		
503	Pickling, cleaning, degreasing, and related occupations		
504	Heat-treating occupations	**55**	**Occupations in processing of chemicals, plastics, synthetics, rubber, paint, and related products**
505	Metal spraying, coating, and related occupations		
509	Occupations in processing of metal, n.e.c.	550	Mixing and blending occupations
		551	Filtering, straining, and separating occupations
51	**Ore refining and foundry occupations**	552	Distilling occupations
510	Mixing and related occupations	553	Heating, baking, drying, seasoning, melting, and heat-treating occupations
511	Separating, filtering, and related occupations		
512	Melting occupations	554	Coating, calendering, laminating, and finishing occupations
513	Roasting occupations		
514	Pouring and casting occupations	555	Grinding and crushing occupations
515	Crushing and grinding occupations	556	Casting and molding occupations, n.e.c.
518	Molders, coremakers, and related occupations	557	Extruding occupations
519	Ore refining and foundry occupations, n.e.c.	558	Reacting occupations, n.e.c.
		559	Occupations in processing of chemicals, plastics, synthetics, rubber, paint, and related products, n.e.c.
52	**Occupations in processing of food, tobacco, and related products**		
520	Mixing, compounding, blending, kneading, shaping, and related occupations	**56**	**Occupations in processing of wood and wood products**
521	Separating, crushing, milling, chopping, grinding, and related occupations	560	Mixing and related occupations
522	Culturing, melting, fermenting, distilling, saturating, pickling, aging, and related occupations	561	Wood preserving and related occupations
		562	Saturating, coating, and related occupations, n.e.c.
523	Heating, rendering, melting, drying, cooling, freezing, and related occupations		
524	Coating, icing, decorating, and related occupations		

563   Drying, seasoning, and related occupations
564   Grinding and chopping occupations, n.e.c.
569   Occupations in processing of wood and wood products, n.e.c.

57   Occupations in processing of stone, clay, glass, and related products
570   Crushing, grinding, and mixing occupations
571   Separating occupations
572   Melting occupations
573   Baking, drying, and heat-treating occupations
574   Impregnating, coating, and glazing occupations
575   Forming occupations
579   Occupations in processing of stone, clay, glass, and related products, n.e.c.

58   Occupations in processing of leather, textiles, and related products
580   Shaping, blocking, stretching, and tentering occupations
581   Separating, filtering, and drying occupations
582   Washing, steaming, and saturating occupations
583   Ironing, pressing, glazing, staking, calendering, and embossing occupations
584   Mercerizing, coating, and laminating occupations
585   Singeing, cutting, shearing, shaving, and napping occupations
586   Felting and fulling occupations
587   Brushing and shrinking occupations
589   Occupations in processing of leather, textiles, and related products, n.e.c.

59   Processing occupations, n.e.c.
590   Occupations in processing products from assorted materials
599   Miscellaneous processing occupations, n.e.c.

MACHINE TRADES OCCUPATIONS

60   Metal machining occupations
600   Machinists and related occupations
601   Toolmakers and related occupations
602   Gear machining occupations
603   Abrading occupations
604   Turning occupations
605   Milling, shaping, and planing occupations
606   Boring occupations
607   Sawing occupations
609   Metal machining occupations, n.e.c.

61   Metalworking occupations, n.e.c.
610   Hammer forging occupations
611   Press forging occupations
612   Forging occupations, n.e.c.
613   Sheet and bar rolling occupations
614   Extruding and drawing occupations
615   Punching and shearing occupations
616   Fabricating machine occupations

617   Forming occupations, n.e.c.
619   Miscellaneous metalworking occupations, n.e.c.

62/63   Mechanics and machinery repairers
620   Motorized vehicle and engineering equipment mechanics and repairers
621   Aircraft mechanics and repairers
622   Rail equipment mechanics and repairers
623   Marine mechanics and repairers
624   Farm mechanics and repairers
625   Engine, power transmission, and related mechanics
626   Metalworking machinery mechanics
627   Printing and publishing mechanics and repairers
628   Textile machinery and equipment mechanics and repairers
629   Special industry machinery mechanics
630   General industry mechanics and repairers
631   Powerplant mechanics and repairers
632   Ordnance and accessories mechanics and repairers
633   Business and commercial machine repairers
637   Utilities service mechanics and repairers
638   Miscellaneous occupations in machine installation and repair
639   Mechanics and machinery repairers, n.e.c.

64   Paperworking occupations
640   Paper cutting, winding, and related occupations
641   Folding, creasing, scoring, and gluing occupations
649   Paperworking occupations, n.e.c.

65   Printing occupations
650   Typesetters and composers
651   Printing press occupations
652   Printing machine occupations
653   Bookbinding-machine operators and related occupations
654   Typecasters and related occupations
659   Printing occupations, n.e.c.

66   Wood machining occupations
660   Cabinetmakers
661   Patternmakers
662   Sanding occupations
663   Shearing and shaving occupations
664   Turning occupations
665   Milling and planing occupations
666   Boring occupations
667   Sawing occupations
669   Wood machining occupations, n.e.c.

67   Occupations in machining stone, clay, glass, and related materials
670   Stonecutters and related occupations
673   Abrading occupations
674   Turning occupations

675 Planing and shaping occupations, n.e.c.
676 Boring and punching occupations
677 Chipping, cutting, sawing, and related occupations
679 Occupations in machining stone, clay, glass, and related materials, n.e.c.

68   Textile occupations
680 Carding, combing, drawing, and related occupations
681 Twisting, beaming, warping, and related occupations
682 Spinning occupations
683 Weavers and related occupations
684 Hosiery knitting occupations
685 Knitting occupations, except hosiery
686 Punching, cutting, forming, and related occupations
687 Tufting occupations
689 Textile occupations, n.e.c.

69   Machine trades occupations, n.e.c.
690 Plastics, synthetics, rubber, and leather working occupations
691 Occupations in fabrication of insulated wire and cable
692 Occupations in fabrication of products from assorted materials
693 Modelmakers, patternmakers, and related occupations
694 Occupations in fabrication of ordnance, ammunition, and related products, n.e.c.
699 Miscellaneous machine trades occupations, n.e.c.

BENCHWORK OCCUPATIONS

70   Occupations in fabrication, assembly, and repair of metal products, n.e.c.
700 Occupations in fabrication, assembly, and repair of jewelry, silverware, and related products
701 Occupations in fabrication, assembly, and repair of tools, and related products
703 Occupations in assembly and repair of sheetmetal products, n.e.c.
704 Engravers, etchers, and related occupations
705 Filing, grinding, buffing, cleaning, and polishing occupations, n.e.c.
706 Metal unit assemblers and adjusters, n.e.c.
709 Miscellaneous occupations in fabrication, assembly, and repair of metal products, n.e.c.

71   Occupations in fabrication and repair of scientific, medical, photographic, optical, horological, and related products
710 Occupations in fabrication and repair of instruments for measuring, controlling, and indicating physical characteristics
711 Occupations in fabrication and repair of optical instruments

712 Occupations in fabrication and repair of surgical, medical, and dental instruments and supplies
713 Occupations in fabrication and repair of ophthalmic goods
714 Occupations in fabrication and repair of photographic equipment and supplies
715 Occupations in fabrication and repair of watches, clocks, and parts
716 Occupations in fabrication and repair of engineering and scientific instruments and equipment, n.e.c.
719 Occupations in fabrication and repair of scientific and medical apparatus, photographic and optical goods, horological, and related products, n.e.c.

72   Occupations in assembly and repair of electrical equipment
720 Occupations in assembly and repair of radio and television receiving sets and phonographs
721 Occupations in assembly and repair of motors, generators, and related products
722 Occupations in assembly and repair of communications equipment
723 Occupations in assembly and repair of electrical appliances and fixtures
724 Occupations in winding and assembling coils, magnets, armatures, and related products
725 Occupations in assembly of light bulbs and electronic tubes
726 Occupations in assembly and repair of electronic components and accessories, n.e.c.
727 Occupations in assembly of storage batteries
728 Occupations in fabrication of electrical wire and cable
729 Occupations in assembly and repair of electrical equipment, n.e.c.

73   Occupations in fabrication and repair of products made from assorted materials
730 Occupations in fabrication and repair of musical instruments and parts
731 Occupations in fabrication and repair of games and toys
732 Occupations in fabrication and repair of sporting goods
733 Occupations in fabrication and repair of pens, pencils, and office and artists' materials, n.e.c.
734 Occupations in fabrication and repair of notions
735 Occupations in fabrication and repair of jewelry, n.e.c.
736 Occupations in fabrication and repair of ordnance and accessories
737 Occupations in fabrication of ammunition, fireworks, explosives, and related products
739 Occupations in fabrication and repair of products made from assorted materials, n.e.c.

74   Painting, decorating, and related occupations
740   Painters, brush
741   Painters, spray
742   Staining, waxing, and related occupations
749   Painting, decorating, and related occupations, n.e.c.

75   Occupations in fabrication and repair of plastics, synthetics, rubber, and related products
750   Occupations in fabrication and repair of tires, tubes, tire treads, and related products
751   Laying out and cutting occupations, n.e.c.
752   Fitting, shaping, cementing, finishing, and related occupations, n.e.c.
753   Occupations in fabrication and repair of rubber and plastic footwear
754   Occupations in fabrication and repair of miscellaneous plastics products
759   Occupations in fabrication and repair of plastics, synthetics, rubber, and related products, n.e.c.

76   Occupations in fabrication and repair of wood products
760   Bench carpenters and related occupations
761   Occupations in laying out, cutting, carving, shaping, and sanding wood products, n.e.c.
762   Occupations in assembling wood products, n.e.c.
763   Occupations in fabrication and repair of furniture, n.e.c.
764   Cooperage occupations
769   Occupations in fabrication and repair of wood products, n.e.c.

77   Occupations in fabrication and repair of sand, stone, clay, and glass products
770   Occupations in fabrication and repair of jewelry, ornaments, and related products
771   Stone cutters and carvers
772   Glass blowing, pressing, shaping, and related occupations, n.e.c.
773   Occupations in coloring and decorating brick, tile, and related products
774   Occupations in fabrication and repair of pottery and porcelain ware
775   Grinding, filing, polishing, frosting, etching, cleaning, and related occupations, n.e.c.
776   Occupations in fabrication and repair of asbestos and polishing products, abrasives, and related materials
777   Modelmakers, patternmakers, moldmakers, and related occupations
779   Occupations in fabrication and repair of sand, stone, clay, and glass products, n.e.c.

78   Occupations in fabrication and repair of textile, leather, and related products
780   Occupations in upholstering and in fabrication and repair of stuffed furniture, mattresses, and related products
781   Laying out, marking, cutting, and punching occupations, n.e.c.
782   Hand sewers, menders, embroiderers, knitters, and related occupations, n.e.c.
783   Fur and leather working occupations
784   Occupations in fabrication and repair of hats, caps, gloves, and related products
785   Tailors and dressmakers
786   Sewing machine operators, garment
787   Sewing machine operators, nongarment
788   Occupations in fabrication and repair of footwear
789   Occupations in fabrication and repair of textile, leather, and related products, n.e.c.

79   Benchwork occupations, n.e.c.
790   Occupations in preparation of food, tobacco, and related products, n.e.c.
794   Occupations in fabrication of paper products, n.e.c.
795   Gluing occupations, n.e.c.

STRUCTURAL WORK OCCUPATIONS

80   Occupations in metal fabricating, n.e.c.
800   Riveters, n.e.c.
801   Fitting, bolting, screwing, and related occupations
804   Tinsmiths, coppersmiths, and sheet metal workers
805   Boilermakers
806   Transportation equipment assemblers and related occupations
807   Structural repairers, transportation equipment
809   Miscellaneous occupations in metal fabricating, n.e.c.

81   Welders, cutters, and related occupations
810   Arc welders and cutters
811   Gas welders
812   Resistance welders
813   Brazing, braze-welding, and soldering occupations
814   Solid state welders
815   Electron-beam, electroslag, thermit, induction, and laser-beam welders
816   Thermal cutters and arc cutters
819   Welders, cutters, and related occupations, n.e.c.

82   Electrical assembling, installing, and repairing occupations
820   Occupations in assembly, installation, and repair of generators, motors, accessories, and related powerplant equipment

821	Occupations in assembly, installation, and repair of transmission and distribution lines and circuits
822	Occupations in assembly, installation, and repair of wire communication, detection and signaling equipment
823	Occupations in assembly, installation, and repair of electronic communication, detection, and signaling equipment
824	Occupations in assembly, installation, and repair of lighting equipment and building wiring, n.e.c.
825	Occupations in assembly, installation, and repair of transportation and material-handling equipment, n.e.c.
826	Occupations in assembly, installation, and repair of industrial apparatus, n.e.c.
827	Occupations in assembly, installation, and repair of large household appliances and similar commercial and industrial equipment
828	Occupations in fabrication, installation, and repair of electrical and electronics products, n.e.c.
829	Occupations in installation and repair of electrical products, n.e.c.

84	**Painting, plastering, waterproofing, cementing, and related occupations**
840	Construction and maintenance painters and related occupations
841	Paperhangers
842	Plasterers and related occupations
843	Waterproofing and related occupations
844	Cement and concrete finishing and related occupations
845	Transportation equipment painters and related occupations
849	Painting, plastering, waterproofing, cementing, and related occupations, n.e.c.

85	**Excavating, grading, paving, and related occupations**
850	Excavating, grading, and related occupations
851	Drainage and related occupations
853	Paving occupations, asphalt and concrete
859	Excavating, grading, paving, and related occupations, n.e.c.

86	**Construction occupations, n.e.c.**
860	Carpenters and related occupations
861	Brick and stone masons and tile setters
862	Plumbers, gas fitters, steam fitters, and related occupations
863	Asbestos and insulation workers
864	Floor laying and finishing occupations
865	Glaziers and related occupations
866	Roofers and related occupations
869	Miscellaneous construction occupations, n.e.c.

89	**Structural work occupations, n.e.c.**
891	Occupations in structural maintenance, n.e.c.
899	Miscellaneous structural work occupations, n.e.c.

MISCELLANEOUS OCCUPATIONS

90	**Motor freight occupations**
900	Concrete-mixing-truck drivers
902	Dump-truck drivers
903	Truck drivers, inflammables
904	Trailer-truck drivers
905	Truck drivers, heavy
906	Truck drivers, light
909	Motor freight occupations, n.e.c.

91	**Transportation occupations, n.e.c.**
910	Railroad transportation occupations
911	Water transportation occupations
912	Air transportation occupations
913	Passenger transportation occupations, n.e.c.
914	Pumping and pipeline transportation occupations
915	Attendants and servicers, parking lots and automotive service facilities
919	Miscellaneous transportation occupations, n.e.c.

92	**Packaging and materials handling occupations**
920	Packaging occupations
921	Hoisting and conveying occupations
922	Occupations in moving and storing materials and products, n.e.c.
929	Packaging and materials handling occupations, n.e.c.

93	**Occupations in extraction of minerals**
930	Earth boring, drilling, cutting, and related occupations
931	Blasting occupations
932	Loading and conveying operations
933	Crushing occupations
934	Screening and related occupations
939	Occupations in extraction of minerals, n.e.c.

95	**Occupations in production and distribution of utilities**
950	Stationary engineers
951	Firers and related occupations
952	Occupations in generation, transmission, and distribution of electric light and power
953	Occupations in production and distribution of gas
954	Occupations in filtration, purification, and distribution of water
955	Occupations in disposal of refuse and sewage
956	Occupations in distribution of steam

List the occupational prospects you generated from your exploration of the *Dictionary of Occupational Titles*.

_____   _____

_____   _____

_____   _____

_____   _____

_____   _____

_____   _____

_____   _____

_____   _____

_____   _____

_____   _____

_____   _____

_____   _____

_____   _____

_____   _____

_____   _____

_____   _____

_____   _____

_____   _____

_____   _____

_____   _____

_____   _____

_____   _____

_____   _____

_____   _____

_____   _____

_____   _____

_____   _____

_____   _____

O*Net Search for Occupations (Exercise 4-3 in Chapter 4)

If you have completed Exercise 4-3 in Chapter 4, you can move directly to the groups of occupations that interest you the most and locate the specific occupational descriptions you want to access, either online or in the book *O*Net Dictionary of Occupational Titles.* (If you did not work on Exercise 4-3, that's okay, but you'll need to look at *all* the groups and determine which occupations you want to consider.) Each occupation has an O*Net-SOC numeric code and has a place in 1 of 23 major occupational groups, called a "job family." SOC stands for Standard Occupational Classification, a system by which the U.S. government classifies all occupations.

Directions for going online. The Internet address is http://online.onetcenter.org/search. Use the "Job Family" Search. (If you have not determined the groups of greatest interest to you, use the "All Occupations" Search.) You can also search by the O*Net-SOC numeric code or by keyword. From the pull-down menu of job families, select one of the 23 groups that interest you most. The next screen will display a list of all occupations within your specified job family. From left to right on the screen come the heads of columns: O*Net-SOC Code, the title of the occupation, and reports (help). For reports, you have the options of "Summary," "Details," or "Custom" reports. For the data you are seeking for your occupational prospects, any of the three options provides information on the following:

Tasks—Specific work activities that can be unique to each occupation.

Knowledges—Organized sets of principles and facts that apply to a wide range of situations.

Skills—Developed capabilities that assist learning and the performance of activities in jobs.

Abilities—Enduring attributes of a person that influence job performance.

Work activities—Summaries of tasks that may be performed across multiple occupations.

Work context—Physical and social factors that influence the nature of the work.

Job zone—Similar experience, education, and training requirements are grouped together into one of the five Job Zones. (Occupations that need little or no preparation are in Job Zone 1, some preparation in 2, medium preparation in 3, considerable preparation in 4, extensive preparation in 5.)

Interests—A person's preferences for work environments and outcomes.

Work values—Wide-ranging aspects of work that are important to a person's satisfaction.

Work needs—More specific aspects of work that are important to a person's satisfaction (not a part of the "summary" option).

Related occupations—Similar to the selected occupation based on knowledge areas, skills, abilities, work environment, and work activities.

Wages and employment link—Because these data are not collected by the O*Net project, O*Net Online provides a link to the America's Career InfoNet Web site, where the wages and outlook information are provided for the user's specified state within the United States.

Crosswalk—Corresponding codes and titles in other classification systems (Custom report only).

The Summary Report gives an overview or "snapshot" of the selected occupation, concentrating on the most important descriptors. The Details Report displays all descriptors for the selected occupation and (where available) a rating of how important each descriptor is to the occupation. The Custom Report lets you choose from 12 different factors to generate a tailored report about the occupation, and with certain selected descriptors you can view minimum cutoff scores.

The descriptors in O*Net have scales—Importance, Level, Context, Extent, and Frequency of the activity. Level and importance can be thought to be the same, but they could be very different. A skill can be *important* for a variety of occupations, but the *level* of the same skill in those occupations can differ widely. Speaking is important for both lawyers and legal assistants; however, lawyers arguing cases before judges and juries are required to have a high level of speaking, whereas legal assistants need an average level of this skill, according to the ratings of the O*Net project.

Each scale has a minimum and maximum numeric value. To make the ratings on the scales more understandable, they are standardized scores ranging from 0 to 100. The O*Net Online Help Web page (http://online.onetcenter.org/help/online/scales) explains the formula for those who are interested.

Circle or check the names of those occupations from O*Net that you want to use as occupational prospects, and transfer them to Exercise 3-15 in Chapter 3. The titles in boldface are occupational groups; you want the specific occupations below them. An asterisk (*) means Summary Report only. After you finish getting the names and/or descriptions of occupations from O*Net Online, obtain a printout if you have a printer attached to your computer. The alternative is to write salient information on an Occupational Worksheet from Appendix H (or use a plain sheet of paper on which to write your notes).

O*Net-SOC Code	O*Net-SOC Title	O*Net-SOC Code	O*Net-SOC Title
11-0000	**MANAGEMENT OCCUPATIONS**	**11-3000**	**Operations Specialties Managers**
11-1000	**Top executives**	___ 11-3011.00	Administrative services managers
___ 11-1011.00	Chief executives *	___ 11-3021.00	Computer and information systems managers
___ 11-1011.01	Government service executives	___ 11-3031.00	Financial managers*
___ 11-1011.02	Private sector executives	___ 11-3031.01	Treasurers, controllers, and chief financial officers
___ 11-1021.00	General and operations managers*	___ 11-3031.02	Financial managers, branch or department
___ 11-1031.00	Legislators*	___ 11-3040.00	Human resources managers
		___ 11-3041.00	Compensation and benefits managers
11-2000	**Advertising, Marketing, Promotions, Public Relations, and Sales Managers**	___ 11-3042.00	Training and development managers
___ 11-2011.00	Advertising and promotions managers	___ 11-3049.99	Human resources managers, all other*
___ 11-2021.00	Marketing managers	___ 11-3051.00	Industrial production managers
___ 11-2022.00	Sales managers		
___ 11-2031.00	Public relations managers*		

*Summary Report only

O*Net-SOC Code	O*Net-SOC Title
____ 11-3061.00	Purchasing managers
____ 11-3071.00	Transportation, storage, and distribution managers*
____ 11-3071.01	Transportation managers
____ 11-3071.02	Storage and distribution managers

11-9000   Other Managers

O*Net-SOC Code	O*Net-SOC Title
____ 11-9011.00	Farm, ranch, and other agricultural managers*
____ 11-9011.01	Nursery and greenhouse managers
____ 11-9011.02	Agricultural crop farm managers
____ 11-9011.03	Fish hatchery managers
____ 11-9012.00	Farmers and ranchers
____ 11-9021.00	Construction managers
____ 11-9031.00	Education administrators, preschool and child care center/program
____ 11-9032.00	Education administrators, elementary and secondary school
____ 11-9033.00	Education administrators, postsecondary
____ 11-9039.99	Education administrators, all other*
____ 11-9041.00	Engineering managers
____ 11-9051.00	Food service managers
____ 11-9061.00	Funeral directors
____ 11-9071.00	Gaming managers
____ 11-9081.00	Lodging managers
____ 11-9111.00	Medical and health services managers
____ 11-9121.00	Natural sciences managers
____ 11-9131.00	Postmasters and mail superintendents
____ 11-9141.00	Property, real estate, and community association managers
____ 11-9151.00	Social and community service managers
____ 11-9199.99	Managers, all other*

13-0000   BUSINESS AND FINANCIAL OPERATIONS

13-1000   Business Operations Specialists

O*Net-SOC Code	O*Net-SOC Title
____ 13-1011.00	Agents and business managers of artists, performers, and athletes
____ 13-1021.00	Purchasing agents and buyers, farm products
____ 13-1022.00	Wholesale and retail buyers, except farm products
____ 13-1023.00	Purchasing agents, except wholesale, retail, and farm products
____ 13-1031.00	Claims adjusters, examiners, and investigators*
____ 13-1031.01	Claims examiners, property and casualty insurance

O*Net-SOC Code	O*Net-SOC Title
____ 13-1031.02	Insurance adjusters, examiners, and investigators
____ 13-1032.00	Insurance appraisers, auto damage
____ 13-1041.00	Compliance officers, except agriculture, construction, health and safety, and transportation*
____ 13-1041.01	Environmental compliance inspectors
____ 13-1041.02	Licensing examiners and inspectors
____ 13-1041.03	Equal opportunity representatives and officers
____ 13-1041.04	Government property inspectors and investigators
____ 13-1041.05	Pressure vessel inspectors
____ 13-1041.06	Coroners
____ 13-1051.00	Cost estimators
____ 13-1061.00	Emergency management specialists*
____ 13-1071.00	Employment, recruitment, and placement specialists*
____ 13-1071.01	Employment interviewers, private or public employment service
____ 13-1071.02	Personnel recruiters
____ 13-1072.00	Compensation, benefits, and job analysis specialists
____ 13-1073.00	Training and development specialists
____ 13-1079.99	Human resources, training, and labor relations specialists, all other*
____ 13-1081.00	Logisticians
____ 13-1111.00	Management analysts
____ 13-1121.00	Meeting and convention planners
____ 13-1199.99	Business operations specialists, all other*

13-2000   Financial Specialists

O*Net-SOC Code	O*Net-SOC Title
____ 13-2011.00	Accountants and auditors*
____ 13-2011.01	Accountants
____ 13-2011.02	Auditors
____ 13-2021.00	Appraisers and assessors of real estate*
____ 13-2021.01	Assessors
____ 13-2021.02	Appraisers, real estate
____ 13-2031.00	Budget analysts
____ 13-2041.00	Credit analysts
____ 13-2051.00	Financial analysts
____ 13-2052.00	Personal financial advisors
____ 13-2053.00	Insurance underwriters
____ 13-2061.00	Financial examiners
____ 13-2071.00	Loan counselors
____ 13-2072.00	Loan officers
____ 13-2081.00	Tax examiners, collectors, and revenue agents
____ 13-2082.00	Tax preparers
____ 13-2099.99	Financial specialists, all other*

O*Net-SOC Code	O*Net-SOC Title

15-0000 COMPUTER AND MATHEMATICAL SCIENCE OCCUPATIONS

15-1000 Computer Specialists

____	15-1011.00	Computer and information scientists, research*
____	15-1021.00	Computer programmers
____	15-1031.00	Computer software engineers, applications
____	15-1032.00	Computer software engineers, systems software
____	15-1041.00	Computer support specialists
____	15-1051.00	Computer systems analysts
____	15-1061.00	Database administrators
____	15-1071.00	Network and computer systems administrators*
____	15-1071.01	Computer security specialists
____	15-1081.00	Network systems and data communications analysts
____	15-1099.99	Computer specialists, all other*

15-2000 Mathematical Science Occupations

____	15-2011.00	Actuaries
____	15-2021.00	Mathematicians
____	15-2031.00	Operations research analysts
____	15-2041.00	Statisticians
____	15-2091.00	Mathematical technicians
____	15-2099.99	Mathematical science occupations, all other*

17-0000 ARCHITECTURAL AND ENGINEERING OCCUPATIONS

17-1000 Architects, Surveyors, and Cartographers

____	17-1011.00	Architects, except landscape and naval
____	17-1012.00	Landscape architects
____	17-1021.00	Cartographers and photogrammetrists
____	17-1022.00	Surveyors

17-2000 Engineers

____	17-2011.00	Aerospace engineers
____	17-2021.00	Agricultural engineers
____	17-2031.00	Biomedical engineers*
____	17-2041.00	Chemical engineers
____	17-2051.00	Civil engineers
____	17-2061.00	Computer hardware engineers
____	17-2071.00	Electrical engineers
____	17-2072.00	Electronics engineers, except computer
____	17-2081.00	Environmental engineers*
____	17-2111.00	Health and safety engineers, except mining safety engineers and inspectors*

____	17-2111.01	Industrial safety and health engineers
____	17-2111.02	Fire-prevention and protection engineers
____	17-2111.03	Product safety engineers
____	17-2112.00	Industrial engineers
____	17-2121.00	Marine engineers and naval architects*
____	17-2121.01	Marine engineers
____	17-2121.02	Marine architects
____	17-2131.00	Materials engineers
____	17-2141.00	Mechanical engineers
____	17-2151.00	Mining and geological engineers, including mining safety engineers
____	17-2161.00	Nuclear engineers
____	17-2171.00	Petroleum engineers
____	17-2199.99	Engineers, all other*

17-3000 Drafters, Engineering, and Mapping Technicians

____	17-3011.00	Architectural and civil drafters*
____	17-3011.01	Architectural drafters
____	17-3011.02	Civil drafters
____	17-3012.00	Electrical and electronics drafters*
____	17-3012.01	Electronic drafters
____	17-3012.02	Electrical drafters
____	17-3013.00	Mechanical drafters
____	17-3019.99	Drafters, all other*
____	17-3021.00	Aerospace engineering and operations technicians
____	17-3022.00	Civil engineering technicians
____	17-3023.00	Electrical and electronic engineering technicians*
____	17-3023.01	Electronics engineering technicians
____	17-3023.02	Calibration and instrumentation technicians
____	17-3023.03	Electrical engineering technicians
____	17-3024.00	Electromechanical technicians
____	17-3025.00	Environmental engineering technicians*
____	17-3026.00	Industrial engineering technicians
____	17-3027.00	Mechanical engineering technicians
____	17-3029.99	Engineering technicians, except drafters, all other*
____	17-3031.00	Surveying and mapping technicians*
____	17-3031.01	Surveying technicians
____	17-3031.02	Mapping technicians

19-0000 LIFE, PHYSICAL, AND SOCIAL SCIENCES OCCUPATIONS

19-1000 Life Scientists

____	19-1011.00	Animal scientists
____	19-1012.00	Food scientists and technologists
____	19-1013.00	Soil and plant scientists*

*Summary Report only

O*Net-SOC Code	O*Net-SOC Title	O*Net-SOC Code	O*Net-SOC Title

____ 19-1013.01 Plant scientists
____ 19-1013.02 Soil scientists
____ 19-1020.01 Biologists
____ 19-1021.00 Biochemists and biophysicists*
____ 19-1021.01 Biochemists
____ 19-1021.02 Biophysicists
____ 19-1022.00 Microbiologists
____ 19-1023.00 Zoologists and wildlife biologists
____ 19-1029.99 Biological scientists, all other*
____ 19-1031.00 Conservation scientists*
____ 19-1031.01 Soil conservationists
____ 19-1031.02 Range managers
____ 19-1031.03 Park naturalists
____ 19-1032.00 Foresters
____ 19-1041.00 Epidemiologists
____ 19-1042.00 Medical scientists, except epidemiologists
____ 19-1099.99 Life scientists, all other*

19-2000 Physical Scientists

____ 19-2011.00 Astronomers
____ 19-2012.00 Physicists
____ 19-2021.00 Atmospheric and space scientists
____ 19-2031.00 Chemists
____ 19-2032.00 Materials scientists
____ 19-2041.00 Environmental scientists and specialists, including health
____ 19-2042.00 Geoscientists, except hydrologists and geographers*
____ 19-2042.01 Geologists
____ 19-2043.00 Hydrologists
____ 19-2099.99 Physical scientists, all other*

19-3000 Social Scientists

____ 19-3011.00 Economists
____ 19-3021.00 Market research analysts
____ 19-3022.00 Survey researchers*
____ 19-3031.00 Clinical, counseling, and school psychologists*
____ 19-3031.01 Educational psychologists
____ 19-3031.02 Clinical psychologists
____ 19-3031.03 Counseling psychologists
____ 19-3032.00 Industrial-organizational psychologists
____ 19-3039.99 Psychologists, all other*
____ 19-3041.00 Sociologists
____ 19-3051.00 Urban and regional planners
____ 19-3091.00 Anthropologists and archeologists*
____ 19-3091.01 Anthropologists
____ 19-3091.02 Archeologists
____ 19-3092.00 Geographers
____ 19-3093.00 Historians
____ 19-3094.00 Political scientists
____ 19-3099.99 Social scientists and related workers, all other*

19-4000 Life, Physical, and Social Science Technicians

____ 19-4011.00 Agricultural and food science technicians*
____ 19-4011.01 Agricultural technicians
____ 19-4011.02 Food science technicians
____ 19-4021.00 Biological technicians
____ 19-4031.00 Chemical technicians
____ 19-4041.00 Geological and petroleum technicians*
____ 19-4041.01 Geological data technicians
____ 19-4041.02 Geological sample test technicians
____ 19-4051.00 Nuclear technicians*
____ 19-4051.01 Nuclear equipment operation technicians
____ 19-4051.02 Nuclear monitoring technicians
____ 19-4061.00 Social science research assistants*
____ 19-4061.01 City planning aides
____ 19-4091.00 Environmental science and protection technicians, including health
____ 19-4092.00 Forensic science technicians
____ 19-4093.00 Forest and conservation technicians*
____ 19-4099.99 Life, physical, and social science technicians, all other*

21-0000 COMMUNITY AND SOCIAL SERVICES OCCUPATIONS

21-1000 Counselors, Social Workers, and Other Community and Social Service Specialists

____ 21-1011.00 Substance abuse and behavioral disorder counselors
____ 21-1012.00 Educational, vocational, and school counselors
____ 21-1013.00 Marriage and family therapists*
____ 21-1014.00 Mental health counselors
____ 21-1015.00 Rehabilitation counselors*
____ 21-1019.99 Counselors, all other*
____ 21-1021.00 Child, family, and school social workers
____ 21-1022.00 Medical and public health social workers
____ 21-1023.00 Mental health and substance abuse social workers
____ 21-1029.99 Social workers, all other*
____ 21-1091.00 Health educators
____ 21-1092.00 Probation officers and correctional treatment specialists
____ 21-1093.00 Social and human service assistants
____ 21-1099.99 Community and social service specialists, all other*

O*Net-SOC Code	O*Net-SOC Title

21-2000 Religious workers
- ____ 21-2011.00 Clergy
- ____ 21-2021.00 Directors, religious activities and education
- ____ 21-2099.99 Religious workers, all other*

23-0000 LEGAL OCCUPATIONS

23-1000 Lawyers, Judges, and Related Workers
- ____ 23-1011.00 Lawyers
- ____ 23-1021.00 Administrative law judges, adjudicators, and hearing officers
- ____ 23-1022.00 Arbitrators, mediators, and conciliators
- ____ 23-1023.00 Judges, magistrate judges, and magistrates

23-2000 Legal Support Workers
- ____ 23-2011.00 Paralegals and legal assistants
- ____ 23-2091.00 Court reporters*
- ____ 23-2092.00 Law clerks
- ____ 23-2093.00 Title examiners, abstractors, and searchers*
- ____ 23-2093.01 Title searchers
- ____ 23-2093.02 Title examiners and abstractors
- ____ 23-2099.99 Legal support workers, all other*

25-0000 EDUCATION, TRAINING, AND LIBRARY OCCUPATIONS

25-1000 Postsecondary Teachers
- ____ 25-1011.00 Business teachers, postsecondary*
- ____ 25-1021.00 Computer science teachers, postsecondary
- ____ 25-1022.00 Mathematical science teachers, postsecondary
- ____ 25-1031.00 Architecture teachers, postsecondary*
- ____ 25-1032.00 Engineering teachers, postsecondary
- ____ 25-1041.00 Agricultural sciences teachers, postsecondary
- ____ 25-1042.00 Biological science teachers, postsecondary
- ____ 25-1043.00 Forestry and conservation science teachers, postsecondary
- ____ 25-1051.00 Atmospheric, earth, marine, and space sciences teachers, postsecondary*
- ____ 25-1052.00 Chemistry teachers, postsecondary
- ____ 25-1053.00 Environmental science teachers, postsecondary*
- ____ 25-1054.00 Physics teachers, postsecondary
- ____ 25-1061.00 Anthropology and archeology teachers, postsecondary

O*Net-SOC Code	O*Net-SOC Title

- ____ 25-1062.00 Area, ethnic, and cultural studies teachers, postsecondary
- ____ 25-1063.00 Economics teachers, postsecondary
- ____ 25-1064.00 Geography teachers, postsecondary*
- ____ 25-1065.00 Political science teachers, postsecondary
- ____ 25-1066.00 Psychology teachers, postsecondary
- ____ 25-1067.00 Sociology teachers, postsecondary
- ____ 25-1069.99 Social sciences teachers, postsecondary, all other*
- ____ 25-1071.00 Health specialties teachers, postsecondary
- ____ 25-1072.00 Nursing instructors and teachers, postsecondary
- ____ 25-1081.00 Education teachers, postsecondary*
- ____ 25-1082.00 Library science teachers, postsecondary*
- ____ 25-1111.00 Criminal justice and law enforcement teachers, postsecondary
- ____ 25-1112.00 Law teachers, postsecondary*
- ____ 25-1113.00 Social work teachers, postsecondary*
- ____ 25-1121.00 Art, drama, and music teachers, postsecondary
- ____ 25-1122.00 Communications teachers, postsecondary*
- ____ 25-1123.00 English language and literature teachers, postsecondary
- ____ 25-1124.00 Foreign language and literature teachers, postsecondary
- ____ 25-1125.00 History teachers, postsecondary
- ____ 25-1126.00 Philosophy and religion teachers, postsecondary*
- ____ 25-1191.00 Graduate teaching assistants
- ____ 25-1192.00 Home economics teachers, postsecondary*
- ____ 25-1193.00 Recreation and fitness studies teachers, postsecondary
- ____ 25-1194.00 Vocational education teachers, postsecondary
- ____ 25-1199.99 Postsecondary teachers, all other*

25-2000 Primary, Secondary, and Special Education School Teachers
- ____ 25-2011.00 Preschool teachers, except special education
- ____ 25-2012.00 Kindergarten teachers, except special education
- ____ 25-2021.00 Elementary school teachers, except special education
- ____ 25-2022.00 Middle school teachers, except special and vocational education
- ____ 25-2023.00 Vocational education teachers, middle school

*Summary Report only

O*Net-SOC Code	O*Net-SOC Title

____ 25-2031.00   Secondary school teachers, except special and vocational education

____ 25-2032.00   Vocational education teachers, secondary school

____ 25-2041.00   Special education teachers, preschool, kindergarten, and elementary school

____ 25-2042.00   Special education teachers, middle school

____ 25-2043.00   Special education teachers, secondary school

25-3000   Other Teachers and Instructors

____ 25-3011.00   Adult literacy, remedial education, and GED teachers and instructors

____ 25-3021.00   Self-enrichment education teachers

____ 25-3099.99   Teachers and instructors, all other*

25-4000   Librarians, Curators, and Archivists

____ 25-4011.00   Archivists

____ 25-4012.00   Curators

____ 25-4013.00   Museum technicians and conservators

____ 25-4021.00   Librarians

____ 25-4031.00   Library technicians

25-9000   Other Education, Training, and Library Occupations

____ 25-9011.00   Audiovisual collections specialists

____ 25-9021.00   Farm and home management advisors

____ 25-9031.00   Instructional coordinators

____ 25-9041.00   Teacher assistants

____ 25-9099.99   Education, training, and library workers, all other*

27-0000   ARTS, DESIGN, ENTERTAINMENT, SPORTS, AND MEDIA OCCUPATIONS

27-1000   Art and Design Workers

____ 27-1011.00   Art directors

____ 27-1012.00   Craft artists*

____ 27-1013.00   Fine artists, including painters, sculptors, and illustrators*

____ 27-1013.01   Painters and illustrators

____ 27-1013.02   Sketch artists

____ 27-1013.03   Cartoonists

____ 27-1013.04   Sculptors

____ 27-1014.00   Multimedia artists and animators*

____ 27-1019.99   Artists and related workers, all other*

____ 27-1021.00   Commercial and industrial designers

____ 27-1022.00   Fashion designers

O*Net-SOC Code	O*Net-SOC Title

____ 27-1023.00   Floral designers

____ 27-1024.00   Graphic designers

____ 27-1025.00   Interior designers

____ 27-1026.00   Merchandise displayers and window trimmers

____ 27-1027.00   Set and exhibit designers*

____ 27-1027.01   Set designers

____ 27-1027.02   Exhibit designers

____ 27-1029.99   Designers, all other

27-2000   Entertainers and Performers, Sports and Related Workers

____ 27-2011.00   Actors

____ 27-2012.00   Producers and directors*

____ 27-2012.01   Producers

____ 27-2012.02   Directors—stage, motion pictures, television, and radio

____ 27-2012.03   Program directors

____ 27-2012.04   Talent directors

____ 27-2012.05   Technical directors/managers

____ 27-2021.00   Athletes and sports competitors

____ 27-2022.00   Coaches and scouts

____ 27-2023.00   Umpires, referees, and other sports officials

____ 27-2031.00   Dancers

____ 27-2032.00   Choreographers

____ 27-2041.00   Music directors and composers*

____ 27-2041.01   Music directors

____ 27-2041.02   Music arrangers and orchestrators

____ 27-2041.03   Composers

____ 27-2042.00   Musicians and singers*

____ 27-2042.01   Singers

____ 27-2042.02   Musicians, instrumental

____ 27-2099.99   Entertainers and performers, sports and related workers, all other*

27-3000   Media and Communication Workers

____ 27-3011.00   Radio and television announcers

____ 27-3012.00   Public address system and other announcers

____ 27-3021.00   Broadcast news analysts

____ 27-3022.00   Reporters and correspondents

____ 27-3031.00   Public relations specialists

____ 27-3041.00   Editors

____ 27-3042.00   Technical writers

____ 27-3043.00   Writers and authors*

____ 27-3043.01   Poets and lyricists

____ 27-3043.02   Creative writers

____ 27-3043.03   Caption writers

____ 27-3043.04   Copy writers

____ 27-3091.00   Interpreters and translators

____ 27-3099.99   Media and communication workers, all other*

*Summary Report only

O*Net-SOC Code	O*Net-SOC Title

27-4000 Media and Communications Equipment Workers

____ 27-4011.00	Audio and video equipment technicians
____ 27-4012.00	Broadcast technicians
____ 27-4013.00	Radio operators
____ 27-4014.00	Sound engineering technicians
____ 27-4021.00	Photographers*
____ 27-4021.01	Professional photographers
____ 27-4021.02	Photographers, scientific
____ 27-4031.00	Camera operators, television, video, and motion picture
____ 27-4032.00	Film and video editors
____ 27-4099.99	Media and communication equipment workers, all other*

29-0000 HEALTH CARE PRACTITIONERS AND TECHNICAL OCCUPATIONS

29-1000 Health Diagnosing and Treating Practitioners

____ 29-1011.00	Chiropractors
____ 29-1021.00	Dentists, general
____ 29-1022.00	Oral and maxillofacial surgeons
____ 29-1023.00	Orthodontists
____ 29-1024.00	Prosthodontists
____ 29-1029.99	Dentists, all other specialists*
____ 29-1031.00	Dietitians and nutritionists
____ 29-1041.00	Optometrists
____ 29-1051.00	Pharmacists
____ 29-1061.00	Anesthesiologists
____ 29-1062.00	Family and general practitioners
____ 29-1063.00	Internists, general
____ 29-1064.00	Obstetricians and gynecologists
____ 29-1065.00	Pediatricians, general
____ 29-1066.00	Psychiatrists
____ 29-1067.00	Surgeons
____ 29-1069.99	Physicians and surgeons, all other*
____ 29-1071.00	Physician assistants
____ 29-1081.00	Podiatrists
____ 29-1111.00	Registered nurses
____ 29-1121.00	Audiologists
____ 29-1122.00	Occupational therapists
____ 29-1123.00	Physical therapists
____ 29-1124.00	Radiation therapists
____ 29-1125.00	Recreational therapists
____ 29-1126.00	Respiratory therapists
____ 29-1127.00	Speech-language pathologists
____ 29-1129.99	Therapists, all other*
____ 29-1131.00	Veterinarians
____ 29-1199.99	Health diagnosing and treating practitioners, all other*

29-2000 Health Technologists and Technicians

____ 29-2011.00	Medical and clinical laboratory technologists
____ 29-2012.00	Medical and clinical laboratory technicians
____ 29-2021.00	Dental hygienists
____ 29-2031.00	Cardiovascular technologists and technicians
____ 29-2032.00	Diagnostic medical sonographers*
____ 29-2033.00	Nuclear medicine technologists
____ 29-2034.00	Radiologic technologists and technicians*
____ 29-2034.01	Radiologic technologists
____ 29-2034.02	Radiologic technicians
____ 29-2041.00	Emergency medical technicians and paramedics
____ 29-2051.00	Dietetic technicians
____ 29-2052.00	Pharmacy technicians
____ 29-2053.00	Psychiatric technicians
____ 29-2054.00	Respiratory therapy technicians*
____ 29-2055.00	Surgical technologists
____ 29-2056.00	Veterinary technologists and technicians*
____ 29-2061.00	Licensed practical and licensed vocational nurses
____ 29-2071.00	Medical records and health information technicians
____ 29-2081.00	Opticians, dispensing
____ 29-2091.00	Orthotists and prosthetists
____ 29-2099.99	Health technologists and technicians, all other*

29-9000 Other Health Care Practitioners and Technical Occupations

____ 29-9011.00	Occupational health and safety specialists
____ 29-9012.00	Occupational health and safety technicians*
____ 29-9091.00	Athletic trainers
____ 29-9099.99	Health care practitioners and technical workers, all other*

31-0000 HEALTH CARE SUPPORT OCCUPATIONS

31-1000 Nursing, Psychiatric, and Home Health Aides

____ 31-1011.00	Home health aides
____ 31-1012.00	Nursing aides, orderlies, and attendants
____ 31-1013.00	Psychiatric aides

31-2000 Occupational and Physical Therapist Assistants and Aides

____ 31-2011.00	Occupational therapist assistants
____ 31-2012.00	Occupational therapist aides
____ 31-2021.00	Physical therapist assistants
____ 31-2022.00	Physical therapist aides

*Summary Report only

O*Net-SOC Code	O*Net-SOC Title

31-9000 Other Health Care Support Occupations

____ 31-9011.00 Massage therapists*
____ 31-9091.00 Dental assistants
____ 31-9092.00 Medical assistants
____ 31-9093.00 Medical equipment preparers
____ 31-9094.00 Medical transcriptionists*
____ 31-9095.00 Pharmacy aides*
____ 31-9096.00 Veterinary assistants and laboratory animal caretakers
____ 31-9099.99 Health care support workers, all other*

33-0000 PROTECTIVE SERVICE OCCUPATIONS

33-1000 First-Line Supervisor/Managers, Protective Service Workers

____ 33-1011.00 First-line supervisors/managers of correctional officers*
____ 33-1012.00 First-line supervisors/managers of police and detectives
____ 33-1021.00 First-line supervisors/managers of fire fighting and prevention workers*
____ 33-1021.01 Municipal fire fighting and prevention supervisors
____ 33-1021.02 Forest fire fighting and prevention supervisors
____ 33-1099.99 First-line supervisors/managers, protective service workers, all other*

33-2000 Fire Fighting and Prevention Workers

____ 33-2011.00 Fire fighters*
____ 33-2011.01 Municipal fire fighters
____ 33-2011.02 Forest fire fighters
____ 33-2021.00 Fire inspectors and investigators*
____ 33-2021.01 Fire inspectors
____ 33-2021.02 Fire investigators
____ 33-2022.00 Forest fire inspectors and prevention specialists

33-3000 Law Enforcement Workers

____ 33-3011.00 Bailiffs
____ 33-3012.00 Correctional officers and jailers
____ 33-3021.00 Detectives and criminal investigators*
____ 33-3021.01 Police detectives
____ 33-3021.02 Police identification and records officers
____ 33-3021.03 Criminal investigators and special agents
____ 33-3021.04 Child support, missing persons, and unemployment insurance fraud investigators

O*Net-SOC Code	O*Net-SOC Title

____ 33-3021.05 Immigration and customs inspectors
____ 33-3031.00 Fish and game wardens
____ 33-3041.00 Parking enforcement workers
____ 33-3051.00 Police and sheriff's patrol officers*
____ 33-3051.01 Police patrol officers
____ 33-3051.02 Highway patrol pilots
____ 33-3051.03 Sheriffs and deputy sheriffs
____ 33-3052.00 Transit and railroad police

33-9000 Other Protective Service Workers

____ 33-9011.00 Animal control workers
____ 33-9021.00 Private detectives and investigators
____ 33-9031.00 Gaming surveillance officers and gaming investigators*
____ 33-9032.00 Security guards
____ 33-9091.00 Crossing guards
____ 33-9092.00 Lifeguards, ski patrol, and other recreational protective service workers
____ 33-9099.99 Protective service workers, all other*

35-0000 FOOD PREPARATION- AND SERVING-RELATED OCCUPATIONS

35-1000 Supervisors, Food Preparation and Serving Workers

____ 35-1011.00 Chefs and head cooks
____ 35-1012.00 First-line supervisors/managers of food preparation and serving workers

35-2000 Cooks and Food Preparation Workers

____ 35-2011.00 Cooks, fast food
____ 35-2012.00 Cooks, institution and cafeteria
____ 35-2013.00 Cooks, private household*
____ 35-2014.00 Cooks, restaurant
____ 35-2015.00 Cooks, short order
____ 35-2019.99 Cooks, all other*
____ 35-2021.00 Food preparation workers

35-3000 Food and Beverage Serving Workers

____ 35-3011.00 Bartenders
____ 35-3021.00 Combined food preparation and serving workers, including fast food
____ 35-3022.00 Counter attendants, cafeteria, food concession, and coffee shop
____ 35-3031.00 Waiters and waitresses
____ 35-3041.00 Food servers, nonrestaurant

____ *Summary Report only

O*Net-SOC Code	O*Net-SOC Title

35-9000 Other Food Preparation- and Serving-Related Workers

____ 35-9011.00 Dining room and cafeteria attendants and bartender helpers
____ 35-9021.00 Dishwashers
____ 35-9031.00 Hosts and hostesses, restaurant, lounge, and coffee shop
____ 35-9099.99 Food preparation and serving-related workers, all other*

37-0000 BUILDING AND GROUNDS CLEANING AND MAINTENANCE OCCUPATIONS

37-1000 Supervisors, Building, and Grounds Cleaning and Maintenance Workers

____ 37-1011.00 First-line supervisors/managers of housekeeping and janitorial workers*
____ 37-1011.01 Housekeeping supervisors
____ 37-1011.02 Janitorial supervisors
____ 37-1012.00 First-line supervisors/managers of landscaping, lawn service, and groundskeeping workers*
____ 37-1012.01 Lawn service managers
____ 37-1012.02 First-line supervisors and manager/supervisors, landscaping workers

37-2000 Building Cleaning and Pest Control Workers

____ 37-2011.00 Janitors and cleaners, except maids and housekeeping cleaners
____ 37-2012.00 Maids and housekeeping cleaners
____ 37-2019.99 Building cleaning workers, all other*
____ 37-2021.00 Pest control workers

37-3000 Grounds Maintenance Workers

____ 37-3011.00 Landscaping and groundskeeping workers
____ 37-3012.00 Pesticide handlers, sprayers, and applicators, vegetation
____ 37-3013.00 Tree trimmers and pruners
____ 37-3019.99 Grounds maintenance workers, all other*

39-0000 PERSONAL CARE AND SERVICE OCCUPATIONS

39-1000 Supervisors, Personal Care and Service Workers

____ 39-1011.00 Gaming supervisors
____ 39-1012.00 Slot key persons*
____ 39-1021.00 First-line supervisors/managers of personal service workers

39-2000 Animal Care and Service Workers

____ 39-2011.00 Animal trainers
____ 39-2021.00 Nonfarm animal caretakers

39-3000 Entertainment Attendants and Related Workers

____ 39-3011.00 Gaming dealers
____ 39-3012.00 Gaming and sports book writers and runners
____ 39-3019.99 Gaming service workers, all other*
____ 39-3021.00 Motion picture projectionists
____ 39-3031.00 Ushers, lobby attendants, and ticket takers
____ 39-3091.00 Amusement and recreation attendants
____ 39-3092.00 Costume attendants
____ 39-3093.00 Locker room, coatroom, and dressing room attendants
____ 39-3099.99 Entertainment attendants and related workers, all other*

39-4000 Funeral Service Workers

____ 39-4011.00 Embalmers
____ 39-4021.00 Funeral attendants

39-5000 Personal Appearance Workers

____ 39-5011.00 Barbers
____ 39-5012.00 Hairdressers, hairstylists, and cosmetologists
____ 39-5091.00 Makeup artists, theatrical and performance
____ 39-5092.00 Manicurists and pedicurists
____ 39-5093.00 Shampooers*
____ 39-5094.00 Skin care specialists*

39-6000 Transportation, Tourism, and Lodging Attendants

____ 39-6011.00 Baggage porters and bellhops
____ 39-6012.00 Concierges*
____ 39-6021.00 Tour guides and escorts
____ 39-6022.00 Travel guides
____ 39-6031.00 Flight attendants
____ 39-6032.00 Transportation attendants, except flight attendants and baggage porters

39-9000 Other Personal Care and Service Workers

____ 39-9011.00 Child care workers
____ 39-9021.00 Personal and home care aides
____ 39-9031.00 Fitness trainers and aerobics instructors
____ 39-9032.00 Recreation workers
____ 39-9041.00 Residential advisers
____ 39-9099.99 Personal care and service workers, all other*

*Summary Report only

O*Net-SOC Code	O*Net-SOC Title

41-0000 SALES AND RELATED OCCUPATIONS

41-1000 Supervisors, Sales Workers

____ 41-1011.00 First-line supervisors/managers of retail sales workers

____ 41-1012.00 First-line supervisors/managers of non–retail sales workers

41-2000 Retail Sales Workers

____ 41-2011.00 Cashiers

____ 41-2012.00 Gaming change persons and booth cashiers*

____ 41-2021.00 Counter and rental clerks

____ 41-2022.00 Parts salespersons

____ 41-2031.00 Retail salespersons

41-3000 Sales Representatives, Services

____ 41-3011.00 Advertising sales agents

____ 41-3021.00 Insurance sales agents

____ 41-3031.00 Securities, commodities, and financial services sales agents*

____ 41-3031.01 Sales agents, securities and commodities

____ 41-3031.02 Sales agents, financial services

____ 41-3041.00 Travel agents

____ 41-3099.99 Sales representatives, services, all other*

41-4000 Sales Representatives, Wholesale and Manufacturing

____ 41-4011.00 Sales representatives, wholesale and manufacturing, technical and scientific products*

____ 41-4011.01 Sales representatives, agricultural

____ 41-4011.02 Sales representatives, chemical and pharmaceutical

____ 41-4011.03 Sales representatives, electrical/electronic

____ 41-4011.04 Sales representatives, mechanical equipment and supplies

____ 41-4011.05 Sales representatives, medical

____ 41-4011.06 Sales representatives, instruments

____ 41-4012.00 Sales representatives, wholesale and manufacturing, except technical and scientific products

41-9000 Other Sales and Related Workers

____ 41-9011.00 Demonstrators and product promoters

____ 41-9012.00 Models

____ 41-9021.00 Real estate brokers*

____ 41-9022.00 Real estate sales agents

____ 41-9031.00 Sales engineers

____ 41-9041.00 Telemarketers

____ 41-9091.00 Door-to-door sales workers, news and street vendors, and related workers

____ 41-9099.99 Sales and related workers, all other*

43-0000 OFFICE AND ADMINISTRATIVE SUPPORT OCCUPATIONS

43-1000 Supervisors, Office and Administrative Support Workers

____ 43-1011.00 First-line supervisors/managers of office and administrative support workers*

____ 43-1011.01 First-line supervisors, customer service

____ 43-1011.02 First-line supervisors, administrative support

43-2000 Communications Equipment Operators

____ 43-2011.00 Switchboard operators, including answering service

____ 43-2021.00 Telephone operators*

____ 43-2021.01 Directory assistance operators

____ 43-2021.02 Central office operators

____ 43-2099.99 Communications equipment operators, all other*

43-3000 Financial Clerks

____ 43-3011.00 Bill and account collectors

____ 43-3021.00 Billing and posting clerks and machine operators*

____ 43-3021.01 Statement clerks

____ 43-3021.02 Billing, cost, and rate clerks

____ 43-3021.03 Billing, posting, and calculating machine operators

____ 43-3031.00 Bookkeeping, accounting, and auditing clerks

____ 43-3041.00 Gaming cage workers*

____ 43-3051.00 Payroll and timekeeping clerks

____ 43-3061.00 Procurement clerks

____ 43-3071.00 Tellers

43-4000 Information and Record Clerks

____ 43-4011.00 Brokerage clerks

____ 43-4021.00 Correspondence clerks

____ 43-4031.00 Court, municipal, and license clerks*

____ 43-4031.01 Court clerks

____ 43-4031.02 Municipal clerks

____ 43-4031.03 License clerks

____ 43-4041.00 Credit authorizers, checkers, and clerks*

____ 43-4041.01 Credit authorizers

____ 43-4041.02 Credit checkers

*Summary Report only

O*Net-SOC Code	O*Net-SOC Title
____ 43-4051.00	Customer service representatives*
____ 43-4051.01	Adjustment clerks
____ 43-4051.02	Customer service representatives, utilities
____ 43-4061.00	Eligibility interviewers, government programs*
____ 43-4061.01	Claims takers, unemployment benefits
____ 43-4061.02	Welfare eligibility workers and interviewers
____ 43-4071.00	File clerks
____ 43-4081.00	Hotel, motel, and resort desk clerks
____ 43-4111.00	Interviewers, except eligibility and loan
____ 43-4121.00	Library assistants, clerical
____ 43-4131.00	Loan interviewers and clerks
____ 43-4141.00	New accounts clerks
____ 43-4151.00	Order clerks
____ 43-4161.00	Human resources assistants, except payroll and timekeeping
____ 43-4171.00	Receptionists and information clerks
____ 43-4181.00	Reservation and transportation ticket agents and travel clerks*
____ 43-4181.01	Travel clerks
____ 43-4181.02	Reservation and transportation ticket agents
____ 43-4199.99	Information and record clerks, all other*

43-5000 Material Recording, Scheduling, Dispatching, and Distributing Workers

____ 43-5011.00	Cargo and freight agents
____ 43-5021.00	Couriers and messengers
____ 43-5031.00	Police, fire, and ambulance dispatchers
____ 43-5032.00	Dispatchers, except police, fire, and ambulance
____ 43-5041.00	Meter readers, utilities
____ 43-5051.00	Postal service clerks
____ 43-5052.00	Postal service mail carriers
____ 43-5053.00	Postal service mail sorters, processors, and processing machine operators*
____ 43-5061.00	Production, planning, and expediting clerks
____ 43-5071.00	Shipping, receiving, and traffic clerks
____ 43-5081.00	Stock clerks and order fillers*
____ 43-5081.01	Stock clerks, sales floor
____ 43-5081.02	Marking clerks
____ 43-5081.03	Stock clerks—stockroom, warehouse, or storage yard
____ 43-5081.04	Order fillers, wholesale and retail sales

O*Net-SOC Code	O*Net-SOC Title
____ 43-5111.00	Weighers, measurers, checkers, and samplers, recordkeeping

43-6000 Secretaries and Administrative Assistants

____ 43-6011.00	Executive secretaries and administrative assistants
____ 43-6012.00	Legal secretaries
____ 43-6013.00	Medical secretaries
____ 43-6014.00	Secretaries, except legal, medical, and executive

43-9000 Other Office and Administrative Support Workers

____ 43-9011.00	Computer operators
____ 43-9021.00	Data entry keyers
____ 43-9022.00	Word processors and typists
____ 43-9031.00	Desktop publishers
____ 43-9041.00	Insurance claims and policy processing clerks*
____ 43-9041.01	Insurance claims clerks
____ 43-9041.02	Insurance policy processing clerks
____ 43-9051.00	Mail clerks and mail machine operators, except postal service*
____ 43-9051.01	Mail machine operators, preparation and handling
____ 43-9051.02	Mail clerks, except mail machine operators and postal service
____ 43-9061.00	Office clerks, general
____ 43-9071.00	Office machine operators, except computer*
____ 43-9071.01	Duplicating machine operators
____ 43-9081.00	Proofreaders and copy markers
____ 43-9111.00	Statistical assistants
____ 43-9199.99	Office and administrative support workers, all other*

45-0000 FARMING, FISHING, AND FORESTRY OCCUPATIONS

45-1000 Supervisors, Farming, Fishing, and Forestry Workers

____ 45-1011.00	First-line supervisors/managers of farming, fishing, and forestry workers*
____ 45-1011.01	First-line supervisors and manager/supervisors—agricultural crop workers
____ 45-1011.02	First-line supervisors and manager/supervisors—animal husbandry workers
____ 45-1011.03	First-line supervisors and manager/supervisors—animal care workers, except livestock
____ 45-1011.04	First-line supervisors and manager/supervisors—horticultural workers

*Summary Report only

O*Net-SOC Code	O*Net-SOC Title
____ 45-1011.05	First-line supervisors and manager/supervisors—logging workers
____ 45-1011.06	First-line supervisors and manager/supervisors—fishery workers
____ 45-1012.00	Farm labor contractors*

45-2000 Agricultural Workers

____ 45-2011.00	Agricultural inspectors
____ 45-2021.00	Animal breeders
____ 45-2041.00	Graders and sorters, agricultural products
____ 45-2091.00	Agricultural equipment operators
____ 45-2092.00	Farmworkers and laborers, crop, nursery, and greenhouse*
____ 45-2092.01	Nursery workers
____ 45-2092.02	General farmworkers
____ 45-2093.00	Farmworkers, farm and ranch animals
____ 45-2099.99	Agricultural workers, all other*

45-3000 Fishing and Hunting Workers

____ 45-3011.00	Fishers and related fishing workers
____ 45-3021.00	Hunters and trappers

45-4000 Forest, Conservation, and Logging Workers

____ 45-4011.00	Forest and conservation workers
____ 45-4021.00	Fallers
____ 45-4022.00	Logging equipment operators*
____ 45-4022.01	Logging tractor operators
____ 45-4023.00	Log graders and scalers
____ 45-4029.99	Logging workers, all other*

47-0000 CONSTRUCTION AND EXTRACTION OCCUPATIONS

47-1000 Supervisors, Construction and Extraction Workers

____ 47-1011.00	First-line supervisors/managers of construction trades and extraction workers*
____ 47-1011.01	First-line supervisors and manager/supervisors—construction trades workers
____ 47-1011.02	First-line supervisors and manager/supervisors—extractive workers

47-2000 Construction Trades Workers

____ 47-2011.00	Boilermakers
____ 47-2021.00	Brickmasons and blockmasons
____ 47-2022.00	Stonemasons
____ 47-2031.00	Carpenters*

O*Net-SOC Code	O*Net-SOC Title
____ 47-2031.01	Construction carpenters
____ 47-2031.02	Rough carpenters
____ 47-2031.03	Carpenter assemblers and repairers
____ 47-2031.04	Ship carpenters and joiners
____ 47-2031.05	Boat builders and shipwrights
____ 47-2031.06	Brattice builders
____ 47-2041.00	Carpet installers
____ 47-2042.00	Floor layers, except carpet, wood, and hard tiles
____ 47-2043.00	Floor sanders and finishers
____ 47-2044.00	Tile and marble setters
____ 47-2051.00	Cement masons and concrete finishers
____ 47-2053.00	Terrazzo workers and finishers
____ 47-2061.00	Construction laborers
____ 47-2071.00	Paving, surfacing, and tamping equipment operators
____ 47-2072.00	Pile-driver operators
____ 47-2073.00	Operating engineers and other construction equipment operators*
____ 47-2073.01	Grader, bulldozer, and scraper operators
____ 47-2073.02	Operating engineers
____ 47-2081.00	Drywall and ceiling tile installers*
____ 47-2081.01	Ceiling tile installers
____ 47-2081.02	Drywall installers
____ 47-2082.00	Tapers
____ 47-2111.00	Electricians
____ 47-2121.00	Glaziers
____ 47-2131.00	Insulation workers, floor, ceiling, and wall
____ 47-2132.00	Insulation workers, mechanical
____ 47-2141.00	Painters, construction and maintenance
____ 47-2142.00	Paperhangers
____ 47-2151.00	Pipelayers
____ 47-2152.00	Plumbers, pipefitters, and steamfitters*
____ 47-2152.01	Pipe fitters
____ 47-2152.02	Plumbers
____ 47-2152.03	Pipelaying fitters
____ 47-2161.00	Plasterers and stucco masons
____ 47-2171.00	Reinforcing iron and rebar workers
____ 47-2181.00	Roofers
____ 47-2211.00	Sheet metal workers
____ 47-2221.00	Structural iron and steel workers

47-3000 Helpers, Construction Trades

____ 47-3011.00	Helpers—brickmasons, blockmasons, stonemasons, and tile and marble setters
____ 47-3012.00	Helpers—carpenters
____ 47-3013.00	Helpers—electricians
____ 47-3014.00	Helpers—painters, paperhangers, plasterers, and stucco masons
____ 47-3015.00	Helpers—pipelayers, plumbers, pipefitters, and steamfitters

*Summary Report only

O*Net-SOC Code	O*Net-SOC Title	O*Net-SOC Code	O*Net-SOC Title
____ 47-3016.00	Helpers—roofers*	____ 49-2011.01	Automatic teller machine servicers
____ 47-3019.99	Helpers, construction trades, all other*	____ 49-2011.02	Data processing equipment repairers
		____ 49-2011.03	Office machine and cash register servicers

47-4000 Other Construction and Related Workers

____ 47-4011.00 Construction and building inspectors
____ 47-4021.00 Elevator installers and repairers
____ 47-4031.00 Fence erectors
____ 47-4041.00 Hazardous materials removal workers*
____ 47-4041.01 Irradiated-fuel handlers
____ 47-4051.00 Highway maintenance workers
____ 47-4061.00 Rail track laying and maintenance equipment operators
____ 47-4071.00 Septic tank servicers and sewer pipe cleaners
____ 47-4091.00 Segmental pavers*
____ 47-4099.99 Construction and related workers, all other*

47-5000 Extraction Workers

____ 47-5011.00 Derrick operators, oil and gas
____ 47-5012.00 Rotary drill operators, oil and gas
____ 47-5013.00 Service unit operators, oil, gas, and mining
____ 47-5021.00 Earth drillers, except oil and gas*
____ 47-5021.01 Construction drillers
____ 47-5021.02 Well and core drill operators
____ 47-5031.00 Explosives workers, ordnance handling experts, and blasters
____ 47-5041.00 Continuous mining machine operators
____ 47-5042.00 Mine cutting and channeling machine operators
____ 47-5049.99 Mining machine operators, all other*
____ 47-5051.00 Rock splitters, quarry
____ 47-5061.00 Roof bolters, mining
____ 47-5071.00 Roustabouts, oil and gas
____ 47-5081.00 Helpers—extraction workers
____ 47-5099.99 Extraction workers, all other*

49-0000 INSTALLATION, MAINTENANCE, AND REPAIR OCCUPATIONS

49-1000 Supervisors, Installation, Maintenance, and Repair Workers

____ 49-1011.00 First-line supervisors/managers of mechanics, installers, and repairers

49-2000 Electrical and Electronic Equipment Mechanics, Installers, and Repairers

____ 49-2011.00 Computer, automated teller, and office machine repairers*

____ 49-2021.00 Radio mechanics
____ 49-2022.00 Telecommunications equipment installers and repairers, except line installers*
____ 49-2022.01 Central office and PBX installers and repairers
____ 49-2022.02 Frame wirers, central office
____ 49-2022.03 Communication equipment mechanics, installers, and repairers
____ 49-2022.04 Telecommunications facility examiners
____ 49-2022.05 Station installers and repairers, telephone
____ 49-2091.00 Avionics technicians
____ 49-2092.00 Electric motor, power tool, and related repairers*
____ 49-2092.01 Electric home appliance and power tool repairers
____ 49-2092.02 Electric motor and switch assemblers and repairers
____ 49-2092.03 Battery repairers
____ 49-2092.04 Transformer repairers
____ 49-2092.05 Electrical parts reconditioners
____ 49-2092.06 Hand and portable power tool repairers
____ 49-2093.00 Electrical and electronics installers and repairers, transportation equipment
____ 49-2094.00 Electrical and electronics repairers, commercial and industrial equipment
____ 49-2095.00 Electrical and electronics repairers, powerhouse, substation, and relay
____ 49-2096.00 Electronic equipment installers and repairers, motor vehicles
____ 49-2097.00 Electronic home entertainment equipment installers and repairers
____ 49-2098.00 Security and fire alarm systems installers*

49-3000 Vehicle and Mobile Equipment Mechanics, Installers, and Repairers

____ 49-3011.00 Aircraft mechanics and service technicians*
____ 49-3011.01 Airframe and power plant mechanics
____ 49-3011.02 Aircraft engine specialists
____ 49-3011.03 Aircraft body and bonded structure repairers
____ 49-3021.00 Automotive body and related repairers

*Summary Report only

O*Net-SOC Code	O*Net-SOC Title
____ 49-3022.00	Automotive glass installers and repairers
____ 49-3023.00	Automotive service technicians and mechanics*
____ 49-3023.01	Automotive master mechanics
____ 49-3023.02	Automotive specialty technicians
____ 49-3031.00	Bus and truck mechanics and diesel engine specialists
____ 49-3041.00	Farm equipment mechanics
____ 49-3042.00	Mobile heavy equipment mechanics, except engines
____ 49-3043.00	Rail car repairers
____ 49-3051.00	Motorboat mechanics
____ 49-3052.00	Motorcycle mechanics
____ 49-3053.00	Outdoor power equipment and other small-engine mechanics
____ 49-3091.00	Bicycle repairers
____ 49-3092.00	Recreational vehicle service technicians
____ 49-3093.00	Tire repairers and changers

49-9000   Other Installation, Maintenance, and Repair Occupations

O*Net-SOC Code	O*Net-SOC Title
____ 49-9011.00	Mechanical door repairers
____ 49-9012.00	Control and valve installers and repairers, except mechanical door*
____ 49-9012.01	Electric meter installers and repairers
____ 49-9012.02	Valve and regulator repairers
____ 49-9012.03	Meter mechanics
____ 49-9021.00	Heating, air-conditioning, and refrigeration mechanics and installers*
____ 49-9021.01	Heating and air-conditioning mechanics
____ 49-9021.02	Refrigeration mechanics
____ 49-9031.00	Home appliance repairers*
____ 49-9031.01	Home appliance installers
____ 49-9031.02	Gas appliance repairers
____ 49-9041.00	Industrial machinery mechanics
____ 49-9042.00	Maintenance and repair workers, general
____ 49-9043.00	Maintenance workers, machinery
____ 49-9044.00	Millwrights
____ 49-9045.00	Refractory materials repairers, except brickmasons
____ 49-9051.00	Electrical power-line installers and repairers
____ 49-9052.00	Telecommunications line installers and repairers
____ 49-9061.00	Camera and photographic equipment repairers
____ 49-9062.00	Medical equipment repairers
____ 49-9063.00	Musical instrument repairers and tuners*
____ 49-9063.01	Keyboard instrument repairers and tuners

O*Net-SOC Code	O*Net-SOC Title
____ 49-9063.02	Stringed instrument repairers and tuners
____ 49-9063.03	Reed or wind instrument repairers and tuners
____ 49-9063.04	Percussion instrument repairers and tuners
____ 49-9064.00	Watch repairers
____ 49-9069.99	Precision instrument and equipment repairers, all other*
____ 49-9091.00	Coin, vending, and amusement machine servicers and repairers
____ 49-9092.00	Commercial divers
____ 49-9093.00	Fabric menders, except garment
____ 49-9094.00	Locksmiths and safe repairers
____ 49-9095.00	Manufactured building and mobile home installers
____ 49-9096.00	Riggers
____ 49-9097.00	Signal and track switch repairers
____ 49-9098.00	Helpers—installation, maintenance, and repair workers
____ 49-9099.99	Installation, maintenance, and repair workers, all other*

51-0000   PRODUCTION OCCUPATIONS

51-1000   Supervisors, Production Occupations

O*Net-SOC Code	O*Net-SOC Title
____ 51-1011.00	First-line supervisors/managers of production and operating workers

51-2000   Assemblers and Fabricators

O*Net-SOC Code	O*Net-SOC Title
____ 51-2011.00	Aircraft structure, surfaces, rigging, and systems assemblers*
____ 51-2011.01	Aircraft structure assemblers, precision
____ 51-2011.02	Aircraft systems assemblers, precision
____ 51-2011.03	Aircraft rigging assemblers
____ 51-2021.00	Coil winders, tapers, and finishers
____ 51-2022.00	Electrical and electronic equipment assemblers
____ 51-2023.00	Electromechanical equipment assemblers
____ 51-2031.00	Engine and other machine assemblers
____ 51-2041.00	Structural metal fabricators and fitters*
____ 51-2041.01	Metal fabricators, structural metal products
____ 51-2041.02	Fitters, structural metal—precision
____ 51-2091.00	Fiberglass laminators and fabricators*
____ 51-2092.00	Team assemblers*
____ 51-2093.00	Timing device assemblers, adjusters, and calibrators
____ 51-2099.99	Assemblers and fabricators, all other*

*Summary Report only

O*Net-SOC Code	O*Net-SOC Title	O*Net-SOC Code	O*Net-SOC Title

51-3000 Food Processing Workers

____ 51-3011.00 Bakers*

____ 51-3011.01 Bakers, bread and pastry

____ 51-3011.02 Bakers, manufacturing

____ 51-3021.00 Butchers and meat cutters

____ 51-3022.00 Meat, poultry, and fish cutters and trimmers

____ 51-3023.00 Slaughterers and meat packers

____ 51-3091.00 Food and tobacco roasting, baking, and drying machine operators and tenders

____ 51-3092.00 Food batchmakers

____ 51-3093.00 Food cooking machine operators and tenders

51-4000 Metal Workers and Plastic Workers

____ 51-4011.00 Computer-controlled machine tool operators, metal and plastic*

____ 51-4011.01 Numeric control machine tool operators and tenders, metal and plastic

____ 51-4012.00 Numeric tool and process control programmers

____ 51-4021.00 Extruding and drawing machine setters, operators, and tenders, metal and plastic

____ 51-4022.00 Forging machine setters, operators, and tenders, metal and plastic

____ 51-4023.00 Rolling machine setters, operators, and tenders, metal and plastic

____ 51-4031.00 Cutting, punching, and press machine setters, operators, and tenders, metal and plastic*

____ 51-4031.01 Sawing machine tool setters and set-up operators, metal and plastic

____ 51-4031.02 Punching machine setters and set-up operators, metal and plastic

____ 51-4031.03 Press and press brake machine setters and set-up operators, metal and plastic

____ 51-4031.04 Shear and slitter machine setters and set-up operators, metal and plastic

____ 51-4032.00 Drilling and boring machine tool setters, operators, and tenders, metal and plastic

____ 51-4033.00 Grinding, lapping, polishing, and buffing machine tool setters, operators, and tenders, metal and plastic*

____ 51-4033.01 Grinding, honing, lapping, and deburring machine set-up operators

____ 51-4033.02 Buffing and polishing set-up operators

____ 51-4034.00 Lathe and turning machine tool setters, operators, and tenders metal and plastic

____ 51-4035.00 Milling and planing machine setters, operators, and tenders, metal and plastic

____ 51-4041.00 Machinists

____ 51-4051.00 Metal-refining furnace operators and tenders

____ 51-4052.00 Pourers and casters, metal

____ 51-4061.00 Model makers, metal and plastic

____ 51-4062.00 Patternmakers, metal and plastic

____ 51-4071.00 Foundry mold and coremakers

____ 51-4072.00 Molding, coremaking, and casting machine setters, operators, and tenders, metal and plastic*

____ 51-4072.01 Plastic molding and casting machine setters and set-up operators

____ 51-4072.02 Plastic molding and casting machine operators and tenders

____ 51-4072.03 Metal molding, coremaking, and casting machine setters and set-up operators

____ 51-4072.04 Metal molding, coremaking, and casting machine operators and tenders

____ 51-4072.05 Casting machine set-up operators

____ 51-4081.00 Multiple machine tool setters, operators, and tenders, metal and plastic*

____ 51-4081.01 Combination machine tool setters and set-up operators, metal and plastic

____ 51-4081.02 Combination machine tool operators and tenders, metal and plastic

____ 51-4111.00 Tool and die makers

____ 51-4121.00 Welders, cutters, solderers, and brazers*

____ 51-4121.01 Welders, production

____ 51-4121.02 Welders and cutters

____ 51-4121.03 Welder-fitters

____ 51-4121.04 Solderers

____ 51-4121.05 Brazers

____ 51-4122.00 Welding, soldering, and brazing machine setters, operators, and tenders*

____ 51-4122.01 Welding machine setters and set-up operators

____ 51-4122.02 Welding machine operators and tenders

____ 51-4122.03 Soldering and brazing machine setters and set-up operators

____ 51-4122.04 Soldering and brazing machine operators and tenders

O*Net-SOC Code	O*Net-SOC Title	O*Net-SOC Code	O*Net-SOC Title
____ 51-4191.00	Heat treating equipment setters, operators, and tenders, metal and plastic*	____ 51-5023.02	Offset lithographic press setters and set-up operators
____ 51-4191.01	Heating equipment setters and set-up operators, metal and plastic	____ 51-5023.03	Letterpress setters and set-up operators
____ 51-4191.02	Heat treating, annealing, and tempering machine operators and tenders, metal and plastic	____ 51-5023.04	Design printing machine setters and set-up operators
____ 51-4191.03	Heaters, metal and plastic	____ 51-5023.05	Marking and identification printing machine setters and set-up operators
____ 51-4192.00	Layout workers, metal and plastic	____ 51-5023.06	Screen printing machine setters and set-up operators
____ 51-4193.00	Plating and coating machine setters, operators, and tenders, metal and plastic*	____ 51-5023.07	Embossing machine set-up operators
____ 51-4193.01	Electrolytic plating and coating machine setters and set-up operators, metal and plastic	____ 51-5023.08	Engraver set-up operators
		____ 51-5023.09	Printing press machine operators and tenders
____ 51-4193.02	Electrolytic plating and coating machine operators and tenders, metal and plastic		

51-6000   Textile, Apparel, and Furnishings Workers

O*Net-SOC Code	O*Net-SOC Title	O*Net-SOC Code	O*Net-SOC Title
____ 51-4193.03	Nonelectrolytic plating and coating machine setters and set-up operators, metal and plastic	____ 51-6011.00	Laundry and dry-cleaning workers*
____ 51-4193.04	Nonelectrolytic plating and coating machine operators and tenders, metal and plastic	____ 51-6011.01	Spotters, dry cleaning
		____ 51-6011.02	Precision dyers
____ 51-4194.00	Tool grinders, filers, and sharpeners	____ 51-6011.03	Laundry and dry-cleaning machine operators and tenders, except pressing
____ 51-4199.99	Metal workers and plastic workers, all other*	____ 51-6021.00	Pressers, textile, garment, and related materials*
		____ 51-6021.01	Pressers, delicate fabrics

51-5000   Printing Workers

O*Net-SOC Code	O*Net-SOC Title	O*Net-SOC Code	O*Net-SOC Title
____ 51-5011.00	Bindery workers*	____ 51-6021.02	Pressing machine operators and tenders—textile, garment, and related materials
____ 51-5011.01	Bindery machine setters and set-up operators	____ 51-6021.03	Pressers, hand
____ 51-5011.02	Bindery machine operators and tenders	____ 51-6031.00	Sewing machine operators*
____ 51-5012.00	Bookbinders	____ 51-6031.01	Sewing machine operators, garment
____ 51-5021.00	Job printers	____ 51-6031.02	Sewing machine operators, non-garment
____ 51-5022.00	Prepress technicians and workers*	____ 51-6041.00	Shoe and leather workers and repairers
____ 51-5022.01	Hand compositors and typesetters	____ 51-6042.00	Shoe machine operators and tenders
____ 51-5022.02	Pasteup workers	____ 51-6051.00	Sewers, hand
____ 51-5022.03	Photoengravers	____ 51-6052.00	Tailors, dressmakers, and custom sewers*
____ 51-5022.04	Camera operators	____ 51-6052.01	Shop and alteration tailors
____ 51-5022.05	Scanner operators	____ 51-6052.02	Custom tailors
____ 51-5022.06	Strippers	____ 51-6061.00	Textile bleaching and dyeing machine operators and tenders
____ 51-5022.07	Platemakers		
____ 51-5022.08	Dot etchers	____ 51-6062.00	Textile cutting machine setters, operators, and tenders
____ 51-5022.09	Electronic masking system operators	____ 51-6063.00	Textile knitting and weaving machine setters, operators, and tenders
____ 51-5022.10	Electrotypers and stereotypers		
____ 51-5022.11	Plate finishers	____ 51-6064.00	Textile winding, twisting, and drawing out machine setters, operators, and tenders
____ 51-5022.12	Typesetting and composing machine operators and tenders		
____ 51-5022.13	Photoengraving and lithographing machine operators and tenders		
____ 51-5023.00	Printing machine operators*		
____ 51-5023.01	Precision printing workers		

*Summary Report only

O*Net-SOC Code	O*Net-SOC Title
____ 51-6091.00	Extruding and forming machine setters, operators, and tenders, synthetic and glass fibers*
____ 51-6091.01	Extruding and forming machine operators and tenders, synthetic or glass fibers
____ 51-6092.00	Fabric and apparel patternmakers
____ 51-6093.00	Upholsterers
____ 51-6099.99	Textile, apparel, and furnishings workers, all other*

51-7000   Woodworkers

O*Net-SOC Code	O*Net-SOC Title
____ 51-7011.00	Cabinetmakers and bench carpenters
____ 51-7021.00	Furniture finishers
____ 51-7031.00	Model makers, wood
____ 51-7032.00	Patternmakers, wood
____ 51-7041.00	Sawing machine setters, operators, and tenders, wood*
____ 51-7041.01	Sawing machine setters and set-up operators
____ 51-7041.02	Sawing machine operators and tenders
____ 51-7042.00	Woodworking machine setters, operators, and tenders, except sawing*
____ 51-7042.01	Woodworking machine setters and set-up operators, except sawing
____ 51-7042.02	Woodworking machine operators and tenders, except sawing
____ 51-7099.99	Woodworkers, all other*

51-8000   Plant and System Operators

O*Net-SOC Code	O*Net-SOC Title
____ 51-8011.00	Nuclear power reactor operators
____ 51-8012.00	Power distributors and dispatchers
____ 51-8013.00	Power plant operators*
____ 51-8013.01	Power generating plant operators, except auxiliary equipment operators
____ 51-8013.02	Auxiliary equipment operators, power
____ 51-8021.00	Stationary engineers and boiler operators*
____ 51-8021.01	Boiler operators and tenders, low pressure
____ 51-8021.02	Stationary engineers
____ 51-8031.00	Water and liquid waste treatment plant and system operators
____ 51-8091.00	Chemical plant and system operators
____ 51-8092.00	Gas plant operators*
____ 51-8092.01	Gas processing plant operators
____ 51-8092.02	Gas distribution plant operators
____ 51-8093.00	Petroleum pump system operators, refinery operators, and gaugers*
____ 51-8093.01	Petroleum pump system operators

O*Net-SOC Code	O*Net-SOC Title
____ 51-8093.02	Petroleum refinery and control panel operators
____ 51-8093.03	Gaugers
____ 51-8099.99	Plant and system operators, all other*

51-9000   Other Production Occupations

O*Net-SOC Code	O*Net-SOC Title
____ 51-9011.00	Chemical equipment operators and tenders*
____ 51-9011.01	Chemical equipment controllers and operators
____ 51-9011.02	Chemical equipment tenders
____ 51-9012.00	Separating, filtering, clarifying, precipitating, and still machine setters, operators, and tenders
____ 51-9021.00	Crushing, grinding, and polishing machine setters, operators, and tenders
____ 51-9022.00	Grinding and polishing workers, hand
____ 51-9023.00	Mixing and blending machine setters, operators, and tenders
____ 51-9031.00	Cutters and trimmers, hand
____ 51-9032.00	Cutting and slicing machine setters, operators, and tenders*
____ 51-9032.01	Fiber product cutting machine setters and set-up operators
____ 51-9032.02	Stone sawyers
____ 51-9032.03	Glass cutting machine setters and set-up operators
____ 51-9032.04	Cutting and slicing machine operators and tenders
____ 51-9041.00	Extruding, forming, pressing, and compacting machine setters, operators, and tenders*
____ 51-9041.01	Extruding, forming, pressing, and compacting machine setters and set-up operators
____ 51-9041.02	Extruding, forming, pressing, and compacting machine operators and tenders
____ 51-9051.00	Furnace, kiln, oven, drier, and kettle operators and tenders
____ 51-9061.00	Inspectors, testers, sorters, samplers, and weighers*
____ 51-9061.01	Materials inspectors
____ 51-9061.02	Mechanical inspectors
____ 51-9061.03	Precision devices inspectors and testers
____ 51-9061.04	Electrical and electronic inspectors and testers
____ 51-9061.05	Production inspectors, testers, graders, sorters, samplers, weighers
____ 51-9071.00	Jewelers and precious stone and metal workers*

*Summary Report only

O*Net-SOC Code	O*Net-SOC Title
____ 51-9071.01	Jewelers
____ 51-9071.02	Silversmiths
____ 51-9071.03	Model and mold makers, jewelry
____ 51-9071.04	Bench workers, jewelry
____ 51-9071.05	Pewter casters and finishers
____ 51-9071.06	Gem and diamond workers
____ 51-9081.00	Dental laboratory technicians
____ 51-9082.00	Medical appliance technicians
____ 51-9083.00	Ophthalmic laboratory technicians*
____ 51-9083.01	Precision lens grinders and polishers
____ 51-9083.02	Optical instrument assemblers
____ 51-9111.00	Packaging and filling machine operators and tenders
____ 51-9121.00	Coating, painting, and spraying machine setters, operators, and tenders*
____ 51-9121.01	Coating, painting, and spraying machine setters and set-up operators
____ 51-9121.02	Coating, painting, and spraying machine operators and tenders
____ 51-9122.00	Painters, transportation equipment
____ 51-9123.00	Painting, coating, and decorating workers
____ 51-9131.00	Photographic process workers*
____ 51-9131.01	Photographic retouchers and restorers
____ 51-9131.02	Photographic reproduction technicians
____ 51-9131.03	Photographic hand developers
____ 51-9131.04	Film laboratory technicians
____ 51-9132.00	Photographic processing machine operators
____ 51-9141.00	Semiconductor processors
____ 51-9191.00	Cementing and gluing machine operators and tenders
____ 51-9192.00	Cleaning, washing, and metal pickling equipment operators and tenders
____ 51-9193.00	Cooling and freezing equipment operators and tenders
____ 51-9194.00	Etchers and engravers*
____ 51-9194.01	Precision etchers and engravers, hand or machine
____ 51-9194.02	Engravers/carvers
____ 51-9194.03	Etchers
____ 51-9194.04	Pantograph engravers
____ 51-9194.05	Etchers, hand
____ 51-9194.06	Engravers, hand
____ 51-9195.00	Molders, shapers, and casters, except metal and plastic*
____ 51-9195.01	Precision mold and pattern casters, except nonferrous metals
____ 51-9195.02	Precision pattern and die casters, nonferrous metals
____ 51-9195.03	Stone cutters and carvers

O*Net-SOC Code	O*Net-SOC Title
____ 51-9195.04	Glass blowers, molders, benders, and finishers
____ 51-9195.05	Potters
____ 51-9195.06	Mold makers, hand
____ 51-9195.07	Molding and casting workers
____ 51-9196.00	Paper goods machine setters, operators, and tenders
____ 51-9197.00	Tire builders
____ 51-9198.00	Helpers—production workers*
____ 51-9198.01	Production laborers
____ 51-9198.02	Production helpers
____ 51-9199.99	Production workers, all other*

53-0000 TRANSPORTATION AND MATERIAL-MOVING OCCUPATIONS

53-1000 Supervisors, Transportation and Material-Moving Occupations

____ 53-1011.00	Aircraft cargo handling supervisors
____ 53-1021.00	First-line supervisors/managers of helpers, laborers, and material movers, hand
____ 53-1031.00	First-line supervisors/managers of transportation and material-moving machine and vehicle operators

53-2000 Air Transportation Workers

____ 53-2011.00	Airline pilots, copilots, and flight engineers
____ 53-2012.00	Commercial pilots
____ 53-2021.00	Air traffic controllers
____ 53-2022.00	Airfield operations specialists

53-3000 Motor Vehicle Operators

____ 53-3011.00	Ambulance drivers and attendants, except emergency medical technicians
____ 53-3021.00	Bus drivers, transit and intercity
____ 53-3022.00	Bus drivers, school
____ 53-3031.00	Driver/sales workers
____ 53-3032.00	Truck drivers, heavy and tractor-trailer*
____ 53-3032.01	Truck drivers, heavy
____ 53-3032.02	Tractor-trailer truck drivers
____ 53-3033.00	Truck drivers, light or delivery services
____ 53-3041.00	Taxi drivers and chauffeurs
____ 53-3099.99	Motor vehicle operators, all other*

53-4000 Rail Transportation Workers

____ 53-4011.00	Locomotive engineers
____ 53-4012.00	Locomotive firers
____ 53-4013.00	Rail yard engineers, dinkey operators, and hostlers

*Summary Report only

O*Net-SOC Code	O*Net-SOC Title
____ 53-4021.00	Railroad brake, signal, and switch operators*
____ 53-4021.01	Train crew members
____ 53-4021.02	Railroad yard workers
____ 53-4031.00	Railroad conductors and yardmasters
____ 53-4041.00	Subway and streetcar operators
____ 53-4099.99	Rail transportation workers, all other*

53-5000   Water Transportation Workers

____ 53-5011.00	Sailors and marine oilers*
____ 53-5011.01	Able seamen
____ 53-5011.02	Ordinary seamen and marine oilers
____ 53-5021.00	Captains, mates, and pilots of water vessels*
____ 53-5021.01	Ship and boat captains
____ 53-5021.02	Mates—ship, boat, and barge
____ 53-5021.03	Pilots, ship
____ 53-5022.00	Motorboat operators
____ 53-5031.00	Ship engineers

53-6000   Other Transportation Workers

____ 53-6011.00	Bridge and lock tenders
____ 53-6021.00	Parking lot attendants
____ 53-6031.00	Service station attendants
____ 53-6041.00	Traffic technicians
____ 53-6051.00	Transportation inspectors*
____ 53-6051.01	Aviation inspectors
____ 53-6051.02	Public transportation inspectors
____ 53-6051.03	Marine cargo inspectors
____ 53-6051.04	Railroad inspectors
____ 53-6051.05	Motor vehicle inspectors
____ 53-6051.06	Freight inspectors
____ 53-6099.99	Transportation workers, all other*

53-7000   Material-Moving Workers

____ 53-7011.00	Conveyor operators and tenders
____ 53-7021.00	Crane and tower operators
____ 53-7031.00	Dredge operators
____ 53-7032.00	Excavating and loading machine and dragline operators*
____ 53-7032.01	Excavating and loading machine operators
____ 53-7032.02	Dragline operators
____ 53-7033.00	Loading machine operators, underground mining
____ 53-7041.00	Hoist and winch operators
____ 53-7051.00	Industrial truck and tractor operators
____ 53-7061.00	Cleaners of vehicles and equipment
____ 53-7062.00	Laborers and freight, stock, and material movers, hand*
____ 53-7062.01	Stevedores, except equipment operators

O*Net-SOC Code	O*Net-SOC Title
____ 53-7062.02	Grips and set-up workers, motion picture sets, studios, and stages
____ 53-7062.03	Freight, stock, and material movers, hand
____ 53-7063.00	Machine feeders and offbearers
____ 53-7064.00	Packers and packagers, hand
____ 53-7071.00	Gas compressor and gas pumping station operators*
____ 53-7071.01	Gas pumping station operators
____ 53-7071.02	Gas compressor operators
____ 53-7072.00	Pump operators, except wellhead pumpers
____ 53-7073.00	Wellhead pumpers
____ 53-7081.00	Refuse and recyclable material collectors
____ 53-7111.00	Shuttle car operators
____ 53-7121.00	Tank car, truck, and ship loaders
____ 53-7199.99	Material-moving workers, all other*

55-0000   MILITARY-SPECIFIC OCCUPATIONS

55-1000   Military Officer Special and Tactical Operations Leaders/Managers

____ 55-1011.00	Air crew officers*
____ 55-1012.00	Aircraft launch and recovery officers*
____ 55-1013.00	Armored assault vehicle officers*
____ 55-1014.00	Artillery and missile officers*
____ 55-1015.00	Command and control center officers*
____ 55-1016.00	Infantry officers*
____ 55-1017.00	Special forces officers*
____ 55-1019.99	Military officer special and tactical operations leaders/managers, all other*

55-2000   First-Line Enlisted Military Supervisor/Managers

____ 55-2011.00	First-line supervisors/managers of air crew members*
____ 55-2012.00	First-line supervisors/managers of weapons specialists/crew members*
____ 55-2013.00	First-line supervisors/managers of all other tactical operations specialists*

55-3000   Military Enlisted Tactical Operations and Air/Weapons Specialists and Crew Members

____ 55-3011.00	Air crew members*
____ 55-3012.00	Aircraft launch and recovery specialists*
____ 55-3013.00	Armored assault vehicle crew members*

*Summary Report only

O*Net-SOC Code	O*Net-SOC Title	O*Net-SOC Code	O*Net-SOC Title
____ 55-3014.00	Artillery and missile crew members*	____ 55-3018.00	Special forces*
____ 55-3015.00	Command and control center specialists*	____ 55-3019.99	Military enlisted tactical operations and air/weapons specialists and crew members, all other*
____ 55-3016.00	Infantry*		
____ 55-3017.00	Radar and sonar technicians*		

Write the names of any occupations you have uncovered in the *Occupational Information Network* or O*Net in the following spaces, and transfer them to Exercise 3-15 in Chapter 3.

_____   _____

_____   _____

_____   _____

_____   _____

_____   _____

_____   _____

_____   _____

_____   _____

_____   _____

_____   _____

_____   _____

_____   _____

_____   _____

_____   _____

_____   _____

_____   _____

_____   _____

_____   _____

_____   _____

_____   _____

_____   _____

_____   _____

_____   _____

_____   _____

_____   _____

_____   _____

_____   _____

GOE Group Checklist

The purpose of the GOE Group Checklist is to save you time in using a big book that covers the entire world of work. The *Guide for Occupational Exploration (GOE)*, 3rd edition, is not intended to be read from cover to cover. Read only those parts of the GOE that have the greatest interest to you; completing this exercise can help you do that.

The GOE Group Checklist lists the 14 interest areas and 133 work groups and subgroups of the *Guide for Occupational Exploration* (3rd edition). Within each of those groups are one or more occupational titles in Part 1 of the GOE and their job descriptions in Part 2. Go to the two or three interest areas that strike you as being the most interesting ones; you may have done this in Chapter 4. Now check those subgroups you believe should be explored by indicating which ones are of greatest interest to you; try to identify at least four or five of them. If you were unsure of which interest area to select, go through all the interest areas and consider each work group or subgroup.

The *six-digit number code* is given first. (The first two digits refer to one of the 14 interest areas. The second two digits are for the work group; those numbers are not needed in this exercise. The six-digit number indicates the name of the subgroup.) After the name of the group, the *number in parentheses* stands for *the number of occupations in the group* that are titled in Part 1 of the GOE and described in Part 2. If you have access to the *Guide for Occupational Exploration*, 3rd edition, you can get an idea of the specific occupations in each work group and subgroup by looking at the Table of Contents on pages v, vi, and vii of the GOE while you are completing this exercise. There are too many of those occupations (about 1,000) to list here.

01 Arts, Entertainment, and Media (13 groups)

___ 01.01.01 Managerial work in arts, entertainment, and media (5)

___ 01.02.01 Writing and editing (5)

___ 01.03.01 News, broadcasting, and public relations (5)

___ 01.04.01 Visual arts: Studio art (4)

___ 01.04.02 Visual arts: Design (9)

___ 01.05.01 Performing arts, Drama: directing, performing, narrating, and announcing (4)

___ 01.05.02 Performing arts, Music: directing, composing and arranging, and performing (6)

___ 01.05.03 Performing arts, Dance: performing and choreography (2)

___ 01.06.01 Craft arts: Graphic arts, hand lettering, painting (3)

___ 01.07.01 Graphic arts (12)

___ 01.08.01 Media technology (7)

___ 01.09.01 Modeling and personal appearance (3)

___ 01.10.01 Sports: Coaching, instructing, officiating, and performing (4)

02 Science, Math, and Engineering (20 groups)

___ 02.01.01 Managerial work in science, math, and engineering (3)

___ 02.02.01 Physical sciences (8)

___ 02.03.01 Life sciences: Animal specialization (4)

___ 02.03.02 Life sciences: Plant specialization (5)

___ 02.03.03 Life sciences: Plant and animal specialization (7)

___ 02.03.04 Life sciences: Food research (3)

___ 02.04.01 Social sciences: Psychology, sociology, and anthropology (4)

___ 02.04.02 Social sciences: Economics, public policy, and history (7)

___ 02.05.01 Laboratory technology: Physical sciences (6)

___ 02.05.02 Laboratory technology: Life sciences (3)

___ 02.06.01 Mathematics and computers: Data processing (7)

___ 02.06.02 Mathematics and computers: Data analysis (6)

___ 02.07.01 Engineering: Research and systems design (7)

___ 02.07.02 Engineering: Industrial and safety (6)

___ 02.07.03 Engineering: Design (4)

___ 02.07.04 Engineering: General engineering (10)

___ 02.08.01 Engineering technology: Surveying (3)

___ 02.08.02 Engineering technology: Industrial and safety (3)

___ 02.08.03 Engineering technology: Design (6)

___ 02.08.04 Engineering technology: General (9)

03 Plants and Animals (7 groups)

___ 03.01.01 Managerial work in plants and animals: Farming and fishing (9)

___ 03.01.02 Managerial work: Nursery, grounds-keeping, and logging (5)

___ 03.02.01 Animal care and training (6)

___ 03.03.01 Hands-on work: Farming (4)

___ 03.03.02 Hands-on work: Forestry and logging (4)

___ 03.03.03 Hands-on work: Hunting and fishing (2)

___ 03.03.04 Hands-on work: Nursery, grounds-keeping, and pest control (5)

04 Law, Law Enforcement, and Public Safety (10 groups)

___ 04.01.01 Managerial work in law, law enforcement, and public safety (5)

___ 04.02.01 Law: Legal practice and justice administration (4)

___ 04.02.02 Law: Legal support (4)

___ 04.03.01 Law enforcement: Investigation and protection (13)

___ 04.03.02 Law enforcement: Technology (2)

___ 04.03.03 Law enforcement: Security (6)

___ 04.04.01 Public safety: Emergency responding (4)

___ 04.04.02 Public safety: Regulations enforcement (15)

___ 04.05.01 Military: Officers and supervisors (10)

___ 04.05.02 Military: Specialists (8)

05 Mechanics, Installers, and Repairers (8 groups)

___ 05.01.01 Managerial work in mechanics, installers, and repairers (1)

___ 05.02.01 Electrical and electronic systems: Installation and repair (14)

___ 05.02.02 Electrical and electronic systems: Equipment repair (11)

___ 05.03.01 Mechanical work: Vehicles and facilities (23)

___ 05.03.02 Mechanical work: Machinery repair 10)

___ 05.03.03 Mechanical work: Medical and technical equipment (6)

___ 05.03.04 Mechanical work: Musical instrument fabrication and repair (4)

___ 05.04.01 Hands-on work in mechanics, installers, and repairers (3)

06 Construction, Mining, and Drilling (6 groups)

___ 06.01.01 Managerial work in construction, mining, and drilling (3)

___ 06.02.01 Construction: Masonry, stone, and brick work (7)

___ 06.02.02 Construction: Construction and maintenance (21)

___ 06.02.03 Construction: General (19)

___ 06.03.01 Mining and drilling (13)

___ 06.04.01 Hands-on work in construction, extraction, and maintenance (13)

07 Transportation (8 groups)

___ 07.01.01 Managerial work in transportation (3)

___ 07.02.01 Vehicle expediting and coordinating (4)

___ 07.03.01 Air vehicle operation (2)

___ 07.04.01 Water vehicle operation (7)

___ 07.05.01 Truck driving (3)

___ 07.06.01 Rail vehicle operation (4)

___ 07.07.01 Other services requiring driving (6)

___ 07.08.01 Support work in transportation (5)

08 Industrial Production (15 groups)

___ 08.01.01 Managerial work in industrial production (3)

___ 08.02.01 Production technology: Machine set-up and operation (31)

___ 08.02.02 Production technology: Precision hand work (19)

___ 08.02.03 Production technology: Inspection (8)

___ 08.03.01 Production work: Machine work, assorted materials (18)

___ 08.03.02 Production work: Equipment operation, assorted materials processing (20)

___ 08.03.03 Production work: Equipment operation, welding, brazing, and soldering (9)

___ 08.03.04 Production work: Plating and coating (4)

___ 08.03.05 Production work: Printing and reproduction (22)

___ 08.03.06 Production work: Hands-on work, assorted materials (13)

___ 08.04.01 Metal and plastics machining technology (6)

___ 08.05.01 Woodworking technology (4)

___ 08.06.01 Systems operation: Utilities and power plant (8)

___ 08.06.02 Systems operation: Oil, gas, and water distribution (9)

___ 08.07.01 Hands-on work: Loading, moving, hoisting, and conveying (14)

09 Business Detail (12 groups)

___ 09.01.01 Managerial work in business detail (3)

___ 09.02.01 Administrative detail: Administration (3)

___ 09.02.02 Administrative detail: Secretarial work (4)

___ 09.02.03 Administrative detail: Interviewing (4)

___ 09.03.01 Bookkeeping, auditing, and accounting (6)

___ 09.04.01 Material control (2)

___ 09.05.01 Customer service (12)

___ 09.06.01 Communications (6)

___ 09.07.01 Records processing: Verification and proofing (5)

___ 09.07.02 Records processing: Preparation and maintenance (8)

___ 09.08.01 Records and materials processing (10)

___ 09.09.01 Clerical machine operation (10)

10 Sales and Marketing (5 groups)

___ 10.01.01 Managerial work in sales and marketing (5)

___ 10.02.01 Sales technology: Technical sales (6)

___ 10.02.02 Sales technology: Intangible sales (4)

___ 10.03.01 General sales (8)

___ 10.04.01 Personal soliciting (3)

11 Recreation, Travel, and Other Personal Services (9 groups)

___ 11.01.01 Managerial work in recreation, travel, and other personal services (10)

___ 11.02.01 Recreational services (9)

___ 11.03.01 Transportation and lodging services (6)

___ 11.04.01 Barber and beauty services (5)

___ 11.05.01 Food and beverage services: Preparing (9)

___ 11.05.02 Food and beverage services: Serving (7)

___ 11.06.01 Apparel, shoes, leather, and fabric care (11)

___ 11.07.01 Cleaning and building services (3)

___ 11.08.01 Other personal services (5)

12 Education and Social Service (7 groups)

___ 12.01.01 Managerial work in education and social service (6)

___ 12.02.01 Social service: Religious (2)

___ 12.02.02 Social service: Counseling and social work (12)

___ 12.03.01 Educational services: Counseling and evaluation (3)

___ 12.03.02 Educational services: Postsecondary and adult teaching (39)

___ 12.03.03 Educational services: Preschool, elementary, and secondary teaching, and instructing (12)

___ 12.03.04 Educational services: Library and museum (7)

13 General Management and Support (5 groups)

___ 13.01.01 General management work and management of support functions (16)

___ 13.02.01 Management support: Human resources (4)

___ 13.02.02 Management support: Purchasing (3)

___ 13.02.03 Management support: Accounting and auditing (4)

___ 13.02.04 Management and support: Investigation and analysis (16)

14 Medical and Health Services (8 groups)

___ 14.01.01 Managerial work in medical and health services (2)

___ 14.02.01 Medicine and surgery (14)

___ 14.03.01 Dentistry (6)

___ 14.04.01 Health specialties (4)

___ 14.05.01 Medical technology (9)

___ 14.06.01 Medical therapy (13)

___ 14.07.01 Patient care and assistance (5)

___ 14.08.01 Health protection and promotion (4)

Follow the number codes of the groups you have checked to find the work groups and specific occupations in the *Guide for Occupational Exploration*. You can also use the index at the back of the GOE to locate the page numbers for the work groups and their occupations.

Specialized training and where it is obtained for the occupation in a group is given in Part 1 of the GOE. The job descriptions for the nearly 1,000 occupations in Part 2 of the GOE have brief information about what people do in the occupation, education needed, average salary, projected growth or decline of workers, occupational values, skills and abilities required, kinds of interactions with others, and physical work conditions. (The number after each job title is its O*Net number, assigned to it by the U.S. Department of Labor.) Add those occupations you want to explore further to your occupational prospect list.

Part 3 of the GOE is a "Crosswalks to Careers" section. A *crosswalk* is a bridge that enables you to move back and forth between ways of classifying occupations or work groups (as is the case here). The GOE identifies the work groups that correspond in each case with work values, leisure activities, home activities, school subjects, work settings, skills, abilities, and knowledge. Using the crosswalks may help you discover new occupational prospects you could have overlooked.

List the occupational prospects you get from the *Guide for Occupational Exploration* in the following spaces and/or in Exercise 3-15 of Chapter 3.

Origami: An Achievement Motivation Game

Your role in this game is that of a manufacturer who builds and sells products. You are in competition with the other players. The instructor will take the role of a government contract agent. There are seven steps in the game.

1. *Learn and practice* making the product by folding a sheet of paper. The instructor or group leader will show you the proper way to make this product, or see the instructions on page 446.
2. *Set a preliminary goal* by estimating how many acceptable products you can make in a 5-minute production period. Check Table G-1 on page 445 for materials cost and selling prices.
3. *A time trial* will be held so you can determine how long it takes you to make one product.
4. Set your *final goal* after you learn the length of time it takes you to make one product. Notice that there are penalties for changing from your preliminary goal (see Table G-2), but revising your goal may reduce losses or increase profits if you have set your preliminary goal too high or too low. Also, you cannot sell more products than the number you stated for your final goal. (For example, if your final goal is 12, you cannot sell more than 12.)
5. The 5-minute *production period* is held. Time remaining will be announced at intervals.
6. *"Sell" your products* to the government contract agent. Only those products judged acceptable can be sold. In the case of paper airplanes, acceptable means
   a. The cabin (in the middle) must be puffed out.
   b. Both wings must come together equally in the middle of the back of the plane.
   c. The wing tips must be pointed up.
7. *Figure your profit or loss.* How many of your products were sold to the contract agent? Check Table G-1 for the selling price. Then subtract the materials cost and any penalty (see Table G-2) to find your profit or loss.

   Example A. Your final goal was to make 15 products. Your materials cost was $440. You made 15 planes in the production period, and 12 of them were sold for a total of $600. Your profit is $160 ($600 – $440 = $160).

   Example B. Your final goal was to make 12 products. Your materials cost was $375. You made 10 planes, and 6 of them were sold for a total of $300. Your loss is $75 ($300 – $375 = –$75).

Source: Adapted from A. S. Alschuler, D. Tabor, and W. McIntyre (1971), *Teaching achievement motivation: Theory and practice in psychological education* (Middleton, CT: Education Ventures).

Example C. Your final goal was to make 15 products. Your materials cost was $440. You made 15 planes, and all 15 were sold for a total of $750. However, there is a penalty of $6 because you changed your final goal by 3—from a preliminary goal of 12 to a final goal of 15. Your profit is $304 ($750 – $440 – $6).

Table G-1 Product Information

Number of Products	Materials Cost	Selling Price	Number of Products	Materials Cost	Selling Price
1	$50	$50	16	$460	$800
2	95	100	17	480	850
3	135	150	18	500	900
4	170	200	19	520	950
5	200	250	20	540	1000
6	225	300	21	560	1050
7	250	350	22	580	1100
8	275	400	23	600	1150
9	300	450	24	615	1200
10	325	500	25	630	1250
11	350	550	26	645	1300
12	375	600	27	660	1350
13	400	650	28	675	1400
14	420	700	29	690	1450
15	440	750	30	700	1500

(Beyond 30, materials cost goes up $10 per unit and selling price increases by $50 per acceptable product.)

Table G-2 Penalties for Changes from Preliminary Goal to the Final Goal

Change in Goal	Penalty	Change in Goal	Penalty	Change in Goal	Penalty
1 more or 1 less	$2	5 more or 5 less	$10	9 more or 9 less	$18
2 more or 2 less	$4	6 more or 6 less	$12	(Add $2 penalty for	
3 more or 3 less	$6	7 more or 7 less	$14	each unit increase or	
4 more or 4 less	$8	8 more or 8 less	$16	decrease of change)	

Contract Worksheet for Origami Game

	Round 1	Round 2	Round 3
1. *Preliminary goal.* How many acceptable products can you make in a 5-minute production period?	_____		
2. *Time trial. How* long did it take for you to make one product? (Indicate minutes and seconds.)	_____		
3. *Final goal.* Based on the time trial, set your final goal for the 5-minute production period.	_____	_____	_____
4. *Penalty.* What is the difference (if any) between your final goal and your preliminary goal?	_____	_____	_____
5. *Number of products made.* How many planes did you make in the 5-minute production period?	_____	_____	_____
6. *Acceptable products sold.* How many products were accepted for sale by the government contract agent?	_____	_____	_____
7. *Figure your profit or loss.*			
a. Selling price of products sold (Table G-1)	$_____	$_____	$_____
b. Materials cost of final goal (Table G-1) Subtract	$_____	$_____	$_____
c. Penalty (Table G-2) Subtract	$_____	$_____	$_____
d. Total of profit or loss	$_____	$_____	$_____

How to Make the Product (Paper Airplane)

Use a standard 8½- × 11-inch blank sheet of paper (or, to conserve paper, use a half-sheet).

First fold: Take the upper right-hand corner and bring it down to the bottom of the paper (1), and fold (1F).

Second fold: Take the lower right-hand point and bring it up to the top of the paper (2), and fold (2F).

Third fold: Take the bottom half of the paper and bring it even to the top of the paper (3) and fold evenly down the middle (3F).

Fourth fold: Bring the *first layer only* (there are three layers) back down to about ¾″ from the bottom (4), and fold (4F).

Fifth fold: Fold about ½″ to ¾″ up this first layer (5F). The wing tip is pointed *up*.

Sixth and seventh folds: Turn the plane over and fold the top layer (6F, 7F) the same way as you did the fourth and fifth folds. Straighten out the wings and make sure they come together equally. Wing tips must be pointed up.

Eighth and ninth folds: Press the middle layer down gently and make folds on both sides at about a 30-degree angle (8F, 9F).

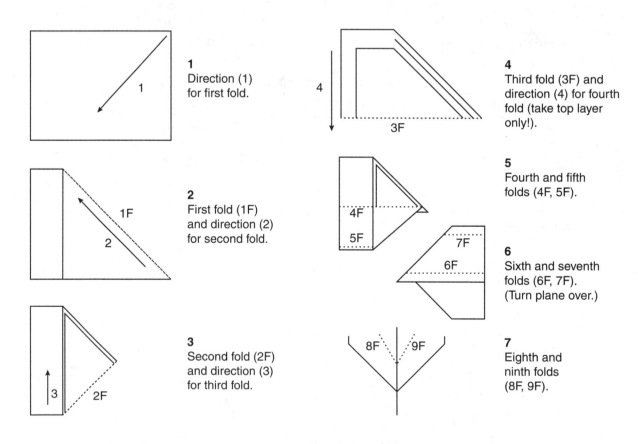

1
Direction (1) for first fold.

2
First fold (1F) and direction (2) for second fold.

3
Second fold (2F) and direction (3) for third fold.

4
Third fold (3F) and direction (4) for fourth fold (take top layer only!).

5
Fourth and fifth folds (4F, 5F).

6
Sixth and seventh folds (6F, 7F). (Turn plane over.)

7
Eighth and ninth folds (8F, 9F).

O*Net Skills, Abilities, and Knowledges

The Occupational Information Network or O*Net, discussed in Chapter 4, has 46 skills, 52 abilities, and 33 knowledge subjects in its database. These skills, abilities, and knowledge areas are listed here with short definitions after each title. Thirty-five skills are used in O*Net's online job descriptions and are organized under six broad categories: *basic, social, complex problem solving, technical, systems*, and *resource management skills*. The 52 abilities are organized into four broad categories: *cognitive, psychomotor, physical strength*, and *sensory abilities*. In most cases, you would use the definition to explain your skill or ability. The subjects making up the areas of knowledge are organized into 10 "domains"—*business and management, manufacturing and production, engineering and technology, mathematics and science, health services, education and training, arts and humanities, law and public safety, communications*, and *transportation*. Check the skills, abilities, and knowledges you believe you have or could acquire with education and training in the spaces provided and save for future reference.

35 O*Net Skills

Basic skills are developed capabilities that help with learning and rapidly acquiring more knowledge.

> (O*Net classifies two broad categories of basic skills, *content* skills and *process* skills.)

Content skills are fundamental skills that are needed to work with or acquire more specific skills.

_____ *Reading comprehension.* Understanding written sentences and paragraphs in work-related documents.

_____ *Active listening.* Giving full attention to the words other people are saying and asking questions as appropriate.

_____ *Writing.* Communicating effectively with others in writing as appropriate for the needs of the audience.

_____ *Speaking.* Talking to others to convey information effectively.

_____ *Mathematics.* Using mathematics to solve problems.

_____ *Science.* Using scientific rules and methods to solve problems.

Process skills are procedures that contribute to the more rapid acquisition of knowledge and skill.

_____ *Critical thinking.* Using logic and analysis to identify the strengths and weaknesses of alternative solutions.

_____ *Active learning.* Understanding the implications of new information for problem solving and decision making.

_____ *Learning strategies.* Using training methods when learning or teaching new things.

_____ *Monitoring.* Assessing the performance of oneself, another person, or organizations to make improvements.

Social skills are developed capabilities used to work with people to achieve goals.

_____ *Social perceptiveness.* Being aware of others' reactions and understanding why they react the way they do.

_____ *Coordination.* Adjusting actions in relation to others' actions.

_____ *Persuasion.* Persuading others to change their minds or behavior.

_____ *Negotiation.* Bringing others together and trying to reconcile differences.

_____ *Instructing.* Teaching others how to do something.

_____ *Service orientation.* Actively looking for ways to help people.

Complex problem-solving skills are developed capabilities used to solve problems in real-world settings.

_____ *Complex problem solving.* Identifying complex problems and reviewing related information to develop and evaluate options and implement solutions.

Technical skills are developed capabilities used to design, set up, operate, and correct problems involving machines and technological systems.

_____ *Operations analysis.* Analyzing needs and product requirements to create a design.

_____ *Technology design.* Generating or adapting equipment and technology to serve user needs.

_____ *Equipment selection.* Determining the kind of tools and equipment needed to do a job.

_____ *Installation.* Installing equipment, machines, wiring, or programs to meet specifications.

_____ *Programming.* Writing computer programs for various purposes.

_____ *Testing.* Conducting tests to determine whether equipment, software, or procedures are operating as expected.

_____ *Operation monitoring.* Watching gauges, dials, or other indicators to make sure a machine is working properly.

_____ *Operation and control.* Controlling operations of equipment or systems.

_____ *Equipment maintenance.* Performing routine maintenance and determining the kind of maintenance needed.

_____ *Troubleshooting.* Determining causes of operating errors and deciding what to do about it.

_____ *Repairing.* Repairing machines or systems using the needed tools.

_____ *Quality control analysis.* Conducting tests and inspections of products or services to evaluate quality or performance.

Systems skills are developed capabilities used to understand, monitor, and improve social and technical systems.

_____ *Judgment and decision making.* Considering the relative costs and benefits of potential actions to choose the best one.

_____ *Systems analysis.* Determining or knowing how a system should work and how changes will affect outcomes.

_____ *Systems evaluation.* Identifying indicators of system performance and the actions needed to improve performance.

Resource management skills are developed capacities used to allocate resources efficiently.

_____ *Time management.* Managing one's own time and the time of others.

_____ *Management of financial resources.* Determining how money will be spent to get the work done, and accounting for these expenditures.

_____ *Management of material resources.* Obtaining and seeing to the appropriate use of equipment, facilities, and materials needed to do certain work.

_____ *Management of personnel resources.* Motivating, developing, and directing people as they work, identifying the best people for the job.

52 O*Net Abilities

21 cognitive abilities. These abilities are mental processes that influence the acquisition and application of knowledge in problem solving.

_____ *Oral comprehension.* Listening to and understanding information and ideas presented through spoken words and sentences

_____ *Written comprehension.* Reading and understanding information and ideas presented in writing.

_____ *Oral expression.* Communicating information and ideas in speaking so others will understand.

_____ *Written expression.* Communicating information and ideas in writing so others will understand.

_____ *Fluency of ideas.* Developing a number of ideas about a given topic, whether or not they are correct or creative.

_____ *Originality.* Developing unusual or clever ideas about a given topic or situation, or to develop creative ways to solve a problem.

_____ *Problem sensitivity.* Recognizing when something is wrong or is likely to go wrong, not necessarily solving a problem.

_____ *Deductive reasoning.* Applying general rules to specific problems to come up with logical answers; deciding if an answer makes sense or provides a logical explanation for why a series of seemingly unrelated events occur.

_____ *Inductive reasoning.* Combining separate pieces of information or specific answers to problems to form general rules or conclusions, including logical explanations for why a series of seemingly unrelated events occur together.

_____ *Information ordering.* Following a given rule or set of rules correctly to change numbers, letters, words, pictures, procedures, and sentences in a certain order.

_____ *Category flexibility.* Producing many rules so each rule tells how to group (or combine) a set of things in a different way.

_____ *Mathematical reasoning.* Understanding and organizing a problem and then selecting a mathematical method or formula to solve the problem.

_____ *Number facility.* Adding, subtracting, multiplying, or dividing quickly and correctly.

_____ *Memorization.* Remembering information such as words, numbers, pictures, and procedures.

_____ *Speed of closure.* Quickly making sense of information that seems to be without meaning or organization; quickly combining and organizing different pieces of information into a meaningful pattern.

_____ *Flexibility of closure.* Identifying or detecting a known pattern (a figure, object, word, or sound) that is hidden in other distracting material.

_____ *Perceptual speed.* Quickly and accurately comparing letters, numbers, objects, pictures, or patterns presented at the same time or one after the other; also includes comparing a presented object with a remembered object.

_____ *Spatial orientation.* Knowing one's location in relation to the environment, or knowing where other objects are in relation to one's self.

_____ *Visualization.* Imagining how something will look after it is moved around or when its parts are moved and rearranged.

_____ *Selective attention.* Concentrating without being distracted while performing a task over a period of time.

_____ *Time sharing.* Efficiently shifting back and forth between two or more activities or sources of information (such as speech, sounds, touch, or other sources).

10 psychomotor abilities. These abilities influence the capacity to manipulate and control objects primarily using fine motor skills.

_____ *Arm–hand steadiness.* Keeping the hand and arm steady while making an arm movement or while holding the arm and hand in one position.

_____ *Manual dexterity.* Making coordinated and quick movements of one hand, a hand together with its arm, or two hands to grasp, manipulate, or assemble very small objects.

_____ *Finger dexterity.* Making precisely coordinated movements of the fingers of one or both hands to grasp, manipulate, or assemble very small objects.

_____ *Control precision.* Making precise adjustments quickly and repeatedly in moving the controls of a machine or vehicle to exact positions.

_____ *Multilimb coordination.* Coordinating movements of two or more limbs together (for example, two arms, two legs, or one leg and one arm) while sitting, standing, and lying down (but not while the body is in motion).

_____ *Response orientation.* Choosing quickly and correctly between two or more movements in response to two or more signals (lights, sounds, pictures, and so on); includes the speed with which the correct response is started with the hand, foot, or other body parts.

_____ *Rate control.* Timing the adjustments of a movement or equipment control in anticipation of changes in the speed and/or direction of a continuously moving object or scene.

_____ *Reaction time.* Responding quickly with the hand, finger, or foot to one signal (sound, light, picture, etc.) when it appears.

_____ *Wrist–finger speed.* Making fast, simple, repeated movements of the fingers, hands, and wrists.

_____ *Speed of limb movement.* Moving the arms or legs quickly.

9 physical strength abilities. These abilities influence strength, endurance, flexibility, balance, and coordination.

_____ *Static strength.* Exerting maximum muscle force to lift, push, pull, or carry objects.

_____ *Explosive strength.* Using short bursts of muscle force to propel oneself (as in jumping or sprinting), or to throw an object.

_____ *Dynamic strength.* Exerting muscle force repeatedly or continuously over time; involves muscular endurance and resistance to muscle fatigue.

_____ *Truck strength.* Using one's abdominal and lower back muscles to support part of the body repeatedly or continuously over time without giving out or fatiguing.

_____ *Stamina.* Exerting oneself physically over long periods of time without getting winded or out of breath.

_____ *Extent flexibility.* Bending, stretching, twisting, or reaching out with the body, arms, and/or legs.

_____ *Dynamic flexibility.* Bending, stretching, twisting, or reaching out with the body, arms, and/or legs quickly and repeatedly.

_____ *Gross body coordination.* Coordinating the movement of the arms, legs, and torso together in activities where the whole body is in motion.

_____ *Gross body equilibrium.* Keeping or regaining one's body balance or staying upright when in an unstable position.

12 sensory abilities. These abilities influence visual, auditory, and speech perception.

_____ *Near vision.* Seeing details of objects at a close range (within a few feet of the observer).

_____ *Far vision.* Seeing details at a distance.

_____ *Visual color discrimination.* Matching or detecting differences between colors, including shades of color and brightness.

_____ *Night vision.* Seeing under low light conditions.

_____ *Peripheral vision.* Seeing objects or movements of objects to one's side when the eyes are focused forward.

_____ *Depth perception.* Judging which of several objects is closer or farther away from the observer, or judging the distance between an object and the observer.

_____ *Glare sensitivity.* Seeing objects in the presence of glare or bright lighting.

_____ *Hearing sensitivity.* Detecting or telling the difference between sounds that vary over broad ranges of pitch and loudness.

_____ *Auditory attention.* Focusing on a single source of auditory (hearing) information in the presence of other distracting sounds.

_____ *Sound localization.* Telling the direction from which a sound originated.

_____ *Speech recognition.* Identifying and understanding the speech of another person.

_____ *Speech clarity.* Speaking clearly so that it is understandable to a listener.

33 O*Net Knowledge Areas—Organized sets of principles and facts applying in general domains.

(*Note:* Start each description with the words "Knowledge of . . ." in all groups. You may want to use the descriptive words rather than the title of the knowledge.)

Business and Management

_____ *Administration and management.* Strategic planning, resource allocation, human resources, leadership technique, production methods, and coordination of people and resources.

_____ *Clerical.* Word processing, managing files and records, doing stenography and transcription, designing forms, following office procedures.

_____ *Economics and accounting.* Dealing in financial markets, banking, and the analysis and reporting of financial data.

_____ *Sales and marketing.* Handling marketing strategy and tactics, product demonstration, sales techniques, and sales control systems.

_____ *Customer and personal service.* Assessing customer needs, meeting quality standards for services, and evaluating customer satisfaction.

Manufacturing and Production

_____ *Production and processing.* Working with raw materials, production processes, quality control, costs, techniques for maximizing the effective manufacture and distribution of goods.

_____ *Food production.* Planting, growing, and harvesting food products (both plant and animal); storage/handling techniques.

Engineering and Technology

_____ *Computers and electronics.* Working with circuit boards, processors, chips, electronic equipment, and computer hardware and software.

_____ *Engineering and technology.* Applying principles, techniques, procedures, and equipment to the design and production of various goods and services.

_____ *Design.* Using design techniques, tools, and principles involved in production of precision technical plans, blueprints, drawings, and models.

_____ *Building and construction.* Using materials, methods, and tools involved in the construction or repair of houses, buildings, or other structures such as highways and roads.

_____ *Mechanical.* Using machines and tools, including their designs, uses, repair, and maintenance.

Mathematics and Science

_____ *Mathematics.* Studying arithmetic, algebra, geometry, calculus, statistics, and their applications.

_____ *Physics.* Studying fluid, material, and atmospheric dynamics, and mechanical, electrical, and atomic structures and processes.

_____ *Chemistry.* Studying chemical composition, structure, and properties of substances and of the transformations they undergo; includes uses of chemicals and their interactions, danger signs, production techniques, and disposal methods.

____ *Biology.* Studying plant and animal organisms, their tissues, cells, functions, and interactions with each other and the environment.

____ *Psychology.* Studying human behavior and performance; individual differences in ability, personality, and interests; learning and motivation; psychological research methods; assessment and treatment of behavioral and affective disorders.

____ *Sociology and anthropology.* Studying group behavior and dynamics, societal trends and influences, human migrations, ethnicity, and cultures and their history and origins.

____ *Geography.* Studying the features of land, sea, and air masses, their physical characteristics, and locations; distribution of plant, animal, and human life.

Health Services

____ *Medicine and dentistry.* Diagnosing and treating human injuries, diseases, and deformities; includes symptoms, treatment alternatives, drug properties and interactions, and preventive health care measures.

____ *Therapy and counseling.* Diagnosing, treating, and rehabilitation of physical and mental problems; career counseling and guidance.

Education and Training

____ *Education and training.* Applying curriculum design, instructing for individuals and groups, measuring training effects.

Arts and Humanities

____ *English language.* Studying structure and content of the English language, the meaning and spelling of words, and the rules of composition and grammar.

____ *Foreign language.* Studying structure and content of a non-English language, including the meaning and spelling of words, rules of composition and grammar, and pronunciation.

____ *Fine arts.* Composing, producing, and performing works of music, dance, visual arts, drama, and sculpture.

____ *History and archeology.* Studying historical events and their causes, indicators, and effects on civilizations and cultures.

____ *Philosophy and theology.* Exploring different philosophical systems and religions; their principles, values, ethics, ways of thinking, customs, practices, and their impact on human culture.

Law and Public Safety

____ *Public safety and security.* Applying local, state, and national security operations for the protection of people, data, and property.

____ *Law and government.* Studying laws, legal codes, court procedures, precedents; government regulations, executive orders, agency rules; democratic political processes.

Communications

____ *Telecommunications.* Handling transmission, broadcasting, switching, control, and operation of telecommunications systems.

_____ *Communications and media.* Using media production, communication, and circulation methods; informing and entertaining by written, oral, and visual media.

Transportation

_____ *Transportation.* Moving people or goods by air, rail, sea, or road, including the relative costs and benefits.

Worksheets for Occupational Information

Worksheets for Occupational Information

Name of Occupation _____   SOC or DOT number _____

   1. Definition of occupation, nature of work, job functions performed

   2. Education, training, experience needed

   3. Personal qualifications, skills, abilities required

   4. Earnings (salary range, benefits)

   5. Working conditions, hours

   6. Location of employment

      a. Work organizations

      b. Geographic areas

   7. Personality characteristics of people in the occupation

   8. Employment and advancement outlook

   9. Personal satisfactions from this work

  10. Advantages and disadvantages of this work

  11. Related occupations

  12. Sources of information

Worksheets for Occupational Information

Name of Occupation _____   SOC or DOT number _____

   1. Definition of occupation, nature of work, job functions performed

   2. Education, training, experience needed

   3. Personal qualifications, skills, abilities required

   4. Earnings (salary range, benefits)

   5. Working conditions, hours

   6. Location of employment

      a. Work organizations

      b. Geographic areas

   7. Personality characteristics of people in the occupation

   8. Employment and advancement outlook

   9. Personal satisfactions from this work

  10. Advantages and disadvantages of this work

  11. Related occupations

  12. Sources of information

Worksheets for Occupational Information

Name of Occupation _____   SOC or DOT number _____

1. Definition of occupation, nature of work, job functions performed

2. Education, training, experience needed

3. Personal qualifications, skills, abilities required

4. Earnings (salary range, benefits)

5. Working conditions, hours

6. Location of employment

    a. Work organizations

    b. Geographic areas

7. Personality characteristics of people in the occupation

8. Employment and advancement outlook

9. Personal satisfactions from this work

10. Advantages and disadvantages of this work

11. Related occupations

12. Sources of information

Worksheets for Occupational Information

Name of Occupation _____   SOC or DOT number _____

1. Definition of occupation, nature of work, job functions performed

2. Education, training, experience needed

3. Personal qualifications, skills, abilities required

4. Earnings (salary range, benefits)

5. Working conditions, hours

6. Location of employment

    a. Work organizations

    b. Geographic areas

7. Personality characteristics of people in the occupation

8. Employment and advancement outlook

9. Personal satisfactions from this work

10. Advantages and disadvantages of this work

11. Related occupations

12. Sources of information

Worksheets for Occupational Information

Name of Occupation _____   SOC or DOT number _____

1. Definition of occupation, nature of work, job functions performed

2. Education, training, experience needed

3. Personal qualifications, skills, abilities required

4. Earnings (salary range, benefits)

5. Working conditions, hours

6. Location of employment

   a. Work organizations

   b. Geographic areas

7. Personality characteristics of people in the occupation

8. Employment and advancement outlook

9. Personal satisfactions from this work

10. Advantages and disadvantages of this work

11. Related occupations

12. Sources of information

Worksheets for Occupational Information

Name of Occupation _____   SOC or DOT number _____

1. Definition of occupation, nature of work, job functions performed

2. Education, training, experience needed

3. Personal qualifications, skills, abilities required

4. Earnings (salary range, benefits)

5. Working conditions, hours

6. Location of employment

    a. Work organizations

    b. Geographic areas

7. Personality characteristics of people in the occupation

8. Employment and advancement outlook

9. Personal satisfactions from this work

10. Advantages and disadvantages of this work

11. Related occupations

12. Sources of information

Worksheets for Occupational Information

Name of Occupation _____   SOC or DOT number _____

   1. Definition of occupation, nature of work, job functions performed

   2. Education, training, experience needed

   3. Personal qualifications, skills, abilities required

   4. Earnings (salary range, benefits)

   5. Working conditions, hours

   6. Location of employment

      a. Work organizations

      b. Geographic areas

   7. Personality characteristics of people in the occupation

   8. Employment and advancement outlook

   9. Personal satisfactions from this work

 10. Advantages and disadvantages of this work

 11. Related occupations

 12. Sources of information

Worksheets for Occupational Information

Name of Occupation _____   SOC or DOT number _____

1. Definition of occupation, nature of work, job functions performed

2. Education, training, experience needed

3. Personal qualifications, skills, abilities required

4. Earnings (salary range, benefits)

5. Working conditions, hours

6. Location of employment

    a. Work organizations

    b. Geographic areas

7. Personality characteristics of people in the occupation

8. Employment and advancement outlook

9. Personal satisfactions from this work

10. Advantages and disadvantages of this work

11. Related occupations

12. Sources of information

Worksheets for Occupational Information

Name of Occupation _____   SOC or DOT number _____

1. Definition of occupation, nature of work, job functions performed

2. Education, training, experience needed

3. Personal qualifications, skills, abilities required

4. Earnings (salary range, benefits)

5. Working conditions, hours

6. Location of employment

    a. Work organizations

    b. Geographic areas

7. Personality characteristics of people in the occupation

8. Employment and advancement outlook

9. Personal satisfactions from this work

10. Advantages and disadvantages of this work

11. Related occupations

12. Sources of information

Index